# Writing for
# Public Relations and
# Strategic Communication

# Writing for Public Relations and Strategic Communication

**William Thompson**
University of Louisville

**Nicholas Browning**
Indiana University Bloomington

cognella®
SAN DIEGO

# Unique Features to Build a Strategic Writer

**This book offers full chapters covering an array of foundational topics ...**

- Synthesizing relevant communication theory (Chapter 1)
- Walking students through the discovery practice leading from research to storytelling (Chapter 4)
- Presenting a practical model of ethical, strategic communication practice (Chapter 5)
- Translating print copy to audio, visual and video (Chapter 8)
- Outlining the principles behind interactive communication (Chapter 9)

**... and sections outlining important analytical literacies ...**

- Data visualization (Chapter 13)
- Search engine optimization tactics (Chapter 9)
- Marketing statistics analysis (Chapter 13)
- Data-driven media and audience-targeting approaches (Chapter 13)

**... and offers three, two-chapter modules thoroughly exploring how-to skills in Part III ...**

*The focus of the modules?*

1. Uncontrolled communication (e.g., media relations, earned media writing)
2. Controlled communication (e.g., internal communication, advertising)
3. Semicontrolled communication (e.g., blogs, social networking sites)

*The reason for two chapters?*

1. The first chapter explains a practical step-by-step procedure to build prose writing and organization skills for uncontrolled, controlled and semicontrolled communication.
2. The second chapter shows how to write for a platform and then deliver that message effectively.

**... and elaborated through special learning features.**

- "Lessons From Life" frame each chapter within real-world experiences
- "What You Know, What You'll Learn" sections anchor new lessons within students' past knowledge
- "Principles in Practice" present extended discussions of contemporary issues
- "Strategic Thoughts" offer in-text prompting for greater engagement with the subject
- "Memory Memos" provide short, standout, in-text summaries of key concepts
- "Click-Throughs" point to interactive online content to help students familiarize themselves not only with common writing formats, but with the thought process behind their creation
- "Scenario Prompts" at the end of the book present original cases, requiring students to address management problems; select and organize information; and hone grammar, style and editing skills while practicing long-form writing

# Brief Contents

# Table of Contents

# Listings of Principles in Practice and Cases in Point

## Principles in Practice

## Case in Point

# About the Authors

### William Thompson

Thompson brought a practitioner's mentality into the academy, working with clients across the United States while he educated PR students at the University of Louisville.

In addition to authoring the book *Targeting the Message: A Receiver-Centered Process for Public Relations Writing*, Thompson has professional writing experience across a spectrum of media platforms. He has scripted and directed six video documentaries, as well as radio and TV commercials and special events. As a syndicated writer, he garnered hundreds of newspaper and magazine writing credits. His media relations efforts have placed client stories in *The New York Times*, NPR's *All Things Considered*, *Time* magazine, and NBC's *Sunday Today*, among others.

Thompson headed the PR division for the Association for Education in Journalism and Mass Communication, the world's largest organization of public relations academicians, and was a long-time editorial board member of the *Journal of Public Relations Research*. He has written or contributed to many scholarly articles and books, and presented in nearly 30 panel or paper sessions at academic conferences.

For contributing to the communication industry's diversity, he received five national commendations from the American Advertising Federation and was given the Southern States Communication Association's Outreach Award. He has also won multiple professional awards for his work in media relations, development, and special event production.

Thompson was voted one of the University of Louisville's top-ten teachers by the institution's student body and is a member of the Kentucky Communicators Hall of Fame.

Jealous for his wife's attention, he does not have a cat.

### Nicholas Browning

Dr. Browning is an associate professor of public relations at Indiana University's Media School. He serves as the school's curriculum coordinator for the PR major and teaches several undergraduate and graduate courses in the sequence, including the introductory *Principles of Public Relations*, the *Public Relations Campaign* capstone, and of course, *Public Relations Writing*. Since 2010, he has taught several sections of PR and strategic writing as instructor of record at three R1 universities: Indiana University, the University of Georgia and the University of Louisville.

Outside the classroom, Dr. Browning labors as a researcher. He currently serves as associate editor of the *Journal of Public Relations Research*, the field's preeminent academic journal. He is the co-founder and director of IU's Strategic Communication Research Lab, a collaborative effort among students and faculty to produce high-quality, original scholarship. His research interests include business and communication ethics, corporate social responsibility, organizational advocacy, and reputation and relationship management. His scholarship has been published in several respected outlets, including the *Journal of Public Relations Research*, *Public Relations Review*, *Journalism & Mass Communication Quarterly*, and the *Journal of Media Ethics*.

Dr. Browning earned undergraduate degrees in communication, English, and psychology from the University of Louisville, and an M.A. and Ph.D. from the University of Georgia's Grady College of Journalism & Mass Communication.

A native of Louisville, Kentucky, he lives and works in Bloomington, Indiana, with his wife, Chelsey—and their four cats, to whom he is allergic.

# Preface

Most multiyear projects start with at least one monstrous miscalculation.

"Once we hire a contractor, that pyramid in Giza will be up in no time at all."

"If we just sail west, we'll definitely hit India. I mean, what else is there?!"

"I think you're exaggerating the problems of fighting a land war in Asia."

This book emerged from the authors' impulse to construct a strategic writing text encompassing the features our colleagues told us they wanted (and that echoed our own classroom frustrations) but couldn't find in any book:

- A writing process arising from theory and planning easily adapted to new platforms
- Opportunities to examine issues of social justice within my teaching
- Greater focus on translating research into writing and practice
- An approach meeting my college/university's emphasis on critical thinking, not merely vocational instruction
- Practical instruction on *constructing* prose, not just *mimicking* another's writing
- Grounding practice in ethics
- A structured, data-driven approach to social media writing
- A vibrant prose voice to energize students

Oh sure, that won't be a problem. We'll get right on that. Be back to you in a week or two. Five years later, here's our answer

Our founding vision compelled us to produce a more complete writing textbook than those currently available in our field. When you scan our chapter titles, we think you'll perceive that we managed that. However, to fulfill our rather bold promise—introducing more material in greater depth with more versatile uses and a longer shelf life, all within the same time frame (one semester—two, if you're lucky)—required unique approaches to thinking about writing, practicing writing skills and teaching students the writing process. We'd like to take a few pages here to elaborate on the unique approaches and features you'll encounter in our textbook.

## Driven by the Wrong Questions

Anyone who's ever worked, taught or studied in the communication field knows it's dynamic. Change has always been the constant of our professional reality. But the march of technology has accelerated that change astronomically. At times, it feels as though we're careening ever faster into an unknowable future for which we're woefully unprepared.

Responsible for educating future PR, advertising and or/marketing students, we hear student demands for increasingly specific skills and tactics. They often evaluate our teaching through the lens of a single question: "Will I use this in my job?"

In response, we see educators scramble to follow every new tactic, new channel—new everything—to maintain the currency of their supposedly aging curriculum. Our struggle becomes, "How do I prepare students for tomorrow's transformed professional landscape?" From our perspective as decorated, oft-wounded veterans of writing classes, we've erred by flirting with the fleeting. We've been responding to the wrong questions, directing us toward flawed approaches that limit the shelf life of the strategic communication education our students receive.

In our view, the question, "Will I use this in my job?" is better translated as "Will I be able to adapt what you're teaching me to what I'll face in my career?"

This book is our attempt to help educators and students alike pump the breaks, grab the wheel and take control of their profession by developing enduring, adaptive skills within the field's grounding principles. Perhaps it's best to begin with a broader question:

## How Does One Create a Strategic Thinker?

That's a question every university and college must answer if its goal is to provide a more holistic, well-rounded education—one that prepares students to be engaged citizens embarking on lifelong growth rather than simply landing a job. It's the subtle but substantial difference between simple vocational training and a more complete and adaptable understanding of what a given profession is—and will likely become.

So what are the concrete results of reframing this key question? Let's say an instructor devotes two weeks of a course, teaching students how to use communication metrics such as Google Analytics, Cision and Meltwater.

Will students use this knowledge in their careers? And does it prepare them to enter the strategic communication profession? Yes … at least in 2022.

But what is the value of this knowledge in 2026? Or 2041? Well, that depends. Who can predict with certainty whether these platforms will even exist in five years, let alone 20? And if they do, it's a fair bet they will have changed, perhaps considerably. And it's likely better, more efficient platforms will take their place. Remember Myspace? Or payphones?

Knowledge of such practical skills is important, but it can come at the cost of adaptability. If students only learn the *how* behind such skills, their value comes with a built-in expiration date. It's the underlying *why* that gives this knowledge legs.

## Fundamental Questions Lead to Universal Answers

Communicating effectively with an audience requires understanding that audience. How do people respond to rational and emotional appeals? How do those responses vary based on individual characteristics? To which media channels do they attend? How can I use the strengths of certain channels to elicit stronger responses? If gatekeepers control access to those channels, how can I most effectively communicate with them? Was my persuasive message ultimately successful? How might I refine it?

These deeper strategic questions were as important in the time of Aristotle as they are in the time of Amazon. If students truly understand *why* they undertake tactical efforts and what they're meant to accomplish, they can discover *hows* to whatever new tools and circumstances they encounter in their future careers.

That's why we focus on theory, research, planning and ethics in the early chapters of this textbook. They ground our understanding of those *whys*, helping students adapt to the frantic pace of the profession. And not only across their careers' decades but also within the mania of a "typical" workday that involves switching platforms, channels, audiences and vocabularies.

And that's just the writing. Messages cannot be effective unless people see them, so practitioners must effectively deploy technical expertise to increase their internet posts' visibility, the terms directing camera motion in video … even the deadline for a monthly magazine in another state.

No matter how you break it down, that's a lot to teach and learn in a single semester. This book is trying to answer that challenge for both students and instructors by presenting a well-defined model emerging from an understanding of the interplay of an organization's communication goals with the logic of how an audience receives and interprets a message.

## The Audience-Centered Writing Process

We call this the audience-centered process, a solid organizational communication approach founded on understanding communication and persuasion theory, research, planning and ethics. Many strategic communication programs have dedicated courses for each of those areas, but few integrate them specifically into the all-important professional skill of strategic writing. This text does.

Some of our colleagues may view this as complicating an already overwhelming course schedule. We believe it simplifies the task each writer faces when encountering each type of writing.

For instance, writing a lede or a hook is easier when you can predict the target audience's motive. Sequencing arguments becomes automatic if you understand how targeted audience members value different arguments as they contemplate a decision.

In our approach, students are given tools to determine what elements are most persuasive and what angles are most newsworthy, which in turn directs students to the sequencing of arguments in the story's body. Easily remembered acronyms and simple checklists help students make quicker, more sound editorial judgments during prewriting, all while actively working on their prose.

The book solidifies that audience-centered process with practical, transferable writing tactics, offering specific, structural tactics for building good prose.

This step-by-step, cumulative learning approach extends through the entire text. For instance, prose emerges from planning. Chapter 6 is devoted to teaching student writers how to integrate audience analysis from a planning document (which they learned to construct in Chapters 2 and 3) into a persuasive document's opening sentence. Chapter 7 extends the logic of the lede to outline how information will be sequenced in the rest of the document, no matter the channel.

Each lesson adds to the next. Our approach recognizes audio, video and social media not as completely different categories requiring students to learn a second, third and fourth "type" of writing but instead as "additive" channels to solid, strategic thought and writing skills.

The final six chapters are arranged into three modules focusing on uncontrolled media (news releases, story pitching, etc.), controlled media (company publications, advertising, etc.) and interactive online media, with a focus on social media. Each module's first chapter details writing processes and formats within a specific type of writing, while the second chapter summarizes the most current applications of communication technology and targeting techniques to deliver cost-effective messages to precise publics.

## Insights Into (Not Just Examples of) Powerful Prose

We present numerous examples of persuasive prose and then closely examine them at the textual level to demonstrate, for instance, how to construct transitions between paragraphs. We even analyze individual word choice and placement within character-limited social media messages and discuss developing and coordinating the author's voice. Many of these examples were written by the text's authors, so we're able to comment not only on structure but also on the writer's real-time thought process while at the keyboard. This approach provides an entire tool chest of skills students can pull from, restructure and employ under deadline pressure as they develop their own prose voices and professional ethos.

## Opportunities to Hone the Craft

The book capitalizes on its web appendix to give students numerous opportunities to learn and employ the communication skills we emphasize. The writing and management assignments structured around a variety of short organizational case study scenarios let students apply instruction from each chapter to specific writing assignments and related management problems. These cases more closely replicate real-life writing situations, challenging students to excise extraneous information, correct style errors, prioritize arguments and deal with issues of ethics and company purpose. Students can gain additional writing practice through the "Strategic Thought" callouts (such as shown on p. 6) in each chapter's text that challenge students with professional applications of the information they are reading and provide instructors with prompts for classroom discussion.

We've also included frequent self-guided learning options for writing instructors to assign. An online appendix contains quick lessons instructors can assign if they discover individual students are still struggling with one or more common writing/grammar problems, such as dangling modifiers or subject-verb agreement.

"Click-Throughs" (such as shown on p. 56) are placed throughout the text and direct students to long-form examples of news releases, advertisements and video scripts housed on the book's dedicated website. These go beyond the mere text to include detailed explanations as to why we, the authors, wrote each piece the way we did, focusing on detailed decisions made—even down to the level of word choice. On this interactive platform, students can fully grasp the seemingly minute details that persuasive writers must consider as they first wrestle with these same issues themselves.

We hope our approach better enables students to master the novel complexity of persuasive writing in the mere semester our departments traditionally devote to teaching students this vital, lifetime skill. More than anything, we hope this book helps you, our colleagues, develop more of the strategic thinkers who fulfill the goals our universities and colleges have set for themselves and which our profession and our world need.

## Acknowledgments

We would like to take a moment to acknowledge the efforts of our colleagues who generously reviewed this textbook. On numerous occasions, their advice left us banging our heads against our keyboards as we labored to address their insightful critiques and more demanding revision requests. As such, our hair is a bit grayer and thinner, but more importantly, the finished textbook is more complete, cohesive and coherent due in large part to their guidance. For that, we are truly grateful.

Sincerest thanks to

Pamela Bourland-Davis, APR (Georgia Southern University; Department of Communication Arts)

Barbara DeSanto, APR, Fellow PRSA (Kansas State University; A. Q. Miller School of Journalism and Mass Communications)

Haley Higgs (Georgia Southern University; Department of Communication Arts)

Kelly C. Gaggin, APR (Syracuse University; S. I. Newhouse School of Public Communications)

Paul T. M. Hemenway (Lamar University; Department of Communication and Media)

Jacqueline Lambiase (Texas Christian University; Bob Schieffer College of Communication, Department of Strategic Communication)

Russell Mack, J.D. (Texas Christian University; Bob Schieffer College of Communication, Department of Strategic Communication)

Deanna K. W. Pelfrey, APR, PRSA Fellow (University of Florida; College of Journalism and Communications, Public Relations Department)

John Powers (Quinnipiac University; School of Communications)

Arien Rozelle (St. John Fisher College; Department of Media and Communication)

Erica Salkin (Whitworth University; Communication Studies Department)

Stephanie A. Smith (Virginia Tech; School of Communication)

Donna Stein, APR, Fellow PRSA (Syracuse University; S. I. Newhouse School of Public Communications)

Patricia Swann, APR, PRSA (Utica College; School of Business and Justice Studies)

Vivian Wagner (Muskingum University; Department of English)

# COGNELLA ACTIVE LEARNING

### Instructions for Students

This book has interactive activities available to complement your reading:

- Click-through activities to illustrate the writing techniques presented in the textbook

- Thinking Through Writing activities to help students strength their critical thinking and sharpen their writing skills

- Self-Edit activities to engage students in the theories and concepts presented in the textbook

- The Grammar/Style Boot Camp allows students to brush up on foundational rules for constructing effective prose.

- A set of flashcards for each chapter

Your instructor may have customized the selection of activities available for your unique course. Please check with your professor to verify whether your class will access this content through the Cognella Active Learning portal (http://active.cognella.com) or through your institution's learning management system.

It is necessary to enroll in Active Learning to ensure your professor receives your scores on any graded content. If you are enrolled in a course at a higher education institution where your professor has adopted this book, enroll with your cohort of classmates by either (1) redeeming a code at https://store. cognella.com/codes/redeem or (2) finding your institution and course and purchasing access in the Cognella Student Store at store.cognella.com.

### Instructions for Educators

If you are an educator, you will need to adopt Active Learning in order for you and your students to gain access. Please contact your Cognella Sales Representative or email adopt@cognella.com if you need to enroll as an instructor in Active Learning.

Please contact adopt@cognella.com with any Active Learning enrollment questions.

## WEB-BASED RESOURCES: ACCESSING QR CODES AND LINKS

The authors have selected some supporting web-based content for further engagement with the learning material that appears in this text, which can be accessed through QR codes or web links. These codes are intended for use by those who have purchased print copies of the book. You may scan them using a QR code reading app on your phone, which will take you to each website. You can also search for the link using a web browser search engine. Readers who have purchased a digital copy of the book can simply click on the hyperlinks beneath each QR code.

Cognella maintains no responsibility for the content nor availability of third-party links. However, Cognella makes every effort to keep its texts current. Broken links may be reported to studentreviews@cognella.com. Please include the book's title, author, and 7-digit SKU reference number (found below the barcode on the back cover of the book) in the body of your message.

Please check with your professor to confirm whether your class will access this content independently or collectively.

cognella®
SAN DIEGO

# PART I

# Think First, Write Second

The best writing is rewriting; that's Hemingway's sentiment, anyway. As ruthlessly obsessive editors, we can't argue with his sentiment. We spent hundreds of hours fine-tuning this text's final version. We've debated issues ranging from the absurdly obscure (Does capitalizing *God* privilege Judeo-Christian-Islamic monotheism?) to the practically relevant (Will our readers, most born in this millennium, appreciate a reference to '70s rock?) to the grammatically germane (Could we use *she* as a genderless pronoun?).

The process was immensely frustrating, yet almost masochistically fun. As you grow as writers, you'll learn to appreciate the impact of subtle editorial choices, or you'll fail in this profession. Simple as that.

And as authors of a writing-focused textbook, we assume you'd anticipate those sorts of detailed discussions on the nuts and bolts of writing generally, as well as the tactical specifics of writing for the PR and strategic communication professions. Don't worry. We won't disappoint.

But we might delay.

You see, from our vantage, the best writing isn't rewriting, despite the importance of editing. The best writing is actually *pre*writing.

In our experience, students and professors alike are eager to dive into writing. While that eagerness is admirable, it can be counterproductive. It sometimes obscures the fact that writing is a process, one that starts long before fingertips meet keyboard. A baptism by fire from a bombardment of writing tasks can leave novice writers burned (or burned out) rather than better trained for having survived the onslaught.

Our advice? Think first, write second. Writing is, after all, a profession, and every other professional takes the same approach. Lawyers first review case precedent, prepare briefs and research arguments; then they suit up for the courtroom. Athletes pore over scouting reports and game tape before facing an opponent. Why should strategic writers be any different?

The truth is, no matter how skilled a wordsmith you may be, you can't write effective, persuasive messages if you're blind to certain basics:

- Why do people think and behave in the predictable ways they do?

- Where can you learn more about your audience to increase your persuasive appeals?

- How do you incorporate that knowledge into a viable plan of action that serves organizational goals?
- How can you leverage research into more powerful persuasion?
- What factors must you consider to execute that researched plan ethically and effectively?

This first unit's five chapters are our attempt to open your eyes to these key considerations. At first, you may view this as something keeping you from the task at hand. Eventually, you'll come to view prewriting as a time *saver*. It enables you to process information, generate ideas and develop arguments more quickly, all of which make the subsequent writing and rewriting stages much easier.

So, as you read this unit, keep an open mind. The road ahead may seem long, but if you absorb all that's offered in the stops along the way, the journey's end will be that much more rewarding.

# Communication Theory in Real Life

## How Marketing, Public Relations and Advertising Work

### LESSONS FROM LIFE   Theories You Didn't Know You Knew

It's 6:30 a.m. Your cell phone's alarm blares. As you stagger out of bed to shut off the alarm, you glance at a news alert: "Dozens arrested, $3 million seized in local drug raid."

Walking to the kitchen, you scroll through social media sites while making coffee. You play a news video posted by a local TV station to Facebook that discusses last night's drug bust. You pick up some details but miss much of the story when your attempt to microwave bacon threatens to set off the smoke detector. Besides, you're more concerned with your weather app's forecast, which helps you dress for the day.

On the bus to campus, you grab your tablet. *The New York Times* app reports your senator, whom you support, accepted political donations from a hate group. The full story reveals the senator's reelection campaign did accept the money but immediately returned it upon learning its source. Moreover, there are no records indicating the senator had accepted donations like this in the past, and the staffer responsible for screening donations had been fired.

Breathing a sigh of relief, you hop off the bus and actually make it to your first class a few minutes early. As you wait for your professor to arrive, many of your fellow students are discussing last night's drug bust. You can't add to the conversation because you missed the details amid preventing your fiery, bacon-fueled death.

Your friend walks into the classroom. "Could I copy your notes from last class?" she asks. You remember she was sick the week before. Of course you let her review your notes. When you missed class last month, she did the same for you.

Your poli-sci professor finally strolls into class. She asks the class about your senator's hate-group donation. One of your peers is quick to judge the senator, condemning her for associating with such despicable people. You spring to the senator's defense, reminding your classmate that the hate-group donation was returned, that it appeared to be a one-time error and that the staffer responsible was promptly fired.

Your political science class ends by 10:30. Though you won't know it until you finish reading this chapter, already you and your friends' interactions can be explained—indeed predicted—using the tenets of five communication theories.

Each tells a part of the story as to why certain information entered your consciousness, while some didn't. They predict why you chose to offer cooperation to some people and oppose others. They explain how you enlisted the resources of others, and why you recognized others' attempts to do the same.

For our immediate task, understanding how humans select information sources, use media and transform information and other societal influences into their own sense of self offers lessons that will guide your writing. Knowing communication and persuasion theory helps identify receptive audiences, then craft prose and sequence arguments to increase your messages' effectiveness.

In the longer term, theory helps you adapt to conditions that neither the authors nor you can imagine. Society will change. Media technology will change. Will there be more encompassing forms of virtual reality (hopefully without the goofy headgear) or implanted microchips beaming images directly to your brain's occipital lobe? We don't know. But we do know the constant: a human mind amid a flurry of social activity will interpret that message.

—*Nick Browning*

## What You'll Learn

- How theory can help you organize, explain and predict patterns of human behavior

- How marketing, advertising and public relations functions are similar and distinct

- How persuasion is the unifying purpose of all strategic communication

## Theories of Media Effects

### The Importance of Theory

You may be saying to yourself, "Wait. Why all this talk about theory? I thought this book was about *writing*." It is, but there's more to writing than just … well, writing. This book is about writing for public relations and strategic communication, which means it's about planning and persuasion, and those activities are grounded in theory.

We recognize you may think theory is disconnected from your everyday life, but if your morning looks anything like what we described in the chapter opening, the relevance of communication theory to you—both personally and professionally—will become obvious.

This book intends to make you into a strategic thinker and advocates a generative writing process. By that we mean many of your writing choices are "generated" by your understanding of the person, who by comprehending and accepting your message, can help your organization reach its goals.

Theory offers the guideposts and informs every persuasive writing task. Theory can predict audience thought sequences and determine which audiences are open to persuasion. Theory helps you analyze the persuaders that will most likely affect those audiences and even direct you on how to best structure your sentences to create long-term opinion changes.

Throughout this book, you'll discover our ambition isn't merely to teach you how to format documents that characterize current strategic communication tactics. Instead, we're trying to teach you to be strategic writers, to think about what you wish to accomplish through your words, to construct effective and ethical messages and to work within the strengths and weaknesses of every medium at your disposal—both those that exist now and formats that haven't yet been conceived.

We can't precisely envision the new communication landscape or the media that will dominate the profession during your career. By understanding theory, however, you can transfer the skills you learn during this single semester to that unknowable future. Theory will establish principles of analysis, research and communication effects that will make every professional task you encounter more comprehensible and more solvable.

That's why we're starting a writing book with a focus on theory and persuasion.

## Persuasion Is Life

At its root, almost any **theory** of human behavior intends to explain and predict how, when and why certain acts of strategic communication are more effective than others. That typically means those acts are more persuasive. **Persuasion** is the art and science of using communication to convince a target audience to adopt a desired attitude, express a desired opinion or act in a desired manner. Many people fear persuasive media messages, concerned that powerful organizations—especially governments and for-profit businesses—act only in their own self-interests and with total disregard for others. If that were true, these groups might say or do whatever they could to convince key **publics** to act in ways that benefit themselves, even if it hurts countless others. You've probably heard this complaint, and usually, it's linked with the perceived power of media to sway public opinion and behavior.

In essence, this fear explains why the **powerful effects model** of media dominates public consciousness and conspiracy plots. It argues that media have direct and immediate effects on audiences, who are in turn virtually unable to resist media's influence. The powerful effects model was the dominant academic view during the 1920s and 1930s but has since fallen from favor.[1] Why? You can explain it through your own experience. You're exposed to thousands of advertisements and promotional messages daily.[2] If you acted on each one, you'd own thousands of cars, fill hundreds of closets and eat dozens of times a day—assuming you could squeeze those meals in between an endless stream of doctors' appointments where you ask whether the latest prescription drug is right for you.

Clearly, we don't react to media messages like lemmings. However, that doesn't mean media has no effect on us. Instead, our reactions to media messages are much more nuanced and more readily explained by **limited effects models**.

## Two-Step Flow: The Value of Opinion Leaders

The limited effects view suggests media influences us within a web of other factors. Our relationships with others is an important one. Sociologist Paul Lazarsfeld helped establish this view by investigating media's impact on voting behavior through monthly surveys of an Ohio county's residents during a presidential campaign.

Lazarsfeld found that media had relatively little direct effect in altering public opinion. In most cases, media messages either reinforced voters' existing positions or were simply ignored. However, there were instances in which media had indirect effects, sometimes contributing to changing audience opinions and behaviors.

Lazarsfeld found not everyone pays equal attention to the news media, and as a result some audience members are more informed than others. Moreover, those paying close attention to political news interpreted and shared that information with those around them. In this way, mass media appears to influence most audience members indirectly through a **two-step flow** of communication: attentive audiences internalize media messages and then pass along those messages—as well as their personal interpretations of the messages—to their less-informed social contacts.[3]

These attentive audiences, or **opinion leaders**, are not limited to the political realm. In fact, opinion leaders come in various shapes and sizes, and we often rely on their field-specific expertise to help us make decisions in our everyday lives. For example, like many of you, we depend on various technologies in our personal and professional lives. But how do we make decisions about our next cell phone upgrade? Or which computer to buy? We rely on opinion leaders. We read product reviews from the experts at CNET or pore over the extensive product testing of the tech writers at Wirecutter.

Many of you go through essentially the same process. Consider the high-paid peers on social media to whom you turn for recommendations on gaming, fashion, music, films, makeup tutorials, social causes or politics. Collectively, they guide millions of buying, entertainment and advocacy decisions daily. Those Lazarsfeld-labeled opinion leaders you probably call *influencers*.

We all rely on opinion leaders in some capacity. That's why as persuasive communicators, understanding how to reach these key audiences is particularly important. If we can persuade them to think well of our organization, its products and/or its services, in turn they may influence countless others in much the same way. We'll talk more about the importance of opinion leaders when we discuss planning persuasive communication campaigns (Chapter 3) researching target audiences (Chapter 4) and crafting persuaders to engage those target audiences (Chapter 6).

### Uses and Gratifications: What We Do With Media

Lazarsfeld's two-step flow model prompted communication scholars and practitioners to question how people interact with media. Until that point, audiences were generally seen as passive, simply absorbing the media content they encountered. By the late 1940s and 1950s, prominent theorists like Harold Lasswell and Elihu Katz had come to a different conclusion: *audiences are active in choosing the media to which they attend.*[4]

Katz flipped the media-research script, emphasizing that we'd mostly been asking, "What do media do to people?" According to Katz, it's better to

---

**Strategic Thought**

Imagine you're planning to buy a new car. Who are the opinion leaders you would consult? Now imagine you're searching for a summer internship. To which opinion leaders would you turn? Are they the same or different from those advising you on your new car purchase?

ask, "What do people do *with* media?"[5] This moment initiated the **uses and gratifications** approach, now widely applied to analyze how media and audiences interact.

Think about this for a moment: How many media options do you have at any given time? Well, if you have cable or satellite television, that's probably a minimum of 100 channels right there. Of course, as we all know, there's never anything on, which is why you have subscriptions to Netflix, Hulu and Amazon Prime. That lets you access thousands more shows and movies. But if you've run through your respective queues, there's always YouTube, which houses millions of videos available at the push of a button. And we've barely scratched the surface. We haven't even mentioned theater, radio, music streaming, podcasts, concerts, newspapers, magazines, books, blogs, Facebook, Twitter, Instagram and the endless wealth of content comprising the rest of the internet.

The bottom line? Maybe you can be passive in *consuming* media, but you're certainly active in *choosing* which media to consume. The uses and gratification approach explains and predicts how and why you make those media choices. Generally speaking, people use media to gratify a variety of needs. Most fall into the following four categories:[6]

**Information**. People want to know what's going on, which is why they pay attention to news in all its forms: politics, science, weather, celebrities. But even if you're not a news junkie, you may still want to know a movie's show time, or the weekend's weather forecast.

**Entertainment**. Sometimes it just feels good to laugh, to be drawn into a dramatic adventure, to emotionally connect with a character or to cheer your school's sports team to victory.

**Escapism**. Other times we come home and just want to forget about life for a while. Media can let us focus on things outside our day-to-day lives.

**Socialization**. Media reflect life's common narratives and provide a point of contact for interacting with others. You may find yourself out of the loop if you missed the Oscars, a hit show's latest installment or the endless news and gossip circulating on an array of social media sites. Media helps you maintain connection points.

Of course, a given media choice may satisfy multiple needs. For example, you may be entertained by the basketball playoffs; it might also help you escape and unwind after a long week of classes; it might give you something with which to chat up your dad before you masterfully transition to begging him for money.

Regardless, we know audiences actively seek media to meet certain needs and they are satisfied with their media experiences when those needs are met.[7] Understanding which media outlets our target audiences turn to often determines the success or failure of any persuasive communication tactic and is crucially important to communication planning and research discussed in Chapters 2, 3 and 4.

### Agenda Setting: What Media Tell Us to Think About

Despite the control we have to determine our media choices, in many ways, we have little say over what media presents to us. Aside from user-generated content, the average reader/listener/viewer consumes media; she doesn't create it, and neither do her peers. Because the power of media over audiences is somewhat limited, content creators don't dictate our reactions to media, but they do control what we are able to consume.[8]

**Agenda-setting theory** is often summarized by political scientist Bernard Cohen's adage: "The press may not be successful much of the time in telling people what to think, but it is stunningly successful in telling its readers what to think about."[9] In other words, what creators of media content deem important often finds its way into their work, which shapes how we as media consumers see our world.

Think of it like dining at a restaurant. As the customer, you control what you eat. You're free to choose your own meal, but only from the menu options the restaurant owner dictates. Our media diets work much the same way. Yes, we are free to choose what we read, watch and listen to, but we can only choose from what's there. Content creators set the media menu.

News editors, producers and reporters in particular have great power. Consider, for example, the job of a news outlet's editor-in-chief. She is tasked with informing her audience about the most important happenings. But what exactly does she deem important? Her decision will be based in part on what information her staff brings to her attention. If she never learns of an issue, she can't direct anyone to cover it. She'll also apply journalistic standards regarding what information is newsworthy, a central principle in generating lede sentences, the art and science of which we'll discuss in Chapter 6. Additionally, her coverage is constrained by her outlet's budget and staff—and perhaps in part by personal biases, both known and unknown. In any case, the editor will choose to publish some stories and discard others. Before news reaches us, it typically passes through these **gatekeepers**, who determine which issues become publicly relevant.

In short, what is important to these gatekeepers often becomes important to audiences.[10] Part of this effect appears unavoidable because it stems from mental shortcuts audiences take in assigning credibility. Although public trust of the news media as an institution has declined in recent decades,[11] many people consider information from established news sources as credible and important simply because an established news source reported it.[12] If it's in the news, we often reason, it probably matters.

The press's agenda-setting power also impacts strategic communicators. One pivotal function of PR practitioners is **media relations**, or the process of establishing respectful, mutually beneficial relationships between the press and the organizations for which we work. These relationships help organizations communicate more effectively with key publics by allowing them to influence the media agenda and thus the agenda of its consumers. Elements of good media relations practice will be discussed throughout this book, although we'll focus most heavily on those skills in Chapters 10 and 11.

## Theories of Message Processing
### The Elaboration Likelihood Model: Diverging Paths

The media affect us in many ways. However, we process the messages presented to us in different ways, with different mental processing routes leading to different effects.

The **elaboration likelihood model (ELM)** focuses primarily on three factors that determine how we process a message: (1) How motivated are we to pay attention to the message? (2) How capably can we understand the message? (3) And what is the nature of the message itself?[13] The answers to these questions determine how likely an audience is to engage with a given message.

These factors may seem rather straightforward, but there are a number of nuanced considerations that complicate matters, especially when considering all three at once. Perhaps a more concrete example is needed to bring this particular theory to life.

### *Relevance and Ability*

Let's say we, the authors, work for a nonprofit organization promoting energy conservation, and we want to persuade you, the reader, to cut your electricity use. Generally speaking, people are most highly motivated to pay attention to messages they find personally relevant. Energy conservation might be important to you if you're concerned about curbing climate change. Or maybe a tight budget compels you to cut your monthly utility bill. Either way, energy conservation would be relevant to you.

The next question: whether you're able to process the message. This step has several components. First, it's vital our audience comprehends what we communicate. As professors, we're fairly well educated and occasionally unbox a big word from the university's vocabulary warehouse. But what good would it do us to employ prodigiously pharaonic and esoteric verbiage if our audience can't extrapolate our communiqué? Translation: Don't talk over your audience's head.

Similarly, we must be certain we send those messages through media you use regularly. All too often, we hear students say they want to structure a "digital-first" communication campaign, relying on a "comprehensive social media strategy." There's nothing inherently wrong with that approach, but there's nothing inherently right about it either. If we're communicating to a technologically illiterate audience, we'd be insane to use Twitter or Snapchat. But since in our present example we're communicating with a younger, more tech-reliant demographic, those are valid media choices. In short, your audience should dictate your media choices, which makes the discussions on audience research in Chapters 2, 3 and 4 very important.

Still, for all we research and plan, there are some factors we can't control that affect our audience's ability to process messages. Maybe you normally check your Twitter feed throughout the day, but your smartphone battery died at noon. Or maybe you were streaming music during your drive home and an ambulance sped by with sirens blaring just in time to drown out our advertisement. As communicators, we must acknowledge that an audience can't process a message if they never receive it.

### Central Route Processing

But let's assume you are motivated and able to process our message about cutting electricity usage. If that's the case, then energy conservation probably matters to you. Perhaps you believe energy conservation is an important step toward fighting climate change. If so, then our communication objective is to reinforce that belief. Conversely, you may believe scientists' efforts to produce more energy-efficient devices will soon solve our problems; as a result, you see no reason to conserve energy now. If so, then our task is to change your belief.

Either way, you don't come to our message as a blank slate but are instead bound within a net of past influences. We can only persuade you that our view is the soundest if we present a strong argument. That may mean providing a series of logical, well-reasoned claims. It might mean making a strong emotional appeal. It could be that some combination of head and heart is most effective (and it usually is). No matter the argument structure we choose, the better the evidence backing up our rational and/or emotional arguments, the more likely we are to persuade you. This process of deep message elaboration is called the *central route*.

### Peripheral Route Processing

However, not everyone will process messages in this way. First, what's personally relevant to you may not be relevant to others, meaning they're less motivated to attend to the same messages. Second, there could be numerous factors limiting a person's ability to process the message, like those we discussed earlier. Third, and perhaps most importantly, people don't have time to think deeply about each message they see and hear.

Human beings strive for efficiency. We try to simplify our lives as much as possible, and one way we do that is by using **heuristic**, practical cues; the message cues that attract our attention to help us make quick decisions.

This is *peripheral route* processing, in which audiences focus mostly on surface-level information.[14] For example, you may not find our message content interesting, but you may be drawn in by our spokesperson. Generally, individuals respond positively to messages delivered by people they like, those they see as charismatic and/or those they believe to be authorities on the matter.

But it's not just the speaker who delivers a peripheral cue. When we see others we value respond to the same message, it can influence us as well. Remember this childhood scold from your mother? "If your friends all jumped off a cliff, would you too?" Much to our mothers' collective dismay, the answer is yes, we probably would. We're social creatures. We want to fit in. And under these pressures, we often model others' behaviors to foster their acceptance. So, regarding our energy conservation message, if we can convince you that your peers care about this issue and are acting to conserve electricity, you'll likely read that as a cue to do the same.

But these efforts sometimes backfire. Persuasion effects stimulated through the peripheral route are often short-lived. Why? Our audiences haven't internalized that given attitude, opinion or behavior. Those who actively engage with persuasive messages and then act, do so because they truly believe it's important to take the action. Those who act based only on peripheral cues may not have considered why a given action is important or, indeed, why they are acting in the first place. As a result, they can be more easily persuaded to reverse their behaviors in the future.

## Inoculation Theory: Immunization to Counterarguments

If we contemplate persuasion from this perspective, we see there are really two tasks involved. First, we want to influence people's attitudes, opinions or behaviors. Sometimes that means convincing others to adopt new positions; sometimes it means convincing others to maintain their current positions. Either way, there's a flip side to the persuasive coin: keeping our target audiences from being swayed by future counterarguments.

So how do we do that? **Inoculation theory** guides us. It asserts that each of us adheres to a number of beliefs, beliefs that are rarely challenged. Because we have little practice defending our beliefs in the face of criticism, they are susceptible to change when we are confronted with convincing, contradictory arguments. However, we can be conditioned to defend our viewpoints when facing criticism.

Inoculation theory echoes the principle of immunization.[15] As children, most of us were immunized through vaccinations against a host of diseases. Vaccines typically introduce weakened viruses into our bodies, teaching our immune systems to produce antibodies necessary to eradicate full-fledged versions of diseases should we ever be exposed. This makes us less susceptible to the disease's effects. On the other hand, unvaccinated individuals don't have these protections. They first encounter these diseases in their full potency, without protection from infection and all its accompanying harm.

Inoculation theory suggests our minds can be immunized in much the same way as our bodies. Like a body that has not encountered a particular pathogen, unchallenged beliefs are vulnerable to attack. However, when people are exposed to opposing views early and prepared with rebuttals, they develop protection against subsequent conflicting information. In short, they're inoculated.

As we'll discuss in Chapters 5, 7 and 12, it's almost always best to present both sides of an argument. First, we have an ethical responsibility to treat issues fairly and to be as honest and forthright as possible. Second, exposing publics to multiple viewpoints, arguing for our position and then letting knowledgeable audiences determine their own opinions, is a highly effective form of persuasion. When people engage with an issue and make informed decisions, the attitudes, opinions or behaviors they adopt last longer. The ELM partially explains this: engaged audiences process messages more deeply, which leads to greater resilience of an adopted position.

But inoculation theory further explains what's happening. When people are exposed to multiple viewpoints, they necessarily weigh them against one another before determining their position. This process exposes individuals not only to the position we as persuaders wish them to adopt but also to competing views. When individuals are introduced to counterarguments early in the persuasion process, they'll be better equipped to defend their own positions, making those positions more resilient over time.[16]

## Cognitive Dissonance: Life in the Bubble

But why do so many of our beliefs go unchallenged in the first place? One reason? Many beliefs are *truisms*, which are agreed-upon and deeply held cultural values. For example, few people would question a belief that it's wrong to murder or that slavery is immoral. Because these beliefs are so widely held, they're rarely challenged.

However, our beliefs often go unchallenged because we (1) avoid information contradicting our worldviews and/or (2) seek information that confirms them. These are two common ways people sidestep **cognitive dissonance**, the state of mental distress that results from simultaneously holding contradictory beliefs or acting counter to our beliefs.[17]

### Avoidance and Rationalization

Humans strive for consistency in our ongoing attempt to make sense of ourselves and the world around us. Above all, we want to view ourselves as rational. To that end, we can easily recognize when something doesn't quite add up. In his early work on cognitive dissonance, Leon Festinger studied how smokers handled the mental inconsistency resulting from smoking while simultaneously knowing it was bad for their health. It's easy to imagine the discomfort. If you knew something was bad for you but continued to do it anyway, how would you feel? Foolish? Ashamed? Saddened? Nobody wants to feel that way, so we try to avoid the contradiction.

In the smoker's case, perhaps she tries to block messages regarding the health risks. If she can avoid information questioning her smoking behavior, then there's less discomfort. Maybe she'll look for evidence that smoking isn't really so bad, making her feel better about smoking in the first place. These preventative steps of avoiding challenges to our beliefs and seeking out information that confirms our existing viewpoints are collectively called **selective exposure**.

But what happens when challenging information gets through? According to Festinger, we have two choices: change our belief or change our behavior. Whichever is least ingrained is the one most likely to change. The smoker will either quit smoking or find ways to discredit conflicting information. You've probably heard such rationalizations: "I can quit anytime I want." "Nonsmokers get cancer too." "My grandfather smoked his whole life, and he lived to be 85."[18]

### Reaching Reluctant Audiences

These behaviors of avoidance and rationalization may help us sidestep cognitive dissonance, but as you might imagine, they present serious barriers for persuasive writers. First, if you hope to persuade people, they must see or hear your message. That can be difficult in a media environment where receivers are not only rewarded for avoiding information challenging their beliefs, but where media fragmentation makes that avoidance increasingly easier. We explore that phenomenon in Principles in Practice 1.1.

**PRINCIPLES IN PRACTICE 1.1    The Social Media Bubble and
the 2016 Presidential Election**

In a bitterly contested race, the 2016 presidential election campaign pitted Hillary Clinton against Donald Trump. They were the two most disliked candidates in the 40 years the Roper Center has tracked favorability. Fewer than half the voting public viewed either candidate positively.[19] It seemed most Americans wanted nothing to do with either, in particular nothing concerning the candidate they disliked more.

In recent years, media fragmentation has made such avoidance simpler. For the last two decades, 24-hour cable news has enabled viewers to retreat to outlets echoing their ideological views.[20] As opposed to the relatively objective and far less opinion-driven news provided by network TV outlets during most of the 20th century, 21st-century cable news provides viewers an effective means of preventing cognitive dissonance. Audiences can attend to news that rarely, if ever, challenges their ideological viewpoints.

But that level of insulation pales in comparison to the so-called filter bubble. According to a 2015 Pew Research Institute study, a whopping 61% of millennials turned to Facebook for news about government and politics; 51% of Generation Xers and 39% of baby boomers did as well.[21]

The way Facebook and other social media sites filter information for their users creates serious concerns. Facebook personalizes the newsfeeds of individual users by analyzing past behaviors. So if you consistently click on stories or outlets taking either a liberal or conservative slant, then Facebook will begin to filter out the information you don't click on. And as we know from dissonance theory, we're most likely to ignore information challenging our beliefs in favor of information confirming them.[22]

In some ways, Facebook's political filter is simply a more robust wall against opposing views than the filter cable news provides. However, it's crucially different in one major way: users are often unaware of it. When a person chooses to watch one channel over another, there's at least a sense she is exercising a content preference. The Facebook filter, however, evolves slowly and unseen. Over time and without conscious awareness, our past media choices cocoon us in difficult-to-penetrate social media bubbles.

As we unwittingly succumb to avoiding cognitive dissonance, we build our own online realities that are barely recognizable to those holding opposing views. During the 2016 presidential election campaign, *The Wall Street Journal* went so far as to construct a side-by-side "Blue Feed, Red Feed," which pulled frequently shared content from liberal and conservative Facebook users and news sites.[23] For many, reading the newsfeeds of those with opposing political views was akin to visiting an alien world they didn't recognize, understand or like.[24]

While more recent attempts to diminish the amount of fake news shared via social media might benefit American democracy, it doesn't address the fundamental challenge social media bubbles pose to persuasive communicators: How do we persuade our target audiences as they become increasingly less reachable?

Second, if you succeed in reaching your audience, how do you convince them to attend to your message rather than dismiss it? For starters, it helps to answer the WIIFM question: *What's in it for me?* As a general rule, people are more likely to take an action if they can easily discern how it benefits them. So if you want to persuade someone to change her behavior, it helps to offer her a reward for doing so. Research has shown such rewards should be set just high enough to encourage behavior change but no higher. Why? Well, if the reward is massive, people will attribute their behavior change to the reward itself rather than internal motives, and such changes can be short-lived.[25]

For example, let's say you work for a bank and offer a two-week promotion during which all new customers receive a $500 deposit in their new checking accounts. In the short term, that's likely to boost your number of account holders, but how long will they remain loyal? Instead, a better strategy might be offering new customers a free financial planning session to help them better budget their money and save for the future. This reward is valuable, but the payoff's long-term nature clarifies how your customers view the reward. Moreover, it demonstrates your organization's commitment to its customers' well-being. Signaling that you value your publics and your relationship with them helps penetrate the selective exposure bubble, making your persuasive attempts more likely to succeed.[26]

As you progress through this textbook, you'll find we consistently stress the importance of building stable, lasting relationships with stakeholders and communicating persuasive messages based on your audience's self-interest. Overcoming cognitive dissonance is just one reason why.

## Theories of Audience Characteristics and Response

By this point, we hope you understand that persuasion—let alone persuasive *writing*—is a difficult task, but certainly not impossible. Indeed, we've seen how theory helps us structure messages so they are better received. However, theory also informs us concerning who to target and why.

### Stakeholder Theory:
### Who the Organization Needs

Generally speaking, practitioners in the PR and strategic communication fields work on behalf of organizations of all kinds: for-profit, nonprofit, government, etc. Organizations have responsibilities to and relationships with a wide array of people. This makes communication incredibly challenging in a practical sense—and in an ethical sense, as we'll discuss in Chapter 5. As practitioners, before we can determine *with* whom we should communicate, we must first understand those publics *to* whom our organizations are responsible.

Consider for-profit organizations. They are often publicly traded, meaning individuals can purchase a share of the company through a stock exchange. These companies then use this money, known as *capital*, to fund organizational activities, such as research and development, building new facilities and a host of other things. In return, these individuals share the organization's profits their investments helped create. These individuals are shareholders, and for-profit organizations credibly answer to them.

However, organizations don't exist in a vacuum. They are part of a larger economic ecosystem. Their decisions impact numerous publics, and those publics' actions can alter organizational operations. These publics are commonly known as **stakeholders** (Figure 1.1), which encompass any individual or group who can affect or is affected by an organization.[27] While investors certainly comprise one stakeholder group, there are multiple others: Customers/consumers, employees, suppliers, distributors, governments, community groups, and others all have a stake in how a company operates.

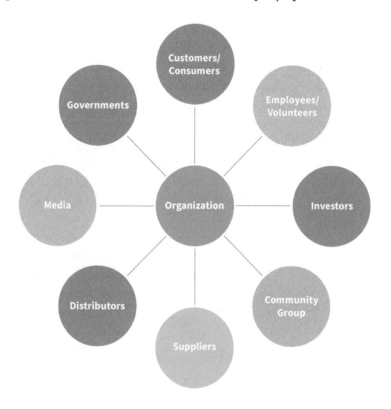

**FIGURE 1.1 Common Organizational Stakeholders.** Strategic communication practitioners have loyalties and responsibilities to a variety of different groups. These are just a handful of them.

Also, you'll notice we didn't say stakeholders had to be friends. An organization's stakeholders include industry competitors, government regulators and antagonist publics. For an oil company like BP, ExxonMobil, EPA regulators and Environmental Defense Fund advocates are all key stakeholders with whom BP must manage ongoing relationships.

## Resource Dependency Theory: Why the Organization Needs Them

Stakeholders are critical to organizational success because they control needed resources. Investors supply capital needed to fund new business ventures; employees provide labor, which lets companies build products or offer services;

and customers purchase those products and services, injecting more money into the business. Governments can regulate companies in ways that help or hinder growth, and consumer-advocacy groups can impact operations by delivering the weight of negative public opinion against an organization. Similar relationships exist for nonprofit organizations: Donors supply capital needed for overhead expenses and providing services; volunteers work to administer those services; recipients of vital services depend upon such organizations to sometimes meet even their most basic needs.

**Resource dependency theory** explains the value of stakeholders. By an organization's very nature, it lacks access to all the resources necessary for success. Organizations depend on stakeholders to supply them—or, in the case of public support, not withhold such a vital resource. For this reason, organizations must acknowledge and manage relationships with stakeholders to keep resources freely flowing. Strategic communication plays a key role here.[28]

### Social Exchange Theory: You Scratch My Back, I'll Scratch Yours

As strategic communicators, it's critical we understand the nature of resource exchange to fulfill our persuasive efforts. The way in which organizations and stakeholders exchange resources does not fundamentally differ from how individuals exchange resources in interpersonal relationships. **Social exchange theory** explains how these interpersonal transactions function.

| MEMORY MEMO 1.1 Rules of Social Exchange[29] |
|---|
| • Based on developed, proven patterns of success |
| • Relies on norms of reciprocity |
| • Rules govern how resources should be allocated |
| • Procedures are set for resource distribution |
| • Relationships collapse if fairness and stability are not maintained |

Social exchange theory conceives of relationships within a given social system as governed by self-interest, norms of reciprocity and rules dictating how resources are fairly exchanged. If exchanges are no longer perceived as fair by both parties, or if the flow of resources becomes unstable, the relationship will dissolve. If fairness and stability aren't restored, or if one or both parties develop better exchange relationships elsewhere, the engagement ends.[30]

Even our closest friendships can be explained by resource exchange principles. Let's say your friend recently lost a close relative. You logically provide comfort (a resource) to your friend in her time of need because she was there for you when you suffered a devastating breakup (reciprocity).

And when you think back to that breakup, you see it was for the best. Remember how you always had to spend time with her friends, but she never made time for you (lack of fairness)? And on the few occasions she agreed to hang out with your friends, she was often late and sometimes didn't even bother to show (instability).

Organizational relationships with stakeholders work similarly. Consider what creates a good employer/employee relationship. The organization wants employees who are hardworking, loyal and productive. Employees want job security, reasonable salaries and benefits, recognition, and a sense that what they do matters. If both parties reliably supply these resources, the relationship will likely continue. However, if the employee fails to produce quality work or the employer fails to offer deserved raises and promotions, the employee is likely to be fired or quit—provided equal or better alternatives exist. The strategic writer should always strive to communicate those better alternatives. We perceive of these exchanges as central to that mutually beneficial relationship, so we'll talk a lot more about social exchange theory in Chapter 2.

## Signaling and Attribution Theories: Everything Says Something, but What Does That Something Mean?
### *How You Communicate Meaning*

It's one thing to secure these resources in equitable exchanges. It's another to ensure that both parties *perceive* their joint advantages, which is where communication activities become essential. Here's an example.

Say your computer is constantly freezing up, so you're looking to buy a new one. In this case, the resource exchange is based on an organization/customer relationship. So what are you looking for in your new computer? It's likely you want a machine that is dependable, easy to use, reasonably priced and a good fit for your normal computing activities. That might mean examining a variety of features—e.g., touch screen, processor speed, storage, RAM.

OK. You know what you want. But how do you know which company can best deliver those desired features? Let's assume you've had your current computer for six years, and though it's at the end of its life cycle, it's been a solid machine. Maybe you examine rankings of customer service scores across brands, or you read reviews from industry experts who've tested various computers. Perhaps you seek the opinions of friends who own different models. All this information signals the quality of the product, the brand and the company—for good or ill. This is the crux of **signaling theory**.[31]

It's not enough that organizations bring valuable resources to the table to initiate exchanges with stakeholders. Organizations must communicate, or signal, to stakeholders why those resources are valuable. In our earlier discussion of the employer/employee relationship, we noted it's important for employers to have a productive workforce, and it's important for employees to be recognized for good work. Successful organizations signal how they value employees not only through words but also through actions. The organization could offer raises or promotions, expand benefits and stock options, acknowledge employee contributions in organizational publications or present formal awards accompanied by bonuses. All these communications and actions demonstrate the value of these resources to both parties, encouraging future exchanges.

Let's discuss resource theories from a strategic communication standpoint. It's important to emphasize that our organization must commit its resources to incentivize audiences before our writing can effectively persuade stakeholders to commit their resources to us. Our communication efforts start by assessing which benefits our stakeholders perceive as valuable and convincing our managers to offer them. It's only then that our writing can motivate our audiences to commit their own resources.

### How Audiences Assign Meaning

As you'll learn in greater detail in the next two chapters, simply because a message is sent and a signal is given, that doesn't necessarily mean it's been received. Moreover, even if the message is received, there's no guarantee the receiver will interpret it in the way the sender intended. While there are a variety of reasons why these communication breakdowns occur, **attribution theory** offers solid explanations.

Signaling theory suggests that every action sends some message. But what exactly is that message? Well, that's a matter of interpretation. It's likely you recall a time in your childhood when a parent came home angry. Perhaps your father frustratingly slammed grocery bags on the kitchen counter or your mother threw her briefcase in the living room corner in disgust. And then, before you could even blink, the anger was directed at you: "Why are all these dirty dishes in the sink?! And the lawn's not going to mow itself!"

Clearly, these words and actions send a message, but what message? Were your parents truly upset with you for neglecting your chores? Or were they just upset because they had a tough day and misdirected some of that frustration toward you? Without asking directly, you can never know the true answer. But if you're like most people, you will assign a meaning to their behaviors based on your past interactions with them, and that judgment will be based on whether you attribute their actions to dispositional or situational factors.

*Dispositional attributions* occur when we explain a person's behavior as stemming from something innate about that individual, such as her personality. *Situational attributions* occur when we explain a person's behavior as stemming from a particular set of circumstances. Essentially, what we're asking is whether a person's behavior is characteristic of who that person is or whether it's the result of external factors.

In the case of your frustrated parents, you'd probably ask yourself a few questions. Is this behavior common for them? Might they be acting that way for other reasons? If your parents rarely voice displeasure with you, and you happen to know they are stressed at work, you'll likely make a situational attribution and assume they did not intend to berate you. However, if your parents consistently express these frustrations about your shirking responsibilities, you'll likely make a dispositional attribution and assume that, yes, they are indeed upset with you.[32]

Similarly, organizations and their stakeholders constantly make attribution judgments about the signals they send one

---

**MEMORY MEMO 1.2** Making Attributions[33]

- *Consensus:* Do others in the same circumstances act the same way as this individual or organization?
- *Consistency:* Does this individual or organization behave like this regularly?
- *Distinctiveness:* Is the comment or behavior unusual for the individual or organization?

another. Let's say an auto plant is one of your hometown's major employers. The manufacturer recently announced plans to move 15% of your town's jobs overseas. Does that mean this car company no longer values your community? Or is there some other reason for this action?

You can assess this quite logically. You may look for industry *consensus* and ask whether other auto plants are outsourcing jobs or if your hometown plant is the exception. You may also search for *consistency* within the company, asking whether this particular auto manufacturer has a history of moving jobs overseas. Additionally, you may assess *distinctness*, which often means evaluating the organization in broader terms, asking whether the outcomes of this action differ from other organizational actions over time. In short, has the company typically been a good corporate citizen?

In general, when individuals or organizations act in a way that is (a) uncommon among their peers, (b) consistent over time and (c) similar across situations, we usually assume the company is just like that. We've made a dispositional attribution. However, if behaviors are (a) common among peers, (b) inconsistent with their behavioral histories and (c) distinctive to the circumstances, then we'll likely assume their actions result from outside factors. In this case, we've made a situational attribution.[34]

A successful strategic writer can anticipate the attributions audiences are likely to make based on the variety of signals they send. In later chapters, we'll examine a number of factors contributing to persuasion. These range from how specific media constrain or enhance a message, and even how minute details like word choice can push your audience toward vastly different attributions.

## Partitioning the Professional and Media Landscapes: Exploring Our Options

To this point, we've discussed several theories of media effects, persuasion and audience response. Understanding these approaches is essential as you hone your skills as a strategic writer for public relations, advertising and marketing—the subdisciplines of **strategic communication**. But applying those strategic writing skills effectively within each of these professions necessarily requires that you understand the differences and similarities of the PR, advertising and marketing functions.

### Distinct Media Usage

Strategic communication practitioners use numerous media outlets—so many that they're virtually impossible to catalog. For that reason, scholars and practitioners alike have devised models to categorize media based on certain characteristics.

#### *Modeling Strategic Communication Fields*

The **PESO Media Model** classifies media as either Paid, Earned, Shared or Owned. While this model was designed for a PR profession evolving in the digital age, we feel it is broadly applicable across several strategic communication fields.[35]

Figure 1.2 illustrates how various media might be categorized within the PESO model. More broadly speaking, **paid media** describe content for which placement was purchased. As we define it, paid media encapsulate most forms of traditional advertising in addition to any sponsored social media content.

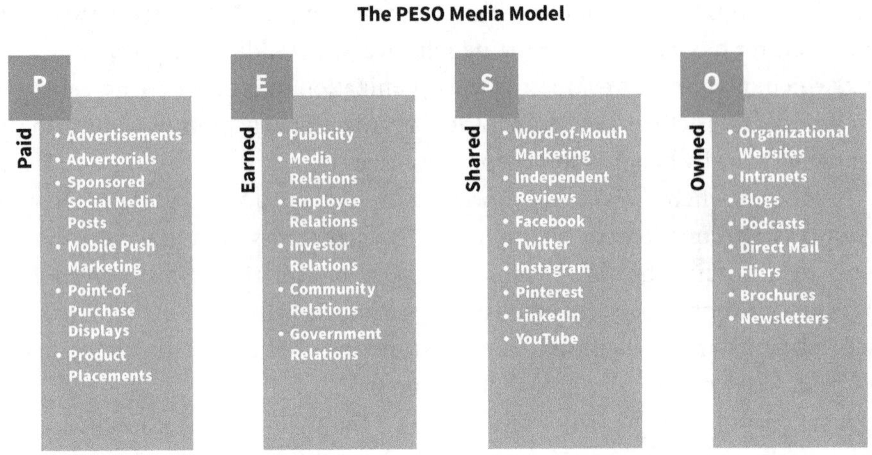

**The PESO Media Model**

| **P** Paid | **E** Earned | **S** Shared | **O** Owned |
|---|---|---|---|
| • Advertisements<br>• Advertorials<br>• Sponsored Social Media Posts<br>• Mobile Push Marketing<br>• Point-of-Purchase Displays<br>• Product Placements | • Publicity<br>• Media Relations<br>• Employee Relations<br>• Investor Relations<br>• Community Relations<br>• Government Relations | • Word-of-Mouth Marketing<br>• Independent Reviews<br>• Facebook<br>• Twitter<br>• Instagram<br>• Pinterest<br>• LinkedIn<br>• YouTube | • Organizational Websites<br>• Intranets<br>• Blogs<br>• Podcasts<br>• Direct Mail<br>• Fliers<br>• Brochures<br>• Newsletters |

**FIGURE 1.2  The PESO Media Model.**

**Earned media** are garnered through publicity or media relations. Entertainment and news media seek to provide content interesting to their audiences, and strategic communication practitioners work to provide this relevant content while simultaneously promoting the organizations for which they work. Efforts to fill these media content holes form the cornerstone of traditional PR practice. **Shared media** are largely synonymous with social media, but in a broader sense, they could also encompass traditional word-of-mouth marketing or independent product and service reviews.

**Owned media** refer to content you distribute through some space that already belongs to you. Organizational websites are an excellent example. Organizational blogs and podcasts, as well as company intranets, would also fall under this umbrella.

Of course, the PESO model is just one way to categorize media. In the late 1980s, Thomas Bivins popularized a simpler view based on the level of control the sender exerted over the message, considering information to be either controlled or uncontrolled. Information is said to be *uncontrolled* when individuals outside the organization exercise editorial control over content. *Controlled* information, on the other hand, is precisely crafted by practitioners and delivered to audiences exactly as we intend.

**MEMORY MEMO 1.3** CUS Media Characterizing Each Strategic Communication Discipline

- Advertising
  - Controlled
- Marketing
  - Controlled
  - Semicontrolled

- Public Relations
  - Controlled
  - Uncontrolled
  - Semicontrolled

Looking back at the PESO model, you can see how the models might overlap. It's easy to see that earned media are uncontrolled. Sure, as practitioners, we control all the information that goes into, let's say, a press release: who launched a local charity and what that charity does, the date and location of the charity's next event, how these charitable efforts will impact an audience and how a reader might get involved. But when it is transmitted through the media, the final product is ultimately beyond our control. We have no say in the message's style or tone, where and when it will be placed or even if it will be placed at all.

Paid media, on the other hand, clearly fall into the controlled category. For example, if our organization purchases a television advertisement, we totally control not only what the final message will be but also when, where and how it will be presented. That editorial control over the message is largely what we're paying for.

But when you look closely at owned and shared media, these classification systems seem to break down. As we said earlier, *shared media* has become a catchall term for social media, so Facebook, Twitter, Instagram, etc., are lumped into this category. However, we could make a case that these are owned media. When you ask someone to follow you on social media, how do you phrase it? Check out *my* Facebook page, *my* Twitter feed, *my* Instagram photos. You curate, manage and, arguably, own that space. The initial information you disseminate is no more "shared" than that of a billboard. It's a voicing of a particular view to an audience that happens to be traveling down that portion of the information highway at that moment. You control those initial information outputs.

Having said that, there's certainly the opportunity for greater interactivity through such online channels. Yes, you may "own" your Facebook feed, but others are free and often encouraged to share information on that site through comments or direct messaging. Moreover, virtually all social media allow audiences to push that content on their own profiles through retweets, pins and other forms of sharing. The content of comments or the nature of who shares, along with how and when sharing occurs, isn't within your control. These information exchanges occur more in a space you monitor than own. In that sense, such media are very much shared.

But what if an organization pays to boost a Facebook post? That's clearly paid, right? But it's posted on a social networking site, which makes it shared media, correct? Or is it really owned since the company controls access to the profile?

You can see how quickly the wheels start falling off when you look at these models more closely.

From our perspective, the PESO model is overly specific in drawing hard lines where blurred ones are more accurate. Moreover, media labeled as shared and owned don't neatly fit into the controlled or uncontrolled categories either, as neither category is specific enough to accommodate the varied characteristics of online channels.

To more distinctly resolve these categorizations, Professor Browning adapted the controlled/uncontrolled model by adding a third category, *semicontrolled*, defined by messages over which the sender and receiver share marked degrees of control. From an organizational standpoint, these messages are arguably the most difficult to manage because of their high degree of volatility. Taken together, *controlled*, *uncontrolled* and *semicontrolled* information forms the three elements of the **CUS Information Model**, which sits at a useful Goldilocks point between the other models discussed earlier. We use this approach to organize Part 3 of this textbook, with Chapters 10 and 11 focusing on uncontrolled media, Chapters 12 and 13 on controlled media, and Chapters 14 and 15 on semicontrolled media.

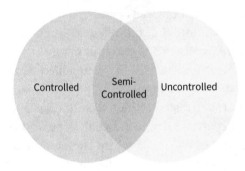

FIGURE 1.3  **The CUS Information Model.** Strategic communication practitioners exercise varying levels of control over messages, which is often predetermined by the media they target.

### Distinct Target Audiences

Beyond the types of media used and the varying levels of control over message content, advertising, marketing and public relations have traditionally differed in regard to the audiences they target.[36] Marketing primarily—arguably exclusively—communicates with customers and consumers. In large part, this reflects marketing's primary function, which is to promote goods and services.

Advertising shares this promotional goal. Thus customers and consumers are advertising's primary audience as well. However, occasionally, advertising is employed to communicate with other niche audiences. Through business-to-business communication in particular, an organization might purchase trade publication advertisements to reach suppliers and distributors. Additionally, publicly traded organizations commonly advertise in both popular and financial media as a way to communicate with investors.

Public relations by far communicates with the widest array of audiences. This is due to the broad function of public relations, which the Public Relations Society of America (PRSA) defines as "a strategic communication process that builds mutually beneficial relationships between organizations and their publics."[37] That's a difficult and diverse task because organizations are responsible to a vast number of stakeholders. Building relationships with each of these groups improves an organization's chance of achieving important goals, as it builds the perception of the equitable resource exchange we discussed earlier.

## Persuasion: The Unifying Purpose

So if we consider only the types of media each profession commonly uses and the audiences each target, the distinctions among marketing, advertising and public relations are readily apparent. Here's a simple definition for each profession:

**Marketing** employs controlled and semicontrolled media to communicate with customers/consumers to influence their opinions of organizational products and/or services and in turn persuade them to purchase those products or services.

**Advertising** employs paid media to communicate with target audiences, most often customers/consumers, to persuade those audiences to adopt an attitude, express an opinion or take some behavior that benefits the organization.

**Public relations** employs controlled, uncontrolled and semicontrolled media to communicate with a wide variety of target audiences to persuade those audiences to adopt an attitude, express an opinion or take some behavior that benefits the organization and ideally benefits members of the target audience as well.

At first glance, these professions appear somewhat disparate, but on closer inspection, you'll see a unifying theme: persuasion. As authors of this text, we contend that *persuasion is the aim of all strategic communication*, regardless of form and irrespective of the subdiscipline under which a specific practice may fall. You will see this theme reiterated throughout this text for two main reasons. First, we find that this understanding of marketing, advertising and public relations more accurately reflects today's professional environment, where the fields more often work in concert than in competition.[38] Second, as educators we feel it profoundly important that you understand exactly how versatile and transferrable many of your strategic communication skills will be, particularly your writing ability.

Our personal educational backgrounds are more firmly grounded in public relations than either marketing or advertising. However, we've found in our professional experiences that our knowledge of public relations, and in particular the foundational elements of persuasive communication, have enabled us to produce successful marketing and advertising content. Moreover, this type of crossover has become more the norm than the exception.

It's not enough to understand how to manage media buys, write creative copy, build relationships with media gatekeepers or design product packaging. Even within the relatively narrow confines of persuasive writing, it's critically important that you understand how to use various media, whether it be paid, earned, shared or owned; print, audio, visual or digital; or communicated to mass, specialized or individual audiences. You have to know it all—or at least demonstrate basic familiarity.

**Strategic Thought**

Look back to the "Lessons From Life" vignette at the opening of this chapter. Now that you've familiarized yourself with a number of communication theories, can you identify exactly which theories were at play in this story? How did they manifest?

Moreover, you must not only demonstrate knowledge of these concepts but also consistently apply that knowledge to deliver results that advance organizational goals. That means meeting objectives through exercising sound strategic thought grounded in functional communication tactics.

But you'll never become a successful writer without first maturing as a critical thinker. You must understand your organization and its stakeholders, your audiences and their interests, your media environment and situational surroundings—as well as a host of other factors too numerous to mention here. That's where theory can help you. If you let theory guide your strategic choices, it will serve as the glue that binds abstract and ambitious organizational goals to concrete and achievable communication tactics. Such knowledge will propel you to a string of professional successes as you embark on any one of a multitude of potential career paths.

## SUMMARY

- To effectively exercise persuasive writing skills, you'll need to understand various theories of human behavior, particularly those relating to media effects and audience response. These theories help connect organizational goals to the communication tactics persuasive writers use to achieve those goals.

- Marketing, advertising and public relations can be categorized in many ways. One is based on the type of media they most often employ, be it paid, earned, shared or owned; or controlled, uncontrolled or semicontrolled. Another is based on the types of audiences with which they most often communicate.

- Despite these differences, advertising, marketing and public relations are all connected by the unifying purpose of persuasion. All strategic writing seeks to either reinforce or alter individuals' attitudes, opinions and/or actions.

### Scenario Prompts: Communication Theory

You'll find Scenario Prompts on pp. 367–386 of this textbook. While they vary in subject and difficulty, they help you hone your critical thinking and strategic writing skills. The following are best suited to this chapter's topics.

Management: 4.3, 6.2, 6.3, 9.1, 10.3, 10.4

# Transforming Communication Theory Into Working Models of Persuasion

## From Abstract Thought to Actionable Ideas

Strategic communicators are paid to persuade people, but some people—even those who work in these fields—think persuasion is a dirty word.

We don't really understand this line of thought. Using false information to manipulate people is bad. Coercion is bad. Blackmail is bad.

Persuasion is life.

Why do you frequent one fast-food franchise over another? Why do you have one romantic partner rather than another? Why are you a Republican and not a Democrat? Why are you in a college classroom now instead of climbing Mount Kilimanjaro?

You were persuaded to do this over that by cost, accessibility, peer pressure, advertising, parental influence, religious experiences, threat of jail, media socialization or billions of other permutations of motives. These motives, calculated within your own limitations in what you were able or willing to exchange to fulfill those motives, are the essence of persuasion.

Yet persuasion, as ever present as it is, continues to be one of the most difficult intellectual activities to explain. I used to begin my introductory communication classes by asking my students this question: What is your first memory? The question usually provoked some lovely tale of a trip to the zoo with a kind grandfather, a family vacation where the student first got to paddle the canoe or getting a puppy.

I'd then relate my first memory. Growing up the fifth of seven farm children, we began working young. One of my first chores was pumping water by hand for 30 or 40 hogs in an outdoor pen. I was probably 4, maybe 5 years old.

I remember my father watching me as I jumped just a little bit to put my full weight onto the pump handle to bring the water 35 feet to the surface. After my father was satisfied with my primitive proficiency at pumping water, he lifted me onto a wide board atop the fence around the pigpen and held my hand as I balanced my way across it.

Thinking they were going to be fed, the squealing hogs rushed the fence. It was then my father started the second, and seemingly most important, instruction. He warned me that if I ever walked along that board by myself and fell into the pen's muck, the hogs would rip open my stomach with their sharp teeth and eat my intestines.

The lesson: Don't ever walk on the board surrounding the hog pen.

So how, I asked my students, can you expect me to react the same way to my first memory as you do? You got a new puppy—I was told I would be eaten by pigs.

Each of us begins with a unique founding story. In turn, every second we experience after, and the hundreds of millions of memories we could have collected from all those incidents, provide the material to construct a totally unique person.

The designation, *you,* comprises a never-to-be repeated conglomeration of memories. *You* never lived before and will never live again. And with every second that comes today, and in the years ahead, *you* will add another layer to that identity.

That's one of the problems of persuasion theory. Any theory that attempts to say, "Do A and B will happen," is inherently limited. While all humans have almost an identical DNA structure, behaviorally, each of us is a one-of-a-kind creature.

To counter those difficulties, this chapter translates Chapter 1's theories into working models that analyze likely behavioral possibilities by individual humans. In most cases, we'll usually end up saying, "It depends." It depends on the audiences' backgrounds, economic statuses, moral platforms and a thousand other individual characteristics.

In fact, we'll argue "it depends" is actually a universal maxim, and your greatest source of potential error is in thinking your experiences are shared by everyone else on the planet.

—*William Thompson*

## What You Know

- Communication theories help explain a broad range of human interactions with both other humans and institutions.

- Effective communication about an issue focuses messages on those likely to respond and uses fewer resources to communicate to audiences uninterested or unable to respond.

## What You'll Learn

- Why communication models should focus on the interests of the audience, not the speaker

- How sequential theories of human decision-making fail to adequately predict behavior

- Why an economic model more perfectly describes communication engagement and decision-making

- Why the most accurate persuasion models suggest individuals take multiple paths to make decisions

## Strategic Communication Management

### Opinions Into Action

With more public relations, advertising and marketing professionals working in all areas of American life—for nonprofit organizations, corporations, citizen advocacy groups and government—the field has never been more competitive. Clients insist that practitioners prove how communication can generate actions and move opinion to create advantages for their organizations.

Action. That's a key word for persuasive communicators. Miller and Levine define **persuasion** as "at a minimum ... generat[ing] some type of cognitive, affective or behavioral modification in the target."[1]

Too many laypeople believe persuasion is the act of communicating a message in the hope of convincing someone to believe something. As we will reinforce throughout this text, that's a **speaker-centered communication process**. But convincing someone isn't enough. The speaker-centered approach focuses on the communicator's actions. We're going to focus on the responses of the audience.

In light of the aforementioned definition, let's examine persuasion from the point of view of an individual audience member. As a communicator, you can talk all you want. You can use complicated arguments or offer cash-back rebates. You can suggest the dire consequences of failing to yield to your words. But, at the least, if your audience has not moved down the path toward expressing a different or more energetic outlook than before, persuasion has not occurred. It's as simple as that.

Among professional communicators, persuasion means motivating a person to take an action. That action might be buying a product, contributing to a local volunteer organization, or voting for a political candidate, among thousands of others.

Thus persuasion constitutes a step beyond simple communication. The mere act of communicating doesn't fulfill your goals as a persuasive writer. If you're issuing a news release only because "that's what we've always done," you're most likely wasting your efforts.

Such mismanagement most often occurs when we focus on communication activities rather than on the goals we want to accomplish by undertaking those activities. To put it in a different light, it would be like an auto manufacturer establishing a goal of making 300,000 cars next year yet having no plan about how to sell them.

Instead, we suggest practitioners adopt a results-focused system for managing communication efforts. Those results should contribute to the goals of the organization that employs us. In essence: persuasion.

## Rethinking How We Measure Success

The idea of coordinating communication goals with organizational goals sounds obvious. But even today, strategic communication professionals often fail to link their communication goals with company objectives. Fundamentally, this means they fail to highlight the positive contributions their communication efforts make to the company's overall performance. Instead, persuasive communicators too often evaluate their success by the number of social media posts they've written, the number of awards their ads won or the volume of articles they placed in popular media outlets. But distinguishing between communication products and communication outcomes is critical.

For business executives who evaluate employees based on how they contribute to company profits, a communication practitioner's attempt to justify her salary by boasting of having written 20 tweets in a week's time seems rather pathetic. A more persuasive claim to prove her value to the company is that one of those tweets targeted a tech journalist, who in turn wrote a feature about the new capabilities of the company's state-of-the-art industrial robot. That story in turn generated five inquiries from potential customers.

To many people, this seems a subtle difference. If the practitioner didn't pitch media contacts, she wouldn't have gotten the story. But if no editor responded, and if no customer was stimulated into action, then technically persuasion would not have taken place.

The remainder of this book will emphasize this singular orientation toward the receiver and the receiver's actions. This approach, which we title the **audience-centered communication process**, reverses the typical approach of many standard communication models.

## Traditional Communication Models: A Reality Check

### Speaker-Centered Models

The audience-centered system assumes persuasive communication isn't encompassed by a person deciding to communicate about an issue. For professional communicators, communication begins by determining why (or even if) a particular audience might respond to our message.

Again, this may seem a trivial difference. Yet PR practitioners too often waste time trying to convince people who have already decided on an issue while ignoring groups interested in and/or important to their cause. Efficient, cost-effective communication requires knowing how to select audiences that have the greatest potential to respond to our communication.

That's not necessarily the focus of many traditional persuasion models. Let's start with Harold Lasswell, as his is the most basic communication model.[2]

Lasswell perceived the speaker as initiating and dictating each step of communication acts.[3] As you can see in Figure 2.1, the model concentrates on what the communicator wants. That's why we call it a speaker-centered model: the audience's only role is to receive the message and respond to it at the conclusion of the communication act.

**FIGURE 2.1 A Speaker-Centered Model.** The only engagement with the receiver is when she responds to the message. Later versions of this model suggested that in cases where the audience misinterpreted the speaker's meaning, it was because characteristics of the message were altered before the message was received. These physical, psychological and sociological factors were called *noise*.

**Lasswell's Linear Model of Communication**

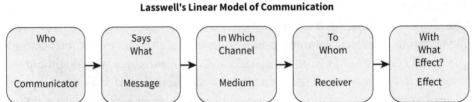

Lasswell's model and its subsequent modifications assert that communication occurs when an individual (a speaker) decides on a message and transmits it through her chosen medium. That medium could be a social media post, a newspaper article, a rock thrown through a window, or millions of other options. The medium delivers the message to a receiver, and communication has occurred.

Or has it? What happens when a manufacturer's PR practitioner decides to convey a message about a stupendous technological breakthrough in microchip technology? The practitioner emails a written story pitch to a news show's producer. Among the producer's hundreds of emails, she sees the practitioner's name, remembers she has gotten a whole string of the company's useless, irrelevant pitches and deletes the email without even opening it.

But what if we examine this relationship from the receiver's perspective. No matter what message a writer wishes to convey, audience self-interest dictates what the writer can hope to accomplish. It's silly to think any message can be written without acknowledging the receiver's characteristics and capacities. For instance, the writer isn't the final arbiter of the medium she employs to deliver her message. Remember uses and gratification theory from Chapter 1? That determination is strictly governed by the media platforms the target audience has chosen for itself.

## Does Everyone Always Communicate the Same Way?

There's another common issue with many traditional communication models. In the quest to simplify the complex act of communication, they make the spurious assumption that every person approaches every situation in the exact same way.

A significant number of social science models suffer from this fault, attempting to explain persuasion through **hierarchy models**. There have been many hierarchy models (see Figure 2.2), but the idea behind each is basically the same: When people determine whether to adopt a new idea, their decision process moves through a rigid sequence of programmed steps termed a hierarchy.

Perhaps the best known such model is **Maslow's hierarchy of needs**, which asserts people meet their needs in a definite sequence. Maslow suggested that until the basic needs for food and clothing are met, people don't spend much time thinking about or working to satisfy their need for housing. Until they have a roof over their heads, they don't pay much attention to having a nice house. According to Maslow, it's only after they have a nice house that impresses their neighbors that they begin to seek answers concerning their relationship with their creator and their place in the world.[4]

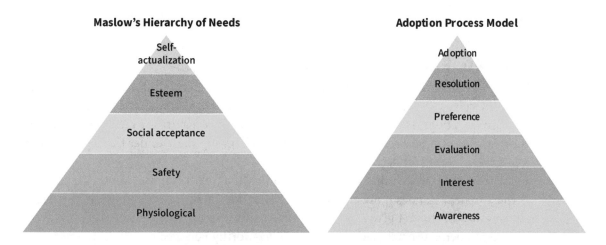

**FIGURE 2.2 Hierarchical Persuasion Models.** We've illustrated these models as pyramids because one must complete the foundational elements at one level before moving to the next. While hierarchical models credibly describe rational decision-making processes, they fail to predict many decision processes based on impulse or emotion.

A hierarchical model more targeted toward communication and persuasion is the **adoption process model**. First formulated to explore how people respond to innovative technology, it then was adapted to examine how people respond to new ideas. It too asserts that people go through a definite sequence as they acquire new information or new attitudes.

The adoption process model states that individuals first develop an awareness of an idea or product and then an interest in it. Then they go through a period of evaluation and trial, from which comes a preference and then a resolution of intention. Finally, they adopt the new idea as their own.[5]

### Skipping Steps: The Flaw in Hierarchical Models

While these models helped advance our understanding of communication, they often fail to predict actual human behavior in run-of-the-mill scenarios. For example, Maslow believes survival, safety and social needs must be satisfied before a person will attempt to satisfy esteem needs. If that's true, why would a college student sell all her possessions and backpack through Asia in search of enlightenment at the feet of a spiritual master? Obviously, all her lower-level needs won't be met, but she is acting—growling stomach, aching feet and all—to satisfy a self-actualization need.

Similar difficulties arise with the adoption process model. When an 11-year-old declares she favors the Republican candidate in the next election or a business executive buys a new brand of gum, it's hard to trace a hierarchical thought process that led from awareness through evaluation to these actions. The child may be repeating arguments her parents have made. The executive buys a brand of gum because she likes the packaging. There's not much climbing through the hierarchy in these decisions. The girl may be reacting based on her parents' party affiliation. The executive acts because the consequences of a bad decision are insignificant; she can afford 50 cents to sample the new gum brand.

### How Are People Persuaded? It Depends

So it seems Lasswell's model incorrectly assumes human communication occurs when a sender decides to talk, and hierarchical models inadequately predict the way people react in many situations. However, there are models that more accurately guide us in our persuasive tasks as professional communicators. We'll group these under the umbrella term **audience-centered models**.

We're sure you're familiar with the old riddle, "If a tree falls in the woods, and nobody is there to hear it, does it make a sound?" Yes, it does make a sound, but the persuasive communicator doesn't give a damn because nobody is there to hear it. You could craft the world's perfect social media post, a Pulitzer-worthy newspaper feature or graphically stunning ad, but if your target audience can't attend to the message, well, you're just a tree falling in a vacant forest.

Audience-centered models, such as the informal one Professor Thompson constructed to guide persuasive writing, adopt a different perspective from those of sender-centered approaches. In so doing, they more ably guide persuasive communicators in making better message choices.[6]

The audience-centered communication process stems from ideas formulated by William McGuire. McGuire drew attention to the aspect of communication that started only after Lasswell's model ended, arguing that successful communication is dictated by the receiver's response. Communication, McGuire reasoned, hasn't occurred merely because the audience receives a message; communication does not occur until the audience decides to "yield" to the message.[7]

In Thompson's audience-centered communication model, as in McGuire's, the receiver arbitrates communication success. However, Thompson's model also integrates the sender/message/medium steps of the Lasswell model. Figure 2.3 shows the audience-centered communication model. A discussion of the basic questions that underlie each step follows and is summarized in Memory Memo 2.1.

## Audience-Centered Model

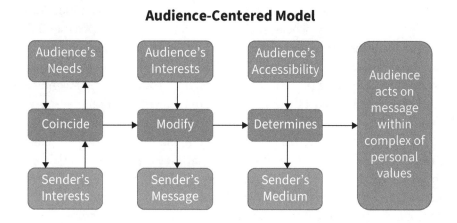

**FIGURE 2.3 Audience-Centered Model.** The audience-centered model starts by considering the capacities, needs and habits of the audience and then sculpts a strategy for engaging strategic publics.

## Steps in the Audience-Centered Model

1. **Does your audience have a reason for listening?** During the communication process, the receiver decides whether to attend to the message. Does the information the sender wants to communicate have any relevance or interest to the receiver? If it doesn't, the audience won't pay any attention.

2. **Does the message have to be changed to influence your audience?** Is the message presented in a way the intended audience can understand, and recognize it as meant for them? Is the vocabulary too complex or too simple? Are the examples relevant to her prior experiences or future

self-interests? If the message isn't designed to draw the right audience, the intended communication won't occur.

3. **Do you reach your audience with the medium you've chosen?** Has the speaker chosen a medium the desired public uses? To cite a most obvious example, if you're trying to communicate to children and you place your message in The Wall Street Journal, you haven't effectively communicated.

4. **Does your audience react the way you predicted?** Has the receiver acted on the message in a way that indicates she has understood the message as the sender intended?

### The Complex of Personal Values

**Strategic Thought**

During the 2016 presidential election, turnout among the voting-age public was 61.4%, on par with the past several presidential election cycles.[8] Consider the complex of personal values of the roughly 40% of the electorate who sat on the sidelines. What past experiences do you think drives the choice not to vote? How did they develop? As a persuasive writer, how would you address them to boost voter turnout?

Even when you've followed all the preceding steps, you still must consider that because your audience's experiences may differ from yours, those individuals may interpret your message differently from the way you would. This individual outlook is what we term the **complex of personal values**. It's an individual's layers of personal experiences, socialization, faults and strengths that inflect her predisposition in assigning a meaning to a communication act. It's what makes cognitive dissonance so powerful: Receivers who don't want to believe your evidence-based assertion will simply ignore your message, misinterpret your message to support their values or search for information that supports their belief system.

Consider the Benetton fashion brand, praised for its years of advertising campaigns that draw attention to societal issues. Yet sometimes even they failed to accurately predict their audience's interpretation of its message. Benetton's marketing executives thought the ad in Figure 2.4 displayed the clothing company's commitment to racial harmony. However, the cherubic, smiling white girl posed with an unsmiling African American boy whose hair has been styled into what appear to be horns, sparked complaints that it communicated a statement of the moral inferiority of Black people.[9]

You can see Benetton following the Lasswell communication model. The speaker decided to communicate, formulated a message and chose a medium through which to transmit that message, which was then indeed accepted and decoded by the receiver. While you might argue communication happened, the persuasive communication act failed. Stimulating a discussion concerning how Benetton was racist appeared to be the exact opposite of the communication objective the company wanted. The lesson: Instead of being obsessed with the information we want to communicate, we should be sensitive to the information our publics are in a position to receive, as well as how their complex of personal values prompts them to adopt a particular understanding of that message.

**FIGURE 2.4 Advertisement from the "United Colors of Benetton" Campaign Intended to Display the Company's Advocacy for Racial Justice.** The strategy was to expose stereotypes equating Blackness with darkness, anger, hatred and, at times, even evil. Thus the very dark-complexioned child has his hair styled to resemble devil horns. In contrast, the white child, oppositely pale-skinned, provokes association with the fleshy angels floating above the holy characters in European Renaissance paintings. While the company's art director later explained that he had hoped shedding light on such imagery would expose the nonsensical nature of those associations, instead the campaign provoked accusations that Benetton was perpetuating that very racial stereotype for shock value and profit.

## Making the Model Work

At this point, you may just want to throw up your hands in frustration. If you can't persuade someone who doesn't want to be persuaded, is persuasion impossible?

It's perhaps not that dire. While acknowledging the limits of persuasion among resistant publics, there are many other publics with as-yet unformed ideas who can be influenced, and others whose personal values can be strengthened so they will act on their beliefs.

Strategic communication demands you determine the audiences most likely to accept and act upon your message. It asks you to formulate a message that prioritizes that audience's motives for accepting new information. It also requires you to calculate the cost-effectiveness of investments you make in communicating to publics.

The audience-centered approach situates you in a frame of reference that makes this job easier.

> **MEMORY MEMO 2.1** Audience-Centered Questions
>
> - Does your audience have a reason for listening?
> - Does the message have to be changed to influence your audience?
> - Do you reach your audience with the medium you've chosen?
> - Does your audience react the way you predicted?

## Targeting People Who Care: Situational Theory

For audience-centered communication to be effective, we need a way to predict when people might be interested in listening and yielding to a message. Equally important, we must find those publics that aren't interested in our message or that can't or won't assess our message fairly.

James Grunig developed a model predicting when people will take these steps. His **situational theory of publics** is summarized in Memory Memo 2.2.

> **MEMORY MEMO 2.2**  Situational Theory of Publics
>
> The best targets for a communication campaign are people who
>
> - see our issue as a problem or opportunity
> - feel the issue affects their lives
> - believe they can do something to solve the issue

Along with its later significant adjustments, the model maintains that if we can identify the people who are likely to communicate about a situation, as well as those people who probably won't, we can design a cost-effective communication plan.[10] That's logical, because we can then devote more time and resources to the relatively smaller number of people whose support can help (or whose opposition can hinder) our institution's activities.

### The Search for Information Seekers

Grunig split communication behaviors into two categories, which he called *information seeking* and *information processing*. Information seekers are individuals eager to receive and accept a message about a specific subject. They often take the message and communicate it to others, thus increasing the original communication's impact and leading additional people to accept that viewpoint. Think back to the two-step flow model from Chapter 1: Information seekers are the people most likely to translate information into action, be it their own or someone else's.

Information processors, on the other hand, exhibit low involvement regarding a given topic. They don't look for information but merely process what's presented to them. They are unlikely to act after receiving information or convey their knowledge to others.

However, a person can be an information processor in one situation and an information seeker in another. Situational theory (hence its name) suggests a person's communication behavior depends on the situation. Another example of "it depends."

When you slump in front of your computer watching the ninth commercial for the same car company during a 60-minute video, you are probably an information processor. You are aware a commercial is running and could possibly name the advertiser if someone asked you. But you are no longer actively gathering information from the commercial, and you're probably not going to share information about the commercial with friends or family.

Let's observe you in your PR classroom instead. You bought the whole seat with your tuition, but you only need its edge. You are poised, eager to receive new information, keen to share your insights with classmates during the discussion. You want to discover more material, knowing that in the long term it will be important to your professional life and, in the short term, it will impact your hopes of graduating. In this, our professorial fantasy, you are an information seeker.

Situational theory readily translates into persuasive writing situations. An office manager, burned out after 14 years in the position, comes home and drops into her recliner's depths. Listlessly scrolling through email messages, her communication efforts with her family, even in response to direct questions, are limited to heaving sighs.

But when she opens an online video showing her college's current field hockey team, she suddenly becomes animated. She discusses the shortcomings of her school's coach, recites brand characteristics of field hockey equipment and, red-faced and panting, demonstrates the prowess she possessed decades ago.

Here is a near full-time information processor—until we awaken her passion for field hockey. When communicating about field hockey, she is an information seeker, attending games, following field hockey websites and trying to recruit new players into the sport. In this one situation, she has translated information into action. While she is a seemingly listless communicator in many other areas, for this topic she is a prime candidate for persuasive messages.

### Predicting Information Seekers

Grunig isolated three elements to help determine whether an individual will be an information processor or an information seeker in a particular situation. He asserts that people are most likely to be information seekers, and thus the best targets for our communication efforts, when they (1) recognize some issue as a problem, (2) feel the problem affects their lives somehow and (3) perceive few barriers that prevent them from doing something to solve the problem.

1. **Problem Recognition: Can You See the Dilemma?** Typically, people must perceive something as a problem before they will become information seekers. Let's say a charity tries to raise money in the United States to fund classes for girls in French-speaking countries in Africa.

    For many audience members, educational shortfalls for African girls don't register as a problem. Yet it is perceived as an enormous problem for those who feel worldwide economic and social improvements depend on encouraging female voices in patriarchal societies—Africa's as well as our own.

    In this situation, as you might expect, those concerned about gender equality are much more likely to become information seekers, gathering information about the African schools and communicating their support to others. People who see the charity's messages but don't think African girls' schooling rises to the level of a problem will receive the charity's ads passively and be less likely to communicate their support (or displeasure) about the project to others. In short, they are more likely to be information processors.

    Recognize that situational theory characterizes "problem" very broadly, encompassing not only negative elements but positive opportunities as well. To a French textbook publishing executive, U.S. charities funding education in French-speaking African regions presents a different "problem," which also influences the likelihood she'll become a communication seeker. She might immediately contact charity officials to determine the project's feasibility and scope so she can pitch her publisher's French-language textbooks.

2. **Level of Involvement: Is It Your Problem?** Additionally, we can predict whether an individual will be an information seeker or processor in a situation if she perceives herself as highly involved in the issue.

   For instance, a dairy farmer may recognize that gang violence in cities is a serious problem. But she doesn't believe she's responsible for the situation or that her small-town life is threatened by urban problems.

   This lack of involvement in the issue would make the farmer less likely to seek information about gang violence and unlikely to communicate with others about the subject. However, urban high school principals with higher involvement levels might seek out information, attend conferences and speak to groups of parents and students about the problem.

3. **Constraint Recognition: Can You Do Something About It?** Finally, the likelihood of people communicating about a situation is affected by whether they foresee factors limiting their behavior and their ability to bring about change. For instance, if a woman watching a television program hears about an investment opportunity that promises a tremendous return, she will probably seek information about the investment only if she has enough money to invest. Otherwise, she will merely process the information, as there is little she can do to take advantage of the situation.

Similarly, if a women's rights activist hears about a march in Washington, she'll likely want to learn about the march, its organizers and even bus transportation and hotel accommodations in the capital. In that situation, she's an information seeker. But if the march is scheduled for a day when she knows she must make a vital presentation to her company's board of directors, she will merely record and process general information about the march and not seek other information about it. When a situation presents barriers to taking constructive action, we usually become information processors.

## Categorizing Publics Based on the Situational Theory

Knowing these three elements, PR practitioners can more accurately target their communication efforts to the information seekers eager to receive information about a situation and act based on that information. By targeting these people who recognize a problem, feel personally involved in the situation and do not see barriers to solving the problem, we have guideposts to select receptive and cost-efficient audiences for our persuasive messages (Figure 2.5).

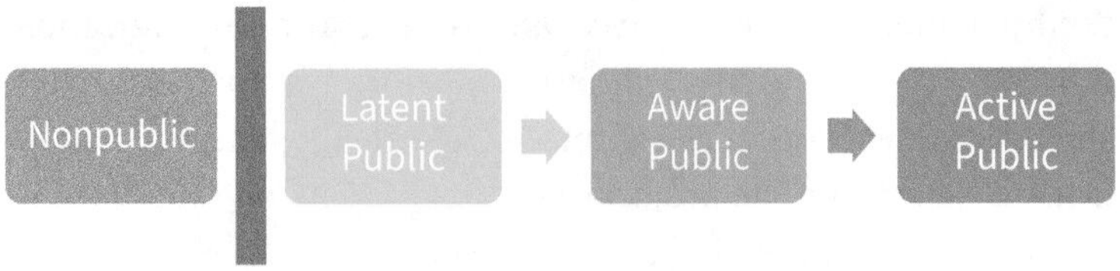

**Strategic Thought**

Were you seriously considering taking an action or buying a product but decided not to because a barrier prevented you? Can you think of things the organization could have offered you to overcome those barriers, prompting you to take the action?

**FIGURE 2.5 Segmenting Publics Using the Situational Theory.** Based on varying levels of problem recognition, issue involvement and perceived constraints, publics can be segmented based on how likely they are to seek information and act on persuasive messages.

After individuals are categorized based on their likelihood of displaying information-seeking behaviors, they can be further segmented into different types of publics. Each of those publics merit varying levels of organizational attention and differ in their response to organizational messages.[11]

The first group is called a *nonpublic*. Anyone who has no interest or stake in an issue falls into this category. While it may at first seem strange to even consider such a classification, recognize that for persuasive communicators, it's just as important to avoid communicating with disinterested publics as it is to effectively communicate with targeted stakeholders. There's no need to waste their time and yours.

We're thus left with three categories of interested publics. The first is *latent publics*. These individuals might conceivably be interested in the issue at hand, but they are uninformed or underinformed regarding it. If offered relevant information, these latent publics can easily become aware publics. *Aware publics* recognize some problem or opportunity. As they increasingly see themselves involved in that issue and when they recognize few barriers to acting, they engage with the issue in some way. They then become *active publics.*

Individuals and groups thus progress from latent to active publics as they display greater tendencies of information-seeking behavior. As publics move toward more active states, they become increasingly attuned to persuasive communication messages and potentially more receptive to what we as strategic communicators have to say.

## Predicting When Messages Become Action: The Learn-Feel-Do Persuasion Model
### Building Uncertainty Into Communication Models

While situational theory offers insights concerning how we can isolate a receptive audience, we still haven't determined how they'll act. Until we model the audience's decision process, we can't fully describe persuasion.

Again, "It depends."

It depends on the type and level of involvement of the person considering the issue or the product. It depends on the importance the person attaches to the issue. It depends on whether the people making decisions rely on emotional or rational considerations as they ponder their choices.

A model developed by the Foote, Cone & Belding advertising agency helps explain factors people use to make decisions by focusing on several of the hierarchical models' inherent problems.

As we detailed earlier, people don't necessarily proceed through every level of the hierarchy before making a decision. Often, their level of involvement and the consequences of making a bad decision dictate the number of steps they take. Also, the hierarchy isn't always in bottom-to-top sequence. The hierarchies generally specify that a person learns about an issue, then develops and internalizes a feeling or belief about the issue and then does something to reinforce or confirm that feeling. However, in some decision processes, those components occur in a different sequence.

To correct some of these faults, Foote, Cone & Belding researchers developed the "**learn-feel-do**" model (Figure 2.6).[12] They believed people approach buying decisions about products (1) according to the importance they attach to their decision and (2) whether the purchasing decision is made to satisfy an emotional or a rational need. In short, there are times when people adopt an opinion about an issue or product without much thinking.

Also, people usually don't make decisions dictated by their emotional needs without logic slipping in to a greater or lesser degree. Similarly, logical decisions are usually colored by emotion. Reinforcing this adage of "it depends," the learn-feel-do model asserts that we should look at this decision-making process as a continuum. People assess how important the consequences of making the wrong decision are and whether they emphasize emotional or rational rewards when they make specific decisions.

**FIGURE 2.6 The Learn-Feel-Do Persuasion Model.** The learn-feel-do model asserts that individuals consider many factors in making a decision, or sometimes don't think about it at all. By analyzing a decision-making process in terms of the rational thought used and the consequences of the decision, practitioners can more accurately predict the decision-making sequence in a specific situation.

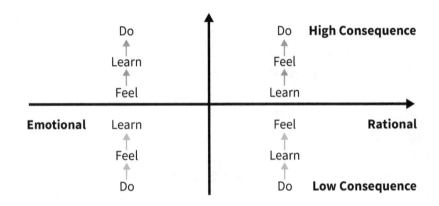

### Patterns of Decision-Making

To represent these variations, the learn-feel-do persuasion model is presented as a grid with two perpendicular axes (Figure 2.6). The vertical line represents the importance of the decision, ranging from situations in which the consequences of making the wrong decision are minor, up to those in which they could be devastating. The horizontal axis represents the degree of rational thought involved in a decision process, ranging from completely emotional to completely rational decisions.

Different decisions entail different strategies for different people. In situations in which the decision is important and rational processes dominant (such as in deciding to buy an expensive machine for a factory), people usually follow a learn-feel-do hierarchy. That is, they learn all they can about competing brands of machines, develop a conviction about the machine they have decided on, and then purchase the equipment. You'll notice this sequence follows the steps outlined in the hierarchy models.

But what happens when someone determines her stand on abortion? It's a very important issue. But emotional and not rational factors often predominate. In those cases, we often have a feeling about what we want to believe before we've developed any balanced knowledge about all the issues involved in the controversy. As Chapter 1's cognitive dissonance discussion highlighted, people often seek information to justify their initial emotional reactions so they can carry out their original intentions with a good conscience. They are using the feel-learn-do hierarchy of decision-making.

Let's look at another quadrant in the model. The lower-left corner illustrates the do-feel-learn sequence, a high-emotion, low-consequence decision in which emotions and the desire to satisfy immediate needs greatly influence the process.

An example of a do-feel-learn behavior process? When a waiter offers you dessert after a satisfying meal. You've been trying to lose a little weight, but the dessert menu excites an emotional response in you, which you justify by telling yourself you've already violated your diet tonight anyway. This decision can be summarized as follows: You anticipate an emotional reward and minimal perceived consequences to making the wrong decision. You do (eat the cake), feel (great about the chocolate rush) and learn (from the scale that you'll never get fit engaging in this sort of behavior).

The last quadrant is the do-learn-feel sequence in the lower right. Again, we have a low-involvement decision, but here thought is involved in the decision-making process. For example, say a woman contemplates whether to attend a free lecture on plastic surgery sponsored by a hospital. She had been considering removing her varicose veins but didn't want to spend the money or risk the pressure she fears the surgeon might put on her during a personal visit. As we've established the context, her thought process might look like this: By attending a free lecture, she can act on a relatively unimportant issue (do), research the more consequential issue (learn), and then develop a conviction (feel).

> **MEMORY MEMO 2.3** Knowing Your Way Through the Learn-Feel-Do Model
>
> - DO happens first in low-consequence decisions
> - DO happens last in high-consequence decisions
> - FEEL happens earlier in emotional decisions
> - LEARN happens earlier in rational decisions

## Reframing Rewards Through Communication

Learn-feel-do analysis will directly influence your writing. If you suspect the audience's primary motivation is emotional, the first words and opening paragraphs should present that emotional reward. You should wait to discuss rational rewards until later in the document. High-consequence decisions will usually require more explanation and a longer document than will low-consequence decisions. Low-consequence decisions often need little elaboration. For instance, a midnight yell of "beer run" in a dorm hallway can drive action quite effectively.

There are other powerful message-creation strategies that emerge from the learn-feel-do analysis. By reformatting an action you can encourage potential targets to think the decision belongs to a different quadrant in the model. For instance, you could separate a very high-consequence decision into a series of less consequential steps.

In the surgery scenario, we ask an audience member to attend a free presentation on cosmetic surgery. But let's say instead we had proposed the woman initially submit a down payment on the surgery. That significant financial commitment transforms the decision into a high-consequence one and likely dampens the audience's response.

Similarly, the practitioner might transform the decision from a high-consequence/ emotional-reward decision into the rational half of the decision matrix. Offering statistics about the surgeon's universally favorable reviews from patients and the offer of a half-price procedure might prompt them to reconceptualize the decision as a rational reward. The persuasive writer can thus proactively recast a persuasion task among the quadrants of the learn-feel-do model, or segment communication campaigns based on the audience's response to particular persuaders.

## Predicting Motives: Social Exchange Theory

We've now analyzed who is most likely to act on a message, and are able to predict what sequence an audience member will follow during a decision process. Our series of audience-centered models now turns to perhaps the most important element in persuasion: What motivates a particular person to act?

As we've repeatedly emphasized, our audience members are bombarded with thousands of messages each day. We've asserted that they generally choose to attend only to those messages that relate to their own self-interests. Think about it. You have only 24 hours in a day. Say your message requires three minutes of the receiver's time to process. Three minutes devoted to a persuasive writer's message is a significant investment, particularly amid scores of other messages struggling for your attention at that very time. Social exchange theory (briefly discussed in Chapter 1) gives us practical and significant insight into the thought process through which readers flip the toggle switch on your persuasive writing: to scan and abandon, or scan and engage.[13]

Social exchange is basically a restatement of pure economic theory. You could buy brand A, B or C of a virtually identical product—say hypoallergenic laundry detergent. Since all can clean clothes without aggravating your allergies, economic theory predicts you would buy the cheapest brand. However, you might buy a more expensive option because of brand loyalty, attractive packaging or a host of other factors. After all, those considerations also count as rewards the product offers you. As such, your buying decision is a calculation of how much value you think you'll get from your purchase minus how much it costs you to gain that value. Presented in its simplified form, your decision can be described like this:

**Rewards – Costs = Worth**

But there is a vital difference between standard economic theory and social exchange theory. Social exchange theory asserts transactions happen in all aspects of life, social as well as economic. It suggests each individual places valuations of rewards versus costs on laundry detergent but also on relationships with people and institutions. Take friendship: As long as the rewards (such as companionship, a study partner, use of a car) you obtain from a relationship with a friend exceed the costs (annoying late-night phone calls, unpaid personal loans, stealing your romantic partner), you're likely to remain friends.

Once that calculation becomes negative, and the costs of maintaining the friendship are more than the rewards, it's likely you'll pull back. Social exchange theory presumes every social interchange can be described as a calculated transaction. Brand and kinship loyalty, as well as adherence to social norms, all have a value from which you can calculate the relative advantages every choice offers.[14]

## Applying Economic Principles to Interpersonal Choices

Let's look at an example. How are you going to spend this Saturday night? Think about it. You will never have this particular Saturday night ever again. This Saturday night, and its rewards, will be gone forever come Sunday morning. Say you've got three choices: study for next week's midterm, go on a date or attend a distant cousin's wedding.

You need to study, but you've got a few more days to cram, and you're willing to risk a few points to have an evening out with your companion. OK, so abandon studying; rewards are greater for the date.

But then you remember your ailing grandmother, who lives in a far-away state. Three months ago, you promised her you would go to a family wedding she was attending. And the wedding couple will furnish free food and an open bar. That would help your equally ailing bank account survive the restaurant tab resulting from your date.

A possible calculation? On this particular Saturday night, you get more value from the status of "good granddaughter." You avoid the guilt you would feel if something happened to your grandmother before you made it home for the holidays. You get free food and alcohol. Going to the family wedding offers more value for less cost than going on your date. Final decision: go to the wedding.

Notice what's happening here? Social exchange theory assumes you're assigning relative values to all types of activities. There's not only your economic calculation of the money you will save by going to the wedding to eat free food. More importantly, you are valuing the social relationship with your grandmother more highly than the emotional and rational rewards from your potential date, who might offer friendship, sexual gratification, or expert help in studying for your test.

There are additional, very personal, rewards you use to justify your decision, and on which you can calculate a relative value. Even the avoidance of punishment is a reward. By attending the wedding, you can alleviate the awful guilt you would feel if your grandmother died before you could see her again. And it's not completely implausible that in the recesses of your thought processes, you may remember your aunt hinting that you might be

Imagine Jane, a single mother working in a low-paying retail job. She's back-to-school shopping with her beloved son, Eric. When Eric sees a Teenage Mutant Ninja Turtles backpack on a store shelf, he jumps with excitement. But it costs $80! What persuasion sequence would you predict Jane will go through in deciding whether to purchase the backpack? Why? How might that calculation change if Jane were a wealthy businesswoman?

in your grandmother's will. The chance of that outcome might be improved by making this effort to see your grandmother. Another data point in your social exchange calculation!

## The Calculating Audience

We speculate social exchange theory confronts you with an unattractive view of human behavior. Nevertheless, social exchange theory is tremendously relevant to the persuasive writer. We've described the writer's central problem: getting the target public to attend to your message from among the thousands people receive each day. Those competing messages issue not only from media but from family, pets, and street signs. Then there are the messages we interpret from black storm clouds or the begrudging crank of our car's fading battery. If we agree to acknowledge one message's presence, then we decide to abandon some other message, at least temporarily, from the overflowing pool filling each second of our lives.

Just as there was only one *this Saturday*, social exchange theory asserts there is only one time in your life that it will be 24.3 seconds after 1:48 p.m. today. Of all the relationships you could have, of all the activities you could undertake, even of all the messages present at that moment, you can select only one—at that moment. You may glance at your vibrating phone, notice that it's an automated call from your pharmacy and then immediately turn back to the professor's lecture. You might be singing along in your car when, a split second later, a police cruiser appears in your rearview mirror, prompting an end to your glorious in-car karaoke as you quickly hit the brake and check your speedometer.

It's useful to think of your mind as a toggle switch. You've got distractions A through quadruple Z in front of you. You must decide which message offers the greatest reward for your investment of time in it. Toggle—you switch to option B. But instantly you're ready to determine if there is another message to which you can toggle that will give you more value than the one you just chose.

And you do this every second of every day.

This may be hard to believe. But think how you can transition so quickly while immersed in study at the library. There may be scores of people whispering around you, the warm glow from dozens of laptops, the smell of coffee in the air. You're not distracted. But if a friend walking in front of you waves or whispers, you're highly likely to notice that one message.

*Know Your Baseline.* Here's how social exchange theory diagrams this complex situation. Every decision is a competition between three reward states. First is the *baseline*, which is the audience member's perception of what she expects out of the relationship with this person, this organization or, in our particular circumstances, our institution's message to her. This perception, which will drive her decision, is established, then changed over time by past interactions and knowledge of this type of event.

For instance, because an online store courteously refunded the purchase price when your new tablet didn't include a key feature, you'll likely be more receptive to the store's message when encountering it in the future. You would likely react less favorably to a message from another computer site—one that disregarded your complaints during previous transactions. This is your baseline for internet-based computer retailers. Of course, you'd have a different baseline for the DMV or your college's financial aid office.

This universal, ongoing calculation of what to expect from the relationship is formed from the hodgepodge of positive and negative encounters, as well as from reports from friends and media coverage. It's then implanted atop an individual's other tendencies and characteristics.

*Learn Your Options.* You compare that baseline of expectations with what economists call opportunity costs, which we term more directly as an *option*. Simply stated, you naturally think of what else you could do with the time, money and other resources that you would devote to this interaction. Would you gain more from another choice available to you?

Could you get the product at a cheaper price down the street? Does this potential employer have a record on civil rights that would be hard to justify to your friends? Do I spend the afternoon watching frolicking otter videos on my social media feed or do I go to the gym? Social exchange theory asserts you would consider all these decisions as if they were purchase decisions. If there is a better option out there than your existing baseline, you'll likely take it.

*Do the Math.* The calculation scale that social exchange theorists formulated helps us understand how a receiver acts moment to moment as she decides on what message to expend time. It predicts how an individual receiver will interpret her relationship with a contact or message and helps us predict the likely outcome of any given *encounter* with a receiver.[15]

Simply stated, the receiver judges every action within a matrix determined by (1) her perceptions of the rewards she received when she has encountered this type of event before, (2) her perception of the rewards she might gain in the situation immediately before her and (3) her perception of rewards if she seeks different options. Whichever option seems to present the greatest reward is what she'll pick.

So if an individual thinks the reward she'll receive from the message in which she is presently engaged (encounter) is greater than her expectations from similar past encounters (baseline), and if it's better than any option she has available at the moment, she'll likely engage.

But what if she thinks the anticipated rewards from this situation (encounter) won't satisfy even the baseline of what she anticipates after her past incidents with your organization? Moreover, what if there's a better option open to her? You shouldn't expect she'll be reading your prose.

Of course, sometimes, neither a given encounter nor any option perceived as available meets even our baseline expectations. These scenarios present serious challenges to strategic communicators, sometimes with life-or-death consequences, as Principles in Practice 2.1 describes.

The "Me Too" movement has been a visible force for change in combating the too-present incidents of sexual harassment and assault.

Preventing both physical and psychological harm is particularly difficult in cases of domestic violence. In these situations, victims—typically women—live with their abusers, often in constant fear. Domestic violence also results in an astonishing number of sexual assault cases: over half (51.1%) of reported rapes are committed by intimate partners.[16]

One commonly asked question is, "Why don't these women just leave?"

From the outside, that seems like a simple solution, but the problem is far more complicated. The National Domestic Violence Hotline, an activist organization helping victims and supporting survivors, describes several reasons why individuals stay with abusive partners.

A major driver is fear. Fear the abuse might worsen if they try to leave but fail; fear for their children's well-being if the family breaks apart. Additionally, victims are commonly dependent on partners to make ends meet, and without financial help from abusers, they may face poverty and/or homelessness. Tragically, for many, abuse just feels normal. Perhaps they were raised in abusive households or over time may simply have become numb to the violence.[17]

The social exchange calculus provides useful insights into each of these reasons for staying in an abusive relationship. For those fearing poverty for themselves and their children, their current situation clearly falls well short of baseline expectations. Their misery is not how they conceived an adult partnership would be. However, they perceive the alternative options as equally devastating, if not worse.

Those who have normalized abuse because of their own family experiences may have baseline expectations of domestic relationships that are so low they may actually view a life of perpetual violence as tolerable. In all these scenarios, staying in the relationship appears to the victim as the most rational choice.

The challenge for advocacy organizations and the strategic communicators they employ is recalibrating those calculations. Or, to use the language of situational theory, to remove the constraints these women feel are ensnaring them in sometimes deadly relationships. Advocates hope abuse victims will internalize a belief that domestic abuse is not normal and that there are better alternatives than their daily reality. In social exchange terms, our communication task is to convince the domestic violence victim that her options are superior to the situation she is in and push her to action.

Some first steps may be to inform domestic violence victims of the social services and legal recourses at their disposal. The stories of fellow victims—now survivors—might prove especially valuable here. Those stories resonate because survivors provide a roadmap for how a person much like them, with a family much like theirs, might pursue a safe, fulfilling life outside the brutal confines of an embattled home.

### Takeaways for Persuasive Writing

From a writing standpoint, we should internalize these lessons from social exchange theory:

1. You communicate to people who have a preexisting opinion about your organization or your organizational category, a perception from which they will view the message you send them.

2. You communicate to people who are looking for an anticipated reward from an encounter with your message.

3. Your audience is assessing the anticipated rewards your message offers and comparing them to rewards an alternative message might offer.

4. Their decision will likely take place within two seconds of when they encounter your message.

5. Each encounter with them will likely reinforce or diminish their previously held opinion of your organization, a perception that will influence your next communication encounter with them.

## Translating Communication Models Into Action

How do these practical extensions of communication models relate to planning real-life persuasive writing tasks? While we'll provide explicit demonstrations of their usefulness in Chapters 6 and 7, there are several principles that will inform the rest of your career.

In our opinion, these models give writers vital audience-evaluation tools to pursue a cost-effective, audience-centered writing process. They demonstrate our writing must be relevant to the audience we are addressing. We must structure our writing to immediately and repeatedly show how the information we're communicating affects our readers' lives. We should reinforce in our readers' minds how they can act on the issues we present.

Using the insights into our audience these models provide, we can design realistic, workable strategies for mounting the types of cost-effective, objective-driven communication campaigns we'll advocate in the next chapter. We can predict how certain people will conceptualize decision processes in certain situations. We can involve and motivate important publics to see the goals they share with our organization. We'll eventually assert that this thought process actually "generates" prose, simplifying and accelerating your writing production.

In sum, we can start to manage communication within an organizational framework: setting realistic goals, integrating those goals into management perspectives and designing effective processes to reach those goals. That's the ultimate purpose of this book: to explore the strategies for effective and efficient public relations and strategic communication that will further persuasive communication in its growth as a management profession—and to provide you with the skills to assure you a prominent place within that profession.

## SUMMARY

- The audience member, not the speaker, controls the reception and interpretation of messages within a complex of personal values, the combination of an individual's personal experiences and socialization.

- Hierarchical persuasion models, such as the adoption process model, don't adequately predict human decision-making because people skip steps in the hierarchy and don't always follow the same series of steps.

- The social exchange theory posits that individuals incorporate prior experiences into their calculations of the risks and advantages of taking an action, including engagements in interpersonal relationships. It provides a quasi-mathematical approach toward assessing an individual's spectrum of emotional and rational motives, helping the writer analyze and sequence those persuaders for best effect in messages.

- The learn-feel-do model suggests individuals undertake different decision sequences through their perception of the consequences of making the wrong decision and whether they anticipate emotional or rational rewards resulting from their action.

### Scenario Prompts: Persuasion Models

You'll find Scenario Prompts on pp. 367–386 of this textbook. While they vary in subject and difficulty, they help you hone your critical thinking and strategic writing skills. The following are best suited to this chapter's topics.

Management: 1.1, 1.2, 3.4, 8.1

### *Figure Credits*

Fig. 2.1: Source: https://www.communicationtheory.org/lasswells-model/.

Fig. 2.2a: Adapted from Abraham Maslow, "A Theory of Human Motivation," *Psychological Review*, vol. 50, no. 4. Copyright © 1943 by American Psychological Association.

Fig. 2.2b: Based on ideas from Everett Rogers, *Diffusion of Innovations*. Copyright © 1995 by Simon & Schuster, Inc.

Fig. 2.4: Copyright © by Benetton.

# Creative Communication Planning

What You Need to Know

---

Some writers view planning as unproductive time, wasted because it's not spent writing. We believe planning refines the writer's thoughts, making the upcoming writing task easier, faster and more apt to compel readers toward the writer's hoped-for purpose. Planning can transform the written piece, even the entire campaign, to be more creative and successful than it would have been otherwise. Need an example?

I was retained by a newly formed alliance of six community choirs to help them recruit an audience for their first-ever concert. The groups displayed various musical styles. In fact, one of the few things they could agree on was that there were only two dates all six groups could perform together: Nov. 11, or Nov. 18.

So, I had choral music and two dates. Did you recognize either of those dates? Not much happened on Nov. 18. Britain and the United States did sign the Hay–Pauncefote Treaty on Nov. 18, 1901, which nullified the earlier Clayton–Bulwer Treaty. It may mark jolly conversations among the Hay and Pauncefote clans, but it doesn't offer many marketing possibilities.

But Nov. 11? On the 11th hour of the 11th day of the 11th month of 1918, World War I ended. In the United States, it's celebrated as Veterans Day.

The date suggested an entire series of very practical marketing decisions. While I had the core of an audience that each group's supporters brought to this concert, the Veterans Day connection gave me an entire other bloc: military veterans, their families and others who wished to commemorate the veterans' service commitment.

Logical decisions poured from this one insight. The choirs' repertoire? Patriotic music, of course. The concert's name: "Singing America's Praises." The location? The city's auditorium honoring the area's dead from World War I, a site containing souvenirs and military memorabilia. The program colors? Red, white and blue, naturally.

The Veterans Day theme introduced media and marketing possibilities. I got distribution lists for members of the area's Veterans of Foreign Wars and American Legion posts. The city's mass media channels, who recognized their obligation to acknowledge the holiday, responded eagerly to news releases.

With veterans as the concert theme, media pitches emerged naturally. In preconcert publicity, I was able to place a story about veterans who sang in the choirs, organize a televised tour of the memorial auditorium's artifacts and history, and place a video documenting an elderly veterans' color squad practicing the precise routine with which they would open the concert.

This is a simple example of planning's value. Planning helps the practitioner fight through limitations and often shows how those very limitations can offer previously unrealized opportunities. It leads you to unanticipated audiences, and by separating your audience into subcomponents, it lets you study them more easily and discover the motives most likely to drive their behavior.

More importantly, it promotes your creativity. Note that this campaign outline couldn't be employed on any other project. That novelty will help you gain more media and audience attention, which will be a major part of your ultimate success.

—WT

## What You Know

- An effective persuasive message must orient the speaker's communication goals within the context of the audience's self-interest.

- Different audiences will perceive the same situation and their potential responses to it in vastly different ways.

- It's possible to predict audiences that will most likely act in a situation and determine the message that will persuade them to act.

## What You'll Learn

- How to write a persuasion platform and objectives

- How strategic communication campaigns can be segmented into specific components, which can be more easily planned for maximum effectiveness

- How individual steps within the persuasion platform plan can be directly integrated into persuasive documents

- How quantifying the effects of communication gives practitioners vastly increased power in organizations

## Creativity and Control

As we will often remind you, our goal is to transform developing professional writers into strategic thinkers. It's a hugely important distinction. A writer transposes what her supervisors say into streamlined prose. A strategic thinker discovers the organization's fundamental issue and designs a communication campaign to propel the organization and its publics toward actions that will help ensure its long-term success.

By its very nature, strategic communication intends to identify a problem and find a way to solve it. For professional communicators, separating "communication" from its amateur meaning of "what comes out of your mouth" is vitally important. *Strategic communication is planned communication.*

When we harp on planning to executives, they inevitably complain that planning sounds wonderful, but they are far too busy to take the time to plan. However, when we start exploring their work processes, we discover that even though they aren't aware of it, they are planning.

Do they have at least a primitive understanding of why it's important to spend more time, now, on this communication effort rather than another? Yes? Then they're planning. Is there a media platform the audience most likely sees and believes? That's all planning.

At some level, **planning** is a part of any project. In some situations, the processes we discussed earlier are sufficient. But there are definite advantages to formalizing the planning process. First, planning lets you do your job better. It structures your thought process, enabling you to think more expansively about your audience and the reasons they might respond to your message.

Planning enhances your creativity too. Instead of shackling you to previous problem-solving approaches, planning can spur sparkling new messages, media strategies and approaches that distinguish your organization's presentation from those of your rivals. Such novelty can stimulate your campaign's success.

Additionally, formal planning creates a document to persuade your own institution's supervisors of a project's importance. It helps convince managers to invest the staff time, money and resources to successfully complete the proposed communication task. Because planning predicts a campaign's **cost-effectiveness**, you and your supervisors can prioritize how you expend your efforts. Tasks most important to the organization's success deserve your best efforts and the institution's resources. Efforts that marginally impact the organization might be expendable. You can argue convincingly only if you've planned cogently.

Finally, planning helps you complete a communication task on time and with the fewest complications. That's because it helps you better understand the sequencing and complexity of the tasks vital to the campaign's success. That's critical in establishing your credibility and professional success.[1]

## How Planning Drives Strategy: The Persuasion Platform

In the previous chapters, we argued that effective communication focuses on satisfying our audiences' needs and capabilities. By analyzing each audience, we can select the most persuasive messages and present them in forms and using media platforms to which audiences are most likely to respond.

We like to think of this as an "organic" process. That is, our efforts do not start with the decision to opt for a campaign placed on a particular media platform. Instead, the campaign "grows" from an understanding of the audience's motives, the media to which they attend, or how a specific time of the year enhances the strength of the message. Any one of those approaches may stimulate a strategy that provides insights into a campaign exactly corresponding to the audience's need to take an action benefiting both themselves and our organization. As we said before: The communicator cannot dictate the campaign; audience-centered communication recognizes that the campaign emerges from the complex interaction of audience motives within a web of time and social environments.

**MEMORY MEMO 3.1** Steps in the Persuasion Platform

- Isolate the institution's problem
- Determine a campaign objective
- Describe the target audience
- Predict the persuasion sequence
- Define the persuaders
- Select the media
- Determine the timetable
- Calculate the budget
- Determine the evaluation process

The **persuasion platform** (summarized in Memory Memo 3.1) translates the theory describing why and how audiences react into a planning system. Professor Thompson formulated the persuasion platform by combining the management-by-objective (MBO) business model envisioned by management strategist Peter Drucker and an advertising planning model initially introduced by A. Jerome Jewler. The platform enables its user to identify and creatively confront organizational issues while providing a framework that actually guides the writing process.[2] It also helps its user calculate cost-effectiveness and evaluate the success of the communication plan. The persuasion platform can also adapt to different tasks, and can be employed quickly and informally for a one-shot writing assignment, or spun into a full-blown, multipart communication campaign.

While planning by itself can't guarantee success, the persuasion platform process helps us gain insights into many communication tasks. We use it to isolate the persuaders that will motivate audiences. With that knowledge, we can develop attention-grabbing headlines or arresting visuals for social media posts.

Instead of diminishing creativity, the persuasion platform can stimulate it. Users have found it identifies what we term **multiple insertion points**. Rather than forcing a sequential planning process, the persuasion platform isolates potential factors around which to organize the communication task and your persuasive message.

For instance, undertaking the process might draw your attention to an audience demographic that would help you amplify your message's impact. Your organization may have preliminarily scheduled a four-part spirituality lecture series at a single church. But as a perceptive communication practitioner, you realize that if you scheduled one lecture at four different houses of worship, you could plug into your own media distribution list and the networks of four other community institutions. Modify the scheduling to focus each lecture's topic on an important upcoming holiday for the church or temple hosting the event, and you've provided even a stronger persuader for audience engagement.

That's the essence of the persuasion platform's usefulness: It simultaneously captures the complexity of communication while focusing on each component. That lets you envision the impact a single step may have on the others.

### Isolating the Institutional Problem

Isolating the problem motivating your organization's communication effort seems like an easy task. Let's say it's September. That's when your nonprofit always prepares its annual giving solicitation that drops in November and December. The conventional wisdom is that year-end drives optimize the moment when donors consider how they'll maximize their tax breaks the following April.

Good idea? Maybe.

However, the essence of planning is to force yourself to ask, "Why?" The holiday season is the peak time for solicitations and the competition from other charities will be fierce. And speaking of the holidays, you're asking donors to dig into their bank accounts at just the time when many have extraordinary expenses arising from gift-giving or family travel.[3]

Holiday concerns aside, it's also worth asking if your organization's goals will grab your target audience's attention at this particular time. Let's say your organization raises money to educate children on water safety. Potential donors' concerns about warm-weather recreation may not be a top-of-mind issue when a foot of snow makes drowning deaths seem remote.

The planning process forces you to question the rationale for this communication plan, to this public, at this time, using this medium, for this investment of staff and money. In the scenario above, you might decide to concentrate your main fundraising activities in warmer months. If you decide on a year-end solicitation, you might want to tie your request to the holiday season while distinguishing yourself from your competition. You could structure your request not as a year-end donation, but by asking the donor to buy swimming lesson gift certificates your organization could distribute as holiday gifts to less fortunate children.

The key lesson? Planning never accepts any tactic as the best approach without considering the alternatives. It compels you to determine whether what you've done in the past worked, what part of it worked and how it can be expanded, improved or abandoned for your next effort.

As we mentioned earlier, the first step in strategic communication is to identify an organizational problem that can be remedied through communication. In the previous sentence, we mean exactly what we say: Not all organizational problems can be solved by communication.

For instance, let's imagine the baby chair your company manufactures collapses because the frame is made of shoddy steel, and three infants are injured. No cleverly written media release or glib talking points can fix the fundamental problem—that in this instance your company produced a defective product that harmed consumers. That can only be fixed by the company manager who chooses the firm's steel supplier. As a communicator, you can smooth the recall procedures, quickly engage with affected families and explain your company's efforts to prevent future problems. However, vital operational problems must be meaningfully addressed to give the communicator any plausible foundation from which to launch an effective communication campaign.

Instead, the strategic communicator examines the historical, social, economic or perceptual elements that caused the problem. In short, we develop a reason for communication before we communicate.

It seems contrary to one of our society's—and, sad to say, too often the profession's—basic perceptions: that communication is good any time, with everyone and about anything.

Utter nonsense. Total insanity.

Misguided or unneeded communication wastes effort and organizational resources. Indeed, it may be counterproductive to an institution's overall objectives.

Let's say you work for a company whose CEO has just overseen a merger resulting in 4,000 lost jobs. But the merger was a financial boon for the company, and thanks to stock options, your CEO suddenly becomes the nation's highest-paid executive. She wants you to publicize these gains in major business publications, financial TV channels and electronic business platforms. Should you try to dissuade her?

Perhaps you should if you don't want to stir up the resentments and protests of the former employees who are now collecting unemployment for the same reason the CEO is on the top of the heap. There's no doubt the communication effort would help the CEO's standing, but does this personal benefit outweigh the potential harm the organization suffers if it appears insensitive? Probably not.

We would forcefully argue against the CEO's instructions. Communication professionals working for an institution have a duty to the institution and its many stakeholders: employees, stockholders, customers and communities that depend on the organization's stability and prosperity (we'll talk more about these responsibilities in Chapter 5). Certainly, there are enough situations where our efforts would serve just such purposes: communicating with certain publics could reverse an attitude threatening fundraising efforts, support sales of a newly introduced product or gain a sympathetic hearing on a rezoning permit from a neighborhood preservation group.

Thus, defining the institutional problem is important for two reasons. First, detailing the institutional problem guides us toward the tasks yielding the most organizational dividends. It keeps us focused on those efforts that will represent the best investment of our time and talents.

Second, it tells you what tasks you shouldn't do, from both practical and ethical standpoints. It lets you avoid tasks motivated more by tradition than any real contribution they make to the organization's success. This helps a practitioner gain power within the organization by demonstrating how her efforts directly contribute to reaching the company's overall goals. Isolating the institutional problem is a vital first step to freeing yourself for creative thought about how to solve the problem.

But that first step is just the beginning. The MBO planning process illustrates how you can build out from that initial problem to an eventual solution. Case in Point 3.1 presents hints on how to construct each of the persuasion platform's 10 steps.

### Determining a Campaign Objective

The campaign **objective**, although a single, declarative sentence, may be the most important component of the communication planning process. It guides your campaign precisely and defines exactly the results upon which you'll be measured, including the date when your efforts will be assessed.

An objective must answer every one of the six criteria listed in Memory Memo 3.2. First, your objective must be focused on solving an objective important to your organization. Second, because you'll be judged by the stipulations in your objective statement, your objective must be unambiguous, incapable of being interpreted multiple ways. Third, the campaign's outcome must be measurable. You're essentially signing a contract with your company stating you'll accomplish something, therefore that something must be quantifiable. Fourth, you need

**MEMORY MEMO 3.2** What's a Good MBO Objective?

- It must solve an institutional problem
- It must be unambiguous
- It must be measurable
- It must contain a deadline
- It must be realistic
- It must focus on outcomes, not outputs

to establish a timetable. Hit your objective in this time frame and you're a success. Miss it, or hit it after your deadline, and you've failed. That's why you always want to observe the fifth requirement, to define a goal that can be realistically met by the deadline your objective establishes. Finally, your objective should focus on a communication **outcome**, not a communication **output**. The eight posts you disseminated represent outputs (i.e., they are your actions); the 100 people who attended your client's restaurant opening because they were exposed to those stories? That's an outcome (i.e., they are audience actions). If you get lost, remember that well-crafted objectives meet the SMARTO acronym qualifications: they are specific, measurable, actionable, relevant, timebound and outcome oriented.

Let's examine some objective statements. Let's say you're concerned that fewer shareholders are reinvesting their dividends in your company's stock. Messages delivered to shareholders along with monthly online investment statements could emphasize the convenience and cost savings of automatic reinvestment might improve the situation.

First, let's look at a poorly written objective for this campaign:

> Make extensive improvements in communication efforts to our corporate stockholders. .

This objective does not have a measurable goal. What are *extensive* improvements? In fact, how can you know what an *improvement in communication* is? Beyond that, there's no deadline defining when the project will be finished. Should we expect improvement by next week, or in a decade? This objective won't help you plan your communication efforts and provides no method to evaluate your success.

Here's another objective that's almost as bad:

> By July 1, mail stockholders one letter from the company president explaining the benefits of automatic reinvestment.

This objective defines a deadline and a measurable goal. That's good. However, it's not measuring an important organizational outcome. Instead, it argues that the project is over once some activity is completed. If you prove you've mailed a letter, what has the company truly gained? Instead, you must link your communication efforts to an organizational goal. Remember, outputs are not outcomes.

Here's the same scenario, but with a well-written objective statement:

> By October 1, increase by 5% the number of current stockholders enrolled in the automatic stock investment plan.

This objective contains all six elements necessary for guiding a cost-effective communication program. It's relevant to what the organization values: reinvestment in company stock. It establishes an unambiguous, measurable goal. In this case, it is probably realistic to anticipate a 5% jump in program participation, though more extensive research into company, competitor and industry records could offer more certainty. There's a deadline when you and your supervisors will evaluate whether your communication campaign has succeeded. Finally, you'll note it hasn't tied us to a tactic or a media platform before we've even started thinking about the audience.

When writing objectives, it is critical to carefully define a component that can be measured. After all, you're trying to assign a number to assess "improved communication," and numbers afford you credibility with your supervisors. To paraphrase one of Professor Browning's mentors: "In God I trust, but everybody else better show me the damn numbers." Fortunately, there are many secondary numerical measures that are valid indicators of improved communication.

For instance, in a campaign announcing a new use for an old product, you could measure the additional number of units sold or the larger sales volume. At a health insurance company suffering from poor customer relations, you might judge the campaign's effects by comparing the average hold time for telephoning customers before your campaign with the time they wait after your plan is implemented.

You can even measure the effects of communication on something as vague as better employee education. Let's say research determines improved training for custodians might help prevent hospital-borne infections contracted in recovery rooms. Your hospital's lab could assess whether the germ count on recovery room surfaces was lower after the custodians received the additional training, job recognition or other efforts your campaign implemented.

In this last scenario, notice that we did not evaluate our communication success by testing whether they retained training information. Although that test might demonstrate custodians knew what we wanted once the training concluded, it doesn't convince us that they applied that knowledge in the workplace. Because we want the result to help the organization solve its problems, the persuasion platform planning process always attempts to measure outcomes addressing our institution's opportunity or difficulty as explicitly as possible.

## CASE IN POINT 3.1   The Persuasion Platform

**Client Problem:**
The client problem is a brief exploration of the difficulties the client wants to overcome. The client problem should not be concerned exclusively with "improving audience awareness" or "increasing sales," but should explore the root causes of the difficulties that keep your client from gaining its desired impact on certain discrete audience groups.

**Objective:**
The objective statement should be one declarative sentence that isolates a single, measurable goal important for the institution to reach. It should also state a deadline and a procedure to determine if that goal has been met. Remember: ONE sentence. If you've written two, you're doing something wrong.

**Audience Analysis:**
*Demographic statement:* The demographic statement identifies the targeted audience by age, income, residence, profession, gender, race, marital status and other factors that indicate the audience's capacity to make a decision. A common mistake is to develop one persuasion

platform to persuade two distinct publics. Because audiences are so different, it won't work. If you want to target two audiences, construct a separate persuasion platform for each audience.

*Psychographic statement:* The psychographic statement uses surveys, marketing statistics, focus group interviews (and sometimes the practitioner's informed but informal psychological analysis) to explore self-image considerations that determine the audience's motive to make a decision that will help your client. Audience psychographics are frequently the most detailed section of your entire persuasion platform.

### Probable Persuasion Sequence:

The probable persuasion is your best prediction of the decision sequence your targeted audience will use in responding to your persuasive message. You'll choose one of the quadrants from the learn-feel-do model detailed in Chapter 2 to (1) predict whether your audience considers this a low- or high-consequence decision and (2) whether the audience perceives that emotional or rational rewards will be most important. It should be a three-word answer.

### Persuaders:

*Main persuader:* The main persuader will be a single declarative sentence derived from the persuasion sequence's prediction. If you indicate that emotion will drive behavior, your main persuader will be emotional. If you indicate rational rewards will drive behavior, your main persuader should provide reasoned incentives to your intended audience. Again, your main persuader should be stated in a single sentence.

*Secondary persuaders:* The secondary persuaders provide the weight of evidence in the decision process. They give audience members extra reasons to act as the client desires. There often are several secondary persuaders, often including both rational and emotional appeals, no matter what motive you expressed in the main persuader.

### Media Choices:

Selecting media forces you to consider the wide variety of mass media, online, advertising, direct mail and organizational and specialized media that will deliver your persuasive message accurately and credibly to your intended audience. Choosing media before you contemplate your plan often limits your creativity in considering the best, most cost-effective media for your purposes.

### Timetable:

The timetable requires the practitioner to contemplate how scheduling will affect the perception of and response to a communication event. The timetable also helps you determine if you can finish a project within the allotted time and provides useful guideposts to keep you on schedule. The information in the timetable will be more useful if presented in tabular rather than narrative form. It's usually constructed by establishing your project's completion date and then working back to the present.

**Budget:**

Budgeting for your campaign is critical. You may discover that realistically the profits realized from meeting your goal can't possibly cover the costs necessary to reach that goal. It provides a valuable warning sign that lets you alert your supervisors of a potential crisis in the making. Sharing that knowledge can also insulate your judgment from being questioned if you're forced to complete the campaign as originally written. It also allows you to adjust your objective or other aspects of the plan to accommodate your predicted outcome. In the case shown in **Click-Through 3.1**, the practitioner estimates her expenditures of staff time and out-of-pocket costs will deliver $1.44 for each dollar spent on the campaign. That 44% rate of return will likely convince your supervisors to approve the project. (Click-Through elements are available in Cognella Active Learning. For details on how to access Active Learning, please see the notice at the front of your book.)

**Evaluation Statement:**

The evaluation statement repeats the measurable goal and the deadline from the client objective statement and describes the method you will use to measure whether you've reached that objective. If you can't measure the outcome, then you haven't written an effective objective statement. It's usually one or two sentences.

## Describing the Target Audience

Once you've established an explicit objective for your communication efforts, you then determine which audiences can help solve the defined problem. Put simply, you need to determine the individuals or groups who can help you meet your overall objective, as well as those who can sabotage that quest.

This is an important step because you can't possibly afford to talk to everyone in the world about your issue. This may confound some clients who suggest that "everyone in the world is a potential buyer of my product."

Utter nonsense. Total insanity.

We'll give you an example. Say you work for a large supermarket. Everyone eats food, so everyone in your city is a potential customer, right? Wrong! Some people are rich (or lazy) enough to hire people to buy their groceries for them. In other households, only one family member makes the food-buying decisions for the whole family. Some may only buy farm-to-table. Many families choose their store based on its accessibility via public transportation. You must decide to whom to direct your message for maximum cost-effectiveness, concentrating on some audiences and ignoring others.

Theory guides us through some initial selections. The situational theory of publics (see Chapter 2) suggests we evaluate different publics based on their capacity to take action. In no case does that mean dismissing those who don't like your organization. Environmental activists, workers battling for a contract or dissident stockholders have the capacity to hurt your company just as much as loyalists can help it. Who are those individuals most likely to take an action? Those who (1) perceive a problem, (2) see themselves as involved in that problem and (3) face few barriers to action. Evaluating a public through these lenses will help you select those most likely to respond to your message.[4]

Using the situational model's three criteria, any public, adversarial or not, can be evaluated. If any public, friend or foe, emerges from this test with a high potential for action, you should consider a communication campaign to answer their concerns and capitalize on their motivations for being involved. That often means developing multiple persuasion platforms reflecting each public's perception of the issue and the persuaders motivating them to act.

### Demographic Analysis

So who are these specific audiences with whom you wish to communicate, and what can you offer them so they'll partner with your organization? Demographic information from your own consumer research, other database sources or active internet tracking through social media all provide valuable insights that help describe your publics' capacities to engage in action.

Where does your audience live? How old are they? How much money do they make and from what source? Do they have children? Are racial or ethnic considerations important in determining who will be interested in your message?

**Demographics** in part determine those people who have the capacity to act on your message. Obviously, if you're selling diamond jewelry for birthday gifts, you need to locate people who have enough money to buy them. If your task is to recruit snowmobile club members, you're likely focusing on publics who live in regions with heavy snowfall.

Yet remember that those making a purchase or support decision may not be the ones paying for it. Think about who pays for a McDonald's Happy Meal. Parents of course. But is that the audience the company targets in its advertising? Nope. Because who makes the decision to go to McDonald's? For Happy Meals, it's those short people in the back seat about a decade shy of voting age. McDonald's follows that wisdom in campaigns placed on animated shows seen by children barely out of diapers.[5] That targeting of age segments continues throughout the human life span. The company directs social media toward college students trying to maximize their time between school and work.[6] Another commercial even promoted McDonald's as a meeting place and as a potential pickup spot for romantically starved retirees.[7] Each is a target audience, and each has a demographically discernable reason for acting.

### Psychographic Analysis

A demographic analysis is hardly enough to determine the audience with whom we should communicate. Although demographics determine whether someone has the capacity to act, they don't necessarily guide you toward those people motivated to do so. Instead, motives are more often revealed by the psychographic traits you discern in your target publics, descriptors that can lead directly to developing the message to persuade that audience.

For instance, if your client sells fur coats, you know your audience has achieved a certain income level. Demographics can show you an audience with the capacity to buy your expensive product. Using this conclusion, you know a story placement promoting your exotic furs in a podcast targeting college students or a weekly newspaper serving poor, rural residents would not be cost-effective. So, you need to communicate your message through media platforms reaching high-income audiences, correct? Yes and no.

We concede such a group would include people who could afford a fur coat. But if you live in a community that hosts a passionate animal-rights movement, you might discover yourself communicating with an equal number of people who think it's morally wrong for anyone to buy fur. If you don't target your audience tightly enough, you spend money and effort communicating to an audience that won't help you meet your sales goal. Just as importantly, you may have energized an audience that might have otherwise remained passive. Instead of selling furs, you might ignite a riot at your door.

**Psychographics** define the attitudinal traits that describe an audience by focusing on probable emotional, self-image and lifestyle factors, such as hobbies, interests and opinions.[8]

Psychographics give you the power to isolate the characteristics distinguishing the individuals who support an idea or a product from those people who reject it. In our professional practice, we've found that in constructing successful writing strategies, it's more important to discover an individual's personal rationale for taking action than knowing her income level. When we target our campaign to a tightly focused group constructed based upon a public's decision motives, our communication becomes more cost-effective and our writing much easier.

Constructing an effective psychographic description involves multiple steps. Internal research, secondary sources and particularly social media metrics provide insights into buying patterns, media use and hobbies (see Chapters 11 and 15). Those are all important starting points in determining what a group does.

But psychographics explore *why* people do what they do. When you construct an audience's psychographic description, you will profit by being expansive, exploratory and, at times, even speculative. Emotions are a dominant factor in a large number of decisions people make. Out of those loves, hates and desires come the basic reasons why people buy products, support causes and adopt ideas.

Once you have determined an audience's demographic identity and behavior patterns, psychographic analysis extends this portrait into the targeted public's perception of itself, your organization and your product or idea. For instance, here's an urban university's psychographic profile of potential students it's recruiting from the state's rural areas.

> These high school students can't wait to escape from their parents' and small towns' oversight. They are adventurous and want big-city life they've never experienced in their small-town high schools. While excited about college and their future, at the same time they are insecure about their rural backgrounds if faced with fellow college students at a distant university with whom they perceive they would have

nothing in common. While independence is essential, they'd be more psychologically comfortable if they enrolled in an institution where there would be peers with somewhat similar backgrounds and a campus close enough so they could return to familiar surroundings for a weekend if city life becomes too disorienting.

You can often begin your psychographic analysis by isolating a core psychological factor affecting your audience's behavior. Say you work for a company selling gold commemorative coins. Maybe your audience considers itself practical. If you respond to that motivation, you probably believe your customers buy a few gold coins as a useful diversification of a broad retirement portfolio. But if you believe your audience's principal motivation is their panic concerning the prospects of political upheaval, there's a different psychological factor at work. Would they convert all their savings to gold, a traditional investment bulwark in torturous times, to relieve the uneasiness they feel? You can see how motivating the same buying behavior emerges from radically different motives, motives that should be reflected in your persuasive writing. **Click-Through 3.1** provides another example of a psychographic analysis and lets you examine a fully developed persuasion platform.

### Predicting the Persuasion Sequence

With each step in the persuasion platform, you enhance your ability to focus your efforts on a specific audience and make reasonable conclusions concerning their motives to act. Now, we can start to use that information to predict the sequencing of your persuasive arguments.

In Chapter 2, we advocated using the learn-feel-do persuasion model to predict how people will approach a decision (refer to Figure 2.6 for a quick refresher). Given your audience's financial profile, would the decision you're asking it to make represent a huge sacrifice? If so, you'll more likely be successful if you present more information before asking your reader to take an action. If the decision you want doesn't demand your public to sacrifice their ethics, money or other things they value, then it's likely a low-consequence decision. Consequently, you can ask your audience to make an almost-immediate decision.

Let's turn to emotion/rationality, the other dynamic in the persuasion sequence model. Are audience members seeking emotional or rational rewards? Answering this question tells you where to situate your audience's probable decision process in the learn-feel-do grid, as well as the sequence in which you'll present your arguments in your writing. Can you ask your audience to make an almost-immediate decision, or do you need to provide a significant amount of persuasive information first? Will your primary persuader offer emotional rewards or rational ones? You now know.

**Strategic Thought**

Identify an example in which a communicator has chosen the wrong medium and/or motivator for the audience she was attempting to reach? What gave away the disconnect? How would you alter the message or media choice to create a more persuasive appeal?

### Deciding on the Persuaders
#### Main Persuader
At this point, you can isolate the main persuader. As you will learn in subsequent chapters, in doing so, you're also sketching an outline for composing prose for every outlet.

Your main persuader is a distilled statement, a simple, declarative sentence that states a single motive for your primary audience's action. What does the persuasion sequence suggest you do? If you have determined that emotional rewards drive persuasion, you've got tremendously valuable information.

Let's say you're marketing a throwback toy train. Anything you say about the product's quality materials, the manufacturer's 80th anniversary or the train's five-year warranty will unlikely be important for the affluent grandfather who wants to present his grandson with the same train he had as a kid. Emotion directly referencing the purchaser's own experience, maybe a soft-focus photo of a 1970s father and son playing on the floor, will be more effective for this high-emotion, low-consequence persuasion process.

Same thing if your learn-feel-do analysis indicates a rational motive. For a start-up florist buying a new delivery van, preserving her small capital stake is likely more important than prestige. Sales copy opening with gas mileage or reliability claims will be more effective than copy that emphasizes choice of paint colors or 0-to-60 claims.

Whether emotional or rational reasons are most important, you've now established the central motive driving the particular audience you described earlier in the persuasion platform. With this, you've already gone a long way toward writing the first sentence of your prose.

#### Secondary Persuaders
The main persuader is important, but there are other motives that may encourage audience reaction to your message. While your analysis may have determined your public will be most engaged by an emotional reason, there may be rational reasons that will bolster their desire to act.

Secondary arguments add evidence to strengthen the audience's belief that the desired action is correct for them. For example, in the earlier model train scenario, the product's quality and warranty are secondary persuaders. They help convince the grandfather that his well-intentioned gift will not disappoint by breaking the day his grandson opens it. Additionally, these secondary persuaders, even if not important enough to include in your message's earliest appeals, help you outline topics found deeper in the piece.

### Selecting the Medium
Only now, with details you've gleaned creating your persuasion platform, can you select the media through which you'll deliver your messages. The choice of media should emerge from your knowledge of audience characteristics and institutional problems and objectives. If you ever receive an instruction that "our company needs to have a presence on [insert social media platform] because it's blowing up right now," you're courting trouble. Lacking a particular media presence is not necessarily a problem. Failing to address an institutional issue always is.

Our media decisions consequently involve considering a variety of media platforms. Yes, public relations is traditionally known for drawing mass media attention to our institution, often through media releases or pitches. But you need to think beyond that. Would a card and informal sales letter delivered through the mail on your recipient's birthday be most effective for introducing your client's retirement specialist to prospective customers? Would hosting a special event create more community involvement and media attention to your institution's anniversary than merely distributing a media release? Do you need to buy advertising placements to guarantee your persuasive message is most accurately delivered to your selected audience?

Don't neglect channels that too rarely enter the profession's calculations. Would a one-on-one visit with pressure group leaders be more effective than communicating through mass media channels? How do you employ internal media such as e-newsletters or intranet blogs? What about promoting your CEO or employees as high-credibility guest speakers to targeted groups?

What about social media? For some audiences, it's perfect. Other publics can't even access social media channels. And if you choose social media, you then encounter other questions. Which platform incorporates the features—such as video, direct messaging or longer character counts—that let you best communicate your persuasive message? Which of these platforms reaches your audience at a time or in a space that lets them respond to your message? Even at that point, does your audience consider information from that platform to be credible?

> **Strategic Thought**
>
> Identify a client and a communication campaign for which you could obtain a number of placements, but which would be of no practical benefit to the client? How would you persuade the client that a more focused media strategy might better suit their needs?

Additionally, assume that no matter how many decades you practice your craft, you'll never comprehensively understand your organization's media universe. Specialized magazines, cable channels, web interest groups and complete media platforms appear and collapse with dizzying speed. Instead, assume that no matter the subject, there most probably is a medium that lets you target highly complex, insider information topeople who passionately care about 1952 GMC pickups, lop-eared rabbits or billions of other unique specific topics.

Picking media is a critical task, which we'll discuss throughout the book, but particularly in the message-delivery chapters (Chapters 11, 13 and 15). However, we again emphasize that channel choices emerge organically via the insights you gain while completing the persuasion platform. You should never select—or reject—a medium before you know why you want to communicate a given message and with whom you wish to communicate.

## Developing the Timetable

Now that you've determined your communication campaign's persuasive approach and tools, you can plan the details. Your initial step, as we discussed earlier in this chapter, is to determine if the campaign's public launch date has a persuasive effect.

Professor Thompson's own experience confirms this. He was helping a little-known composer who wished to draw attention and sales to his quartet's recordings. The composer hired Professor Thompson to create a release directed to the composer's local media announcing his latest works, which included two songs about snowy days. Instead of distributing the press campaign immediately, Professor Thompson convinced the composer to not transmit the materials until winter's first big snowstorm. When a forecast called for six inches, Professor Thompson shipped the media packet to all the city's TV stations.

On most such days, governments, businesses and schools shut down, so the stations' usual sources of local news, which likely would have pushed the lonely composer off the air, were no longer competition. On this day, the composer was competing against only the stimulating live cut-ins of the station's most-junior reporter standing in a blinding blizzard, repeatedly acknowledging to the audience that she was, in fact, standing in a blinding blizzard. Riveting.

> **MEMORY MEMO 3.3** A Timetable Is Vital to Planning
>
> - It helps you capture the advantages of timing communication events
> - It helps you determine if you've got enough resources to finish on time
> - It establishes guideposts that let you monitor your progress

In this situation, the composer's story and news of his snow-themed compositions had a much better chance of making it to air. And so it was. All day long, the city's TV stations trudged to his house or interviewed him remotely, with each playing clips of the wintery compositions and discussing his blizzardly inspiration for the works. The composer ended the day with all the city's TV stations developing a package and hundreds of viewers downloading his compositions. A simple change of dates transformed the campaign's chance of success.

Thinking about timing helps in other ways. Does your event compete with similar events, with mega-events like the Super Bowl or religious holidays? There are also seasonal components to launching campaigns. Are you promoting snowshoes in July? Sometimes anniversary dates, days of the week, or even the hour of day can make a difference. Would you schedule a news conference at 6 p.m. in the evening? It would be a tough sell because so many television reporters are at the station producing the newscast. Even if it were a huge announcement that might tempt the station to schedule a live shot about the news conference, starting at exactly 6 p.m. causes difficulties. You could anticipate the newscasts' hosts might want to open the newscast and introduce your news conference's subject before cutting to the live reporter at 6:02 p.m.

Once you've considered these types of decisions, you'll usually work backward from the launch date to build your campaign's timetable. How many days or weeks before your announcement should the media be informed? What scheduling coordination is necessary between a mass media announcement and your release of the information on social media channels? If you need to create support materials, how many more days must you add to the production schedule? Will auditoriums have to be rented or seating and stages obtained and erected? Do other departments have to approve your campaign plans or perform tasks? How long will that take? The Gantt chart in Figure 3.1 illustrates the process.

Gantt charts allow you to establish important milestones for communication activities, estimating how long each activity will take to set reasonable timetables to ensure you meet

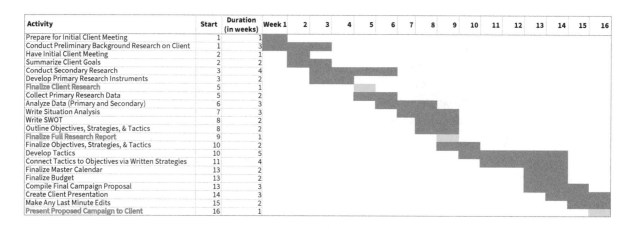

| Activity | Start | Duration (in weeks) | Week 1 | 2 | 3 | 4 | 5 | 6 | 7 | 8 | 9 | 10 | 11 | 12 | 13 | 14 | 15 | 16 |
|---|---|---|---|---|---|---|---|---|---|---|---|---|---|---|---|---|---|---|---|
| Prepare for Initial Client Meeting | 1 | 1 | | | | | | | | | | | | | | | | |
| Conduct Preliminary Background Research on Client | 1 | 3 | | | | | | | | | | | | | | | | |
| Have Initial Client Meeting | 2 | 1 | | | | | | | | | | | | | | | | |
| Summarize Client Goals | 2 | 2 | | | | | | | | | | | | | | | | |
| Conduct Secondary Research | 3 | 4 | | | | | | | | | | | | | | | | |
| Develop Primary Research Instruments | 3 | 2 | | | | | | | | | | | | | | | | |
| Finalize Client Research | 5 | 1 | | | | | | | | | | | | | | | | |
| Collect Primary Research Data | 5 | 2 | | | | | | | | | | | | | | | | |
| Analyze Data (Primary and Secondary) | 6 | 3 | | | | | | | | | | | | | | | | |
| Write Situation Analysis | 7 | 3 | | | | | | | | | | | | | | | | |
| Write SWOT | 8 | 2 | | | | | | | | | | | | | | | | |
| Outline Objectives, Strategies, & Tactics | 8 | 2 | | | | | | | | | | | | | | | | |
| Finalize Full Research Report | 9 | 1 | | | | | | | | | | | | | | | | |
| Finalize Objectives, Strategies, & Tactics | 10 | 2 | | | | | | | | | | | | | | | | |
| Develop Tactics | 10 | 5 | | | | | | | | | | | | | | | | |
| Connect Tactics to Objectives via Written Strategies | 11 | 4 | | | | | | | | | | | | | | | | |
| Finalize Master Calendar | 13 | 2 | | | | | | | | | | | | | | | | |
| Finalize Budget | 13 | 2 | | | | | | | | | | | | | | | | |
| Compile Final Campaign Proposal | 13 | 3 | | | | | | | | | | | | | | | | |
| Create Client Presentation | 14 | 3 | | | | | | | | | | | | | | | | |
| Make Any Last Minute Edits | 15 | 2 | | | | | | | | | | | | | | | | |
| Present Proposed Campaign to Client | 16 | 1 | | | | | | | | | | | | | | | | |

**FIGURE 3.1** **Planning Backward Using Gantt Charts.**

the final deadline. Here is an example Gantt chart Professor Browning uses in his PR campaigns course to map the 16-week process of developing a six-month-long communication campaign.This routine is tremendously important. It lets you determine whether the task is feasible with the time and staff you can devote to it. With that early warning, you have a cushion of safety so you can assemble the personnel and resources you'll need to meet your deadline. Once your timetable is established, you'll have frequent signposts to check that you're on schedule and help guarantee you'll reach your organization's objective.

## Calculating the Budget

At this point, you know what you want to accomplish, and you've outlined how you'll best undertake the task. Your next step is to determine how to pay for the campaign and, just as importantly, whether your campaign's anticipated outcomes justify the expenditures. Campaign costs include staff wages and fringe benefits, printing, advertising and space acquisition costs, facility rental and a host of other expenditures.

Although specific tactics for estimating a campaign's cost-effectiveness will have to wait until later in this book, you can gain enough information to compare costs by computing how much money it costs to communicate with each prospect or how much you must spend to drive a desired action, gain a contribution, make a sale or drive a click-through to a page collecting an email or IP address. It's even better if you can determine how many dollars in communication costs you have to spend to obtain $1 in revenue.

Establishing a budget is too rarely considered a mandatory part of the communication campaign. Yet a budget allows you to justify your efforts in contributing to your organization's goals. If your calculations indicate your campaign costs only 8 cents to drive an action yielding $1 in net revenue, you can very forcibly argue that you have a legitimate claim on the company's resources. Conversely, if your budget predicts you'll be spending $1.05 to gain the same $1 of revenue, you know you may need to restructure your campaign or even abandon it. In fact, dumping a campaign that is likely doomed to fail is a solid strategy and lets you use your organization's resources of money, talent and time to best effect.

### Determining the Evaluation Process

The persuasion plan's final step is to state how you'll determine whether you've met your communication objective. The evaluation is generally a one- or two-sentence statement that repeats the objective and deadline statement and indicates the procedure you'll use to measure your performance. For instance, if you're trying to fund an endowment, it might be as simple as calculating the total dollars pledged. In other situations, you might use the site-generated count of individuals who clicked through your organization's home page to enroll in paperless billing. In another situation, you might compare the before-and-after performance time a worker takes to finish a task after she has received specified training.

It's vital to build evaluation into the communication process. Judging the success and payback of every major organizational communication effort provides important data on techniques that do and don't work. It helps you, your colleagues and your organization to improve your performances in this campaign and subsequent campaigns.

## How Planning Drives Prose

As you study this chapter, the issues we're asking you to consider may seem very remote from your rationale for taking this course: learning how to write effective, persuasive prose. You'll find many communication practitioners who will agree with you. In our experience, too many communication professionals dismiss planning as isolated from the act of writing.

Utter nonsense. Total insanity.

We vehemently argue against such suppositions. We've found that creating persuasive prose of virtually any length or type of prose is inescapably intertwined with the process of planning.

As you'll discover in Chapters 6 and 7, your plan's audience analysis will tell you who will be most receptive to your message. Defining the main persuader will tell you what is most likely to motivate them. Those two elements will comprise the first sentence of your piece. The third paragraph will usually amplify and explain why that persuader is important.

Each of the secondary persuaders you've outlined in your persuasion plan will dictate the first sentences of subsequent paragraphs, often in exactly the sequence of importance you've determined in the persuasion platform.

The final section defines precisely the actions, time, date, cost, location and procedures through which the audience can get the benefits you promised in the very first sentence.

In this chapter's introduction, we asserted that planning did not make the writing process more burdensome. We instead argued that planning makes the writing process faster, more organized and more effective. We'll explore just these dynamics in the writing- and application-focused chapters later in this book.

## Planning and the Currency of Power in the Organization

A final point. This book focuses on empowering you within the organizations for which you will eventually work. That may seem the foundation for all your courses within the discipline, but we want to remind you of the distinction between competency and power.

**Strategic Thought**

We discussed how the persuasion platform allows for multiple insertion points to modify a planning process for greater success. Think of a campaign in which simply changing the launch date in combination with an audience and/or a main persuader might yield much better results? What were the dynamics that made your campaign work better?

In many organizations, professional communicators are viewed as ancillaries to top decision-makers. In those organizations, the practices of public relations and strategic communication are too often viewed as a social activity that promotes the company as a benevolent player among its community or workers.

Planning processes let you surmount these limitations while building respect and power for you and your fellow communication practitioners. Planning compels you to define objectives for your efforts that directly relate to the company's other bottom-line goals. Being able to demonstrate that communication contributes to the organization's purpose provides a common vocabulary that helps communication practitioners buy their way into the company's ruling coalition. That's why we claim communication planning mints the "currency of power."

## SUMMARY

- An objective statement must solve an institutional problem, be measurable, be unambiguous, be realistic, state a specific deadline and focus on outcomes rather than outputs.

- The persuasion platform's nine steps guide practitioners to consider all elements of the communication process: selecting audiences and predicting their needs and characters and then selecting persuasive messages and media that will most effectively move those audiences to action.

- Individual steps in the persuasion platform predict prose placements in the final document: The main persuader and targeted audience will appear at the outset; the secondary persuaders will be found later in the body copy; the reader action needed to fulfill the objective will be in the final paragraph.

- Planning helps the practitioner gain control over resources and commitment within the institution. It provides a mechanism that proves the value of organizational communication activities, establishes priorities for the most beneficial persuasive tasks and helps practitioners finish projects on time.

### Scenario Prompts: Communication Planning
You'll find Scenario Prompts on pp. 367–386 of this textbook. While they vary in subject and difficulty, they help you hone your critical thinking and strategic writing skills. The following are best suited to this chapter's topics.

Management: **2.1, 2.2, 3.1, 7.5, 8.2, 9.9, 10.5** / Writing: 4.1, 4.4, 8.5, 9.9

# Market Research and Targeting

## How You Come to Know

Over the years, I've heard students admit they were in my classroom because they feared the math courses demanded of STEM majors (that's science, technology, engineering and mathematics for the uninitiated).

I should know. I'm one of them. In my first college semester, I supplemented my impressive SAT math scores with four months of studying to score a D in freshman calculus.

Flash-forward four years when I'm an English and journalism graduate. I was working for a state association of local government administrators fighting a gasoline sales tax sponsored by the state's highway department. The proposed tax would have raised tens of millions of dollars. However, the state highways would consume every cent, even though local jurisdictions felt their road budgets were seriously underfunded.

I was assigned to write a story justifying the local administrators' pleas for some of the tax revenue. But I really didn't have much to write about. What percentage of the state's roads were maintained by the state, its counties or cities? Nobody knew. Were more of my state's gasoline taxes retained by the state than in other states? Nobody knew. Not the librarians, the economists or any of the other experts I consulted.

If my state's local roads were underfunded, voters might be persuaded they should defeat the tax increase. But my only evidence was a bunch of county officials complaining the tax allocation "wasn't fair."

Because no one knew, I had to discover it myself. For days, I sat at my desk with a handheld calculator poring over columns of tiny numbers on U.S. Department of Transportation statistics. Seven days, 50 states and 4,400 calculations later, I could rank-order the states in terms of the percentage of gas tax revenue allocated to the state highway department. Just one simple statistic.

Those many hours on the calculator found my state was the nation's second stingiest in sharing its gas tax money with its counties. With that one fact, I could finally employ my storytelling skills. A news release I wrote generated scores of media hits that helped my client defeat the state gasoline tax vote. Two years later, a new ballot initiative passed that gave the counties and small cities over half of the revenue the new gas tax would raise.

Such intense research may not coincide with your conception of strategic communication. But as we'll argue throughout this book, the strategic communicator cannot be a passive conduit for information that's already known. We are supposed to be experts in what will persuade audiences. As a result, one of our jobs is finding and employing research in our writing to support persuasive communication claims.

This chapter will suggest an expansive role for research in your career. We'll position the organization as a *message-making machine*. As strategic communicators, information is what we produce.

We don't do research just because we're supposed to do research. We do it because it gives us a better chance of success.

—WT

## What You Know

- Strategic communication involves understanding your organization's underlying objective.

- Solving client problems necessitates solving their audiences' problems.

- The strategic communicator, as the organization's persuasion specialist, must discover the persuaders that move its audiences to action.

## What You'll Learn

- How secondary research, undertaken by governments or private institutions, is a well of knowledge enabling you to study your organization's operations

- How statistical data offer few practical benefits unless combined with other statistics that can be logically compared

- How the benchmarking process studies the approaches a different organization takes that let it function better than your organization

## More Than a Researcher ... a Thinker

In this chapter, we assume you are relatively conversant with research methods.

We're not going to talk about how to write and conduct surveys, to calculate $z$-scores or to perform a Spearman correlation or an ANOVA—as much as Professor Browning would like to, nerd that he is.

This chapter's task is to help you use research to transform yourself into a strategic thinker. As we emphasized in our first three chapters, strategic communication writers don't merely convey information; they must also understand what information may persuade their target audiences to take action and why. Coupled with those insights is the capacity to explain to your organization's leaders why your reasoning is sound, and your action plan should be adopted.

### The Nature of Truth

That task is more difficult than you might imagine, particularly in the so-called **post-truth** era in which we live. Post-truth is a loaded term, so it merits some unpacking. Generally speaking, post-truth claims impair our ability to determine with any accuracy what's happening in the world around us. Sellers of such claims employ a variety of tactics: hyperbolic statements; distractions from verifiable claims; evasion and silence in the face of criticism. If you make a bogus claim when you know it to be false, it's lying, but at least the liar must first know the truth to subvert it. If, for your own ends, you persist in talking when you don't know what you're talking about, it's **bullshitting**, a technical academic term advanced by philosopher and Princeton University Professor Harry Frankfurt's seminal essay, *On Bullshit*. For real. With a citation and everything.[1]

Anyway, most post-truth claims ultiamtely boil down to attempts at **gaslighting**, a practice in which, over time, the cumulative effects of all the nefarious tactics listed above cause us to question the very nature of the daily reality we observe. In the end, such continuous second-guessing often leads people to give up on discovering the truth altogether.

So, in this environment, how do you determine what is *the* truth?

As a strategic communication practitioner, you will be among your organization's experts in determining the answer to that question. Such a judgment isn't necessarily encompassed by merely stating the facts truthfully and openly. The question often becomes, "Which facts?"

Here are consecutive headlines from one city with two daily newpapers:

Newspaper 1: *County schools' statewide tests scores decline.*

Newspaper 2: *County schools' state ranking rise after tests.*

Both can't be true, right? Well, actually they are. The first headline highlights the grim fact that local schools' raw scores on a statewide achievement test were lower than the previous year. The second shared the encouraging news that the statewide tests discovered local schools ranked higher among all the state's schools. However, this happened because other districts' scores fell more precipitously than did this county's schools.

It's a lovely illustration of Professor John Keane's assessments that "'reality' is multiple and mutable" and "what counts as truth is a matter of interpretation."[2]

So back to the test score claims, how do you interpret these truths, these multiple realities? This is a critical judgment call for a strategic communicator. If both these messages are true, on which do you think your PR campaign should focus?

First, there's your point of perspective as a communication professional. Are you working for the school district, or are you working for a lobbying group trying to divert funds from public schools to charter schools? The charter school pressure group might emphasize the public school's declining test scores. Discrediting the public schools might help the charter schools' cause.

So, the public schools' communication professionals would naturally choose to concentrate their message on their schools' higher ranking, right? Maybe. Maybe not.

If the public school district's budget had been cut the year the lower test scores occurred, its PR practitioners might recommend embracing the falling scores statistic. Linking the falling scores with a smaller budget could strengthen the district's campaign for greater funding and bolster the district's contention that any charter school funding would cannibalize a precariously underfunded public school system.

Which one should you choose? As we've repeatedly said through the first three chapters … it depends.

But there's one assertion we can make. Your professional goal is to become your organization's expert in forging its most productive message. There's no one else better trained in understanding human motivation or the power of words to engage that commitment. By extension that means you can't necessarily depend on others to tell you the message best able to accomplish that. You must be able to evaluate the potential messages you could convey, messages that are often not apparent to even your organization's leaders. That is where your capacity to evaluate research for its impact on your target publics becomes vital.

There's one more factor dictating your need to design research and evaluate data. Most organizational cultures reward those who deliver good news. You, the strategic communications professional, are often the only employee who has a vested interest in finding faults through which your organization may be attacked. Why? Because you will be on the front lines in defending your organization from your competitor's strategic communicator, who will likewise be undertaking research to find what best communicates her most persuasive message. That message will usually be opposed to the one you'd most like to convey.

In communicative conflict, just as in war, there can be only one winner, and this preparation is often your primary means of survival. You need to recognize your organization's best persuasive messages and develop your campaign using research that often starts as just a pile of raw data. Then you also must evaluate that same data from your competitor's standpoint to predict the campaign they might develop so you can counter it with your own.

Such "adversarial" public relations is rarely acknowledged, but it is a central component in practicing political communication and in social, racial and economic advocacy campaigns. To illustrate how research can be transformed into strategic thought, we've presented ourselves with a daunting social problem. We'll assign ourselves the task of assembling a cohesive argument that the United States should and can address its vast income inequality, and counterarguments against those who do not think it's a problem.

This chapter's "Principles in Practice" will challenge you with your own project in converting columns of seemingly unrelated statistics into a coherent communication strategy for an organization encountering a crisis.

### The Lay of the Land

Before we move on, we once more emphasize: Many practitioners have the same stomach-churning response as communication students when confronted with a research task. Because so many of us entered strategic communication because of our storytelling and language skills, we often feel insecure when we discover statistics will often be vital to our daily duties. But statistics are as much about storytelling as they are about math.

As researchers, we too often think we're finished when we find a number. The more important issue is determining what that number means. Remember Professor Thompson's work with his state's gasoline tax? All the data needed to answer his client's question were available, but only as isolated numbers individually describing money raised by gasoline taxes and miles of roads maintained by counties and cities in 50 states. However, those numbers told a story, once they were transformed into a tale of who got cheated and who did the cheating. Good researchers don't just crunch numbers; they specialize in crafting compelling narratives.

## Secondary Research: Discovering What Others Have Found

But before you can craft your message, you must determine what that message is.

Although it is sometimes necessary to do independent, original research, many of the issues facing persuasive communicators are urgent. You often won't have the time to design and administer a survey or conduct and analyze focus groups.

Luckily, you can usually gather enough information to intelligently solve the immediate task by examining secondary sources, previously compiled marketing research, public opinion polls, governmental reports, census data and other research. In this chapter, we'll limit our efforts to analyzing **secondary research**. However, the same approaches will guide an analysis supplemented by **primary research**.

### Government Statistics: Tax Dollars Researching for You

There are thousands of sources for secondary research. One of the most prolific information compilers is the U.S. government. You're likely most familiar with the U.S. population census the federal government conducts every decade. But the Census Bureau counts more than people.

It compiles information on population growth, industrial production, the average time people within individual communities spend commuting to their jobs—among literally billions of other pieces of information. Dig deep enough and there are even statistics on how many people during past years were murdered by strangulation (there's a separate breakdown for murder by asphyxiation, as well as drowning, poisoning, firearms, knives, beatings and falls). That's how specific the Census Bureau gets.

In fact, the Census Bureau zooms in on the American population to the level of block statistics—over 11 million zones. With this, you can view characteristics of the United States' 325 million residents at the level of individual city blocks. You can assess each block's statistics on age, race, income, number and relationship of household members, rate of homeownership and much more. If every block had an equal population, that would be the equivalent of having detailed, comparable demographics on every group of 30 people in the entire country. Think of the value this would provide for a small-business owner who needed guidance on where to site her business, where to place her advertising or what merchandise her business should stock.

In fact, census statistics are a tremendously valuable starting point for many clients' communication campaigns. There are censuses of retail trade, wholesale trade, manufacturing, transportation and agriculture. Like the population block statistics, each economic census offers very focused information. Want to know how many gas stations are in a particular ZIP code? It's in there. You need to discover what percentage of the average shoe store's expenses are spent on packaging materials and containers? You can find it and help your client assess her performance against competitors. In addition to shoe stores and gas stations, there are specific business intelligence break-outs for over 1,100 additional different business classifications. These business statistics are even more useful. Now the Census Bureau's recently developed North American Industry Classification System lets you compare your U.S. client directly to those in Canada and Mexico.

The U.S. census statistics are only the beginning. The federal departments of Commerce (home to the Census Bureau), Labor, Energy, Education, Interior, Justice and others collect and publish copious amounts of data. State, county and local governments also compile thousands of reports each year on subjects as diverse as air pollution, welfare reform, technological advances and housing. The government also keeps detailed public records on most court cases, along with births and deaths.

We don't offer this information to suggest that to finish a communication task you'll always need to know the number of residences with indoor plumb-ing in a particular city block. This merely illustrates how much information the government collects.

### Publicly Available Data From Private Institutions

But the government isn't the only secondary research game in town. Several private institutions collect data on everything from product usage to public opinion, and some are incredibly generous in sharing that information.

There are too many to name here, but among our personal favorites is the Pew Research Center. Pew primarily collects public opinion data concern-ing nationally and internationally significant topics. If you want to discover opinions on education, drugs, health care, immigration, etc., they've got it. Changing trends in parenthood practices, the average person's knowledge of cybersecurity or how Americans prepare financially for retirement? It's there. Pew is a particularly useful source for researching media usage patterns, infor-mation we'll employ in Chapter 15's social media discussion.

Whether the source is public or private, secondary research's value is undeniable. During your career, someone in your organization will preface a statement by saying, "If we only knew … ." The important thing to remember is there's a good chance somebody has collected statistics from which you can build a credible answer to the problem you face, and that those raw numbers are available to the public. You just need the persistence and the skills to find them.

### Comparability

But before you can write a compelling narrative, you must have a story. A word to the wise. One statistic is not a story.

**Census Bureau**
*QuickFacts*

https://www.census.gov/
quickfacts/fact/table/US/
PST045219

You can glance at the vol-ume of statistics the Census Bureau collects by referring to the *QuickFacts*.

**Pew Research Center**

https://www.pewresearch.
org/

Pew compiles public opinion data on a wide array of topics.

Data are of little use if there is nothing with which to compare the numbers. This introduces the idea of comparability, simply the ability to be compared. Is a 78% favorability score toward your company's environmental actions good? You really can't say. If the favorability index was 92% a year ago, then something is wrong. If companies in your industry have a 62% favorability score on the same questions, then you apparently are doing something right … at least for now.

However, this is still a rather imperfect measure. What if your 78% favorability index results from averaging a 95% approval from people over 65 with a 22% favorability index for consumers under 35? One age group loves you, the second one … not so much. Upon what issues and to whom should you devote the bulk of your communication efforts?

This demonstrates the value of **cross tabulations** (or cross tabs). They let you compare variations in response from different subgroups, such as gender, age, political party or cat lover. For instance, the practitioner can discover whether the company has been more successful in publicizing its recycling efforts than its pollution control measures. As in the earlier example, analyzing cross tabs can also show whether certain publics lag in understanding the company's commitments. This guides you in deciding what story to tell and to whom to direct it.

But the strategic thinker extends the principle of cross tabulations beyond comparing apples to apples. You might think of it as comparing apples that have an orange orbiting them to other apples that have their own orbiting oranges. Here's an example: You could compare communication or marketing goals expressed in a company's mission statement (a message) with their fulfillment (a behavior).

In one case Professor Thompson supervised, an art glass company proclaimed in its mission statement that it wanted to become one of its category's top-three companies in non-U.S. sales. An independent researcher tested the company's actions to see if they tracked with the company's words. She compared the company's respective number of contacts with international media and the marketing dollars it invested in trying to capture non-U.S. accounts. She then compared those data with the same contacts used to win U.S. customers. Turned out the company directed only 6% of its media relations contacts to international media and only 3% of its marketing dollars. Pairing that data with the company's sales records, it was little wonder that over 90% of the company's products were sold within seven states surrounding its headquarters.

In isolation, these numbers don't say much. But taken together? They clearly demonstrated a disconnect between the company's stated goal and the tactics it employed. Some serious reorientation appeared in order, all due to the researcher's resourcefulness in conceiving how seemingly dissimilar data points could be made comparable.

**PRINCIPLES IN PRACTICE 4.1A   A $70 Million Lesson in Public Faith**

Systematic research can often suggest problems organizations may encounter and suggest coherent strategies they can undertake to lessen their impact. The following postmortem study on the Wounded Warrior Project (WWP), a nonprofit group enlisting public support for U.S. military personnel suffering mental or physical injuries from post 9/11 military interventions, shows how even a tremendously successful organization can suffer immense damage from tone-deaf actions.

By most accounts, the WWP was a stunning success. In CEO Steven Nardizzi's first five years as the project's leader, WWP's contributions and its expenditures on targeted veterans jumped 1,200%. Nardizzi accomplished this by instituting high-profile business practices into a nonprofit environment.

Copying performance metrics analysis and employee motivation tactics from the best performing corporate performers, Nardizzi instituted aggressive branding tactics, high-energy employee meetings and ambitious fundraising goals for the rapidly growing group of employees necessary to achieve his growth objectives.

Nardizzi capitalized on multiple revenue streams. The huge public presence WWP gained from its advertising budgets, events and media relations campaigns made the organization's logo a valuable commodity. WWP licensed the right to print the Wounded Warrior Project logo on other organizations' products. WWP amassed millions of dollars in interest from its accumulated earnings. Even selling donor contact information added to the coffers.

WWP's corporate-management orientation was complemented with the usual practices of for-profit governance. Top-performing WWP employees received significant raises. Nardizzi's own salary more than doubled over five years, likely in response to the organization's 735% revenue increase during that period. On the other hand, WWP employees—some of whom were veterans—who failed to meet fundraising quotas or other performance metrics were dismissed.

However, there were troubling signs. While some charity oversight groups gave WWP stellar reviews, others categorized its performance as middling, focusing on what those critics viewed as below-average disbursements to veterans from the organization's current-year revenue. Additionally, a number of disgruntled former employees voiced their concerns over Nardizzi's management of WWP.

Even when the public began questioning the organization's expenditures and employment practices, WWP continued its aggressive business model and advertising, seemingly ignoring public perceptions that WWP's mission was drifting from its original intent. Despite the apparent success, actions that would appear normal in a for-profit company were viewed as self-serving, wasteful and disrespectful to the wounded veterans for whom this nonprofit organization raised contributions.

In early 2016, media reports stimulated by disgruntled WWP employees erupted, accompanied by a video of a company-wide, team-building session. The report, first aired on CBS, showed about 500 WWP employees in a high-end resort renting for a reported $3 million, cheering as Nardizzi rappelled down the hotel wall into the session's opening ceremonies. In the resulting media furor, WWP made ineffectual attempts to counter the accusations of profligate spending. Within two months, Nardizzi was fired, and in the remaining eight months of the WWP's fiscal year, contributions declined $70 million and net revenue was down 60% from the previous year.

But it needn't have happened.

Nardizzi and the WWP organization had excellent evidence it never deployed in its defense. The table below presents the relevant statistics from the postmortem. Remember we said that as writers, our supposed skill is storytelling? What arguments could you have made from these columns and columns of numbers that would have helped WWP avoid or mitigate the crisis it faced?

### TABLE 4.1A Wounded Warrior, Part I

| | A | B | C | D | E | F | G | H | I | J |
|---|---|---|---|---|---|---|---|---|---|---|
| 1 | Executive Compensation & cost effectiveness measures | | | | | | | | | |
| 2 | Year | CEO pay | FY revenue | pay/ %rev | Y/Y rev $ diff | Y/Y rev grow | employ # | rev per emp | FY prog outlay | Y/Y exp grow |
| 3 | | | | | | | | | | |
| 4 | 2009 | | $ 26,102,000 | | $ 26,102,000 | | 86 | $ 303,512 | $ 12,801,000 | |
| 5 | 2010 | $ 199,171 | $ 40,943,000 | 0.49% | $ 14,841,000 | 56.9% | 125 | $ 327,544 | $ 15,637,000 | 22.2% |
| 6 | 2011 | $ 320,000 | $ 74,059,000 | 0.43% | $ 33,116,000 | 80.9% | 147 | $ 303,512 | $ 31,782,000 | 103.2% |
| 7 | 2012 | $ 312,000 | $ 154,959,000 | 0.20% | $ 80,900,000 | 109.2% | 248 | $ 624,835 | $ 55,387,000 | 74.3% |
| 8 | 2013 | $ 375,000 | $ 234,683,000 | 0.16% | $ 79,724,000 | 51.4% | 340 | $ 690,244 | $ 91,221,000 | 64.7% |
| 9 | 2014 | $ 473,015 | $ 342,066,000 | 0.14% | $ 107,383,000 | 45.8% | 481 | $ 711,156 | $ 148,641,000 | 62.9% |
| 10 | | | | | | | | | | |
| 11 | | 137% | 1210% | -72% | 311% | 68.8% | 459% | 134% | 1061% | 65.5% |
| 12 | | | | | | | | | | |
| 13 | | | | | | | | | | |
| 14 | | A is WWP fiscal reporting year | | | | | Columns B,C,D,E,G,H and I display cumulative | | | |
| 15 | | B is Nardizzi's pay in each of the designated CALENDAR years | | | | | percentage change over period. | | | |
| 16 | | C is Total WWP revenue during FY designated | | | | | | | | |
| 17 | | D is Nardizzi's annual income as % of WWP revenue | | | | | Columns C,F and J display average annual | | | |
| 18 | | E is the year-to-year % growth in WWP revenue | | | | | percentage change. | | | |
| 19 | | F is the year-to-year % growth in WWP revenue | | | | | | | | |
| 20 | | G is the FY number of WWP employees | | | | | | | | |
| 21 | | H is WWP revenue per employee | | | | | | | | |
| 22 | | I is WWP expenditure on programming (charity) | | | | | | | | |
| 23 | | J is year to year % difference in WWP programming expenditures | | | | | | | | |

Source: Calculations based on data from IRS 990 forms filed by the Wounded Warrior Project. Internal Revenue Service (2011–2015). Form 990: Return of Organization Exempt from Income Tax: Wounded Warrior Project Inc.3

## Using Data to Discover the Story: An Analysis of U.S. Income Inequality

In the authors' consultations about the important lessons we wanted this book to convey, we devoted hours concerning how we might start students on learning the process of becoming a strategic thinker.

For the most part, practitioners agree there's an important distinction between *tactics* and *strategy*. Again, employing our adversarial model, tactics refer to winning a battle; strategy focuses on winning the war by fulfilling our organization's ultimate goal. However, as much as our colleagues toss the strategic communication term around, we'd argue the profession is closer to a definition than it is to an understanding about how to do *strategic*.

Not to get all Zen on y'all, but acquiring the power of strategic thought is predicated on superior knowledge.

That doesn't mean you necessarily have to be more intelligent. You just need better information than your competitor. Beginning from sublime ignorance, through research, you'll progressively establish why an issue is a problem and who is affected by it. You can discover what it would take to solve the problem, who gains by maintaining the status quo and overwhelm the objections your adversary can summon to quash your position. It's kind of organic—a question leads to an answer, which leads to a question and, subsequently, more specific bits of information that further solidify your argument.

To illustrate, we'll lead you through the discovery process of a topic to which we bring opinions but no prior knowledge: Is U.S. income inequality a problem? If it is, what could we do about it?

Here are the ground rules. As we start this section, we have not established a research plan, nor determined even the outline of an argument we wish to eventually communicate. We're just as likely to discover there is no legitimate argument for our position as one supporting it.

We're doing no original research, conducting no interviews, traveling to no research library … every bit of information is from secondary sources accessible via a home laptop. We'll compare and combine data, but we'll restrict ourselves to the addition and primitive algebra that fifth-graders (and this textbook's senior writer) can muster. Here we go.

### The Power of the Particular

You must always be aware that you're a thinker, not a transcriber. Your choice to include this statistic, rather than that one, links your credibility, and that of your client, to the accuracy and applicability of the fact you presented. You've got to know, and be able to translate, the subtleties of statistics to your audience.

Here's a quick head-scratcher to introduce our examination of U.S. income inequality.

U.S. 2019 mean household income: $98,088

U.S. 2019 median household income: $68,703[4]

The United States has a **mean** household income of $98,088? An average income of almost $100,000 a year? That's not our ZIP codes' lived experience, and it likely isn't yours. Something seems off.

We don't want to overly stress the role of intuition in statistical analysis. However, the seasoned statistical storyteller doesn't automatically dismiss her intuition when a number sounds really odd. A look at the median income, which is about $30,000 less than the mean, offers a hint to what the real story may be.

Quick! What's the difference between the mean and the median? Overcoming flashbacks of your research class—the horror … the horror—you may recall both are indicators of central tendency. Maybe you're able to recall that the **median** is the point at which there is an equal number of cases below as above.

In this example, the median U.S. household income is $68,703. Half of households earn more, half earn less. That seems a closer representation of American life than our ~$100,000 mean.

But you should immediately think: Why is the mean income 40% higher than the median? Remember a lecture concerning a *negative skew*? A negative skew suggests there are many more instances of low incomes among the people in our data set. In order to understand the data set, and by extension our research problem, our first data points tell us we have to examine the far edges of our statistical range.

### The Wisdom of the Outliers

In fact, the statistical storyteller rarely finds insights in the middle of the data distribution. Knowing the average person, the average house, the average wage, whether defined by mean or median, generally makes poor prose. The average person doesn't climb Mt. Everest. We write about those who do.

Knowledge often hides among the averages. Between 2019 and 2020, economists predicted U.S. median income would rise by 6%, while the people among the top 1% of earners would have an 8% increase.[5] While the highest earners seem to be doing slightly better, these statistics make it seem like nearly everyone was going to experience significantly higher earnings.

This is the problem with measures of central tendency like means and medians. Even the median, which is generally considered to yield a more accurate data profile, can hide huge malformations. In Figure 4.1, we specifically look at the income growth an individual in the 25th percentile of U.S. income experienced from 2000–2019.[6] The rapidly climbing line was the rate of income growth for the top 5% of U.S. earners.

Examining the **outliers**, those data points appearing on the very ends of the data set, immediately highlights divergences the mean and median did not tell us. Figure 4.1 confirms our earlier suspicions, that the rise in median income was hiding a huge gulf in how our economy rewards rich and poor.

Drilling down into the outliers, we begin assembling a compelling story. In Figure 4.2, the data set's lower end reveals just how poor the poorest in society are. The bottom 2% report they have no net income at all! (And yes, for those of you wondering why we didn't offer

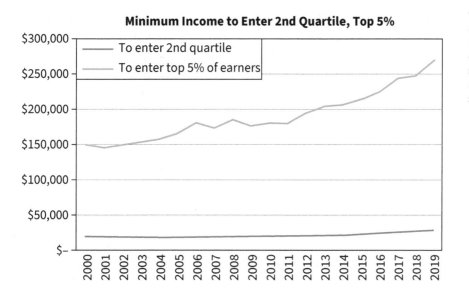

an income **mode** along with a mean and median, the most frequent income value in the United States is ZERO.)

Climbing the income ranks from that dreary finding, we discover that not a single household within the poorest 13% of American households makes enough money to reach the poverty level, even for a person living alone. Each of those centiles represents 1.3 million households—a total of 16.8 million U.S. households.[8] If you live with your partner or parent, the poverty threshold is at the 18th percentile. A household of three? You need to make as much

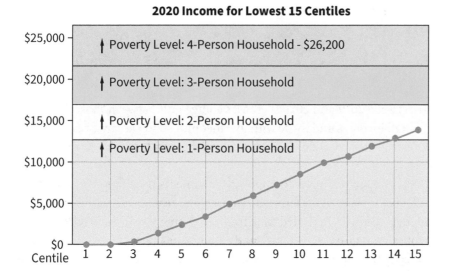

money as families in the 23rd percentile. The perfect American family of two partners and two children? The four of you would need to make more than 29% of American households. That's approximately 39 million American households cut off from the American dream.

It's just as shocking to examine the other set of outliers, the highest earners in the income spectrum. Figure 4.3 shows the minimum income you need to enter each level of the top 10% of American incomes.[11]

Of course, you're really no one if you're not in the top one-half of 1% of American earners. It's only then your annual income is above $1 million. But to those about half a percentile above you, making a million a year barely qualifies you as a peasant. To dip your toes into the waters of the 99.99 percentile, you'd have to earn 29 times more than a meager, once-over millionaire from the 99.5%.

**FIGURE 4.3  Minimum Annual Income Within the Highest 10%.** A detailed look at the top is just as telling as our look at the bottom. Even among the wealthiest 10% of Americans, there are enormous income gaps.[12,13]

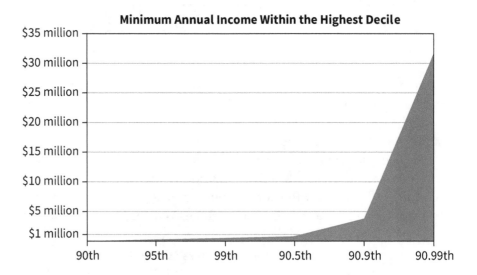

Minimum Annual Income Within the Highest Decile

## Timing Tests for Accuracy

Our research has indeed isolated a problem. The outliers confirm that in the year between 2019 and 2020 there was a huge gulf between those Americans with high incomes and those with low incomes. And we can already imagine riveting stories we could uncover to pair a human face with these shocking statistics.

But we open ourselves to opposing arguments if we stop here. Might the pandemic or some other temporary blip have created this gap? Perhaps if we viewed it within an extended time frame, this single year was itself an outlier. Of course, because you can track and compare behaviors across time, you can also verify that the evidence you see this year seems logical. If the same trend, either up or down, extends across several time periods that suggest this year's data is correct.

This tactic is called **trend analysis**. In our simplified version, we have tracked the percentage of the nation's total annual income earned by each quintile (i.e., 20% chunk) from 1980 through 2019. When charting the data, a sustained pattern justifies presuming that such a pattern would continue, barring some drastic policy change.

**Distribution of National Income by Quintile**

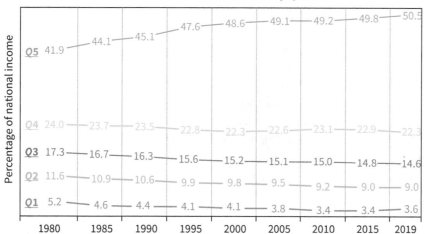

FIGURE 4.4 **Distribution of National Income Over Time.** When you examine longitudinal data—that is, information collected over a period of time—you can discover the current state of income inequality continues an established trend.[14, 15, 16, 17]

So is income distribution in the United States becoming more equitable? We again employ cross tabs to peer within the data. The trend lines in Figure 4.4 display the proportion of each year's total income collected by the members within all five quintiles between 1980 and 2019. The good news is that the incomes of the three lowest quintiles are becoming more alike. The bad news is they're compressing toward the bottom. In 1980, there was a 12.1% difference between the income controlled by the third and first quintiles. By 2019, the gap had closed to only 11%.

The surprising news is that even the fourth quintile, what most of us would deem the upper middle class, lost some of its income relative to the nation's top earners. The winners? The top 20%'s proportion of the United States' total income jumped nearly 10 percentage points during these four decades while all other income levels lost position against them.

## The Complexity of Time

At this point, we know Americans in the highest income brackets make tons more money than those in the lowest levels. We can confidently assert the groups' respective incomes have been diverging more and more. But the number we have now, detailing the percentage of wealth concentrated within quintiles, seems complicated and remote. Those characteristics don't enhance its persuasiveness. It would carry more heft if we knew how many dollars have flowed uphill to those richest Americans.

This is a more difficult research problem because of the passage of time. When you're calculating wealth, time is another variable for which you must control. Every year, inflation affects money's purchasing power. In 1980, the United States' entire national income amounted to about $3 trillion.[18] But nowadays, $3 trillion doesn't buy what it used to. Accounting for inflation, 1980's $3 trillion of buying power equals $9.2 trillion in 2019 money.[19]

Of course, the economy also has been expanding since 1980. By 2019, the nation's entire annual income was $21.6 trillion, split among the five quintiles. But how was that $12.4 trillion of additional national wealth split? While it might seem logical that all income groups would gain or lose relatively equitably against inflation, you can anticipate the answer. As Figure 4.5 demonstrates, $7.1 trillion went to the top 20%, while $2.7 trillion went to the 60% at the bottom.

These series of calculations are vitally important to the strategic thinker. Every subsequent data point eliminates another off-the-cuff rationale our opposition might introduce to support their viewpoint. It's difficult to argue that our conclusions are biased. We used the U.S. government's own statistics. And it can't be explained away because we didn't factor in time or inflation. Our research has begun to insulate us from better-funded, even smarter, adversaries.

**FIGURE 4.5** Quintile % Gain Against Inflation: 1980–2019. Over this nearly 40-year period, the richer you were, the richer you became relative to those poorer than you. The real inflation-adjusted income of America's wealthiest 20% rose 58% during that period. The poorest 20% gained only 2% against inflation.[20, 21, 22, 23, 24]

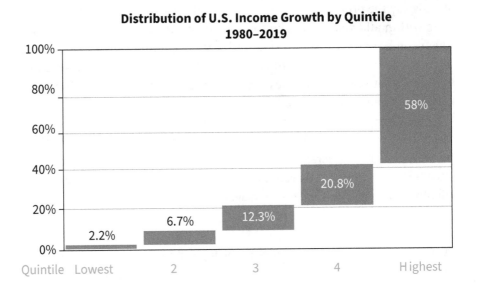

**Distribution of U.S. Income Growth by Quintile 1980–2019**

Figure 4.6 offers us a soul-sickening bit of proof that this isn't a one-time event but a vividly American problem reflecting many other pathologies in our society.

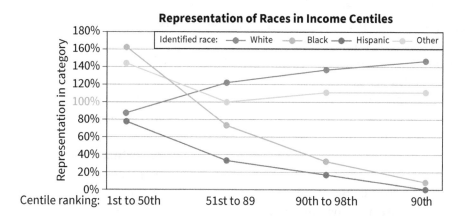

**Representation of Races in Income Centiles**

Identified race: White    Black    Hispanic    Other

Representation in category: 180%, 160%, 140%, 120%, 100%, 80%, 60%, 40%, 20%, 0%

Centile ranking: 1st to 50th    51st to 89    90th to 98th    90th

**FIGURE 4.6 Racial Differences in U.S. Income.** Though we're often uncomfortable facing it, the data demonstrate that people of color are over-represented in lower-income brackets and under-represented among the wealthier classes.[25, 26, 27]

In what at first seems to be just numbers, we affirm a painful racial judgment concerning those who have and those who have not in our nation. In Figure 4.6, the green line represents a perfect match between a proportion of the population, and a equivalent percentage of the income class. In a case of statistical perfection, African Americans, who comprise 13.4% of the U.S. population would also comprise 13.4% of each income category.

That's not the case. Black and "Other" Americans (American Indian or Alaska Native, Asian, Native Hawaiian or Other Pacific Islander and "Some Other Race") were over-represented in the whole bottom half of income among the population.[28] People who identify as White are under-represented among those in the lowest 50 centiles.

But notice as each racial classification progresses to higher incomes. Black and Hispanic populations become a smaller proportion at each decile. Conversely, White representation increases as the income categories become higher. "Other" races' representation initially dips as incomes increase but then stabilizes to approximate their proportion of American society as a whole. And the highest category, the 99th centile? African Americans are enormously under-represented and there are not even enough Hispanic Americans to register among the group. At the same time, White Americans are over-represented by nearly 50% among the most prosperous earners.[29]

Race is merely one of the demographic identifiers that correlate with income inequality. Age, education and other factors also signal potential problem areas.

And with this realization, the strategic communicator starts to envision the coalitions she can build and the opposing arguments she can deflect.

### Benchmarking

You've confirmed there's a problem and can knowledgably dispute most anyone who claims there isn't. Congratulations. You've now added your little yip to the din of people moaning about a problem for which they can't offer a remedy.

We can already hear an opponent's response: "Yeah, that's awful. It's always been that way. Now let me go back to scrambling for what's left after the rich stop eating."

One thing we've learned in our professional work: There's nothing that more completely changes an argument's course than offering an answer for exactly the problem your adversary just claimed is incapable of being answered.

But how does one find potential solutions? Despite our insistence that you've got the makings of a powerful strategic thinker, you may believe solving an institution's problem is well above your pay grade or should at least be left to those folks in the corporate suite. We're not economists nor do we have the capacity to solve staggering issues of the relationship between power and wealth. But there's one useful research approach that helps you apply the successes of others to your problem.

It's called **benchmarking**. The benchmarking process starts by discovering an organizational function or metric your organization wishes to improve. You then search for other organizations that perform the same activity, but do it much better than your organization. The benchmarked organizations don't have to resemble your organization in size or industry. They just need to perform the same operation you're looking to improve.

At that point, you investigate the processes the higher-performing organization employs that seem to contribute to its success in that one area: funding levels, performance monitoring, automation, whatever. You then evaluate whether introducing those potential innovations into your own company's operations would help you duplicate the same success your benchmarked organization experienced.

### Benchmarking Revenue

To start our benchmarking process, we looked for another country that is comparable to the United States yet is significantly more economically equitable. We settled on Norway. Table 4.2's highlighted columns offer the two key metrics for our choice.[30]

**TABLE 4.2** Income in the United States and Norway

|  | Population | Median Income | Income Rank | Equality Rank |
|---|---|---|---|---|
| United States | 328 million | $68,700 | 9th | 107/159 |
| Norway | 5 million | $82,500 | 5th | 9/159 |

Norway has many fewer people than the United States but is similar to the United States in its median per capita income, and it's driven by a diverse economy, including energy, manufacturing, mining, fisheries, shipping and tourism.[31]

One key difference? Norway is ranked ninth in the world in income equality out of 159 countries tracked; the United States is ranked 107th, slightly lower than Iran, but encouragingly, higher than Uganda.[32]

What does Norway do differently than the United States that may explain its more egalitarian society? Norway devotes 5.9% of its gross domestic product (GDP) toward "income support to working-age populations." That roughly translates to what Americans call welfare: income supplements to aid nonelderly citizens whose circumstances keep them from earning a living wage. The United States devotes 1.9% of its GDP to the same group. If the United States spent the same percentage on income support as Norway, it would require adding $850 billion to the $407 billion it currently spends on such programs.[33]

Let's get to benchmarking. We examine an outside organization (in this case, the government of Norway) to define a key metric (percentage of GDP spent on income support) related to an objective our organization would like to emulate (international top-10 position for citizens' income equality).

Yes, we acknowledge the United States has issues of culture, history and race that Norway doesn't face. But on the other hand, Norway copes with a harsh environment and largely inarable topography the United States largely doesn't possess. We also acknowledge that benchmarking multiple factors and understanding how they interact is critically important to making sound policy decisions and countering arguments against our position.

However, for the sake of this example, we recognize this key comparison, the percentage of GDP spent on income support, potentially represents a powerful argument concerning Norway's success. Reduced to its essential element, to reach our goal of enhanced income equality we need to find $850 billion more to fund an income-support system for America's 328 million citizens.

We now look for systems in the Norwegian government that we might copy to bring us success. What's a big difference between Norway and the United States? Well, one is that Norway's maximum income tax rates kick in way sooner than those in the United States. In Norway, households begin to pay the highest tax rate of 39% on any earnings over $132,000.[34] Presently, a U.S. household pays the maximum federal rate of 37% on any income over $622,000.[35] That income ranks those earners among the top one-half of 1%.[36] There are only about 642,000 U.S. households that fall into that bracket.

This suggests a significant distinction in the way each country thinks of taxes. Norwegians begin to pay the highest tax rate on the first kroner they earn above 160% of the country's median income. In the United States, that rate doesn't apply until the first dollar after a person's income is 905% above the median. And it's not that the United States is overtaxed. The United States ranked 33rd in total tax burden among the 37 economically developed nations, a point enhancing the power of our argument.

What would happen if we instituted Norwegian tax rates into the United States federal tax code (Figure 4.7)? The wealthiest 30% of U.S. households would pay a Norway-like 37% on every dollar of income above $110,000. Instituting the highest tax rate for incomes 1.6 times the median income would result in 38.6 million more U.S. households offering a fuller measure of gratitude for the security, lawfulness and liberty America offers them to earn and protect their ample salary. Of course, the tax rates for 70% of households would not change.

**FIGURE 4.7  Norway's Marginal Tax Rate Applied to the United States.** By taxing the top 30% of earners at a rate similar to Norway, the United States could raise more than enough tax revenue to cover equivalent income-support programs.[37, 38, 39]

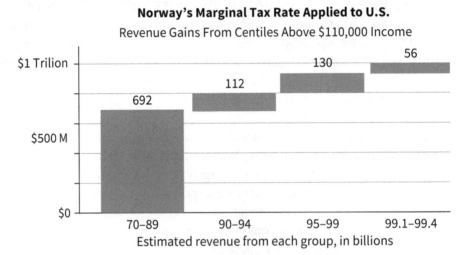

**Norway's Marginal Tax Rate Applied to U.S.**

Revenue Gains From Centiles Above $110,000 Income

Estimated revenue from each group, in billions

In bottom-line numbers, that change alone would put about $945 billion into the federal budget in 2020, a 17% boost to federal funding. We said we needed $850 billion to replicate Norway's income supplement budget. We made that much, with $95 billion to spare.

## PRINCIPLES IN PRACTICE 4.1B   Just Numbers, Right?

**TABLE 4.1B** Wounded Warrior, Part II

|    | A | B | C | D | E | F | G | H | I | J |
|----|---|---|---|---|---|---|---|---|---|---|
| 1 | Executive Compensation & cost effectiveness measures | | | | | | | | | |
| 2 | Year | CEO pay | FY revenue | pay/%rev | Y/Y rev $ diff | Y/Y rev grow | employ # | rev per emp | FY prog outlay | Y/Y exp grow |
| 3 | | | | | | | | | | |
| 4 | 2009 | | $ 26,102,000 | | $ 26,102,000 | | 86 | $ 303,512 | $ 12,801,000 | |
| 5 | 2010 | $ 199,171 | $ 40,943,000 | 0.49% | $ 14,841,000 | 56.9% | 125 | $ 327,544 | $ 15,637,000 | 22.2% |
| 6 | 2011 | $ 320,000 | $ 74,059,000 | 0.43% | $ 33,116,000 | 80.9% | 147 | $ 303,512 | $ 31,782,000 | 103.2% |
| 7 | 2012 | $ 312,000 | $ 154,959,000 | 0.20% | $ 80,900,000 | 109.2% | 248 | $ 624,835 | $ 55,387,000 | 74.3% |
| 8 | 2013 | $ 375,000 | $ 234,683,000 | 0.16% | $ 79,724,000 | 51.4% | 340 | $ 690,244 | $ 91,221,000 | 64.7% |
| 9 | 2014 | $ 473,015 | $ 342,066,000 | 0.14% | $ 107,383,000 | 45.8% | 481 | $ 711,156 | $ 148,641,000 | 62.9% |
| 10 | | | | | | | | | | |
| 11 | | 137% | 1210% | -72% | 311% | 68.8% | 459% | 134% | 1061% | 65.5% |
| 12 | | | | | | | | | | |
| 13 | | | | | | | | | | |
| 14 | A is WWP fiscal reporting year | | | | | Columns B,C,D,E,G,H and I display cumulative | | | | |
| 15 | B is Nardazzi's pay in each of the designated CALENDAR years | | | | | percentage change over period. | | | | |
| 16 | C is Total WWP revenue during FY designated | | | | | | | | | |
| 17 | D is Nardazzi's annual income as % of WWP revenue | | | | | Columns C,F and J display average annual | | | | |
| 18 | E is the year-to-year % growth in WWP revenue | | | | | percentage change. | | | | |
| 19 | F is the year-to-year % growth in WWP revenue | | | | | | | | | |
| 20 | G is the FY number of WWP employees | | | | | | | | | |
| 21 | H is WWP revenue per employee | | | | | | | | | |
| 22 | I is WWP expenditure on programming (charity) | | | | | | | | | |
| 23 | J is year to year % difference in WWP programming expenditures | | | | | | | | | |

Source: Calculations made based on data from IRS 990 forms filed by the Wounded Warrior Project. Internal Revenue Service (2011–2015). Form 990: Return of Organization Exempt from Income Tax: Wounded Warrior Project Inc.[40]

Actually, these numbers might have been used to refute virtually every one of the organization's critics.

Was Nardizzi paid too much? Tracking five years of his calendar-year salary (that's column B) between 2010 and 2014, his salary did more than double. The organization's total revenue (column C) for the same time? Up 750%. In fact, you could surmise that he was more overpaid in 2010 than in 2014. Look at column D. In his first year, Nardizzi's salary alone consumed about one-half of 1% of the organization's revenue. By 2014, that percentage, even with his higher salary, had declined by a factor of 3.

Further research would have established interesting anecdotal support: Even in WWP's hometown of Jacksonville, Florida, the CEO of the Gator Bowl Association, which produces an annual college football bowl game, claimed a $375,000 salary from his nonprofit's revenue—about $30,000 higher than Nardizzi—despite earning $320 million less than WWP.

What about WWP's worker management skills that might have brought on employee complaints? It's difficult to assess supervisor attitudes or empathy by looking at numbers. However, column E tracks the organization's huge growth in employees, which climbed 200% in just five years. Such rapid employee expansion might typically create inefficiencies resulting from lesser productivity from new hires or lost work time instead devoted to training. Yet WWP, no matter the complaints expressed by former employees, kept increasing the revenue yielded from each employee, as seen in column F. That's rarely an indication of low employee morale.

And the criticism from charity watchdogs that WWP didn't devote a sufficient percentage of its current-year revenue to the charity's recipients? Look at column C. You'll notice that WWP had a problem few charities suffer from. During Nardizzi's five-year tenure, the organization averaged a 70% revenue increase every year. WWP's annual revenue gains were so big that it would have been irresponsible to commit the organization to expenditures two years hence, which would be a normal timeline for an organization that needed to plan programming and find charity partners to help its targeted veterans. But when you compare WWP's program expenditures during the fiscal period two years after each new record-setting revenue, WWP's gifts very closely tracked and sometimes surpassed the organization's revenue two years previously.

The storyteller's possible tale? Nardizzi was an up-to-date leader for this generation's veterans. Nardizzi's integration of best business practices straight from top-performing American corporations made him a hero to this cadre of young wounded veterans whose concerns were remote to traditional veterans' organizations dominated by the service members of wars that ended 40-plus years ago. The productivity and revenue gains the organization displayed highlighted the coming approach that charities might consider adopting if they really want to more completely fulfill their missions.

And why were workplace practices—like annual motivational retreats, demanding performance goals matched with performance-centered salaries and capitalizing on multiple revenue streams—bad when employed successfully by a nonprofit but celebrated when used by corporate players? After all, is the duty of a corporate CEO to deliver the best stock market returns through exemplary performance less important than an organizational leader who is attempting to offer benefits to the nation's veterans, injured during their service?

Of course, in retrospect, there's no guarantee that explaining Nardizzi's rationale through a well-designed communication campaign would have changed the organization's eventual course. But they would have established that the organization was a consciously, even conscientiously, directed organization that did not undertake these actions solely through the selfishness or thoughtlessness of its managers.[41]

## Benchmarking Expenses

If we don't want to find our $850 billion exclusively through revenue increases, we could also benchmark to raise the funding by cutting another part of the federal budget.

Again, we look for a function the Norwegian and U.S. governments share but to which each invests dramatically different resources. We could have chosen health care, where the United States has the world's most expensive system. It spends 43% more per capita on health care than the nation ranking second and 160% more than the worldwide average.[42]

However, the defense budget still represents 54% of the U.S. governmental discretionary spending budget. One goes where the money is.[43]

The distinctions between the two countries are stark. Defense spending in Norway totaled 3.4% of government expenditures in 2020. The United States spent 15.9% of its governmental budget on defense.[44] Calculated another way, Norway spent 1.5% of its GDP on defense; the United States 4.9%. The United States alone accounts for 38% of the world's total military expenditures.[45]

So what would happen if we statistically reexamined the United States' defense expenditures?

We think of the United States as an essentially pacifist state. We perceive ourselves as the "world's policeman," the thin line that protects the boundaries between peace and chaos. However, statistically, we can argue that the United States is one of the world's most militarized societies. Figure 4.8 starkly communicates the fact, comparing U.S. spending to China, the world's second-largest military power. The third column represents all the rest of the world, which includes such military powers as Russia, Saudi Arabia, Israel, Germany and Britain.

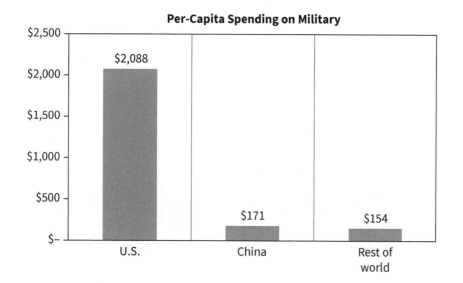

**Per-Capita Spending on Military**

FIGURE 4.8 **Per-Capita Spending on Military.** The United States spends more per citizen on defense than any other nation and by a wide margin.[46, 47, 48]

Each U.S. citizen pays 12.2 times more for the country's military than a person in China, the second-largest economy and presumably the nation's most formidable strategic threat, invests in its military.

We can deliver more statistics arguing the U.S. military is overbuilt. Table 4.3 shows some miscellaneous financial data that validates an argument for changing the nation's priorities from war-making to making its citizens' lives more equitable.

**TABLE 4.3  Some Comparative Numbers on Military Spending[49]**

|  | Military Budgets: Billion $ | % Military Spending to Gov Budget | Military Spending as % of GDP | Military as % of Population | $ per Active-Duty Service Personnel | Reserve and Active-Duty Military |
|---|---|---|---|---|---|---|
| United States | $786 | 16.6% | 3.4% | 0.67% | $604,615 | 2.2 million |
| China | $261 | 7.6% | 1.8% | 0.16% | $109,940 | 2.5 million |
| Russia | $65 | 24.0% | 10.0% | 6.9% | $72,222 | 2.9 million |
| Rest of World | $905 | 3.5% | 1.8% | 0.4% | $38,012 | 23.7 million |

Most people would view each comparison as jaw-droppingly oversized. The United States spends more than twice as much of its annual governmental budget on the military as its largest competitor. The United States, with the world's largest gross domestic product, still spends nearly twice as much of its annual wealth on defense than China.

And to those who suggest the United States trusts its defense to a small percentage of the population? Well, they're correct. The country's armed forces constitute a bit more than one-half of 1% of the citizenry. On the other hand, an American citizen is four times more likely to be in the armed forces than a Chinese citizen. And while tanks, missiles, planes and ships cost every nation lots of money, how is it that the United States spends 5.5 times more on each active-duty military member than China or 14 times more than the militaries in the rest of the world?

What's the risk? This is a critical question in our persuasion campaign since we're suggesting to U.S. citizens that they trade what they now perceive as safety for a commitment to an egalitarian society.

Yes, the United States trails China in a few categories of military might. Most critically, China has 800,000 more members of the military than the United States. However, when the trained military reserves for both nations are added to the total, the United States only trails by about 340,000 total members. China sometimes has more pieces of equipment than the United States. For instance, China possesses much more artillery and more fighter planes than the United States, both of which the United States have increasingly supplanted by drones. China's navy has more ships, but China's excess is largely in smaller and auxiliary ships. Likewise, China's navy has 76 submarines to the United States' 71. However, all U.S. subs are nuclear powered, while China has only nine (see Table 4.4).[50]

**TABLE 4.4  Comparing Chinese and U.S. Armaments**

| Weapons Category | Carriers | Helicopters | Aircraft | Battle Tanks | Nuclear Warheads |
|---|---|---|---|---|---|
| USA | 20 | 4,889 | 12,304 | 6,393 | 6,500 |
| China | 2 | 1,170 | 4,182 | 1,000 | 280 |

Are these statistics evidence that we've been frightened into spending the nation's wealth on the military? We can't prove that. However, to the persuasive communicator, it poses a telling contradiction. How can we believe our military's personnel and our technologically superior equipment and weapons make the United States the world's most deadly strike force … but simultaneously we tremble before existential threats from what we tell ourselves are far less able soldiers and fewer, less capable weapons?

To a storyteller commissioned to advance income equality, it might be argued there are superfluous federal budget expenditures that could be redirected to another cause.

It's been several pages, so let's go all Zen again. The strategic thinker, like the master of self-defense, allows the weight and velocity of her opponent to help achieve her goals. Understanding the arguments your opponents employ to convince themselves guides you to the rewards you'll need to offer them in your own persuasion process. Persuasive writers often do the same, listening carefully to their adversaries' stated wishes and then giving them precisely what they asked for—just in a different package than they envisioned. Your research is guided by listening closely to your adversary's reasoning and anticipating the hard questions they'll be asking you in a future debate.

So what would our approach be? Defense experts demanding higher and higher budgets have asserted that the United States must be able to fight two wars at the same time. Starting with President Lyndon Johnson in the 1960s, political leaders from both parties have forcefully argued for this "two-war doctrine."[51]

Here's how we give them their two-war funding and still gather money for our income-support plan. For the sake of our argument, we agree to agree with defense analysts that the United States defense budget should enable the nation to fight two wars simultaneously. We think this is a defensible conclusion: If the United States matched the defense funding of both countries it assumes to be its most likely adversaries, then it could fight those two wars (Figure 4.9). At least some portion of funds above that level could be considered extraneous to U.S. defense strategy.

How does the math work? The United States spent $786 billion on defense in 2019. China countered that with its $240 billion military budget and Russia anted up another $65 billion. If the United States matched the military funding for the two countries it perceives to be the most formidable threats, there would still be $463 billion remaining from the United States' current defense spending. That's short of the total $850 billion we need to replicate Norway's income-support funding formula.

FIGURE 4.9 **Fulfilling the Two-War Doctrine.** Were the United States to simply match the spending of its two most threatening adversaries, there would still be a massive excess of funds.[52]

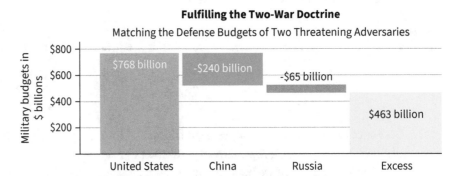

**Fulfilling the Two-War Doctrine**

Matching the Defense Budgets of Two Threatening Adversaries

However, note that we've only benchmarked one category of the U.S. federal government's $4.4 trillion budget. And note we've made a feasible argument that frees nearly a half-trillion dollars on the cost side, to which we can add the $945 billion we envisioned by implementing the Norway-like tax hikes.

At this point, we've got a powerful, persuasive argument. Through a brief analysis conducted from Professor Thompson's arm chair, we now have a financial pool of $1.4 trillion from which we could negotiate a softening of either our tax or defense suppositions and still fully fund the $850 billion we need for the United States' new income-support program. We've imagined story lines, conceived political partnerships and equipped ourselves with hard-nosed economic arguments, as well as appeals to human decency. So operates a strategic thinker.

## For Real?

This is admittedly a fanciful exercise. Our goal was to argue a seemingly impossible task: constructing a logical solution that would reverse a century-long transfer of wealth from lower- and middle-income Americans to the nation's top earners. Will we two professors be able to yank hundreds of billions of dollars from the clinging grasp of America's kleptocracy? Do we think we'll be able to pluck a half-trillion dollars from the military-industrial complex? We sincerely doubt it's going to happen.

However, we wanted to demonstrate the exercise of strategic thinking. We presented ourselves with a vexing social problem: income inequality in the United States. Truthfully, we didn't know the research steps we would take to analyze the problem. Initially, we didn't even know the size of the problem. We didn't know about Norway's commendable success in battling inequality, nor its tax structure. Until we benchmarked what portion of its GDP it devoted to income support, we didn't know the goal we could propose if the United States were to tackle the issue. The prodigious amount of government funding used to tackle income inequality dictated that we find the federal government's largest pool of money in its discretionary budget, the U.S. military. And no, offhand, we didn't know the proportion of China's obsolete tanks, though we're certain that piece of trivia will make you the life of your next party.

Instead, we've shown you a process. At this point, you should be mentally recording the potential audience blocs with which specific messages will resonate, and what media platforms you might use to reach them. Your choice of funding to solve your problems automatically introduces you to the groups who will be opposing you. Your confidence should be bolstered because you know the answers to many of the questions with which your adversaries will confront you. You have a solution for a problem they may not even know exists. And you're ahead of them in other ways. You have a familiarity with research sources your competitor can only start learning after you drop your campaign.

It's about the process. We can't answer the research questions with which you'll be confronted in your career in persuasion. But we can tell you to trust the research process.

## Acting Ethically

Chapter 5 is next, where we'll focus on communication ethics in greater detail, but we thought we'd get a head start as we conclude our discussion about research. We know all this talk of research methods and statistical analysis may seem overwhelming for some of you. But like most practitioners, we believe in the value of research, and not just because it's an effective tool to help you craft more audience-relevant messages. Understanding how data are gathered and analyzed lets you evaluate the credibility of information presented to you, both about your organization and issues relevant to its operations.

Sometimes researchers make honest mistakes that bias their findings; sometimes, it's more nefarious. Our advice? Trust your gut. If a figure doesn't add up, an opinion poll seems off or a research finding doesn't feel right, look deeper. Maybe there are issues with the sample or the survey that explain how unexpected results were arrived at, possibly as the result of researcher mistakes or purposeful malpractice. Maybe the data you have only paint part of the picture, as the mean and median income figures did in our example. Knowing these issues, about the story behind the story, about these things no one else knows, can be a powerful tool for a strategic communicator. Moreover, now that you know the ins and outs of research, you have a responsibility not only to conduct research ethically yourself, but also to ensure that others do.

## SUMMARY

- The time constraints of strategic communication jobs frequently allow only for time to conduct secondary research, which can still offer an enormous amount of relevant information to your tasks.

- Outliers, those values on the extreme ends of your data set, often provide more valuable insights than measures of central tendency.

- The benchmarking process, in which you examine best practices for a particular function, lets you develop persuasive arguments supporting your recommendations.

### Scenario Prompts: Market Research

You'll find Scenario Prompts on pp. 367–386 of this textbook. While they vary in subject and difficulty, they help you hone your critical thinking and strategic writing skills. The following are best suited to this chapter's topics.

Management: 1.5, 3.3, 9.2

# Ethical Issues for Persuasive Writers

## A Guide for Doing Good and Making Moral Choices

**LESSONS FROM LIFE** **What I Know About Communication Ethics, I Learned From My Gallbladder**

When I was 26 years old, my gallbladder nearly ruptured. If you're like me, you haven't given much thought to this little bile-storing organ but trust me: When you wake up in the middle of the night with sharp, stinging pangs in your abdomen, you become uncomfortably well acquainted with the little basta … uh, bile producer.

After several hours, I grudgingly agreed to an emergency room trip, which I had avoided because I wasn't sure I could afford an ER visit—despite having health insurance.

For agonizing hours, I saw patients in the more highly regarded triage categories—heart attacks, strokes, stab wounds—treated. Finally, a nurse escorted me to a semiprivate room, where my gallbladder was awarded that night's "most likely to rupture" sash and tiara.

"We'd like to go ahead and remove your gallbladder," the ER doctor said.

"I'd like you to remove it," I replied, with the relieved sigh only a morphine drip can induce.

About then a hospital billing agent entered the room. I will never forget her beside-mannerless greeting: "Mr. Browning … sorry to hear about your ailment. Today's visit will be $900. Cash, check or charge?"

"Charge, I suppose," I stammered. "But where did you get the $900 figure?"

"Well, that's the average cost for an ER visit, and we prefer to receive the payment upfront," she explained. "I have some forms to go over with you. Mr. Browning, what is your occupation?" I told her I worked in a health insurance company's communication department. "That's a relief!" she answered. "You'll at least *understand* everything I'm about to tell you."

She briefed me on what I assume were the standard billing procedures, and she was right: Despite the morphine drip, I understood every jargon-filled sentence.

My ER misadventure provokes a variety of moral issues: Is it right that even those with insurance should worry so much about health care costs? Should care be rationed based on need? Should the doctor have presented less invasive alternatives *before* jumping to a surgical solution? And if she had, could I have made an informed decision while under the influence of powerful drugs—or provide adequate consent on medical and billing documents for that matter?

What disturbed me most was the notion that I would understand the value and limits of my health insurance *only because I worked for an insurance company!* In my view, this represents a profound ethical communication failure by the insurance industry, health-care providers, the education system and our civic leaders.

Consider how insurance options are often explained to the two-thirds of Americans who buy insurance through their employers or on the individual marketplace.[1] Health benefit summaries are alphabet soups of PPOs, HMOs, HDHPs, PCPs, HSAs, FSAs—and that's just a few alphabetic permutations.[2] Few readers can even *identify* those acronyms, let alone *understand* their complexities and interrelationships.

How can people be expected to make an informed—literally life-and-death—decision about something they can't hope to understand? "Surely this is wrong," you may find yourself thinking. I'd agree. But why is it wrong? And how might you more adequately and rightly communicate those messages when you face such challenges? Those are the difficult, yet immensely important questions this chapter will address.

—*NB*

---

## What You Know

- Theory helps us organize our social world so we can better explain and predict others' actions.

- According to stakeholder theory, organizations and the strategic communicators who represent them have responsibilities to numerous publics.

- Research and planning are essential first steps in determining which messages will be most persuasive and effective.

- Inoculation theory contends that communicating the benefits, as well as costs, of taking a given action is an effective way to create lasting behavioral change.

## What You'll Learn

- How the most relied-upon ethical theories can help you categorize actions as either right or wrong

- How ethical obligations to stakeholders often conflict, creating difficult yet solvable moral dilemmas

- How to apply moral theory in your language choices to ensure persuasive messages are ethically constructed and delivered

- How adhering to moral principles such as justice, trust, wisdom and truthfulness leads you to construct messages that are not only more ethical but often more effective

## PR Ethics? Is That Even a Thing?

Deep down, we can understand why many people mock the very notion of PR and business ethics. Ethically conducted business rarely commands newspaper headlines. However, multiple news cycles can be dominated by stories of fraud, embezzlement, deception, product failures, and inappropriate or insensitive language choices.

While PR practitioners occupy a variety of roles, crisis communication and damage control are by far the best known. They're practically synonymous with our profession. When a crisis strikes, you can bet at least three people will soon meet: the CEO, a lawyer and a PR practitioner. The PR professional has three roles during a crisis: (1) ensuring faulty messaging doesn't make an already bad situation worse, (2) developing strategies to rehabilitate organizational reputation and (3) putting fail-safes in place to prevent repeat crises.

There's nothing wrong with taking corrective action, in either a practical or a moral sense. However, it's worth noting that PR and strategic communicators are most visible to the public during times of crisis, which often result from nefarious or negligent organizational behavior. Given this common association in the public's mind, unfair as it may be, it's no surprise our profession's image is ethically tainted.

Sadly, the public rarely sees our daily successes. Our greater ethical accomplishments occur when we help organizations avoid crises altogether, or the times we help management build mutually beneficial relationships with stakeholders, or the times we push companies to adopt socially responsible practices that benefit both their key publics and their bottom lines.

A professional's moral desire to do good and be good often drives such successes. Indeed, good strategic communicators incorporate ethical considerations into their daily practices, and numerous professional organizations—the Arthur W. Page Society, the Public Relations Society of America (PRSA), the American Advertising Federation, the International Association of Business Communicators, etc.—have developed ethics codes to guide practitioners. While flawed, these guidelines nevertheless demonstrate a concerted effort among communication professionals to understand what is right and to act accordingly.

Though such understanding is not easily achieved, it is critical. Learning the terminology and exercising the thought patterns of moral philosophies will help you recognize what is right and what is wrong. More importantly, moral education will help you understand *why* something is right or wrong.

It's also important in creating prose. Knowing the what and the why helps you more convincingly urge your clients into ethical action and more forcefully advance their positions in public communication.

Ethical stances are often manifested in the writer's seemingly simple, day-to-day activities of choosing one word rather than another. We make deliberate choices about the words we use—and for that matter, the words we don't use. We choose them for specific reasons to elicit desired outcomes. Word choice is an ethical exercise. Therefore, understanding the intent behind those choices and their outcomes builds moral character we can employ when confronted with more profound ethical challenges.

## Inherently Fraught With Ethical Issues
### Moral, Immoral and Amoral

In Chapters 1 and 2, we discussed the numerous publics to whom strategic communicators are responsible. These stakeholders place countless demands upon us and the organizations we represent. Professor George Cheney illustrates these demands with a clever and insightful play on words: "Practitioners are routinely responsible ("response-able") to multiple publics."[3]

Virtually every organizational action provokes effected stakeholders to demand some response: Employees expect to know why their organization changed its retirement account contributions; shareholders expect justification for withheld dividend payments; managers expect an explanation for why quarterly sales were down when advertising budgets went up; customers expect an answer for how a recalled product made it on the shelves in the first place.

Practitioners routinely respond to these stakeholder questions, and our actions demonstrate the ethical approach we use to formulate our responses.

Sometimes these justifications are pragmatic and largely **amoral**, meaning they lack any deep ethical component related to moral rights and wrongs. Perhaps quarterly sales were down because consumers reduced spending during an economic slump. Neither you nor your organization did anything wrong.

However, such justifications and the prose we use to explain them are often imbued with ethical concerns. **Ethics** represent a process for making decisions and taking actions based on considerations of moral rights and wrongs. For example, one reason to recall defective products is to avoid harming consumers. Intentionally hurting others is generally considered wrong; therefore, we are ethically obligated not to. Why is the product recall necessary? Well, that could result from some unintentional, unforeseeable and innocent mistake—which most would view as *amoral*—or from knowingly marketing a shoddy product—which most would view as *immoral*.

At this point, you may be thinking, "I just have to do right by all my stakeholders, and I'll be fine."

Oh, young writer, were life so simple! Every organizational decision comes with a host of consequences, some knowable, some unintended and many controversial. Because resources are finite and stakeholder interests frequently conflict, organizations often find themselves playing zero-sum games in which one stakeholder group benefits at the direct or indirect cost of another.

You saw these calculations playing out during the 2020 coronavirus pandemic. Does the small business owner choose to pay the rent on her property or pay her employees? In reopening schools, how do governments balance the inherent health risks to students, faculty and staffs with the long-term costs to young people improperly educated or socialized? Should the local food bank be closed to ensure volunteers' safety when the people they serve may starve as a result?

## Your Everyday Words and Actions Matter, Every Day

COVID-19 admittedly represents an extreme case of conflicting stakeholder interests, but equally difficult organizational decisions occur daily. Moreover, these choices reveal the morality of the organization and all its employees. Their character and their views on professional and personal moral duties are invariably intertwined in these determinations.

**Strategic Thought**

In 2009, the federal minimum hourly wage was $7.25. In 2021, it was $7.25. At 40 hours a week, 52 weeks a year—so no vacation—that totals $15,080.[4] Activists have sought to raise the minimum wage, with the most commonly floated figure being $15 an hour, or $31,200 a year.[5] Imagine you work for a publicly traded company considering a minimum wage increase. Is this a moral or amoral decision? Why? How would different stakeholders (e.g., employees, customers, investors) be affected, either positively or negatively? How would you best explain this new policy to each public?

Every day of your career, you must explain these decisions to both the winners and losers of organizational policies. In many cases, that means ethically justifying the reasoning behind these choices and their impacts. As a strategic communicator, understanding moral decision-making and communicating your rationales are vital components of your professional preparation.

## Studying Ethics:
## It's Really Not so Bad

By now, you know we're going to talk about ethical theory, and we can sense your intense desire to hurl this book against the wall. We're not surprised. Professor Browning has been reading and writing on ethics for nearly two decades, and he's shattered his fair share of book spines.

Studying ethics and morality can sometimes be frustrating, even overwhelming. So before we begin discussing what are often complicated concepts, we urge you to keep this in mind: Nobody expects you to be Aristotle … or for that matter, even a philosophy major.

Take comfort that such feelings of moral ineptitude are common among seasoned professionals as well. Professor Shannon Bowen's survey of PR practitioners revealed many felt their lack of education and experience in ethics left them ill-equipped to help organizations in ethical decision-making.[6] Despite this perception, PR professionals generally exhibit above-average levels of moral reasoning.[7] If you understand even the basics of moral theory, you're well on your way to becoming an ethical and effective persuasive communicator—perhaps better prepared than those practicing today.

## What Does It Mean to Act Rightly?

Theories of moral philosophy differ in meaningful ways, but they share many commonalities as well. One such similarity regards the issues they address and the questions they seek to answer. From our perspective, every ethical theory in some way addresses the five questions summarized in Memory Memo 5.1. As we begin exploring these theories, remember these questions and consider how various approaches compare. Remember as well that we simply don't have the time or space to study dozens of ethical theories. Instead, our discussion will focus on three prominent moral philosophies summarized in Table 5.1: utilitarianism, deontology and virtue ethics.

**MEMORY MEMO 5.1** Five Questions Moral Philosophies Attempt to Answer

1. How do we perceive the nature of right and wrong?
2. How does that perception shape our internal consciences?
3. How do our consciences influence our decision-making?
4. How do other external factors similarly influence our decision-making?
5. How, if at all, do our decisions lead to moral behavior?

**TABLE 5.1  Prominent Moral Philosophies**[8]

| Approach | Actions are good if ... | Key Concepts | Key Figures |
|---|---|---|---|
| Utilitarianism | ... they produce the best outcomes for most people involved. | • Greatest good for the greatest number<br>• Hedonic calculus | • John Stuart Mill<br>• Jeremy Bentham<br>• Henry Sidgwick<br>• Peter Singer |
| Deontology | ... they are undertaken out of moral duties and adhere to universal ethical rules. | • Moral duty<br>• Good will<br>• Categorical imperative | • Immanuel Kant<br>• William David Ross<br>• Thomas Nagel<br>• Frances Kamm |
| Virtue Ethics | ... they are characteristic of how virtuous persons typically act. | • Virtue<br>• Character<br>• Practical wisdom<br>• Golden mean | • Aristotle<br>• Philippa Foot<br>• Rosalind Hursthouse<br>• Alasdair MacIntyre |

## The Importance of the Greater Good: Mill's Utilitarianism

Let's begin with **utilitarianism**. It's likely the ethical approach you're most familiar with. Try to create the greatest good for the greatest number.[9]

In broader terms, utilitarianism is a *consequentialist ethic*. That means it evaluates an act's goodness based on the outcomes it generates. Utilitarians generally consider human happiness and well-being as the ultimate good, treating all human beings as equal in this respect. Therefore, actions are deemed good insofar as they contribute to human happiness and well-being. The greater that happiness is and the more people who share it, the "more good" an action is.

### Calculating the Good

As Chapter 2's discussion of social exchange theory suggested, matters of morality can to some degree be understood mathematically. When we adopt a utilitarian perspective, "greatest good" and "greatest number" are relative terms. The latter is pretty easy to quantify: How many people did my action affect? This is the principle of *extension*.

But how exactly do you quantify goodness? "Something that makes people happy," you might say. Fair enough. But what if you're faced with the blissful decision of choosing between two options, both of which make equal numbers of people happy? Which option should you choose? Numerically, there is no difference, so to determine which one is better you need to know which option generates more happiness.

Eighteenth-century philosopher Jeremy Bentham formalized morality math with what he called the *hedonic calculus* (*hedonic*, as in *hedonism*, the pursuit of pleasure). Extension and the six other principles outlined in Memory Memo 5.2 help us calculate the level of goodness in different ways.

*Intensity* suggests we consider how much happiness the action generates. For example, if your boss offered you a 3% raise, that would certainly make you happy. But not as happy as a 5% raise. Thus a bigger raise represents a more intense good.

*Duration* asks us to consider how long the happiness that results from our action will last. Consider the old proverb: "Give a man a fish and you feed him for a day; teach a man to fish and you feed him for a lifetime." Clearly, if someone is hungry and you give him food, you've made that man happy. But that happiness only lasts until hunger returns. However, if you enable him to provide his own nourishment, then he's happy for the foreseeable future.

> **MEMORY MEMO 5.2** The Hedonic Calculus
>
> - *Extension:* How many people will be affected?
> - *Intensity:* How much good does this generate?
> - *Duration:* How long will that good last?
> - *Certainty:* How likely is it that good will occur?
> - *Propinquity:* How soon will that good occur?
> - *Fecundity:* How likely is it this good will spawn future goods?
> - *Purity*: How likely is it this good will NOT spawn future evils?

But the future is only so foreseeable. When we act to generate some desired outcome, there's no way to guarantee that result. Nevertheless, some outcomes are more probable than others. Thus how *certain* we are that our anticipated results will happen may dictate whether we take the action.

Think back to the early days of the coronavirus outbreak, around March 2020. Because the virus was new, scientific knowledge about prevention was far from settled. Experts weren't certain wearing masks in public would effectively combat the spread.[10] However, they were certain that personal protective equipment (PPE) was vital in safeguarding health care workers and that we faced a national PPE shortage at the time. Advising the public to wear masks would likely strain an already thin supply chain for PPE. In hindsight, we now know face coverings effectively combat COVID-19 spread.[11] However, in early 2020 the relative certainty of the harm to health care workers outweighed the uncertainty of the public benefit. Hence the decision advising against widespread mask usage.

The remaining three principles are in many ways expansions of those we just discussed. *Propinquity* asserts that, all things being equal, the sooner we can deliver happiness to others, the better. Note, however, that this is not a wholesale argument for immediate gratification. If you jump the line at the deli counter, you'll happily get your sandwich sooner but at the expense of the customers now behind you whose gratification you'll delay. This is wrong. However, if the deli owner takes advance orders to speed the line's flow, then we all get our lunches sooner. The owner's choice enhances the communal good.

*Fecundity* and *purity* consider potential domino effects that various actions may spark. For example, most people would likely agree that imparting knowledge and career skills is a good action because it prepares students for fruitful careers. As professors, we believe helping students master persuasive communication skills will make them more employable and likely happier over their lifetimes. Writing this book extends the effects of our deed, meeting the test of fecundity. Huzzah for us!

However, if you use these skills to urge impoverished Indonesian children to smoke cigarettes or lobby Congress to permit haphazard nuclear proliferation, then suddenly you've diminished the goodness from our original act of imparting wisdom. In hedonic calculus terms, the authors dedicated an entire chapter of this book to ethics to help ensure you practice persuasive communication thoughtfully and deliberately to preserve the fecundity and purity of our instructional actions. So damn it, don't let us down!

### The Flaws of Utilitarianism

Of course, utilitarianism is not without its flaws. One of the most common critiques is that because of its focus on serving the greatest number, utilitarianism tends to favor the needs of the majority over those of minority publics.[12] Others point to the uncertainty of outcomes as a serious problem: Because we can never be completely sure whether a predicted outcome will occur, it's difficult in the moment to know whether a utilitarian decision is good or bad. Moreover, relying solely on outcomes to evaluate ethicality means (a) an act's morality can only be judged after the fact and (b) the actor's intent has little bearing on the action's ethicality.[13]

The most compelling criticism? Utilitarianism requires a calculation unique to each scenario you face.[14] Over a lifetime, this could constitute billions of one-off judgments. Moreover, because the variables in each scenario change, you're limited in your ability to generalize ethical standards from one situation to the next; the exact same action may be ethical in one situation and unethical in another. For example, say your significant other asks you how her hair looks. At this instant, it resembles a nest built by a particularly careless bird. If you plan to spend a quiet evening alone, the moral choice may be to lie, thus preserving her self-esteem. However, if she's preparing for a job interview, the moral choice is to tell the truth. Although it may hurt her feelings in the moment, it will likely prevent the more intense pain of social embarrassment. In a sense, because utilitarianism doesn't provide widely or readily applicable standards of actions, it is a weaker moral system.

### The Importance of Duty: Kant's Deontology
#### Playing by the Rules

**Deontology**, on the other hand, represents a strong, rules-based view of ethics. Immanuel Kant, deontological ethics' most pivotal figure, viewed morality as stemming from universal obligations he labeled *duties* (deontology roughly translates from the Greek as "the study of the necessary"). Within such a view, certain choices and actions may not be justifiable regardless of their outcomes. The well-worn example of the transplant illustrates this point:

> A surgeon currently treats six patients. Five are dying of organ failure, and one healthy patient has fully functioning organs that, if transplanted, could save the lives of the

other five patients. Should the doctor allow the five sick patients to die, or kill the healthy patient and harvest her organs to save the other five?

For a strict utilitarian concerned solely with outcomes, there's a solid argument for murdering the healthy patient and harvesting her organs. In addition to being one hell of a horror movie pitch, this action results in the greatest happiness for the greatest number of people. However, from a deontological perspective, such an action would be unquestionably wrong, primarily because it violates the universal duty to not murder.

But how are such moral duties determined? Deontologists believe that, when free from external pressures and conflicts of interests, individuals can exercise their reason to develop universally applicable standards of conduct. Kant said the ethicality of such standards can be tested by evaluating them through the criteria comprising the categorical imperative.[15] These are the categorical imperative's two most essential questions:

1. Would I want every person to always act as I am about to?

2. Am I treating everyone involved with respect for their full humanity, or am I simply using them as means to an end?

The first question tests whether your action can be universalized, while the second measures whether you're treating others as persons rather than objects. Actions are considered moral when they are (1) universally applicable and (2) respect others' humanity.

Let's say you're driving to campus when some jerk cuts you off in traffic. After using your superior language skills to instantly sculpt an enormously creative expletive, your first thought is, "I'm going to kill that guy!" Then you remember it is wrong to murder. *It is wrong to murder* pretty much qualifies as one of Kant's moral duties tested by the categorical imperative. The world would be a better place on the whole if we all agreed not to murder one another. After all, murdering pretty thoroughly violates the murdered person's humanity. In the traffic example, you're murdering the jerk to satisfy your immediate anger. In the transplant example, you're murdering a woman to harvest her organs, forfeiting her life as a means to save others.

### The Flaws of Deontology

A decision-making process based on universal moral rules opens the door for several criticisms of deontology. We'll examine two.

Deontologists rely on universally applicable rules to make decisions. Their advantage? Rules inform moral choices across a variety of situations. Therefore, it makes sense to devise rules that are more general than specific. Paradoxically, while more general rules apply to a wider array of situations, a situation's particular circumstances may expose flaws in what we presumed were universal rules.

## PRINCIPLES IN PRACTICE 5.1    The PRSA Code of Ethics

**PRSA's Code of Ethics**

https://www.prsa.org/about/prsa-code-of-ethics

PRSA, like most professional organizations, has an official code of ethics, perhaps the field's most widely referenced set of moral guidelines. It was first adopted in 1950. The most recent revision was approved in 2000.[16]

PRSA's code can be criticized for a variety of reasons. Many argue it has no teeth because PRSA can't meaningfully enforce it. The only penalty for violating the code is expulsion from PRSA, but you don't have to be a member to practice public relations. Moreover, there appears to be little specific action guidance in the code.[17] Donald Wright's condemnation of professional codes of ethics is easily among the harshest:

> In reality codes of ethics in public relations are more cosmetic than anything else. They're warm and fuzzy and make practitioners feel good about themselves, but they don't accomplish much. They don't even come close to being meaningful tools for ensuring accountability. They don't achieve what they're set out to do and most are filled with meaningless rhetoric and are not taken seriously by the majority of those who practice public relations.[18]

In our view, such critiques are fair, but only up to a point. The PRSA code does articulate useful professional values:

- *Advocacy:* Responsibly advance the interests of your clients.

- *Honesty:* Be truthful in your communications.

- *Expertise:* Continue to enhance your professional skill set.

- *Independence:* Be objective in and accountable for your counsel.

- *Loyalty:* Be faithful to the client.

- *Fairness:* Respect and support the opinions and rights of stakeholders.

These are all useful guidelines, but like most rules-based ethics, the PRSA code is deontologically driven: professional values are assumed to represent universal moral duties. That's a problem when conflicts arise.

Imagine how consistently difficult it is to act as a loyal advocate while remaining independent and fair to all stakeholders. If your client is dumping toxic waste into municipal waterways, can you remain both loyal to your client and honest with the public?

Or what about the far less inflammatory scenario the Centers for Disease Control and Prevention (CDC) faces when it recommends vaccines? In 1998, Dr. Andrew Wakefield published findings suggesting childhood vaccines cause autism. These findings were largely fabricated, leading the academic journal to retract his article and Britain to revoke Wakefield's medical license.[19] Subsequent studies showed no discernable link between vaccinations and autism.[20] Further, Autism Speaks, a prominent advocacy group representing autistic individuals and their families, has condemned all misinformation propagating this false link.[21]

The PRSA value of fairness asks us to "respect all opinions and support the right of free expression." But does that include respect for misinformation? And if so, how can the CDC honestly and effectively advocate for the American public's health without disrespecting members of the anti-vaccination crowd?

The PRSA code offers no useful guidance in dealing with such conflicts. Frustratingly, the organization acknowledges that such clashes may arise. PRSA's advice? Practitioners should "build trust with the public by avoiding or ending situations that put one's personal or professional interests in conflict with society's interests." Avoiding conflicts of interest is a sound policy,[22] but it doesn't help you resolve a conflict of which you're already a part. Moreover, walking away from these situations simply removes you from the conflict, which doesn't solve the problem. If anything, to turn your back may actually constitute shirking your moral obligations rather than fulfilling them.

So what should you do? We believe the simplest solution is to reframe the problem. In this case, the problem is that PR professionals treat the PRSA code as a set of deontological duties. Instead, we might do better to conceive of the code as a collection of virtuous guidelines. Virtue ethics don't rank virtues, inherently valuing one over another. Instead, virtue ethics encourages us to exercise practical wisdom to understand that at times, situational factors require certain principles to override others.

So, while combating the misinformation many vaccination opponents propagate may disrespect that stakeholder group's free expression, it does allow the CDC's PR team to loyally advocate for their organization. Moreover, to combat misinformation with facts is an exercise of honesty, which demonstrates concern for and fidelity to the CDC's numerous stakeholders. It certainly seems a worthwhile trade-off, and it reflects a more practical approach toward ethical codes.

Recall the jerk in traffic. Notice how we constructed the categorical imperative: *It is wrong to **murder**.* To murder has an explicit meaning: the unlawful, unjustified, inhumane and typically premeditated killing of another.[23] Were we to construct the imperative more widely, we might have said, *It is wrong to **kill**.* While killing is certainly an ugly business, there might be situations in which it is reasonable. From a deontological perspective, some killings might even fulfill moral duties, such as protecting one's family from harm (self-defense) or preventing genocide (so-called "just" wars).

But for the sake of argument let's say a prohibition against killing others is our moral duty, as is protecting one's family. Then how should we act in a scenario where the only way to protect our families from harm is to kill armed assailants? This brings us to a second, and much more serious problem of deontology: With its rigid rules, *deontology provides no way to adequately resolve conflicts of moral duties.*[24]

This presents a particular problem for strategic communicators. Every day, we're responsible to a variety of stakeholders, and our duties to each group regularly conflict. Remember the coronavirus dilemmas discussed earlier? We might reasonably assume the small business owner has a moral obligation to her landlord (i.e., honoring promises) and to her employees (i.e., fairly compensating work). Similarly, the food bank operator is morally bound to feed the hungry *and* prevent volunteers from contracting a deadly disease, both satisfying the maxim to preserve life. But what happens when you can't fulfill duties to all stakeholder groups? Deontologists don't provide satisfactory answers, and as Principles in Practice 5.1 illustrates, that's a real problem for strategic communicators.

### The Importance of Character: Aristotle's Virtue

#### Moral Wisdom

Though conflicts in ethical responsibilities may be relatively rare, they are inevitable. In fact, they are more common in strategic communication professions than in many others. Because deontologists see all moral duties as equally important, they struggle to deal with these conflicts.

Proponents of **virtue ethics**, espoused most notably by Aristotle, assert such struggles stem from a person's reluctance to employ her moral wisdom. Speaking bluntly, philosopher Alasdair MacIntyre frames the issue: "For Kant, one can be both good and stupid; but for Aristotle stupidity of a certain kind precludes goodness."[25] MacIntrye is asserting that deontologists seek universal rules. However, applying those rules require no special consideration of the situation or the action's consequences. Learning and adhering to rules requires minimal moral intelligence, or what virtue ethicists call **practical wisdom**. To an extent, then, deontologists often act without thinking; they simply follow a rule. That's a luxury utilitarians and virtue ethicists aren't permitted.

As we said before, universally applicable rules give deontologists an edge over utilitarians in making everyday, low-stakes, moral decisions: they don't have to perform a complex calculation of consequences to apply an ethical rule. However, the back-end cost is an inability to deal with conflicting moral duties, primarily because deontology sidesteps complex, situational calculations. Virtue ethics splits the difference by employing practical wisdom to gradually and deliberately develop moral principles of character.

#### Moral Character

Take a look at Figure 5.1. Honestly, for all our discussions of right action, none of the three moral philosophies we discussed define ethicality at the moment of action. Utilitarians focus on outcomes, while deontologists focus on intentions in taking action.

Virtue ethics is unique in that its focus is on the moral agent, the person acting. More specifically, the focus is on her **character**. The foundation of virtue ethics is that an individual who regularly nurtures a disposition for ethical behavior will consistently do the right thing.[27]

As you might expect from the name, the key elements of virtue ethics—practical wisdom, character, learning to live well—are all interconnected via **virtue**. Philosophers Rosalind

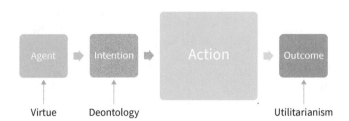

Virtue　　Deontology　　　　　　　　Utilitarianism

FIGURE 5.1 Browning's Anatomy of Moral Decisions. While ethicists often talk of moral action, defining an action as moral has less to do with the act itself and more to do with considerations made before and after. Utilitarians judge acts to be ethical if they generate positive outcomes. Deontologists view acts as ethical if they stem from moral duties, which we might think of as good intentions. Virtue ethicists consider an action ethical if it's something a virtuous person would characteristically do and if acting in that manner strengthens the agent's overall moral character.[26]

Hursthouse and Glen Pettigrove define virtue as "a disposition, well entrenched in its possessor [...] to notice, expect, value, feel, desire, choose, act, and react in certain characteristic ways."[28] Those who possess and act upon these virtues to promote the well-being of one's self and others are said to have sound moral character.

So a virtue is essentially any character trait that, when possessed and acted upon, promotes our own happiness and well-being, as well as that of others. Writing over 2,000 years ago, Aristotle proposed four cardinal virtues: prudence, justice, courage and temperance.[29] In the centuries since, ethicists have debated which traits truly are virtues. After two millennia of arguments, the list in Memory Memo 5.3[30] constitutes the most commonly accepted virtues.

### Moral Education

Possessing and acting from these virtues is much harder than following rigid rules. As virtue ethicists propose, and evolutionary psychologists support, human beings are naturally social animals. Being able to live in groups and work cooperatively has contributed to our species' survival and success.[32] So, according to modern virtue ethicists, we're preprogrammed to develop virtuous character. But our inborn drive must be honed through trial and error.

| MEMORY MEMO 5.3 A Working List of Virtues[31] | |
| --- | --- |
| • Prudence | • Wisdom |
| • Justice | • Charity |
| • Courage | • Truthfulness |
| • Temperance | • Civility |
| • Trust | • Ambition |
| • Understanding | • Decency |

Here's another way to look at it. Learning the virtues is like learning to walk. Most of us are born with that innate ability, but we don't emerge from the womb, high-five the obstetrician and stroll on our merry way. We learn to hold up our head, to sit, to stand, to crawl and eventually to walk. Still, we're far from done. Toddlers seem to fall down more often than not, and even 6- and 7-year-olds are less than graceful. At this point in your life, you might consider yourself an expert walker, but how many times have you stumbled in the last month?

### The Golden Mean

And so it is with the virtues. Just as they do in learning to walk, children learning to exercise virtues encounter growing pains.

Consider the virtue of trust. It has two components: learning to trust others and learning how to be trusted. Toddlers trust others almost implicitly, which scares the hell out of parents; they know not everyone is trustworthy. So "stranger danger" kicks in, and children overcorrect by avoiding contact with anyone they don't already know. As we age and encounter others, we learn to recognize social con artists by more judiciously building and exercising trust. The more interactions we have with someone, and the more that person demonstrates truthfulness, wisdom, decency and civility—themselves all virtues, incidentally—the more we trust her.

Virtue ethics emerges, cumulatively, from experience and nurturing. It requires that we use our practical wisdom to test, then understand when, how and if the exercise of certain virtues in specific situations promotes personal and social well-being. This links it closely to the concept of social exchange we discussed in Chapter 2. Each additional experience an individual has with a particular person, institution or situation presents another data point to assess how likely good outcomes emerge from that type of encounter.

So, though trust is a virtue, by no means should we employ it universally. It's easy to see an overabundance of trust exposes us to harm from people who might predictably take advantage.

However, if the pendulum swings too far in the other direction, we close ourselves to others, limiting our ability to work cooperatively for our own and others' benefit. In this sense, the virtue of trust—like all virtues—represents a **golden mean** existing between two vices, in this case gullibility (an excess of trust) and paranoid cynicism (a deficiency of trust).[33]

### Moral Heroes

As a final yet critical point regarding education in the virtues, we must consider the role of moral heroes. It's common to face new challenges for which we're unprepared. Recall Chapter 1's discussion of opinion leaders. For advice on computers and technology, Professor Browning turns to his sister, a relative expert in the field. Morality is no different. Virtue ethics asserts that we learn by experience. So, when faced with the ethical uncertainty of unfamiliar scenarios, it's often best to talk to someone who's been there before: a **moral exemplar**.

We all have people we admire and emulate for their knowledge and expertise. When we, the authors, first began our careers as university professors, there was a lot we simply didn't know. We've each grown into our roles with guidance from respected colleagues who themselves faced and overcame similar challenges. Now, as we've matured into capable professionals, we increasingly find ourselves serving as moral exemplars to others entering the academy. Thus, the torch of virtue is carried and passed on.[34]

## Moral Meaning From Multiple Perspectives

Should you choose to read moral philosophy closely, you'll notice major conflicts arise from small, nuanced differences in thought. To be sure, it's important whether we consider ethicality through the lens of utility, duty, character or some other principle. As communication ethicist Wendy Wyatt notes, these varying ethical perspectives pose different questions: "An option that satisfies the requirements of all questions […] is the ideal. […] Of course, ethical dilemmas are often thornier than this, and an ideal option is just that: ideal."[35] Ethical dilemmas are indeed more thorny, and each moral theory may have its own unique way of resolving them. Even as a novice student of ethics, you should be prepared for these quandaries. Know that to some degree they are inevitable.[36]

Certainly, different ethical approaches will offer different guidance amid moral dilemmas you'll face in your personal and professional life. However, more often than not, they closely align. Most ethical perspectives, for instance, would advise against blaming a colleague for your own mistake, lying in a press release, revealing your organization's trade secrets and so on.

Perhaps it's best to take a pluralistic approach, to view our choices through lenses of multiple moral theories. That way we have a better understanding not only of what these varying approaches prescribe but also when certain moral considerations might trump others.[37] Similarly, everyday moral moments present opportunities for us to examine our reasoning in obvious and often low-stakes situations. Training ourselves to respond consistently and appropriately in these moments prepares us for more challenging ethical issues we may face in the future and make it that much more likely we'll act rightly, despite the pressure.[38]

## Communicating Through Moral Dilemmas

So let's take a look at one of those more challenging ethical moments and evaluate a company's strategic and communicative response.

Following the 2020 death of George Floyd at the hands of Minneapolis police, the United States erupted in a wave of racial justice protests in a size and scope arguably unseen since the 1960s. Individuals, governments and corporations felt pressured to take action.

On June 17, 2020, Quaker Oats announced it would remove the name and likeness of Aunt Jemima from its popular breakfast-line brand. The character is based on the "mammy" archetype prominent through the antebellum and Jim Crow eras. Aunt Jemima packaging initially portrayed her as a formerly enslaved, overweight Black woman, subservient and jovial in the kitchen. Aunt Jemima was introduced at the 1893 Chicago World's Fair, played by Nancy Green, herself born a slave in Kentucky. At the exposition, she prepared pancakes for fairgoers while regaling them with stories and songs about her poeticized plantation life.

**Aunt Jemima's Rebrand**

https://www.prnews-wire.com/news-releases/aunt-jemima-brand-to-remove-image-from-packaging-and-change-brand-name-301078593.html

See how Quaker Oats framed the Aunt Jemima rebrand in this press release announcing the change.

As you can clearly see, there's a deep racist history to the character and, by extension, the brand. In a news release announcing the change, Quaker Foods North America vice president and chief marketing officer Kristin Kroepfl explicitly acknowledged that history and cited a need for change:

> As we work to make progress toward racial equality through several initiatives, we must also take a hard look at our portfolio of brands and ensure they reflect our values and meet our consumers' expectations. [...] We recognize Aunt Jemima's origins are based on a racial stereotype. While work has been done over the years to update the brand in a manner intended to be appropriate and respectful, we realize those changes are not enough.[39]

Looking at Quaker Oats' actions, would you say they are ethical? And were they effectively communicated to reflect some ethical intention?

That first question is tougher to answer than you might think. We can't enter the minds of executives at Quaker Oats or PepsiCo, its parent company, but we can draw some inferences about their motives based on what we can see.

Racism is now, forever was, and forever will be wrong. However, in 1893, when Aunt Jemima debuted, it was certainly socially accepted in many circles. The North had abandoned Reconstruction efforts in the 1870s, leaving southern African Americans to their own devices. In search of opportunity, many relocated to the Northeast, Midwest and West during the Great Migration of the early to mid-20th century. They were met with a resurgence of the Ku Klux Klan, race riots, murders, massacres and other forms of violence. Segregation, voter suppression and systemic oppression were commonplace for Black Americans. Although the 1860s' 14th and 15th amendments had codified equal protections and voting rights for African Americans, it wasn't until the Civil Rights and Voting Rights Acts of 1964–65, nearly a century later, that these rights were again meaningfully enforced.

Notice what happened. Racism was not eradicated, but over time it moved from a socially acceptable to a socially scorned ideology. So while we could understand how a racist figure like Aunt Jemima was created in the 1890s, it is still puzzling how such a figure could have endured until 2020.

It's not as though Quaker Oats was unaware of the brand's bigoted roots. Kroepfl acknowledged as much in her statement. Among the brand updates she referenced were dropping the mammy kerchief and giving the Black character "a contemporary look, adding pearl earrings and a lace collar,"[40] as the official brand history describes. That was in *1989*.

So for at least the past 30 years, Quaker Oats knew it had a racism problem but took minimal action. From our perspective, profit most likely drove inaction. We're not claiming the company took any pleasure in retaining a racially compromised brand image. What we're saying is that the economic costs and risks of rebranding outweighed those resulting from boycotts and reputational damage.

Rebranding is dicey. Corporate graveyards are filled with businesses that failed in the effort. Even as parent company PepsiCo contemplates the brand's future, the practical challenges are immense. Consider the average consumer of Aunt Jemima products. She probably has no intense emotional reaction to the logo. In all likelihood, she simply finds the product reliable or better tasting than the alternatives. As such, she would probably continue buying it under its new name, Pearl Milling Company.[41]

But how do you educate that consumer about the name change? Most likely through a costly, intensive, integrated communication campaign. Still, there's no guarantee that consumer will receive or even comprehend the message. And any rebranding efforts to retain the brand's current customers risks reminding consumers of the brand's original, racially poisoned position. Beyond that, any rebranding presents our hypothetical consumer a ready opportunity to switch to another brand entirely.

So for years, the economically safer option was likely trudging on with a highly compromised and controversial brand. The deciding factor in abandoning Aunt Jemima was almost certainly the resurgent Black Lives Matter movement. However, our ethical judgment rests upon the balance point of how demands for racial justice influenced the organization's decision-making.

Utilitarians assessing the action by its outcome would likely praise PepsiCo executives. While we might question the company's motives, it seems abandoning a figure who normalized racial stereotypes makes society at least nominally better than it was before.

Deontologists would argue such action respects others' humanity by discontinuing the use of bigoted imagery to sell breakfast foods. However, they would also ask whether Quaker Oats was acting out of a sense of duty to promote equality and human dignity or because of financial motives.

Maybe. Maybe not.

The press release certainly checks the rhetorical boxes in signaling an ethical commitment. However, Quaker Oats and PepsiCo may have used the cultural moment to jettison the brand when they knew they would receive some praise for the action, along with an incalculable amount of free publicity.

From a virtue ethics perspective, judgment is equally difficult. On the one hand, it's hardly courageous to make a change only when institutions face immense pressure to address systemic racism. To retain the brand image for so long, unnecessarily perpetuating a hurtful stereotype, is not particularly charitable either. Still, to abandon a racist moniker of the past demonstrates prudence and decency and perhaps even a sense of understanding about the pain caused during decades of insensitivity.

Additionally, a virtue ethicist would try to assess the company's general character to evaluate the action more completely. While walking away from Aunt Jemima is long overdue and certainly represents a step in the right direction, acting with basic decency is literally the least a company can do. The rebrand is nice, but alone it does little to advance the more important struggle for racial equality.

This is where the communicative effectiveness of the original press release comes in. The PR team didn't simply stop at a name change. The main copy of the release is 652 words long. Only 265 of them were spent on the rebrand. The bulk of the release focused on PepsiCo's efforts to advance diversity and inclusion, in particular a $400 million, five-year

**PepsiCo and Racial Equality**

https://www.pep-sico.com/about/diversity-and-engagement/racial-equality-journey-black-initiative

PepsiCo made measurable commitments to advancing racial equality, a necessary follow-through to show sincerity of purpose.

program to serve Black communities, as well as a renewed focus on good corporate citizenship.

These were smart choices. PepsiCo demonstrated seriousness of purpose by connecting the efforts for diversity and inclusion to its core principles, making them harder to ignore in the future. Moreover, the diversity plan includes several specifics:

> Increasing our Black manager population by 30%. Adding 100 Black associates to our executive ranks. [Committing] $25 million to establish support for students transitioning from 2-year to 4-year programs and scaling our efforts to support trade/certificate and academic 2-year degrees through community colleges.[42]

Notice that these statements carry the hallmarks of good objectives you learned in Chapter 3: they address institutional problems, are unambiguous, are measurable, contain deadlines, are realistic and are outcome oriented. PepsiCo embraces accountability here, and for all the questions we may currently have regarding motives, in the future we'll know the answers about the company's resolve. Finally, for our purposes here, this example illustrates that ethical behavior doesn't just happen. At some level, it's something you actively choose—perhaps even plan for—in every decision you make, from those addressing major social issues of the time, down to the simplest word choices you make in an everyday email.

## Thinking Through Language: Everyday Ethics for Persuasive Writers

Up to this point, our discussion of ethics has been the view from 40,000 feet up, primarily focused on your ability to assess the moral dilemmas inherent in a situation. Such skills undeniably help you influence the organizational action you will be required to write about.

However, such considerations are also inescapable when you are facing the screen, writing. Virtually everything you say or write, the manner in which you conduct yourself and how you represent the profession are imbued with ethical considerations, some small, some large.

We've argued that the primary role of strategic communicators is to persuade publics. Many people are uncomfortable with that assertion, primarily because they are concerned that persuasive tactics can lead to immoral ends.[43] While they most certainly can, they usually don't. Public relations gets a bad rap regarding the manner in which practitioners advance client interests. While bad actors exist, their unethical behavior is not emblematic of the field.[44]

As a profession, we're probably not as ethical as we'd like to believe, but we're certainly not the evil, shameless purveyors of untruths our harshest critics claim. Still, there's no doubt we could be better. One of the most common ways our ethicality comes to bear is in the language we use, the reasons we choose it and the manner in which that language will likely affect our audiences. Thinking through these language choices is a good place to start incorporating ethical thought into a persuasive writer's everyday tasks.

## How Words and Ethics Impact One Another

Avoiding offensive language may seem like an obvious and easy ethical choice for persuasive writers to make. Racial and ethnic slurs, for example, hurt not only the groups to whom they refer but others as well; they should never appear in professional writing.

Easy. We're done, right? Well, not so fast.

Consider that what constitutes offensive language varies across individuals, audiences, cultures and time periods. A quick revisit to Aunt Jemima will illustrate that point. Here's the copy for a 1920 print ad appearing in The Saturday Evening Post, in which Aunt Jemima exclaims:

> Lawzee! Mekkin' pancakes is th' mos' impawtines thing ah does, that which dere aint' no better, effen ah does say so! Jes mah flour and water, on de griddle and—whuf! Dey's done honey! Grab em![45]

Damn! That's some top-tier racism right there, right? Fast-forward to the 1940s and the ad copy is less jaw-droppingly awful, but still abrasive:

> Whe-e-e-e how folks enjoys scrumptious Aunt Jemima pancakes![46]

In both ads, African Americans were portrayed as simpletons, exemplified in Aunt Jemima using non-normative English. With the benefit of hindsight, these language choices clearly appear to us as racist and thus offensive. However, the predominantly white audiences of the era, to whom such messages were targeted, wouldn't have batted an eye. In fact, copy portraying Aunt Jemima speaking more eloquently would likely have bewildered those audiences more.

While admittedly this is an extreme example of shifting cultural mores, the legacy of now-racist, then-not, terminology remains with us today, even among unquestionably well-meaning organizations. The National Association for the Advancement of Colored People (NAACP)—founded in 1909—and the United Negro College Fund founded in 1944—feature word choices cringeworthy to us, but acceptable and preferable given the options of the Black men and women who established them.

All this is to say that language is constantly on the move. This evolution is readily apparent in other arenas. Once it was perfectly acceptable to refer to individuals as *crippled*. The term came to be seen as offensive and was replaced with *handicapped*, which itself became offensive and was dropped in favor of *disabled*. Recently, to refer to someone as *disabled* has become taboo. The preferred nomenclature of the moment is *people with disabilities*.

And notice even how we phrased that. The Associated Press (AP) specifically advises writers to avoid phrases like *suffering from* or *afflicted by* when referring to people with disabilities. The implication is that such individuals are defined as victims more so than autonomous people capable of leading full lives. Recalling our discussion of deontology, you can easily see how narrowly defining people violates the moral maxim of respecting their full humanity.

We also think the AP is spot on with other guidance here—namely (1) if a person's disability isn't relevant to what you're writing, don't include it; defining a person primarily by her disability is disrespectful. And (2) when possible, you should avoid referring to a person as *disabled* but instead be specific with your language. Better to say someone is deaf, blind, mute or paralyzed, or has Down syndrome, ADHD or PTSD than to treat disability as a uniform classification.

Lastly, recognize that some language that isn't inherently offensive may appear so through no fault of its own. For instance, this should be a perfectly innocuous sentence:

> Drinking alcohol while pregnant can retard your baby's brain development.

As a verb, *retard* simply means to delay progress or impede development. Unfortunately, as a noun, it has been used as an insult to those perceived as stupid or even to mock those with mental or learning disabilities. As a result, even the correct use of such words makes audiences squirm. So it's best to substitute with a synonym.

### How Should I Put This ... ?

Of course, when you really think about it, synonyms are more myth than manifest. No two words in the English language truly have the same meaning. That's why throughout this book, we'll emphasize the importance of word choice. This word instead of that word can make a crucial difference in how organizational actions are judged and whether they are judged fairly.

Let's say the manufacturing plant you work for has agreed to significantly shrink its carbon footprint by opting for cleaner energy sources. Would it be more honest to say you're *cutting emissions*? Or *reducing air pollutants*? How about *eliminating wasteful by-products*?

Technically each statement may be true; that is, their dictionary definitions, or *denotations*, are more or less the same. But some clearly paint a better picture of the organization because of the different emotions they may evoke. This second layer of meaning is called *connotation*, and how we as practitioners use or misuse this layer of meaning is a key determinant in the ethicality of our language.

Thus, the most transparent and ethical descriptor in the case of our manufacturing plant example rests on several factors. According to the PRSA Code of Ethics, loyalty to the client is a key professional value, but so too are fairness and honesty.[47] Defaulting to more direct language often guides us toward making ethical choices in our writing, as do principles of clarity and completeness. There's an old saying that a half-truth is a whole lie. What we wrestle with as persuasive writers is when euphemisms become half-truths.

First, we must ask ourselves whether we're omitting details critical to the audience accurately understanding the situation. Second, we should consider whether our descriptions of events constitute fair representations of the events themselves.

So let's return to your manufacturing plant's new-found desire to go green. To decide on the most truthful account, we need to know a lot more about the plant. Is this reduction of carbon emissions a voluntary move on the part of plant managers, or is the plant being forced to comply with environmental protection laws? How much carbon has the plant emitted? For how long? And how do those numbers compare with the industry average?

These, as well as numerous other factors, provide needed context. As you progress through your careers, you'll find brevity is highly valued. While succinctness is often a good thing, it sometimes comes at the expense of clarity. But remember, you have an obligation to preserve content critical to a fair representation of the facts. If you praise your organization as an industry leader in environmental stewardship, but fail to mention it adopted clean energy policies only after government coercion and decades of unfettered pollution, you're lying—a lie of omission, but a lie nonetheless. By most accounts, such behavior is unethical: Remember that truthfulness is highly prized as a duty and virtue that more often than not leads to ethical ends—not to mention that it represents a key professional moral principle.

Organizations, much like individuals, tend to emerge as the heroes of their own stories. As persuasive communicators, we often operate as organizational storytellers. What we say and write will help shape organizational policy, for good or for ill. What we say and write will create an image of the organization, one that closely resembles reality or one that callously distorts it. What we say and write will shift the public discourse about various facets of the organization, either in the direction of fairness and transparency, or bias and opacity. While we have a professional obligation to represent our organizations in a favorable light, we have an equal if not overriding moral obligation not to leave stakeholders in the dark. Without a developed understanding of ethics, we have no hope of meeting the latter duty.

> **Strategic Thought**
>
> In college football, whenever a field goal or extra point is kicked, insurance giant Allstate now comes to mind. In 2005, Allstate initiated its Good Hands Field Goal Net Program, brandishing its logo on field goal nets provided to 90 U.S. colleges and universities. For every successful field goal, Allstate donates to each institution's general scholarship fund. As of 2017, contributions totaled roughly $3.4 million.[48] Until recently, TV announcers would state the exact donation total. Now, the announcers simply state that Allstate has donated millions. How are these claims different? Is one more truthful than the other? Might they be perceived differently? If so, how?

## SUMMARY

- Understanding ethical theories, such as utilitarianism, deontology and virtue ethics, helps make sense of the moral issues facing both your organization and you as a practitioner.

- Strategic communicators often have competing loyalties to different stakeholders. Understanding what those ethical obligations are and why they matter will help you resolve moral conflicts more amicably.

- The way in which you use language reflects the moral values of your organization and yourself, so persuasive writers should avoid language that is offensive (i.e., sexist, racist, exclusionary), unclear or dishonest.

- While our culture often views effective and ethical public relations as polar opposites, in reality, the moral language and messaging choice is often the most effective one as well.

### Scenario Prompts: Ethical Persuasion

You'll find Scenario Prompts on pp. 367–386 of this textbook. While they vary in subject and difficulty, they help you hone your critical thinking and strategic writing skills. The following are best suited to this chapter's topics.

Management Problems: 1.4, 7.3, 8.4, 10.1

# PART II

# How to Write Strategically

Over the decades, we've taught over a thousand students in our respective PR and strategic communication writing courses. In that time, we've been forced to confront virtually every possible prose deficiency left uncorrected in our students by their middle and high school language arts teachers.

No, we're not condemning every eighth-grade English teacher in America. We're acknowledging the immensity of their jobs. To paraphrase Tolstoy, every bad writer is bad in her own way. Diagnosing and addressing each pupil's unique distortion of English usage during a school year is a Herculean task.

Of course, you didn't make our jobs any easier. If you hadn't slept through middle school grammar class, you'd have known what adverbs and adjectives were long before arriving on a college campus.

But perhaps we've been a bit harsh. Maybe you do know the parts of speech. But what about the distinction between subjective and objective case? Or the relative power of active voice verb constructions? Or what exactly a demonstrative is?

Unwittingly, you've employed these elements in your own writing, often successfully, sometimes not. But could you explain why your phrasing was good or bad?

So you're *capable* of producing good writing. Fine. But because you lack the tools to reflect deeply on what you write or read, you're inefficient at *reproducing* that success on demand.

We're not like your earlier instructors. They just hoped you could spit out a coherent sentence. We work under the dark cloud of your ambition to be a professional writer. If you get your wish, you'll be trusted to produce quality prose, every time, under deadline pressure. If you can't do that, you lose your job, your family goes hungry, and your car doubles as your home. We don't want to be held responsible.

Writing professionally presents a challenging but doable task. You're already partly there. This book's first unit walked you through human motivation, organizational imperatives and other building blocks of persuasive arguments. Part 2 will give you the tools to guide your decision-making. It breaks down the writing process (e.g., a full chapter on writing a first sentence) so you can understand and explain why you chose to eliminate some information, then organize the remaining elements so your prose appeals to your target audience.

You'll learn how to reverse-engineer prose so you'll be better capable of overcoming the unknown in your career. Even now, we can guarantee you'll be asked to produce a message in an unfamiliar format, targeted to an audience you don't know, sent through a medium you've never written in. What to do? Anchor what you don't know in what you do. Analyze how and why you've been successful in distinct but related tasks. Break down the successes of others in each new arena to their component parts, then repurpose those scrap pieces to fit your objective.

While every strategic writing task includes unique demands, they all share basic, universal commonalities. In each case, your goal is to convey relevant information to a target audience, craft a message that accounts for the medium's strengths and limitations and then deliver that message to your audience at a time and place when they're likely to attend and respond to it.

Thankfully, fairly basic rules govern this strategic writing game. In this unit, we'll teach you how to play it. In the next unit, we'll help you take the field.

# Reaching the Right Audience Right Now

## The Audience-Centered Process and Writing the First Sentence

Let's talk about your media life. This may be easiest if you think about your daily routine as if you're recording a point-of-view show where you're the star. In your room, your camera/eye may see a poster of a favorite band, your laptop, an empty pizza box, a family photo and a snoring roommate. A beat-up pair of branded athletic shoes may be on the floor alongside your wrinkled Spider-Man bed comforter (because, let's be honest, who doesn't like Spider-Man?). There's a text message from your mother on the phone and beside it an old celebrity magazine a friend left. You've got your chemistry book open from where you were studying last night.

Your textbook's diagrams of atomic bonds are a blur at this point. You ignore your mother's text to read one from a high school classmate from whom you're hoping to get a ride home this weekend. Your laptop needs recharging, and as you fiddle with the cable, you see instructions on the backside about how to open the battery unit. Out your window, there's a billboard for an expensive foreign beer above a stop sign. There's a chalk drawing on the sidewalk promoting last weekend's frat party.

You may view this as your junky college living, but it's all directed communication as well. Every one of the messages above started with someone who wished to communicate with you. That person was trying to predict what you'd want or what you'd like to learn about. Each message was placed in a spot where you'd be likely to notice that information at the precise moment in which you'd be most likely react to it.

Let's look more closely at what's happening here. Did you pay attention to all the messages present within your environment? No way. Your roommate finished off the pizza, so there's no need to even look at the box. The chemistry test was this morning, so that's old news. As much as you love Mom, she can't offer you a lift home. Your laptop battery works fine. The party was last weekend, and neither you nor its hosts can afford the beer from the billboard.

You could notice those messages, but you don't. They aren't relevant to you now and they don't justify the time it would take to attend to them. Human perception strives for efficiency, so we use past experience to determine which messages to pay attention to, and which ones to ignore. You've driven down your street to the corner so many times, you don't even notice the stop sign anymore. Stopping is now more habit than remembering what a red octagon means.

You may be in college, but in our scenario you're functioning at reptilian-brain level. We have at least some awareness of all the messages we encounter but act only on some. Researchers explain it this way: When humans encounter certain messages—say the billboard advertising a beer you can't afford—the messages are instantaneously processed and superficially analyzed and then abandoned because they're not interesting or relevant to the audience. Other messages, like your classmate's offer of a ride, are similarly processed, analyzed and deemed important. Those messages are transferred to a conscious process level.[1] Once there, you decide what action to take: immediately reply to your classmate's text.

Fundamentally, the study of communication focuses not only on our understanding of the messages we process, but also how we *don't* bring to the conscious level most messages we receive each day. That's the challenge this chapter discusses: How can our persuasive message be one of those that gets noticed and breaks through to the higher conscious level of the people we wish to influence?

*—WT*

## What You Know

- Social exchange theory predicts how individuals make decisions regarding opportunity costs and the actions they ultimately take.

- A receiver's self-interest determines whether she'll attend to a message.

- Employing communication theory helps predict the decision process your audience will use to evaluate your persuasive message.

## What You'll Learn

- How audiences determine the small percentage of messages they will focus their attention on

- What news values are present in all information and how to evaluate which aspects will interest a particular audience

- How to evaluate a lede sentence for its potential to draw and then persuade a target audience

- How audience capabilities and wants dictate changes in a lede sentence

## Scan, Then Abandon or Engage: The Realities of Message Acceptance

The first sentence of any writing task is arguably the most important one of the entire piece. Known as the **lede** sentence, it establishes the basic structural outline you will use to build the rest of the document. In many situations, it will signal the order in which other topics will be discussed in the body of the story.

The lede sentence has another purpose. The lede's information and structuring should be designed to compel our intended audience to elevate our message to a more conscious level of their minds. Too many writers somehow forget that the first requirement of any form of persuasive writing is to compel a specific audience to read what we write.

As we noted in this chapter's "Lessons From Life," each day your audience faces thousands of competing messages, from social media, friends, business associates, food labels, tattooed arms, whatever. Every one of us is constantly judging which messages to attend to, sometimes after only a glance or reading just a few words.

Obviously, garnering that initial attention is critical to your communication goal. That's why we'll spend an entire chapter on how to write a single sentence, the lede sentence, in a process we call **audience-centered writing**. The basic premise of audience-centered writing is that effective persuasive communication consciously matches audience to information. It focuses on audience traits and audience needs to generate persuasive prose and story structures, maximizing those few seconds during which the receiver makes the decision to attend to or abandon a message.

## The Race for Your Audience's Attention: The Audience-Centered Model

### Redirecting Your Focus From Organization to Audience

What's the practical meaning of this to a professional communicator? It means we as writers have a few precious moments—a few precious *words*—to attract our intended readers' attention and convince them our message is important to their lives.[2] If we don't accomplish that task immediately, the reader abandons the entire message. That's a formidable writing challenge. However, knowing what's happening inside the receiver's mind helps us structure a message that will succeed in engaging our audience.

We are proposing something much more sophisticated than **clickbait**, the gratuitous use of compelling information to grab attention. Internet messages constantly shout (falsely) that a popular TV or film star has died, or that a politician is in the midst of a pseudo-scandal. Admittedly, the gullible often click through, only to be exposed to dubious "news" and pop-up ads. However, if your attention is drawn by your adoration of Beyoncé or your state's senator, you'll be disappointed if confronted with advertising for stackable food containers or high-power flashlights. Sure enough, the writer got eyeballs looking, along with the justifiably pissed-off brains behind them.

We are advocating a change in the power dynamic of the writer/audience relationship. Instead of a writer thinking she can manipulate her audience to attend to the message, we suggest the audience's needs should dictate what the writer presents to the audience.

That seems simple, but it contradicts some of communication theory's founding logic. In Chapter 2, we discussed Lasswell's communication model. With appropriate dismay, we labeled it a **speaker-centered model**: the audience's only role is to receive the message and respond to it at the conclusion of the communication act.

As you begin to construct a persuasive strategy, it's important to examine the relationship from the opposite perspective. No matter what message a writer wishes to convey, audience self-interests dictate what she can hope to accomplish. No matter what message the writer conceives, it's silly to think it can be written without acknowledging her audience's characteristics and capacities. For instance, the writer can't arbitrarily decide what medium she will employ to deliver her message. That determination is strictly governed by the media platform to which the target audience regularly attends.

**FIGURE 6.1  The Audience-Centered Model.** The audience-centered model starts by considering the capacities, needs and habits of the audience and then sculpts a strategy for engaging key publics.

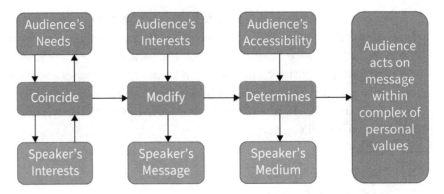

However, if you stand the Lasswell model on its head, you can much better understand the dynamics of the persuasion process. The **audience-centered model** asserts that knowledge of the audience determines each step in the communication process.[3] In Figure 6.1, you'll notice the focus on audience. The writer must:

1. **Choose an audience whose interests intersect with the institution's needs.** Why would an internet matchmaking service advertise in a glossy bridal magazine? Or why would a football equipment retailer try to get an article about itself placed on a public access cable program intended for seniors? If this very first precept is not met, the writer can indeed transmit a message. However, it's going to be hard to persuade the wrong audience.

2. **Craft a message that speaks to audience needs and interests.** A family of four and a young couple beginning a serious relationship may have vastly different reasons for booking a weekend at a ski lodge in the Rockies. Effective messaging accounts for differences through more tailored persuasive appeals.

3. **Select a medium that reaches that audience.** As a writer, you could choose any media platform you like. However, if your targeted audience doesn't use that media channel, you've just wasted your institution's resources.

4. **Understand that audiences don't react in a vacuum.** Each of the audience's members has a lifetime history of experiences that predicates their particular response to a particular message. We call that lifetime of past experience a **complex of personal values**. Members of your audience may hate or love technology and anchor their responses to your start-up tech company within that bias. They may welcome the convenience brought by a new big-box retailer while worrying about negative effects on local businesses. While it's difficult to completely know an individual's complex of personal values, knowing that it's a factor gives you the opportunity to consider it, and perhaps adjust your audience analysis accordingly.

In essence, if you wish to persuade, your audience's circumstances outrank what your organization hopes to gain from its relationship with a particular public. It's only by finding the common interests your institution shares with your audience or the benefits your institution can offer them that you can more surely guarantee your messages will be read.

## Social Exchange and the Calculating Audience

And how do we determine the audience's motives for engaging with our organization? We again refer to our Chapter 2 discussion of social exchange theory.

Social exchange theory is central in a receiver-centered writing process. It redirects the writer's focus from what the writer wants to what the audience will consider adequate rewards for their attention to the message. Social exchange theory considers not only economic factors in this calculation, but also friendship, esteem, entertainment, convenience, and other social and psychological aspects. To quickly summarize our earlier discussion, social exchange theory asserts that individuals are drawn to whatever offers the best payoff within the spectrum of available options.

Social exchange theory also reminds us that our message exists in a competition with a flood of other messages, all pleading for attention from our audience. Some competing messages come from strategic communication colleagues working for other organizations. But that competition could also originate from a parent's crying child, an interesting book or the no-holds-barred performance by a sports star or musical artist: anything that pulls a potential audience away for our message.

From a writing standpoint, we should learn these lessons from social exchange theory:

- You communicate with people who have a preexisting opinion about your organization or industry, a perception from which they will view the message you send them.

- You communicate with people who are looking for an anticipated reward from an encounter with your message.

- Your audience is assessing the anticipated rewards your message offers and comparing them to rewards an alternative message might offer.

- Their decision will likely take place within two seconds of when they encounter your message.

- Each encounter with an audience will likely reinforce or diminish their previously held opinion of your organization, a perception that will influence future communication encounters with them.

**Strategic Thought**

What's your own complex of personal values? What predispositions concerning politics, movies, celebrities or fashion do you bring to your consideration of messages you encounter? If you have trouble believing you have a complex of personal values, think about sports teams that you support and those you hate. How did you develop those biases?

**Strategic Thought**

Can you recall a time when you exchanged what others perceived as too much money for an emotional reward? Can you justify the valuation you placed on the emotional reward?

## Writing Organically

The key phrase in our discussion of social exchange theory might be "within two seconds." That's probably a generous estimate of the time your potential audience will commit to judging whether your message offers greater rewards than some alternative.[4] As strategic communicators, the only reward we can offer in that tiny window is information, most importantly the information that gains the attention of the precise audience we wish to reach.

The audience-centered process rests on the belief that there's no such thing as uninteresting information, only information we have communicated to uninterested people or in uninteresting ways. For that reason, the audience-centered approach relies on strategically thinking about every step in the model. What group of people have interests that can be fulfilled by the resources our organization offers? What message will reward the reader? What media does our target audience frequent?

All these questions are focused on what the audience needs, not what our organization wants. With such an assessment, prose structures, from the first few words of the lede to the sequence of paragraphs in the document's body, naturally flow. We call it a generative writing system to express the idea that prose organically grows, or is generated, from a knowledge of your audience and to what they'll be most likely respond.

## You Really Want All the News Fit to Print?
## The 5W1H Writing Formula

Before we can discuss our approach to writing the lede sentence, it may be useful to analyze how a common writing formula actually discourages mere browsers from becoming attentive readers.

Traditionally, journalists and public relations writers have been taught the **5W1H system**. If you took a high school media writing course, it's a formula you likely learned. It's thought that by answering the six questions of Who?, What?, When?, Where?, Why? and How?, you've covered the basic information your readers should know about your event or issue. It's what a club's publicity chairperson would use. On bulletin boards, you will find announcements structured like this:

**WHO:** Cathy Smith, Rose Expert

**WHAT:** Presents Private Garden Consultations

**WHEN:** Tuesday, Sept. 15

**WHERE:** Women's Civic Club, 1119 Main St.

**WHY:** To benefit Kalibash Youth Day Camp

**HOW:** $25 Donation Requested

It's not illogical to use the 5W1H formula to formulate a poster. However, it doesn't necessarily translate into an effective lede. We found early in our careers that when we convert the 5W1H formula to prose, it frequently produces sentences that (1) are needlessly long, (2) include information that isn't useful in generating reader interest and (3) bury behind a wall of words the very information that would generate interest. That actually discourages our target audience from attending to the story.

Here's an example showing how a 5W1H lede can go wrong:

> Assistant prosecuting attorney Trish Korman Bennett announced Wednesday that Anthony J. Edwards, the city's director for emergency preparedness, pleaded guilty to the June 1 ax murder of assistant city manager Kenneth J. Breakstone, whom Edwards said he killed at Breakstone's home after an argument over secretarial assignments in city hall.

You can instantly see the problems. In a hectic world that each day scatters thousands of messages in front of us, this lede sentence squanders the two seconds readers will invest as they decide to abandon or attend to the story.

The sentence's first 18 words identify people our readers probably don't know, or even care to know. There's not a single detail revealing what the story is about. Those first 18 words imply the story could concern the city's emergency siren system or Bennett's political ambitions. Those subjects won't lure too many readers into the story.

Very persistent readers eventually find some really shocking news: a city worker murdered another official—and with an ax! That's information that would draw a vastly larger audience to read the story. However, would a busy executive, gulping down breakfast before heading to her office, read far enough to discover it? Probably not.

The vital step 5W1H misses? Filtering what information is best able to capture the attention of the audience you want to draw.

## Choosing News Your Audience Wants to Know: The TIPCUP Filter

Our previous example demonstrates that information a writer omits from the first sentence is as important as what she includes. To help students judge what information will encourage a target audience's attention, Professor Thompson developed the **TIPCUP Filter**.[5] The TIPCUP acronym helps you remember the six factors that make information interesting to a target public. They are listed in Memory Memo 6.1.

As the term *filter* implies, it lets us predict what information will or will not interest our target audience by filtering such information through various layers of questioning. Elements most likely to draw an audience are included in

*Use This*

**MEMORY MEMO 6.1**  The TIPCUP Information Analysis Filter

- *Timeliness*: Do I need to know it today?
- *Impact*: Will it change what I do?
- *Proximity*: Did it happen around me?
- *Conflict*: Am I interested in the battle?
- *Unusualness*: Is it the first, last, or only time it's happened?
- *Prominence*: Do I know who it's about?

the lede. Information that doesn't draw an audience is reserved for deeper in the story or perhaps abandoned altogether.

### Timeliness: Do I Need to Know It Today?

A surprising amount of the information that interests people appeals to them only because they haven't heard it before. An auto wreck that killed a man yesterday may spark coverage on the television newscast tonight or in tomorrow morning's paper. However, it's unlikely to be covered further because another accident will have replaced it in the public eye.

Remember that timeliness relies on the freshness of information. New speculations about the death of aeronautical pioneer Amelia Earhart would still draw attention nearly a century after she disappeared during a flight over the Pacific Ocean.

But gaining attention using the timeliness filter usually requires a quick response, and often institutional planning, so you can respond when a timeliness opportunity presents itself. For instance, let's say your firm produces dry ice. A Friday afternoon power failure in your city threatens to last well into the weekend. In this case, your company can't afford to wait until Monday to interact with the public. By then their refrigerated food, as well as your news angle, will be spoiled.

### Impact: Will It Change What I Do?

Another reason people are interested in certain information is that it affects how they conduct their lives. This self-interest is illustrated every time a public school asks voters to approve higher property taxes to build new schools. For homeowners who must pay those higher taxes and parents who may decide to enroll their children in private schools because of the public school's crumbling buildings, this issue is critically important. Virtually every messaging channel, from social media to billboard advertising, will be mobilized to support each side's opposing messages.

Impact is arguably the most powerful motivator for interest. Let's say a senior citizens' advocacy organization encourages a national television news producer to air a story concerning a community on the far coast that uses visiting nurses to curb health care costs. That issue is likely relevant in your community. If you're working for a local seniors' organization, you'd profit from notifying local outlets serving older adults to share the network video. It may build support to replicate the program in your area. In short, the power of impact.

### Proximity: Did It Happen Around Me?

People are interested in many events simply because they happen close to them or involve someone from their community. It's easy to see this at work. If a bomb scare forces one of your city's high schools to evacuate, the story might prompt the local outlets to respond immediately. However, the evacuation almost certainly won't be covered nationally, or even by media in another state.

But remember when earlier in the chapter we stated there is no such thing as completely uninteresting information? Here's a situation that shows this. A couple living in the suburbs of a large city has triplets. The happy news certainly won't be covered by the metropolitan newspaper or the local television station. It's unlikely to be covered by the suburb's weekly newspaper. However, if the mother works at a small manufacturing plant with an employee e-magazine, the triplets might be the homepage story. In the same way, a social media posting of the babies' photos will likely be the most eagerly consumed news flash of the year by the newborns' grandparents, aunts, uncles and cousins. As we said—there's no unimportant news; you simply may not have found the right audience yet.

In public relations, proximity is among the greatest attention grabbers, and it's often the easiest to exploit. Too often, we practitioners neglect the perfect placement, say in a rural weekly newspaper, because we want credit for getting a story in major-city media. Yet the rural outlet may be the optimum placement. For example, the U.S. Army would send a news item to the hometown paper of every boot camp graduate. In Professor Thompson's small-town newspaper, stories on boot camp graduates, complete with photos, were frequently front-page news. For the U.S. Army, striving to find volunteers to enlist, this pool of rural high school graduates accessible through weekly newspaper stories was a low-cost method for promoting the military's career and training prospects. When appropriate and cost-effective, your story placement chances increase dramatically when you include a reference to proximity in your lede sentence.

## Conflict: Am I Interested in the Battle?

People are interested when people or groups come into conflict with each other. Some struggles are ritual, like sports. Others are deathly real, like war. Yet conflict means more than just physical confrontation. We can see struggle in political contests, environmentalists contesting a mining company's desire to develop a wilderness area, or a company fighting a hostile takeover by another firm.

Another form of struggle, and thus potential reader interest, is illustrated by accident and disaster coverage, where victims fight against Mother Nature's whims. For whatever dark reason, people like to peer at the misfortunes of others. That's essentially the business model of reality TV. The same morbid curiosity explains high audience attention to plane crashes, industrial accidents and other instances where blood is spilled. As the old news adage goes: "If it bleeds, it leads."

Although it's commonly perceived that PR and marketing practitioners prefer to portray their clients sailing on a calm sea of passively positive public opinion, remember the inherent interest in conflict can be a great force you can engage to awaken an important audience's attention and incite their support for an organizational policy. For instance, a company's effort to fend off unauthorized uses of a protected patent or a nonprofit's fight with a governmental organization over infant adoption processes could energize latent publics to support the organization.

### Unusualness: Is It the First, Last or Only Time It's Happened?

Consider one of the classic definitions of news, first offered by writer Jesse Williams (and since attributed to many others): "When a dog bites a man, that is not news. But when a man bites a dog, that is news."[6]

Such unusualness is a frequent component of PR and marketing writing. We are often asked to publicize projects such as the city's first drone delivery of groceries, the production of a local factory's last car before retooling or the work of the only stained-glass artisan in the state. These "firsts," "lasts" and "onlys" are relished by editors, broadcast news producers and internet audiences.

But again, we remind you of the difference between clickbait and genuine motivation. Sure, you can title your pitch letter to an editor under the heading: "Nude photos of U.S. senator revealed!" However, if the story you're trying to place in the editor's publication concerns a clothing drive for the homeless, you've made the editor angry and damaged your credibility as an information source. It's a horrible mistake even if you put it in an internet pop-up ad. You paid money to gather people who are interested in embarrassing a senior politician, not those likely to respond favorably to a homeless clothing drive. The lesson? If you choose unusualness as the method by which you're collecting readers, the novelty must be directly relevant to your communication objective.

### Prominence: Do I Know Who It's About?

If a young mother from your community goes to the local Walmart, it's not news.

However, if a young mother picks up a few disposable diapers at a discount store clear across the country—and she happens to be the star of a hit movie—you'll see multiple versions of the incident on your social media posts, in your local newspaper and on national entertainment news. What's the difference? The doings of celebrities, no matter how inconsequential, fascinate many people.

The lure of prominence is not necessarily limited to film stars. If your city's mayor is charged with driving under the influence, the coverage will be much more extensive than if a lower-level office worker were arrested for the same offense.

The same principle applies to public relations and other forms of persuasive writing. A charity banquet for the local animal shelter probably won't get much attention from anyone except those passionately interested in protecting cats and dogs. But if the host of a popular TV animal training series is the banquet's guest speaker, the media coverage and social media interest you could prompt increases dramatically. For that reason, the celebrity's name may deserve to be included in a prominent place in your lede.

**Strategic Thought**

Analyze the top story on your school newspaper's homepage. How many TIPCUP elements did it include? Were any omitted? Why did they frame the story as they did? Were any opportunities missed?

## Who You Are Determines What You'll Read
### One Person in Many Publics

In the previous section, you may have noticed how often we used very specific audience descriptors to indicate how each element of the TIPCUP filter would define the most prominent news value in each scenario. We mentioned small-town high school graduates, environmentalists, health care professionals, parents of public school children. Each one had a specific audience.

That's why we spent so much of Chapters 2 and 3 talking about audience and why we call our analysis process audience-centered writing. Your audience's interests will determine which of the TIPCUP filters you choose to begin your lede. In turn, that choice will outline the rest of your piece.

To prove the point, here's a purely ludicrous scenario. Let's say the crown prince of Monaco is visiting your city today. He's riding in a Shriner motorcycle unit in a benefit parade raising restoration funds for the 70% of the city destroyed by a flood. The prince's motorcycle crashes into the Luxembourg national float. The Luxembourg prime minister suffers a concussion when he falls from the float onto the street. The two countries declare war on each other.

Every one of the TIPCUP elements is in this story. In your community, you could choose *timeliness*, *proximity* and/or *prominence*. *Unusualness?* His royal highness performing precision driving routines. The parade's fundraising will have a significant *impact* on the mud-encrusted city. Moreover, *conflict* is everywhere. Luxembourgian blood pollutes our sewers and war clouds darken these formerly peaceful little principalities.

But say you're the social media editor of the nation's flour millers trade association, which is in that same city. There's not a single aspect in this story that interests your readers, at least in their role as flour manufacturers. Audience is critical.

Audience dominates all the other criteria we use to value information for our lede. That's because the innate qualities of the individuals receiving your message profoundly alter the gratifications they receive from devoting their time and mental energy to your communication. While people who grind grain into flour might enjoy reading about precision motorcycle riders, they do not anticipate, nor do they appreciate, receiving that information through a forum supposedly devoted to helping them more successfully manage their milling businesses.

We said before there is no such thing as uninteresting information, just information presented to the wrong audience. This contradicts many beliefs we hold about our society. In fact, we probably should call it socie*ties.*

**Strategic Thought**

Describe yourself demographically, then psychographically. What media would be effective in communicating to the demographic groups to which you perceive you belong? Are these different from media platforms that would reach your psychographic groups?

Each of us belongs to many different publics: homeowners, doctors, students, stamp collectors, Manchester United fans, French-Canadians who enjoy traveling in Africa. However, no person can be defined by membership in a single audience.

You are a student and belong to that public. However, you may also be president of a political club, a homeless shelter volunteer, a part-time employee at an online warehouse and the local polka band's accordionist. The person next to you in class joins you as a student at your university, but has a completely different and equally complex set of self-identifiers that dictate her interests in certain information. As Figure 6.2 illustrates, even this text's two authors, who share many professional and some personal interests, differ vastly in substantial ways. This complex of personal values provides the perspective through which we judge our own self-interests and determine our reactions to communication events.

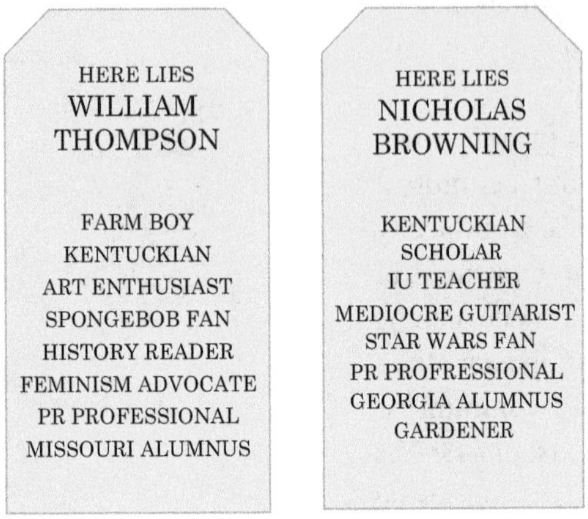

Every individual has a different combination of interests and attributes. As we discussed in Chapter 3, these personal characteristics can be defined through demographics and psychographics. Demographics classify people through quantitative information, such as their age, sexual identification, where they live, educational level and how much money they earn. In most cases, it's very difficult to select your demographic characteristics. You can't change your age or your birthplace, and it takes a lot of effort to increase your educational level or how much money you make.

Compare that to psychographics. Psychographics describe how people define themselves—their political views, spiritual beliefs, personal values and interests. Psychographic elements are a much more powerful indicator of an audience's interest in a specific subject. Our nearly constant use of the term "individual's perception" during our social exchange theory discussion shows just what an important force an individual's understanding of her own self-identity is.

HERE LIES
WILLIAM
THOMPSON

FARM BOY
KENTUCKIAN
ART ENTHUSIAST
SPONGEBOB FAN
HISTORY READER
FEMINISM ADVOCATE
PR PROFESSIONAL
MISSOURI ALUMNUS

HERE LIES
NICHOLAS
BROWNING

KENTUCKIAN
SCHOLAR
IU TEACHER
MEDIOCRE GUITARIST
STAR WARS FAN
PR PROFRESSIONAL
GEORGIA ALUMNUS
GARDENER

**FIGURE 6.2  The Two Authors' Abridged Audience Profiles.** Note how the authors' tombstones display audience characteristics that sometimes converge and sometimes diverge. It's apparent they would be in the same public for some messages but not for others.

## Analyzing Audience Demographics and Psychographics

Together, demographics and psychographics give essential clues to constructing an effective communication campaign that will be relevant to a number of different audiences.

Let's explain this with another scenario. You're a PR practitioner for a client whose company has developed an advanced desktop blood diagnosis machine affordable for even a small medical practice. While a media pitch to a medical journal's editor would likely focus on the device's faster diagnoses and lower cost, any interest from the editor of the inventor's college alumni publication will only begin when you list her major and graduation year. If you're developing a fact sheet to prompt a consumer health blog post, it might be better to emphasize the machine's convenience and novelty. A report to the innovating company's stockholders would probably concentrate on the profits expected from the new product.

The predictive power stemming from understanding the audience's self-identity has other uses as well. Those identity factors not only suggest the specific portion of the issue in which the audience is interested, but even the way the material itself should be presented. A social media campaign trying to recruit dropouts to enroll in a high school equivalency program would have a simpler vocabulary than a university's media release touting its discovery of gravity's effect on a subatomic field. Your audience for the equivalency program might not even be able to read on an eighth-grade level, while the audience for the scientific breakthrough will probably have completed two decades of formal education.

The audience analysis also is central to media choices. Say you were a practitioner representing an estate attorney striving to get people older than 80 to hire her to modify their wills. Will the lawyer's audience be accessible through social media, or would a direct mail campaign, expensive as it is, actually be more cost-effective than a Facebook marketing effort?

Sometimes that change of perception between different audiences results in even more radical outcomes. At times it can cause groups of people to take the same set of information, yet define the event's meaning in very different ways. On an anniversary of the attack on New York's World Trade Center, there were many tributes and remembrances concerning the tragedy. Some commentators mourned their work colleagues who died Sept. 11. Others commemorated the efforts of first responders, the passengers on the four planes that went down that day, or the crews who labored in dangerous conditions to clean the site.

One commentator affiliated with PETA had a different perspective on the solemn anniversary. PETA's Joe Taksel reminded us "of all the cats, dogs, birds, hamsters, fish, and other companion animals who waited in vain for the return of their loving guardians who lost their lives that day."[7]

Taksel related how PETA's staff and volunteers mobilized to reach pets left in residences in the lower Manhattan neighborhoods that in the days after the Twin Towers attack were cordoned off by police. Unfortunately, the organization's efforts were largely fruitless, and many, many animals died.

Taksel ended his essay with a call for peace and understanding, whatever one's DNA signature. "Let's resolve to open our hearts as much as we can to everyone," he wrote, "regardless of race, color, species, gender, creed, nationality, or religion—every day."

None of these tributes are inappropriate responses. Instead the scenario reminds professional communicators that we cannot be mired within the boundaries of our own background. It's our job to be the people within our organization who can envision the breadth of responses a particular situation

**PETA's Disaster Response**

https://prime.peta.org/2020/09/helping-animals-when-tragedy-strikes/

People for the Ethical Treatment of Animals (PETA) has a long history of helping animals in times of tragedy, shifting the focus from human to animal suffering to appeal to their mission—and their audience's primary interests.

might inspire. At that point, we design the most effective communication plan to engage the appropriate audiences with our message by offering them the rewards that motivate each to action.

That's the outline of the audience-centered writing model. Now let's summarize its practical implications as we translate the model into real-life writing tasks:

- Every individual in our society is faced with thousands of messages each day. From those thousands of messages, a person chooses to attend to only a few.

- Individuals decide whether to attend to a specific message based on their perceptions of interests and self-interests.

- The competition for attention is intense for each message. As professional communicators, we increase our odds of grabbing attention for our messages through a systemic process of analyzing the audiences we wish to persuade.

- Once that analysis is complete, writers must integrate the information most likely to engage their target audience members so individuals immediately recognize the story is important to them.

## Generating Effective Persuasive Writing: The Audience-Centered Writing Process

Professional writers we encounter often mock the process of constructing writing models, implying that talking about writing is just pleasant conversation for people who can't write.

How do your authors define the real test of writing theory? Does it tell you what to do when you face a writer's block or when you encounter some unfamiliar writing task?

When you are a professional writer, you aren't paid to sit and wait for a creative inspiration. You're paid to write and sometimes do it in a room with 25 other people yelling while you work to meet a deadline that's—let's check the clock—22 minutes from now. The audience-centered writing process presents the writer with a sequence of questions that helps generate prose in virtually every circumstance.

We described it before as a generative writing system: It helps you refine your thinking, thus making it easier to generate the first few words of each paragraph. By helping you analyze your audience, you'll know what information will most interest your potential reader. The model then helps you prioritize that information so you can craft the lede sentence. Once you've got the basic pattern established in the first few words, you'll actually structure an approximate sequence for the rest of the paragraph, then the rest of the piece.

That's perhaps more important than you can possibly imagine now. To capture your intended audience, the first sentence, those first couple of seconds of your encounter with each reader, is the most important in the entire piece. At the same time, for most beginning writers, the first sentence is the most difficult to write. That's understandable, since the lede must draw the correct audience, as well as outline the rest of the document.

The audience-centered process breaks down the writing of the lede sentence into three fundamental steps. These steps are the same for virtually every document you're asked to write.

Before you begin writing, you should (1) know for whom you're writing, (2) determine what that specific audience is interested in and (3) tell them that information as quickly as you can. Another scenario may help illustrate this.

Let's say you are the communication specialist at the KonkreteWeave Carpet Corp. plant located in Portsburg, a city mired in an economic slump. KonkreteWeave researcher R. P. Scallion has developed a stain-proof carpet fiber in the company's labs in the Lesser Antilles. The breakthrough? Scallion rediscovered a 4,000-year-old Egyptian method of dipping raw fabric in a high-temperature bath filled with Saharan salts.

Beginning Jan. 1, the Portsburg factory will exclusively produce the carpet fiber. The plant will hire 900 more workers to meet the demand. Scallion said the new product will soon dominate the industry and be manufactured in plants throughout the world. You're asked to write a media release announcing the finding to the local metropolitan news outlets.

The traditional 5W1H formula for writing ledes discussed earlier might yield something like this:

> KonkreteWeave Carpet Corp. has announced that company scientist R. P. Scallion has discovered in tests over the past six years at the company's research laboratories in the Lesser Antilles that a new, no-stain carpet can be made by soaking carpet fibers in a high-temperature salt bath, giving consumers a much-desired feature in their new carpet purchases.

All the 5W1H questions are answered. However, this is a speaker-centered lede. It's good at communicating self-congratulatory information that will delight your company's board of directors. It's difficult to imagine more than a few Portsburg citizens paying attention.

A better approach? Understanding the rewards you can offer an audience for its attention will help generate a more compelling lede. Prioritize the information presented based upon the audience you want to read this. Eliminate some details and push the most relevant information to the very beginning of the lede.

### Know Whom You're Writing For: The Audience Analysis

Throughout the early chapters of this book, we've emphasized the importance of audience. As you might anticipate, your first step in constructing a better lede sentence for Konkrete-Weave is to assess the audience characteristics discussed in Chapter 3. In essence, if our assigned task is to place a story in Portsburg media, what is the greatest reward we can offer those potential readers and viewers? Let's walk through a likely audience analysis in Konkrete-Weave's persuasion platform, constructed through formal analysis and good strategic communication intuition in Figure 6.3.

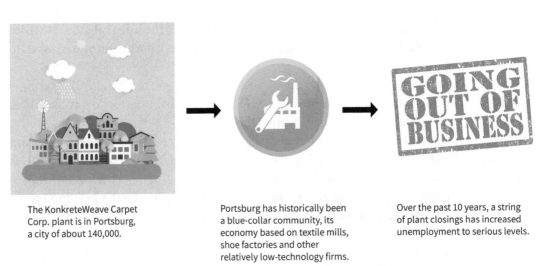

The KonkreteWeave Carpet Corp. plant is in Portsburg, a city of about 140,000.

Portsburg has historically been a blue-collar community, its economy based on textile mills, shoe factories and other relatively low-technology firms.

Over the past 10 years, a string of plant closings has increased unemployment to serious levels.

The plant closings have shattered the spirit and pride of Portsburg's leaders and citizens. Unemployed workers fear tumbling into poverty.

Those still employed fear their jobs will soon disappear. Even people who should feel more secure, like the retired who have comfortable pensions or adults working in white-collar jobs, are worried.

They're concerned about the effects of the high unemployment on housing values, the city's tax base and their community's quality of life.

**FIGURE 6.3  Portsburg Demographics and Psychographics.**

### Know What They're Interested In: The TIPCUP Analysis

The persuasion platform distilled a simple profile of what is important to our audience. Now we evaluate the story components through the TIPCUP filter. To do this, we estimate the strength of the information in each of the six TIPCUP categories on the basis of how much it rewards our audience's engagement with the message. The question: Which of the following TIPCUP components help draw Portsburg's media audience? A logical thought process might resemble this:

*Timeliness:* Not really important. The project has taken six years to complete. The news there will be a new carpet fiber would be as interesting two weeks from now as it is today.

*Impact:* Vital. Portsburg is filled with unemployed factory workers. Announcing 900 new jobs by year's end is tremendously important to this struggling community.

*Proximity:* Another very important element. If the new jobs were in another county or another state, Portsburg readers would not care. However, it's intensely important because of the community's high unemployment.

*Conflict:* None.

*Unusualness:* A bit. It's the process's first modern use. However, to most of our target audience, the technology's discovery is less important than the new jobs it creates.

*Prominence:* Nope. There is no person connected with the story whose name Portsburg residents would recognize.

### Tell Them Quickly: Generating the Lede Sentence

Knowing what story elements are most important to our readers, the receiver-centered writing process practically generates the lede sentence. Memory Memo 6.2 outlines the basic process: Take only the TIPCUP elements you have determined are important to your audience. You'll want those—*and only those*—tucked into the first 10 words or so of your lede. This is what we'll designate the *No. 1 position.* In KonkreteWeave's case, we determined those are impact, unusualness and proximity.

Next, choose words that communicate each of your selected TIPCUP concepts to your readers. For instance, proximity for our readers would be conveyed by *Portsburg, hometown* or *local.* Impact for this defined audience might be stated using words like *unemployment* or *jobs.* Timeliness might be suggested by the words *soon* or *Jan. 1* or *next year.* Unusualness could be communicated by using words like *breakthrough, ancient Egyptian* or *new.*

Noting that proximity and impact are more likely to draw our projected audience's attention, we prioritize them over unusualness and timeliness. The sentence generated by using the audience-centered process might look like this:

> Portsburg's unemployment problems may lessen Jan. 1 when KonkreteWeave's local plant hires 900 new workers to start making a breakthrough carpet fiber.

Now, reduced to the individual TIPCUP elements:

> Portsburg's (PROXIMITY) unemployment problems may lessen (IMPACT) Jan. 1 (TIMELINESS) when KonkreteWeave's local plant hires 900 new workers (IMPACT AGAIN) to start making a breakthrough (UNUSUALNESS) carpet fiber.

The receiver-centered process has helped you generate a lede sentence fulfilling the vital roles of virtually any persuasive message. It immediately alerts its intended audience that the coming message will be about them. Within its first 10 words, it has delivered the information you prioritized as most likely to capture your reader's attention and keep them reading.

---

**MEMORY MEMO 6.2** The Audience-Centered Writing Process

- Formulate your audience's demographic and psychographic profile
- Evaluate your story information through the TIPCUP filter
- Choose the TIPCUP elements that stimulate your audience's interests
- Find words that illustrate each TIPCUP element you've chosen
- Prioritize the TIPCUP elements important to your target audience
- Write the lede sentence, using the most important TIPCUP elements first
- Refine and tighten the lede sentence

## CASE IN POINT 6.1   Checking the First 10 Words

Here's a quick check to see if your lede is on the right track.

Count 10 words into your sentence. If you can read 10 words and can't discover at least one or two TIPCUP filter items you isolated, you most likely have some problems.

ORIGINAL: *Original introduces uninviting topics and unknown speaker* → Taxpayers United president Jody Carlin said the group's study of the Second Street Bridge accident determined that "bad concrete" caused the bridge collapse.

REWRITE: *Rewrite concentrates on scandal in the first few words and involves the correct audience. Specific names not drawing audience eliminated.* → "Bad concrete" caused the Second Street Bridge Collapse, according to a taxpayer's advocacy group.

**Compare the First 10 Words**

ORIGINAL → Taxpayers United president Jody Carlin said the group's study of ...

REWRITE → "Bad concrete" caused the Second Street Bridge collapse, according to ...

Case in Point 6.1 establishes a rule that encapsulates the process: In the lede's first 10 words, define an audience and define a benefit for that audience.

Although the receiver-centered writing process helps writers produce an effective lede sentence, there's no one single correct sentence. There are many ways writers can accomplish the persuasive task:

About 900 new Portsburg jobs will be created by Jan. 1 when KonkreteWeave begins manufacturing a breakthrough new carpet fiber in its local plant.

Or:

About 900 more Portsburgers will have jobs next year when KonkreteWeave begins making a revolutionary carpet fiber in its local plant.

Or:

The new year will relieve Portsburg's job problems when KonkreteWeave's local plant adds 900 workers to make a breakthrough, no-stain carpet fiber.

Although each lede sentence is different, all concentrate the story's most important elements within the sentence's first 10 words. Those elements define the audience we want to reach with this persuasive message and present a benefit important to those readers' self-interest.

## You Want Different Audiences? You Need Different Ledes

It's important to recognize that a lede is a direct expression of your strategy for reaching the greatest number of people within a target public united by a specific interest. It's not a static, unchanging construction. As we discussed earlier, if the audience changes, the lede will likely change as well.

For instance, what would happen if you were communicating about the plans for KonkreteWeave's factory to the readers of a science blog? First, the audience analysis suggests a transformed readership. Instead of blue-collar workers in a specific city, our persuasive message would now be directed at an international audience of scientists. Even though they are scattered throughout the world, their science training has fostered a strong bond within which personalities and reputations have developed. Additionally, the scientific process dictated by their experimental process suggests a new scientific finding might redirect many other scientists' research.

In Figure 6.4, you can see what a new audience analysis, even with the same set of news elements, might be.

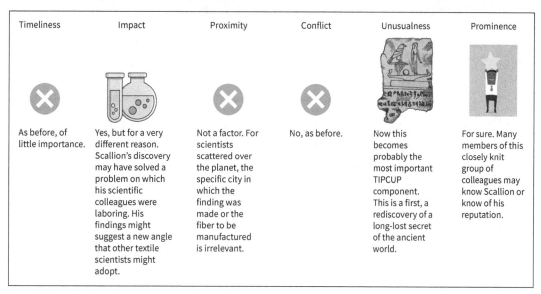

| Timeliness | Impact | Proximity | Conflict | Unusualness | Prominence |
|---|---|---|---|---|---|
| As before, of little importance. | Yes, but for a very different reason. Scallion's discovery may have solved a problem on which his scientific colleagues were laboring. His findings might suggest a new angle that other textile scientists might adopt. | Not a factor. For scientists scattered over the planet, the specific city in which the finding was made or the fiber to be manufactured is irrelevant. | No, as before. | Now this becomes probably the most important TIPCUP component. This is a first, a rediscovery of a long-lost secret of the ancient world. | For sure. Many members of this closely knit group of colleagues may know Scallion or know of his reputation. |

**FIGURE 6.4 Scientist TIPCUP.**

As we did in our previous example, we employ only those elements we've deemed most important in drawing our audience of scientists and giving them a reason to continue reading: impact, prominence and unusualness. Again, selecting words that illustrate those concepts, a logical lede might look like this:

Solving an ancient chemical mystery, KonkreteWeave researcher R. P. Scallion found Egyptian carpets resisted stains because they were soaked in high-temperature salt baths, a process to be duplicated on an industrial scale in a KonkreteWeave factory.

Notice the differences between the local newspaper lede and the one intended for the science blog. True, we are communicating information about the same event. However, the difference in our audience analysis suggests this audience of scientists will demand different rewards if we are to draw their attention. The analysis helps us predict the audience's probable interests, its reading level and the differently perceived importance of the event.

Our two examples show evidence for all three of these factors. The research scientists want to know about a colleague's contributions to a perplexing technical problem. Conversely, Portsburg's newspaper readers have more interest in the jobs that may help their city recover from its economic trauma.

You can see differences in reading level too. The most important determinants of reading difficulty are the average sentence's number of words, number of multisyllabic words and punctuation marks. There is a striking difference between the KonkreteWeave ledes. The lede targeting scientists demanded seven more years of education, according to **readability formulas**. You can see the calculations in Case in Point 6.2.

## CASE IN POINT 6.2    Readability Formulas

There are a lot of different readability tests. One website lists 17.[8] There are some that supposedly test all writing. Some specialize in writing for readers who are 10 years old or younger. Some are designed to assess readability for texts concerning medical topics. Some determine how hard it is for non-English-speaking readers to understand a selection of prose.

Some of the more recognizable readability indexes are the Flesch Reading Ease Formula, the SMOG Readability Formula and the Gunning FOG Index. Many of you will be in jobs in which your employers will specify a readability formula, so it's useful to know the presumptions from which they spring.

Let's first look at how the FOG Index assesses the two sentences we developed for the KonkreteWeave story. Here are the two sentences, one for the local Portsburg media and the other for a scientific journal, as calculated by the FOG Index:

1. Portsburg's unemployment problems may be softened Jan. 1 when KonkreteWeave's local factory hires 900 new workers to start making a breakthrough carpet fiber.

2. Solving an ancient chemical mystery, KonkreteWeave researcher R. P. Scallion found ancient Egyptian carpets resisted stains because they were soaked in high-temperature salt baths, a process that will be duplicated on an industrial scale at a KonkreteWeave factory.

- 23 Words
- Two words of more than two syllables
- Reading level: sixth grade

- 37 Words
- Seven words of more than two syllables
- Reading level: first-year college

You can clearly see how we've crafted ledes that reflect audience capabilities, the first broadly accessible and the second more technical in nature. However, you need to be careful when employing any readability formula. They can be fooled in different ways if you unknowingly challenge the premises of their calculation process. For instance, take two sentences, each seven words long:

I saw an elephant in the refrigerator.                I saw two quarks in the hadron.

Because so many of the readability formulas assume multisyllable words are harder to understand, the FOG Index calculates that you'd have to be a college sophomore to understand the concept of looking at the elephant. The same FOG Index calculated that the seven-word sentence discussing particle physics could be understood by second-grade pupils.

Other readability tests, like the New Dale-Chall Readability Index, define a lexicon of "familiar," longer words. In the Dale-Chall formula, those 3,000 words, which include *elephant* and *refrigerator,* are counted as a single-syllable word before calculating the readability score. Because of that assumption, Dale-Chall calculates a more reasonable kindergarten reading score for the elephant sentence, and predicts a high school senior could understand the quark sentence. However, Dale-Chall has problems as well. It predicted that both KonkreteWeave ledes, for the local media and the science journal, had the same readability level: early college.

**How Accessible Is Your Writing?**

https://readabilityformulas.com/free-readability-formula-tests.php

This website conducts multiple readability calculations at once.

Do we have a recommendation? In most cases, the FOG Index predicts what seems to be a justifiable measure of readability. Perhaps the best approach is to run your prose through multiple readability tests and then determine a consensus among all the scores. Sounds difficult, but it's actually quite easy. The QR code to the right links to a calculator that tests seven different readability formulas simultaneously. Use it to test the readability of your own writing.

## The Constants: Define the Audience, Tell Them Their Benefit

The audience-centered approach gives writers a process through which their knowledge of key publics greatly assists their writing production. Because of that, the same steps can be used to address any audience in any type of writing.

Let's say your task is to create an internal memorandum to KonkreteWeave's CEO about the new fiber's expected benefits. The same principles apply. Instead of jobs or innovation for its own sake, your lede is likely now about profits, market position and so on. Even if your audience is only one person, you let her motives to read dictate what you'll write.

And you still need to place that information within the first few words of your first sentence. If you're already thinking that you could capitalize upon the audience-centered writing process to expand your reach by changing the lede, you're correct (although you're anticipating topics in chapters yet to come).

So we're back to considering communication competition, with which we began this chapter. The essence of good writing is to give your intended audience a reason to be interested in what you wish to communicate and a reward for reading what you write. In the next chapter, we'll examine how the audience-based writing process provides a structure for the rest of the written piece.

## SUMMARY

- Although people have some subconscious awareness of most messages they encounter, they dismiss the vast majority of them and save their attention for a few messages they perceive as rewarding their time in reading them.

- The TIPCUP filter—**T**imeliness, **I**mpact, **P**roximity, **C**onflict, **U**nusualness and **P**rominence—analyzes each communication situation from the context of a specific audience, determining what elements of the scenario will most likely draw that audience's attention to the piece.

- The first 10 words of a good lede sentence define an audience and then provide a benefit that will be important for that audience.

- Audience characteristics will also determine necessary changes in the complexity of vocabulary, the choice of media platform and other modifications.

### Scenario Prompts: Developing Lede Sentences

You'll find Scenario Prompts on pp. 367–386 of this textbook. While they vary in subject and difficulty, they help you hone your critical thinking and strategic writing skills. The following are best suited to this chapter's topics.

Management: **6.1, 7.4** / Writing: 5.8, 6.8, 9.11

### *Figure Credits*

Fig. 6.3a: Copyright © 2014 Depositphotos/odis.

Fig. 6.3b: Copyright © 2016 by MikeRenpening. Reprinted with permission.

Fig. 6.3c: Copyright © 2015 Depositphotos/camen_dorin.

Fig. 6.3d: Copyright © 2017 Depositphotos/prettyvectors.

Fig. 6.3e: Copyright © 2014 Depositphotos/zoo-co.

Fig. 6.3f: Copyright © 2020 Depositphotos/Tdubov.

Fig. 6.4a: Copyright © 2017 by janjf93. Reprinted with permission.

Fig. 6.4b: Copyright © 2017 by Memed_Nurrohmad. Reprinted with permission.

Fig. 6.4c: Copyright © 2013 by OpenClipart-Vectors. Reprinted with permission.

Fig. 6.4d: Copyright © 2016 Depositphotos/seamartini.

# Building a Persuasive Case

## Generating Body Copy Using the Audience-Centered Process

---

**LESSONS FROM LIFE**     **A Noble Calling**

I've been quite lucky. I've been paid to be a writer my entire professional life. However, that comes with a certain sense of dissatisfaction.

In high school I thought the natural result of my writing would be a long string of screenplays adapted from my collected works. Armored trucks would deliver bags of money from triumphant first-week movie grosses. People would clamor for a reading, an autograph, a lock of hair. Now, at an age when I don't have enough excess hair to waste on some excited fan, I admit I didn't really understand the profession.

Never did any of those fantasies include sitting by myself in a lonely room and struggling to get prose onto paper, or as technology later dictated, pixels into the online ether. That's the cruel reality of writing, in any form.

Only when I went to the University of Missouri's journalism school did I understand. Phil Norman, a grizzled editorial veteran, was not impressed with my prose. I think he recognized I was trying to overcome my farm-boy intellectual insecurity by weaseling long, obscure vocabulary into even longer, more obscure sentences.

He called it "mama prose," writing so unfathomably terrible that only my mother would suffer through reading it. The type of writing he was trying to foster, he explained, existed to help people understand information that lets them live their lives.

Anything detracting from that purpose is counterproductive. In a brutal, semester-long tsunami of red editor's ink, Professor Norman truncated my sentences, substituted simple synonyms for my complex word choices, slashed prepositional phrases … and put me on the road toward becoming a decent writer.

As a writer of journalism, PR, advertising or marketing prose, you should recognize that no one camps outside bookstores eagerly awaiting your media release. No one drags herself through 300 dreary pages because a college professor's distant voice tells her she might be rewarded if she sustains her effort. Our writing must provide instant fulfillment for a much simpler purpose: to help people interact with the institutions and people in their lives. From that, hopefully, they can sculpt a better existence.

In some ways, or at least during internal monologues I convene to justify my career, it's a pretty noble calling. You are exchanging knowledge between your organization and the people around it in the fastest, most forthright and most comprehensible manner you can.

That's what we hope this chapter will foster. We think persuasive writing is a challenging, intellectually engaging task for which some of you will be rewarded throughout your lives. It's not been so bad … though an armored truck of money here and there would have been nice.

—WT

## What You Know

- Readers make rapid decisions about whether messages offer enough rewards to continue reading.
- Messages emerge organically from an assessment of the audience's needs and capacities.
- An audience's evaluation of a decision's consequences and its likelihood of satisfying emotional or rational rewards dictates the placement of persuaders in a document.

## What You'll Learn

- How to position persuasive information within a story to assure the most important elements will be communicated, no matter how brief the reader's attention
- How the nature of your evidence dictates the argumentation pattern you'll employ
- How to structure transitions between story elements
- How employing tactics to increase your audience's reading speed improves information transfer and comprehension

## Writing Created by Your Audience's Needs

What did we keep saying in the previous chapter? It's your assessment of your audience's interests and priorities that will generate your prose. We'll extend that same lesson in this chapter.

Strategic communication writing is primarily created to persuade a targeted public to act. That's a simple statement, but we're dismayed by how many persuasive writers don't follow that principle. Instead, they produce copy that may flatter their senior managers' egos or display their own prose skills. But that's not why people pay us to write.

Professional persuasive writers must concentrate on communicating information efficiently to specific publics in a way that demonstrates how organizational resources can help satisfy their needs. It's in that way, not the glow of pride you create in your CEO's mind or your creative writing teacher's heart, that we meet the organization's management goals.

This chapter outlines writing strategies to address those needs. You'll employ the same planning and analysis routines that prioritized the arguments most likely to interest your target audience in the first sentence. But now we'll extend that approach to demonstrate how it can guide you to sequencing entire documents, thus leading your readers toward accepting your message.

However, rather than reciting rules about writing, we'll continue to reinforce a communication philosophy founded on your knowledge of your audience's needs for particular information delivered in a particular way. In essence, it's a heuristic process for storytelling. That said, it's not intended to make all strategic communication writers or writing alike. There are no formulas for universally good writing (though adhering to certain principles can help prevent objectively horrific writing). Instead, our audience-centered approach will point you toward your own writing style, one that involves and motivates your readers. It's one you can employ in a wide variety of persuasive writing tasks, both ones that exist now and those that may develop in the future.

## Relevant and Fast:
## What People Want From Persuasive Messages

People read PR, advertising and marketing communication not as entertainment. Instead, it's a tool to find information about an institution with which they interact, or might soon.

Two imperatives grow from that philosophy. First, remember your audience members are reading to gather information important to their lives.[1] That fact compels you as a professional persuasive writer to structure information within the story in a logical flow, one letting your readers readily see relationships among the arguments you include. That logic also compels you to build a story structure prompting readers to retain and later retrieve the information you present.

Second, your readers want to gain that information as quickly as possible. Again, look at it from their points of view. They are faced with processing and responding to thousands of messages every day. Even if they are interested in your message, they have limited time to devote to it.

If your writing is unnecessarily long, or you offer important information in such a way that it's hard to understand or access, your readers will quit reading—of course, assuming they even start. That's why you must know the places within stories where readers make decisions about attending to the message. It's equally important to use a simple and direct prose style, as well as vocabulary accessible to your intended audience. Additionally, you must structure your information within the piece to motivate your readers to continue reading.[2]

Memory Memo 7.1 summarizes the fundamental principles that should motivate each and every piece of your persuasive writing. All the prose rules discussed in this chapter derive from your readers' needs for comprehension and economy. That's vital because prose rules don't exist simply as random, disconnected edicts issued by some embittered middle school language arts teacher (and yes, we've had personal experiences with the category). Instead, they stem from and should promote continued engagement by serving your readers' communication needs. In short, they foster audience-centered writing.

> **MEMORY MEMO 7.1** Audience-Centered Writing Musts
>
> - Make certain they have communicated their message by ensuring reading comprehension
> - Use as little of their readers' time as possible by enhancing reading speed

## Inverted Pyramids:
## Matching Writing Structure and Reader Involvement

In the previous chapter, we examined how people approach the decision to attend to a message. They're usually receptive for the moment during which they're deciding whether the message contains information interesting to or involving them. If it does, they devote a bit more time to reading a little further. If it doesn't, they'll abandon the piece. That's why we emphasized placing such information in the lede's first 10 words.

However, readers continue making these decisions about whether to keep reading throughout the piece. Think of your own experiences when you've clicked on a web story and discovered it's 9,000 words long. After a couple of ad-encrusted pages, you abandon the quest for knowledge or entertainment. You read until you thought the trouble of continuing to attend to the message wasn't worth the time you would invest. The same thing happens on different media platforms, whether it's print, audio, visual or even face-to-face. You've probably even neglected your dinner companion's conversation when it seemed to offer fewer rewards than perusing your cell phone's content.

This is a fact of life in persuasive writing. There's no message you can write that is so clever or compelling that all people will feel it's worth their time to read it. Recognizing this reality, your task becomes to communicate as much vital information as possible in your message's first sections, reserving less important facts for deeper in the story. This ensures the greatest number of readers will be attracted, and that even those readers who abandon the piece midway through may understand the most important facts.

The **inverted pyramid**, journalism's most prominent information-structuring formula, recognizes this truth.[3] Depicted as an upside-down pyramid in Figure 7.1, it concentrates the most important information at the top of the story. Through this tactic, we let readers to immediately grasp the story's most compelling aspects. If they're not interested in the topic, they abandon it. But if we can correctly predict what our audience will most value, we begin engaging our target public more deeply.

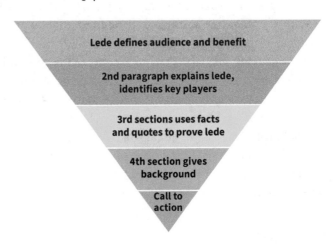

**FIGURE 7.1  The Inverted Pyramid.** The inverted pyramid visualizes a story structure that reflects reader habits.

Lede defines audience and benefit

2nd paragraph explains lede, identifies key players

3rd sections uses facts and quotes to prove lede

4th section gives background

Call to action

In later paragraphs, the inverted pyramid reinforces the lede sentence by coherently offering quotes, statistics and information that guides the reader through our argument. Less important information is placed lower in the story, where dedicated readers can find historical background and miscellaneous information about the issue. The inverted pyramid works on the principle that you must (1) capture the attention of your target public (2) before you can convince them with the arguments that will ultimately (3) persuade them to act. The exact way your target public can act to obtain those benefits is in the inverted pyramid's final section.

The inverted pyramid works the same if the story is a 10-second radio ad or a 20-minute vlog. You first indicate why the audience would profit by attending to your message. You next deliver your arguments, and in so doing move the audience to action. Then you tell them how to act: Visit this website. Buy this product. Attend this event at this address. In most professional persuasive writing, the inverted pyramid comprises the following five parts:

### Lede Paragraph

After you analyze your communication purpose and your audience, you write the lede using the TIPCUP filter components your audience analysis found most compelling. The vast majority of ledes will be a single sentence. Chapter 6 covered lede writing in detail, so we won't rehash that here.

### Briefly Explain the Lede

An inverted pyramid's second paragraph explains the lede. In most instances, it establishes the program or organization's official name you introduced in the lede and highlights a single piece of information that lends credibility to the claim you made in the lede. Sometimes it will offer the name of an important person who was the subject of the lede. Other times, it's a compelling statistic. However, this paragraph should be short. It is not intended to summarize your entire story.

### Justify the Lede

The middle paragraphs comprise the inverted pyramid's third section, which can vary from a single sentence to many paragraphs, depending on the audience and document's communication purpose. It's where you offer quotes, facts, chronologies and other information to prove the statement you made in your lede. If the lede announced a concert, this section is where you'd tell what groups will be playing. If your first sentence of your company's annual report narrative announces big profits from a new product, this is where you would offer projections and quotes from marketing experts to justify your optimism.

You'll usually sequence your supporting your argument in the same order as they were introduced in the lede sentence. This practice is called **parallel structure**. Your lede signals to your readers what the piece is about, typically listing elements of the story in the order of their importance. You should follow this sequence in the body copy so your lede not only captures the piece's most important aspects but becomes a road map foreshadowing the overarching structure.

You typically use only one new idea in each paragraph. (Later in this chapter, we'll offer more guidance about setting priorities and structuring information within the pyramid's third section.)

### Background

After you've built the pyramid's middle portion, the fourth section presents a historical overview of the event or issue your piece discusses. For instance, if you work for a government agency announcing a new law's implementation, you might include the measure's legislative history. A story on a leukemia cure might include information about earlier folk cures or how the new therapy was developed.

### Call to Action

The pyramid's fifth section includes the information necessary for your reader to act—to attend your event, buy your company's new product, follow a new law or contact the hospital offering the new leukemia cure. This is where you would put the company website URL, links to official social media accounts, telephone number or brick-and-mortar business address. This section, usually only a paragraph, might also include the time and place for a rally, the range of ticket prices for a lecture or other specific information important for the reader acting upon your information.

Writing students sometimes question why we recommend waiting until the final paragraph to inform our audience about such important details. Why not give the ticket price and the event date and location in the first or second paragraph so readers could instantly act on the information? For one, if your reader is interested in the event or issue discussed in the piece, they're probably interested enough to read further to feed their curiosity.

But let's say a particular reader is marginally interested in your issue. Immediately discovering an item's high cost, or that the event happens on a night she works or at a place outside her usual traveling range would diminish her probability of attending. But what if that reader encounters all the information reinforcing why she can't miss this event? *IF* she reads those arguments and is enthused, she may then decide to cut back other expenses, rearrange her work schedule or carpool to the distant site so she can attend.

Final scenario: Imagine if your reader previously wasn't interested in the issue. In that case, following the inverted pyramid method, you've used every word in the few seconds the reader is willing to devote to your issue to present your best persuaders. You've allocated that precious prose space to build her desire to keep reading. In the end, you might be able to persuade her to take the action. You can almost be certain that knowing an event's date won't be as convincing.

### CASE IN POINT 7.1    Inverted Pyramid News Release

| | |
|---|---|
| *Intended target identified within first few words* | Local home and business owners will pay higher premiums because of increasing arson rates, according to a fire department-commissioned study. |
| *Lede justified with single fact and full identification of source* | Metro fire insurance rates increased 19% during the past year, largely due to arson, reported Metro fire chief Robert McKintreck. |

| | |
|---|---|
| *Statement of position story will prove* | McKintreck said city residents are already paying larger insurance premiums to cover fires being set for profit, often in cases of suspected insurance fraud. |
| *Most important support for position* | Of the 82 local fires last year known to be arson-related, two-thirds involved small businesses that were losing money. |
| *Secondary support for position* | Another 20% occurred in rental homes and apartments, often buildings so old and run-down that they could no longer be profitably rented. |
| *Background to further understand issue* | FBI statistics show the Metro's problem was mirrored in other cities. Nationally, arson rates rose 28%, and fire insurance premiums rose a similar 30%. |
| *Call to action* | McKintreck said the statistics demonstrate that the Metro Council should increase funding for arson test equipment. |

## The Logic of the Prose: Predicting Your Reader's Decision Sequence

As we mentioned before, the body of the persuasive piece must prove what you said in your lede. And because persuasive writing asks readers to take a particular action or adopt a position important for the organization, it's vital to sequence the arguments in a way your audience can most easily understand and retain them.

How do we do that? In Chapters 2 and 3, we presented working models based on Chapter 1's communication theories. You'll remember the persuasion platform isolated a number of questions about your audience to guide your message creation.

What's the best way to predict whether someone will graduate from a communication processor into an information seeker? Grunig's situational theory gives insights to the arguments individuals use in making that change.[4] Situational theory argues there are three steps a person must take to become an information seeker—that is, a person most likely to convert knowledge into action. The person must:

1. understand that something is a problem,

2. view herself as involved in the problem, and

3. think she can overcome barriers that might prevent her from acting on the problem.

You see how this approach is reflected in the audience-centered writing process. The lede sentence establishes both the benefit to be gained (step 1 in situational theory) and the person who could gain that benefit (step 2). The body of the inverted pyramid documents the rationale for taking an action. Finally, the call to action explicitly defines the ways in which the audience can take action to gain the benefits promised in the lede (step 3). Notice the arc through the story: problem and then solution. This will become important in structuring your writing.

The learn-feel-do model further refines the audience thought process, recognizing how arguments must change when audience perceptions change. We adjust our persuasive sequence depending on whether our target public views the decision as primarily emotional or rational in nature. In addition, the model suggests that if our audience believes they will experience horrific consequences if they make the wrong decision, our readers will employ a different decision sequence than if their decisions have few or minor negative consequences. In many ways, the learn-feel-do model rests on principles of cognitive processing reflecting those outlined in Chapter 1's discussion of the elaboration likelihood model.

This learn-feel-do model will be valuable in our writing as well. Which of many possible rewards will most likely persuade our audience? Predicting whether that most powerful motivator will be rational or emotional helps determine which argument receives the premier spot in our story. Will readers perceive high or low consequences from making the wrong decision? Knowing that helps determine the complexity and length of arguments you need to build their confidence before acting.

### Matching Audience to Argument: Integrating the Situational Model

In his situational model, Grunig suggested including information that would move your audience through a three-step hierarchy so they are more likely to become information seekers:

1. **Demonstrate the Problem.** Show your audience how significant the problem is. Provide examples, emotional anecdotes and/or statistics supporting your argument. Use comparisons that make them recognize the situation you describe is really a problem.

2. **Show How Readers Are Involved.** Now your readers recognize this as a problem, tell them exactly how it is THEIR problem. Does it attack their belief structure? Will it make them money? Does it endanger their health? Are there examples of how people just like them have been or will be affected by the issue? How are similar communities affected by the problem?

3. **Overcome Barriers.** Now you reverse direction. After you've established the problem's severity and your audience's connection to the issue, you then tell them the specific tasks they can perform to change the situation. They might join a protest march, donate on a website, report for a health screening, buy a certain stock or change their work habits. Break down the obstacles they believe prevent them from acting. Detail any financial or technical help, free transportation or other assistance that might encourage your audience to respond.

## What Comes First: Integrating the Learn-Feel-Do Model

The learn-feel-do model suggests persuasive messages should be sequenced based on the audience's comprehension of the situation.[5]

### Rational or Emotional?

Does your audience think they'll receive rational or emotional rewards from taking the action you'll recommend?

If you think they'll decide the issue on emotional criteria, you should introduce your main arguments by presenting personal anecdotes and human-interest stories. This likely will indicate how those whom readers care about will be affected by the problem. After you have your audience's emotions engaged, you can then quote statistics, give histories and provide technical facts that lend rational credence to those emotional reactions.

However, if your audience appears more likely to decide your issue based on rational factors, your initial argument should be more logic-based. You'll probably be more successful if you concentrate the strongest technical evidence early in the story, then use emotional persuaders as secondary reasons deeper in the piece.

### High Consequence or Low Consequence?

At the same time, you have to predict whether your audience would perceive the decision as high consequence or low consequence. This is important because it will change the level of detail you will need to include in your writing.

For instance, let's say you're producing an internet advertisement offering a free, three-month digital magazine subscription. You could legitimately anticipate this offer's audience would consider it low consequence. It doesn't cost them anything. Because you're delivering it digitally, trial subscribers aren't enlarging their carbon footprint. Thus you, in your persuasive writer role, might ask them to subscribe without including hundreds of words fully explaining the magazine's content, its editors' illustrious backgrounds or the magazine's discount for multiple-year subscribers.

However, when your audience perceives significant threats if they make the wrong decision, different rules apply. When a company's employee portal describes a new set of disciplinary and dismissal procedures for salaried employees, personnel will want much more detailed information. Your audience will likely not only want relatively complete details in your electronic publication, but also additional access to contractual information and legal documents via your company's website or in writing. Case in Point 7.2 summarizes how the learn-feel-do model guides your writing.

**Strategic Thought**

Consider an issue affecting your campus or community. What information could you offer a defined group of students that would convince them they are affected by the problem? What information might help them see they can overcome obstacles that might keep them from solving the problem?

**CASE IN POINT 7.2    Learn-Feel-Do Affecting Macro-Story Structure**

The learn-feel-do model offers you an overarching sense of the story's structure and length. If you're asking an audience to make what they will perceive is a decision presenting few negative consequences, your story can usually be shorter. If it's a high-consequence decision, your argument will likely be more effective if you present multiple reasons for taking the action. The learn-feel-do sequence also informs you of what your main persuader, and consequently the focus of your lede, will be.

- Emotional/High Consequence ⟶ Main emotional persuader + many secondary persuaders

- Emotional/Low Consequence ⟶ Main emotional persuader + few secondary persuaders

- Rational/High Consequence ⟶ Main rational persuader + many secondary persuaders

- Rational/Low Consequence ⟶ Main rational persuader + few secondary persuaders

## Supporting Arguments Dictate Story Structure

So far, we've discussed some insights into your message's overall sequencing. We can predict whether the story will begin with emotional or rational arguments. We have a pretty good idea concerning how detailed and lengthy your piece must be if you want to persuade your audience to act.

At this point, we need to consider structures that will help organize information deeper within the story. This is a much more significant problem than you might imagine. You've received critical guidance from the persuasion platform and the TIPCUP filter. You now know which argument is most likely to persuade your audience and hence to appear in the lede and third paragraph.

However, you must make sequencing decisions throughout the piece, which become more critical and frequent as your document length increases. How will you decide where your secondary persuaders will appear in the story? And, if one of your persuaders contains several arguments, in what order would you sequence those arguments?

The **position-evidence relationship** helps make these decisions more coherent to the writer. The position-evidence relationship describes a sequence for persuasive arguments in which the writer states a position, then provides evidence for that position.[6] Memory Memo 7.2 summarizes these structures.

**MEMORY MEMO 7.2**  Different Information? Different Argument Structures

| | | |
|---|---|---|
| Lists | use | Order of Importance |
| Recommendations | use | Problem-Solution |
| Procedures or Histories | use | Chronology |

These argument patterns often interlock within your document as you present different arguments justifying the action you wish your reader to undertake. In Case in Point 7.3, the writer presents a list of reasons for the law firm to undertake the action and then a schedule a meeting contracting the campaign's initial actions. Both of those position-evidence structures are lodged within a surmounting structure outlining the problem and detailing actions to solve the problem.

There are three major ways to structure the position-evidence sequence. You choose a specific one because of the nature of the evidence you're introducing. Remember we talked about an organic writing process? Here, the evidence you're offering actually dictates the argumentation patterns you'll use to present the information.

---

**CASE IN POINT 7.3    Overlay of Argumentation Patterns in a Sales Letter**

October 17, 2021

To: Johnson Legal Services

From: Joe Schmo

*An order-of-importance structure featuring … :*

You asked about a social media advertising campaign targeted to reach area residents who are seeking legal advice on divorce. I can say with certainty that our firm can target residents who live within a certain distance of each of your three law offices.

It's possible to selectively target ads to selected geographic regions, down to ZIP code level, through Facebook and other social media. I judge it would be relatively inexpensive.

1. *Client's most pressing goal*

Importantly for you, you can select additional key demographics for individuals who your past experiences indicate as most likely to be seeking divorce representation. For instance, you can select for gender, age, marital status, homeownership and approximate net worth.

2. *A possible secondary benefit*

I also found other monitoring approaches could extend your prospecting campaign into other services your firm offers. For instance, the technology lets you detect social media posts that include keywords like "estate," "inheritance" or "family business." When your selected keywords pair with other audience markers, those individuals would receive pop-ups presenting services like wills, or small-business start-ups and incorporation.

3. *A chronological argument structure*

So you can better plan your marketing budget, I propose a year-long plan. This lets you use cash flow from your growing practice to fund expanding advertising efforts. I foresee this initial timetable:

- Jan. 1: complete comprehensive assessment of your current public communication efforts
- Jan. 20: complete assessment of your firm's geographic market isolating audience characteristics
- Feb. 5: perform live test run of proposed interactive ads
- Feb. 15: develop social media content to drive traffic to your websites
- March 1: mount fully operational campaign among all selected channels

4. *Background*

Our firm's success in over 20 tightly targeted social media campaigns, in which our clients experienced nearly 60% growth in billed income, should assure you that you're making a wise choice.

5. *A call to action*

I hope you'll share our conversation with your partners and call or email me if you have additional questions. I'm looking forward to meeting all of you to discuss how we can implement these exciting capabilities into your firm's marketing efforts.

## Lists of Information? Use Order of Importance

You're already familiar with a form of the order-of-importance structure. Essentially, the inverted pyramid illustrates this structure. You place your most important arguments first, and then sequence the rest of your persuaders in descending order. If your reader only reads your first four paragraphs, you can be assured you've presented what you felt were your best persuaders.

Let's say a media release's lede announces an insurance company has been recognized as its community's best corporate citizen. The position statement is *the manufacturer is a good corporate citizen.*

How do you justify that position? In the release's body copy, you're likely to begin by telling how the company contributed 2% of its profits to local charities. What's next? A related, yet less-formidable persuader, detailing how company employees volunteered more than 3,000 hours of time toward local nonprofit organizations. In the last section, you present what you consider your least formidable argument, which is that your company cut its carbon footprint 40% in the last two years.

Order of importance is a useful argumentation structure, but it's the best choice only when you are presenting a list of reasons. If that's not your approach, there are other argumentation patterns.

### Is Your Evidence an Event Sequence? Use Chronology

In introducing this evidence-sequencing section, we indicated that the body of your document is essentially a prediction concerning how your audience will cognitively process information. Think of times when someone has told you a story but forgot to include an incident or step that's essential to the tale. You struggle to make any sense of it. Even when your conversation partner finally adds the missing detail, you're confused. In essence, this is because you're forced to reassemble the story in your mind, placing the missing information in its proper place.

That's exactly why it's logical to use chronology when you're presenting evidence that involves sequential events. That could be a legislative process, the history of an organization to mark its centennial, the steps to assemble a product—any situation in which it helps your audience understand your argument if they know what happened first, what happened next and what happened after.

Let's say you're working for an environmental group striving to end the ivory trade threatening the extinction of elephants and rhinos. You're compiling supporting information for your organization's website section titled "How We Help." A month-by-month narrative detailing how governmental lobbying and personal activism that brought successive nations into the ivory-ban movement would likely be the most effective way to structure this narrative.

### Got Recommendations? Use Problem-Solution

In persuasive writing, which is almost always devoted to moving your reader to adopt a position or take an action, you're likely to use a problem-solution sequence.

Imagine a city councilwoman reveals city employees are taking what she considers an excessive number of sick leave days. In analyzing an employee survey, it's discovered that because sick leave doesn't accumulate, employees lose any days they don't use by year's end. Predictably, the city workers may claim they're ill merely to escape the feeling they're being exploited.

That's the problem. What's the solution? You present the councilwoman's recommendation to introduce a new city compensation plan that promises cash bonuses for employees who don't take all their sick leave time.

The problem-solution pattern replicates the reader's cognitive process. It shows the justification for a complicated decision-making sequence and helps reveal the logic of your client's position to the audience.

## Structures Within Structures

Again we emphasize using these argument patterns as a guide. You can plan and structure the evidence to support the position statement you established in your lede sentence. It then directs you in sequencing sometimes complex and lengthy evidence to most effectively support your position. This approach also helps you envision your audience's priorities so you can sequence your arguments in the body of your story. In essence, it provides the underlying framework of a well-organized and coherent presentation of your client's viewpoints.

While position-evidence outlines how evidence is structured, virtually every piece you write will incorporate more than one of the three evidence-position sequences. It's tremendously useful as you approach each of the arguments you wish to make and need a scheme to quickly organize it within your story. You can also review that structure-within-a-structure in Case in Point 7.3.

## Tests in the Text:
## Keeping Your Reader Reading

The position-evidence sequence steers us as we sequence the story's arguments. But once you've established the argumentation pattern outlining the entire piece, there are additional parameters that improve your chances of persuasion. These help your readers grasp your evidence more easily by matching your prose to the steps your audience will likely use to process your story.

### Grouping Like Information Strengthens Arguments

Your readers can better comprehend information when you keep similar information in close proximity.[7] Say you are writing a newspaper op-ed for your company president about the need for more governmental stimulus to attract new businesses to the community. She wants to make two main points: (1) business licensing and permit processes should be streamlined, and (2) county property taxes should be lowered.

Her audience will be much better able to follow her logic if you place all the arguments supporting the relaxed licensing processes in one section of your story. Then, turn and elaborate on the reasons for lowering property taxes. If you jump around, with one paragraph about business permits, the next discussing taxes and then another about city licensing processes, you'll confuse your audience.

This is the same logic we discussed concerning a reader's problems tackling a historical background or sequence of events when it's not presented in chronological order. In both cases, the hopscotch game you're asking your readers to undertake hinders their comprehension because they must remember and reassemble scattered information. The constant diversion from one argument to another and then back has another ill effect: It diminishes your arguments' strength. Instead of an overwhelming concentration of points validating each position, you've presented little clumps of isolated reasons, which is less persuasive.

### Smoothing Break Points Keep Readers Involved

In Chapter 6, we discussed how and why people decide to continue reading a story. The places where these decisions seem most likely to occur, where the reader, listener or viewer is most likely to abandon the message, are what we call **break points**.

The very first break point, as we suggested in the previous chapter, occurs in the document's very first sentence. During the first few words, readers decide whether the topic interests them. Generally, you'll find break points at the start of every prose structure. At the beginning of a story, the beginning of the story's major sections and at the start of paragraphs and sentences, readers decide whether to remain in the communication act. These later break points work exactly like the lede's break point. The reader will grant you but a few words in which to justify her decision to continue reading.

This means you must be aware of these break points and work to make the linkage as smooth and relevant to your reader as possible. The easiest approach? Concentrate the most important information within the first few words of whatever new assertion you are making.

You might think of effective writing as the difference between a sprinting and a hurdling event. You want your reader to glide through the story to the end without impediments, not make them jump a 42-inch hurdle every 30 feet. Making use of transitions to smooth these breaking points—or removing the hurdles, as it were—effectively helps you achieve this goal.

### Transitions Help Readers See Links Between Arguments

Knowing how to construct a transition is a useful method to heighten reading speed and demonstrate the connections between your arguments. **Transitions** are bridges between the sections of the story that show your readers the relationship between what they just read and what they're about to read. As such, they are vital to enhancing your readers' comprehension and empowering your persuasive case.[8]

You can think of all transitions as *memory cues*. In essence, a transition places the information your readers have already received in the context of what they are about to read. In our opinion, writers of all skill levels are not nearly as conscious of carefully constructed transitions as they should be.

So how do you write a transition? Again, it's a fairly routine exercise that a series of guidelines can help you master. Here are four simple approaches that have a remarkably broad series of applications.

#### *Repeat a Word, Phrase or Concept*

The simplest transition plucks a keyword, phrase or concept from the previous paragraph, and places it within the first few words of the next paragraph's topic sentence. Here's an example of how many options this method offers the writer.

Let's say you have this paragraph:

Persuasive writers must know the specific characteristics of the media through which they are communicating. Understanding that background will help you deliver the message most likely to interest each outlet's gatekeeper.

The transition to the subsequent paragraph, which will present research sources helping you justify that insight, could be structured in a variety of ways. If you select *writer*, you might get this transition:

A *writer* can gather that knowledge from audience research, which many media outlets conduct to guide their editorial and advertising decisions.

Or choose *characteristics* …

You can often find those *characteristics* by reviewing audience research that many media outlets conduct to guide their own editorial and advertising decisions.

Maybe *gatekeeper* …

Media *gatekeepers* conduct their own audience research to guide their editorial and advertising decisions, research that can help persuasive writers refine their own stories.

You could even note *knowledge* and transform that into a related concept: *insights* …

The *insights* letting you more closely match a target medium's needs can often be gained through audience research that media outlets conduct to guide their own editorial and advertising decisions.

### Definite Modifier or Demonstrative Adjective

Sometimes you can use a definite modifier or demonstrative adjective to signal a transition. Even at the distance we are from you, we can hear the student mind grinding away to remember what those are, so let's review.

Contrast the definite modifier *The* with *A* in the phrases "A woman mailed her letter" versus "*The* woman mailed her letter." *A* only specifies that some woman took the action. *The* implies you know the precise, although unnamed, woman who mailed the letter.

Now let's look at *That*, a demonstrative adjective: "*The* woman mailed the letter" versus "*That* woman mailed the letter." In this illustration of a demonstrative adjective, *that* affirms you can identify which woman mailed the letter. Other demonstrative adjectives are *this*, *these* and *those*. Each alerts you to the explicit connections between the topics in the two paragraphs. Basically, it's just another form of a memory cue.

### Connectives

There's a third way to build a transition. Connectives are words like *plus*, *and*, *besides*, *also*, *therefore*, *moreover*, *in addition*, *another*, *additionally* and *furthermore*. These indicate an additive relationship, in which you're offering another reason supporting your argument.

There are other kinds of connectives for other purposes. If your succeeding argument contradicts your previous line of thought, use connectives that are words of opposition. These are words like *but, although, however, otherwise* and *conversely*. If you wish to assert a cause-and-effect relationship between two paragraphs, such connectives as *consequently, thus, hence* or *as a result* signal this linkage to your readers.

### Time-Related Concept

There's a final form of transition—the time reference. Words and phrases such as *meanwhile, soon, before, after, in the past* and *in three years* communicate that you've changed the time frame in which your writing is centered. Position them in the first few words of your subsequent paragraph, and your readers can more easily follow your line of reasoning.

Case in Point 7.4 shows how these various transitions can be successfully employed in a short news release.

## CASE IN POINT 7.4  Transition in Action

|  |  |
|---|---|
|  | Harper-Madison University President Kelly Swain will remain the institution's president through her retirement in 2025, the school's board chair announced Thursday. |
| *Repeating* Swain *and* board chair *from paragraph 1 in paragraph 2 links the two paragraphs. A repeated-word transition.* | "We feel lucky we'll be keeping an executive with Dr. *Swain's* talents for the foreseeable future," said board chair Dave Gardner, after announcing Swain had signed a multiyear contract. "It's largely through her leadership that this university has been climbing through the national rankings." |
| *Another repeated-word transition: repeating* Gardner *as linkage to the most important reason for the decision.* | Gardner noted that during Swain's term the university funded a $150 million endowment, which more than doubled the school's previous funding. |
| *A two-item list of arguments signaled by using a connective transition,* in addition. | In addition, Swain "has fostered mutual benefits between the university and the city's business and industry leaders," Gardner said. |
| *A tone transition.* Although *signals a deviation from information in the previous paragraph.* | Although Swain's contract did not expire until June, Gardner said the school did not want to lose her. "She's become a top candidate whenever a leadership job comes open." |
| That *explicitly directs attention back to the competition in the previous paragraph.* Competition *is a concept cue that reflects the previous paragraph's main subject.* | That competition, Gardner said, compelled board members "to demonstrate they were committed to her" through a contract extension. |
| Long contract *is a repeating word/concept transition.* | Swain's long contract came less than two months after the Higher Education Congress named her one of the nation's top-10 presidents at medium-sized institutions. |

### When Do You Use Transitions?

It's probably simplistic to suggest that you need to write a transition for every single paragraph in the relatively short pieces that persuasive writers compose. However, we would suggest this be your default position: "Why wouldn't I write a transition introducing this new paragraph?"

By consciously constructing transitions, you can more quickly organize your prose and arguments much more effectively. They'll provide an informal working outline of your story as you write it, alerting you to problems in your logic patterns and guiding you to the argument that should come next. Our experience has demonstrated that if you can't use one of these transition structures to seamlessly link one paragraph to another, it's likely you've ordered your paragraphs poorly and should sequence them differently to improve flow and enhance comprehension. This is an immensely valuable insight because it signals when your entire story structure is misaligned.

More importantly, transitions are signposts to your readers, displaying how your arguments are related and providing a template upon which they can construct their own memory of the story's assertions.

Nonetheless, you deserve a more sophisticated answer to the question, "When do you need a transition?" In short, you should link paragraphs with a coherent transition each time you have a change in any of the four T's—topic, tone, time and talker.[9] Let's review how those four transitions are integrated into a company backgrounder blog on forthcoming tax legislation.

#### *Topic*

You need a transition to bridge between paragraphs when you switch topics within your story. Let's say you've devoted the blog's first section to the savings in capital gains taxes accompanying an organization's increased investment in new industrial equipment. You now think it would reinforce your argument if you discuss the tax incentives offered for employee retraining. To help your reader see the logical connection between the two topics, you need a transition. Here's an example in which the writer repeats words and concepts from the previous paragraph (*investments, rewarded, tax*) and connects them to the changed topic (*human capital*) in the second paragraph's opening sentence.

> Mining and manufacturing companies that *invest* in new equipment can claim *tax* credits for their expenditures, according to new IRS regulations. Our company, which last year purchased over $2 million in machinery covered by the IRS rules, would *receive* nearly $250,000 in additional tax benefits if we continue to upgrade our manufacturing equipment.

> *Investments* in human capital are also *rewarded* under the new *tax* laws. IRS officials our company consulted speculate the president's campaign promises will be transformed into generous tax allowances for employee training programs. News reports discussing the training tax breaks predict 30% of all employee education expenses could be deducted.

### Tone

You're working on the same piece. After discussing all the benefits the tax legislation will offer your company, you now need to acknowledge the company operations that might face higher tax bills because of the new law. Before you switch in tone from positive to negative, alert your readers through a transition. In this case, the oppositional connective *however* cues your reader you're changing the tone. Notice as well that the repeated concept from the previous paragraph, *new tax laws*, is echoed in *new regulations.*

> Investments in human capital are also rewarded under the *new tax laws*. IRS officials our company consulted speculate the president's campaign promises will be transformed into generous tax allowances for employee training programs. News reports discussing the training tax breaks predict 30% of all employee education expenses could be deducted.

> *However*, the *new regulations* don't contain universally good news for the company. Our research recommends that profits from the firm's overseas operations be restructured. If Congress implements the budget committee's recommendations, the company's foreign divisions could see its tax liabilities rise about 5%.

### Time

You've completed your analysis of the current situation. Now, as you move into the inverted pyramid's background section, you must alert your reader that you're changing the chronological framework. Because you are reorienting the discussion from the present to the past, you use a transition to guide your reader into the proper chronological frame. In this case, you are using a clear time marker, *previous*, to explicitly tell readers to expect a different chronological orientation.

> However, the new regulations don't contain universally good news for the company. Our research recommends that profits from the firm's overseas operations be restructured. If Congress implements the budget committee's recommendations, the company's foreign divisions could see their tax liabilities rise about 5%.

> The regulations mark a dramatic change from those governing the *previous* administration's tax policy, according to the manufacturing industry's governmental affairs director. "These regulations abandon the emphasis on short-term profit strategies the previous president advocated," said Jerry Horsly of the Continental Factory Federation. "It's clear this approach reduces employers' incentives to reduce costs by hiring overseas labor."

### Talker

In this background section of the blog, you choose to validate your argument by quoting two experts. But unless you specifically and immediately signal the change of speakers, your reader will assume you're still quoting the first speaker. You must write a transition alerting your audience that someone else's opinions are being offered when you introduce the new paragraph. In this case, you use the term *other experts* to definitely inform your readers that someone else is talking.

> The regulations mark a dramatic change from those governing the previous administration's tax policy, according to the manufacturing industry's governmental affairs director. "These regulations abandon the emphasis on short-term profit strategies the previous president advocated," said Jerry Horsly of the Continental Factory Federation. "It's clear this approach reduces employers' incentives for reducing costs through overseas labor."

> *Other experts* also suggest we should be changing our tax tactics. "We can't compete unless we begin to capitalize on the potentialities of North American-based workers and the newest technology," said Lawrence Chikon, CEO of the Industrial Technology Council. "These new tax laws portend the realities that will govern our business strategy during the next decade."

### Reading Speed Contributes to Persuasion

A reminder from this chapter's first paragraphs: Persuasive writing's No. 1 goal is to communicate information coherently, simply and quickly. Audience-centered writing demands we adjust prose to fit the audience's needs. No one searches for our work to supplement their pleasure reading. That means we need to make our writing as short as possible, with few pauses and hesitations.

Such economy contributes two things to our communication effectiveness. First, it requires less of our readers' time to absorb our entire message. That's important when our message is competing with so many other messages for our audience's attention. Second, it supplies fewer break points where they might decide to abandon the message.

In addition to our just-concluded advice concerning transitions and logical argumentation structures, there are thousands of writing tips that will help you clean your prose of its redundancies, extra words and punctuation. Those inefficiencies increase your audience's reading time and more often than not, decrease your audience's capacity to understand your arguments.

## Writer's Block? Return to Your Audience

On most days during your professional writing career, you'll discover time is your most precious commodity. By using the general principles outlined in Chapters 6 and 7, you don't have to wait for inspiration. We've advocated our methods as a generative-writing system that prompts the first few words of your lede, and the first few words of each subsequent paragraph.

Our purpose in these past two chapters is to convince you that an audience-centered approach to persuasive communication provides a rational thought structure you can always consult when you're faced with a writing problem.

Our students from decades ago who are now experienced persuasive writers no longer consciously think about what goes first in their lede. Experience and habit generally guide them in writing a lede or sequencing paragraphs. However, they tell us that when they get stuck, they think back to these self-tests.

Difficulty writing a lede sentence? The TIPCUP filter guides you.

Issues constructing an argument? The evidence you're presenting dictates whether to select a chronology, order-of-importance or problem-solution sequence.

Can't compose a transition into a new paragraph? Look to the prior paragraph's theme.

Writing doesn't require some mystical artistic transformation. It's predicated on understanding audience needs and applying communication principles to meet those needs.

Continued practice and constant concentration on your audience's needs will help you develop your writing skills so you'll excel in all forms of persuasive writing.

## SUMMARY

- The inverted pyramid is a traditional journalism writing structure that recognizes readers will remain in a communication event only as long as it satisfies their needs. It sequences information to communicate the most important information to the reader first, even if she spends only a few seconds with the article.

- The position-evidence relationship defines a logical argumentation pattern based upon the type of evidence presented. Order of importance is a good way to present lists. If a writer is offering a recommendation, problem-solution is recommended. A chronology is better in communicating sequences.

- Transitions use memory cues to alert readers to shifts between topics, tones, times or talkers. Transitions are established within each paragraph's first few words by (1) repeating a word, phrase or concept, (2) using a definite modifier or demonstrative adjective, (3) using a connective that signals a continuation or modification of a concept or (4) introducing a time-related concept.

- Keeping similar information within a single section, concentrating important information at the beginnings of sentences and paragraphs, and modifying sentence structures and vocabulary increases reading speed and comprehension while encouraging readers to continue attending to the message.

### Scenario Prompts: Drafting Body Copy

You'll find Scenario Prompts on pp. 367–386 of this textbook. While they vary in subject and difficulty, they help you hone your critical thinking and strategic writing skills. The following are best suited to this chapter's topics.

Management: 3.5 / Writing: 8.6, 9.7, 9.10

# Adding Sensory Channels

## Realizing the Power of Audio and Video Storytelling

A persuasive writer encounters great pleasures and stupendous challenges because of the job's stunning variety. Among the reasons to eagerly confront your job every morning (and sometimes late nights) is the fact that you'll write for almost every audience, medium and topic imaginable.

In my career, I've written speeches for international conferences and fourth-grade curriculum guides. I've written media releases, documentaries and fundraising solicitations for botanical gardens.

I wrote a charity's tongue-in-cheek television script selling yard-sized children's playhouses via a Sunday morning real estate showcase. ("The spacious 3-foot by 3-foot balcony overlooks the living area and its towering 7-foot-tall cathedral ceiling.")

People have paid me to write about ballet, sewage plants, organized labor, fine art, Catholic mysticism, cartoons, Japanese children's crafts and commodity markets. I even wrote the bulk of a lawyer's opening statement for a felony gambling trial.

Aside from a message in a bottle, I've written for virtually every medium, some of which did not exist at the beginning of my career.

To return to my primal farm lexicon, it was a hoot. I was trained as a print journalist, but when I now contemplate writing about one topic (the police beat, say) for one audience in one medium—every day—it sounds terribly dull. Luckily, I like being forced to understand a topic in a few hours or a few days, and I like the challenge of adapting my writing to whatever new audience, topic or medium placed before me.

OK, that's the fun part of the equation.

But that fun is simultaneously terrifying. Can you downshift from writing a formal presentation on development partnerships in the morning to a script on child prodigies for third graders in the afternoon? There are distinctions of style and presentational format with each change between print, audio, video or face-to-face. You must integrate different vocabulary, sentence length and complexity, medium and sophistication of illustrations.

It's a problem for every professional in our field. In journalism school, we took from four to six courses in writing specifically for print media. But as a student of strategic writing, you're being asked to shift from writing for print, to multichannel, to organizational writing, to advertising copy and to be conversant in each area after a single semester.

When I started teaching writing, the task seemed impossible. My ultimate solution? I focused on similarities among all the varieties of writing. Thus, my students could cling to some basic precepts as I jostled them among all the writing skills they needed to master.

In essence, writing is writing. Words are delivered through ink on paper or pixels on a screen. The words can be spoken in person or spoken by a person on video. And the face seen talking during a video looks just like a person delivering a speech to an audience.

During those face-to-face or audio-oral presentations, someone could play a sound recording or music to emphasize her messages. During those face-to-face or video-oral presentations, someone could flash a photograph or data slide on a screen, demonstrate a process or show another video.

But at the center of it all is persuasive intent.

So, we're not going to spend multiple chapters convincing you to forget everything you've learned about print writing so you can succeed at multichannel writing. Instead, we advocate you take the power of solid prose writing, and overlay the distinct power of sound to reinforce your message when presented in a podcast. Then, when you are presented the task of writing for video presentations, you take solid prose, the reinforcement of audio, and add motion.

Not three separate skills, just three progressive layers of communication channels in mutual support of one task: delivering your client's communication outcome.

*—WT*

---

### What You Know

- Individuals use different media channels for their own purposes and their own rewards.

- The first few seconds of any message needs to communicate information that engages the audience in the remainder of the message.

- Persuasive writing sequencing mirrors the cognitive approaches the audience uses.

### What You'll Learn

- How multichannel media supplements additional channels atop strong prose writing

- How to exploit the strengths and minimize the weakness of multichannel media

- How to incorporate the audience-centered writing process into multichannel media

## Writing for Audio and Video Channels: The Same but Different

Many people in the profession think writing that incorporates audio and visual channels is completely different from writing for print media. That's a vast exaggeration. Writing is communication, and communication—no matter what the medium—is governed by many of the same principles and procedures.

There are, however, important differences across the media for which you write. To this point, we've grounded persuasive writing in the integration of the audience's needs and the writer's objectives. That applies equally in audio, video and print writing. However, this book strives to help you adapt your writing techniques for different media, to exploit the strengths of a medium and minimize the accompanying weaknesses.

In **multichannel writing**—which we characterize as writing for those electronic transmission channels such as radio, television, film, documentaries, audio and video news releases, podcasts or blogs—there are both formidable weaknesses and significant strengths. Some of the distinctions are outlined in Table 8.1.

**TABLE 8.1  Advantages and Disadvantages of Multichannel Media[1]**

| Audio | |
|---|---|
| **Advantages** | **Disadvantages** |
| • Relatively inexpensive to produce | • Listener can't review message |
| • Message can be delivered anywhere | • Time restrictions limit message |
| • Adds power of sound to text | • Listener may not be engaged in message immediately |
| • Narrator's personal characteristics add to power of message | • Can't use visuals or print to reinforce message |

| Video | |
|---|---|
| **Advantages** | **Disadvantages** |
| • Combines power of motion, sound and dialogue | • More expensive to produce |
| • Narrator's appearance and mannerisms add to message's power | • Time restrictions often limit message |
| • More effective in communicating emotional persuaders | • Viewer must make efforts to review message |
| • Print can be added to reinforce message | • Viewer may not be engaged in message immediately |

This talk of the weaknesses of multichannel communication may surprise you. For decades, we've had to endure both celebrations and condemnations of the power of messages delivered through audio and visual sensory channels, especially television. For instance, **cultivation theory** posits that there are significant differences in how people perceive the world depending on whether they obtain most of their information from television or primarily from other media.[2] Hence television's disparaging nicknames, such as "boob tube" and "idiot box."

We don't believe people lose all critical thinking capacity when they encounter **multichannel media**. Media that engage either audio and/or video sensory channels do have great power.

However, they also have profound weaknesses. Let's talk about their strengths first. Multichannel media uses words and so duplicates the print medium's capability to communicate language. But multichannel incorporates additional sensory channels that print media does not possess, channels that persuasive writers must integrate into their creative processes.

Audio should take the heart of a print message and add sound—voice, on-site recordings, sound effects and music. Video should take the print message, add the strengths of audio and then supplement those communication methods with visuals and motion.

We say "should" because all too often writers merely take a prose message and think they've created an effective audio message by having an announcer read it into a microphone. For video, they record the announcer as she reads the message out loud on camera. That may *technically* be multichannel production and distribution, but it's poor multichannel writing.

## PRINCIPLES IN PRACTICE 8.1    Video Changed the Radio Star

MTV launched on Aug. 1, 1981, airing its first music video, The Buggles' "Video Killed the Radio Star." Explicit in the title is the worry that technological advancements in one media platform render useless those channels that came before. Obviously, video didn't kill radio. Similarly, radio didn't kill print, and the internet isn't poised to kill television—at least any time soon. Instead, media platforms evolve with and adapt to new innovations, building on old conventions before developing their own. The delivery of news illustrates this change perfectly.

Newspaper and magazines long dominated as news delivery media, and then a new competitor emerged. Detroit station 8MK launched the first U.S. radio news broadcast in August 1920. The station was owned by a local newspaper, The Detroit News, which feared radio might challenge its dominance in providing news content to the city, prompting its expansion into the new medium. The broadcast amounted to little more than a reading of election returns.[3]

It wasn't until the 1930s that the unique, additive elements of audio were implemented to create more engaging messages. From 1933 to 1944, President Franklin Roosevelt broadcast a series of fireside chats, in which he spoke directly to the citizenry, bringing his personality and charisma to bear.[4] And of course, there's perhaps the most famous radio broadcast of all: Orson Welles' 1938 dramatic interpretation of H. G. Wells' "War of the Worlds," which offered vivid detail by using sound effects and exasperated quotations from "on-site" reporters covering the fictional Martian landing.[5] Those innovations were integrated into real radio newscasts. Any regular NPR listener can attest that including rich quotations and other on-the-ground sound effects enhance the narrative.

Originally, television was simply an outgrowth of radio. The major radio stations—ABC, NBC and CBS—expanded into television. NBC radio reporter Lowell Thomas broadcast the first regularly scheduled TV news program in 1940, which was just a video airing of his radio program.[6] To some extent, television news still relies on this format, with a familiar anchor—or *newsreader*, as the British say—reading news from a teleprompter into the camera. However, TV news has since adapted to include multimedia charts and graphs to visualize data, **b-roll** to provide a backdrop to the narrative and live footage to underscore the happenings of the moment.

Just as writers struggled to refine each new medium by integrating new sensory channels, we've been able to redefine older media to fit new media landscapes. Print news could no longer compete with the immediacy provided by radio and television reporting. Instead, print shifted to providing greater depth in reporting complex and nuanced issues. Radio, once heavily reliant on episodic entertainment programs, found it could not compete with the rich visuals television added to comedic and dramatic storytelling. Instead, radio refocused and specialized, creating channels dedicated to local and national news and the genre-specific music format we know today.

The internet's rise has seen each of the legacy platforms struggle with online's increased interactivity. It's now common practice for journalists and other on-air personalities to engage with individual audience members via social media, a trend that shows no signs of slowing.[7] The online world has also led to a growing trend of **convergence**, in which many of the old distinguishing factors among traditional media platforms have fallen away.[8] For example, it wasn't long ago that if you wrote for a newspaper, print was your whole life. Now, newspapers post print content online, often accompanied by audio, video, infographics and other features.

As the media environment changes, it's no longer possible for persuasive writers to embark on successful careers with mastery of a single message channel. You must be capable in each channel that exists now, and become conversant in future media as they emerge throughout your career. In our view, the most efficient way to do so is to take advantage of what you already know and adapt when change inevitably arrives. Recognize what elements of print writing transfer to audio, apply them and then adjust your writing to account for the strengths and weaknesses the aural channel provides. Repeat the process for video, and again for digital.

It's hard work, precisely because video didn't kill the radio star. Far from it. It simply gave her more to consider, and more to do.

As in the case of all writing, multichannel writing exploits the strengths of the medium and tries to minimize its weaknesses, as outlined in Memory Memo 8.1. Those strengths are, for audio, the power of sound; and for video, of sound and then motion. Engaging those additional sensory channels is key if you wish to reinforce the impression of the words or even to create new impressions that words alone are not capable of delivering. If you don't use that power, you've merely got an overly expensive and usually less effective version of print communication.

> **MEMORY MEMO 8.1** Writing for Audio and Visual Media Should Emphasize Each Channel's Strengths
>
> - Sound, sight and motion
> - The receiver's relationship with the person delivering the message
> - Its portability and pervasiveness

We urge writers to consider multichannel writing not as a completely separate type of writing, but as an "additive medium." For us, it's a process of overlaying additional communication channels on solid prose. That approach preserves the print medium's ability to transmit information efficiently while adding the emotional and persuasive power of multichannel media. As Principles in Practice 8.1 describes, it's a process with a long tradition.

## Exploiting the Strengths of Multichannel Media

Although multichannel media are not the all-powerful communication narcotic we have often been led to believe, there are many persuasive tasks that multichannel media accomplish very efficiently. As with all communication, the intelligent practitioner begins by examining the communication objective she wants to reach and selecting an effective medium to accomplish those tasks.

### Involve the Senses

In some ways, multichannel has powerful advantages over print. With multichannel you can involve other senses in communicating your message: letting your audience hear the excitement of a crowd before a concert or witness a test proving your product is better than its competitors. With audio, you can hear the pop of bacon sizzling, the crack of a rifle firing or the happy squeal of children playing.

In video productions, we can add sight and movement atop those sounds. The emotional power on the human psyche of seeing a whimpering child or a basketball player soaring high above the rim for a dunk fuels interest and involvement.

> **Strategic Thought**
>
> Compare the memorability and persuasiveness of emotional and rational appeals. What types of messages are better portrayed in different media? Are some more suited for audio? Video? Print? Why?

### Exploit Strengths of Personal Media

Multichannel writing, because it is often delivered by people with whom we become familiar, has many of the advantages of more personal media. We grow to trust the judgments of our favorite personages and often perceive we have a form of relationship with them. We like this personality or think another is funny or sincere or committed. The perception that we know and have a relationship with a multichannel personality provides extra persuasive power for a message.

This **parasocial relationship** can compellingly reinforce a message. An early-morning conversation between Professor Thompson and his mother-in-law, Jean, illustrates this phenomenon. Katie Couric was at that time on NBC's "Today" program. And at the precise moment of this story, which Professor Thompson was experiencing at 7:15 a.m. on a winter's day in snowy northern Iowa, Couric was enjoying a tour through sun-drenched wine fields in California's Napa Valley.

Looking at Couric in short-sleeves and sunglasses, Jean asked, "Don't you wish you could be there now?"

Professor Thompson: "You'd need a flashlight. Right now it's 5 o'clock in the morning there."

A spirited discussion ensued in which Professor Thompson's in-law insisted all of "Today" was live programming. When Professor Thompson insisted there were indeed prerecorded segments, Jean used her ultimate argument for the show being live: "But Katie would never lie to *me*." Clearly, Couric was in Jean's eyes not just a trusted source, but almost a friend.

### Embrace the Inescapability

Perhaps multichannel media's most profound power is its seeming pervasiveness. We wake up in the morning to our phone alarm playing a favorite song; check our text messages, email and social media feeds while lying in bed; eat breakfast while watching television news; and drive to work or school listening to a favorite disc jockey, podcast or audiobook. We perform many of our daily tasks to the accompaniment of streaming music, only to come home at night and perhaps put in several hours in front of the monitor watching streaming shows with our family and friends. For many people, some glowing rectangle is a constant background in their waking lives.

## Overcoming Multichannel's Weakness: The Passive Audience

That word "background" suggests multichannel's most profound shortcoming. Think how many times you've heard someone say she switches on the television "for some background noise." It's there, but we often aren't attuned to it.

That's because multichannel media are often passive. With print media, you have to commit time and mental energy in order to receive the message. You can't drive to work or vacuum the house and read the newspaper at the same time. You can't take your daily jog and study a textbook.

Print media demand the receiver's active participation. Multichannel media just sort of happen, whether or not you're engaged in receiving and processing the message.

Think of your attention level to your car radio as you drive to school. For the safety of the world and its people, let's hope you're paying more attention to the cars merging into traffic ahead of you than analyzing the intricate bass line of a song you're hearing. Of course, when the traffic report comes on, you may actively process that information, adjusting your route to avoid a tie-up. When there's news of your favorite band you'll probably pay much closer attention than you do while the disc jockey is prattling to the meteorologist. That's natural. As we've explained earlier, we're very selective about the communication events to which we attend.

Thus, even though the multichannel message is always there, it doesn't mean we're always paying attention. The relative likelihood that people who see a print story that interests them will at least consider reading it doesn't apply to multichannel media.

**Strategic Thought**

What sounds could you use to illustrate an audio story on homelessness? What sounds might help communicate a story on housing values?

Multichannel communication is received continuously by the brain at some very low level. But it isn't transferred to a conscious level unless there is some audience interest that becomes involved, an assertion we've maintained for every type of media channel we've discussed so far—and will discuss. Hence, that greater power of multichannel media (its pervasiveness) is accompanied by a massive weakness. Because your audience isn't consciously attending to your message a good portion of the time, it's the multichannel writer's initial task to break into the reverie induced by this steady hum of noise and motion.

Therefore, the audience's attention must be captured immediately. Print gives the reader an opportunity to review the message if she didn't understand or attend to it initially. A multichannel message speeds past the receiver's eyes or ears, never to return. Even when multichannel is delivered via internet channels, it's often much more cumbersome to review exactly the information that will clarify the message. We're used to scanning print media to find the specific paragraph providing just the message we want. That's not so easy in multichannel contexts.

It's also more difficult to act on information delivered through multichannel media. What steps do you have to take to record a phone number or a hard-to-fathom web address or street location? For the writer striving to create effective messaging, overcoming the transience of multichannel media presents a major obstacle.

## The Important No. 1 Position: TIPCUP Multichannel Ledes

Multichannel writers struggle to capture the attention of a passive audience very likely engaged in some other activity and not highly involved in the medium. But as we dismiss our complete rapture with multichannel's superior persuasiveness we also have to acknowledge its power. We often realize we are entranced by video images, watching raptly as fast-paced commercials flip visuals before our eyes and imagination. We recoil from an image of the rapid strike of a snake in a YouTube video. We unconsciously tap our toes to songs and advertising jingles on radio.

How do we transform a passive processor into an active participant? By integrating the same persuasive, audience-centered writing principles we've already discussed into multichannel messages, and then adding the power of sound and motion.

Such a process starts by recognizing that we have to drag our audience's attention into a multichannel message, to awaken them from passive engagement and enlist their active attention. Remember the No.1 position we discussed in the previous two chapters? Although we are in different media, our task is still the same: to capture the attention of an elusive audience so we can successfully communicate. Just as we've asserted before, concentrating elements of interest into that No.1 position of our multichannel's lede will more likely attract the public we need to reach.

Using the TIPCUP elements, we can judge the information most likely to interest a specific audience. Is the element *impact*, as it would be for animal activists regarding news about new ways of testing cosmetics without animals? Is it *prominence*, such as the news of a Hollywood actor's participation in a civil rights demonstration? Is it *unusualness*, such as a first-time use of a revolutionary technology that could reduce air pollution?

No matter which TIPCUP element you highlight, your task is virtually the same as in the simplest news release. You must signal to your targeted audience that this given message is intended for them by placing the most important information into the No. 1 position. As before, you are looking for words that communicate one or more TIPCUP components to your audience, and you are looking for ways to place the most important filter into the No. 1 position.

But in multichannel writing, we must contend with a big conundrum. We know when people read newspapers, or magazines, or letters, they are involved in the message. It may take them only a second to decide whether the message affects them or not, but for that moment, we can be relatively certain they aren't perusing social media, cooking dinner or settling a fight among the children. There aren't any such assurances with multichannel media. In fact, multichannel audiences are notoriously inattentive. Let's see what happens when a print lede sentence is introduced to a typical multichannel audience.

> Keffin County residents who use a private trash hauling service can get a $1,000 tax refund if they sign up today, the county's tax assessor announced.

You might notice a problem. A person eligible for the refund who is only half-listening to the message through a multichannel medium would probably only start actively attending to the message when she hears the $1,000 refund mentioned. But by that time, 14 words into the story, she has already missed a vital piece of information: who is eligible for the refund. If the receiver has no way to review the No. 1 position, she is less likely to respond to the message. For the persuasive writer, no response represents a failure.

How to solve this? Follow Memory Memo 8.2 as we present some ways to incorporate the additional sensory channels offered via multichannel media to draw the target audience into our message.

> **MEMORY MEMO 8.2**  Strategies for Involving Receivers in the Multichannel Lede
>
> - Use trigger words to alert your desired audience that the story is for them
> - Use setups as auditory headlines to give the audience time to attend to the story
> - Use sound effects to draw the receiver's attention before starting text

## Trigger Words

There are several specialized ledes used in broadcast writing to overcome this problem of receiver passivity. All use what's called a *trigger word* to alert the target audience that the story is intended for them. The trigger word or words suggest the story's significance in the No. 1 position, so the audience is primed to listen to the second sentence. Here's how to use trigger words to convert the above lede into a stronger multichannel lede:

> There might be a *one-thousand-dollar* tax refund in your future.

> Keffin County residents who use a private trash hauling service can get a thousand-dollar refund if they sign up today, the county's tax assessor announced.

Or:

> The county is *giving money back* to people who take care of their own trash.
>
> Keffin County residents who use a private trash hauling service can get a thousand-dollar refund if they sign up today, the county's tax assessor announced.

In both cases, the writer initially provides a motive before announcing the audience that can get the reward. When the writer gains the audience's active attention, she can then provide the vital information concerning how someone becomes eligible.

### Setups

As you can see, we're attempting to counter the audience's passive engagement with multichannel messages. We alert listeners to the story topic that is approaching and let them decide whether to attend to the message. You might consider them multichannel versions of newspaper headlines: a few brief words informing your audience what to expect in the following story.

In fact, another type of multichannel lede is structured exactly like a headline. These multichannel ledes, called *setups*, are usually incomplete sentences without articles like *a*, *an* or *the*. A setup for the above story might look like this:

> *Tax refunds for some Keffin County residents.*
>
> County residents who use a private trash hauling service can get a one-thousand-dollar tax refund if they sign up today, the county's tax assessor announced.

### Opening Sound Effects

And, of course, never forget that multichannel messages offer additional sensory channels to grab your target audience's attention. In keeping with our philosophy of capitalizing upon a medium's characteristics, one of the ways to signal a multichannel story's topic is to introduce the story with a sound effect. For instance, we might signal the topic of the Keffin County tax story by opening the story with the distinctive beeps of a trash truck backing up or the cha-ching of a cash register to emphasize the topic and audience benefit of the story.

## Break Points:
## Using Memory Cues to Build Transitions

Multichannel prose must also lead the receivers from one topic to the next as effortlessly as possible. That's quite a task because often multichannel pieces are not freestanding stories, as print stories usually are.

Think about your local newscast. Broadcast stories are shorter, and the coverage in your city's newscast might bounce from a city police roundup of white-collar criminals to hurricane coverage from Indonesia, war in Africa and a local dog show. That's a broad range of subjects, and receivers could very easily get lost in the jumble of topics. The multichannel writer who is writing a company-wide video blog featuring institutional news must simplify the audience's cognitive task with a transition signaling when the topic changes.

Sometimes you can find relationships between topics leading naturally from one story to the next. For instance, a story on your company president's trip to Europe to sign a merger agreement could be linked with another story on the hiring of a foreign researcher by using the common term, "overseas," in a sentence like this:

> The company also thinks it will profit by another *overseas* acquisition.

Two stories, one announcing a company history book released for a 75th anniversary and another highlighting a company donation to restore your city's remaining Art Deco office building, might be linked like this:

> And XYZ Corporation funds will help a city landmark look as it did on the day our company was founded.

Finding these thematic elements to tie individual stories together is often very useful, but there are some situations when they shouldn't be used. In fact, some of the worst moments of broadcast journalism arise from embarrassingly awkward attempts to link stories. We're sure you've heard an exchange like this on your local radio or television news as the anchor introduces the weather forecast:

> I hope it's not going to be as warm here over the weekend as in those Mideast hot spots, Joan.

There are alternatives to such utter humiliation. The memory-cue transitions discussed in Chapter 7 work as well when you are moving between stories in broadcast writing as they do when you are moving between paragraphs in print writing.

If you are making a shift in time or topic, alert your audience with a memory-cue transition in the first few words of the new story. For instance, if you're moving between events that happened the same day, this might work:

> *While* our company's management team was in Europe, local workers received awards for their community activism.

It's the same if you are moving between stories about two different individuals. Again, the single word *while* has immense power:

> *While* President Jones was signing the merger agreement, retired president Smith declared his candidacy for a state house seat.

Even though you're using different channels, the principle in constructing a multichannel transition is exactly the same. In each case, you are merely alerting your audience that they should be ready for another topic and orienting them to its theme.

## Multichannel Prose: Keeping the Receiver Involved

The need to overcome the multichannel audience's problems of attention continuity isn't limited to the opening lines of stories. It creates problems you'll confront throughout.

### Simplifying Prose: Helping Receivers Who Can't Review

Because you don't have the option of letting your audience review a sentence in case they initially miss its meaning, you have to simplify. You must simplify vocabulary, choosing more understandable and accessible words for the broad audience that multichannel media usually draw. You must simplify and shorten sentences too.

#### *Putting the News First*

You even need to simplify sentence structures. Don't separate subjects and verbs from each other, because receivers relying completely on aural memory can forget the sentence's subject by the time they encounter a verb. For instance, this is a bad multichannel sentence.

> The contract provision, which will be discussed in Thursday's negotiations, would enforce stricter worker safety rules.

In fact, you need to be careful whenever you use a dependent clause in multichannel writing. As you can see from the example above, they usually don't work in the middle of a sentence. Don't put them at the beginning either.

> Because of new financial tracking software, forecasting the company's future performance will become much more accurate.

A sentence structure like this forces your audience to remember the qualifying information, then place it in context of the sentence's main point when they finish hearing the statement. As we've discussed before, try to shape your writing to reflect the way your audience will cognitively process the message. Communicate the sentence's main topic and then offer the reader any qualifying information.

> The contract provision would enforce stricter worker safety rules. It will be discussed in Thursday's negotiations.

Here's another example:

> Forecasting the company's future performance will become much more accurate because of new financial tracking software.

#### *Simplifying for Comprehension*

You should also adjust your prose to acknowledge the great reliance you're placing on your audience's memory as they process the story. Avoid strings of numbers and even the names of sources if they aren't imperative to understanding or giving credibility to the story.

**MEMORY MEMO 8.3** Overcoming the Audience's Difficulty in Reviewing Multichannel Messages

- Put important content first, then place qualifying information later in the sentence
- Simplify sentence structures and vocabulary
- Emphasize multichannel's person-to-person communication
  - Use less formal language
  - Use more facial and voice inflection cues

Instead, simplify complex numbers into more understandable concepts. Eighty-two million Americans could be translated into "one of every four Americans." If a source's name is not as important to establishing credibility as the position she holds, give only her title. Of course, simplifying the information you're presenting not only helps lessen the burden on your audience's memory but also eliminates words. That is critically important when you're trying to cut an 800-word print article to 80 words for a multichannel audience.

In case you forget any of these elements, you can review them in Memory Memo 8.3. There's also a useful guide to audio script formatting in Case in Point 8.1.

## Showing Your Strengths: Immediacy and Personality

Although we've been discussing how to overcome the weaknesses of multichannel media, you can accentuate the medium's strengths by consciously integrating two elements.

As we mentioned before, one of the strengths of multichannel is its immediacy. That is emphasized in multichannel writing by using present tense and present perfect verb tenses. For instance, when you attribute a statement to a source in multichannel copy, you usually would use "she says" (present) or "she has said" (present perfect).

**CASE IN POINT 8.1    Audio Script Format**

Note: If this copy were being prepared for a narrator to read, it would be set double or triple spaced.

# my pr firm

123 Main Street/Hometown, Any State/12345/505 555-1234

**Title of Story**

| Time | Sound effects | Narration: Victor Voice Talent |
|---|---|---|
| 0:00 | NATURAL SOUND-2 seconds | |

Sound of old-fashioned radio being tuned.
Narrator's voice flashes in, then comes in clearly.

| | |
|---|---|
| **0:02**  **TALENT NARRATION** | Audio feature stories often begin with a sound effect. It helps draw listeners' attention to the story before the narration begins so they don't miss any important information. Second, if it is chosen carefully, it can identify the subject and audience for a story. Because the sound of the narrator's voice and sound effects are all you've got to communicate your ideas, you need to use them wisely. Here's public relations practitioner Moe Howard to tell you how the listener's needs are factored into radio writing. |
| **0:24**  **HOWARD ACTUALLY (12 seconds)** "It's true that the broadcast writer has to think about the capabilities of the people listening. Since they can't review any facts, radio stories have less complex and shorter sentences. The writing should be more conversational to take advantage of the listeners' identification with the human being reading the copy." | |
| **0:36**  **TALENT NARRATION** | What about the announcer reading the story? How does copy change to reflect the person reading it aloud? |
| **0:41**  **HOWARD ACTUALITY (14 seconds)** "The broadcast writer needs to double-space the copy and use special broadcast style rules when writing the script. That makes it much easier to read. Just as importantly, the writer needs to give the narrator some help with other sounds so he or she doesn't have to carry the whole story alone." | |
| **0:55**  **TALENT NARRATION** | And how do you use sound to tell your story? |
| **0:58**  **HOWARD ACTUALITY (8 seconds)** "You need to use all the sound resources you can to communicate, switching back and forth among the narrator's voice, actualities from other speakers and sound effects that help tell your story." | |
| **1:06**  **TALENT NARRATION** | The multiple-column format you're looking at helps you accomplish that. The first column is the running time—the total the story has run so far. It reminds you if you've used a particular narrator's voice or sound effect too long, or if you haven't given enough time for a sound effect to be understood. And since radio reports are usually very short, it also reminds you if you've run over your limit. |
| **1:27**  **SFX: Blaring horn (1 second)** | |
| **1:28**  **TALENT NARRATION** | Newly out of time, this is Victor Voice Talent reporting. |
| **1:30** | |

**Strategic Thought**

Think of your reaction to a YouTube personality you really dislike. What sort of personal image does she attempt to project? How does that change your perceptions of the information or entertainment she presents?

Another strength of a multichannel message is its ability to add the effect of a speaker's personality and humanity to your communication effort. That power is exploited in a number of ways in multichannel writing. First, persuasive writers can select on-air announcers with whom their target audiences can identify and who bring credibility to their information. For instance, a pharmaceutical company's video news release on an advanced breast cancer detection system might be better narrated by a woman than a man and a doctor rather than a layperson.

You need to capitalize on other personal characteristics. In addition to age, race or gender, the announcer's clothing or accent can also contribute to drawing in and then communicating to a certain audience.

There are other ways to exploit multichannel's strengths associated with interpersonal communication. Multichannel writers generally use more informal, conversational language than print writers; more contractions, such as *don't* or *can't*; and shorter sentences.

However, that informality and casualness have to be perfect when read by an imperfect person. Because you are employing a fallible human being to read your copy, you must make major changes in preparing copy for multichannel tasks. Case in Point 8.2 discusses some of the changes you integrate into multichannel copy to accommodate the perils of trusting someone else to read it aloud.

## CASE IN POINT 8.2    Multichannel Copy Style Rules

While most of this chapter emphasizes how good multichannel writing resembles good text writing, the nature of the medium makes some adjustments necessary. The style rules governing multichannel copy preparation derive from the reality that the copy is intended to be read aloud by a narrator or on-camera presenter. Because of that, multichannel copy is written to appear precisely as it would be spoken. Here's how that manifests itself.

### Abbreviations

Because it is difficult for an announcer to instantly recognize and translate abbreviations into their spoken form, abbreviations are generally not used. There are a few exceptions. For organizations and countries known by their initials, make sure you write them exactly as they would be spoken. Thus, U.S. Senate becomes the *U-S Senate*. FBI is written in broadcast copy as *F-B-I*. Maintain exact oral pronunciation in your broadcast copy. NAACP is written in broadcast copy as *N-double A-C-P*. But when an acronym is pronounced as a word, don't use hyphens. Thus, broadcast copy uses *NATO* and *NASA*.

### Symbols

Symbols are also difficult for an announcer to convert into spoken English. Again, spell out all symbols in exactly the way they would be pronounced. Thus, in broadcast copy $7 is written as *seven dollars*.

### Numbers

The style rules for handling numbers are different for broadcast, too. Write out the numbers one through ten, just as you would in print copy. Also write out eleven, as the narrator might mistake it for two letters. Use figures for 12 through 999. But write the words *thousand, million* and *billion.* It sounds confusing but it becomes simpler if you realize you're writing broadcast copy to duplicate spoken language. Thus, 2,603,000 is written *two million, 603 thousand.* That principle extends to decimals—8.6 is written *eight-point-six.*

Although there are some exceptions to the preceding rules (for addresses, times, sports scores and stock reports), you'll still adhere to the need for exact spoken language. For that reason, 1124 Hite St. becomes *eleven-24 Hite Street.* Dates are also converted into spoken style. Dec. 7, 1941, is written *December seventh, 19-41.*

### Phonetic Spelling

Broadcast copy preparation is intended to make the announcer's job as simple as it can be. Part of that task is to provide guidance on pronouncing unfamiliar words. Pronouncers are placed in parentheses after the word. Accented syllables are capitalized, as in this example: Mackinac (MAK-ih-naw) Island hosted the festival. Obviously, if your copy contains too many pronouncers, review it. You may need to simplify it for your spokesperson. Here are the symbols used in broadcast copy:

#### *Vowel Sounds*

| | | | | |
|---|---|---|---|---|
| ah—father, hot | ee—feet, machine | eye—time, ice | oh—note, oval | u—put, took |
| a—bat, apple | eh—get, bed | ih—pit, middle | oo—food, tune | uh—shut, puff |
| aw—raw, fought | ew—few, mule | | ow—how, clout | |
| ay—fate, ace | | | | |

#### *Consonant Sounds*

| | |
|---|---|
| g—got, beg | s—seem, civil |
| j—general, job | sh—machine, show |
| k—kick, cap | z—disease, visit |
| ch—chain, butcher | zh—vision, measure |

## Overlaying Sound Onto Copy

This chapter's introduction described multichannel writing as "additive." The writer doesn't abandon solid prose principles. She just capitalizes on the strengths contained within each additional sensory channel. Any multichannel message neglecting those powerful tools could likely be communicated more effectively through print media. If your multichannel writing is merely reciting copy into a microphone or having a talking head speaking it on a screen, you're missing key opportunities.

### Your Audio Toolbox

**Strategic Thought**

Why is there a difference in how much information people retain from print and multichannel media? Does the involvement of other sensory channels overcome the inability to review?

In audio-only formats, the components to create this sensory addition to your message are voices, recordings at a site (called an **actuality**), sound effects and music. Each can play an important part in making a more powerful communication piece.

At its simplest, sound can draw the reader's attention from whatever she was doing. The drawn-out explosion that characterizes a rocket launch, followed by the words "We have liftoff," could draw attention to a story about a moving company's use of satellite technology to monitor a family's household goods across the country. The scream of an African lion is an attention-grabbing opening for a story on efforts to stop zoos from capturing wild animals. In Click-Through 8.1, you'll see how a radio news release signals a story about water with the squeaking sound of a shutoff valve to pull inattentive listeners into the piece.

### Sounds That Establish Time and Place

Sound can also be used to indicate to an audience that a particular piece is intended for them. Cows mooing might signal an audio piece is for farmers. The high-pitched whine of stock cars whizzing by might draw auto enthusiasts or the squeaking of sneakers on hardwood might attract basketball fans.

Sound can also be used to create a mood or establish a time period for a story. Big band music quickly signals a story about World War II. The ringing of a single church bell might alert listeners to a story on small-town life. A cacophony of bells might set the tone for an audio piece on the Vatican.

Music and sounds can even be used to identify concepts in audio writing. For instance, a copier company's radio ad might have its high-speed copier identified by pulsing, majestic, harmonious symphonic music, while its slower competitor is represented by out-of-key music played by a single tuba.

The most important and powerful use of sound is to help tell the story you need to tell. Any words you use to describe the agony of babies born to addicted mothers are overwhelmingly reinforced by the wailing of scores of abandoned babies in nurseries devoted to their care. You are better able to persuade listeners that industrial machinery noise is harmful if instead of spending the entire report saying, "The machinery is loud enough to damage your hearing," you devote several seconds of the soundtrack to the narrator yelling over the equipment's racket.

### Integrating Voices

The two-column audio script format shown in Case in Point 8.1 and Click-Through 8.1 will help remind you to integrate sound into your radio writing. One column contains the narrator's words, and the other makes sure those sound effects, music and other auditory cues reinforcing the narrator's speech are integrated into the story. You'll see how the two-column format reminds you not to let one source speak too long and to stitch sound effects and actualities into the story.

You should also be conscious of integrating voices into your radio reports. Just as in print stories, outside sources bring credibility. They demonstrate that someone else supports the conclusions you are making in the story.

Also, as in print stories, additional sources help relieve the tedium of listening to only one voice. Even more important, the audience can often perceive the source's emotion or sincerity from his or her speech, which makes the report that much more persuasive.

### Relevance, Not Noise

Integrating these auditory elements into copy is indispensable in exploiting the power of the medium. But while sound elements are key, it's equally important to use sound, music and voices with a purpose. As in all communication, every word and sensory element must contribute to one central communication objective.

For example, if your piece concerns ways doctors use your company's new technology to set broken legs, but your report begins with sounds from a football game (which you include because it's an activity in which a person might get a leg broken), you've already got two problems.

It's very likely that you discouraged the audience you wanted—the doctors who might adopt this procedure—from attending to the message. They won't immediately understand the message is intended for them. Second, you're going to confuse the sports audience you've drawn by presenting a story on medical technology when they expected a story on football.

That integration of messages is equivalent to "keeping like elements together," a guideline that is just as important in multichannel audio writing as in print communication. You are just adding an audio channel to a message in which those same basic principles of communication apply.

However, remember you are relying solely on the audio channel to communicate your message. Your audience can neither see what you're discussing nor review the message. For that reason, your prose needs to be more descriptive. Use wordplay and alliteration to make the language more interesting and involving to an audience totally reliant on auditory cues for understanding the story. Click-Through 8.1 demonstrates how to use a memory-cue transition to link the story's final words (which feature some alliteration) with the preceding sound effect.

Lastly, remember that you need to describe, where relevant, whether your speakers are old or young, whether they are factory workers or business executives, whether the action of the story is taking place in a factory or a wheat field and so on. If a sound effect is not obvious, identify it to your readers. If you are alternating between speakers, you need to identify each source every time she speaks, unless the voice is very distinctive. In other words, you must replace visual elements with descriptive writing and sound effects to recreate those visual elements of the story. Use the checklist in Memory Memo 8.4 to see if you're accomplishing that task.

> **MEMORY MEMO 8.4** Integrating Sound Into Audio Writing
>
> - Use sound cues to draw the target audience into attention
> - Use sound to establish the story's mood or time period
> - Use sound to help tell the story

## Overlaying Motion Onto Copy

When you write for video, you're trying to apply all the strengths of print and audio writing while adding the power of sight and movement. You want to employ every persuasive force of the print medium: the power of printed words and photos, subtitles and lists, graphs and charts and quotes and written excerpts. To that, you want to add the capability of sounds, voice and music to create a mood, add credibility, stimulate attention and draw a targeted audience.

### Motion, Not Sight

Once you have these elements of words and sound in a video piece, you can think about pictures. That's different from the way most of us think about constructing video stories. Too often we believe pictures are enough to make good video productions. That attitude is what contributes to the general vacuousness that characterizes too much of what we see on social media, and even television.

For video to be as effective as possible, your writing needs to incorporate all three sensory channels into its presentation. That's why it's impossible to talk about video as if it's entirely independent of other communication media.

Once you have the strengths of print and audio in place, you can create a tremendously effective piece by adding motion. It's the combined impact of each successive sensory channel that makes a piece ultimately engaging. Showing a slow-moving column of peasants trudging through a narrow cemetery gate as they mourn an assassinated warlord creates a stirring picture. Showing that video to the audio accompaniment of hecklers from a rival political party makes for powerful drama. In a different way, showing fast cuts of the

> **MEMORY MEMO 8.5** Writing Video Copy
>
> - Assure you've developed effective text and sound to which you can add visuals
> - Coordinate the communication effects of text, sound and motion
> - Assure you're adding motion and not merely sight to your message
> - Don't distract from powerful images with text unnecessarily describing the video

hyperkinetic energy of auditions for a clown college to the accompaniment of upbeat pop music provides an experience you can't achieve with the video alone.

You notice we talk about the power of video as the power of motion, not of sight. That's intentional. You can use the power of sight in print prose with photographs, charts, sidebars and illustrations. The major element video adds is motion. Memory Memo 8.5 may help guide your thought process to guarantee you're using this sensory element effectively.

For that reason, you shouldn't be content merely to pose an announcer in front of scenery and shoot video of her reading copy. That's not what video is for. In fact, magazine photographers wouldn't be able to keep their jobs if they tried to illustrate articles with such boring visuals.

Instead, you need to emphasize motion in the imagery accompanying your story. For a story on a famous rock band's concert in your town, illustrate it with ticket holders sprinting toward the stadium gate for the best seats. Visualize a story on taxes by following legislators through a day as they meet with special interest lobbyists, encounter protesters outside the Capitol, and finally take their places in the chamber to vote.

## Video Shorthand

There are thousands of such procedures and possibilities for visual storytelling. There are volumes and volumes written about video techniques and the mental images they can evoke. It takes directors years of study and experience to begin to master them. But as we referenced during our discussion of audio techniques, we have an audience that's been wonderfully trained by movies to know what some very simple shots mean.

Want examples? What is happening when a shaky handheld camera follows a character down hallways or across dark alleys? From your experience with horror movies, you probably know the character is most likely in extreme danger of a gruesome and bloody demise. What's happening when a man and a woman run toward each other in slow motion? They're usually in love. When two men approach each other in slow motion, there is usually going to be a fight employing rather savage forms of martial arts.

There are thousands more of these cinematic conventions. Video shots without Steadicam stabilization usually suggest realism or tension. A camera shot swiveling on its base indicates speed. Black-and-white shots give a gritty, documentary feel to a scene. Shooting a subject from below emphasizes size and power. Shooting someone from above communicates a sense of vulnerability and timidity. Some basic terminology describing these techniques is included in Case in Point 8.3.

**CASE IN POINT 8.3     Glossary of Video Terminology**

Video production has its own language. Writers need to understand it to communicate different camera angles and movements. Although there are thousands of different combinations of visual techniques that can create innumerable emotional effects, these constitute the basic building blocks for video writers.

**Camera Shots**

The manner in which you frame a shot can encompass a vast setting or focus intently on a single subject.

*Long Shot (LS):* Shows the entire setting. Sometimes called an establishing shot because it establishes the location for the rest of the action.

*Medium Shot (MS):* Far enough from subject so we can see the subject, as well as the setting behind the action.

*Close-Up (CU):* The subject fills the screen. This shot emphasizes one specific subject without distractions from the background.

*Extreme Close-Up (ECU):* The camera focuses on one specific item—the detail in a picture, a serial number on a product or a healing wound on a finger. Don't be afraid to use close-ups and extreme close-ups. They provide variety and help your viewers concentrate on what you want them to see.

**Placing and Moving the Camera**

The way you place and move the camera can emphasize certain emotional effects.

*Eye-Level Placement:* Putting the camera at the eye level of a normal person establishes the viewer in the same emotional position as the person in the shot.

*High-Angle Placement:* In addition to being a standard angle for establishing shots, a high-angle shot creates a psychological impression belittling the shot's subject.

*Low-Angle Placement:* As you might guess, a low-angle shot emphasizes the power and dominance of the scene's subject.

*Panning:* The camera base remains stationary while the camera swivels. A pan recreates the position of a spectator.

*Truck:* A truck shot has the camera rolling sideways to stay alongside the action. This is the perspective you have while you're looking at the driver in a car traveling beside you on the highway.

*Zoom:* While the camera base remains stationary, the zoom lens rotates to bring the image closer or move it away. With a zoom, you can rapidly change the viewer's orientation to the subject.

*Dolly:* On a dolly, the camera approaches or pulls back from the subject. This gives the same impression as walking toward a scene and is a more natural movement than a zoom.

### Transitions Between Shots

As in print writing, video transitions help show the viewer the links within your story and demonstrate your argumentation pattern.

*Cut:* A cut is an instantaneous switch from one scene to another. It is by far the dominant transition used in news coverage.

*Dissolve:* When you need a softer transition between shots (for example, to suggest romance during a wedding scene) you might consider a dissolve. A dissolve also is used to evoke dream sequences, passages of time, and other more disjointed transitions in a sequence.

*Wipe:* In a wipe, the screen appears to peel or erase the image and substitutes another one on the screen. A wipe lets the viewers view one image as another image is entering the screen and suggests a more direct linkage between the images in the transition.

### Special Effects

Because they can sometimes overwhelm the message, special effects should be used sparingly. However, the following are commonly used to recreate some of the communication effects of visuals in print media.

*Supertitle (SUPER):* A supertitle is lettering superimposed on the screen to identify a speaker or present statistics or other information. It should be used to bring the power of print to reinforce an aural or visual message.

*Split Screen:* This is a wipe that stops halfway across the screen. It's used to compare before-and-after scenes and other transformations.

*Key Insert:* In a key insert, an image is placed over another scene. Thus, you could show a product and then place a corporate logo onto the image.

### Feature Stories Told in Multichannel

Writing copy for video production closely follows the principles outlined for print and radio media. After establishing your thesis in the first few seconds of the piece, you've got to precisely explain the issues you'll explore. That's the same routine you would follow in the first two paragraphs of a print story. The video feature story lede in Click-Through 8.2 illustrates this conception.

Click-Through 8.2 was prepared by a brokerage firm to showcase its advice for a changing stock market. Notice how the writer uses a thematic visual, the lonely Santa Claus, to anchor the beginning and end of the package. It's also interesting to see how she uses cash register sounds as an aural asterisk to draw attention to her three main points about the weakening economy. Finally, note how she mixes graphics and live action to involve the viewer.

The same principles apply to the body of the story. As we discussed during audio writing, don't let one scene or one speaker dominate for too long. The three-column format is used as a reminder to fill all the sensory channels available.

Remember as well that you still have the responsibility to create solid argumentation structures using chronology, order of importance or problem-solution. In addition, you have to link each of them together with memory-cue transitions that orient your viewers to what they'll be seeing next.

## Coordinating Channels With Your Message

Be conscious of how easy it is to confuse your viewers, who are receiving information simultaneously through several sensory channels. For example, you shouldn't show scenes of your institution's president jogging in a company-sponsored charity event while the narrator is talking about the president's problems coping with a recession in your industry. Viewers will be confused because the information they're receiving from the auditory channel doesn't support the visual message. Similarly, if you display a slide or supertitle of a quotation on screen, the voice-over should repeat the words on the screen exactly. Again, any deviation confuses viewers and distracts them from the message you're trying to communicate.

Much of video writing is essentially the same as for the other media we've discussed. In fact, the major distinction is not so much a matter of knowing what to write as knowing what not to write.

It bears emphasizing that video is powerful because of its ability to focus the effectiveness of sound and motion in communicating a message. All too often, words disrupt that process. It's true that in audio and in print you need words to create a vision in the receiver's mind. For instance, in a radio story, you might reinforce the cracking voice of an elderly nursing home resident by mentioning her weathered face and uncertain walk.

But such prompting is unnecessary in video. If you are showing video of a blizzard, it's both redundant and infuriating to have a voice-over telling the viewers they are looking at a blizzard. If you are attempting to communicate the emotion of a local sports hero's retirement, don't say "it was an emotional time for Old Bucko" as you show footage of the retirement ceremony. To communicate that sentiment, it's probably going to be much more effective to have no narration as you show Old Bucko fighting back the tears as he basks in the roaring cheers of the home crowd one last time.

Instead of describing the scene, the words should supplement the power of the video. Use words to identify speakers and explain the context of action the video is showing, but don't try to compete with the power of your image. If it's necessary to orient the viewers to a scene, make the points before the film begins or against scenic shots. If you are talking when the filmed action is at its height you may detract from the visual's strength and confuse your viewers as they attempt to absorb complex information from two channels at once.

Again, we suggest a scripting format that reminds writers to incorporate all three channels into their video writing, as well as to coordinate sound, visuals and words in their video writing. You'll see an example of this scripting format in Case in Point 8.4.

# my pr firm

Client: Practitioners of the Future
Title: "Video Writing Format"

Time:    1:06
Date:    Aug. 16,
Writer:  Thompson

| effects | video | dialogue |
|---------|-------|----------|
| :00<br>black screen<br>THOMPSON VO |  | THOMPSON: The first step in writing any video document is to recognize that broadcast is an additive medium. By that I mean that you must take the same written prose that is so important in print writing... |
| :06<br>FX: Oscilloscope voice pattern<br>SFX: scratchy noises simulating oscilloscope pen on paper<br>THOMPSON VO | | ... and add audio in the form of voices... |
| :08<br>GRAPHIC: word "SFX"<br>SFX: whistle<br>THOMPSON VO | **SFX** | ... or sound effects. |

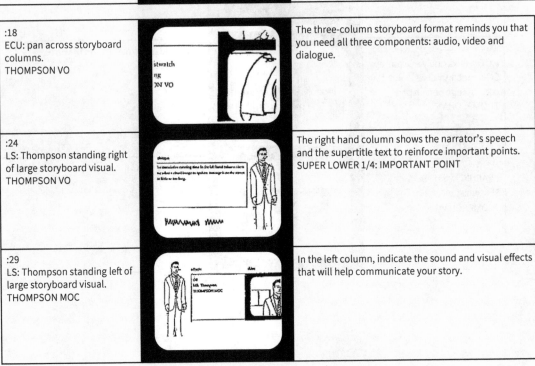

| :09<br>GRAPHIC: plus sign<br>THOMPSON VO | | To that potent mix you add ... |
| :12<br>MS: Thompson<br>THOMPSON MOC | | ... video. But it's not nearly enough simply to have sight, like my talking head. |
| :15<br>FX: word "Motion" flashes across screen<br>SFX: spinning tires<br>THOMPSON VO | | Instead, video only becomes effective when you have motion. |
| :18<br>ECU: pan across storyboard columns.<br>THOMPSON VO | | The three-column storyboard format reminds you that you need all three components: audio, video and dialogue. |
| :24<br>LS: Thompson standing right of large storyboard visual.<br>THOMPSON VO | | The right hand column shows the narrator's speech and the supertitle text to reinforce important points.<br>SUPER LOWER 1/4: IMPORTANT POINT |
| :29<br>LS: Thompson standing left of large storyboard visual.<br>THOMPSON MOC | | In the left column, indicate the sound and visual effects that will help communicate your story. |

## No Different—Just More

It's important to remember that as we move from one medium to the next, from print to audio to video, we don't completely alter the principles that guide good writing. Instead, each medium represents an additional communication channel supplementing the power we've already gained from the others. Using that knowledge, we can exploit the vast communication power of multichannel media most effectively.

### SUMMARY

- Multichannel writing is an additive process, supplementing the principles that guide print writing with the power of sound, visuals and motion.

- Multichannel media don't require audiences to be consciously engaged in the message, necessitating writers to incorporate techniques to capture attention and overcome memory issues.

- Incorporating the audience-centered writing process into multichannel writing involves concentrating on stimulating the attention of your target audience and incorporating memory cues into the more frequent transitions in multichannel writing.

### Scenario Prompts: Adding Sensory Channels

You'll find Scenario Prompts on pp. 367–386 of this textbook. While they vary in subject and difficulty, they help you hone your critical thinking and strategic writing skills. The following are best suited to this chapter's topics.

Management: 4.2 / Writing: 5.7, 8.8, 9.12

# Fostering Interactivity

## Engaging Your Audience

It's 2011. A major American guitar manufacturer, Gibson, was being investigated a second time for violating the Lacey Act, a federal law protecting endangered animals and plants. Gibson's Nashville facility had been raided by the U.S. Justice Department, and agents confiscated exotic woods from Madagascar and India.[1]

Gibson CEO Henry Juszkiewicz initiated a fierce PR counterattack, asserting the law was vague and the government's action arbitrary. In the run-up to the 2012 presidential election, anti-Obama media and Tea Party groups echoed Juszkiewicz's position, describing the federal agents enforcing Fish and Wildlife regulations as "government jackboots" engaging in "Gestapo-style" raids.[2]

Juszkiewicz fostered this anger, enlisting Gibson-endorsing artists to support him. Seventies rocker Ted Nugent was among the most vocal Gibson backers. "This is an illegal Gibson guitar; the game warden told me it was illegal," Nugent told a Texas concert audience. "Those spineless, soulless pieces of shit from the Wildlife Agency should take me down now. I vow that I will use our freedom to get these dirty cocksuckers out of the White House."[3]

When Juszkiewicz attended a Nashville Tea Party event six weeks after the raid, I was sufficiently alarmed to respond to a Gibson-sponsored Facebook support site. One afternoon, I wrote a message indicating the wood seizure was not a political attack against the company, but due to the company's alleged illegal importation of exotic woods.

*Send.*

I was eager to see the response to my message. Ten minutes later I checked the site again. My comment wasn't in the message stream.

I typed my message again. *Send.*

This time I left the Gibson site open. My message was posted for about five minutes, then disappeared before my eyes.

I typed my message again, now also asking why the company kept deleting my comment. I saved my message, then hit *send*.

In a minute or so it disappears.

A few more repetitions, and the person manning the Gibson site and I are in a posting war. I post. She deletes. I post-she deletes. IpostShedeletes. Post … Delete. Pos … Delet. Po … Del. P … D.

Another 10 minutes of rapid-fire Ctrl+Vs, and I decide to spare the hapless Gibson employee on the other end of the internet from a crippling repetitive motion injury.

Why am I telling you this story? Because this chapter concerns what should be one of the most valuable aspects of being on the web: its interactivity. The internet provides what persuasive communicators have forever said we wanted: a low-cost way to involve our organization's stakeholders in real-time discussions of what they want our company to be.

So, while I acknowledge Gibson might not want to share my negative opinions with all their customers, their actions were extremely counterproductive. The company's web monitor spent the better part of an hour deleting my posts. In much less time she could have simply responded, affirming why the company felt its prosecution was unfair. A polite, well-reasoned answer would certainly have provided me some evidence they considered my opinion valid, even if unwanted.

But Gibson wasted another, greater opportunity. If alongside my comment, they had explained why they felt my viewpoint was misguided, their arguments might have been adopted by site visitors, who could then have used that reasoning in conversations with others. That would have extended their message.

That's why we have devoted this chapter to interactivity. When you plan any online persuasive communication, whether directed toward external or internal publics, you must consider how you would obtain and use feedback. If you haven't, you've abandoned some of your potential communication power.

And Gibson suffered one more loss by deleting my negative post in 2011. If they had replied, this story would have ended, and I likely wouldn't be sharing news of Gibson's environmental transgressions all these years later.

—*WT*

## What You Know

- Writing doesn't require you to start from scratch. You can overlay basic principles of multichannel communication onto what you learned from writing just print.

- The TIPCUP filter lets you focus on the most newsworthy elements to increase the likelihood that gatekeepers will publish information your target audiences will access.

- Audience feedback is a useful research tool that helps you hone future messages to better target key stakeholders.

## What You'll Learn

- How the internet is an all-of-the-above channel that utilizes principles of print and multichannel media with an added focus on interactivity

- How to optimize your online content so target audiences can find it more easily

- How, by adding CAN to TIPCUP, you can generate a *Conversation* about your organization or a related issue among those who have an *Affinity* for the organization to *Nurture* important relationships and boost the likelihood those stakeholders will share that content with others

- How to employ interactivity to solicit audience feedback and respond in real time, improving relationships with key stakeholders

## The Reality of Interactivity

For decades, strategic communicators have yearned for interactivity. If your earlier classroom work included an introductory course in strategic communication or public relations, you likely learned about two-way symmetrical communication, the final, aspirational stage in James E. Grunig's four models of public relations (Figure 9.1).[4] To remind you of lectures of yore, Grunig postulated four models of public relations practice.

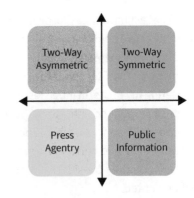

**FIGURE 9.1  Grunig's Four Models.**
James E. Grunig conceptualized public relations practice as varying in its direction of communication (one- vs. two-way) and level of consideration for publics' well-being (asymmetric vs. symmetric).

Grunig characterized two of his models as one-way. The **press agentry model** of practice features an organization communicating for its own ends, with virtually no concern for public engagement in the message or for the truth of the information communicated. The second approach, the **public information model**, displayed greater organizational responsibility to stakeholders; when organizations felt it necessary to communicate, messages would be truthful. But it was still the organization choosing to communicate, and the public's desire or need for information entered less into the equation.

Grunig also described two additional models, which he designated as two-way, marked by varying degrees of concern for audiences' right to engage in communication with an organization. The first of these, the **two-way asymmetrical** model, described how some practitioners studied and tested their target publics' characteristics and motives to learn how to best persuade them. While the practice allows for some measure of stakeholder feedback, the relationship is asymmetric because such campaigns don't require deep consideration of the public's needs before committing to an institutional action.

Finally, Grunig proposed a fourth model, one he considered ideal. The **two-way symmetrical model** suggested that when designing a communication campaign, the needs of an organization and the needs of its stakeholders merit equal consideration. Expanding upon the audience research the asymmetric model employed, organizations pursuing the symmetrical approach would more actively engage with its publics as it developed its plans. It would also design procedures to encourage and capture public responses so subsequent company actions could be honed to improve relationships with its publics. Essentially, in exchange for the organization's permission to talk to a stakeholder and to be listened to, the stakeholder has an equal right to communicate with and be listened to by the organization and thus directly shape organizational policy and actions.

As we suggested earlier, the two-way symmetrical model is aspirational. Grunig himself posed a question that undermined its credence: "Is it unlikely that a large organization with more power than its publics would ever deliberately choose to practice symmetrical public relations?"[5]

Our view? Yes, it's damned unlikely.

But with the rise of internet communication and social media we can more realistically acknowledge that the two-way symmetrical model isn't completely impractical. Maybe it was just premature.

Now organizations are confronted by publics, both internal and external, who don't wait on organizations to desire communication with them before they speak out. Publics have relatively low-cost ways to share opinions, so organizations no longer have phenomenal financial advantages over publics' ability to communicate.

So, in our opinion, organizations have adopted practices more akin to symmetrical communication because their publics now have communication power more closely approaching that of the organization. This new dynamic has made it necessary for strategic communicators to forthrightly plan for and integrate interactive communication into their approaches.

## New Elements of Online Communication

This isn't to say that interactive communication is novel. Even in the 1980s, an advertiser who faced a boycott by activists because of its billboard's sexist message was essentially forced to engage with that audience. However, to a large degree, the possibility for enhanced two-way communication—even symmetrical communication—owes a great deal to the advent of the internet. While these advancements have arguably caused fundamental changes in the strategic thinking about effective persuasive messaging, the tactical adjustments to your writing styles are comparatively more minimal.

You may remember that in the previous chapter, we talked about sound and motion as the additive channels placed atop solid prose to create compelling multichannel messages. When we discuss interactivity, we're adding time and technology considerations, which you must integrate within your message delivery, monitoring and response systems. These additive layers enhance your capacity to engage the right audience with your content and react more substantively and promptly to the audience feedback needed to create meaningful two-way communication.

Let's deal with the technology first. Even we, the old masters of printed prose, chippers of cuneiform onto stone tablets, must now become aware of the technical elements of designing a system that encourages interaction and a commitment to listening to and engaging with the publics we've drawn together.

### All of the Above: Using Text, Audio and Video Together

In discussing the relative characteristics of print and multichannel messages, you discovered how to maximize the strengths and mitigate the weaknesses of your message; nevertheless, traditional media channels dictate certain parameters.[6] A printed newspaper or magazine can display text and still images, but not audio or video. Radio takes those words and adds audio, while foreclosing your ability to review a print message. Television takes the strengths and weaknesses of audio, adds visuals and motion, but demands sometimes stunning financial investments for production and distribution.

The web represents the first all-of-the-above medium. Online news stories covering a politician's official statements offer much of what the print version would: pulled quotes, descriptive information about the event and expert analysis. However, these elements are often supplemented with raw video of the statement. Moreover, if the statement focused on a major tax policy, the news outlet may provide an image depicting the timeline of various parties' standing on the issue, or an interactive infographic that prompts readers to plug in basic income information to see exactly how the new policy would affect them.

The internet provides you the ability to account for the weaknesses of one sensory channel by supplementing it with the strengths of another. In this way, you're able to generate greater engagement and interactivity with target audiences. Not only can you deliver messages through the most effective and appropriate sensory channels, but you now can accommodate the audience's preference for how and when they want to receive information.[7]

## Digital Time and Space: Infinite and Finite All at Once

One of the paradoxes of "new" media is that in many ways, it's old. While opportunities for interactivity have undoubtedly increased, online communication hasn't invented a single new sensory channel to carry messages and foster engagement. And you've still got an audience of information consumers who seem to have only become more impatient.

So it's necessary to consciously consider how old-school humans fit into new(ish)-style media. For instance, we often hear that online communication is essentially free and boundless. Indeed, internet communication allows for a theoretically infinite number of messages of infinite length.

That's unlike traditional media, which are often rigidly fixed or timed. Newspapers and magazines have a finite number of column inches, the content for nightly TV newscasts run just over 20 minutes and advertisements rarely run over two pages for print or 60 seconds for multichannel media.

True, some online media restrict message length. As of this writing, Twitter limits tweets to no more than 280 characters. Other sites have limits as well, but many of them are so large it's difficult to imagine how they'd be reached. Facebook, for instance, allows for posts of just over 63,000 characters. To put that in perspective, that's roughly the length of this book's first chapter—so realize your raving relatives' posts could be even longer!

However, if your company is willing to pay for the server space, your website can host as much content as you want. You could generate a 100,000-word blog, produce a six-hour video or host a 24/7 podcast.

That's not to say you should yield to the impulse. You've got a new media channel, but the same old receivers. Novice writers, while not exceeding a medium's character limits, sometimes outstrip their audience's patience.

So we return to conciseness, a constant in our writing approach. It's among the more difficult skills to learn. As French intellectual Blaise Pascal once wrote, "I have made this [letter] longer than usual because I have not had time to make it shorter." Indeed, brevity takes a great deal of effort, either in planning to write more densely at the outset or exercising disciplined editing on the back end.

That brevity becomes particularly important for generating interactivity online, largely because your competition for audience attention has expanded exponentially. There are literally millions of websites vying for the same eyeballs you are, so you have no hope of attracting—let alone retaining—an audience if you can't quickly communicate the most critical aspects of your message. This task is all the more complicated given the limited attention span of online audiences. Like all the other media we've discussed, you've got about two seconds to attract and retain social media audiences before they abandon your message and search out another.

To encourage interaction, you must also account for another technical issue: time. Think about your own interpersonal interactions. Maybe you and a friend have a one-hour break before your next classes. Your conversation can't run longer than an hour because that's all you've got. Operating under the assumption you're not an insufferable egomaniac, we're betting you'll split speaking time with your friend.

Strategic writers must think similarly when communicating with audiences online. If they hope to generate interactivity through back-and-forth commenting or sharing, writers must reserve time for that exchange. Your audience only has so much time to read, listen to or watch your content, and you must set aside time for those activities, as well as any interactions that follow. Seems complicated, but that calculation is simpler than you might think.

The average U.S. adult can read and comprehend about 300 words per minute.[8] Let's say your company blog's analytics informs you the average user spends five minutes on the site. At most, your audience can read 1,500 words of content (300 words per minute $x$ 5 minutes). Do you want your post to eat up all 1,500 words? Or would you be better off writing about 700 words and leaving time for readers to peruse comments and perhaps leave their own?

## Making Your Content Accessible

Of course, the length, quality or sensory majesty of your content means nothing if that content isn't easily accessible. Your audience can't engage with content if they don't know it exists, so you have to consider how stakeholders navigate the digital world to make your content more easily discoverable.

> **Strategic Thought**
>
> What was the last piece of news you read? How did you find it? Why did you engage with it? How much of it did you *actually* read? How far did you get before you quit? What led you to abandon the piece? How might you conquer these same barriers to attention in your own writing?

### Searching or Browsing

Regardless of where your organization houses its digital content, audiences will typically discover it either through **searching** or **browsing**.[9] To search online means to look for a specific thing. To browse means to look with some goal in mind, though that goal may be more general. The distinction between searching and browsing is similar to that between buying and shopping. When you enter a store to *buy* something, you know exactly what that something is; all that's left is to find it. When you enter a store to *shop*, you want to satisfy an as-yet-unknown desire, so you have less direction, and you'll need to make more comparisons between your options.

When you design online content, you must realize audiences will come upon it both through searching and browsing, so you need to organize and categorize your content so they can easily find it using either process. Each website, blog or social network has unique ways for you to make content easier for users to find, and most of those tools are under your control (we'll discuss these in greater detail in Chapters 14 and 15). But how do your target audiences initially get to those sites? Probably through using a search engine, most likely Google. Therefore, it's critical you understand how to craft your content so it's more highly ranked by these sites.

### Search Engine Optimization

Odds are, when you conduct a Google search, even though you're given thousands—sometimes millions—of results almost instantaneously, you won't look beyond the first page in browsing or searching for information. That's why **search engine optimization (SEO)** is so important.

SEO is the process of producing, altering or overhauling content so search algorithms rank the site higher in their results. Memory Memo 9.1 lists several common factors that influence search rankings. Generally, sites that are regularly updated, use commonly searched keywords and phrases, and feature a high quality and quantity of incoming and outgoing links perform better in web searches.[11]

These SEO factors often coincide with the content's relevance, but not always. Certain sites have, over time, established themselves as "search kings" for generic terms, and they're notoriously difficult to unseat from that throne.

But what if you're looking for something more specific? For example, let's say Professor Browning is interested in purchasing a new guitar. So he goes to Google and types in "Fender," a popular guitar brand, and out pops 487 million results. These sites feature all things Fender: message boards

---

**MEMORY MEMO 9.1** SEO Factors[10]

- Speed
  - Sites that load quickly rank highly on search engines

- Size of the site
  - Sites with more pages often rank higher

- Accumulated page value
  - However, you can't just have a ton of pages; those pages have to be valuable based on other SEO criteria

- Age of the domain
  - Older sites are often more trusted and thus more visited

- Long-term versus temporary traffic
  - Sites with steady traffic over time rank higher than those with several peaks and valleys

- Quantity and quality of incoming links
  - The more people who visit your site coming from other highly ranked sites, the higher your rank will be

- Quantity and quality of outgoing links
  - More links to reputable sites raise your site's profile

- Link diversity
  - You can't just have a ton of incoming and outgoing links from the same sites; exposure to multiple sites helps your ranking

from Fender guitar players, tips on repairs and customization, official histories of the brand and so on. But Professor Browning doesn't want that. He wants to buy a Fender. Well, here are what some more specific searches look like:

- "Fender Telecaster"—39.9 million results
- "Fender American Professional Telecaster"—4.72 million results
- "Fender American Professional Telecaster for sale"—2.33 million results
- "Fender American Professional Telecaster for sale in Bloomington, Indiana"—48,000 results

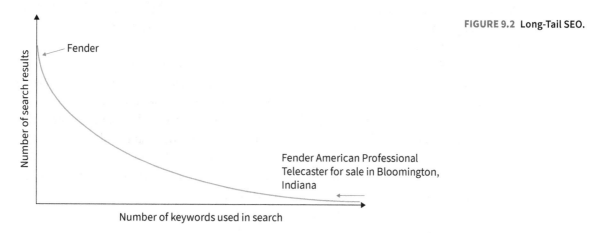

FIGURE 9.2 Long-Tail SEO.

You just witnessed the advantage of long-tail searches. **Long-tail SEO** is a method of optimizing several specific keywords and phrases to improve search engine rankings for more engaged audiences.[12] Figure 9.3 shows how this term gets its name: the increasingly targeted "long tail" of the curve that emerges when searches become more and more specific. It may not be possible for an organization, particularly one that's small or local, to ever rank highly in more general Google searches. But for these organizations, such general relevancy may not be necessary, or even desirable, so long as they show up in more specific searches.

Back to our example. Let's say you worked for a local music shop near Professor Browning's home in Bloomington, Indiana. If he were browsing the web for general information about Fender, would your shop's website be the best place for him to look? Probably not. But as he learns more about Fender guitars and their different makes and models, he becomes ready to make a purchase. This is where your Bloomington store benefits by appearing in the long tail. Incidentally, the first result in that long-tail search is a Bloomington guitar store, Melody Music Shop. Because Melody emphasized localized and specialized keywords in its content, it actually outranks other national sellers like Reverb, Guitar Center and even eBay. As is the case with traditional media, success in new media doesn't depend on how large an audience you attract, but whether you attract an audience that helps you achieve your organizational goals.

## Creating a Relationship With Your Audience

As you'll find in your career, attracting audiences is only half the battle (maybe less). The real challenge is retaining them, and retention is important because it's extremely cost-effective. Marketing research has found that attracting new customers is between five to 25 times more expensive than retaining existing ones.[13] In interactive, online spaces, it's critical for organizations to build, maintain and manage relationships with a variety of stakeholders, because attracting new ones is so difficult.

### Roots in Interpersonal Communication

Whether organizations communicate with you offline or online, their communicators should work to duplicate a conversation's give-and-take with individual members of its publics. It's vital to building relationships and moving audiences to act.

**Relationship management** between an organization and its publics is a process of understanding what each party expects from the other, and then delivering on those expectations in a way that establishes trust and fosters continued commitment. Organizations show that commitment by involving themselves in shared interests with key stakeholders, often investing time, money and other resources to add value to those stakeholders' lives.[14]

At first it may sound strange that an organization can have a *relationship* with you. It should. Realistically, what would that even look like? Is Coca-Cola going to take you out for dinner and a movie? Are you going to have a deep, emotion-laden conversation with Charmin? Are you throwing back happy hour drinks with M&Ms? Of course not. But think for a second how each of those brands market and promote themselves to their audiences.

Coca-Cola rarely creates commercials asserting its product's quality. Instead, the company focuses on the connections people make with one another while enjoying an ice-cold Coke: taking road trips, cooking with loved ones or decorating for the holidays. In many ways, Coca-Cola isn't selling a product. It sells the promise of the interpersonal connections you'll establish *around* that product. That's why Coca-Cola's tag line is "Open Happiness," not "Drink Coke."

Charmin and M&Ms work in the interpersonal realm as well, but they do so through anthropomorphizing, which is a fancy way of saying they rely on spokespersons that possess human-like characteristics. When you think about Charmin, sure, you think about toilet paper, but you also picture the human-like family of bears featured in their promotional materials and on the product label itself. And when you think about M&Ms, you don't picture just the candy but the color-coded characters the company so painstakingly created (Figure 9.3).

FIGURE 9.3 **Meet Ms. Brown.** M&Ms is so dedicated to the personas of the different colored candies that designers and copywriters built each one a website profile. Ms. Brown, for instance, is depicted as a confident, intelligent, sassy, sophisticated professional woman. Her persona is unique among her compatriots, Red, Yellow, Orange, Green and Blue; interestingly, Ms. Brown is the only one granted a courtesy title. Regardless, each one espouses attributes appealing to different segments of the M&Ms audience, who presumably can see themselves in these candy caricatures.

All of these are efforts to humanize organizations, to make stakeholders feel as though they're interacting interpersonally with the company. And the way we see it, all communication is based on human interaction, whether that communication is between individuals, organizations, or organizations and stakeholders. For instance, imagine you've just returned from a beach vacation, and you're on TripAdvisor rating various establishments, like an airline and a hotel. Your review of the airline might read something like this:

> Had a flight from New York to LA with Sky Airlines. I was supposed to have a short layover in Atlanta, but because my flight out of New York was delayed, I missed the second leg of the trip. Though I was frustrated, Sky Airlines booked me on the next flight to LA, upgraded me to business class and gave me a $200 voucher for my next trip! Would recommend Sky Airlines to other travelers.

And the hotel:

> Arrived at Stays Hotel to find they gave away my reservation because I was 30 MINUTES late on check in! Though they refunded my money, the manager was very rude and would not make any effort to find alternative accommodations for me. Would NOT recommend!

So you've got one good experience and one bad one, but what's at the foundation of those experiences? Did you ever interact with Sky Airlines or Stays Hotel? Kind of, but not with the organizations as such; you interacted with *individuals* who worked for and represented those organizations. In both instances, you had reasonable expectations for the services each would

**Strategic Thought**

What is your university's mascot? How do the mascot's characteristics and actions anthropomorphize the university's brand and communication with students and alumni? Who else represents the university brand (e.g., coaches, professors, alums, students)? How do various publics engage with or view these individuals? What do their actions say about your school?

provide. The difference in your experiences was the ability of those employees to relate to your concerns on a person-to-person level and do what they could to retain your business and thus preserve the relationship.

In this sense, when you evaluate the quality of your relationship with Sky Airlines and Stays Hotel, you're not really evaluating the organizations so much as your interactions with individuals who represent them. Jason Falls and Erik Deckers, authors of *No Bullshit Social Media*, say it better than we ever could: "People don't buy products from a building. They don't buy from a logo. They don't even buy from a company. People purchase products and services [...] from other people. And those people are human."[15]

## Building Relationship Online: Understanding Lifetime Value

Whether organizations communicate with you off- or online, establishing the feeling of interpersonal connections is vital to building relationships and eventually moving audiences to act. Driving action may be your ultimate goal (e.g., buy my product, attend my event, sign my petition) and online interaction with your target audiences can help you achieve it. But remember: you're playing the long game here. Yes, organizations will expect online communications to yield eventual returns on investment, but you can't view online interaction—especially on social media—purely through a return-on-investment (ROI) lens. Doing so leads many social media managers to abuse their audiences, lose their trust and ultimately, tarnish valuable relationships.

Think about it this way. As we mentioned before, Professor Browning is a guitarist—a mediocre one but a guitarist nonetheless. Let's say he "likes" a local music shop on Facebook. What sort of content management approach is likely to engage him? Well, imagine that the local music shop does nothing but post promotions and advertisements. Every damn day it's the same thing: 20% off this! Free strings with the purchase of that! Labor-Day-Blowout-Extravaganza-Musicpocalypse!

Unfollow those guys, and quickly. Why? They failed to provide anything of interest. Think about it. Even the most ardent guitar player isn't buying every day. You only want or need so much of any given product or service. At a certain point, you're good, at least for the moment.

If you want people to engage with your organization, you must provide them with something valuable beyond a transaction. In the case of the hypothetical music shop, it would have retained Professor Browning as a follower of its social media content if it shared steps for keeping a guitar sounding like new, videos detailing basic guitar maintenance or tips from expert guitarists on how to become a better musician. While it's true that none of this content *directly* leads to a sale, it does so *indirectly* by preserving a relationship with a valued customer, which the shop can leverage when she's ready to buy new gear.

In their book, *Content Rules*, Ann Handley and C. C. Chapman put it this way: "Good content shares or solves; it doesn't shill. In other words, it doesn't hawk your wares or push sales-driven messages. Rather, it creates value by positioning you as a reliable and valuable source of vendor-agnostic information."[16] Put more simply, successful online communicators focus on relationships more so than transactions. They understand that stakeholders have a **lifetime value** to the organization that extends far beyond a single interaction or purchase, which can only be harnessed if the relationship is properly nurtured. As such, they also focus on becoming trusted sources of pertinent information for their audiences, an idea we'll revisit in Chapter 14.

## TIPCUP + CAN

When producing that original content for the web, the TIPCUP filter will again be helpful to you in determining what interests your audience. But some elements are particularly important for online communicators, such as timeliness, impact and proximity. We'll use Twitter to illustrate our point.

Regarding *timeliness*, issues vary in their level of personal and social importance from moment to moment. One of the most noticeable examples of this phenomenon in online communications is Twitter's trending topics. These change at least weekly, often daily and sometimes hour to hour. If your organizational content or key messages connect to trending topics, making this connection known by employing trending hashtags greatly increases the chances it will be seen. That's just like when we included timely elements in media relations writing to tempt gatekeepers to pick up the story.

Similarly, *proximity* is also critical. But here we mean it more in a social rather than geographic sense. Think friend of a friend. For example, let's say you're hunting for a job at a local PR agency. While researching the firm on LinkedIn, you notice three of your connections are linked to that firm. Maybe they've worked for the agency directly or their employers have hired that agency in the past. Either way, you might ask these people for an introduction or a recommendation. Good online content capitalizes on these connections too. Twitter mentions using the @ symbol are a great way to do so. Maybe there are potential audiences interested in your message, but they don't follow you. However, they might follow an organization you've partnered with, so mentioning that @partner when it's relevant instantly widens your audience.

But of all the TIPCUP elements, *impact* is perhaps the most important. People are self-interested, especially online. Researchers estimate that just over 40% of individuals' Twitter posts are me-focused, meaning people often talk about their immediate emotions or what's happening to them in the moment.[17] In a space where users are so obsessed with the self, your content has a better chance of gaining traction if you can relate your message to your audience members and their personal interests. Unfortunately, organizations are themselves often me-centric, constantly talking about themselves or their products as opposed to displaying the value they can add to their stakeholders' lives. Just as you must fight the temptation to focus on the organization in your controlled and uncontrolled media messages, you must do the same in the internet's semicontrolled space.

However, the web's inherently interactive nature means there are additional elements beyond TIPCUP you should consider. First, does your content foster *Conversation*, either between your organization and key stakeholders (a **dialogue**) or among stakeholders interested

**Strategic Thought**

When organizational leaders say they want to engage with stakeholders in creating lasting and meaningful relationships, what does that mean? What do those relationships look like? What characterizes those interactions? What elements are necessary for such a relationship to be considered good by the organization? By the stakeholder? Are they the same?

in your content, products or services (what marketers call a **multilogue**)? Second, does your content harness existing enthusiasm or *Affinity* your online fans already hold? And lastly, does your content *Nurture* or build relationships or connections you can later leverage? The process of creating quality, online content that fosters interactivity relies on adding this CAN to our TIPCUP.

Principles in Practice 9.1 discusses explicit examples of organizational efforts to generate conversation, play on an existing affinity and nurture relationships through participatory media. By engaging stakeholders in the creation of content itself, savvy strategic communicators often employ each of these critical CAN elements. But while such efforts sometimes have a big payoff, they occasionally backfire when you forfeit some control over the message.

## PRINCIPLES IN PRACTICE 9.1    The Victorious, the Vicious, the Viral

As we've emphasized throughout the chapter, people won't be sharing your message because they want to do you a favor. They only endorse and forward content to their contacts because they think they or the message's recipients will profit from it. When users share information about a company or cause with their social contacts, it's for the rewards they get, often a self-perception of helping someone or displaying their own talents and experience.

You often see companies structure those rewards more overtly. Some sponsor a contest. If you share the firm's internet message, then you're entered in a prize drawing. If you've received such a message from a friend, you've probably already determined this strategy's weakness. While there may be some slight reward for the person sharing the post, most of her friends receiving the message understand they're being exploited. They aren't interested in the promotion, so their inboxes have been needlessly flooded.

A more successful approach to prompt message sharing? Some companies offer to devote a portion of their sales to a nonprofit or charitable effort and request the nonprofit and its supporters share the message with their internet contacts. The difference? In this case, the initial sender likely gains a sense of helping a cause close to her heart. The friends who receive the message are more apt to forward it, either because it shows support for their friend or because they share loyalties to the same cause.

Some very successful sharing campaigns have been prompted by communicators who allow users to participate in content design. Such an approach gives them a more compelling reason to share. One such effort supported "Straight Outta Compton," a 2015 film detailing the rise of the Southern California rap scene. The campaign, nicknamed "Straight Outta Somewhere," developed a personalizable meme in which viewers could place their own location and photo into the frame the movie employed in its marketing campaign. During its first week up, the site had 7 million visitors and the meme was downloaded nearly 6 million times. Every minute during that week, the movie's marketing firm claimed there were 15,000 #Straightoutta tweets and retweets.[18]

The meme shortly took on a life of its own, and "Straight Outta" parodies using the meme proliferated: *Straight Outta Luck, Straight Outta Patience, Straight Outta Beer.* Here's Professor Thompson's entry, created to poke fun at himself for buying a home in an "active-seniors" community in preparation for his retirement.

This highlights an important point about interactive communication. If you accept the benefits that come with interactivity, you also must accept its unpredictability. In the case of the Straight Outta's viral outgrowth, even the silly responses reinforced the movie's branding. With individuals' messages and photos bracketed within the movie's main marketing image, audiences far beyond the marketers' most ambitious goals were introduced to the movie.

However, this unpredictability can turn negative just as quickly. U.S. President Donald Trump's penchant for Twitter frequently provided examples of the peril accompanying a social media campaign. Take the #ThankYouTrump effort.

In the first week after he was sworn into office, massive rallies across the nation protested his initial actions. To counter the opposition's energy, Trump supporters scheduled and promoted a Twitter rally, asking people to tweet what most gratified them about the new Trump presidency, using #ThankYouTrump. Within hours the hashtag was hijacked by the president's detractors, who used the forum to ridicule the new chief executive. Among the vitriol and vulgarity, we managed to find one we can reproduce here: "#ThankYouTrump for making George W. Bush seem smart, Richard Nixon seem honest, & Warren G. Harding seem competent."[19]

But that's part of the interactivity game. In fact, it's likely the most valuable part. Interactivity, with its real-time praise and abuse, is a moment-by-moment assessment of your client's performance. If your client acts in a way your public rejects, it's best to know that as quickly as possible. Conversely, if your organization takes a stance or introduces a product that engenders internet love and affection, that's knowledge you can immediately use to your benefit.

## Fostering Interactivity

Online channels differ in their relative capacity for interactivity, and some rules for developing dialogue are channel-specific (more on those in Chapters 14 and 15). However, you can observe certain general guidelines across platforms.

### Help, Don't Hawk

Audiences want information that's relevant, helpful and in some way improves their lives. Yes, from time to time that means providing information about products and services. But not often. For example, David Meerman Scott, an expert on social media marketing, argues that only about 5% of social media content should include direct promotions. You earn the right to overtly persuade or sell to audiences only after you establish trust through content that engages them.[20] So most of your content online should either be shared from other sources—which is common on social media—or produced to engage your audiences.

The Home Depot does an excellent job of producing material that helps its customers. Rather than using its website just to sell products, Home Depot provides a variety of home improvement resources to help current or potential customers. The company shares project ideas on Pinterest, details home décor concepts on its blog and hosts a variety of do-it-yourself (DIY) videos to walk viewers step by step through more advanced projects.

Of course, each of Home Depot's posts and videos features products you can purchase in its stores. However, its strategic communicators understand not only the importance of engaging with customers beyond mere transactions, but also the purchasing path many of them take. People don't just buy lumber and nails. They decide they want to build a deck, search for information on how to do so and then buy the necessary supplies. By creating walk-throughs like "How to Build a Simple DIY Deck on a Budget," Home Depot attracts audiences interested in the project, tells them how to proceed and, as you might expect, conveniently provides a list of necessary materials they can purchase in their nearest store.

**Home Depot How-To**

https://blog.homedepot.com/how-to-build-a-diy-deck-on-a-budget/

By helping its customers, Home Depot ultimately makes it easier to sell to them.

### Connect, Don't Interrupt

You can clearly see how Home Depot uses *impact* in connecting to potential audiences interested in DIY home improvement. What may be less obvious is how Home Depot employs *timeliness*. First, if you browse their DIY sites, you'll see they highlight certain content based on the season. For example, in November and December, you'll find videos on making your own holiday centerpieces or tips for outdoor Christmas decorations.

Looking deeper, you'll notice good online communicators think of timeliness more broadly. They interact with their audiences at the audiences' convenience, not that of the organization. To understand this principle, compare Home Depot's online communication to the television commercials it airs.

We've got nothing against the TV ads. They demonstrate products, promote sales and tie together thematically. But viewers don't see this content as a valued message so much as an interruption. Nobody seeks out a TV ad. They seek out a primetime college football game, which the ad interrupts.

In fact, advertising buyers are confronted with an almost impossible task. In Home Depot's case, a nationally broadcast football game placement for winterizing supplies sales seems a smart choice. Men are likely to be a greater proportion of the individuals who will install home winterizing; men are a greater segment of the college football audience. Football games are broadcast in the fall when the need for winterizing materials should be heightened.

But there are flaws in the logic. Many in the game's audience don't make decisions about home winterization. For renters, landlords are often responsible for weatherizing. Some viewers are wealthy or physically challenged, meaning their contractor chooses the source of the weathering materials. Consider also that games are also broadcast to regions with mild winters, so their houses don't need to be weatherized.[21] As a strategic communicator, you've transmitted a message that likely has a concentration of your target customers but is also accompanied by many individuals who consider your message irrelevant.

Compare this to Home Depot's online presence. In most cases, its audience algorithm has likely screened out those individuals who don't own a home, who hire contractors for demographic reasons or who live in warm-weather climates and don't need winterizing products. Only those who are match likely customer profiles will see internet ads.

But Home Depot has an even more valuable communication tool. Traditional advertising and media relations placements depend upon the strategic communicator's ability to predict audience characteristics and habits in order to deliver the message when the audience member wants to hear it.

The interactive nature of internet use often places this decision in the consumer's hands. Home Depot hosts a series of informational tools establishing the company's DIY credibility and developing the consumer's perception that Home Depot provides a more efficient buying experience than the company's competitors. With that reputation established, instead of searching out the customers, the customers come to them precisely when they think Home Depot can give them precisely what they want.

How? The company has content waiting for the consumer for just the moment the consumer needs that information, 24/7. Say a nurse got off from her hospital shift at 1 a.m. This is the only available time she has to solve her winterization problems.

What product does she need to stop window drafts? A company-produced video gives advice. Which brands offer added features and at what cost? A comparison guide lets the consumer see the product descriptions side by side. Which stores in her area stock her choice? An inventory lists how many items are in each store. Could she have them delivered to her house? Payment and shipment information are on the store site. In short, Home Depot's online content connects with audiences at a moment in which they're interested in what the organization offers and ready to act based on what they see.[22]

### Build, Don't Stagnate

And while Home Depot's online DIY messaging certainly does attract audiences unfamiliar with the brand, it likely builds on the *affinity* of existing customers. The situational theory of publics, which we introduced in Chapter 2, helps explain this process. As you'll recall, situational theory segments audiences into one of four groups. Active publics are the most involved with an issue and/or organization and thus the most likely to seek out information, followed in lesser intensity by aware publics, then latent publics. Nonpublics aren't interested in this specific issue and thus don't seek information at all.

In this case, fans of Home Depot represent an active public. They're the ones who regularly shop at the store and are most likely to seek information about or from Home Depot directly. Aware publics, who may be interested in home improvement more generally but are not necessarily followers of Home Depot's content, may also find the company's DIY information through more general searches.

Regardless, Home Depot employs a variety of means to use its content to propel audiences to the situational model's higher levels. The active publics are already consumers, and thus likely to purchase products in store. Additionally, because they are fans of the organization, they are also likely to share the content with their online connections to demonstrate usefulness within their social networks.[23] Aware publics may operate similarly. In both instances, we hope the shared material will make its way toward latent publics who may discover the content through social ties, though they may never have otherwise seen it. In this way, you can also see friend-to-friend *proximity* at work, moving audiences up the escalator.[24]

### Listen, Don't Just Speak

It seems obvious, but it's worth reiterating. You can learn a lot about key stakeholder groups just by listening, and online communication offers numerous chances to monitor how stakeholders feel about or interact with your organization so you can adjust your behavior to better answer their needs. It's a process that every competent online communicator engages in, but it's not as easily observable as many other activities; there's a clear online record when an organization speaks, but only implicit indicators of when an organization listens. When managed correctly, this open record offers organizations the chance to communicate authentically, ethically and effectively.

While it's important to listen to and monitor all stakeholder groups, employees perhaps more than any other audience segment value being heard. Most Americans spend between 40 and 60 hours a week at work. That's basically a third of your life. And nobody wants to believe her life is wasted. Generally speaking, employees want to work for organizations they feel positively impact their communities, and in turn they want to meaningfully impact how those organizations are run. So let them. Listen. They know things you don't.

So much of employee communication is one-way and top-down when it should be two-way and bottom-up. For example, let's say you work in the communication department for a large insurance company. Many organizational policies will be set at the top levels and communicated downward to frontline workers, such as those who handle customer complaints or communicate changes in health coverage. While it's important to have a consistent policy across an organization, it's worth asking, "Should the managers at the top be driving that policy?"

From our perspective the answer is no, or at least not entirely. Who knows more about customer interactions with the organization: a CEO who may never have interacted with a single policyholder in her life or trained professionals who communicate with them daily? Probably the latter, so it would be wise for the company to implement formal feedback mechanisms. These might occur offline through employee forums or less formal, face-to-face interactions, or they might occur online through email communication or comments on articles posted on the company intranet.

### Respond, Don't Just Monitor

Whether you're communicating with customers, employees, investors or any other stakeholder group, monitoring is not enough. It's not a conversation if only one person is talking, and responsiveness is key in building relationships via online communication. Virtually every digital platform has some built-in capacity for organizations and their publics to engage in two-way communication. That means anytime a stakeholder reaches out to you, she expects a response. Real- or near-real-time responses (within 15 minutes) signal that you care about this person and you're engaged with her concerns.

Quick responses are valued across the board, but nowhere is it more important than customer service. Delta Air Lines was among the first organizations to harness social media for real-time customer service, launching @DeltaAssist in 2010 with six employees. Now the company fields customer service complaints through its Twitter account, @Delta, and its social media team numbers over 40.[25] In monitoring social media, Delta noticed many frustrated passengers were publicly voicing complaints against the airline over delays, cancellations and booking errors. The @DeltaAssist account was intended to field these complaints, respond quickly and resolve situations when possible.

Delta's Twitter responses were so effective that the company quickly set the standard for online customer relations. In many instances, a passenger would voice a concern before her flight took off (i.e., I paid $15 for in-flight Wi-Fi just to learn it's unavailable), and by the time she landed, find the issue was resolved (i.e., Delta refunded the $15 Wi-Fi charge to a credit card). Not only did these quick responses generate customer loyalty and preserve important relationships, but because the interactions took place on social media, satisfied customers were already in a space where they could share their positive experiences with their followers, which improved Delta's brand image more broadly.

## Traditional Media Platforms and Interactivity

During this chapter, we've primarily discussed interactivity as an internet activity. However, recognize that organizations have necessarily had to interact with stakeholders since human communication has existed. A city zoning board holding a public hearing to listen to public comments concerning a contentious development is a form of interactivity. So is a university's president's choice to either negotiate with or arrest students engaged in a sit-in protest in the president's office. Letters to the newspaper's editorial page are a form of interactivity too. Throughout time, organizational actions have prompted audience reactions, to which organizations have had to respond.

However, now all these public reactions—and more besides—invariably spill onto social media and the internet more broadly. The internet has enhanced the communication power controlled by publics so it more closely equals that held by organizations. Buying and erecting a billboard to protest an organization's stance takes money, and just as importantly, time. A consumer responding to a corporate action by writing a letter to the editor must produce a carefully composed, cogently written piece, and then hope it passes through a gatekeeper to appear in the newspaper.

Internet reactions to organizational actions aren't hindered by any such barriers. There are few gatekeepers who can prevent a critical communication from being posted. It costs the poster virtually nothing to share her message with other individuals. And, as we've all witnessed, the comment doesn't have to be coherent, well phrased or even accurate to be seen by thousands—or even millions—of people. Stakeholders react, hit a few keystrokes, and milliseconds later, it's in your organization's inbox, and potentially the social media feeds of many of your key constituencies.

The lesson? The internet didn't initiate interactivity, but its features made the frequency and the pace of interactivity more frenetic, forcing strategic communicators to plan their interactive responses more carefully and execute them more quickly. We'll deal with that challenge directly throughout the remainder of this textbook, and you'll most likely confront it daily for your entire career.

**Strategic Thought**

How does social media help support activism? Can you cite examples in your community?

### SUMMARY

- The internet enables you to leverage the various strengths of print and multichannel media to create easily understood messages likely to generate conversation and interactivity between an organization and its stakeholders, or among stakeholders themselves.

- By employing SEO tactics, you can make your content more easily accessible to your target audiences, particularly with more specific, long-tail searches.

- While TIPCUP elements remain important in crafting online content, you must also consider that online content *CAN* do a great deal more to generate a <u>C</u>onversation about your organization or a related issue among those who have an <u>A</u>ffinity for the organization to <u>N</u>urture important relationships and boost the likelihood those stakeholders will share that content with others.

- Employing channels that foster interactivity between your organization and key stakeholders lets you solicit critical feedback necessary to respond adequately to stakeholder concerns and nurture long-term, mutually beneficial relationships.

### Scenario Prompts: Fostering Interactivity

You'll find Scenario Prompts on pp. 367–386 of this textbook. While they vary in subject and difficulty, they help you hone your critical thinking and strategic writing skills. The following are best suited to this chapter's topics.

**Management: 7.1** / Writing: 3.8, 6.9, 7.9, 8.7

### *Figure Credits*

Fig. 9.3: Copyright © by Mars Inc.

IMG 9.1: Photo: Copyright © 2007 by Chris Stanbury. Meme was generated by http://www.straightouttasomewhere.com/.

# PART III

# Executing Tactics to Serve a Goal

By now, you've probably noticed we tend to start at *why* we're writing long before we get to the how-to-do-it part. This unit concentrates on the *how*. But even here, we anchor ourselves in the *why*.

We've organized this unit into three, two-chapter modules covering uncontrolled, controlled and semicontrolled communication. For instance, Chapter 10, the first chapter of our uncontrolled communication module, focuses on how to write mediated messages, which we offer to gatekeepers in prospect of their outlets disseminating those messages to their audiences. Chapter 11, the module's second chapter, offers tactics improving your chances of getting that information delivered. No point in writing a message if your audience never sees it, right?

But we can't offer you these tools without redirecting your focus to the *why*. Recall that lecture from intro about goals, objectives, strategies and tactics? Here's a helpful diagram to refresh your memory of their relationship:

This GOST diagram looks like a hierarchy, but it's best to think of it more like a flow chart. Every organization has *goals*, or stated aspirations they'd like to achieve. *Objectives* are smaller, measurable components that, when realized, mark significant progress toward some goal. There are various approaches or *strategies* one might employ to advance an objective, which themselves are carried out through specific communication acts or *tactics*.

In a nutshell, this figure represents every organization: a collection of individuals working toward shared goals. Logically, if the GOST interconnections break down, so too does the organization. That's why it is critically important that goals, objectives, strategies and tactics intuitively flow from and feed into one another.

But as they say—or more specifically, Hamlet said—"there's the rub." In the capstone campaign courses both of us have led, we find too many students struggle because they adopt a tactic-focused approach rather than a goal-oriented one.

It usually goes something like this: Student thinks tactic *y* is really neat. Organization wants to achieve goal *x*. But student thinks tactic *y* is really neat, so student does tactic *y*. See the problem? This hypothetical student never bothers to ask whether tactic *y* serves goal *x*, let alone situate the tactic within any overarching strategy helping her accomplish a goal-oriented objective.

That's why you must first consider the goals and objectives you wish to accomplish, and only then choose a tactic. While we hope you find the detailed, deep dives into tactics that follow valuable, keep in mind how each tactical node fits within the broader strategic web. Seeing those interconnections and mastering the rules that govern good writing across formats makes you a more efficient, effective and employable writer. That's been our goal in crafting this textbook.

- Module 1: Uncontrolled Media

  - Chapter 10: The Audience to Reach an Audience: Applying Audience-Centered Writing to Media Relations

  - Chapter 11: Delivering Uncontrolled Messages: Reaching Media Gatekeepers

- Module 2: Controlled Media

  - Chapter 12: When the Organization Controls the Message: Advertising and Internal Communication

  - Chapter 13: Delivering and Evaluating Controlled Messages: The Power of Personalization

- Module 3: Interactive Online Media

  - Chapter 14: New Media, Old Tricks: Creating Online Content

  - Chapter 15: Say Something, Then Be Ready for Anything: Delivering Semicontrolled Messages

# The Audience to Reach an Audience

## Applying Audience-Centered Writing to Media Relations

For several summers, I marketed a nationally prominent horse show. It was important enough to sell out the last two of the event's six days, when the champions were chosen.

Saturday's championship scored local saturation-level media coverage, but only after the show closed. Coverage prior to the event or for the competition's early-week qualification rounds was usually limited to a sports-section table listing the results.

Perhaps you already see my strategic problem. I knew the after-event media relations report would look impressive. There would be lots of TV features, huge newspaper photos and features and mentions in other media. And most of them would engage potential audiences after the show closed. That left me with great media coverage to propel ticket sales on days when I didn't have any tickets to sell. By Sunday, the whole show was over for another 51 weeks.

This is a cautionary tale. Media relations has long been identified as one of PR practitioners' main tasks, so we judge ourselves by how many stories we place or the prestige of the outlets in which they appear. But as strategic communicators, our true task is accomplishing the client's goals. Sometimes that involves getting a story placed in *The New York Times*, or sometimes just on the PTA Facebook page.

In my case, I was supposed to sell tickets for an event, so I had to determine how to win coverage on the event's opening Monday, not the Sunday following the event.

After tracking media my whole professional life, I recognized the pace of the media calendar. I knew Sunday night newscasts and Monday morning newspapers usually had fewer stories competing for the available **news hole**—the amount of time or print space available for news. There were few government or business stories to compete with because they weren't working on the weekends. The Sunday night broadcast news often ended with an upbeat human-interest feature.

I remembered a student had told me she worked with a nonprofit using therapy horses for children with special needs. She was frustrated her cause hadn't been able to draw attention to expand its impact.

Her problem became my opportunity. Imagine young riders dressed in their stunning riding costumes sharing their majestic horses during a Sunday afternoon to help young people with varying challenges.

In short, a feel-good piece with fantastic visuals that reaffirms our faith in the generous impulses of today's youth. Or from the media's perspective, a great-looking fluff piece under the closing credits. Or, selfishly, a marketing piece showcasing the club's picturesque grounds and interviewing a teenager who urges everyone to see her compete Monday evening. Oh, and here's how you can buy tickets.

It may sound crass, but it's a win-win-win. A nonprofit struggling for attention showcases its important work. A media outlet fills that night's news hole with emotions that communicate service to the city. And I get a pre-event story that helps me sell tickets.

In short, the editor or producer is just an audience with needs, serving an eventual audience both you as a persuasive communicator and they, as journalists, serve.

—WT

## What You Know

- The audience-centered process prompts temporary engagements between sender and receiver.

- Properly structuring information within the lede and body copy helps attract and retain a target audience.

- Individualizing writing for specific target audience subsets increases attention from that segment.

## What You'll Learn

- What criteria media gatekeepers employ to screen public relations messages

- How a tool chest of different media relations formats simplifies gatekeepers' ability to integrate public relations messages into their coverage

- How to structure an emotionally engaging focus feature story

## Our Route to Readers

### The Role of Gatekeepers

This pod's two chapters discuss creating and delivering messages through *uncontrolled media*. As you recall from Chapter 1, we consider information to be uncontrolled when individuals outside the organization exercise editorial control over content submitted by a strategic communicator.

Uncontrolled information is almost always delivered through **external communication** channels. While organizations need the support and commitment of management, employees and stockholders, there are people and groups outside the institution who are often just as important to an organization's success.

External communication presents challenges because there are intervening individuals and organizations through which our information must pass before it reaches people important to our mission. **Gatekeepers**, the editors, producers, reporters and writers who control the flow of information through these journalistic outlets to their audiences, have an enormous influence in determining the persuasive communicator's earned media success.

It's a relationship with problems. Gatekeepers can alter your messages' tone or totally omit your information from their outlets, inhibiting your ability to communicate with vital publics. Journalists' power over PR messages makes practitioners suspect journalists are anti-business and antagonistic toward the PR practitioner's role in disseminating information.

### Rocky Relationships

Unfortunately, it's a situation persuasive communicators helped create and perpetuate. Too often, we've flooded editors and news directors with information totally unsuited to their audiences. We've sent releases about freeway traffic control devices to small-town editors, and hints on applying eye shadow to financial news bloggers.

At one point or another, we've violated every style and grammar rule, often delivering editors poorly written copy. We've also been guilty of ignoring the formats in which journalists expect information. Journalists have expended hours transforming our work into something readable and presentable.

It's no wonder the relationship between journalists and PR practitioners is sometimes filled with mutual distrust. Yet bad as it sometimes is, it's the environment in which you'll be working. However, you don't need to aggravate it by displaying a lack of knowledge and professionalism.

In this two-chapter pod, we translate audience-centered principles to media relations, in which the editor, reporter or producer is deciding whether to attend to the message we send. We detail what journalists expect from the writing they publish, whether it comes from their own staffs or from a strategic communicator. Only if we satisfy that gatekeeper's needs can we hope to access her audience.

## Your Audience-Centered Relationship With Gatekeepers

Effective communication with journalists follows the same principles governing all other communication. To be effective, all messages must answer the needs of the audience for whom it is intended. In the case of journalists, they need information their audiences will find important.

How to accomplish that task? First, we must understand how gatekeepers perceive their duties toward their audiences. Second, we must format that information so journalists can easily integrate it into their work. In other words, what information do they think their audiences need and how can we structure our writing to make delivering that information easier for journalists?

## Media Releases: Not a Magic Bullet

### Critical Thinking Comes First

Chapter 2 suggested any communication process's first step is determining audience wants or needs. But remember the gatekeeper is the initial audience that uncontrolled communication must convince. For instance, if a news site focuses on business news, its editors are uninterested in food or fashion news, unless it relates specifically to the business aspects of those fields.

## News Release Alternatives

As sacrilegious as this sounds, *news releases are not the automatic answer to every communication need.* Many other options can be remarkably effective in stimulating news coverage, as Memory Memo 10.1 reminds us.

News releases have value in certain situations—when you are making routine announcements about institutional changes or special events, for instance. Releases can also provide background information for reporters preparing feature stories.

However, the news release format is often a poor choice. If you announce a worker's promotion to a publication that prints a few lines for the 20 or 30 local executives being promoted, it's counterproductive to send a four-page biographical release. You're only creating more work for yourself and for an editor. If the outlet uses three or four lines and a photo, create a four-line announcement and submit it with a photograph.

If you submit information for a calendar section, it's harder for both you and the editor if you bury those dates in narrative prose. Instead, send a tabular calendar announcement with that important information listed prominently. Click-Through 10.1 provides an annotated example of a calendar announcement.

If you're sending a **public service announcement** (PSA) to a radio station that no longer broadcasts full PSAs but instead weaves a few seconds of information into their announcers' between-segment dialogue, provide information in a way they can use. Case in Point 10.1 illustrates a full PSA format listing information at the bottom that can be adapted by announcers as brief filler material. In addition, the listing can be integrated easily into website, newspaper and magazine calendar sections.

# my PR firm

*123 Main Street / Hometown, Any State / ZIP / 505-555-1234*

PUBLIC SERVICE ANNOUNCEMENT
Start date: (date PSA should begin)
Stop date: (last date PSA should run)
(Descriptive title)
Reading time: X seconds

For information contact: (your name)
For information contact: (your name)
Work phone: (your phone number)
Work email: (your email address)

Nonprofit groups use PSAs to obtain publicity from radio and television stations.

The PSA's narrower margins and shorter sentences make it easier for an announcer to read it on the air.

A PSA can vary in length, but longer PSAs are less likely to be used. Note that you include the PSA's reading time in the top margin.

The reading time of a PSA must be determined because it must fit into a station's programming schedule. It takes about 10 seconds for an announcer to read 25 words.

-30-

If the intent is to get coverage by a photographer, a quick summary with the event's time, date, photo subject and significance is both easier for you to produce and for the photographer to use than a news release. By matching the photographer's needs with your pitch, this teaser provides enough information for the photographer to decide whether to cover the event and write any caption or "cutline." Case in Point 10.2 illustrates the formatting of a **photo op teaser**, while Click-Through 10.2 shows a full example.

# my PR firm

*123 Main Street / Hometown, Any State / ZIP / 505 555-1212*

Photo Opportunity Tip Sheet
Day of the week, Date
Time of event

Contact
Your name
Phone number
Email

## Title of Event Photographer Will Cover

WHO:   Here you should describe exactly what the photographer could cover. Essentially, this is a summary lede with some additional detail.

Remember: photography is a visual medium. As such, you should play up any striking visual elements. Will your events feature brightly colored costumes? Candid action shots? Will the tone be happy or somber? All these elements will help the photographer prepare and set the appropriate mood.

WHEN:   Repeat the date and time. For outdoor events, make sure to have a backup date or location scheduled for inclement weather.

## Scheduled Activities ~

5:05 p.m.   You typically want to begin the first activity slightly after the start time, so 5:05 p.m. works well for a 5 p.m. start.

5:15 p.m.   Events move along pretty quickly, with a number of different activities, so you'll want to use the schedule to break those up conveniently for the photographer. Consider a wedding reception schedule as an example.

5:30 p.m.   The newlyweds enter the room.

5:35 p.m.   Then shortly thereafter have their first dance.

5:45 p.m.   Then the obligatory bride-father and groom-mother dances.

6 p.m.   And most importantly, the cutting of the cake, because … well, it's cake.

6:15 p.m.   Then there are the best-man and maid-of-honor toasts.

6:30 p.m.   These are all iconic, powerful images, each occurring at rigidly scheduled moments. Letting photographers know exactly when these moments will occur helps them position themselves to grab the best photos. At times, this rigid schedule lets a photographer cover another event, yet still visit your location for a specific shot.

WHERE: It's useful to place location descriptors for each of the scheduled activities (e.g., the mansion entrance, to the left of the main stage). Some even include a detailed map of the event grounds.

The *where* comes last because it's the least pressing concern. In the *who* and *when* sections, you're able to outline what's actually happening at the event. This lets photographers judge whether the event is newsworthy and whether the images are potentially dynamic enough to merit attention. TIPCUP and order of importance are just as critical in structuring teasers as in a release.

If you intend to stimulate a feature story, send a **query letter** or **email pitch** instead of a news release. Rather than communicating with multiple journalists, sending a query letter to an individual writer can be much more persuasive, particularly when you're asking for expansive coverage. PR professionals employ query letters frequently so we'll be discussing tips for writing them later in the chapter. For now, just remember the most important thing is to match the message to the coverage you expect to garner.

## Writing the News Release

### When the News Release Is Enough

Although we feel practitioners write too many news releases, they are useful in certain situations. Specialty internet sites and small-market newspapers and broadcast outlets often accept and place print and audio or video news releases (called ANRs or VNRs) announcing an institution's events, promotions and achievements.

In larger markets, releases might prompt or provide background for a feature story. In addition, some outlets print or display news releases when they communicate routine procedural information. Your local newspaper undoubtedly includes releases concerning changes in the trash pickup day. Health care reporters for your city's television stations may routinely include in their own stories the footage from a video news release.

Let's say your situation suggests it's worth writing a news release. Because releases are used by uncontrolled media, they should adhere to the format the media uses. For print media, the acceptable format is that journalism classic, the inverted pyramid. Let's briefly review that format (for greater detail, refer to Chapter 7).

# my PR firm

*123 Main Street / Hometown, Any State / ZIP / 505 555-1212*

NEWS RELEASE

(date)

FOR IMMEDIATE RELEASE

(Descriptive title)

For information contact: (your name):

Work phone: (your phone number)

email: (your email address)

CITY, State Abbr.—A media release's body copy is double-spaced, with a five-space indentation beginning each paragraph. This lets the gatekeeper estimate the release's printed length in her publication if she chooses to publish it. The double-spacing offers room between lines for copy-editing marks if she chooses to print a copy before reviewing and editing it. It's also easier to read.

Writers should not hyphenate a word at the end of a line, nor break a paragraph at the end of a page. If the PDF of a release continues beyond a single page, write the word *more* at the bottom of a page if another page follows.

When distributing your release to media gatekeepers, do not send it as an attachment. Many editors and reporters won't open attachments for fear of viruses. Just paste the document in the body of your email. As you work with gatekeepers, you'll begin to learn each editor's individual delivery preference for media inquiries.

At the end of the release, center the symbol "-30-" below that story's final line. It signals the editor has read to the end of the piece.

-30-

The inverted pyramid recognizes that many people are unwilling to attend to your whole message. The task then becomes communicating as much vital information as possible to your readers, even if they stop reading after one or two paragraphs. The inverted pyramid meets the audience-centered test because it adapts writing structures to the way readers will be using the medium.

When a practitioner decides a news release is a cost-effective method of garnering publicity, it's still vital to target specific messages to each important public. The release in **Click-Through 10.3** directed toward veterans' organization newsletters was only one in the campaign. Other specialized releases went to historical preservation group sites and fine arts editors.

### Applying the Inverted Pyramid

To write an inverted-pyramid story, begin by analyzing your purpose and your audience. Once you know why you're writing, compose the lede using the TIPCUP principles outlined in Chapter 6. The lede in **Click-Through 10.3** engages veterans' interest within the first few words, defining them as the audience and outlining their benefit:

> Billvilles's veterans will be honored when the city's Memorial Auditorium is rededicated.

The pyramid's second paragraph explains the lede. In most cases, it completes any information omitted from the lede that is needed for cursory storytelling. Here's where you include the names of critical individuals or organizations that didn't make it into the lede. If you've introduced a play on words or any other creative element in the lede, explicitly restate your main idea for those readers who didn't understand at first.

The inverted pyramid's third section presents information supporting the lede's argument. If your lede says new taxes would hurt your industry, you offer the evidence for that contention. That might be employment statistics, quotes from economists or government studies.

Develop a structure that demonstrates the logic of your arguments and that matches a mental template you predict your audience will use to process your information. If you're presenting a sequence of events, you should probably use a chronology. To show how your proposal may correct a perplexing situation, a *problem-solution* argumentation pattern may work best. If you're simply presenting a list of reasons justifying your proposed action, *order of importance* is a logical choice (refer to Chapter 7 for more details).

Limit yourself to one new idea per paragraph and keep paragraphs short. As we discussed before, concentrate enticing information in the break points—those first few words of each paragraph where readers often abandon the piece. Readers will also be more likely to push through the break points if you offer smooth memory-cue transitions showing how each paragraph's ideas are linked with prior ideas.

The pyramid's fourth section provides background helping the reader gain perspective on the current issue. For instance, a release announcing a charity fundraiser could include the total amount raised in previous campaigns.

The fifth section includes procedural information important for audiences ready to act. This call to action states explicitly what that action is. It could be a URL relaying product details, event times or a senator's office address to stimulate attendance at an upcoming rally.

In this chapter's opening vignette, Professor Thompson's created equestrian exhibition likely qualifies as a **pseudo-event**. As you'll recall from your grade school Greek course, *pseudo* roughly translates as *false*. So a pseudo-event literally means *false event*. Most introductory PR textbooks regard pseudo-events with predictable disdain, defining them as creations concocted for the sole or primary purpose of garnering media attention.[1]

That presents a conundrum for the media relations practitioner whose job is—you guessed it—garnering positive media coverage to benefit her organization. So are all events that generate media coverage pseudo-events? And are pseudo-events universally unethical?

In a word, this is an overgeneralization. In truth, many events earn the *pseudo* label because media critics—often journalists—believe PR efforts aren't worthy of the media's attention. Perhaps, but maybe that's often just journalists dodging their shared responsibility in the matter.[2]

News becomes news when gatekeepers deem it so. That's why successful media relations require you to temporarily slip into a journalist's persona. We've encouraged you to think (the TIPCUP filter) and write (inverted pyramid style) like news media members.

Journalists are predictable in what they cover. The very standards and norms that establish their field's credibility also, well, *standardize* what is newsworthy. Anticipating what will draw journalists' interests—that is, what will garner coverage—is a critical skill for strategic communicators.

Consider how predictably topics are featured based exclusively on the *timeliness* TIPCUP element. Take Thanksgiving week. Every year local and national news media run stories on charity work, walk-throughs on food preparation and tips on scoring the best Black Friday deals. In many cases, this year's stories duplicate last year's coverage because these stories align thematically with the holiday and draw audiences.

So perhaps a PR practitioner for a veteran's lobbying group organizes a series of turkey dinners for homeless veterans in the 11 largest U.S. cities—drawing on this Thanksgiving coverage while tying in a Veterans Day (Nov. 11) angle—to garner media coverage and support for her group's efforts. Is it wrong for her to advance her organizational interests by attempting to fill a predictable, existing news hole?

While you could certainly argue this fictitious practitioner is more immediately concerned with news coverage than homeless veterans, drawing attention to their plight is certainly a step toward addressing it. Similarly, Professor Thompson's primary reason for partnering with equestrian therapists was to increase his show's revenue, but that coverage likely boosted the local therapy organization's profile. Recalling Chapter 5's ethics discussion, there are clear utilitarian justifications for such pseudo-events, and there's a sincerity about them if they meaningfully connect the organizational mission to audience interest.

Finally, it's worth noting the oddity with which the term *pseudo-event* is applied most often to one-offs in media coverage when more egregious, repeat violators are largely overlooked.

The Oscars is perhaps history's most successful pseudo-event. For almost a century, the Academy of Motion Picture Arts and Sciences has hosted a media circus that by its very definition is a pseudo-event. Network television dedicates its resources to what essentially is a multiweek advertisement for virtually every cinema industry. Nominally the Oscars honor the best films, but that's debatable. Of the American Film Institute's top-five films of all time, only two took home the best picture.[3] While what is the best film is subjective, what numerous studies confirm is that just being nominated for an Oscar—or most any award—boosts box office revenues.[4]

So why do the Oscars really exist? Is its goal less noble than an organization advocating for veterans' well-being? And does an equestrian show organized by a lone PR practitioner that gains a 600-word feature and a 30-second segment on the local TV news merit the moniker of pseudo-event if the Oscars don't?

## Feature Stories:
## Greater and Deeper Coverage
### The Value of the Feature

With the inverted pyramid, you answer the reader's need for fast comprehension of the story's most important elements. As such, the inverted pyramid is used in virtually every other type of PR writing, including the **feature** story.

Whereas the news release is structured to deal with breaking news, to cover events and to make announcements, those event-oriented messages don't encompass all the types of external communication that can help meet organizational goals.

If your nonprofit institution's objective is to recruit more volunteers, you could issue a simple release to local media. Your release, if it runs at all, most likely would be reduced to a brief announcement. It's unlikely you would gain any mention of the important community contributions your volunteers have made or the personal rewards they gain. Local media won't run that information because they don't have enough space or time to do that for every organization. Even if they could, doing so would violate their duty to be objective and independent. Those are the realities of journalism.

But there's another reality here. You need volunteers and depend on a communication campaign to recruit them. However, without background

> **Strategic Thought**
>
> Compare a feature story and a news release in their impact and ability to motivate people to action. Under what conditions would each be your wiser choice? Are there times when both would be effective?

concerning your organization's philosophy and commitments, your appeal for volunteers won't be very effective.

What if you could get the newspaper or TV station to produce a story about an older woman who has been a volunteer for the organization for 40 years? That story of her dedication to the cause would communicate all your organization's positive qualities—everything you wanted to tell the public to strengthen your call for volunteers.

That's what a feature can do. As Memory Memo 10.2 highlights, a feature can communicate those intangible factors of an organization that can't be captured in a news release. Feature stories can show the personality, the passion, the humor and the commitment propelling an organization toward its goals. For many PR communication tasks, those are the most important story components we need to tell our publics. Thus, in formulating a media relations campaign, we should often concentrate on obtaining feature stories from a few sources important to our target publics rather than attempting to send releases to scores of outlets.

> **MEMORY MEMO 10.2**  Feature Coverage Versus News Releases: Features ...
>
> - Better communicate intangibles concerning an organization and its people
> - Gain credibility by being told from a journalist's perspective
> - Are generally longer than coverage from releases
> - May save staff time since journalists often write them

It's feasible to conduct a media relations campaign focused on feature story placement. Feature stories are a prominent component of virtually every medium, including newspapers, internet news services, radio and television. In magazines, virtually all the stories are features except for departments (those short sections that recur each month). Newspapers battling with broadcast media for breaking news use features to provide their readers a more in-depth look. Internal media, such as employee intranets, newsletters and even annual stockholder reports use the feature form frequently.

## What Is a Feature Story?

It's hard to define what a feature story is because there are so many different types, but they can be divided into two basic kinds: a news feature and a special feature.

A news feature probes behind the scenes to explore the social and ethical ramifications of daily news events. For instance, a story examining the political effects of legalizing a controversial new birth control drug would be a news feature; it could focus on the drug company scientists working to develop safer contraceptives, or follow anti-abortion activists on their weekend protests at family planning clinics.

A feature can also concern a topic that isn't breaking news. Such special interest features include stories like the history of parsley or an interview with a popular entertainer. Stories on exotic beach resorts fit into the same general interest feature category, as does the humorous story structured like a consumer report rating the best snow sleds for adults.

There are many opportunities to place feature stories in media outlets. Historical features might highlight the 50th anniversary of a company's local plant or a horrible epidemic that led to establishing a local research hospital. An airline's communications practitioner might pitch a story on South American mountain climbing, to which her airline flies, of course. How-to features, like a story pitched by a security firm on choosing burglar alarm features, are also common.

As you can see by the subject matter range, feature stories aren't defined so much by their topic as their method of presentation. Because of their format, feature stories aren't used for **spot news** coverage. No medium has the space and no editor has the staff time to make every news item a feature. Whereas a spot news story usually answers little more than the who, what, where, when, why and how of an event, a feature story involves much more research, sometimes extensive database or document searches and hours or even weeks of interviewing subjects and following them through their normal activities.

Finally, feature stories are generally united by their more descriptive language, including such literary devices as metaphors and similes, which help bring readers an in-depth understanding of the topic and the people involved in it. While spot news stories and news releases rely exclusively on independent sources to verify the stories' facts, feature stories generally allow reporters to draw some form of supported judgment from the information they collect. In a feature story, a writer might suggest that a particular issue is the most important one of the next decade or even that a celebrity is vastly overrated.

However, before the enthusiasm of respectively touting or trashing your most and least favorite causes overtakes you, note this caveat: These must be *supported* judgments. You must have facts gleaned from your research or interview sources to back your opinions. The only difference is that in a news story with a persuasive communication use, you need sources to build your case and then you must get someone else to voice your conclusion. In a feature story, you need sources to build your case, but then you may choose to voice your own conclusion from those facts.

## Writing the Feature Story

Although some writing texts assert the feature story employs a completely different prose structure, we find more similarities with inverted pyramid writing than differences. We'll review several types of features employing inverted pyramid format, but with a modified style for opening and ending.

### The Feature Lede

The feature lede doesn't begin with the news release's rapid-fire recital of all the elements of self-interest, Instead, features more often develop reader interest with inventive language or interesting situations. Also, unlike inverted-pyramid style, which don't include summary statements, features generally include some sort of resolution.

**Strategic Thought**

What type of evidence do you think is necessary if you're asserting that you made a "supported judgment" about a topic or a person in a feature story? How would you define differences in these standards between spot news stories and feature stories?

There are many types of feature ledes placed atop an inverted pyramid. The summary lede is most similar to the news release lede. A summary lede immediately introduces an important fact identifying the story topic and involving the reader's interest or self-interest. Sometimes the lede merely identifies what the story will be about:

> Three recent high-rise disasters are forcing hotels to reevaluate their fire warning and protection devices.

Sometimes the facts are much more shocking:

> Sex isn't dirty anymore—it's dangerous.

Some feature stories begin by describing the situation in which the story will take place. Sometimes, you'll see these referred to as narrative ledes:

> Imagine a lawn, beautifully green, mowed a uniform inch-and-a-quarter high, stretching unbroken by household fences or subdivision streets from Maine to California, from Washington state to Florida.
>
> That's a fantasy for people who like yards. I don't.

This is also a description lede:

> Outside a tidy South Miami house bordered by yellow flowers crouch six police officers wearing camouflage jumpsuits, their faces mottled with black paint. All clutch AR-15 semi-automatic rifles against their chests.

Among the easiest feature ledes to write are question ledes and quotation ledes. If they grab reader interest with a provocative question that has some relation to the reader's life, question ledes can be acceptable. Here's one recruiting participants for a marriage counseling class:

> How do you rate as a lover?

Here's another question lede, this one inviting people to a charity's amateur sleuth weekend:

> Could you kill someone in cold blood?

These two question ledes have some merit. They use shock to lure a logical target audience for the PR message into the story. But all too often question ledes sound more confounding than compelling. For instance, if you were a stamp collector, would you know this story was targeted to you?

> What do Walt Disney, baby buggies and killer whales have in common?

This last question lede is effective only when qualified with additional information—namely, that the U.S. Postal Service will feature all three on commemorative stamps. Without an element of shock or intrigue, the question lede has little allure. In such situations, ask the question in your head, and just write the answer as a summary lede:

> Commemorative stamps featuring Walt Disney, baby buggies and killer whales will be issued by the U.S. Postal Service this year.

While all these ledes have their place in journalistic writing and persuasive tasks as well, there's one type, the focus lede, which seems best suited to the persuasive tasks we face in strategic communication.

### The Focus Feature

The focus feature's effectiveness stems from our tendency to be overwhelmed when we face enormous problems. However, if we can reduce a problem to how it affects one human being, each reader can develop sympathy and empathy that lead to understanding. There but for the grace of God, go I.

Here's an example. ChildFund International annually raises about a quarter billion dollars to help poor children. However, it doesn't base its campaign on asking you to help the millions of children who need to be schooled, clothed and fed. Instead, the fund, whose advertising tagline is "Change the world, one child at a time," asks you to help one child, a child much like one you know. Flashing pictures of individual children with pleading expressions convince us to forgo a cup of coffee a day to help *this* child. The organization intensifies this identification by offering online tools letting donors select an individual child to sponsor. Among the options is birth date, so you could sponsor a child with the same birthday as you, a friend or family member.[5]

This is a sound strategy considering what we know from the situational theory of publics. One barrier to action is constraint: If we feel our action can't meaningfully solve the problem, we don't act at all. And while it may be true we can't individually solve global crises—at least not quickly—we can chip away at them. That's the power of ChildFund's appeal. By asking us to focus the tangible help we can provide on a single child, the organization removes that constraint and a barrier to action.

That's the power the focus feature structure harnesses (Figure 10.1). If we can show a huge problem through the eyes of one human being, we can get people to care about the problem and believe they can do something about it.

In **Click-Through 10.4**, you can study in full a focus feature that examines farm safety through an incident in which a child witnesses his father being hurt in a serious accident. In the next few pages, we'll extract sections from this story to illustrate how to build a focus feature.

The focus feature has the inverted pyramid at its heart, but it starts and ends with a focus on one individual, a person who through her own struggle or triumph represents all the people affected by the issue. Here's the first sentence of the farm safety story from **Click-Through 10.4**:

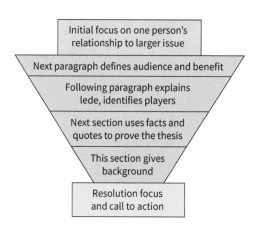

FIGURE 10.1 **The Focus Feature Inverted Pyramid.**

Larry Milchewski was a little boy of 7, isolated on the vast western Nebraska plains, when he saw the violence of the farm for the first time.

### The Critical Incident

By the end of the first paragraph, we're already involved in Milchewski's personal tragedy. This is what we call a **critical incident**, and the persuasive effect of many feature stories will be strengthened by including one. A critical incident is an identifiable instance in a person's life in which she is confronted with the manifestations of a much larger reality. In Milchewski's case, the critical incident is the story of his father's death, a memory that draws us into caring about the issue of rural health care.

"I remember it was a warm, late spring twilight and I was sitting on the tractor's fender," Milchewski said. "My dad was rushing to get several more rounds plowed before we lost the sun behind the hills surrounding our bottom ground."

As the tractor picked up ground speed, suddenly and without warning, the hitch holding the plow onto the tractor's underside shattered. No longer anchored to the tractor, the plow pivoted on the lift arms, swung out of the ground and, in a rapid arc, that half-ton of cast iron and steel came down on Milchewski's father in the seat beside Milchewski.

"I still get sick thinking about the sound," Milchewski said. "There was this loud snap, this chilling scratching of metal against metal. I saw the blur of the plow fly in front of my face, and then the plow recoiled like a cannon and fell back onto the ground."

Although Milchewski, inches away from his father, was unhurt, the plow's impact snapped eight of his father's ribs and drove his face into the 3/8-inch iron spokes of the steering wheel.

"Dad had the presence of mind to shut down the tractor, but when he turned to me there was blood covering his face," Milchewski said. "He spit some blood out of his mouth, then told me to run and get my two older brothers who were working in another field about a half mile away."

The three boys were able to pull their father off the tractor. They placed him as gingerly as possible in the family's pickup truck. But without an ambulance service and with the nearest hospital 60 miles away, the boys' father died at the town's doctor's office.

It's vital for a critical incident to show one human's personal relationship to the larger issue. In a story on a back-to-nature movement, the critical incident might be a humorous experience of a city-bred business executive trying to milk a cow. For a report on racism against Asian Americans, it might be a childhood reminiscence of the first day in a new school. Remember that you're not writing someone's life story, just the critical incident that led them to a larger truth.

Telling the critical incident requires the more informal language of storytelling. Unlike the news release, the focus feature demands attention because of a shared empathy and interest in another person's life rather than the audience's self-interest in the subject.

In a focus feature, you don't stuff the story's most important elements into the first sentence. Instead, introduce the focus individual. Identify her with a title or description. Whatever you do, don't talk about groups of people. As soon as you begin to talk about a group of people or a situation, your readers instantly lose their ability to empathize with an individual.

Within the first sentence, also try to mention one important element that helps frame the story topic. In the paragraph we included earlier, you'll see that after the first sentence we know Milchewski has farm ties and a tragic story to tell. There's nothing in the focus lede that defines the self-interest the TIPCUP news formula demands. Our attention to the story is instead dictated by our curiosity about another person's life and our shared humanity.

The remainder of the initial focus is different from the release style too. Because you are telling a story, the critical incident will almost always be structured chronologically: What happened first? Then what happened? What did that cause?

The most common problem writers experience in composing the critical incident is that they tend to omit important intervening events. That makes it difficult to develop empathy for the individual or understand the motivation for her feelings or actions.

Sometimes that initial scenario demands one paragraph, sometimes five or six. You're trying to establish the sense of a person so your readers can identify with her, so include details that personalize the focus individual and add to your readers' understanding and empathy. It's also important to link the critical incident's paragraphs with strong transitions. By concentrating on the "what happened next" questions of the chronological structure, you'll do that naturally.

However, some writers also try to develop a theme that unites the story. Look at the opening of a story on a group of people who were fooled by a prank call:

> The holidays came early for Holly Gingiss when she received a call Tuesday night telling her she had won a new car, a car she could pick up the next morning at a local car dealership.
>
> "Waiting for my car was just like being a kid on Christmas Eve," Gingiss said. "I couldn't sleep at all that night."
>
> That holiday feeling ended early Wednesday morning when she, along with 28 other people, showed up in front of Foss Ford only to discover they had all been victims of a prank caller.

The writer developed a theme from Gingiss' quote, "a kid on Christmas Eve." From that initial suggestion, the writer has drawn a unifying concept of "holidays," with which she introduces each paragraph in the initial focus. You'll notice the similarities of this technique with the memory-cue transitions we discussed in Chapter 7. Memory Memo 10.3 summarizes important considerations in writing a focus feature lede.

### Transition to Larger Issue

After the initial focus is completed and you've finished telling the critical incident, you're ready to transition to the larger issue.

This is a simple, nearly mechanical step that demonstrates how the critical incident and the person you described in the initial focus relate to the story's main issue. The transitions invariably use phrases like "Friedman is just one of the 3 million Americans who suffer from this disease" or "Bhutto's mechanical flyswatter is on display alongside 200 other wacky inventions at the French industrial trade show."

In the transition, you are making an explicit tie between your focus subject and the main issue. Although there are slight variations (notice in the hoax story the transition is " ... she, along with 28 other people"), a significant number of the transitions to the larger issue use form use some variation of words *one of.*

Here's the same principle at work in the farm safety story:

That's Milchewski's horror story. It's a frightening experience that is shared in some fashion or another by virtually every person who's been around farming for very long.

But now there's evidence that there aren't going to be so many of these horrible stories to tell in the future.

### The Body of the Focus Feature

Once you've established the transition, you're basically writing an inverted pyramid. First, there's a **nut paragraph**, which functions like a news release's lede paragraph, in which you tell the reader what the story is about. In the farm safety story, notice that the nut paragraph is a summary lede and could stand independently as the first paragraph of a news release.

According to government experts and National Safety Council reports, farming has become safer because of better equipment design, more professional emergency medical services in rural areas, and a greater awareness among farmers of the dangers all around them.

As you might expect, the nut paragraph is followed by information contextualizing the story, exactly what the inverted pyramid's second paragraph accomplishes.

In subsequent paragraphs you prove the nut paragraph's assertion, presenting those anecdotes, quotes and statistics that fit one of the pyramid's argument structures (order of importance, problem-solution, chronology). Background and procedural information are saved for later paragraphs.

### *The Ending of a Feature Story*

The focus feature's final element brings closure and is the second major difference between a feature story and straight news style.

In a focus feature, the **resolution focus** returns the reader's attention to an individual. By so doing, it exploits the powerful empathy inherent in the focus feature to suggest solutions the reader can participate in. Sometimes the resolution focus returns to the same person whose story you told in the initial focus, sometimes to a different person involved in the same issue. The same principles you employed in selecting the initial focus apply to the resolution focus. You're looking for a quote or a scenario involving an individual in order to effectively resolve the discussion of the larger issue. As such it serves the same purpose as the call to action in a release.

Obviously, a resolution focus sometimes presents itself when the individual involved in the initial focus has solved the problem affecting her at the story's outset. Sometimes the ending focus will come from a quotation that suggests a new governmental policy or a new social or personal action that will resolve the conflict.

The farm safety story returns in its final section to Milchewski's emotional response to seeing farmers' children attending his safety meetings. Here's that story, showing the last paragraph of the inverted pyramid and the memory-cue transition into the resolution focus:

> "That's why the new labeling requirements for pesticides and farm chemicals the council has gotten are so important," Newberg said. "The public has to be made more conscious of health hazards that might not kill you in one horrible accident, but whose long-term consequences are just as deadly."
>
> That new attitude toward safety may be the biggest improvement the council can claim, according to Milchewski. "That's where I've personally been most successful," he said. "Every time I go out to a farm group to speak and talk about my father dying on that tractor, I look at the boys and girls in the audience. They've already seen so many near-tragedies that they can immediately project themselves into a situation where they've almost lost a parent. And the parents know of times when they've almost left their kids as orphans."

In Milchewski's case, he hoped his involvement might help effect a solution. At other times, the resolution focus is simply a discouraged shoulder shrug with the discovery that there isn't any resolution—at least yet. The phone hoax story mentioned earlier ended with a dejected "winner," her body bent down in cold rain, trudging back to her old, dented car.

Finally, remember virtually all PR writing is persuasive writing, so it's necessary to integrate a call to action into the focus feature's final section. Establish the important lesson you want the audience to take away from the story or suggest an action the reader can follow to remedy the situation. An effective way to accomplish this is to integrate a powerful quote showing your source's courage, commitment and passion into the feature's final paragraph. You'll see this in the farm safety story:

"It's that new awareness I'm most proud of," Milchewski said. "Farmers have to be involved enough in the political process and in their own personal actions so there will never again be another kid who is forced to see his father killed in a farm accident. We just can't accept that nightmare as a normal part of farm life anymore."

## Interview Attribution

Many writers have one more problem to overcome in producing features: They have trouble deciding what to quote. We've observed student writers filling paragraph after paragraph with interminably dull quotes. It's almost as common that writers endlessly paraphrase, with only a few quotes salting pages of prose.

Both approaches are wrong. As a working writer, you have a distinct prose voice—certainly professional and correct, and hopefully lively. But your voice, charming as it may be, gets tedious after a while. In the same way, your source's voice grows tiresome if left blathering too long. You want to balance your own voice with that of your interview sources so your reader can enjoy both of them.

## What to Quote

Which quotes do you pick? That's a question with no easy answers. When you quote someone, you want to bring the essence of her personality into the story. You want to show another human being dealing with the day's problems and prospects.

What does personality-revealing language mean in the real-life decisions of selecting what to quote? Here's one: In general, don't quote procedures. For instance, this is a bad quote:

> "If our city has over 100 applicants for the supplemental rental program, the federal housing office will approve a waiver for new housing construction," Percy said.

This is just as bad:

> "The children who are entering kindergarten need to have their doctors give them their measles shots before they'll be allowed to attend," Downs said.

Neither quote displays humanity or humor or life. They showcase bureaucracy and tedium. As a writer, you should distill the precise information your audience needs to know, especially when you can say it more quickly and interestingly than your source. So generally, paraphrase procedures.

**Strategic Thought**

What are some of the ethical issues involved with using quotations from interviewing? For instance, what if the speaker uses inappropriate or taboo language? What if the speaker uses poor grammar? Do you change the quotation so it is standard English, or retain it exactly as the person said it? Would you follow the same rules on quoting poor grammar if the interviewee were well-educated?

However, you'll often get quotes that contain colorful language or reveal a pleasant, or even a disagreeable, personality trait. If that occurs, consider using the quote. Let's look at the preceding quotes for instances in which you could quote those very same sources.

You'd definitely quote this gem from Percy:

> "Those idiots at the federal housing office won't let us build a single new apartment house until we've got 100 families screaming for places to rent."

Similarly, use Downs' words if she gives you this:

> "When measles took that little Wichita boy last year, I vowed not a single 5-year-old child would enter our school's doors without being vaccinated."

Those quotes sing with human exuberance and passion. They introduce personality and a welcome new voice into your story.

There's another time when you need to quote: When the information revealed in the quote is so unbelievable that your credibility would be doubted if you paraphrased it. That holds true even if you're quoting procedural information.

Let's say a national crime expert offers you this quote:

> "The media cited 250,000 child kidnapping cases last year, but my search of police files found only 88 children were kidnapped by strangers during the last 12 months."

That is news so unexpected that you need to verify the accuracy of your reporting by quoting it.

## Integrating Quotations Into a Feature Story

Now that you know a little bit about selecting quotes, you need to know how to weave them into your story.

One common mistake is relying too much on the phrase *when asked* to introduce quotes. Using "when asked" unnecessarily puts the writer into the story by making her a conscious presence in the reader's mind. It also detracts from the quote's power. Consider a paragraph with this opening:

> When asked why he keeps trying to escape from prison, Jones replied, "I look at every prison wall like it's Mt. Everest. I climb over it because it's there."

You've buried a wonderful quote that could glue your audience in the story for at least another paragraph. "When asked" doesn't offer the reader any hint of the intriguing quote to follow.

There's a better way to do this. As television's "Jeopardy" illustrates, any question can be rephrased as a statement. Thus, instead of saying "when asked," you could turn the question-like phrase into a statement:

> Breaking out of jail is like a mountain-climber's quest, Jones said. "I look at every prison wall like it's Mt. Everest," he said. "I climb over it because it's there."

Rephrasing the introduction to the quote in this way allows you to emphasize the information that keeps readers interested in the story. You'll note it uses the same principle as the memory-cue transitions discussed in Chapter 7.

Final thought. Every quote, just like every word in a story, must push the story to its logical conclusion. There will be times in your professional writing life when you'll be presented with a wonderful quote brimming with backwoods wisdom, a mother's love or the hard-edged glint of a corporate manager. Although it might be a wonderful quote from the story's main source, if it doesn't have anything to do with the story you're writing, don't use it. Everything must add to the story's central effect. If it doesn't, drop it. Memory Memo 10.4 helps remind you of this, as well as your responsibilities in handling quotes.

## Multichannel News Releases and Features

Practitioners often prepare news releases for multichannel, as well as print outlets. Even though they're called video news releases, VNRs are prepared more like the feature stories discussed in this chapter. However, they integrate Chapter 8's multichannel writing principles into feature structures.

It's still important to find a critical incident, except now it's imperative to find one you can illustrate with sound, vision and motion. Just like print writers, multichannel writers need to examine their source materials critically for those quotes that display the speaker's passion and commitment about the subject.

You must support your thesis with sound arguments: Now you need to find sound effects or visuals to accompany and reinforce your reasoning.

Transitions are just as important, except now you weave identifying sound effects or video footage into the announcer's narrative.

Even the basic structural elements of multichannel releases and features are the same. Focus feature structures are as common in audio and video features as in print. But now you are presenting your stories in dramatically abridged versions. A 1,200-word print feature may be truncated to a 400-word video feature running for only one minute and 45 seconds. The same feature story prepared for a radio newscast might last only 35 seconds.

Given those time limitations, it's even more important to exploit all the opportunities sound and motion offer. Reviewing Chapter 8's script and storyboard format guidelines will help you focus the powers of the particular medium you're using. In Click-Through 10.5, you can see how the farm safety print feature was adapted to a multichannel format.

## Writing Query Letters

As a persuasive writer, you'll often be writing feature stories for internal publications and web-distributed channels. You might succeed in placing feature stories you've produced into small-city newspapers and broadcast stations and in some specialty magazines and websites.

However, most feature stories seen in major daily newspapers and in bigger circulation magazines are written by staff members. The same is true for feature stories produced by major broadcast outlets. You've still got an excellent chance of placing feature stories in those media outlets, but you often employ other strategies to introduce editors to story ideas they'll assign to their own writers.

If you've established a good professional relationship with an editor, you might be able to phone her (yes, people still make phone calls), briefly describe the proposed feature and hope she'll assign it to a reporter. If you haven't worked with that editor before, you should take a more formal approach. A query letter, or a direct pitch, usually delivered via email, is your best bet.

---

### CASE IN POINT 10.4   Standard Format for Pitches/Query Letters

**Subject Line**: 60–70 Characters Describing the Story Pitch Is Typically Best

Dear Reporter's Name:

Query letters work best when there's a personal relationship. If you're not on a first-name basis with the reporter you're targeting, it helps to hyperlink to some of her past work. This lets her know you understand what she covers and how your story pitch fits her beat.

If that relationship already exists, then jump right in. Start with something akin to a feature story lede that highlights the story topic and connects it to some audience interest. Statements like "I thought your readers might be interested … " or "Your viewers may want to know … " or "Policy changes could affect many of your viewers … " accomplish this goal well.

The next paragraph resembles the news release's second paragraph. It explains major players and concepts referenced in your introductory paragraph to provide needed context.

From there, you briefly fill in the narrative gaps and provide compelling statistics, facts or quoted anecdotes that drive home the importance of the topic and the story surrounding it.

As you finish the query letter, think of yourself as a salesperson. By this point you've hopefully engaged the reporter's interest. Now you must seal the deal by outlining ways in which you can help her write the story. Do you have any photos, actualities or b-roll? Or maybe just access to interview subjects? Would facility tours be helpful? Basically, anything she needs to do the story well, you should try to provide.

Generally, because features require more resources to produce than spot news, they're pitched as exclusives, meaning you're reserving this story for this reporter. But you can't wait on reporters for very long because you have your own time constraints. Let her know you'll be contacting her soon to gauge her interest or provide further details. If she's noncommittal, don't be afraid to move on.

Sincerely,

Your name and email signature

P.S.—Include postscripts. They stand out from the letter and thus draw attention. If you have any important elements you want to reinforce or an extra kicker to introduce, this is the place.

A **query letter** is a composite creation, essentially an abridged feature story of three-to-five paragraphs melded to a sales letter, which is sent via email, direct messaging on social media or whatever medium a particular gatekeeper prefers. The query letter tells an editor or reporter what your story idea can offer, how information about the subject will fulfill the needs of her audience and how she can obtain the story.

Case in Point 10.4 illustrates the structure and purpose of a query letter, while Click-Through 10.6 shows a full-text example. A pitch essentially begins with a feature story lede attached to a statement acknowledging the gatekeeper's self-interest. Because there is so little space, a query letter usually does not use a focus feature's initial focus structure but a more traditional feature lede. Here's the first sentence from Click-Through 10.6:

> I thought your health-conscious readers might be interested in St. Vincent's newest health care worker, one that is a super laboratory technician, nurse and consulting physician.

The second paragraph is equivalent to the second paragraph in a news release. It explains the lede and the story explicitly so the editor will know precisely what the rest of the letter will contain.

The next one, two or three paragraphs summarize the body of the feature story, giving a few snappy facts, statistics or attributed opinions supporting the statements you've made in the first and second paragraphs.

---

**MEMORY MEMO 10.5** Guidelines for Writing Query Letters

- Establish story lede and journalists' benefit in first sentence
- Explain the lede completely in the second paragraph
- Give highlights of feature story in middle paragraphs
- Restate benefit to audience and present call to action in last paragraph

Up to now, you've merely shortened a feature story into three or four paragraphs. Now the structure transforms into a sales letter. The next paragraph usually contains a very explicit statement telling how the story's information can satisfy the gatekeeper's responsibilities to her audience.

Because a query letter is persuasive communication, the end is reserved for call-to-action specifics. In this case, there's information detailing how the gatekeeper can develop such a wonderful story for her audience. Usually, this paragraph names the person or organization particularly knowledgeable in this field (including your client, of course) and offers a reporter an interview or other research opportunities. The final sentence usually states that you'll follow up on the query letter soon.

Here's how our example involved the editor's self-interests and includes call-to-action details:

> If you think your health-conscious readers might want to know about this high-tech health care professional that will serve them during their next hospital stay, I'd be glad to help you contact St. V's doctors and technicians, who are finding new computer health applications every day. I'll follow up within the next several days to check on your plans.

You can review query letter guidelines in Memory Memo 10.5.

## Working With Media Gatekeepers

The news media will continue to be an important outlet for persuasive communicators. However, we need to recognize journalists' goals and how they function if we want to improve our relationships and our performance. We must limit the excessive number of news releases many of us have been flooding onto their laptops and smartphones. Instead, let's concentrate our efforts on delivering story ideas that help them fulfill their duties to their readers and complement our organizational goals.

Our task with gatekeepers is the same as our task with any other audiences: to target our messages precisely to fulfill their goals and our goals. With the writing techniques you've learned in this chapter and the delivery techniques you will discover in Chapter 11, you'll be improving your own, as well as your colleagues' future relationship with journalists.

### SUMMARY

- Because gatekeepers can effectively limit information from reaching consumers through uncontrolled media, it's necessary for practitioners to anticipate the gatekeeper's needs and provide that information in an easily usable format.

- There are alternatives to media releases that can more readily meet a gatekeeper's needs for information, like query letters, photo opportunity teasers and calendar announcements.

- The focus feature captures the audience's interest and involvement by capitalizing on readers' ability to empathize with an individual. The focus lede concentrates on an individual's involvement in a critical incident in which a person confronts a larger issue. That critical incident and an ending resolution focus employ an inverted pyramid structure to pose the story's main arguments.

### Scenario Prompts: Crafting Uncontrolled Messages

You'll find Scenario Prompts on pp. 367–386 of this textbook. While they vary in subject and difficulty, they help you hone your critical thinking and strategic writing skills. The following are best suited to this chapter's topics.

**Management: 7.2 / Writing:** 1.6, 1.7, 1.11, 2.4, 3.6, 4.5, 5.5, 5.6, 6.5, 6.6, 6.7, 7.6, 9.4, 10.6, 10.7

# Delivering Uncontrolled Messages
## Reaching Media Gatekeepers

---

## LESSONS FROM LIFE    Managing the Uncontrollable

Media relations is traditionally the most predominant task occupying a PR practitioner's day. It's also one of the most exhausting, and often the one most fraught with peril.

In my personal hall of infamy? How about when my live event was to be covered by three local TV stations. Unfortunately, an ill-timed water main break in a small suburban city and its resulting mud puddle lured all three stations' remote crews away from my client's coverage. The result: my hours of hard work turned into no coverage.

There was the time when a concert headliner had to make a last-minute cancellation. I was told by her music booking agency that the substitute musician forced to fill in for that night's concert was an Argentinian guitarist who didn't speak English. The Spanish-speaking translator I recruited within the next three hours was of little use when the metro newspaper's music critic turned up to interview a Brazilian cellist who spoke only Portuguese.

Media relations is one of those pursuits in which hard work is necessary to do it right, but in which fickle communication gods can bring it all to naught.

But when it works, it can be very fulfilling. There was the time I conceived, produced and promoted at my very proper music conservatory an all-classical music cartoon festival—on April Fool's Day. I promoted an evening of chamber music, which I purposefully scheduled against the NFL championship—timing the concert downbeat exactly to the kickoff—and billed as an activity for people who hated the Super Bowl. I got lots of media from reporters tired of decades of writing Super Bowl hype, and a profitable audience.

You may not rate these moments as glorious triumphs. I can certainly guarantee many of you taking this course will far surpass what I've done. However, I hope you can claim what I'm most proud of—that your organization was better because you were its communicator that day.

—WT

---

## What You Know

- Audiences comprise subgroups that take the same action, but for different motives.

- The TIPCUP filter is used to compose lede sentences designed to attract specific target publics.

- Relationships with media gatekeepers are more productive when persuasive messages are matched to their outlet's needs.

**What You'll Learn**

- How to incorporate audience-centered writing tactics to engage different media outlets in covering your organization's message

- How a spectrum of reference works provide insights into audience characteristics of individual media outlets

- How to use database searches to quickly compile tightly focused media lists for targeted communication campaigns

## Building Stories From the Outlet Up

In previous chapters, we've learned the basic techniques of writing effective strategic communication pieces. It remains important to fit the message to the audience to which it is directed; to fashion efficient, well-structured prose; and to make sure your writing style and presentation do not detract from your communication purpose.

The same principles apply to delivering PR messages to the external media. TV news directors, newspapers, blog writers and other media professionals need and want writing intended for their specific audiences. Your job as a strategic communicator is to research your subject and research the media covering your subject so you'll know all the outlets interested in your message and their specific needs. You'll also need to know the technology available to help tailor those messages to specific media, to help you select the appropriate platform and then deliver it effectively.

This chapter explores your relationship with and responsibilities to the media. We'll examine how to use research and technology to target, and then deliver, your PR messages. It's a strategy that will build your credibility with journalists, which will make your communication campaigns more effective and improve your long-term relationships with media professionals.

## The Zero-Sum Game

First thing: media relations is a zero-sum game. Every medium has a finite news hole every day. Your local TV station's evening news program might be 30 or 60 minutes long. Let's say the station's news hole (which is the program's duration, minus the sports, weather, commercials and announcer banter) will accommodate three longer news packages and four one- or two-sentence news items read by the anchors.

If you've pitched that day's fourth most important or watchable feature, your client's story doesn't make that evening's news. That's a zero-sum game. If someone else wins, you lose. The same news-hole limitation prevails for print media and around-the-clock news networks. Even internet-based news sites are limited by bandwidth and site formatting constraints, not to mention the money and staff time they can invest in producing content.

It's like you're a grocer trying to sell fish whose expiration date is that very day. If your competitor next door has a better product, you'll end the day throwing away fish that you paid good money for eight hours earlier.

In fact, it's useful to think of your news releases and story pitches as products. As a strategic communicator, you create a product similar to those other communicators manufacture. You're in competition with all of them for those precious few slots in the specific media outlets that enable you to communicate with your client's audience. To win, you must have a story the gatekeepers serving your public want to buy.

## The Media Relations Relationship

True, there's an inherent tension between journalists and PR professionals. However, we need each other to survive.[1] Media commentator and consultant Julia Hobsbawm made what she viewed as a "conservative" estimate that 50% to 80% of news and business stories emanate from media relations sources.[2] The media would have to hire many more reporters to obtain anything close to the coverage they currently provide through the help of PR practitioners.

As that relationship of mutual benefits suggests, your success in media relations depends on your ability to create a professional environment in which your media relations efforts help journalists do their jobs better. That means guiding editors, producers and reporters to stories that genuinely interest or help their audiences and provide that information in a way letting them accomplish their jobs most efficiently.

When you consistently deliver services mindful of the media's needs, you create a warm relationship with your contacts, and you'll be able to fulfill your organization's communication objectives effectively.

But as a newly minted strategic communicator, you must understand that the practitioners who preceded you haven't necessarily burnished your profession's reputation. Journalists are naturally frustrated by the sheer volume of news releases that daily flood their inboxes. A Los Angeles Times editor said he got about 500 media pitches every workday.[3] Editors regularly complain about the complete disregard for a local angle in news releases and about the bad writing and poor attention to journalistic style. They say there's too much self-serving puffery instead of news in many news releases—and they're right.

> **MEMORY MEMO 11.1** Outlining a Successful Media Relations Relationship
>
> - Media decision-makers: Adapt messages and delivery routines to accommodate their interests and work schedules
>
> - News hole: Plan events and news release timetables to coincide with slow news days
>
> - Market dynamics: Modify delivery systems to capitalize on placement opportunities in smaller markets or media outlets with specialized needs

### Receiver-Centered Media Relations: Knowing Your Audience's Audience

It helps to look upon your relationship with media gatekeepers as a communication act, distinct from yet interdependent with your final goal. Applying the audience-centered communication model we introduced in Chapter 2, you'll remember we first must find situations in which the information we have to communicate coincides with the journalist's interests and needs. Why are they interested in your information? They aren't trying to do you a favor by running information from your release; they are trying to deliver important information to their audiences.

That means you need to evaluate the audience each journalist serves. What are the audience's interests? How much discretionary income do they possess? Where do they live? From that information, and more like it, you can begin to predict the messages that will satisfy those needs.

After you decide on a message, you select an approach that most effectively transmits your message to the publics you need to fulfill your institutional objectives. In our opinion, this is where many PR people need to think more creatively.

## Beyond the Shotgun: Strategic Communication Delivery

Now that you know a little about your relationship with media members, we can begin to talk about operating within that role. Already, you've discovered there are several important components to be considered in designing any successful strategic communication campaign.

First, it's important to know the characteristics of the audience with whom you are trying to communicate. Second, you should prioritize the information in your message important for that audience and structure your information to most effectively involve that audience with your message. Third, you must employ a delivery system that credibly presents your message to people to whom it is important. Finally, the delivery system should do all this in the most efficient way possible.

### The Tool Chest

However, before you can build an effective media relations program, you must understand the tools at your disposal. Logically, when you possess a wider variety of tools, you can build more elaborate things. In media relations, you can employ scores of delivery approaches to reach hundreds of thousands of media outlets. This is your tool chest, which we believe many practitioners too rarely exploit.

Too often, they don't look upon media relations as a dynamic process, with strategies subject to change with each project. For instance, it's not uncommon for practitioners to compile one media list for all their companies' media announcement distributions. Usually, the list includes every outlet the organization perceives could offer a conduit to an important audience or coverage to the company. Once compiled, it's quite typical to ship every release to the entire list. This is called the **shotgun approach**, referring to its unfocused and over-broad delivery. The same release might go to a reporter at a major metropolitan newspaper, the producer of news programming at a rock music station, a popular blog writer and the editor of a locally focused magazine.

But if there's one aspect of persuasive writing we hope you have internalized, it's that for each strategic message, there are multiple audiences, each influenced by distinct motives. As a result, it's difficult for us to envision a campaign we could construct in which one release fit the needs of every audience in an organization's group of publics.

## The Non-Mass Media

The shotgun strategy is valid only if you believe there are no differences among communication media outlets. Some media critics tend to support that position, pointing to the decreasing number of competitive newspapers in big cities and the increasing number of media outlets owned by massive conglomerates.

There's also the perception, voiced by both conservative and progressive pundits, that the media has a single voice—a consistency of message and outlook—that deprives some viewpoints from gaining access to the media. They claim there's no discernable difference between a television station in Seattle (population ~750,000) and a small newspaper in rural Lincoln County, Georgia (population ~8,000).[4] They claim the media now speak with one, harping voice. They cite media conglomerates' frequent purchases of newspapers, television stations and magazines to support their position.

So, is there a single-voiced mass media? There's surprisingly little evidence to support that viewpoint. In fact, we would argue that during the past 40 years, media content has become much more diverse, not less.

Yes, few medium-sized cities have competing daily newspapers. A limited number of conglomerates own the remaining city dailies and even small-market weeklies. A few media corporations own the majority of the nation's television stations.

However, think of your own media habits. Where do you get news informing your passions and interests? Do you still subscribe to a newspaper? Is network television your exclusive source for news? Do you turn to social media as a news aggregator?

Consider basic cable content. Among our cable channels, we can find the latest commentary on the Nikkei stock market index in Japanese. Want updates on Armenian political happenings? How about entertainment programming in Hindi? They're all on basic cable, along with networks completely devoted to cooking, crime, celebrities, history, science fiction, real estate and other specific subjects. That's nothing your parents or grandparents could access.

And what about blogs and internet coverage? A single blogging platform, Tumblr, reported in December 2020 it was hosting 512.6 million blogs. That's the equivalent of one out of every 15 people on Earth—every man, woman and newborn; every Nepalese Sherpa; every ailing senior in a care facility—writing or sponsoring a blog on Tumblr.[5]

Admittedly, certain individuals and organizations manage more than one blog. Nevertheless, that many blogs mean subjects get very specific. It seems every special-interest club or school organization has its own internet site. There are multiple outlets informing you about replacing your car's radiator, using a curling iron, or styling your Emo look.

Then things can get really hyper-targeted. Do you have an unquenched desire to learn about people arrested in New Castle, Pennsylvania, between 1930 and 1960? Check out smalltownnoir.com. Wonder how medieval experts would solve your own contemporary problems, like battling a hangover or determining if someone is dead? Consult askthepast.blogspot.com.

In short, while it's true that mass media ownership has become concentrated, simultaneously the variety of topics available to media consumers has exploded. That leaves you, as a strategic communicator, with a vast array of choices regarding message placement.[6]

## Targeting Specialized Audiences

It makes sense to target your publics more precisely. All too often, strategic communicators have produced one single release on an event or issue and expected it to satisfy the needs of every editor, every producer, every industry blogger. But as we've seen, those media people represent increasingly specialized audiences who look to us for more and more specialized information. What are the implications of these fundamental changes in the media market?

**Strategic Thought**

Do specialized media have more credibility than general media? What other elements help form a message's credibility? What is the connection between message credibility and audiences accepting and acting upon your message?

First, you need to realize that each of those media outlets—broadcast and cable stations, online news services and blogs—is a resource from which you can build your communication campaign. You should view each of those outlets not merely as email addresses to send your organization's releases but as representatives of individuals united by a common interest or quality.

Such increased specialization makes every outlet more valuable, because now you can increasingly target only those audiences for whom your information is vital. Because of the increasingly narrow audiences media outlets serve, it's more likely you can predict what information a specific publication or multichannel outlet wishes to communicate to its audience. Where previously you might have distributed scores, maybe even thousands of news releases, you can now ship releases to only those outlets interested in your message. That can help you cut the cost of your campaigns and nurture valuable relationships with critical gatekeepers.

---

## PRINCIPLES IN PRACTICE 11.1   PR's Place in the New Journalism Model

Is the press release dead? Scholars and practitioners have been writing the media release's obituary for about as long as either of us can remember.[7] Those death knells became increasingly rampant with the growth of online media.

In truth these prognosticators are mostly reiterating what seasoned practitioners have known for years: a press release isn't the be-all-end-all of media relations.[8] Sometimes a press release is an effective medium for delivering your message to your target public, sometimes not. Understanding gatekeepers' needs at a particular moment guides the media relations strategies and tactics of successful professionals.[9]

But what about the internet? Hasn't it revolutionized the way PR practitioners communicate to and with journalists? Well, yes and no. The widespread use of email beginning in the 1990s increased the immediacy with which practitioners can reach journalists, and the growth of social media as both a means to interact with journalists and break news directly has certainly created new possibilities.[10]

More importantly, these new technologies have transformed the economic model in which journalists operate. News outlets, particularly newspapers, have seen many of their advertising revenues shift to online and social media channels. Many outlets have responded by slashing their reporting staffs, a trend the U.S. Department of Labor expects to result in 32% fewer journalists working for newspapers, broadcast and online in 2026 than were employed in 2005.[11]

Since there will presumably be at least as much news and information to communicate in 2026, journalism is adopting different news-gathering models. As major dailies shed reporters while adding internet distribution, the remaining journalists assume new and more diverse roles. Newspaper reporters, while still gathering and writing stories for the print edition, are trained to capture audio and video for the outlet's website.

Another response? Work the remaining reporters harder. A study of journalists working for newspapers with circulations under 50,000—which represents 98% of all papers—reported many regularly working over 50 hours per week.[12]

A third model? Some publishers simply stop anticipating that in a digital world they can make a profit. Instead, entrepreneurs are starting nonprofit news organizations to supplement or supplant local news coverage with donor-funded journalism.[13] These organizations actively raise donations from their communities, freeing themselves from depending on subscriptions and sometimes even ad revenue. Examples are Mississippi Today, 48 Hills in San Francisco and the Honolulu City Beat. Noncommercial news organizations also thrive on the national level, with Mother Jones, PolitiFact, ProPublica and NPR among the more prominent voices.

The common thread? While the number of online news platforms expands, the number of warm bodies in newsrooms declines. So how do news-gathering organizations reconcile the math?

You get a hint by looking at employment projections. During the coming decade when the U.S. Commerce Department estimates journalism employment will go down 9%, the agency predicts the number of public relations specialists will increase 9%.[14]

A good guess is that journalists will rely even more on PR practitioner content, much of it coming from news releases. You can already spot those trends. For instance, both print and online news outlets often include sections that don't include bylines, labeling them "news digests." In many cases, those items are complete or abridged news releases. TV reporters introduce and bracket their comments around PR-produced video.

Public relations' subsidization of news coverage introduces issues of objectivity and judgment concerning what defines news. For instance, will we become increasingly likely to hear only about issues that affect the political fortunes and financial health of those people who can afford to employ PR professionals? Who will tell the stories of economic dislocation, political injustice or governmental corruption?

Those are significant questions. At minimum, the emerging situation demands that strategic communication writers master the form and standards of journalistic writing and produce copy with the knowledge that it may very well be the unmediated version our fellow citizens will perceive as journalistic news. So, no, the press release isn't dead, and the time you spend learning to write them effectively is worthwhile.

Specialization also means you can increase your message's credibility. For computer programmers, information they receive from publications like Extreme Technology or Network Computing will be much more believable than the same information appearing in a metropolitan newspaper. That additional credibility is a bonus to any communication campaign. To take advantage of this media specialization, we must deliver sophisticated, well-researched information desired by the editors, producers and writers creating content for each outlet.

The vital lesson you should draw here is that there are people interested in every conceivable topic, and they have coalesced in organizations and around media outlets focused on their passions. As a strategic communicator, your default assumption should be that your specific audience is out there. Your task now becomes a research effort to find them, and an economic and strategic decision concerning whether your communication efforts to reach them will be cost-effective for your organization.

## Media Databases
### Knowing Your Options

How do you find, and then reach, all the people to whom your message is important? What media outlets offer the most credibility for your message to the audience with whom you most want to communicate?

There are many reference databases that can help with that task. One of the most complete reference works for finding newspapers, magazines, and broadcast and cable systems in the United States and Canada is the Gale Directory of Publications and Broadcast Media.

The Gale Directory indexes more than 59,000 radio, television and cable systems—as well as publications, association magazines and newspapers—by the cities in which they are located. Thus, if you want to find nearly every media outlet in Chicago or in Eufaula, Alabama, it's possible to do that with the Gale Directory. Its listing of each radio and television station's original programming also assists in booking guests on talk shows and locally produced segments.

Need something more specialized? The Standard Periodical Directory classifies more than 58,000 publications either by type (newspapers, company publications, etc.) or by subject matter (genetics, cosmetics, babies, horses, etc.). It delves more deeply into topic-specific publications than the Gale Directory. The Standard Periodical Directory also gathers contact information on college newspapers; professional, scientific and technical journals; as well as directories and databases. It's particularly useful in locating newsletters, listing over 16,000, including email-distributed versions.

If you're looking for even more specialized publications, there are resources to help you with that too. Oxbridge Communications, publisher of The Standard Periodical Directory, also produces references explicitly compiling information for newsletters, magazines and catalogs. The Oxbridge Directory of Newsletters lists more than 13,000 North American newsletters, digests, updates and bulletins, indexing them by subject area. That makes it easy to find the names and addresses of newsletters, along with a detailed description of the publications' editorial interests, circulation and editors.

The subject categories listed in the newsletter directory are even more specific than those found in The Standard Periodical Directory. For instance, there are 10 subject categories listed under the general term "politics."

Oxbridge has consolidated the databases of its newsletter directory with The Standard Periodical Directory and two other publications, The National Directory of Catalogs and The National Directory of Magazines. That lets you expand your project-specific media campaign to reach additional target publics.

Need to conduct communication campaigns with self-identified enthusiasts for a particular vocation or avocation? The Encyclopedia of Associations is a multivolume reference source listing contact information for more than 23,000 organizations, associations, fraternal clubs and lobbying groups. Also published by Gale, it includes a truly broad scope of associations. There are large, well-known organizations like the American Bar Association, which conducts research and educational projects for its 410,000 members. It also

**MEMORY MEMO 11.2** Selected Resources for Media and Audience Research

| | |
|---|---|
| Encyclopedia of Associations | List of over 20,000 associations, purposes and publications |
| Gale Directory of Publications and Broadcast Media | List of print and broadcast outlets and cities' economic activities |
| Oxbridge Directory of Newsletters | Highly specialized, low-circulation web and print publications |
| Simmons National Consumer Survey | Consumer lifestyle and use of products correlated with media use |
| The Standard Periodical Directory | 20,000 U.S. and Canadian niche publications in 260 categories |
| MRI Survey of American Consumers | Product use and lifestyle data, with additional breakouts for Hispanics and youth consumers |
| National Directory of Magazines | Broad-based collection of 58,000 U.S. and Canadian magazines, newspapers, journals, newsletters |

**Strategic Thought**

Envision a media relations campaign for a bicycle company. How could you structure separate approaches segmented on age, income or geographic categories? What motives would you emphasize for each subcategory? What media outlets could you employ to most effectively reach each segment?

includes less celebrated groups, such as the Missouri-based American Council of Spotted Asses, which maintains a breeding registry and conducts competitions for this rare type of donkey. Most important for strategic communicators, it lists each organization's communication outlet and their distribution frequency.

### Harnessing Technology

All these media reference sources can help power your media relations efforts, letting you precisely target your public and isolate their motives for acting. However, you might see a practical problem in using these reference books. If you have 80,000 media outlets here, another 15,000 newsletters there and 78,000 more there, most with multiple editors, producers and writers—you start to have a huge problem keeping track of it all. With this wealth of resources, it's daunting to examine every one for possible media outlets for your client's messages.

Technology can help. Virtually every media directory exists in a database format accessible to computer searches, which tasks the search engine, not you, in examining each reference database looking for specific topics.

For example, let's say you are looking for all publications that have a major focus on raising chickens or that serve areas where chicken ranches are a significant industry. If you were conducting a manual search, that would mean examining the cross-indexes in all the reference books for publications about poultry and then examining individual entries to determine if the publication covers chicken ranching. That would give you a list of the most obvious publications that deal with raising chickens.

It would be nearly impossible to manually search for publications in areas that grow chickens. However, a database search of the references could scan each source looking for mentions of the word *chicken*. By using a database search, the strategic communicator could obtain a complete list and description of all publications or locations that have an identified interest in chickens. From that much shorter list, the practitioner could examine each entry to determine the most appropriate outlets for a given strategic message.

### Audience by Outlet

Knowing the media resources available to us still won't do us much good unless we know what those editors and producers want, and they in turn expect we will deliver the stories they need. As stated earlier, a generalized release that's sent to a metropolitan magazine editor, a television news producer and a small-town newspaper editor often won't get the response it should because each of those journalists is looking for something specific, some news that will interest or help her audience.

Therefore, a practitioner needs to know the special characteristics of the medium with which she is communicating. A knowledge of those characteristics will enable you to deliver the specific message to the specific target audiences.

Again, research will provide many of the answers. There are several research services that compare audience penetration, market share and other factors among print and broadcast outlets. Databases such as the Simmons National Consumer Study or the Survey of the American Consumer (compiled by Mediamark Research and Intelligence, or MRI) can give you additional information about a media outlet's characteristics and the habits of its audience.

Their research is amazingly detailed. Both track media usage by the consumers of approximately 6,000 brands in more than 500 product categories, including personal care products, candy, financial products and satellite radio. Using this data, you can determine whether more people who prefer roll-on deodorant to aerosol watch NBC's highest-rated comedy than the network's most-watched drama.

Simmons and MRI analyze audiences to such a degree that you can tell what publication or specific television show is seen by the greatest number of unmarried women over the age of 25 who don't have a high school education and work in service-industry jobs. A strategic communicator designing a campaign to recruit students for a high school diploma equivalency program would find this specific information invaluable.

The services track other demographic and lifestyle data as well. You can determine whether people who listen to talk radio are more likely to buy Ford or Dodge pickups. What type of jobs are held by people who buy life insurance? Do consumers who read Fortune magazine take more business trips than those who read Forbes? During their off time, do they tend to hike, or boat or go bowling? It's absolutely stunning what you can find.

You can readily see how an advertiser might use this data. But what about the person working in media relations? Initially, the data tell you what audience the outlet serves. Are there income characteristics, job categories, gender identifiers or age distinctions that might make one media outlet more open to your story pitch than another? Is there an unanticipated main persuader for a particular outlet's users?

But there are more insights you can obtain. By studying the lifestyle habits and media choices across your brand or product category, patterns will emerge. For example, let's say you discover the customers for your company's charcoal briquette brand have high user numbers among publications and cable TV programming celebrating nature and environmentalism. That might suggest testing whether your media relations campaign could open a new market niche by emphasizing how your charcoal brand is formulated to create fewer pollutants than competing brands. You can examine an evaluation process using the Simmons statistics in Case in Point 11.1.

## CASE IN POINT 11.1   Simmons Marketing Statistics

Marketing statistics, such as those found in the Simmons National Consumer Study (aka, Simmons OneView), provide valuable information in defining audiences and messages for strategic communicators. The product-use statistics can help you construct a demographic profile of your audience.

However, we find the most intriguing insights are contained in the media-use statistics. By isolating high and low index numbers in the *Index* line, practitioners can build a psychographic profile of a product's users, isolating interests and avocations people reveal and express through their media choices. If you'd like more detailed guidance on interpreting the data contained in the other Simmons columns, that's contained at **Click-Through 11.1**.

Let's illustrate that power with an example. Say you're trying to develop new ways to market an old favorite: ketchup. Table 11.1a displays some data points that give us a solid start, just as they appear in the program itself.

### TABLE 11.1A  Reading Simmons Statistics

| | | Total | Four or More | Three | Two | One | Less Than One |
|---|---|---|---|---|---|---|---|
| | Sample | 23,793 | 1,013 | 1,416 | 4,291 | 7,650 | 7,184 |
| | Weighted (000) | 238,469 | 9,880 | 14,233 | 39,821 | 76,378 | 74,627 |
| TOTAL U.S. | Vertical % | 100.0% | 100.0% | 100.0% | 100.0% | 100.0% | 100.0% |
| Bought Containers of Ketchup Last 30 Days | Horizontal % | 100.0% | 4.1% | 6.0% | 16.7% | 32.0% | 31.3% |
| | Index | 100 | 100 | 100 | 100 | 100 | 100 |
| | Total % | 100.0% | 4.1% | 6.0% | 16.7% | 32.0% | 31.3% |
| | Sample | 7,452 | 178 | 269 | 1,021 | 2,413 | 2,722 |
| | Weighted (000) | 71,302 | 1,442 | 2,247 | 9,176 | 22,009 | 27,567 |
| EDUCATION: College Degree or Higher | Vertical % | 29.9% | 14.6% | 15.8% | 23.0% | 28.8% | 36.9% |
| Bought Containers of Ketchup Last 30 Days | Horizontal % | 100.0% | 2.0% | 3.2% | 12.9% | 30.9% | 38.7% |
| | Index | 100 | 49 | 53 | 77 | 96 | 124 |
| | Total % | 29.9% | 0.6% | 0.9% | 3.8% | 9.2% | 11.6% |

*Source: MRI-Simmons*

The top section of the table establishes a baseline for a certain behavior, in this case, ketchup use. Here we focus on U.S. adults who bought ketchup in the past 30 days. The wonderful thing about Simmons is that it allows you to dive deeper into understanding the composition of that very general audience. If you look to the bottom section, you see how we can drill down to U.S. adults who bought ketchup in the last 30 days *and* who also hold a college degree. This sort of audience analysis can help you determine whether an audience segment—educated adults—is one you should target if you're trying to elicit a specific behavior—buying ketchup.

There's a lot going on in these reports, but we'd like to focus mostly on the *Index* line, which tells us how likely it is a certain audience segment, in this case, college graduates, will buy ketchup. The *Index* line value compares the percentage of college graduates with the ketchup-buying behavior of all adults. Scoring is akin to that of intelligence tests, in which an IQ score of 100 means 50% of the population scored higher than 100 and half lower. The 100 thus designates the median.

Here's an important clarification. A high index number isn't identifying the largest *portion* of the market. Instead, a high index indicates people within a specific category take some action at a higher *rate* than people in other categories. In effect, a high index number in these tables demonstrates a higher concentration of ketchup users—not a greater number of people—are present in a subcategory.

Ho-hum, you say? Be prepared to be excited. By isolating the characteristics connected with high and with low index numbers, a practitioner can determine the possible motives of audiences that drive them to buy the product. Take a look at Table 11.1b, and we'll show you what we mean. We've color-coded the data so you can readily see high (≥ 120) or low (≤ 80) index numbers.

**Using Simmons OneView**

https://www.youtube.com/watch?v=YI2sMhFKUhk

MRI hosts online tutorials on using Simmons OneView. Your university may also subscribe to this service; if so, you can likely find additional help from dedicated research librarians.

**TABLE 11.1B** **Demographics of Ketchup Buyers**

| INDEX: KETCHUP BUYERS | Four Or More | Three | Two | One | Less Than One |
|---|---|---|---|---|---|
| Male | 111 | 103 | 100 | 103 | 94 |
| Female | 90 | 97 | 100 | 97 | 105 |
| College Grad | 49 | 53 | 77 | 96 | 124 |
| High School Grad | 118 | 137 | 113 | 100 | 90 |
| Age 18-24 | 137 | 164 | 125 | 99 | 66 |
| Age 25-34 | 104 | 138 | 113 | 93 | 93 |
| Age 35-44 | 142 | 112 | 111 | 102 | 89 |

**TABLE 11.1B** Demographics of Ketchup Buyers

| INDEX: KETCHUP BUYERS | Four Or More | Three | Two | One | Less Than One |
|---|---|---|---|---|---|
| Age 45-54 | 125 | 94 | 99 | 112 | 90 |
| Age 55-64 | 35 | 75 | 97 | 102 | 116 |
| Age 65+ | 72 | 45 | 67 | 93 | 131 |
| Income <10K | 272 | 190 | 124 | 75 | 69 |
| Income $10K-$15K | 167 | 144 | 98 | 102 | 85 |
| Income $15K-$20K | 214 | 75 | 109 | 81 | 99 |
| Income $20K-$25K | 177 | 79 | 114 | 69 | 106 |
| Income $25K-$30K | 102 | 132 | 118 | 95 | 99 |
| Income $30K-$35K | 59 | 98 | 103 | 106 | 90 |
| Income $35K-$40K | 105 | 180 | 85 | 92 | 90 |
| Income $40K-$45K | 49 | 50 | 96 | 94 | 112 |
| Income $45K-$50K | 140 | 81 | 102 | 93 | 86 |
| Income $50K-$60K | 94 | 87 | 101 | 109 | 99 |
| Income $60K-$75K | 64 | 77 | 86 | 114 | 103 |
| Income $75K-$100K | 94 | 125 | 106 | 98 | 99 |
| Income $100K-$150K | 64 | 78 | 93 | 108 | 102 |
| Income $150K-$250K | 64 | 80 | 105 | 105 | 112 |
| Income $250K-$500K | 59 | 89 | 67 | 110 | 122 |
| Children <2 years | 161 | 167 | 123 | 103 | 67 |
| Children 2-5 years | 179 | 120 | 138 | 104 | 81 |
| Children 6-11 years | 192 | 150 | 164 | 90 | 74 |
| Children 12-17 years | 169 | 168 | 140 | 113 | 66 |

*Source: MRI-Simmons*

We have consolidated and abridged the index numbers here because the actual statistics go on for literally scores of pages! Let's focus on the *Four or more* users, because the category most closely corresponds to the idea of active publics, i.e., those who buy a boatload of ketchup. High index numbers indicate people most likely to act, while low index numbers signal relative inaction.

First, let's look at low numbers. These are important because they identify characteristics of people least likely to engage in a desired behavior. In our case, affluent and well-educated people, as well as older adults, seem unpromising marketing targets for ketchup.

Knowing audiences that are not part of our marketing focus is important, but it's tremendously helpful to discover the traits of those who are. In this example, very high ketchup usage coincides with families with children and people with lower incomes. Young adults also appear to be high-value marketing contacts.

**Table 11.1c  Media Use of Ketchup Buyers**

| INDEX: KETCHUP BUYERS | Four Or More | Three | Two | One | Less Than One |
|---|---|---|---|---|---|
| Bassmaster | 228 | 124 | 133 | 111 | 54 |
| Bon Appetit | 84 | 83 | 89 | 76 | 137 |
| ESPN Magazine | 155 | 145 | 123 | 111 | 68 |
| Esquire | 151 | 187 | 89 | 103 | 73 |
| Family Circle | 77 | 78 | 93 | 116 | 106 |
| Good Housekeeping | 74 | 61 | 102 | 99 | 115 |
| GQ | 171 | 135 | 111 | 103 | 76 |
| Guns & Ammo | 132 | 128 | 105 | 108 | 77 |
| Hot Rod | 141 | 117 | 110 | 96 | 75 |
| Low Rider | 237 | 218 | 137 | 85 | 50 |
| Men's Fitness | 131 | 135 | 121 | 82 | 83 |
| Woman's Day | 104 | 103 | 111 | 102 | 100 |
| ABC Family | 166 | 137 | 123 | 96 | 80 |
| Adult Swim | 151 | 127 | 135 | 100 | 70 |
| BET | 275 | 168 | 120 | 99 | 59 |
| Cartoon Network | 197 | 211 | 119 | 97 | 64 |
| Chiller | 251 | 194 | 107 | 101 | 65 |
| Cinemax | 294 | 146 | 110 | 84 | 76 |
| Disney Channel | 198 | 138 | 131 | 93 | 75 |
| ESPN | 111 | 96 | 100 | 100 | 92 |
| Fox News | 88 | 102 | 95 | 109 | 100 |
| Hallmark | 111 | 111 | 108 | 99 | 97 |
| Home & Garden | 75 | 69 | 99 | 101 | 114 |
| Lifetime Movie | 194 | 187 | 113 | 89 | 78 |
| Nick At Nite | 238 | 206 | 126 | 98 | 58 |
| Nickelodeon | 192 | 204 | 130 | 95 | 66 |
| Teen Nick | 284 | 266 | 108 | 88 | 50 |

*Source: MRI-Simmons*

As a burgeoning ketchup marketer, you now have an idea of who your audience is, but how do you reach them? Well, Simmons can help here too. Table 11.1c provides data on media-use patterns of ketchup users. Looking at cable and TV broadcast, heavy ketchup usage is associated with programming directed toward African Americans, as well as networks that primarily air children's shows. However, it's in print media, with their more tightly focused readership, that we can find additional audience insights.

Though children in the household correlate with high ketchup usage, in Table 11.1c we discover that media directed toward traditional homemakers, magazines like Woman's Day, Family Circle and Good Housekeeping, actually have relatively small concentrations of heavy ketchup users.

Instead, there appears to be another stream of motivations. The high index numbers for magazines associated with young adult male audiences (Esquire, GQ and Men's Fitness), automobile enthusiasts (Hot Rod and Low Rider) and outdoor sports magazines (Bassmaster, Field and Stream, Guns & Ammo) suggest promising options for ketchup marketers.

Taken together, what does all this data mean? Earlier, we said you could use index numbers to predict reasons motivating people to be heavy ketchup buyers. Here's our analysis: The audience appears to be split into two parts. Yes, households with children at home buy lots of ketchup, which both Simmons demographics and broadcast and cable index numbers had suggested.

But some media-use information defies what we thought we knew about people who used the most ketchup if we relied on demographic measures. Based on the index figures for print media, we see a concentration of younger male adults among heavy ketchup consumers, which supports the view that ketchup is a convenience product to enhance meals made by incompetent male cooks.

The cluster of fitness and male lifestyle media suggest those male ketchup buyers are still dating. A ketchup brand's marketing might reason that single men could enhance their dating market value if they prepared easy-to-make food for potential romantic scenarios like outdoor concerts, sporting events or beach visits. It's almost certainly worth a focus group to explore a potential new product niche.

The high index numbers among outdoor sports magazines offer another intriguing hint. It's likely that men going on extended hunting and fishing trips take easy-to-prepare food, which often means buying multiple containers of ketchup. Would wrapping your ketchup brand in camo packaging for hunting season drive brand shifting among sportsmen, who might value the novelty of a ketchup bottle that elicits engagement with their hunting buddies? What about a ketchup with sports-team-licensed labeling, promoted for tailgating?

Each of these analyses introduces data-supported speculations and shows how marketing statistics can drive creativity and instill insight into your persuasive messages.

## Factors in Media Relations Decision-Making

How do you find audience characteristics for media outlets not taking part in these analytic services? Although the evidence isn't quite as scientific as in formal audience surveys, every media outlet offers major clues about the characteristics of its audience.

### "Reading" an Outlet

What can you infer about a publication's audience by examining the publication? Let's look at two senior citizens' magazines that seem pointed toward the same audience: older adults. For the one with advertisements for ocean cruises and luxury household items, it's reasonable to conclude its primary readers are healthy and free of financial worries. The other publication includes a monthly feature on how to make inexpensive meals and advertisements for basic medical products or free transportation services. You can bet that magazine has concentrations of readers with much lower incomes.

#### The News Hole

Studying media outlets offers other insights as well. For instance, because more newspaper advertising is sold for certain days, the news hole is generally smaller in media distributed on Mondays, Tuesdays, Wednesdays and Saturdays.

Although local television newscasts are generally the same length every day, you'll notice that on certain days there are usually fewer breaking news events. Although heavy news days vary depending on the schedule of local government meetings, Saturdays, Sundays and Mondays are generally slow news days in most cities. Releasing your news on those days might boost your broadcast coverage if your information is marginal enough to be pushed out of the media by more prominent events.

There's also a timing strategy for limiting public reaction to uncomfortable tidings. For instance, President Trump's White House communication staff were noted for their Friday-night news dumps. Some of the administration's most controversial actions, like the travel ban on Muslims or the ban on trans military members, as well as multiple firings and pardons, were announced after-hours Friday in the hope fewer people respond to news over the weekend.[15]

#### Large-Market Versus Small-Market Placement

You'll also quickly develop an awareness of the differences between your ability to place information in major metropolitan print and broadcast outlets, and the newspapers, TV and radio stations in smaller markets. Because of smaller staffs, fewer production dollars and, quite frankly, less local news, smaller markets are more willing to accept and place information from institutional sources.

Thus, a story that wouldn't be placed in a major metropolitan newspaper might very easily be run verbatim in a community weekly. Photos that would never appear on a big-city outlet's website might make the home page in a small-city daily or weekly. A taped video news release that a television station in a major market would never run might be a prominent feature during a small-city newscast.

Don't discount those outlets merely because they aren't in a major market. Those consumers, those votes or those voices outside metropolitan areas can be just as valuable—and at times more valuable—to you and your organization's success.

### "Reading" an Editor, Producer, Writer or Reporter

Media outlets have institutional purposes, but they're still managed by humans, each with her own passions and prejudices. As a result, it's not possible to completely understand your media choices without contemplating the goals of the people who produce them. Media relations, no matter how carefully planned, can only succeed when you structure your presentation to meet the needs of the editor and the audience you both serve. That means more than personalizing the story for those readers. It also means adapting the methods and even the times you present the story to gatekeepers.

As you continue to interact with individual media outlets, you'll learn how each operates, which editors have the authority to assign stories and which writers can pick and choose their own stories. In multichannel media, you'll discover whether a producer or the host decides who will be interviewed on the broadcast and webcast talk shows your important publics watch.

You'll even learn their work schedules so you can send your pitch to appear at the top of their email feeds when they get to work. (For instance, we often schedule media releases for distribution to local television producers and assignment editors shortly before 5 a.m., when many of their workdays start.)

All editors, whether working in newspapers, magazines, broadcast media or on the web, have daily peak work periods. During those hours, they'll be concentrating on fulfilling their production responsibilities. It's only common sense that a communication professional presenting her story pitch during those peak times will get an icy reception—unless your story has some critical timeliness element. Thus, schedule your presentations to key media people when your presence won't be so unwanted. Memory Memo 11.3 highlights journalists' peak times and deadlines for non-breaking stories.

Even if you're merely sending a release for an item to be placed in a community calendar section of a newspaper or radio station, consider the medium's deadline schedules. Those deadlines vary widely, but it's not uncommon for daily newspapers that publish schedules in their Sunday edition to require all calendar items by Tuesday or Wednesday of the preceding week.

| **MEMORY MEMO 11.3** Peak Times to Avoid and News Deadlines to Hit | | |
|---|---|---|
| **Outlet Type** | **Peak Times** | **Non-Breaking News Deadlines** |
| Daily Newspapers | Late afternoon and early evening | 4–5 days before running |
| Weekly Community Papers | 1–2 days before publication | 1–2 weeks before running |
| Monthly Magazines | 1 week before publication | 3 months before running |
| Drive-Time Radio | 1 hour before through airtime | 2 days before running |
| TV Evening News | 2–3 hours before broadcast | 5 days before running |

When you anticipate coverage by a reporter or camera crew prompted by a news release, observing those deadlines becomes even more important. Although an assignment editor can send a reporter or camera crew for breaking news at almost a moment's notice, most stories don't warrant that type of response.

For nonemergency news items, you must deliver a media release concerning your event far enough ahead of the deadline so a reporter can be assigned, interviews scheduled and conducted, and the story completed before the deadline. Sometimes it's also necessary to include time for the reporter to find additional background information or visuals. That often stretches the required delivery date for news releases to three weeks or more before the optimum time for your story to run.

Also recognize that feature stories or stories by columnists or special correspondents require even more time. Reporters who specialize in humorous or special features might have scheduled the specific stories they will produce for weeks in advance. Magazine feature story deadlines can be four to six months before publication. That means you'll be pitching end-of-year holiday stories to magazine editors during early summer.

Media relations execution is complicated, but there's one overarching rationale: You structure your presentation knowing that you have to meet the gatekeeper's needs before you'll be able to communicate to that gatekeeper's audience.  That means you adapt to the circumstances of the outlets you hope will cover your event, because they will rarely adapt to yours.

## Getting Maximum Coverage: Story Splitting

As a strategic communicator, you have the tools that will help you target individual messages to individual audiences. You've already learned one way to target audiences. In Chapters 6 and 7, we discussed strategies to determine what would interest particular audiences and how to construct lede sentences and inverted pyramid structures to emphasize that information. But although the structure of a news release demands that it focus on one main topic, that doesn't mean a media relations professional has to send the same release to every media outlet.

For one thing, the growth of specialized media makes a single-release approach ineffective. Moreover, most stories have more than a single interesting aspect, which means you'll have to focus multiple releases on multiple persuaders to cater to those aspects as well as the audiences most attuned to them.

Let's look at an example.

A coal company announces the use of a new, university-developed technique to replant trees on exhausted strip mines. Where previously there were gaping, ugly gashes in the mountains, there are now grassy slopes with saplings. The company is donating the land to the state parks department and building a new backpacking trail that will meander through the growing forests.

### *What Is Interesting About This Story? Who Is Interested in It?*

We can predict environmental bloggers would be interested in the commitment this company has made to restoring the wilderness it disrupted. Backpackers and campers will want to know about the new recreation area being developed. A TV science program might be interested in the application of new technology to address this troubling deforestation problem. Newspapers in the towns and cities around the restored mine will be happy that tourism dollars might replace some of the wages lost when mining operations closed. The university's social media channels will revel in the knowledge that its academic research efforts are paying off for the state's citizens. The newspaper in the small town where the inventor grew up will be interested in the success of the local high school's alumna. And those are only some of the possible stories within this one event.

We call this technique isolating newsworthy elements and directing them to multiple audiences and outlets **story splitting**. Virtually every situation has at least some varied set of news elements.

Taking each of the story's facets and structuring several specialized releases tailored to specific media outlets seems like a simple, reasonable goal for strategic communicators, but our colleagues frequently dismiss the tactic. They argue that customizing releases is impractical because writing multiple releases is too time-consuming and labor-intensive.

However, the task of individualizing releases for particular groups isn't overwhelming because it doesn't necessarily mean rewriting the entire release. Because the audience-centered writing process is built around the inverted pyramid, it's very likely the main body of individualized news releases on a single topic will remain fundamentally identical from release to release, even if releases are directed to different audiences. TIPCUP compels writers to concentrate information important to a specific audience within the story's first few paragraphs. The writer adapts the first paragraph to target the individual editor or producer for whom it is intended. The rest of the release, concentrating on background information about the event, can stay essentially the same. Figure 11.1 outlines the process.

## Automating Individualization: Field-Formatted Releases

Technical tools can be used in other ways to simplify the individualization of news releases. Often, situations arise in which many people receive a similar honor or award. An announcement of a college's graduates or military promotions often involves thousands of individual names whose owners hail from thousands of communities.

Many hometown publications might be interested in a local citizen's achievement. Similarly, an internet outlet might be interested in communicating information about an enthusiast and her innovations in its specific field of interest. However, no editor has the time to search through thousands of names for news of the people who might interest the outlet's readers. Comparable time pressures prevent strategic communicators from individualizing thousands of media releases to increase the possibility of their being used.

Nonetheless, most word processing programs let media relations practitioners individualize releases on a vast scale. The writer can create a standardized news release

Feb. 5, ___    Contact: Flo Davis
574-555-1234
Flo@afe.org

Feb. 5, ___    Contact: Flo Davis
574-555-1234
Flo@afe.org

<u>Classical Works by Women to be Performed</u>

Women's History Month will be celebrated in song by the Actus Feminam Ensemble during a March 6 Warsaw University concert devoted entirely to chamber music composed by women.

The Buffalo-based Actus Feminam Ensemble has helped resurrect and restore women's music to its proper place in the repertoire. The group recently released a recording devoted to music written by Baroque-era women.

<u>OEHS Teacher in WU Women's Music Concert</u>

An Oxbridge East High School teacher will be the featured vocalist in a free concert devoted entirely to chamber music composed by women.

OEHS choir director Linda DeRungs will join fellow members of the Actus Feminam Ensemble to perform in a Women's History Month concert at Warsaw University.

DeRungs has helped resurrect and restore women's music to its proper place in the repertoire. She and the other Actus Feminam members recently released a recording devoted to music written by Baroque-era women.

Thousands of women, most of whom were ignored by the men who wrote music history, have created a treasure trove of technically excellent, emotionally compelling music through the centuries, works that Actus Feminam has discovered. In research trips through Europe and North America, Actus Feminam members have unearthed over 235 diverse chamber music works written by women, most of which were unpublished and had to be prepared directly from the original manuscripts.

That original scholarship has turned Actus Feminam concerts into important events. In virtually every performance the group's four instrumentalists and one vocalist bring to light a work that has languished, unperformed in European archives for hundreds of years. The works are performed on original 17th century instruments or historically accurate recreations. Performances are accompanied by short talks describing the works' histories.

The concert will include three 21st century premieres of works by Isabella Leonarda, Hildegard von Bingen and Marianne Martinez. Leonarda, an Italian, was the 17th century's most published composer, active from her early 20s until she was 80 years old. Germany's von Bingen was credited with inventing the medieval morality play in the early 1100s. Martinez, a Spanish ambassador's daughter, was Vienna's first woman Kapellmeister, or conductor. She studied under Haydn and played piano duets with Mozart.

The March 6 concert by the Actus Feminam Ensemble is free and open to the public. Held in Warsaw University's Koenig Concert Hall, it will begin at 8 p.m. The concert is part of the university's month-long series of lectures, films, plays and art exhibits focusing on women's history.

-30-

**FIGURE 11.1 Story Splitting.** The story-splitting tactic simplifies obtaining coverage from fundamentally different media outlets. The highlighted text shows copy shared by both releases. The lede on the left targets a women's magazine directed primarily toward women who live in the city staging the concert. The second lede targets a suburban newspaper where one of the group's members teaches. While the community paper is unlikely to cover the metro's arts, a local's involvement offers news value. The writer could target additional outlets by modifying the lede's main persuader and the second section explaining the lede.

(for instance, announcing the members of a college's first-semester dean's honor roll), leaving blanks where the individualized information would go. These blanks, called *fields*, are for information like name, gender, city, state, etc.

After just the few words are entered in a database that lists information on an individual, the word processing program will insert all the information into the appropriate fields, then email the release to the individual's corresponding media outlet. You can see how to develop this mail merge release in Click-Through 11.2.

## Media Relations Strategy: Controlling the Controllable

So how can you make uncontrolled media relations more controlled?

Control as many things as you can. There will be times you'll only be able to react, not plan. For instance, Professor Thompson couldn't plan for the time a guest speaker's live body mic broadcast his romantic green-room reunion with his new bride to a gathering auditorium audience, including the city's music critic. Shit happens, as the old saying goes.

However, you can plan an event or story to assure some things you want to happen actually do happen. Such an approach guides you to consider how to structure the event, announcement or news conference to maximize the interest of the media and their ease in covering it by influencing the event's location, date, time, participants, visuals, music and more.

For example, Professor Thompson delayed the grand opening for a restaurant named Napa River three days so it would coincide with California's Napa Valley harvest festival 2,200 miles away. A live video feed of the California harvest festival explicitly proclaimed the parallel between Napa Valley and the restaurant's aspirations to be the city's only outlet for Northern California cuisine.

You could also structure a campaign designed to match story to medium. Professor Thompson worked with an author who wrote a book on how towns, cities or regions were defined by factory whistles, cathedral bells or other sounds. The author dubbed these *soundmarks* and likened them to how citizens perceive landmarks that identify their neighborhood. Recognizing the audio concept also depicts a radio network's relationship with its listeners, Professor Thompson pitched the story to NPR, which produced a long feature on the author and his ideas for its evening national news show. It prompted a sell-out audience for the author's lecture the next day.

So no, you can't control everything about your media relations efforts. But as a thoughtful communicator who knows her event and her media market, you can structure a scenario that will give your project the best chance of being selected for that day's media attention.

## Matching Delivery Strategies to Organizational Objectives

After discussing all these delivery methods, we need to make an important clarification. It may seem this chapter concentrated on how to reach the maximum number of media outlets, without regard to your organization's communications goals. Remember that in employing the tactics and technologies, we have highlighted that our purpose is to fulfill our communication goals by providing specific information to media connecting us to our target audiences.

It's true that every event or issue has many possible publicity angles and that publicity could be obtained in many different media outlets. By researching your subject, you can find all the facets and all the outlets. But not every story you could generate from those angles advances your communication goals. As we stressed in Chapter 2, you should analyze your communication needs and then design a strategy to meet those goals. Your campaign effectiveness should not be judged by how many placements you get (what practitioners call outputs), but in how well the placements you do get inform and persuade the audiences important to your communication objective (what practitioners call outcomes).

That management philosophy reinforces a responsible attitude toward the journalists who have the power over whether our media relations efforts will succeed or fail. In practice, that means finding situations in which the needs of journalists and our organization's communication goals coincide. By carefully selecting media and the messages we want to communicate, we can maintain our organization's credibility and ensure our releases will not be subject to an editor's automatic swipe into her digital wastebasket.

> **Strategic Thought**
>
> What is the potential harm in trying to obtain the maximum number of media messages without regard to your organization's communication goals?

## SUMMARY

- Story splitting helps obtain the broadest possible coverage by crafting a release for each persuader that comprises a story and matching each with the medium most interested in that story element.

- Reference works such as The Standard Periodical Directory, The Gale Directory and the Encyclopedia of Associations explore the audiences served by a wide variety of media outlets.

- Database searches of media characteristics permit practitioners to quickly compile tightly focused media lists for targeted communication campaigns.

### Scenario Prompts: Delivering Uncontrolled Messages

You'll find Scenario Prompts on pp. 367–386 of this textbook. While they vary in subject and difficulty, they help you hone your critical thinking and strategic writing skills. The following are best suited to this chapter's topics.

Management: 2.3, 3.1, 3.2, 3.3, 5.2, 8.3 / Writing: 3.7, 6.4, 7.10

# When the Organization Controls the Message

Advertising and Internal Communication

I love dogs. Always have.

My parents adopted our first real dog, a strangely pugnacious cockapoo I named Louie, right before I began eighth grade.

You probably thought it odd I called Louie our first *real* dog, but it's appropriate. When I was 4 my dad brought home the first dog I remember: Spuds MacKenzie.

The name likely doesn't register for you, but everyone in the late '80s crowd knew Spuds. The bull terrier was Bud Light's spokesdog, their "official party animal" as the popular ad campaign put it. The ads portrayed the lovably ugly Spuds surrounded by beautiful women at beaches, barbecues and concerts. He became one of America's most recognized figures, even prompting a revival of the bull terrier breed.[1]

At this point, I should clarify: My dad didn't actually bring home the real Spuds MacKenzie. My family is a blue-collar bunch, and Spud's security team limited access to the real thing. We weren't exactly in his league.

But during the Spuds ad campaign years, my father was as a routeman for a bread company owned by Anheuser-Busch, maker of Bud Light. When the company was trying to boost morale or reward sales achievements, he sometimes got fun swag. This time it was a life-size, plastic, Spuds bar lamp (Figure 12.1), which quickly became a favorite toy.

**FIGURE 12.1  Spuds MacKenzie Swag.** What makes for a great cooler for an adult of legal drinking age doesn't always translate when you use it as a school lunchbox.

Remember, it was the '80s. Boomer parenting standards were a bit looser. We trick-or-treated unsupervised, rode bikes without helmets and played with matches. And hell, I wasn't even in kindergarten. I didn't know it was a bar lamp. Spuds was the cool, fun-loving dog from TV—and my friend.

I wasn't alone. It seemed the individuals most affected by the campaign were dog-loving kids.

The thousands of grade school and junior high kids wearing Spuds T-shirts—in addition to other branded material, like the Spuds MacKenzie cooler I still use—focused the wrath of anti-alcohol groups onto Anheuser-Busch. Quite appropriately, the company was asked whether the cute-dog campaign convinced adults to buy beer, or was intended to create a market of unwitting children and teenagers. The company was lambasted in the U.S. Senate, in editorial pages and at school meetings. After one of the most extensive ad campaigns in history, Bud Light's ads had helped launch the product but had provoked one of history's biggest consumer protests of a marketing campaign.

This is an important lesson at the start of a chapter focusing on what we dub controlled communication. There's a lot we can control with this messaging: what is said, how it's said and when, where and how often it's said. Ultimately, however, we can't control the audience's reaction.

But that doesn't mean we're helpless. Persuasive communication is ultimately about solving problems, which requires developing solutions and packaging them in ways to prompt audiences to accept our view and/or take a desired action. While we can't guarantee an outcome, by analyzing research and past experiences we can anticipate how audiences will likely respond and adjust accordingly. For me, at least, that's always been the fun part.

Cheers!

*—NB*

## What You Know

- Institutional decision-making requires clearly understanding the motives of a variety of stakeholders.

- Multichannel platforms require writers to overlay additional sensory channels on a solid persuasive message.

- All persuasive writing is focused on solving an institutional problem.

## What You'll Learn

- What the capabilities and limitations of different channels of controlled communication are

- How to create conceits for advertising headlines and multichannel commercials

- How to focus marketing objectives on solving institutional problems

- How internal messages, even though controlled, demand the same standards of persuasive communication

## Controlled Communication

Several times, we've asserted our belief in what we call adversarial public relations. A zero-sum game, we termed it in the media relations chapter. If you successfully pitch a magazine cover story, that means some other practitioner didn't get that cover story.

In these next two chapters, we focus on controlled communication, that writing in which you control all aspects of the message and how you present it to your audience.

Controlled communication. Sounds so powerful, so imposing. For those who believe in the media's omnipotent capacity to compel people to do what they otherwise would not, it would appear to be the culmination of communication's supposed raw power. Controlled communication tactics, which include internal documents, speeches, presentations and advertising, are united by one premise: in exchange for the institution buying or outright owning the message's distribution channel—whether that's a conference room, a website or advertising time on a television station—the organization dictates exactly the format and wording of the message an audience receives.

Many colleagues with whom you'll be sharing office and cyber space in the near future will assert their right to employ controlled communication to communicate the strict company line. This thirst to control often overcomes public relations' usual aspirations for a back-and-forth conversational exchange between an organization and its stakeholders. In direct contradiction, some practitioners think an existing link with an internal audience (say, employees) excuse them from applying the best practices of persuasion communication they'd exert for an external audience.

Our study and practice urge us to remember the importance of feedback and dialogue. Regardless of platform or message type, you fail your clients if you don't observe the principles of honest communication. Even though you control every aspect of the message and its presentation, you and your clients suffer if you abandon sincerity and respect for your audience, whether it's external or internal.

In short, controlled communication isn't a reason to throw away judgment and forget the principles we've discussed. It has rules and structures, and it adheres to the same theories of human communication and the vision of ethical practice. And, unlike many of the writing tactics we've discussed thus far, it targets internal as well as external audiences.

## Advertising

### Strategy and Creativity

It's probably easiest to start from the outside and work our way in. Advertising is perhaps the most widely recognized form of external, controlled communication. It represents the most public, and expensive, presentations of an organization's external communication efforts.

Advertising copywriters are usually perceived as inhabiting a poorly patrolled playground for unconventional creatives. But advertising is controlled communication, and the very price organizations pay for that control means organizations expect a significant return on their investments. That means the strategic, results-centered focus of all the writing forms we have discussed apply to advertising as well.

### Attention Among a Crowd of Competitors

Instead, writing advertising copy means entering the same battle, but with some crucial differences.

Some of those differences make the task easier. Because advertising purchases space or time to promote a product, service or idea, your message is ensured of gaining access to a medium through which a receiver can encounter it. Unlike a news release, advertising doesn't have to pass the gauntlet of an editor's judgment concerning her audience's needs and desires before it can reach its intended audience.

However, an advertising message must overcome other, formidable barriers to gain a public's attention and action. One problem is the sheer volume of advertising messages against which an advertisement is deployed. According to Media Dynamics, Inc., each American encounters over 130,000 advertisements each year. In that roar of advertising claims and counterclaims, it's not surprising the same study estimated the average person engaged with only about 3% of those ads.[2]

It's not just the number of messages that creates an enormous challenge for the advertising copywriter. Even if people notice the message, there's no guarantee they'll believe it. Indeed, researchers found people are more skeptical of advertising messages than information disseminated through news media or by word-of-mouth.[3]

Therefore, unless an advertisement is carefully conceived and creatively executed so it can emerge from the cacophony, your lonely little commercial merely contributes to the confusing clutter of messages audiences routinely doubt or ignore. What's worse yet is that your client has paid thousands (maybe even millions) of dollars to be cast into the wastebasket of audience minds.

## The Advertising Conceit

How does an advertisement gain attention amid this confusion of voices? Some argue that commercials more outrageous in their premises, more outlandish in their presentation, and more overstated in their production are more noticed. The underlying claim? The main task of communication is capturing attention.

Yet those people should be reminded of the basic premise underlying all persuasive communication, including advertising. Persuasion, by its very definition, is moving people to act. Without an eventual action, attention does not help us.

However, those attention-grabbing messages against which advertisers compete do change the way advertising writers conceive and structure their messages. The advertiser must introduce the message more creatively than she would for other strategic communication writing tasks. But that attention-getting device (what we call a **conceit**) must be closely related to the eventual message the advertiser will present. The conceit must logically lead to the benefits the audience will gain by buying a product, using a service or adopting an idea. To help formulate that conceit, many advertising writers begin their writing by composing a persuasion platform.

## Integrating the Persuasion Platform Into Advertising Writing

Chapter 3 details how a persuasion platform helps you develop a plan for solving an organizational problem. In advertising tasks, the persuasion platform helps stimulate the creativity that leads to a conceit, which is a novel approach to presenting an advertising claim. Generally, the conceit appears in the headline and illustration of a print ad or the scenario of a multichannel ad.

The platform stimulates the writer's creative process by first isolating the one major selling idea the product or service can promise the intended audience. Then the platform places that main selling idea within the filter of audience characteristics to try to create a new presentation. This conceit invites the target audience's attention while forcefully communicating the most important message to tempt that audience to act.

It's the same basic planning process recommended for every persuasion task we've faced in other strategic communication duties. There are just a few distinctions we need to discuss, distinctions that respond to the different problems faced in marketing and advertising activities.

### Isolating the Institutional Problem: What Are You Trying to Do Beyond Selling?

The persuasion platform's section detailing the client's problem briefly touches on all those historic, social, economic or perceptual elements that have caused the problem affecting our client's organization. We develop a reason for communication before we communicate. That's as important in advertising as it is in all other institutional communication.

Let's say the appliance company for which you're writing copy has just been purchased by another company. The new company has poured money into a retooling effort to correct your product's awful service record. How would you structure an ad campaign for this situation? Would you picture a spokesperson gazing lovingly at a refrigerator and saying how wonderful it is? Would you have the company's new CEO come on screen and say how fortunate he feels to lead such a stellar company?

Neither of us think any of those will work because neither attacks the basic problem: people know you've made a lousy product in the past. To succeed, you've got to overcome that reputation, and hiding behind slick advertising that ignores your former transgressions won't accomplish that.

When you realize your problem, your options become clearer. In the most extreme cases, perhaps you need to bury the problems along with the brand name and start over. That's what Charter did when it purchased Time-Warner Cable. According to a 2016 letter from the New York Attorney General's office, "Time-Warner has earned the miserable reputation it enjoys among consumers." So Charter rebranded itself and Time-Warner as Spectrum Communications, which seemed to immediately change the consumer viewpoint.[4]

### Determining the Objective: Solving the Problem

Once you've established the problem, it's important to formulate an advertising objective solving that specific problem. We're often trying to extend understanding and commitment to additional consumers. However, when the advertising project is in the formative stage, it's best to think of the persuasion problem as a challenge to change the mind of one typical individual in the target audience. Most advertising experts recommend that during the creative stage, ad copywriters discuss the product in one of the following ways:

1. Establish a use

2. Stimulate trial

3. Position the product

4. Build brand awareness

Each of these objectives roughly correlates to one of the quadrants in the learn-feel-do model discussed in Chapter 2. We'll analyze each of the objectives within that model.

### Establish a Use

If your audience is likely to respond to highly rational arguments, your most logical goal is to try to establish a use—or a new use—for the product. Selling a lawnmower to a homeowner, heavy manufacturing equipment to a corporation president or salt to a cook all involve the user's considerations of cost or efficiency. For this type of product or idea, you're going to use a hard, no-nonsense appeal.

This is probably the simplest advertising appeal because you're showing your audience how buying the product will benefit them in the most direct, practical ways. It can be effective for new products with new functions because it emphasizes the function and not the brand name. Thus, online ads promoting a collapsing hanger set that saves closet space might barely mention the product's brand name.

It can also be effective for an established product with a unique feature. That explains the number of commercials touting "improved cleaning power" or a "new, easy-pull starter."

It can be equally effective when promoting a new use for an established product. Think of the plight of Arm & Hammer baking soda. A one-pound box of baking soda makes, according to Betty Crocker's calculations, over 4,600 chocolate chip cookies.[5] You can't make much money if you're selling an inexpensive product that lasts for years.

What to do? Find new uses for the product, a task at which the Arm & Hammer researchers have been extraordinarily successful. The company promotes baking soda in toothpaste and antacids. In addition, a product that makes delightful cookies also can balance your swimming pool's pH level, clean plastic lawn furniture, or remove acid from car battery terminals. In the most remarkable selling job, they've been able to convince consumers to buy a full box of the product, then pour it down their drains as a deodorizer. These are all examples of convincing the customer of the solid benefits of using the product in novel ways.

### Stimulate Trial

If you predict the persuasion sequence will involve low-consequence decisions, your most likely selling objective may be to stimulate trial. Encouraging a consumer to experiment with a new product works best when the ramifications of making the wrong decision are small.

Stimulating trial is a logical objective for a campaign selling $2 raffle tickets for an animal shelter's fundraiser. Conversely, if you want to convince a town's residents to approve locating a nuclear reactor in their vicinity (a high-consequence decision), you're ill-advised to try to stimulate trial.

Trial works well for all sorts of products. We're equally willing to try a new brand of soap or cereal that largely satisfies rational appeals, as well as inexpensive jewelry, candy or toys that satisfy emotional cravings. It's also appropriate for public issues campaigns asking people simply to sign a petition or mail a postcard to a legislator. And remember that you can reduce a high-consequence decision into one of low consequence. You can isolate a risk-free step toward persuasion, such as asking a potential investor to attend a retirement adviser's group seminar that also includes a high-end meal. What's important is that the consequences of making the wrong decision be manageable.

### Position the Product

Positioning is a way of communicating the market segment a product intends to fill. This approach generally works best in decisions that are of high consequence. For the high-income auto buyer trying to decide whether to buy a Mercedes or BMW, the decision generally doesn't turn on performance, maintenance records or even price. Commercials for these products attempt to convince us of the statement we make to the world when we buy a particular luxury automobile. From their commercials, we understand BMWs are intended for younger people who want to display an unharnessed sophistication. A Mercedes, on the other hand, seems to appeal to older buyers who want to communicate stability and dependability to others.

Such positioning often includes *image campaigns.* That's when a company claims it gives good service just like its competitors, but it cares for the environment or community in ways its competitors can't match.

### Build Brand Awareness

These are also campaigns for products that have been on the market for years. You see them for products in a marketing environment where there are few distinctions among products offered by competitors and little new information to offer consumers. Almost all decisions about these types of products are based on emotionalism.

The classic example of this is the decades-long cola wars between Pepsi and Coca-Cola. After years of advertising and consumer trials, there is little left to say about either product. Each of us knows how they taste, and early in our lives we usually establish a favorite. The task of a brand image commercial is to keep the brand name in the consumer's consciousness and reinforce the positive attributes the user associates with the product.

### Predicting the Probable Persuasion Sequence

After you've isolated the demographic and psychographic factors motivating the target audience's behavior, you need to discover the probable persuasion sequence. This helps the writer decide whether emotional or rational appeals will most effectively motivate the audience to take the desired action. The most common persuasion sequences for each advertising objective are listed in Table 12.1.

**TABLE 12.1  Probable Persuasion Sequences[6]**

| If the Objective is … | then the persuasion sequence will be … |
| --- | --- |
| to establish a use … | learn-feel-do or do-learn-feel |
| to stimulate trial … | do-feel-learn or do-learn-feel |
| to reposition the product among its competitors … | feel-learn-do or do-feel-learn |
| to build brand awareness … | feel-learn-do or do-feel-learn |

### *The Main Persuader: What Can You Say That No One Else Can?*

The main persuader is the central concept driving the creation of all the advertisement's copy. It's introduced in the headline, repeated in the body copy and reinforced at the conclusion. In short, the main selling idea is the one message you judge will most effectively convince the target audience to take the desired action.

Sometimes the message is simply that the product's new ingredient makes it a good buy. At other times the central message is the product's reputation for quality or that people will view you with respect if you own it. Sometimes the main selling idea might be to convince buyers they are saying something about themselves—that they are sophisticated, or frugal or technically knowledgeable—when they use the product.

The main selling idea distills the many hundreds of things you could say about the product into one central idea. For that reason, it's usually best to refine the main selling idea to one declarative sentence. For instance: A paint's one-coat covering capacity saves time. Or: Drinking an all-natural beverage shows you care about the planet's chemical dangers. Or: Buying a certain car brand demonstrates you value your children's safety.

In each of these cases, the main selling idea in your persuasion platform isn't a slogan or a headline (although don't be surprised if your main selling idea is the germ for a good headline). Instead, it is a selling strategy, a persuader you believe your target audience will value as it decides whether to attend to your message.

### *Composing the Creative Strategy Statement:*
### *How Can You Say It Differently?*

The persuasion platform should develop the main persuader into a conceit summarizing the main conclusions. Will an emotional or a rational appeal be more effective with your audience? How can you structure the message to best emphasize those appeals to your audience? Can you expect your audience to make a snap judgment about the issue or must they contemplate before they decide to accept or reject your proposal?

After that, you determine the form of your advertising strategy. What do you want the audience to think or feel? If you're trying to position the product, how should your audience feel about competitors? Will you use humor? How sophisticated will you make the language to communicate with the intended audience?

The strategy statement is often a free-form, stream-of-consciousness play of ideas and thoughts until a central conception for the ad comes into focus. It's a way to generate a creative expression of your main selling idea to a defined public.

Developing this creative conceit is hard work. There are very few new advertising claims left. Neanderthals who beat their dirty furs on rocks and today's detergent manufacturers both claimed their method effectively cleaned clothes. Advertisements for the Pony Express offered the fastest delivery across North America; air-freight companies make the same promise today.

So you need to largely abandon inventing a new advertising claim. Instead, you want to emerge with a new conceit, a way of communicating your claim that makes it different from the way the message has been communicated hundreds of times before.

For instance, a restaurant chain's selling point might be they have more breakfast choices than other fast-food chains. The chain could have said simply, "You can order more types of breakfast here than from our competitors." While that statement is a good main selling idea, it isn't very effective at drawing attention amid the sea of ads swelling around consumers.

A conceit for this advertiser might be, "Breakfast should be a break," showing the upbeat transformation of commuters bored with their every-morning breakfast routine at other franchises. Connecting it with another alliterative claim, "30 days of delicious decisions," the ad could rapidly display a month's worth of different breakfast entrees. The chain establishes the dining varieties they offer and suggests their breakfasts can provide a highlight in a grinding 9-to-5 workweek.

At its best, your advertising strategy statement should forcefully convey the main selling idea in a new and interesting way, while at the same time suggesting the product will fulfill a psychological need. It is from this conceit that the advertisement is built.

## Static Advertising

What we'll call **static advertising** comprises advertising in magazines and newspapers, as well as web banner ads, billboards and transit advertising in which the advertising message is presented in a still, fixed form.

Static advertising has many of the same strengths and weaknesses that print has in accomplishing other persuasive tasks. It's usually the best choice when trying to communicate complicated rational arguments about a product. Because it is in a fixed, static medium (unlike multichannel or interactive media), audiences can study the product and review complex claims at their own pace.

In Chapter 8, we asserted that print readers must be more active participants in receiving messages. People listening to their car radio while dodging traffic or watching television while eating a meal are likely more passive in attending to broadcast messages.

Static advertising has certain weaknesses, too. Most important, beyond visuals, static has none of the sensory elements radio or television advertising possesses that enhance emotional appeals. You can't see a product work, as on television, or hear a soothing voice talking, as on radio.

### Writing Static Advertising: Steps in Moving an Audience to Act

A static ad, like all persuasive communication, is intended to state a proposition, explain the proposition and then give reasons supporting the proposition. Echoing our definition of persuasion, it offers a specific action the audience can take to gain the benefits the message promises. Virtually every static ad comprises five elements that move the reader through just those steps:

1. The headline-visual
2. The bridge
3. The statement of benefits
4. The wrap
5. The logo and baseline

#### The Headline-Visual:
#### Grabbing Attention While Keeping the Focus

One of the most important tasks for advertising copywriters is to compose persuasive prose. Yes, people like to look at pictures. However, it's important to think of advertising visuals as something more than attention-grabbing images.

Contrary to many of the advertising maxims you may have heard, the best advertising illustration isn't necessarily the one that attracts the most people; it's the one that attracts the *right* people. The right people are the ones who are legitimate prospects for helping you accomplish your organizational goal. So your purpose is not to get attention; once again, it is to get results. The headline and visual working together, as in Figure 12.2, makes a great start.

You're hoping to create a synergy between headline and visual, a melding of illustration and text that generates a response greater than the effect either one would have individually. Your intent should be to knit the visual and the words to convey a unified message growing from

**FIGURE 12.2 The Headline-Visual Dynamic.** It's vital to build your headline and visual as one unit, tightly linked in its message. This is a great example. The creative team has identified its audience of sexually active young adults and riveted their attention with this provocative photo. But they extend the visual's impact by a creative illustration of the headline's main selling idea: caution and transparency in exploring past sexual relationships with your partner are essential. What better way than being entwined in four pairs of arms to show that each time you have sex, you are risking an STD from any of your partner's past partners?

your main selling idea and creative strategy statement. That said, there are only a few general guidelines we can offer you in choosing illustrations because, in advertising, virtually anything can work in the right situation.

FIGURE 12.3  **A Tough Sell Succeeds: This Transit Ad for the Lung Cancer Alliance Undertook a Formidable Task.** The organization's research found many people perceived lung cancer sufferers were responsible for their disease, largely because of lung cancer's close association with tobacco usage. The advertisement reverses that superior attitude and confronts the poor reasoning suggesting that any defined class of people deserves to die. The ad reversed common approaches trying to establish disgust with smoking—diseased lungs, yellowed teeth and oxygen-hose-plugged noses. Instead, here's a prosperous-looking businessman to whom we might assign a mildly negative characteristic, in this case, smugness. The ad's copy then turns the table on its audience: Do you possess such moral superiority that you're willing to sentence another human to death because you interpret their behaviors or attitudes as distasteful? This harsh rebuke to the audience is intended to create a broader alliance of anti-smoking activists with donors who now identify lung cancer as a disease, not a moral failing.

Think of your illustration as an extension of your headline, and the headline as extending your illustration. They should support and complement each other. Thus, you should avoid illustrations that are not an integral component of your advertising copy.

An example of this principle marred the introductory ad campaign for the Infiniti luxury automobile, launched just months after its fellow Japanese luxury nameplate, Lexus. In a series of ads narrated by actor Michael Douglas, dreamily photographed video of rocks, trees, streams and birds were used to proclaim the natural inspirations that stimulated the engineering and design of what was at the time Japan's surprising entry into the luxury car market.

But there wasn't even a glimpse of the car. Consumers were confused and unimpressed. Even decades later, advertising analysts blamed the campaign for Infiniti's indistinct brand image and lagging sales compared to Lexus. One critic claimed Infiniti's campaign "overdid the Zen imagery well into self-parody."[7] The moral of the story: Keep your communication objective in focus, and don't disrupt the single-mindedness of the message that escorts the audience from the visual into the copy.

Because effective advertising copy often illustrates how the consumer's life will be bettered by using a product/service or adopting an idea, illustrations showing consumer transformation are often quite effective. Show how the product works better than its competition, how the consumer's life is made better by adopting your ideas or how envious the neighbors would be of the purchase your audience has the chance to make. This consumer transformation is as powerful a motivator in the visual as it is in the body copy. The transit ad in Figure 12.3 powerfully urges transformation from callousness to caring.

Another guideline for advertising illustrations amplifies a central rule for writing advertising copy: Avoid advertising clichés. If readers have seen it before, it probably won't draw their attention from the din of advertising around them.

### The Headline: The Lede Sentence of an Advertisement

Because the headline should complement the visual, many of the same principles apply. Having said that, we still caution you that just as in choosing a visual, there are few rules dictating how to create an effective headline. There is no minimum number of words a headline must contain, nor are there any prescriptions defining what a bad headline is. Consider the success of Chick-fil-A's "Eat Mor Chikin" slogan. Its short phrasing, purposeful misspellings and the childlike font in which it often appears perfectly complements the images of mischievous, self-preserving cows the headline usually accompanies.

Remember the headline essentially serves the same role as a news release's lede sentence. It's the limited opportunity your readers give you to involve them in the story. Within those few words, you've got to interest a reader who's been assaulted by hundreds of thousands of advertisements in the past. To do that, you need to introduce a stimulating idea that involves the reader's self-interest or curiosity in the main selling idea, and you need to structure it within a format they haven't seen before.

There are many types of headlines. Some offer a benefit:

> What does Cerengetti have to do with this rabbit? Absolutely nothing!

This ad for a cosmetic company that doesn't use animal testing is paired with a picture of a wild rabbit and the story of the company's commitment to not hurting animals in their testing and manufacturing process. You can view the full ad and our analysis in Case in Point 12.1.

## CASE IN POINT 12.1  Crafting a Static Advertisement

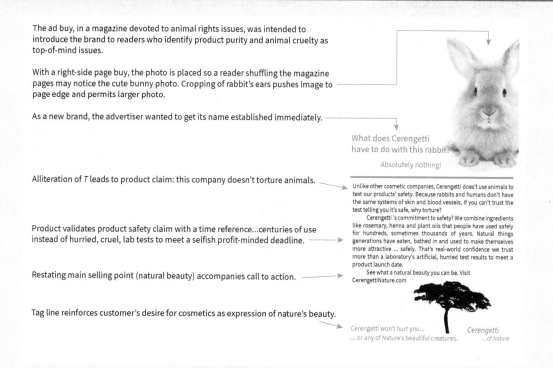

The ad buy, in a magazine devoted to animal rights issues, was intended to introduce the brand to readers who identify product purity and animal cruelty as top-of-mind issues.

With a right-side page buy, the photo is placed so a reader shuffling the magazine pages may notice the cute bunny photo. Cropping of rabbit's ears pushes image to page edge and permits larger photo.

As a new brand, the advertiser wanted to get its name established immediately.

Alliteration of *T* leads to product claim: this company doesn't torture animals.

Product validates product safety claim with a time reference...centuries of use instead of hurried, cruel, lab tests to meet a selfish profit-minded deadline.

Restating main selling point (natural beauty) accompanies call to action.

Tag line reinforces customer's desire for cosmetics as expression of nature's beauty.

What does Cerengetti have to do with this rabbit? Absolutely nothing!

Unlike other cosmetic companies, Cerengetti doesn't use animals to test our products' safety. Because rabbits and humans don't have the same systems of skin and blood vessels. If you can't trust the test telling you it's safe, why torture?

Cerengetti's commitment to safety? We combine ingredients like rosemary, henna and plant oils that people have used safely for hundreds, sometimes thousands of years. Natural things generations have eaten, bathed in and used to make themselves more attractive ... safely. That's real-world confidence we trust more than a laboratory's artificial, hurried test results to meet a product launch date.

See what a natural beauty you can be. Visit CerengettiNature.com

Cerengetti won't hurt you...
... or any of Nature's beautiful creatures.

*Cerengetti*
*...of Nature*

There are headlines that select a specific audience:

Impotence.

This one-word headline for a hospital's sexual dysfunction clinic is quietly effective in drawing the attention of men who desire help for a sensitive problem.

There are headlines that offer news:

On July 12th, there'll be a South Seas port in the center of Iowa.

This ad for a Polynesian arts and food festival offers information about an exotic entertainment option for the landlocked residents of a medium-sized Iowa town. A pig and a cow bedecked with leis necks communicate the Polynesian concept and the local angle.

There are headlines that show the problems you'll encounter if you don't use the product.

There'll be a lot of red faces in your family if you don't use High PF sunscreen.

This ad, using an appeal called the reverse benefit, pictures three sunburned children and suggests you'll be considered a better parent if you buy this sunscreen brand.

In all these headlines, you see informational appeals very similar to the TIPCUP formula outlined in Chapter 6. Three of the headlines show reader impact, whereas the Polynesian festival ad combines proximity, unusualness and timeliness factors.

The commonality? Each of these headlines offers a conceit, a way of provoking curiosity that will tempt the audience to delve into the advertising copy.

You should consider approaches to escape clichés and discover a conceit. One is through wordplay. By rhyming, repeating or alliterating (echoing vowel or consonant sounds), you make the same claim a little more engaging to read, and give an advertisement a touch of the fun we had as kids listening to our parents read children's books to us.

Advertising copywriters also often use what we call **reversals**, which contrast the first example in a headline with the second example, often in an oxymoronic way. For example, an outdoor clothing company employs a reversal when it claims its clothes are "For the outdoors inside each of us," juxtaposing the opposites *outdoors* and *inside*.

Another technique of creating a headline conceit is the **pun**. A pun exploits multiple meanings of a term, or of similar-sounding words, for an intended effect. Puns allow you to communicate multiple ideas at once. For example, while promoting hearing aids sales during the holiday season, Professor Browning developed "Hear for the Holidays," using the headline in several static and multichannel advertisements. The pun communicates not only the importance of a person's *physical* presence (i.e., *here*) during holiday gatherings, but the *emotional* presence the season's sounds engage (i.e., *hear*). After all, what would Christmas be without sleigh bells, carols, children laughing, and on into elf-initum (we like wordplay)? And the possibilities for imagery? Virtually endless!

In all these cases, you've introduced more interest to the headline. So even if the headline's introduction of the subject's self-interest isn't enough to prompt someone to read it immediately, the wordplay's entertainment and curiosity value might. Additionally, you're hoping to introduce multiple meanings that not only announce the benefit but add an emotional statement about the product or service and its creator.

### The Bridge: Explaining the Lede

The problem with most conceits is that no matter how clearly you think you have established the true meaning, a portion of your audience just won't get it. That's where the bridge comes in.

The **bridge** is the advertising equivalent of the media release's second paragraph. The bridge lets you explain the headline and directly state the main selling idea in terms your audience can understand. Here's where you use plain language to tell readers what you're going to prove in the body copy. It's generally a one- or two-sentence paragraph.

### The Statement of Benefits: Justifying the Actions You Want

The main body of the advertisement presents the statement of benefits. The statement of benefits is, again, very much like the third section of an inverted pyramid, in which you engage facts, testimonials and histories to prove your thesis. In this case, the thesis is contained in the bridge.

The benefits stated in an ad are usually segmented much like those in a news release. Information supporting certain points is grouped together. For instance, an auto advertisement might spend the first section of the benefits statement supporting the car's reliability, the next discussing its performance, and the final section talking about its low price. Transitions are important, and memory-cue transitions are useful in showing readers the linkages among the product's many benefits.

### The Wrap: Reminding Your Audience Why They Started Reading

The final section of body copy in an ad is called the wrap. The wrap is the persuader, the invitation that moves the consumer from absorbing information into taking action—to buy a product or adopt an idea. Very much like the inverted pyramid's call to action, the wrap restates the main selling idea and then gives the reader a specific call to action, a way of gaining all the benefits the advertisement promises.

The wrap then presents a definitive suggestion to the reader—that she visit a website for information, call her legislator or visit a brick-and-mortar store. The wrap should explicitly move readers from merely processing facts to gaining the desired outcome.

### The Logo and Baseline: Completing the Call to Action

An ad's logo and baseline generally reestablish the brand name and reinforce the main selling idea. The logo area often pictures the product's store packaging and the company's logo so the consumer will be able to identify it on a retail shelf or online shopping site. The logo and baseline components often contain a link to the institution's website, email, phone number or street address so readers who have decided to act will know how to accomplish that. Finally, a baseline generally employs a corporate slogan to reinforce the ad or corporation's emotional image.

## Modifying Print Principles for Multichannel Advertising Writing

In static advertising, you are trying to display a product proposition that engages your audience's attention and self-interest, presents evidence your proposition is true and moves people to take a definitive action to benefit them and your client. Because the writing principles are fundamentally the same, this section will explore the peculiarities of **multichannel advertising**, which includes controlled audio and video advertising presentations delivered via the internet and other electronic means. We'll then discuss the implications as you write for each medium.

Multichannel advertising is often portrayed as an all-powerful motivator. Yes, those ever-present radio, television and internet ads have some degree of power in creating and socializing us. However, like every other communication medium, multichannel advertising has significant weaknesses.

Even though multichannel advertising sometimes seems like it invades every corner of our lives, it is characterized by the audience's passive engagement. In short, it doesn't command our full attention. That passivity creates problems, because if listeners and viewers discover halfway through a commercial they're interested in the message, they can't review the ad. They can't simply turn a page and see the ad again, as they would a magazine. Yes, technically they could rewind their DVR or YouTube scroll, but when was the last time you watched an ad on a loop? We thought so. For that reason, complicated messages are sometimes not as effective in multichannel media.

Multichannel advertising does, however, have one major advantage over print: You can involve additional sensory channels in communicating your message, letting your audience hear the excitement of a crowd before a sale or witness how your product is better than its competitors. Just as in all static advertisement writing, when you're developing a multichannel advertisement you need to exploit multichannel media's powers and minimize its weaknesses. If your multichannel ad consists of simply reading copy you prepared for a static ad, then you have failed. We'll look at those distinctly different strategies in the following sections.

### Writing Audio Advertising: Creating a Visual With Sound

Radio has been called "the theater of the mind." Out of the fabric of words, sounds and voices, the human brain can construct fabulous stage pieces transporting the listener into an environment that would be very difficult and very expensive to create otherwise: A pilot can land a plane on the city's biggest outdoor restaurant deck; a business executive can be transported from urban office to redwood forest in two seconds; an orchestra can be in the car's backseat to showcase a high-end auto stereo system.

That's a lot of power at your disposal. The theater of the mind doesn't depend on what you can imagine but on what you can *make* your audience imagine. Using words, sounds and voices, you create a mental image of the characters who populate your world, transporting listeners to that environment.

All this requires what we'll call *translation skills*—the ability to translate a striking visual concept into sounds that evoke that world for your listeners. Thus, audio advertising, like all static advertising, starts by establishing a central conceit. This should communicate a main selling idea that's important to your intended audience and unusual enough to draw your audience's attention to the advertisement.

Establishing that central conceit seems harder to do in audio than in any other medium. However, we've already discussed a skill that will help you. In static ads, we introduced the headline-visual conceit, a powerful image making people envision the characters who are talking and the places they inhabit. Once you've visualized a scene that would help your audience understand your main selling idea, the fun begins, because in audio advertising, you aren't limited by what you can photograph—or even Photoshop. The scenarios you can establish are virtually unlimited because you're using the imaginative power of the listener's mind.

We'll give you an example. A rural county's economic development commission wanted a radio ad targeted toward relocating businesses. The commission decided to highlight the county's solid financial advantages and pleasant country lifestyle. Obviously, a magazine ad could have shown an idyllic country farmscape, a clean-cut worker or a photo of a well-dressed business executive. But an audio ad isn't limited by reality.

The commission's radio commercial was structured as a media interview in which the writer blatantly establishes an absurd scenario. With farmyard sounds in the background, a reporter's first comment is, "I've never interviewed a cow wearing a business suit before." The cow, answering in a firm, authoritative voice, lists the county's many benefits. It's a fun, unique concept that shocks the audience from its inattention immediately but always keeps the image of the advertiser (an efficient, business-centered group) and the commercial's message (the benefits of locating in a rural area) upfront.

At other times, sound effects are enough to establish the scenario. The sound of a car's screeching tires, followed by an explosion of glass and the crunching of metal, is quite enough to communicate a car wreck to an audience. Music is often a potent imaginative stimulus too. Balinese finger cymbals and Japanese kotos accompanying an airline's theme music quickly and powerfully helps communicate the company's expanded service to Asia.

Click-Through 12.1 shows how even simple sound effects can add to an audio ad's effectiveness. The commercial to raise funds for a nonprofit organization opens with a suspense lede and the special effect of a child crying, which draws the attention of its targeted audience. Notice how the sound effects and text show a transformation from crying to laughter as a result of the consumer responding to the call to action.

**Strategic Thought**

Let's say you've been asked to develop an audio ad for a new laptop or tablet with a long-lasting battery. You want to communicate the versatility of uses for the products, the capacity to accomplish those tasks anywhere and the ability to work for hours without recharging. What scenarios can you create to communicate the attributes? What sounds would bring those scenarios to life in listeners' minds?

There's one surprising thing about an audience's reaction to audio advertisement: They will believe almost any outrageous scenario you establish. A man going to work naked because he's not using a one-hour dry cleaner or even a space alien buying tie-dye sweatshirts at a local T-shirt shop both seem plausible in audio ads.

What an audience will *not* buy is a commercial filled with actors who sound like radio announcers—acting as if they are in a normal situation—reciting unrealistic dialogue composed of hackneyed advertising claims. Have a listen:

> JOE: "Hello, Harry. I haven't seen you for months. And now to see you here in the Terrace Restaurant of the Ambassador Hotel. What a surprise!"
>
> HARRY: "Joe, what could be more natural? The Terrace Restaurant of the Ambassador Hotel is just the place for business meetings. I've got a big client over in one of the leather-upholstered booths, and he is so impressed by the surroundings and the food. I'm sure he's going to sign that big contract today."

If on our meager professors' salaries we could afford to buy the rights to the facepalm emoji, we'd put it here.

Atrocious as it is, this commercial offers a lot of clues about writing an audio commercial's body copy. First, either create a visual concept in which it's natural to talk about your client's products or create one so unbelievable your audience will accept that in your imaginary world people actually talk like that. Second, when composing dialogue, write like your audience talks. Use contractions, slang and jargon where appropriate. For the sake of credibility, be very careful not to put a trite, overused advertising cliché into a speaker's mouth.

Other things to remember? It's usually good practice to write short. Generally, writing about 60 words in a 30-second commercial will give your actors a better chance to capture the realistic rhythms of natural speech and milk the copy for humor and drama.

You should also mention the company's brand name often. Because there's no chance to review the copy to establish the company name, it's necessary to keep repeating it. Three mentions in a 30-second ad are common. And remember, the need to communicate visually in audio presentations also extends to establishing a picture of the product. Often you'll include some description of the packaging in the call-to-action section at the end of the commercial.

Finally, all advertising has the same basic goal. Good advertisements communicate the real-life benefits of the product. By the commercial's final words, your logical prospect should understand not only how the product will help her but also offer her a more positive self-image. That's a powerful combination, no matter the medium in which it's communicated.

## Writing Video Advertising: Using Every Sensory Channel That's There

As we emphasized in Chapter 8, a multichannel presentation is an additive effort, layering audio and movement onto static channel characteristics. It too is a passive medium, so it's not possible to review these advertising claims. That means you need to arrest your audience's attention immediately to involve them in your message.

But video has the strengths of capturing all the sensory attributes of the other advertising media we've discussed. Like a static ad, a video commercial can present information through pictures and written text, capturing the graphic nature of print. Like audio, product attributes can be established through voices, music and sound effects. However, video engages with movement and captures all the storehouse of rational and emotional associations we've gained from a lifetime of watching movies and television.

Involving all those senses simultaneously in an advertising message is the challenge of video advertising copywriting. Making decisions about camera angles and camera movement, sound effects and music, accents and actors, charts and captions are added to basic skills in presenting benefits in your copy.

### Creating a Visual Memory: The Central Visual

The initial steps in creating a video commercial are remarkably similar to any other advertisement. Your persuasion platform should lead you to a central visual conceit demonstrating your product's main selling idea to your target audience. It should do this by first involving and then persuading the audience.

That central visual conceit, like all other conceits, should be a striking, unique presentation to engage an audience that's become jaded after viewing thousands of other commercials. You can probably remember the small number of ads that, when you first saw them, startled you with the originality of their presentation, and then presented a selling idea that established and solidified your knowledge of the product's main benefit.

We recall a tire company's commercial claiming its tires maintained traction on wet roads better than any other tire. That's a common claim, but the commercial's central visual conceit memorably planted that claim. In the commercial, an exotic European sports car sped down rainy, narrow, mysteriously dark streets onto a wet dock by the harbor. There, workers attached grappling hooks to the car's body to hoist it aboard the ship.

The ship's crane pulled cables tight to lift the car into the ship, but the tires adhered so well, even on the wet dock, that the car's body ripped from its axle and undercarriage. That's a great central visual conceit, one that captures attention and communicates a selling point important to the product.

In static and audio advertising, that central conceit is usually at the beginning of the ad. However, the conceit in a video ad can occur most anywhere, even at the end, as in the tire ad from the previous paragraphs. The challenge of writing a video ad is to fit all the visual, aural and language stimuli into a narrative structure that will effectively communicate the visual conceit and the main selling idea.

Here's where you unfold the staggering variety of options you have in designing a video commercial. You could structure the ad to demonstrate

<aside>
**Strategic Thought**

Reconstruct a video advertisement you remember. Analyze it in terms of a central visual and describe how the central visual helped you remember the selling idea.
</aside>

your product or to show an elegant, romantic or efficient lifestyle of which your product is a part. A user or a celebrity could offer a testimonial or compare your product to its competitors. You could present a problem, illustrated by tragic or humorous situations your product could solve.

Once you decide how to structure your presentation, you're still faced with an astounding range of choices, all of which affect your writing strategies. Will you cast young or old narrators? Sophisticated, down-home or someplace in between? On camera or off camera? If on camera, what message can you convey by their clothing, their hair color, their ethnicity? Each decision will affect the dialogue you write so it fits your characters.

How long is it going to be? How are you going to shoot the commercial? Sometimes black and white is appropriate because it conveys a documentary's credibility or the gritty realism of a film noir detective movie. Is the commercial going to be animated or use live action? Are you going to use hard or soft focus?

### Adding Visuals and Sound to Text

After deciding on the commercial's structure, theme and presentation, you're ready to write copy. However, remember that as in all creative work, sometimes part of the ad copy or even a great camera angle emerges after you've started the process. The sequence isn't as important as the result. You'll recall from Chapter 2 that we're not big fans of rigid, hierarchical sequences.

Your goal is to write believable dialogue for your actors while demonstrating the product's main selling idea. You want to break your ideas into short, simple sentences and repeat your main selling idea and the product name often. At the end of the commercial, try to convince the customer to take the desired action. To accomplish that, you need to write a wrap summarizing your main points, then include specifics so the customer can act on the offer. By now we hope this process sounds familiar.

However, there are some writing modifications you must make because of the medium. Above all, think visually—not only in the scenes you choose to show in your ads but also in the copy you write. Be sure you don't overwrite the copy. In many places, your visuals can communicate many of the adjectives you're tempted to use. Words will simply distract from the visuals or sound effects.

Of course, there will be instances in which you can reinforce the visuals with words. When you make that decision, be certain your words and descriptions merge precisely with the visual. For instance, if your ad copy is discussing your company's reforestation efforts, you shouldn't be showing a visual of your factory smokestacks or of your corporation's president shaking hands with your state's senator. Creating two conflicting messages, one visual and one aural, will confuse your viewers as they try to choose which sensory channel to process. Coordinating your visual and aural messages is simplified by the storyboard format from Chapter 8, which matches narration, sound effects and visuals.

There may also be places where you want to really punch your message home by not only using the visual and aural channels but also by adding print in the form of **supertitles** on the screen. Used sparingly, supertitles can be effective in reinforcing your main selling ideas. Employ them when you have a list of product benefits or when you want to establish the brand name or a corporate baseline slogan forcefully. But when you do use supertitles, again be sure your voiceover is exactly the same as the supertitle so you won't confuse your viewers.

## Scripting the Video Commercial

Once you've written the copy, it's necessary to merge prose with video's technical capabilities. Again, it's vital to remember that movement, not mere visuals, is the medium's greatest strength. You need to employ movement or you're doing nothing more than filming someone reading a print ad.

It's helpful to think of the camera as a character in your commercial's narrative. Does the camera represent one of the participants in the commercial, for instance, an office worker who runs through the office trying to avoid a coworker who has bad breath? Once you've established that viewpoint, you've restricted yourself to only those shots a human could experience. In certain situations this human viewpoint is very persuasive because viewers feel they are involved in the action, as though the characters are speaking directly to them.

However, if the camera is a disinterested observer, you can use a wide variety of shots and camera movements. The camera as objective observer can witness the tension between husband and wife over his grass-stain encrusted slacks, then record the next-door neighbor's advice on which laundry detergent to use and float away to a far-off research laboratory to hear a scientist explain the technical reasons why one detergent is best.

After you've picked a viewpoint, you can decide on specific shots and specific camera movements. The commercial's subject can be photographed in every way, from an extreme close-up to a long shot from the top of a building or an airplane. Long shots are often used at a commercial's opening to establish whether the commercial is set at the beach or in the mountains, at the office or in a restaurant.

Then, depending on what's being communicated, closer shots are used. A commercial for a women's fashion line might use a medium shot to show the overall design of a dress, then move in for an extreme close-up to show detailing on a pocket or collar, and then pull back to a close-up of the model's face to show how pleased she is with the store's low prices for stylish fashions. And though it may sound odd, an ad for quilted toilet paper could use almost the same series of shots. Just further evidence of video's adaptability. (If you need to review video terminology, refer to Chapter 8's online materials.)

After you've reached this stage, you consider the contributions music and sound effects can make to your persuasive efforts. Use aural cues to accentuate the mood you're trying to create or simply draw the viewer's attention to the commercial. It's even possible to differentiate the quality of two products you're comparing, as was demonstrated in a television ad for a small, four-wheel-drive car. The ad characterized the tiny car as a small version of an expensive SUV by playing "Hungarian Rhapsody" every time either vehicle appeared (to avoid mistakes, that's Hungarian, as in Liszt; not Bohemian, as in Queen). When the expensive SUV was shown, the music was played by tubas. When the smaller car was pictured, the rhapsody was performed by flutes. Clever idea.

Creating advertising is a long and complicated process that is beyond the capacity of a book like this to cover fully, but we can examine how a writer thinks as she is creating an effective ad.

In Click-Through 12.2, we walk you through the strategic decisions that accompany each choice in a commercial's production. You probably never imagined a 30-second video advertisement would involve 12 separate camera setups, but it's one of our field's most carefully engineered compositions. The casting, the music, the camera angles and movements—all are considered for their contribution to the message's persuasion effect. That in itself is a measure of how much planning and composition goes into producing a video ad. It's what you can do when you're writing for controlled communication.

## Internal Communication

By now, you can appreciate the complexity and difficulty in executing a successful advertising campaign, regardless of the medium you choose. Though less noticeable than advertising, **internal communication** represents an incredibly important controlled communication investment. Advertising is controlled because practitioners pay for placement; internal communication, on the other hand, is controlled because practitioners own the distribution channels. From the low-tech office bulletin board to high-tech intranets and internal social networking sites, organizations possess a variety of means to communicate with employees, the stakeholder group arguably most pivotal for organizational success.

### Energizing Insider Commitment

Employees and volunteers form the backbones of corporate and nonprofit organizations.[8] When they feel valued, listened to, productive and deeply connected to the organizational mission and vision, they are often its most vocal advocates.[9] When they feel unappreciated, ignored, useless and disconnected, their resentment can spell disaster for the organization.[10]

In a well-managed internal communication program, you're trying to create employee buy-in and belonging that encourages commitment, knowledge sharing and energy to solve institutional problems. Executives, too often isolated from the factory floor, the small investor's home or the middle manager's cubicle, cannot marshal the total expertise needed to run a massive organization without their employees and stakeholders' help and insight. That's not an indictment of management—it's just a recognition of human limitations.

An honest appraisal of institutional strengths and weaknesses improves every management process and consequently forms the cornerstone of a well-conceived internal communication program. An organization's leaders integrate the concerns of many publics into their management plans. They must recognize the company's inherent capabilities and how they match their customers' emerging desires. Finally, they need to understand how changes in society itself, and its concern for the environment or civil rights or consumer affairs, may change the fundamental expectations of the organization.

Many of those insights begin within an organization's internal publics, who collectively represent a much broader and diverse audience than can be encompassed by the institution's management team.

Too often, institutional leaders forget a basic fact when they undertake internal communication: People do not become immune from the underpinning logic of persuasion theory simply because they've walked into their office or onto a factory floor. Paying them to be there doesn't make them less human.

In fact, they are audiences whose support and engagement you truly need. They want to feel like a message is directed to them, they want to be recognized for the contributions they make to the organization's success and they don't have any more patience for irrelevant information than when they are at home. These are employees who the organization depends upon for its profits, its customer service and network security. And woe to the employer who thinks she should devote all her persuasive efforts to clients and scant attention to employees and other internal publics.

Here's the guiding principle: Internal communication means the organization owns the communication medium. Internal communication does not mean the organization owns the audiences inside the organization.

### Indiana University: A Brief Case Study

Consider Indiana University (IU), the institution that pays Professor Browning's salary, a majestically underwhelming pittance of the university's $4 billion budget.[11] Its internal audiences start with the system's 110,000+ students and 22,000+ employees.[12] That alone is a population larger than all but about 500 U.S. counties.[13] Other internal publics include its alumni network of over 700,000 living grads scattered around the world. Then there are donors and fans of the university's sports teams.

The university produces publications, websites, training videos, signage, recruiting materials, application forms, billboard advertising and registration checklists, as well as institutional self-tributes for televised sports programming. That's all controlled communication, and it's largely directed at internal audiences, or audiences the university hopes become internal audiences.

IU (which, in lieu of paying Professor Browning more, has been kind enough to let you view its internal communication products) mounts a structured effort to maintain the university's brand image across its many communication outlets. It has a detailed brand strategy that defines its key publics, brand personality and "reasons to believe."[14] As you can see in Figure 12.4, it's a thoughtful declaration of traits the university wishes to convey about itself to its audiences.

There are specified fonts, rigid guidelines concerning IU's trident logo's use, and a list of all the colors its designers can employ in their communication products. Among the universe's infinite variety of colors, IU's designers have eight colors at their disposal. Of

**FIGURE 12.4** Indiana
University Brand Guidelines.

INDIANA UNIVERSITY

# Brand Guidelines

STRATEGY & MESSAGING    DESIGN    DOWNLOADS    TOOLS & RESOURCES    REQUESTS & APPROVALS    CONTACT

Brand Architecture
Audience
Voice & Tone
Personality & Values
Strategy
Messaging
Editorial Style

Home / Strategy & Messaging
BRAND ARCHITECTURE

## The IU master brand architecture

All of the elements discussed on this website started with the creation of the IU
brand architecture.

The architecture identifies the qualities that make us who we are, both in our
own minds and in the eyes of our community. It shows us what assets we can
leverage to reach our audience and reminds us how to connect with them on an
emotional level.

### Core target

Prospective students who
value the strength of a
world-class education in a
supportive and caring
environment.

### Insight

Choosing the right college is
one of the most important
decisions I will make in my
life. I want to choose the
place that will best prepare
me for a lifetime of success.

### Key benefit

The world-class academic
institution committed to the
lifetime potential of each
and every student.

### Reasons to believe

- World-class education
- Quintessential college experience
- Strong career development
- Great faculty-student engagement
- One of the largest alumni networks
- Global perspectives/experiences
- Experiential learning environment
- Excellent research opportunities
- Exposure to diverse point of views
- Flexibility/choices to finish degree
- Strong value for my dollar

### Brand assets

- IU degrees
- IU red and trident
- History and tradition
- Breadth of academic offerings
- Extraordinary faculty
- Multiple campuses
- One of the largest alumni networks

### Brand personality

- Smart
- Welcoming/approachable
- Global citizen
- Supportive
- Confident
- Exploratory

### Brand values

- Commitment to the individual
- Integrity
- Respect/commitment to diversity
- Research and exploration
- Global citizenship
- Service to the world community
- Academic freedom

course, there's crimson and cream (the school's colors), but only six specific other shades can be used as highlights in its print materials. Designing for online? You only get three.[15]

That control produces some excellent communication products. You can see how the university's internal communication staff manages a complex issue—guiding its valued, long-time employees through the anxiety-provoking, life-changing process of investing in their retirements. It starts early in the university's 26-page booklet detailing the multiple investment approaches and deadlines for consulting a financial adviser, enrolling in a plan or changing their investment funding. On page 4, the writer and designer establish a 1 … 2 … 3 format to break down complex details into easier-to-digest capsules, an approach they used throughout the document.[16]

For instance, deeper in the booklet (pp. 13–16), the university's designer employed the institution's limited palette to coherently explain the retirement plan's investment options using a color-coded decision tree. Designating a color to each of four investment options, the writer and designer let readers radically simplify their task. Once they choose an investment plan, they can follow sections coded with that color through the rest of the booklet to focus any additional procedural decisions on that one plan. You'll see the booklet ends with a checklist, consolidating the employee's needed actions and restating a timeline in a one-page format.[17]

You see the hallmarks of good persuasive communication in these materials. For instance, notice similarities with our earlier assertions that good writing tries to replicate the audience's thought process. By sequencing information to track the audience's anticipated decision process, you greatly improve their capacity and willingness to follow your message. Frequent heads and subheadings help your audience track the outline of your argument and locate and reexamine information for review. Use visual cues like bullet points, boldfaced or underlined copy to draw attention to important points or arguments. Side-by-side comparisons enable your audience to employ their mental energy for analysis, not to remember options that might be separated by pages of information.

The underlying techniques of good writing remain the same as you transition between audiences and communication platforms. It's true even when you're not actually writing. For instance, here's one example in which we didn't think Indiana University's communicators made the best choice. Figure 12.5 reports the results of a COVID-19 survey the university presented to its staff members.[18]

**IU's Retirement Plans Transition Guide**

https://hr.iu.edu/benefits/pubs/misc/IU_TransitionGuide_IU_FINAL.pdf

This transition guide carefully walks employees through complex changes in retirement plans and benefits.

Remember our rule about ledes? You've got a couple of seconds to grab an audience's attention. Figure 12.5a duplicates the first five survey responses the university's communication team posted in their report to university employees. Likely, these responses are presented in the order they were asked in the survey. But if the goal is to communicate the greatest concerns employees expressed in conducting regular duties during the pandemic, this presentation order isn't particularly effective. Why? It buries the lede.

It's not until we reach the ninth of 14 questions that the issue provoking the greatest concern, feelings of anxiety or isolation, comes up. In Figure 12.5b, you'll see the difference

**FIGURE 12.5A** Organizing Data Reporting.

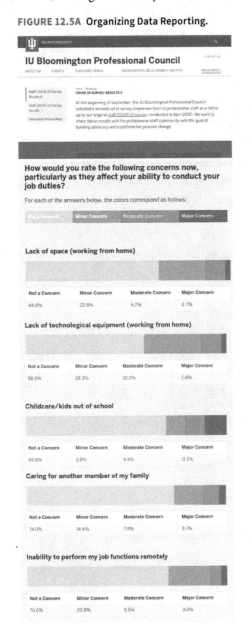

**FIGURE 12.5B** Organizing Data Reporting.

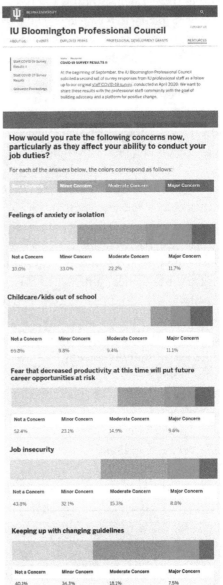

in urgency when we present the survey answers in order of importance, one of the organizational structures we introduced in Chapter 7. The audience receives the most important news from the survey within seconds, and as they scan the rest of the list, they quickly understand the diminishing importance employees assigned to other issues. Even if they abandon the survey results after the first page, our employees still recognize their colleagues' most troubling concerns.

Of course, internal communication isn't always about information as consequential as financial planning, pandemic response or safety measures during a crisis. Oftentimes you'll be asked to communicate much more banal, targeted information through controlled channels. But just because it's ordinary doesn't mean it's unimportant.

There's nothing particularly flashy about IU's Media School intranet, but there doesn't have to be considering what it's designed for. Every organization must communicate procedures employees need to follow, but they can't be expected to memorize all of them. How do you book a conference room for a meeting? What form do you submit to be reimbursed for travel expenses? When are upcoming organizational events and happenings?

Intranets serve as easily accessible repositories for such information. When pages are easily navigable and content clearly presented, employees can efficiently interact with the organization with minimal frustration. Additionally, when employees are more self-sufficient, organizations can dedicate fewer resources to internal management functions.

Finally, intranets have become increasingly used to highlight employees' professional and personal accomplishments, typically in the form of newsletters and updates. Remember, recognition serves as a powerful motivator, and a short article about the month's most prolific sales team, the employee who spearheaded a new company-wide recycling initiative or even the heroic Adonis who won the hotdog eating contest at the company's Labor Day picnic can make employees feel special and valued.

Some organizations extend this approach to include personal announcements like anniversaries and birthdays—even pet profiles. While you may not care that Carol from accounting just welcomed her first grandchild to the world, she and her accounting colleagues probably do. So God help you if you forget to include her blessed event in the monthly roundup.

Two conclusions you should draw from this brief discussion of internal communication. First, you employ precisely the same tools governing effective communication as for other media forms. Second, internal communication reaches vital audiences upon which your organization's success depends. Even though the executive suite may think that a paycheck compels an employee to read whatever the company writes, you should exercise the same attention to the rules of persuasive writing as you do in attempting to persuade audiences

**Run. Hide. Fight.® at Indiana University**

https://www.youtube.com/
watch?v=xU6_kB7RMg0

Remember that internal communication can also employ multichannel writing tactics. Take a look at Indiana University's video informing employees and students about active shooter response protocols and then read our take on the approach in **Click-Through 12.3.**

that you don't pay to listen to you. We'll have many more tips about how to engagingly present information to both internal and external publics in Chapter 13.

## SUMMARY

- Controlled communication constitutes messages that don't have to pass through a media gatekeeper before reaching an audience. While practitioners can be assured their institution's message will reach a public unabridged and without distortion, the speaker cannot control the audience's perceived meaning of the message.

- To overcome the audience's inattention to advertising, writers develop a conceit, a new and creative method of presenting an advertising claim.

- Internal audiences are vital to an institution's success, and communicators should employ persuasive communication's best practices to engage and involve them in the organization's success.

### Scenario Prompts: Crafting Controlled Messages

You'll find Scenario Prompts on pp. 367–386 of this textbook. While they vary in subject and difficulty, they help you hone your critical thinking and strategic writing skills. The following are best suited to this chapter's topics.

**Management: 4.1, 10.2** / Writing: 1.9, 2.8, 3.9, 3.10, 5.3, 5.4, 5.9, 8.5, 9.8, 10.10, 10.12

### *Figure Credits*

Fig. 12.1a: "Spuds MacKenzie" artwork is Copyright © 1986 by Anheuser-Busch, Inc.

Fig. 12.2: Copyright © 2015 by One Life.

Fig. 12.3: Copyright © 2012 by Lung Cancer Alliance.

IMG 12.1a: Copyright © 2012 Depositphotos/Djemphoto.

IMG 12.1b: Copyright © 2011 Depositphotos/lakalla.

Fig. 12.4: "Brand Guidelines," Copyright © by Indiana University.

Fig. 12.5a: "IU Bloomington Professional Council," Copyright © by Indiana University.

Fig. 12.5b: "IU Bloomington Professional Council," Copyright © by Indiana University.

# Delivering and Evaluating Controlled Messages

## The Power of Personalization

Like most people who become writers, I originally wanted to write fiction. I wanted to create beautifully written novels of manners like Edith Wharton. Or Arthur Miller—he was funny looking too—but he somehow convinced Marilyn Monroe to marry him. That's not a bad way to live life.

But then you confront the troubling reality of fiction. The fiction writer has to imagine an entire world populated with characters. During several discouraging fiction writing classes I found inventing things was much more difficult than reporting on reality.

Yet the strategic writer soon learns what the fiction writer knows: You've got a better chance to convince someone if you have a better story than your competitors. That often means you've got to discover the story that best expresses your clients' position (consequently, our major reason for emphasizing research throughout this book). That's particularly important in controlled media. You control the message, but you pay for the privilege through advertising, distribution and marketing production costs. That accentuates the importance of telling a compelling story quickly and communicating it coherently.

A few years ago my consulting firm was competing to dethrone the agency of record for a children's health charity that had amassed about a billion dollars in assets during nearly a century of service. It was a formidable challenge. The charity's current agency had a long-time history with the organization and included members of the fraternal group that was the charity's main base of support.

The contract became competitive when the charity's young new accountant started calculating some primitive metrics. The most shocking news? Nearly 50% of the donations stimulated by the charity's solicitation were $5 or less. In essence, after investments in materials, postage and other distribution costs, the charity actually lost money with every one of those donations.

Initially, I thought my firm could win the contract by asserting the prose for the organization's marketing materials was poorly written and unpersuasive. No help there. The competing firm's copy was generating an acceptable response in driving larger donations.

After exhausting my back-of-the-envelope explanations, I got permission to test the charity's two major mailing lists. What I called the "built list" was assembled over the course of decades by the charity. The "bought list" was a list of prospects my competitor purchased to expand the charity's reach and replace many aging and dead donors on the built list.

First problem? The organization wouldn't approve my request to send a survey to a random sample of their prospect and donor lists. Second problem? My competitor had combined the lists and distributed a single solicitation to the total list. Long story short,

I didn't know if there were significant audience differences between the two lists.

Faced with this dilemma, I submitted each of the lists to Lifestyle Selector (which is now incorporated into Equifax, an audience analysis company we'll discuss later in this chapter). Lifestyle Selector not only collected demographic data like age and income but also information on lifestyles (crafts, types of exercise, interest in pets, reading, etc.) from which a practitioner can extrapolate more meaningful psychographic characteristics.

The Lifestyle Selector results were revealing. The charity already knew the members of the built list were aging. Our research confirmed this. Many donors were 60+ years old. Fortunately for the charity, the income of the built list was extraordinarily high. In the built list, each income tier over $90,000 had a concentration at least 50% greater than the population as a whole.

But my analysis of the bought list, the one the charity's agency of record purchased to supplement the built list, won my firm the contract. The Lifestyle Selector analysis showed the bought list skewed much older and far less wealthy than the built list.

The reason for all the $1 and $3 donations now became clear. The other consultant had compiled audience members who apparently cared for children's welfare (the bought list had high index numbers for "supporting health charities," "donate to charitable causes" and high responsiveness to

mail order appeals). Those were all sound considerations. However, the resulting audiences' financial constraints meant they could donate only tiny amounts. And the bought list added prospects, who were intended to refresh the charity's solicitation list with younger people to replace the built list's aging and dying members, actually *increased* the total list's average age.

This was very persuasive information for my firm's pitch for the job. But you can understand how difficult it is to explain in prose. So here is the devastating graphic reinforcement we used to win the job.

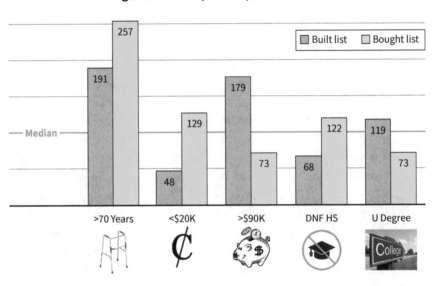

**Bought List: Older, Poorer, Less Educated**

My firm recommended the charity emulate the in-bred wisdom of the built list, which had already identified the characteristics of those who gave to their organization. We built a customer twin profile, using the combination of characteristics of past donors to find potential new donors, ones who reflected the demographic and psychographic profile of the built list. The difference? We modified the customer twin model to target people in their 40s and 50s who were on track to exhibit the same characteristics that the donors on the charity's built list currently possessed in their 60s, 70s and 80s.

That's what this chapter is about. Effective strategic communication is enhanced when you have the best story, even if you have to discover it yourself. And though sometimes that story is extremely complex, the best communicators know ways to present information clearly, often relying on graphics, so they can best use that tiny bit of time that most forms of controlled communication let us have with their audiences.

—WT

## What You Know

- Communicators are involved in a competition for the attention of target audiences.

- Internet applications permit tracking of individual consumer behavior patterns.

- Communicators should employ available sensory channels to construct multichannel messages.

## What You'll Learn

- How purchase and media tracking techniques let you develop a precise, cost-effective comparison for communicating with specific individuals

- How approaches that calculate an individual's lifetime value to a company can justify devoting greater resources to communicating with certain individuals

- How practitioners can employ graphics to more effectively communicate complex data and capitalize on the brief period of audience interaction

## Tight Targeting in Strategic Communication

We began this book by asserting the strategic communicator's role is to solve institutional problems through targeting specific messages to individuals or publics that could solve those problems. In this chapter, we'll examine how advertising, marketing and other forms of controlled communication provide advanced methods that help practitioners reformulate their communication tasks and assess their communication successes.

Disseminating successful controlled communication messages rests on the same basic principles as communicating through uncontrolled channels. Through audience analysis, you gain insight into which individuals will be most receptive to your message and most likely to act. Then you select media to which that audience attends and communicate through those channels.

The distinction here between controlled and uncontrolled communication is … well … the control. Because you either own the communication channel or are paying for placement, there's no gatekeeper to account for or please. When you don't have to work with, through or around gatekeepers, you exercise not only greater control over the eventual message, but you also wield the power to communicate extremely efficiently by hyper-targeting very specific audiences. Such meticulous message delivery is made possible largely thanks to advances in technology and market research.

Technology already has had a profound effect on the way strategic communicators practice their craft and, indeed, in the way organizations are managed. It enables us to more accurately isolate and reach the members of target publics most likely to respond to a specific message.

We can now assess the results of communication, replacing short-term goals with parameters that force us to view their effects over several years of communicating, or not communicating, with a particular public or individual. Sometimes that assessment method examines the lifetime of the members of that public.

Having the ability to examine the long-term ramifications of communication radically changes the procedures we use to plan communication campaigns and may have a startling, positive impact on the way organizations are administered. That makes our ability to translate MBO procedures into strategic communication tasks much more practical and effective.

Although all the media and methods discussed in this chapter may not yet have been applied extensively in strategic communication tasks, it's only a matter of time before they are used in one form or another in our duties. These, and undoubtedly many more, will be available to you and your colleagues soon. Let's first look at new media options.

## It's Everywhere! It's Everywhere!

**New media** is a term that's thrown around quite a bit, and the moniker has numerous, often competing, meanings. For our purposes, new media simply refers to any media message distributed through computer networks like the internet. So, ironically, new media isn't really that new, but practitioners continually find novel, innovative ways to use these channels.

New media offers communicators a variety of outlets in which to place their messages, and advertisers in particular have been quick to take advantage. Indeed, advertisers now place messages on video feeds that play while you get gasoline, while you're checking your social media, while you sit in physician waiting and examination rooms and at eye level while you're doing your business at restroom urinals.

However, these technological advances in advertising have, in many cases, simply created new forums in which to place what are basically traditional advertising messages. The more radical changes technology has fostered stem from new techniques for analyzing customer data and testing adverting effectiveness.

Here's one. Does your car have a factory-installed GPS (global positioning system)? Your car is pinging out your location, which then generates your trip directions. When your car slows or stops on the freeway, you are one of the data points that alerts everyone's traffic readout app that they might want to avoid the unfortunate route you took.

But GPS has uses beyond that. One firm links the traffic flow feature to change roadside digital billboards from simpler, more visual messages when traffic is speeding by, to more text-heavy copy when traffic is creeping or stopped.[1] Other marketing companies have tied consumer databases to mobile transit advertising on buses and cabs that will change advertised products to fit the demographics of each neighborhood through which they travel.[2]

It gets even more specialized. Several companies mount cameras hundreds of yards before you reach a billboard. Software recognizes and identifies oncoming brands and model years of cars. Automaker advertising urging a car purchase is triggered on the billboard when older-model cars approach. When a clump of brand-new cars travel past the sensor, a different product is advertised. Your cell phone is also wired into this network. Your phone is constantly emitting a distinctive code linked to your demographic and buying pattern data. When the ethnic, income or homeowning pattern of cell phones coming toward a billboard changes, the ads can instantly change to target that particular audience.[3]

Consider that all these changes stem from one technology (GPS) in one medium (billboards). That's just a small sample of the technological capacity you can access to personalize your message, a discussion we'll continue throughout this chapter.

> **Strategic Thought**
>
> What's the strangest venue in which you've encountered an advertising message? Did the placement decision improve or interfere with the ad's persuasive appeal?

## Measuring Communication: New Ways to Test Persuasion Effects

PR practitioners have not always looked to advertising to find ways to target audiences and evaluate communication success. That's not to say advertisers haven't expended tremendous effort and money to guide and evaluate their campaigns. For most of their history, however, advertisers have been as relatively inefficient as other strategic communicators in developing systematic methods for directing communication campaigns.

For instance, most research evaluating advertising effectiveness asked consumers if an advertisement generated a positive attitude about the product, or if they could remember the product name associated with a slogan, or if they had read most of an advertisement. That's hardly enough evidence on which to gauge whether a communication campaign has been effective.

Such tests don't prove there's a direct correlation between the selling message and the sale. A product pitched as "made by Americans for Americans" might elicit positive responses from extremely patriotic people. However, if you're trying to sell champagne, where the perceptions of French elegance and quality are important factors, Americanism isn't going to help. Similarly, if your tests find most people can remember the name of the product when confronted with a slogan, it proves only that the advertiser has successfully fulfilled a memory task, not created a sale. And, of course, all these connections only matter if consumers can remember them at the point of purchase and consider them more important than other persuasive factors, like price.

As you'll remember from Chapter 2, these secondary measures of communication aren't true measures of persuasion. For a professional communicator, persuasion has only occurred when the receiver acts as a result of encountering a message.

In some instances, even sales figures don't give a true picture of an advertising campaign's effectiveness. In mass-market advertising campaigns, in which there may be print ads, coupon incentives, in-school promotions and sponsored internet videos running simultaneously, it's virtually impossible to isolate the sales effect of a single part of the advertising campaign.

### Did It Really Work? Tracking Back-End Performance

Other advertising tests, largely adopted from direct marketers and speeded by the tracking capabilities of online interactions, are beginning to establish a solid research base that can more surely evaluate advertising and communication expenditures. One evaluation procedure applied to advertising and direct marketing help determine **back-end performance**. Examining back-end performance lets a business know not only how many people responded to a particular marketing message but also whether an individual consumer is a repeat customer of the company.

That's important to many communication tasks because marketers often go to enormous expense to recruit a prospective consumer to initially commit to a product. Magazines offer trial issues of their magazines, tote bags, gift subscriptions or other premiums to boost circulation. Many other marketers provide deep discounts, rebates and other incentives to entice the consumer to try the product. Each goodie cuts into the marketer's profit.

Because of that substantial outlay just to get a customer, many prospecting campaigns don't make money from the customer's initial order. To break even, the company first must satisfy the customer with the initial purchase. At that point, the company may be positioned to make a profit if the customer buys the product again, buys other company products or recommends the company's products to other prospective buyers.

For such marketers, merely calculating the initial response to a communication campaign can result in an inaccurate assessment. There have been many cases in which customers like the free premium so much that even though they didn't want the product, they would order it just to get the premiums. After the customers have the premiums, they never order the company's products again.

This has created some problems for marketers who merely examine the results from **split-run tests**. Split-run tests let advertisers determine which of many different options for advertising—illustrations, copy, design formats, premiums or even ink colors—deliver more sales. Advertisers can make these judgments by changing one element in the advertisements delivered to one portion of a distribution list. By comparing the sales figures of audiences who receive the different versions, it's possible to predict which version will be more effective in delivering a response from a particular distribution list.

Split-run tests are effective in determining which advertising strategy will be most effective in stimulating a customer to initially respond to an advertisement. But by concentrating only on one response, the tests neglect the capacity of some members of our publics to contribute more to our eventual success. One customer might respond to our initial ad, then never buy another product from our company. Obviously, that customer is much less valuable to us than the customer who buys the product after encountering the initial advertisement and then continues buying over time.

## CASE IN POINT 13.1   Payback Periods for Back-End Performance

Tracking back-end performance compels us to consider the long-term implications of our communication management decisions. Although it was first used by direct marketers to compare the efficiency of different mailing lists, it can also test the payback from offering a premium to encourage sales, or determine whether an employee-retention program would contribute to overall productivity. This back-end performance calculation projecting a financial service company's long-term profits demonstrates the profitability of communicating with different audiences changes dramatically if we extend the payback period. Admittedly, this back-end calculation is very simplified. A more sophisticated analysis might include comparisons of account maintenance costs, the effects of inflation, bad debts and income from new customer referrals.

| age of enrollee | number of enrollees | solicitation costs per 100 enrollees | income generation in year 1 | year 1 profit | income generated through year 5 | 5-year profit | income generated through year 25 | 25-year profit |
|---|---|---|---|---|---|---|---|---|
| 60 | 100 | $500 | $6,000 | $5,500 | $30,000 | $29,500 | $37,000 | $36,500 |
| 35 | 100 | $2,000 | $2,400 | $400 | $16,800 | $14,800 | $203,000 | $201,000 |

Companies study back-end performance in combination with the payback the company might yield from its relationship with an individual customer after one or two years—or even five years. You'll see in Case in Point 13.1 how tracking buying behavior for an extended period changes the marketer's judgment about which audience is most profitable to communicate with.

**Strategic Thought**

Why should extending the payback period for communication activities improve a company's management?

### Relationship Marketing: Calculating a Receiver's Lifetime Value

Because these long-term marketing assessment strategies are so important, many marketers now refer to such practices as **relationship marketing**, thus emphasizing the long-term profits from a continuing relationship instead of a one-time transactional payoff. Relationship costs and relationship marketing are intriguing ways to track direct-response marketing. As you probably already realize, relationship marketing describes the goals of strategic communicators more broadly: to use cost-efficient processes to gain and sustain the support of publics necessary for a company's immediate and long-term success.

> **MEMORY MEMO 13.1** Relationship Marketing
>
> 1. Orients the organization toward ethical behavior and long-term goals
> 2. Justifies extra communication spending to reach the best prospects
> 3. Helps prioritize communication tasks

To formalize and quantify a concept as nebulous as a relationship, marketers have developed a calculation called **lifetime value**. The concept of lifetime value means that some people, over the duration of an information campaign or even the duration of their lives, are more valuable to communicate with than others. If we concentrate our communication efforts on those people who have the ability to substantially help or hurt our institution, we have a chance of getting much better paybacks from our communication campaigns than if we use an equally costly campaign intended to reach everyone.

#### *Different Consumers, Different Value*

Let's consider an example from marketing to illustrate lifetime value. Say Corn Co. sells canned corn. Makes sense, right? In planning its advertising campaign, Corn Co. obviously wants to concentrate its commercials, advertisements and other promotions on people who buy canned corn.

In analyzing the broad market for a product like canned corn, which most families buy, the company's marketers probably rationalize that their most likely target audience will be the adults tasked with food shopping for their households. That audience for messages about canned corn will include a 26-year-old head of family with three small children who is barely able to make ends meet, an affluent 44-year-old woman with three teenage daughters, and an extremely wealthy 73-year-old retired widow. They all buy canned corn, so all are part of the target audience.

That's what a traditional marketing campaign might conclude. However, a campaign using lifetime-value principles doesn't give equal weight to these three customers. Instead, lifetime value argues that at different times in her life, a consumer's loyalty has a different value to a company. Instead of analyzing that customer's value to the company in terms of what she can buy during the next three weeks or three months, lifetime value tries to project the customer's value to the company during her lifetime. By estimating how many purchases customers might make during shopping trips for the rest of their lives, we can determine how much we should invest in communication efforts to win their loyalty.

For Corn Co., it's easy to see that a 73-year-old retired widow doesn't have much lifetime value to the company. No matter how rich she is, there's only a limited amount of canned corn she can buy during her golden years. The analysis of the other two women is much more interesting.

Normal advertising campaigns usually focus on high-income, middle-aged people because they generally have the most buying power. But it's easy to see that although the 44-year-old woman may now be buying a lot of canned corn to feed her three teenage daughters, within a few years her children will have left the house. At that point, even though she has another 30 or 40 corn-buying years on the planet, the amount of value she has to Corn Co. will decrease dramatically.

The young, struggling homemaker with her three small children is another case altogether. She's got another 15 to 20 years in which she will be making food decisions for four or five family members, and then 30 or 40 more years in which she'll still be buying canned corn, although in much smaller quantities. In the eyes of a lifetime value marketer, she's the richest consumer lode to mine because the buying decisions she makes now could establish a pattern that would keep her buying the company's products for the next half-century. Additionally, you can't ignore the brand loyalty she may instill in her children, which could manifest in another generation of purchasers. Corn Co. for life!

Because of the immense payback value she represents, lifetime value marketers can justify quite generous expenditures to communicate with that 26-year-old about canned corn. Although general advertising expenditures might be cost-effective for the 44-year-old customer, Corn Co. can offer the young mother free samples of its product, free recipe books, generous coupons and other premiums. If it can win the product loyalty of that woman, it can balance the costs of those enticements against the value of what she will buy for decades.

### Lifetime Value and Issues Management

Lifetime value represents a healthy trend for American business. It shifts the emphasis away from short-term profits and back to products, conduct and messages that will pay off for the company for a long time to come. That is also the essence of the value strategic communication represents to an institution. It's our job to build an environment of public support that's only obtained through a long-term commitment to corporate responsibility, ethics and ultimately to our stakeholders themselves.

But lifetime value is more than an ethical reminder with which to educate corporate executives. It also is a tool we can use to plan our campaigns and justify higher-than-average expenditures to reach particularly valuable target groups. Let's look at how lifetime value concepts can be applied to strategic communication situations.

Let's say you work for a company that, because of a history of pollution, has gotten a bad reputation among environmentalists. Consequently, every time the company needs a permit to do business or expand, a group of young environmentalists seems to camp in legislators' offices to lobby against your company's plans.

However, new management has brought with it a new, more conscientious attitude. The company has begun cleaning up the environmental problems it caused. As a strategic communicator, you wrote about the company's environmental turnaround in the company's newsletters and corporate reports. You gained prominent local media coverage on the company's pollution control innovations and bought advertisements in the state capital's newspaper during the legislative session extolling your company's new attitude toward lawmakers. Unfortunately, all your efforts haven't changed the minds of the young environmental activists, who still harass the company at every turn.

Lifetime value concepts might tell you that communication with townspeople where the company is located, even with the legislators and regulators who vote on the government permits, won't be the most cost-effective way to communicate. The townspeople and stockholders already know how your company benefits the community. The legislators are nominally responsive to voters and other pressure groups, but they aren't necessarily the people to whom you should devote the greatest communication resources.

Instead, lifetime value concepts suggest that over their lifetimes, those dedicated young environmental activists are going to make the company's existence miserable. They not only can mire the company in sustained legal and regulatory battles, but they are capable of stimulating a lot of negative media coverage for the company. Worst of all, they might be causing havoc for the next 40 years—or perhaps longer thanks to their healthy vegan diets!

Lifetime value argues that it might be wise to spend substantial resources now to communicate with the members of that environmental group. Those tactics might include more interpersonal communication: plant tours for group members and informal emails and personal consultations between environmental leaders and company management. These channels will likely require costly and extensive staff time from you and your company's executives, but they could ultimately prove cost-effective.

Relationship marketing is a useful perspective from which to examine strategic communication and budgeting. It compels us to think about the people with whom it is important for us to communicate if we wish to solve organizational problems. It segments those publics from the general mass of people who comprise a society and forces us to rank the importance of those publics. Once we've established those rankings, we can prioritize our expenditures for communicating to each of those groups, basing our budgets on the importance of their support to the institution's success.

By extending the period during which we look for a payback on our communication efforts, lifetime value forces organizations to confront the short-term and long-term advantages and disadvantages of company initiatives and communication campaigns about those initiatives. That's a very positive outlook for institutions that are planning to survive and prosper in a fast-changing environment.

## Data-Driven Marketing: Targeting Advertising Messages to Individuals

Extending lifetime value principles to granular levels, we introduce **data-driven marketing**. It's called data-driven marketing because it's possible only because of the vast amount of information marketers collect and warehouse about consumer purchases. Data-driven marketing can as easily be applied to several strategic communication tasks.

Marketers have easy access to your buying decisions. Buying an item via the internet provides another personal data point stored somewhere in the cloud. Buy an item in a store with a credit card, and there's a sales slip and a resulting data trail recording who you are, the exact item you bought, the exact time you bought it and if you bought it at a store you usually don't patronize. Those individual store and internet purchases provide a lot of information about your lifestyle and habits. If you order gourmet cookware, exercise equipment, jazz recordings and books on mystic philosophy, marketing experts can begin to piece together a portrait that helps them predict certain other actions you might take.

## We Know What You've Bought: Universal Product Codes

It's easy to see how all your movements on the internet could be tracked. Once you connect to an organization's website, the connection between your computer and the organization's servers is noted and recorded. But a brick-and-mortar store discovering who you are may seem more difficult. In truth, it's not drastically different.

Next time, look at your supermarket and department store cash register receipts that list and describe purchases when your items are scanned. These receipts are generated by the Universal Product Code (UPC) bars printed on product packaging. Those UPC bars were originally intended to tell store inventory managers what items were almost sold out so the store could restock its inventory.[4] However, marketers quickly found other uses for that information. Because so many purchases are made or validated with credit or debit cards, retailers have a record of the customer's name and address. Even cash purchases can be linked by those organizations savvy enough to enroll customers in rewards programs. What did you think that little perks card was for anyway?[5]

All those payment methods and rewards programs give retailers and marketing and public relations practitioners the opportunity to directly link an individual name with specific retail purchases. That pattern of purchases provides wonderfully detailed information that allows communicators to develop comprehensive profiles of current customers. Those profiles also let practitioners predict potential customers with whom to communicate their messages.

In addition, profiles give marketers opportunities to conduct communication campaigns based on lifetime-value principles. Let's go back to the canned corn example. Let's say you are marketing Corn Co. canned corn. You discover from cash register receipts and bank or credit card usage that Mary Jones buys Corn Co. canned corn and Jane Smith buys Kentucky Kernel Inc. canned corn. If you're designing a marketing communication campaign this is extremely important information. Because Mary Jones is already buying your product, you may want to reinforce her present buying behavior, but you don't need to communicate basic product quality or features with your advertising claims. On the other hand, Jane Smith is a person you need to convince of your product's merits.

Offering free product samples, online recipes or cents-off coupons to Mary Jones, your existing customer, simply cuts into your revenues. She would just spend less on purchases she would make anyway. However, those incentives to buy your product could move Jane Smith to become a loyal, long-term Corn Co. customer. Advances in data mining and monitoring let you isolate people who don't buy your products and give them—and only them—coupons and other inducements. That ability to concentrate your financial and communication resources on just those individuals you need to convince is quite valuable to your organization.

### We Know Who You Are: New Capabilities to Target an Audience of One

We have a greater ability to target specific audiences today. As we've seen, we can reach a very selective audience through digital media and direct marketing. But until recently, targeting in traditional advertising has depended on whatever special interest the media outlet served. At least at the moment, it's only on new media channels like YouTube, not television, that it's possible to target video commercials so they'll go only into homes owned by white-collar professionals, or people who like to fish or any other market segment.

But the mass media are striving to catch up. General interest magazines, trying to compete with the targeting capacities of internet marketing, have been employing more and more technology to give that kind of selectivity to advertisers. Decades ago, marketers thought themselves clever because they could buy magazine advertising that appeared only in certain regions of the country. Thus, it was possible for a beer company that marketed its product only to certain states to buy advertising that had the prestige of a national magazine but was limited to only a certain geographic area.

Now even general interest magazines like Time have gone beyond this selectivity. Computer-coordinated binding and addressing equipment let advertisers bind specific advertisements into individual copies of those magazines. That means that if your company sells expensive boats, you could bind an advertisement for your $165,000 cruisers into copies of Sports Illustrated magazine mailed to high-income individuals who own a boat valued at $60,000 to $100,000 and who have certain psychographic traits that make you think they are looking for more status items in their lives.

### We Know What You're Like: Multivariate Analysis and Customer Twins

The intersection of consumer tracking capacity and massive computing power lets us collect and study vast amounts of information about millions of individuals. This extensive information on individual consumers includes demographic, psychographic, lifestyle and purchasing behaviors, which are collectively called **multivariate descriptors**.

Here's how the services that compile multivariate descriptors function.

Marketing research services like Equifax have collected data on hundreds of millions of individual consumers. In addition to standard demographic information such as name, address, phone number, household income, and number and age of family members, the services have collected extensive psychographic information, including data on hobbies, reading interests and past purchases.

Let's examine Equifax's approach. By tracking public records as well as buying and charitable behaviors, Equifax has developed a lifestyle profile for each of about 210 million people.[6] Thus, a practitioner is able to identify if a specific individual has a pet, plays tennis, goes boating, collects stamps, enjoys gourmet cooking, goes to baseball games, or even dabbles in the occult.

At the simplest level, the capacity to capture all these audience characteristics provides you with the ability to build a distribution list of people who pursue particular activities. For instance, if you want people who invest in real estate, you can get a list of the U.S. consumers who might be likely prospects for your organization's e-newsletter on real estate limited partnerships.

You can also find more tightly focused concentrations. Let's say, for example, that you are assembling a prospect list for an Atlanta caterer who specializes in bat mitzvahs. With a list of multivariate descriptors, you can select a mailing list that comprises only the parents of 12-year-old Jewish girls with mailing addresses in the ZIP codes in and surrounding Atlanta.

But there are even more intriguing things you can accomplish with this multivariate list. Let's say you are working for a national nonprofit agency striving to place teenage orphans with new families. Because there aren't any mailing lists specifically comprising people who want to adopt teenage children, you have to look for other methods to find an audience interested in your message. You try to think about some characteristics of the foster families who are already involved in your program, but there don't seem to be any obvious ones. The foster families come from all sections of the country and represent many different income levels, faiths and races. So how can you find promising prospects? You can use what's called a **back-through run**.

Here's how a back-through run works. With the Equifax data, you can submit your entire list of families who have already adopted a teenager. A computer searches the company's entire list and selects every one of your foster families that appears on the Equifax list.

The computer then compiles all the lifestyle and demographic characteristics of the families who have already adopted children and takes that information to create a composite profile of people who have participated in your program. That portrait might reveal a concentration of foster families from certain age groups, occupational groups or lifestyle interests not readily noticeable to you. That profile is valuable in itself, because it gives the adoption agency's writer an idea of appropriate vocabulary, as well as persuaders and premiums to use in its recruitment materials.

But more important is that the group of psychographic and demographic qualities that characterizes the agency's present customers can be used to expand its list of prospects by running the typical adopter profile *back through* the database. Taking those characteristics, a computer program selects every consumer in the entire Equifax data bank who

---

**Strategic Thought**

Name a specialized service or product that could be marketed effectively with a back-through run. What marketing approaches would you need to employ to duplicate the same results using traditional advertising channels?

---

**MEMORY MEMO 13.2** Steps in a Customer Twin Back-Through Run

1. Compile all customers who have taken the desired action
2. Develop a profile of those customers from a multivariate list
3. Search the multivariate list for other customers who echo that profile
4. The resulting list represents customer twins of those who have taken the desired action

exhibits a significant proportion of that cluster of characteristics held by people who have already adopted a teenager. That list of so-called **customer twins** contains potent prospects for the next recruitment campaign the agency mounts. That's an exact way of picking an audience for your message, which Memory Memo 13.2 summarizes.

## Infographics

Of course, once you isolate an audience to communicate with and a medium to communicate through, you still have to produce a message. Because this textbook is first and foremost about writing, we've focused on producing that content through the written word. Even in discussing multichannel media, our aim was to provide you with the tools to script audio and video, not record and edit.

With controlled communication messages, however—particularly those conveying complex information or targeted to internal decision-makers—the ability to generate compelling, easily digestible visuals is often the difference between success and failure.

**Infographics** is a general term for these types of visual displays of information. As the name implies, infographics are graphics that use visual elements to present information. There is solid evidence such presentations do enhance audience comprehension, even among highly educated publics. In one study, researchers offered one group of economists raw data and a standard statistical analysis; a second group got the data, analysis and a graph; and a third group of economists received only the graph illustrating the data. Over 60% of the economists in the first two groups incorrectly answered a question about the data. The third group? Only 3% of those economists gave a wrong answer to the same question.[7] That's the power of infographics (Figure 13.1).

**FIGURE 13.1 Infographics.** In its simplest form, an infographic displays numerical information types of data using icons and other spot illustrations. These help immediately identify the focus of the data being transmitted.

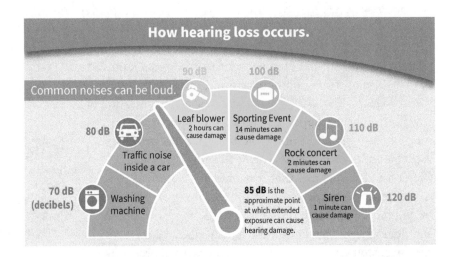

In their most simple forms, infographics are simply more organized, visually stimulating ways to present detailed information. For instance, in Figure 13.1, the CDC portrays information about hearing loss by linking each major increase in decibel level with a spot visual that identifies a commonly encountered noise of that intensity. It communicates the information much more quickly and memorably than if the CDC had offered only numbers.

Another of these compelling infographics is called a **word cloud**. A word cloud is nothing more than a calculation of the relative frequency of word use within a piece of text. Readily available internet applications can then represent those frequencies graphically. The words that appear most often are displayed in the largest font sizes, and words appearing less frequently are progressively smaller.

The final product of a word cloud often vividly illustrates the focus of a document or speech, and frequently reveals an emphasis that listeners or readers may not have even noticed. To illustrate the concept, in Figure 13.2, we've developed a word cloud of the text from Chapter 6 of this book. That chapter, which focused on a strategic communication document's first sentence, is well summarized by the most prominent words in the word cloud: *audience, information, attention, lede, message* and *writing*.

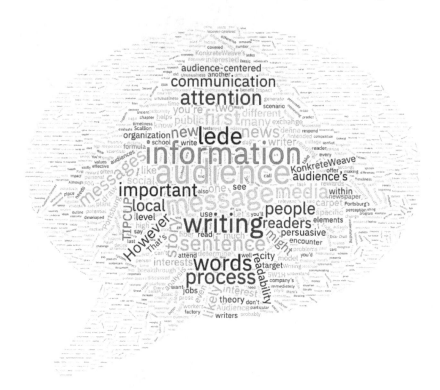

**FIGURE 13.2 Word Clouds.**
Word clouds visually summarize a subject by illustrating the relative frequency of words appearing in a piece of copy.

## Data Visualization

So, one way to increase the effectiveness of your communication is to illustrate it with graphics. However, you cheat yourself, your organization and your audiences by merely better illustrating information.

What if you could extract additional information to share with your audiences? That's the value of **data visualization**. This more limited term for portraying information reminds writers that graphic tools can go beyond illustrating knowledge to their audiences. They can also discover insights that they themselves did not know.

While such visualization approaches can be technically very complex, there are others that are quite accessible to the novice strategic communicator. We're only going to examine three of these methods, which you can develop using the graphic functions of computer programs you likely own already (Adobe's Creative Cloud Suite and even Microsoft Office programs jump to mind).

**FIGURE 13.3 Heat Maps.** Heat maps can represent thousands of data points. In this case, we see the levels of prescription opioid use in 3,144 counties in the United States.

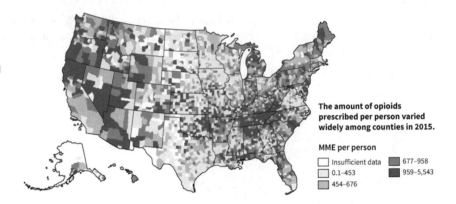

The amount of opioids prescribed per person varied widely among counties in 2015.

MME per person

- Insufficient data
- 0.1–453
- 454–676
- 677–958
- 959–5,543

### Heat Maps

You can quickly compare the geographic concentration of an issue with a **heat map**. The intensity of individual values is represented in varying colors. In Figure 13.3, the counties colored black indicate instantly where the per capita rate of prescribed opioids use is highest. Extremely high concentrations of opioid prescriptions (over 1,000 doses per person per year!) are apparent along the Appalachian Mountain counties in West Virginia, Kentucky, Tennessee and northern Alabama. You can also see how the problem overwhelmingly affects rural counties, both across the South, in the far northern Midwest and in rural counties in the West. Major metropolitan areas, such as Chicago, New York, Los Angeles and Houston and Minneapolis, have lower levels of opioid use.

### Venn Diagrams

A **Venn diagram** (Figure 13.4) shows the possible logical relationships between a defined collection of different characteristics. Each characteristic is represented by a certain geometric figure (usually circles). When the circles overlap, they create subsets of the total data that detail where characteristics are shared between and among audiences.

In Figure 13.4, the Venn diagram visualizes a simplified audience analysis for Home Depot's do-it-yourself winterization campaign, which we discussed in Chapter 9. The circles represent people under 70 years of age (red), people with annual household incomes between

## Winterization Marketing Campaign

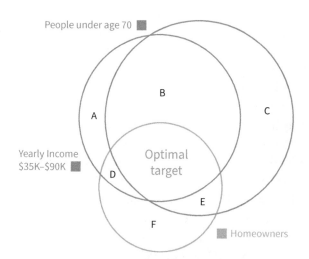

**FIGURE 13.4 Venn Diagrams.** Here's a simplified Venn diagram illustrating a multivariate marketing campaign. In this case, we have chosen three audience characteristics we wish to simultaneously capture in our target public. We could have added additional overlays—e.g., one for ZIP codes where the average wintertime temperature is below 50 degrees.

$35,000 and $90,000 (purple) and people who own homes (green). The circles are different sizes to communicate information about the relative numbers of each set. The largest set constitutes everyone under 70 years old. There are fewer people within our targeted income range: enough money to buy winterization supplies but not so much income they would likely hire a contractor to perform the work. The smallest circle represents the smallest set of people, those who own their homes.

When these three sets of data are superimposed, they clarify our arguments concerning the individual consumers who are the best prospects for our winterization campaign. The Venn areas labeled subsets A, B and C represent individuals who don't own a home. Those are nonpublics since they, as likely apartment dwellers, are unlikely to make buying decisions concerning home improvement projects.

Subset D is the group of people who own homes, but because they are older (70+ years old) and face physical limitations, it's more likely they would rely on others to winterize their homes. Subset E? It contains those homeowners who have incomes outside our specified range: either financially secure enough to have the work done by a contractor, or too poor to be able to afford winterization supplies. The final component, Subset F, comprises those people who own a home, but neither are in our defined age group or in our income group. These are older people who are either very poor or quite wealthy. Again, another nonpublic.

Our prime audience is that segment where all those characteristics merge in individual consumers: physically active adult homeowners who would be receptive to DIY winterization supplies, able to afford insulation and other supplies, but hesitant to spend their finite income on a professional contractor. The Venn diagram is a powerful aid in explaining this decision to our audiences.

*Cartograms*

Because we too often become habituated to considering a problem in only a single dimension, we often must take special efforts to overcome our locked-in perceptions. That's been commonly recognized in U.S. political elections, in which election maps used by politicians and media portray the voting totals by counties, usually communicating the Republican Party votes with the color red, and Democratic votes with blue.

This fails to portray that a county can have a geographic size that isn't proportionate to its population. For instance, New York County, which basically corresponds to the island of Manhattan, comprises just 33.6 square miles. Yet New York County alone has a larger population than 11 individual U.S. states.

Here's another illustration. Dallas County, Texas, containing the state's second-largest city, has 2.67 million people within its 909-square-mile area. Further west, King County, Texas, is almost exactly the same size, 913 square miles. But King County has only 277 residents.[8]

Nonetheless, in a 2020 election results map, an overwhelming triumph for Donald Trump among King County's 159 voters generated a red dot on the Texas election map exactly the same size as the blue dot representing Democratic candidate Joe Biden's triumph, in which he won 65% of the 922,000 votes counted in Dallas County.[9] If the two counties had been represented according to their voting importance rather than their geographic size, Dallas County's blue dot would have been nearly 6,000 times larger than King County's red dot.

Notice how difficult it is to envision these relationships when they are conveyed in prose. That's why **cartograms** (Figure 13.5) are so useful. Cartograms are maps in which the map's geography is distorted to emphasize an alternative comparison, say voting strength, population or income.

Let's consider another political subject. Although the United States hearkens to the axiom of "one person, one vote," the real representative power of voters in different states varies widely for two reasons. First, every state, no matter how small its population, is apportioned at least one member among the 435 House representatives. But this is not exact math. So Montana, whose 2019 population is estimated at slightly over 1 million people, gets one House member. Rhode Island, which had 9,000 fewer people in 2019, got two representatives in the House in a lingering echo of the 2010 congressional reapportionment.

There are also voting power discrepancies in the U.S. Senate. Because of a 1792 constitutional compromise, each state, no matter its size or population, is represented by two senators. As a result, each of California's two senators represent about 20 million people. Each of Wyoming's two senators represent about 290,000 people. Looked at another way, each Wyoming resident's vote derives the same power in the U.S. Senate as approximately 70 Californians.[10]

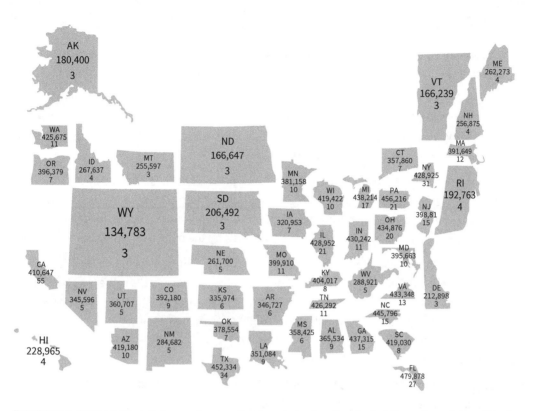

**FIGURE 13.5 Cartograms.** A cartogram is a map that is scaled not on the physical dimensions of the political subdivisions it portrays, but upon the intensity of another statistical unit. In this case, that's the relative congressional power of individual voters in the 50 United States. The label for each signifies how many citizens each state's congressional delegation represents. So a Wyoming voter has 3.4 times the influence in electing a member to the U.S. Congress than a Texas voter.

Figure 13.5 illustrates how those relationships appear when they are approximated in a cartogram.[11] This map, which represents the 50 states not based on their land area but on the relative voting power each resident holds in electing representatives and senators, instantly conveys the disparities. Wyoming, Alaska, Vermont and North Dakota are shown proportionately much larger, indicating the greater voting strength wielded by individual voters in those states. Conversely, individual voters in Texas, California, Florida and North Carolina get much less power per resident. An intelligently designed cartogram can quickly communicate significant insights into data while at the same time presenting even more detailed information for those who wish to spend time studying the map closely.

The lesson? As we discussed in Chapter 4, here again you see the very process of finding new ways to communicate information about your organization and its audiences provides novel insights into powerful messages to animate your storytelling. That self-knowledge is fully as useful in motivating people inside the organization as it is to outside publics. It reveals new audiences, potent persuaders for those audiences, startling information to entice their attention, and visuals that quickly convey your organization's message to time-starved

## CASE IN POINT 13.2  Pareto Charts

Data visualization is not only useful in communicating information to audiences but can also help us discover problems and offer powerful insights into how to solve them.

A Pareto chart is one accessible approach the strategic communicator can use to search for the problems, which if solved, will yield the highest return. The singular, *Pareto chart*, is actually misleading since the process normally comprises several charts that progressively examine more specific subsections of the data.

A Pareto chart highlights the most important components of an issue to ensure they receive the greatest and most immediate attention. The frequencies of the individual values are shown by bars in descending order. Then there's an ascending line that represents the cumulative total of the values portrayed by the bars.

The Pareto charts we're presenting here explore U.S. workplace dangers. In the first manifestation, we chart the causes of all deaths in the workplace. Here, there's an instant surprise, which is made quite apparent in the graph we generate. Most workplace deaths are not caused by machinery or falls, as we might expect. Instead, most occupational mortality occurs because truck drivers, salespeople, construction workers and others are involved in traffic accidents while on their jobs.

But when you start to drill into the data to determine how you could lower worker mortality, you find even more unexpected results. As shown in the next two charts, the largest number of male workers die due to roadway incidents, falls, and equipment accidents, as we would have predicted from our initial chart. But when we perform the same data operation on women in the workplace, we discover a very different result. The leading cause for workplace deaths among women? Homicide.

We might initially think that women must be victims of armed robbery since how else would you be murdered at your place of business? However, when you extend the Pareto chart one further layer, you find a stunner. Most murders of women in the workplace are not by robbers, nor by the colleagues and clients with whom they spend a vast majority of their workplace hours. No, 40% of the murders of women in their place of employment are committed by their spouses, domestic partners or relatives.[12]

This completely reorients our perspective on workplace safety, particularly concerning women's safety. While safety railing and guards near dangerous equipment and yellow paint highlighting slip-and-fall dangers are important, a workplace safety program that wants to confront the chief cause of women's occupational deaths may need to reorient or supplement its efforts.

**Case in Point 13.2a**

What Kills U.S. Workers in the Workplace?

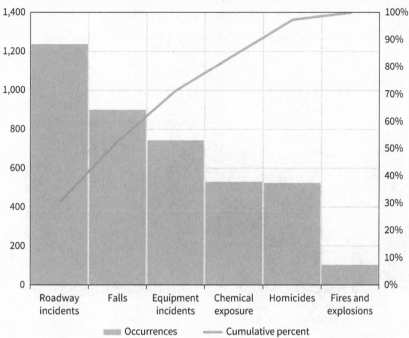

Occurrences     Cumulative percent

**Case in Point 13.2b**

What Kills Men in the Workplace?

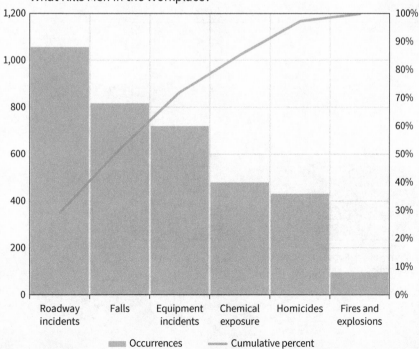

Occurrences     Cumulative percent

### Case in Point 13.2c

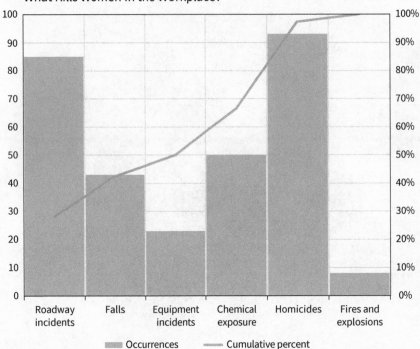

What Kills Women in the Workplace?

### Case in Point 13.2d

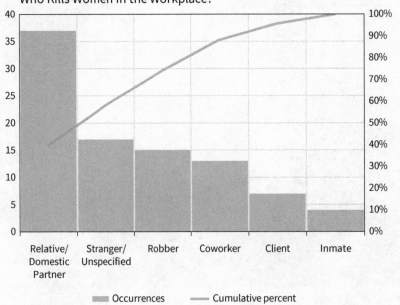

Who Kills Women in the Workplace?

audiences. It's also likely more data-driven and requiring more technological capacity than you might have first thought when you entered this course.

However, it's the wave on which we are riding. That's good, because at long last it provides us with the information and the tools to guide our efforts and predict our successful outcomes.

## SUMMARY

- Back-end performance evaluates communication effectiveness by judging not just the responses to a particular marketing message but also whether individual consumers continue to buy from the company.

- Multivariate marketing statistics can help compile a composite profile of people who use certain product categories. After that profile has been established, it's possible to compile a list of "customer twins," consumers who share characteristics with customers who've already bought a certain product.

- Infographics help communicate complex information through visuals that speed audience comprehension.

### Scenario Prompts: Delivering Controlled Messages

You'll find Scenario Prompts on pp. 367–386 of this textbook. While they vary in subject and difficulty, they help you hone your critical thinking and strategic writing skills. The following are best suited to this chapter's topics.

Management: 2.3 / Writing: 1.10, 2.5, 4.6, 4.7, 7.7, 7.8, 9.3, 10.9

### *Figure Credits*

IMG 13.1a: Copyright © 2013 Depositphotos/blueringmedia.

IMG 13.1b: Source: https://commons.wikimedia.org/wiki/File:Cent_Sign.svg.

IMG 13.1c: Copyright © 2012 Depositphotos/lhfgraphics.

IMG 13.1d: Copyright © 2019 Depositphotos/Blankstock.

IMG 13.1e: Copyright © 2012 Depositphotos/pincasso.

Fig. 13.1: Source: https://www.cdc.gov/vitalsigns/hearingloss/.

Fig. 13.2: Generated using https://www.wordclouds.com/.

Fig. 13.3: Source: https://www.cdc.gov/vitalsigns/opioids/index.html.

Fig. 13.4: Source: U.S. Census Bureau

Fig. 13.5: Adapted from: https://archive.nytimes.com/www.nytimes.com/interactive/2008/11/02/opinion/20081102_OPCHART.html.

Case 13.2a: Source: https://www.bls.gov/news.release/cfoi.t02.htm.

Case 13.2b: Source: https://www.bls.gov/news.release/cfoi.t02.htm.

Case 13.2c: Source: https://www.bls.gov/news.release/cfoi.t02.htm.

Case 13.2d: Source: https://www.bls.gov/news.release/cfoi.t02.htm.

# New Media, Old Tricks

Creating Online Content

When it comes to digital, there's likely a generational divide between us. My family lacked internet access until I was in high school. I'm not sure how many kilobits our download speed was (yes, kilobits, not gigabits), but the screeching, AOL dial-up signal remains seared into my brain. Google it. It's haunting.

My first interaction with computers was in grade school, when my peers and I couldn't imagine, let alone log onto, a publicly open World Wide Web. Hell, we devoted our energies to fighting over the *one* Macintosh with a color display.

But the majority of you "digital natives" have always had internet-enabled devices. Electronics are an extension of your identity—and almost like an extension of your physical being. You know the devices and platforms. So crafting effective, online persuasive content should be a cakewalk, right?

Yeah … not so much.

It's like what they say about chess: Knowing how to move the pieces isn't knowing how to play the game. Too often I work with students who believe just because they manage two fashion blogs, a podcast and half-a-dozen personal social networking accounts that they're ready to manage an organization's web presence. Familiarity with the technology is a leg up, but there's a lot more to it.

Employers can make the same error in mistaking youth for technical acumen. Early on I worked on a wine company's account. Their brand image included a well-recognized and beloved mascot for whom they considered creating a profile on Myspace (Think Facebook before Facebook.) As the conference room's youngest resident, my colleagues immediately sought my input. Fortunately, my communication classes had taught me to first pose strategic questions:

"Myspace lets 16-year-olds create accounts. Would a wine company presence on this platform provoke any legal issues regarding underage drinking?"

"Your mascot is portrayed by an actual person; he's not just a caricature. Do we need additional permission from this individual to use his likeness? Will the profile focus on the character or the individual playing him? And who would manage the profile and create content?"

And last, but certainly not least,

"Why do you want to have a Myspace presence in the first place?"

Intent is an especially difficult question because it's too rarely considered. Sadly, social media campaigns frequently begin with a desire to engage tactically rather than think strategically. "Everybody's doing it" is not a valid reason to invest organizational resources into any communication activity. Many organizational leaders rush to create a footprint on the latest social networking site (SNS) or integrate content into the latest mobile app. Sometimes those are great strategic choices. Sometimes not.

Social media is not free. True, many companies don't charge your organization to create a profile. However, if you want to advertise posts or gain access to specialized features, there's often a cost. You have to hire someone to create the content, distribute it, monitor feedback and respond appropriately. These are monetary costs, but there are also opportunity costs. Every minute spent nurturing a social media presence is a minute that could have been spent developing messages for other media channels that might be more effective.

That said, in many situations an insightful blog and a well-curated Facebook profile are great tools. But like every tool, their uses are specialized. You wouldn't use a wrench to drive a nail. Don't be trapped into assuming web and social media are skeleton keys unlocking all your strategic communication goals. Just like every other modality we've discussed, they have their uses. The hardest part is recognizing them.

—NB

## What You Know

- The audience-centered model focuses communication efforts on matching client messages to target audiences and appropriate media.

- Brevity, clarity and direct language strengthen the persuasiveness of content distributed through print and multichannel contexts.

- Persuasive messages gain credibility if channeled through respected journalists and media outlets.

## What You'll Learn

- How to think like a publisher and operate as a brand journalist creating audience content independent of media gatekeepers

- How to create content for online channels that is easily discoverable, useful to your target audience and structured to build and nurture important relationships

- How to repurpose existing content and add elements fostering interactivity, making messages effective across semicontrolled, online media

- How to reinforce your organization's credibility by creating blog content showcasing your organization's expertise and commitment to key stakeholders

- How brevity, clarity and direct language are even more essential given the special—and spatial—limits and restrictions on many social networks

## A Lifetime of Learning

Over the next two chapters, we discuss the nuts and bolts of writing for interactive, online media, both in general terms and for specific platforms. You'll notice our focus will be more on the general than the specific. That's because we as authors and you as an aspiring professional face extraordinary challenges when it comes to online communications, particularly **social media**.

Why? The modern internet is so new that we all only kind-of-sort-of know what we're doing. The Telecommunications Act of 1996 arguably sparked the World Wide Web's pervasive adoption and commercialization, so we've had only a few decades to learn how the internet works. Compare that to mass printed media and newspapers, which scholars and practitioners have studied for nearly 600 years.

And that doesn't even account for online communication's rapid changes since the late '90s. The web of 1996 is virtually unrecognizable today (type "spacejam.com" into your browser and you'll see what we mean). Increased broadband access has transformed the amount and type of content users can find. The first Apple iPhone, released in 2007, revolutionized how and where we access online content. Then there's the explosion of social media. Early sites like LiveJournal (founded in 1999), Friendster (2002) and Myspace (2003)—some of which still exist—largely gave way to the giants we know now: LinkedIn (2002), Facebook (2004), YouTube (2005), Twitter (2006), Tumblr (2007), Pinterest (2010), Instagram (2010), Snapchat (2011) and TikTok (2016). Of course, these dates only identify each platform's founding. They have undergone myriad iterations since that time.

These rapid changes challenge us all. As authors, we feel it's our role to teach writing skills you can employ *throughout* your strategic communication careers. But how can we teach you to write for constantly evolving platforms, or for media that don't even exist yet? We want to provide knowledge with a longer shelf life, so our approach throughout this textbook—in particular these next two chapters—is to focus on writing principles that have staying power and which you can transfer across platforms.

But that means you'll be filling in the gaps. Learning isn't something you stop doing once you graduate from college. Our field changes, and so do the communication channels around us. It's survival of the fittest, so you learn and adapt, or watch your career wither and die.

## Congratulations on Your Career in Publishing!

You probably began this course thinking it would focus exclusively on writing. Hopefully, you've realized that to be a successful strategic communication *writer*, you've got to think like an *editor*. You've got to predict an editor's audience, interests and workplace routine, recognizing those instances in which media and organizational goals coincide. Then you think beyond a single editor and understand the motives of all the media gatekeepers you target. But with the advent of the internet and social media, becoming a successful strategic writer now requires thinking not only like an editor, but a *publisher* as well.

Consider a newspaper publisher's responsibilities. She oversees all the processes ensuring the paper goes out daily. Should she redesign it to appeal to younger audiences? Will the presses break during the production run? Which syndicated stories will supplement her local staff writers? Can she use visuals to better explain her messages? How will she market her publication to recruit new subscribers?

When organizations commit to communicating online, they face strikingly similar challenges. Communication and information technology (IT) professionals must secure the website domain, then design both its mechanics and graphics so content displays properly on an array of internet-enabled devices. Someone has to write and post original content, as well as compile and share relevant material from other sources. Someone must create multichannel materials supplementing the organization's messages.

In other instances, someone must monitor and promptly respond to issues raised on public discussion pages. Someone is tasked to quickly resolve tech issues if the site is hacked or affected in any way. Someone must analyze the site's visitors and determine whether it's attracting key stakeholders.

No-cost media? No, indeed.

Just as writing effectively for uncontrolled media forced you to think like an editor, in the semicontrolled space that dominates much of the internet, you're adding a publisher's responsibilities to your job's portfolio.

## Build It, Be Found and Be Useful

Let's begin your reeducation with the Costner rule. In 1989's *Field of Dreams*, Kevin Costner's character builds a baseball field and dead MLBers emerge to once again play the game they love. You're probably familiar with its most famous line: "If you build it, they will come." Many internet content producers operate on the Costner rule, reframed as the "content is king" mantra: Supply the web content and the audience will come.

Malarkey. Hogwash. Bullshit. Don't believe our conclusion? *No Bullshit Social Media* authors Jason Falls and Erick Decker echo our feelings about the Costner rule: "If you build it, they will not come. You have to build it, tell everyone it's there, and then be there when they show up."[1]

It's simple. If your audience doesn't know your site exists, and subsequently never see it, then what good is wonderful content? And as before, you really want your key stakeholders to know where to find you online.

Whatever your online writing task, producing content is a three-pronged process.[2] You must have (1) a *presence* in a digital space where your target audience is (2) likely to *discover* you, and once discovered, your content must have (3) *utility* for the audience if you hope to hold their attention, build relationships and ultimately drive them to action. In Chapter 9, we focused on presence and discovery. Here, starting with Figure 14.1, we'll dive deeper into utility.

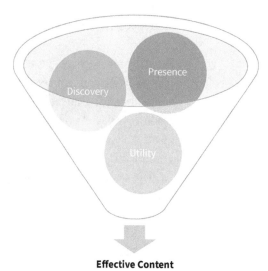

**Effective Content**

**FIGURE 14.1  The Content Funnel.** In Chapter 9, we reviewed SEO as a way to make your content discoverable. In Chapter 15, we'll discuss ways to foster an online presence specifically targeted to key stakeholders. We'll focus on how effective content demonstrates the ways information and engagement you foster improve your audiences' lives.

## Developing Effective Content

In the previous four chapters, we discussed ways to develop content for uncontrolled and controlled media. We primarily relied on the audience-centered model and TIPCUP filter to select that content and determine its structure. Those concepts also apply to semicontrolled communications. However, there are additional considerations complicating the process of crafting and disseminating digital messages. A refresher on the PESO model might help.

As you'll recall from Chapter 1, PESO categorizes strategic communication messages as either **P**aid, **E**arned, **S**hared or **O**wned. In Chapters 10 and 11, we discussed media relations, which delivers messages through gatekeepers, who assess whether the message merits attention from their audiences. In demonstrating that value, we *earn* coverage.

In Chapters 12 and 13, we discussed controlled media, in which the organization has complete say over the message without reliance on, interference by, or input from gatekeepers. Often, that message control resulted because we *paid* for placements or *owned* the channels through which internal messages were delivered.

Online media can't be easily characterized within PESO. Yes, much of it is delivered through *owned* channels. Organizations own their website and blog domains, and **social networking** usernames. However, organizations don't completely control online messages. Online audiences are free—and often encouraged—to engage in two-way communication with organizations. Moreover, others often *share* content about organizations, whether it's organization- or user-generated. Because many organizational internet sites are shared with audiences, we label them *semicontrolled platforms*.

### Repurposing Information From Other Sources

Immediately you can see the immense challenge presented by online communication. You have a host of channels (e.g., organizational websites, intranets, blogs, social networks) reaching a variety of different audiences (e.g., customers, employees, investors, community groups), all of whom expect frequent updates, new information and opportunities to engage. That means you need a lot of content, as well as time to respond to stakeholder feedback.

The task may be daunting, but it's not impossible. First, consider that not all online content has to be original, or even produced by the organization. This is especially true for SNSs, where experts believe up to 85% of posts should be created by and shared from other sources.[3] Monitoring traditional and social media helps immensely, as does mining your own existing content. Let's review the **Click-Through 10.3** news release as an example. As a refresher, here's the lede sentence and second paragraph:

> Billville's veterans will be honored when the city's Memorial Auditorium is rededicated during "Singing America's Praises," a Veterans Day concert presented by five major area choruses on Saturday, Nov. 11.
>
> Memorial Auditorium, which was originally named the War Memorial Auditorium in memory of World War I veterans when it was completed in 1929, will be rededicated

in a patriotic performance featuring over 300 performers. The event will be punctuated by displays of color guards from area military units and a series of patriotic readings accompanied by a special dramatic presentation.

This release promoted MixedMedia, comprising six independent choirs. Assuming MixedMedia and the member groups each have social media followings, there's an abundance of content the groups could share online, related specifically to this performance or to their separate initiatives. Potential concertgoers reveling in their patriotism might enjoy local news stories profiling exceptional veterans. Information about the auditorium's rededication, recent renovations or upcoming events could draw the venue's regular attendees. The groups 300+ singers might post videos of past shows. And that doesn't even scratch the surface of available web content appealing to the chorus' fans: tips for improving your singing voice, a top-10 musicals list, a guide to holiday caroling. It's all out there, easy to find and easy to share.

Of course, you must produce your own content, but not necessarily from scratch. Focusing on new media channels doesn't mean abandoning traditional ones. Every target audience member can't be reached through the same channels. Some may be heavy social media users, while others are ardent newspaper readers. Nevertheless, because they're each part of your target audience, they likely share common interests in your organization, its products and services. That means the same content themes will appeal to several segments, so your "original" online content might already exist in some traditional form.

Again, consider MixedMedia's performance at the Billville Veterans Day concert. It's not difficult to imagine the news release reworked as a **blog** post. In fact, we've converted it to one in Click-Through 14.1. We adapted the lede to create a more conversational tone, which reads like a focus feature's narrative opening. We made the language more informal, often by including first- and second-person pronouns, as well as contractions, and cut the drier background information to focus more on the concert and the veterans.

But when you compare the release and blog language, about 70% is unchanged. So yes, we technically created original content for a blog, but we'd already done most of the work. Repurposing content in this manner lets us efficiently expand our reach and connect with new audiences through different media.

Of course, there are other ways to redirect existing content. For example, any time you or someone from your organization delivers a speech or presentation or appears at some public function, record it. You may be able to use the video in its entirety or pull smaller snippets to share on your company website, intranet or YouTube channels. You might also draw on existing content for inspiration, then modify the piece for use on other channels.

**Strategic Thought**

Look back to the photo-op teaser featured in **Click-Through 10.2**. What elements could you expand to create a 300-word blog post? What would the focus be? How would that differ from a 200-character social media post?

### The Strategic Communicator as Brand Journalist

Hopefully, you're beginning to see how effective content drives online behavior. Traditionally, PR practitioners work in the media relations realm, persuading journalists to produce stories. Online communication largely removes gatekeepers from the equation. When communicating directly with target audiences, your role shifts from simply contributing to content creation toward outright developing and publishing.

Most of what you'll do in this realm is more related to **brand journalism** than traditional public relations. At the prose level, brand journalism isn't all that different from traditional journalism: you tell stories you think will interest audiences. The main difference is that, unlike traditional journalists, brand journalists don't approach their topics from a stance of unbiased objectivity, but instead tell stories promoting some aspect of an organization, its brand or its products/services.

Whether that story relies solely on words or includes some multichannel component, the rules of sound writing outlined throughout Part 2 still apply here. However, there are added considerations, which vary across platforms.

## Internet and Intranet Sites

Let's start with the organization's website, the cornerstone of many companies' online communications. Many larger organizations also establish an **intranet**, essentially a private, inward-facing website accessible only to an organization's employees. Superficially, intranet and internet sites function in roughly the same way. The major difference is that intranets are used exclusively for internal communication.

### PRINCIPLES IN PRACTICE 14.1   Dollar Shave Club, From Viral to Value

Shaving sucks. Men hate it, but many endure this painful and frustrating grooming habit. If you buy a cheap razor, it's a good bet you'll nick your face beyond recognition. Premium razors won't scar your face, but replacement blades will bleed your life savings.

Enter Dollar Shave Club. The online razor distributor ships blades to your house for as little as $3 a month, compared to the $15–$20 you'd spend on store-bought blades. While the product quality and price point are certainly key elements of the brand's success, they're only part of the reason the 2012 startup grew to 1.1 million subscribers and a $615 million valuation … in just three years![4]

First, they employed a familiar problem-solution message strategy: Premium razors offer unnecessary features at a steep price. Dollar Shave Club can provide a quality alternative for less. Simple. But look at the way it was crafted and marketed. Dollar Shave Club made a single launch video, first promoted exclusively online. Its success stemmed largely from its entertaining nature, featuring Mike, the founder, touring the factory.

The comedic value alone attracted audiences, prompting viewers to share it online, which explains why the video had over 27 million views by the end of 2020.[5]

Still, the launch video was just a gateway. The low price point and minimal trial risk prompted thousands to sign up. And this membership concept has undoubtedly contributed to the company's success. Dollar Shave Club actually *feels* like a club. Members receive promotional emails from time to time, but more often the content Dollar Shave Club hosts on its website adds value beyond the product.

For example, the site features an entire section on grooming, with articles on everything from shaving tips to avoid cutting yourself, to advice on matching your facial hair stylings to your face's shape. Understanding its core audience is men, Dollar Shave Club creates and hosts general content about men's health and fitness, with articles ranging from the practical ("Can You Make Your Mood Better by Dressing Up?") to the truly absurd ("Men Sniff Their Fingers After Scratching Their Balls Because It Makes Them Feel Alive").

Hosting and aggregating content its customers—excuse us—*members* find valuable transforms dollarshaveclub.com into a destination not just for purchasing products, but for discovering impactful and interesting information. Doing so engages members, builds trust, nurtures relationships, retains customers, and ultimately drives sales and profits. Not bad for a dollar.

**Dollar Shave Club Launch Video**

https://www.youtube.com/watch?v=ZUG9qYTJMsI

Their blades aren't any good. They're f\*\*king great!

For both internet and intranet sites, the journalistic focus remains. While it's true that websites are often used as sales platforms, the best-run sites are successful because they provide more. Dollar Shave Club, which Principles in Practice 14.1 discusses, is just one example. Their communication successes stem from viewing the website as a source for relevant information rather than a straightforward marketing and sales tool. Indeed, as organizations convert to this viewpoint, many have hired former journalists to manage their web content.

This approach lets organizations establish themselves as experts for their target publics. Recall Chapter 9's Home Depot discussion, whose website hosts DIY videos on home repair and renovations. This strategy positions Home Depot as a pivotal source not just for tools and home improvement supplies but also renovation and repair tips. People not yet ready to buy are drawn to the site, but once inspired by tutorial videos, they're more likely to visit a Home Depot location or its online store to purchase DIY project materials.

## Content Considerations for Websites

Still, great content can turn sour when developed without considering the advantages and constraints of the medium. Memory Memo 14.1 summarizes some unique considerations for developing and presenting online content.

> **MEMORY MEMO 14.1** Presenting Website Content
>
> - Cultivate an organizational voice
> - Maintain a consistent tone across elements
> - Harness the power of images
> - Keep content current
> - Promote feedback and interactivity
> - Help visitors share content via social media

### Cultivating Voice

First, it's important that organizations cultivate a unique voice for their online communication. *Voice* refers to the manner in which the organization writes and speaks. Each of us has our own voice, a distinctive way in which we produce prose. Ever wonder how professors so easily spot plagiarism? What you copy from Wikipedia sounds nothing like you.

Over time, that style or voice becomes representative of the writer or, in this case, the organization. Unfortunately, establishing a corporate voice is particularly difficult because multiple individuals speak on an organization's behalf. Getting them all on the same page regarding tone and style is immensely challenging. Remember your last group project? How hard was it to assemble a 10-page paper so it read as though one person wrote it, not three? Yeah. It's that problem, times like a zillion.

Still, establishing voice is a must. It not only defines how stakeholders view the organization, but it makes the organization seem like a singular entity rather than an awkward assemblage of disconnected individuals. As we've said repeatedly, principles of interpersonal interaction are woven into the fiber of all meaningful communication, but they only work when interactions appear to be one-to-one, or at least one-to-few. Some organizations' gargantuan footprints signal them as distant and unapproachable. A unified, unique and unwavering voice helps erode such barriers and create environments where meaningful interaction seems plausible.[6]

### Choosing the Right Tone

As important as it is to develop an organizational voice, ensuring your voice adopts the correct tone is just as crucial. Your tone should match and reflect what your organization is and what it represents. Consider Kentucky for Kentucky (KFK). The organization promotes the Bluegrass State's people, places and products, and it once petitioned the state legislature to adopt the more appropriate state motto: "Kentucky Kicks Ass!"

We're serious. And so are they.

The folks at KFK are passionate about increasing tourism and helping local artists sell their wares. But with a slogan like "Kentucky Kicks Ass," you can't expect their outreach to be overly stodgy. The prose of the site's "about us" section reinforces that playfulness (Figure 14.2):

**FIGURE 14.2** Kentucky for Kentucky Homepage.

> Kentucky's influence is big and it is strong. In the USA and all over the world, the contributions of the Commonwealth are too many to count and too varied to describe. We were the first to sing Happy Birthday, to slap high fives, and the only people with enough sense to know that chicken ain't chicken until it's breaded and fried. We're the perfect mix of class and crazy. We invented and perfected bourbon, the king of spirits. We run moonshine through the mountains. In May, we Run for the Roses.
>
> We wrote the book on cool by birthing Clooney, Depp and Hunter S. Thompson. We shocked the world with Ali, led a divided nation with Lincoln. Like Daniel Boone and Wendell Berry, we are explorers and visionaries. Our vibe is inimitable. America taps its steering wheel to the honky-tonk twang of Dwight Yoakam and Gary Stewart. We are Bill Monroe, Lee Sexton, The Judds and My Morning Jacket. We are Loretta. And we're damn proud of it.

The playful prose styling and nearly nonstop name-drops of Kentucky's cultural icons are sensible content choices because they work together to establish a unique voice and an appropriate tone. Collectively, they have enabled the group to amass a substantial following among proud Kentuckians. And we should know. As a native Kentuckian, Professor Browning has dropped more cash than he'd care to admit on KFK apparel, in large part because the organizational messaging engaged him.

### Capturing Your Image

And that messaging goes beyond just words. Look at KFK's homepage image: a bearded man sporting a "Y'ALL" sweater (a play on the famous "YALE" university apparel) crazily waving Kentucky's state flag. Behind him are other brazen Kentuckians running through the street, one hoisting a Col. Sanders statue. Apart from the photo's oddity, here are two critical things you should notice.

First, the image tells a story aligning in content and spirit with its accompanying prose. There's no disconnect between the two. They support one another to tell a singular narrative, much like the unified central conceit we asserted in Chapter 12 was necessary for advertising success.

Second, this clearly isn't a stock photo. The image makes you see—perhaps even feel—the authenticity, which in turn makes you feel as though you're getting a true glimpse into the organization. Stock photos don't do that. Does a staged photo of people of every gender, ethnicity and creed striking dominant poses really *say* anything about the organization? Of course not. It's soulless. That's not because the photo itself is bad, but because it wasn't mindful of a particular organization's purpose, culture or values. Take a look at Figure 14.3 and you'll see what we mean.

**FIGURE 14.3 When a Picture's Worth Zero Words.** While stock photos certainly have legitimate uses, they're rarely worth prominent space on your organizational website. This stock photo could just as easily appear on the homepage of a bank, real estate agency or insurance company. That means it doesn't say anything unique about the business or brand, and that's a serious problem.

### Keeping Content Current

Whether your content is print or multichannel, it's important to keep it current. For instance, if your organization hosts an annual fundraiser, be sure your site is displaying the upcoming event's information, not last year's. It's crucial to keep employee information updated too. When employees change positions, leave the company or get married and change last names, your site should reflect that. Such information is especially important to your organization's large investors, major customers or the press. You should also periodically check your prominent outgoing links. "Error 404: Page Not Found" isn't the destination your site visitors wanted.

### Connecting With Stakeholders

These key contacts are just one interaction node. There are various ways to connect with stakeholders online, but we'll touch on some commonplace ones.

Let's start with the most overlooked: Frequently Asked Questions. FAQs show you recognize there are times when stakeholders aren't interested in two-way interactions. Sometimes, they just want information, and there's no reason to waste your time and theirs simply to learn operating hours, or that your company has a 30-day return policy or that open enrollment for health benefits ends Nov. 30. FAQs signal your organization knows its audiences well enough to anticipate their needs and have the answers ready and accessible before the questions are even asked.

Of course, you can't anticipate all your stakeholders' needs, or perhaps they require more detail than a FAQ section can provide. A clearly labeled, easy-to-find "contact us" section is vital. It should include contact information for both general and specific inquiries. If you allow your audience to self-select the proper contact point, you saved time filtering questions and likely improved your response time.

And don't be afraid to go old school here. List a physical address as well as, believe it or not, an array of telephone numbers. Audiences prefer different communication modes, so cater to their wishes. Always remember, strategic communication decisions are based on your audience's preferences, not yours.

Alternatively, you might want to include digital modes of contact beyond just email. Hiring managers, for instance, might list their LinkedIn profiles since that's a reasonable point of contact for job seekers. Additionally, some people use Twitter as a news aggregator, and reporters are increasingly open to pitches through mentions or direct messaging. This has prompted many media relations practitioners to include their Twitter handles in their employee profiles.

### Chaining to Social Media

Finally, some sites operate under more specialized models, giving them additional options for fostering feedback, dialogue and at times even multilogue. Warby Parker is one such case.

Warby Parker sells eyeglasses and related accessories, largely through its website. The site is attractive, easily navigable and ripe with unique features, like a photographic tool allowing customers to measure pupillary distance for better fitting eyeglasses. Exciting, right?

Actually, very. Warby Parker operates like the mullet of the internet: business in the front, party in the back. Its public-facing website is professional, which communicates the quality and reliability a consumer should expect in that space. Its social media channels are more conversational, playful and focused on the lives of consumers and other key stakeholders.

The company does a great job tying products and service features to its social media channels. Example: #WarbyHomeTryOn. Warby Parker will ship prospective consumers up to five pairs of eyeglasses to try at home to find the perfect pair. Many soon-to-be customers are eager to crowdsource opinions from followers, tagging selfies with #WarbyHomeTryOn, which not

**Strategic Thought**

What sort of questions did you have about your university or college before you enrolled? What about now that you're a current student? What might you imagine faculty and staff are most likely to inquire about? Develop two FAQ sections for your school, one targeted to students and the other to faculty and staff. Which FAQ section was hardest for you to develop? Why?

only solicits fashion feedback but also promotes the brand in ways as creative and unique as the individual consumer.

That's possible because Warby Parker's social media team actually reads user content, which generates stellar customer service and response via Twitter, and thus more extensive outreach. For instance, the company encourages followers to create Instagram content referencing Warby Parker. Then the social media team combs through posts to feature their favorite photos in a monthly blog.

Warby Parker's willingness to have fun and engage consumers and fans keeps feeding the machine. Consider Warby Barker, a designer eyeglass site for dogs planned as a one-off 2012 April Fool's joke. It was such a hit that the @warbybarker Instagram is still kicking with fresh content years later.

Though not all organizations can match Warby Parker's creativity, many websites let consumers interact with the organization through their blogs or social networking accounts. Ideally, each organization's digital forum should connect to all others, letting stakeholders easily access different content on a variety of platforms. While websites often serve as the organization's home base, blogs and social networks offer audiences more personal and interactive engagement.

**Warby Barker**

https://www.warbybarker.com/

The "Canine Collection" features stylish eyeglasses, and for more a sophisticated pooch, the single-lens dog-ocle.

## Blogging Toward Expertise
### Media Relations With Bloggers

Before we detail writing your own organizational blog posts, it's worth noting the multiple ways blogs are relevant to strategic communicators.[7] Remember, people will talk about your organization online without asking your permission. Blogs and SNSs managed by others will often post stories and information about your organization. Sometimes the interplay reflects well upon you, sometimes not. However, in all cases, this content affects your organization's reputation. Therefore, it's usually a good idea to monitor blogs for mentions of your company just as you would traditional media in order to track changes in stakeholder moods.

There's another important reason to monitor blogs: identifying online opinion leaders relevant to your organization. The blogosphere constitutes its own ecosystem, and the public has come to view blogs as valuable information sources—perhaps in part because traditional media news sites increasingly look like blogs.[8] Like traditional journalists, bloggers are eager to tell interesting stories, and sometimes those stories relate to your organization and its operations. By monitoring blogs and identifying opinion leaders within targeted industries and sectors, you're effectively building an online media contacts list. Just as you would with traditional media outlets, you can pitch bloggers story ideas and provide photos, videos, infographics and other material. Similarly, if you establish a good working relationship with the blogger, you can suggest company employees as expert sources.

## Managing and Writing a Blog

While blogs help with media relations and monitoring, many organizations also create their own blogs and posts to directly engage stakeholders. Often when we think of direct engagement and interactivity, we think of SNSs. While these sites have multiplied over the years, blogs still serve as important organizational communication tools that offer several advantages over SNSs.

Most importantly, blogs allow organizations to more fully control their content. Yes, most bloggers allow interactivity via comments, or even drive interactivity by encouraging readers to engage with writers via SNSs. However, organizational communicators always initiate the conversation on their blogs. On SNSs, they sometimes can only react to existing conversations.

This content ownership also influences the way search engines index blog content. Typically, when stakeholders view your SNS content, that traffic is attributed toward the social network as a whole, not your organization's feed. On the other hand, websites and blogs credit traffic directly to your organization. That's not an insignificant distinction. Recall in Chapter 9 we discussed SEO and the importance of ranking on the web search's first page. In many cases, strategic communicators use blogs to establish their organizations as thought leaders within an industry or about a given topic—and sometimes both. If your content isn't well indexed, it can't be found; and if it can't be found, your prose serves no purpose.

But how to ascend the search rankings? Retreat to our old friend: audience-centered communication. Too often, novice and even advanced writers, instead of writing about what their audiences will find useful, write about their company. Sometimes a product-centric blog works, assuming the product lies at the heart of meaningful social interaction, has a variety of unique uses, or is just intrinsically cool. But if high school taught us anything, it's that not everyone can be cool. Hence the dilemma of Allstate Insurance Co.

### Discovering a Story Where You Think There Isn't One

Insurance is decidedly uncool. For most people, its conversation value varies between mundane and soul-deadening. Nevertheless, most of us need it. So how do you translate insurance's importance and impact to generate interest? Well, you certainly don't do it by creating blog posts about uninsured/underinsured motorist (UM/UIM) coverage, personal injury protection (PIP) or other alphabet-soup topics. While insurance clients should consider UM/UIM and PIP coverage, that's something they'll reluctantly investigate only at the moment of purchase.

Still, Allstate sees value in maintaining and building relationships with current and potential customers, and The Allstate Blog (blog.allstate.com) certainly helps. It's apparent the company uses the blog to remain a resource for consumers beyond the insurance purchasing and claims processes. The organization does so by going back to basics. From our perspective, the impetus for Allstate's blog could easily have begun by answering three strategic questions:

1. What do we make and/or do?

2. What are customers' psychological motivations to buy our products/ services?

3. What do our customers have in common?

Essentially, this is a rudimentary form of audience analysis, which we discussed most prominently in Chapter 3. The answers here are fairly basic. Allstate sells personal property insurance for vehicles and homes, which customers purchase to protect their assets, bringing them peace of mind and feelings of safety and security. Though Allstate caters to numerous stakeholders we could segment in several ways, they all share one characteristic: they own something they wish to protect.

### Positioning the Post

Knowing just those three things can go a long way. For instance, many of Allstate's customers purchase insurance for their cars and trucks. It's logical they'd be interested in information about safe driving. Enter "Distracted Driving: Understanding Your Fellow Drivers," a post featuring an easy-to-read infographic about U.S. drivers' cellphone use. Or perhaps something more basic, like "How to Deal with Foggy Windows." It advises drivers on how to defog windows, increase visibility and reduce accident risk. Practitioners call these posts **evergreens** because their relevance isn't time bound.

Yet stories and blogs about current events can inject the audience-drawing element of timeliness. Allstate recognizes this, so you see November blogs posts like "Building Your Car's Winter Emergency Kit" and "How to Prevent Pipes from Freezing: Steps to Consider." Following these tips can save car and homeowners a lot of time, money and grief. Additionally, providing these resources demonstrates Allstate values its customers' well-being while reducing its own payouts on accident claims.

### Writing Like You Already Know How

Once you've established a purpose and an audience, writing blog posts does not fundamentally differ from many other forms of writing we've discussed. The ease with which you can convert news releases to blog posts demonstrates this point. Let's look closer at the Allstate blog post on preventing frozen pipes in the QR Code link, and you'll see what we mean. Take a look at the lede:

**"How to Prevent Pipes from Freezing: Steps to Consider"**

https://www.all-state.com/blog/prevent-pipes-from-freezing/

Allstate goes beyond simple transactions to provide stakeholders information when they need it and can use it.

For anyone living in an area where temperatures regularly dip below freezing, a few precautionary steps to help protect your plumbing can be a cost-effective way to help avoid cleaning up after a burst pipe.

Read on to find out what the *Insurance Institute for Business and Safety* (IBHS) says you can do to help stay ahead of the freeze.

Look familiar? This opening includes many of the elements of media release ledes. First, it immediately calls out to a target audience: those who live in colder climates. Right away, residents of New England and the Midwest know this article is for them, while Floridians might understandably stop reading. That's as it should be. Next, the writer identifies several TIPCUP elements. The most obvious is impact: You could save thousands of dollars by preventing frozen pipes. The second paragraph adds credibility by citing an expert organization (IBHS). Lastly, there's conflict, as the narrative pits the homeowner against Mother Nature: Winter is coming; prepare for the fight.

We also find familiar writing tactics in the body copy. You'll notice the writer employs a problem-solution argument structure. The lede establishes the problem (frozen pipes cost you money), and the body outlines various solutions, which are presented chronologically. First, you learn what to do *before* the cold season to protect your pipes. Next, you see more preventative action you should take *during* the winter. Finally, you learn how to check whether your pipes froze and, if so, what to do *afterward* to safely thaw the pipes and solve the problem.

Continuing with the post's structure, you'll notice something else at play: It's a working document. There are prominent subheadings throughout, and the bulleted format makes it easy to differentiate and find the one that solves your problem.

This structure makes perfect sense for a how-to blog post. In some ways, the entire post is a call to action, and it concludes with the more formal call to action you've seen in virtually every piece of writing we've discussed thus far. In this instance, it's a reminder not to overestimate your own abilities.

> **MEMORY MEMO 14.2** Tips for Blog Writing
>
> - Leverage your expertise
> - Write about current events
> - Don't just blog about products and services
> - Be authentic and personable
> - Categorize and tag posts
> - Ensure RSS capability
> - Imbed social sharing tools
> - Make it easy to contact you

### The Added Element of Discoverability

So the general process for blog writing should be nothing new for you. However, there is one major difference: You have to include elements in the prose that will generate site traffic, particularly from search engines. This operationalizes our Chapter 9 discussion of SEO and the importance of content not only being well written but also discoverable.

First, consider what Allstate's article is about: How to prevent frozen pipes. The post is 469 words long, fairly standard for a blog post, which typically range from 300 to 700 words. Of those 469 words, nine are some version of *freeze* or *frozen*, and another 16 are *pipe* or *pipes.* While it's generally good to vary your vocabulary, in social media you can improve SEO by regularly including keywords. For this blog, roughly 5% of its written content would match a keyword search for "frozen pipes."

Speaking of SEO, you'll notice this post links to external sites and sources: the IBHS, the Department of Energy, the American Red Cross and Consumer Reports. Including outgoing links to highly trafficked and well-recognized sites improve search rankings. There are also several practical reasons to include links. First, you should always support your claims with evidence, and linking to credible sources is an excellent way to do so. Second, these sources might provide detailed information that some audience members may find relevant, but which you simply don't have time or space to include. In this way, links serve as a for-more-information call to action, which engaged audiences may find helpful.

But remember, you should ALWAYS direct links to open in a new browser tab or page. Doing so will keep your site active in the user's browser rather than redirecting her from your page. Most blog sites allow you to select this hyperlink option from a dropdown menu, but the XHTML code is pretty simple. Links are inserted using what's called an anchor tag, which would look like this for the American Red Cross:

```
<a href="https://www.redcross.org">American Red Cross</a>
```

However, the above code would direct the user to the Red Cross homepage in the same window, which you do NOT want. To force the link to open in a new tab, you just need to add a small piece of code:

```
<a href="https://www.redcross.org" target="_blank">American Red Cross</a>
```

Nitpicky, but this little piece of code prevents audiences from leaving your site, and that's critical to maintaining at least a chance of retaining their attention.[9]

Another way to help readers find your content is to **categorize** and **tag** your posts. Categories organize posts within a blog, typically by topic. Think of them like a table of contents. For instance, The Allstate Blog lists the pipe-freezing post under the category "Home." That category offers broad information that targets homeowners, with the timeliest posts jumping to a "featured" or "recent stories" list.

*Meta tags*, on the other hand, are specific to each website or blog post. They aren't immediately visible to visitors, but they're included in the site's code to help search engines properly index the site. You can view any site's code by right-clicking in a blank portion of the page and selecting "view page source." Once you do, you'll see seemingly indecipherable XHTML code. There's more going on here regarding meta tags and SEO than this text can cover, but two meta tags, *title* and *description*, are universally agreed to be most important.

Search engines scour the entire source code to index your site, but these two meta tags are the easiest way to influence the indexing's outcome. Here's what those tags look like in the Allstate post:

<title>**How to Prevent Frozen Pipes | The Allstate Blog**</title>

<meta name=**“**description**”** content=**“**Learn how to protect your pipes ahead of a freeze: what to do when the temperatures actually drop and how to thaw pipes if they do freeze.**”/>**

You'll notice that this language doesn't match that of the blog's actual title or opening sentences. It doesn't have to and arguably shouldn't. Meta tags just provide additional information to boost search engine results.

The title and description tags are especially important not only for these reasons but also because they preview site content to a potential visitor. When you conduct a Google search, the results spit out links followed by page content summaries, typically generated from title and description tags. Think of them as the lede before the lede. If you can't capture attention and convince the user to click through to your site, the prose behind that link, however beautiful, is essentially worthless.

Aside from individuals finding your blog organically through web searches, some may encounter this content through other means. One is through an **RSS feed**, which operates like a news aggregator. It recognizes when new web content is available and alerts subscribers so they can quickly find it. Because many blog readers frequent the same sites—much like subscribers to traditional media channels—bloggers should ensure their posts have RSS capability.

Another way we often discover content is through word-of-mouth (WOM), called **electronic word-of-mouth (eWOM)** when spread online. eWOM often spreads through social media, which we'll discuss further in the next chapter. For now, just recognize you can transform a loyal or engaged reader into a promoter of your brand if you make it easy for her to share your content; therefore, you should imbed social sharing tools into your blog posts.

These tips for blog writing are summarized in Memory Memo 14.2 and brought to life in The Blogger's 10 Commandments metablog post, featuring an expanded set of tips for writing effective blogs.

**The Blogger's 10 Commandments**

https://prwritingprose. blogspot.com/2020/12/ the-bloggers-10-commandments.html

We came down from the mount to bring these tips to you, our chosen people!

## The Emergence of Social

Writing social media prose for SNSs may seem like a simple task, but it's extraordinarily complex. There are different platforms with different rules and different users, all factors you have to consider. There's the challenge of social media's adaptation itself. It's hard to establish enduring rules for a constantly changing game. Finally, there's the challenge of brevity. You've got roughly two seconds to capture the attention of an online audience, then it's a battle to hold that attention over similarly short increments.[10]

*(1) Two seconds to catch audience*

*(2) Always Changing*

*Primary factors ① know your audience ② how do They use the medium? ③ what rewards do They want?*

- Using plain language
  - Quickly engage the reader
  - Use concrete nouns (i.e., things we can see, hear, smell, taste or touch)
  - Use strong action verbs, as opposed to various versions of *to be*
    - am, is, are, was, were, be, being, been
  - Limit the use of jargon
  - Write in active voice
  - Keep messages short
  - Write in a friendly but professional tone
  - Choose words with a single meaning
  - Use measurements familiar to your audience
  - Choose familiar terms, and use them consistently
  - Use acronyms with caution
  - Use numbers when they help you make your point
- Incorporating social marketing tools
  - Highlight the positive aspects of your message
  - Remember to answer, "What's in it for me?"
  - Encourage your readers to take specific actions
    - Tie those actions to specific products or services when appropriate
- What social media content should be:
  - Relevant, useful and interesting
  - Friendly, conversational and engaging
    - Write in the first or second person (I, my, we, us, our, you, your)
    - Use contractions
    - Remember, UR not texting, so save moronic abbreviations for L8R
- Easy to understand and share
  - Put relevant, intriguing information at the beginning of your post
  - Keep messages short but relevant
  - Test your message on a cold reader: Could someone get it in less than two seconds?
  - Provide enough context so your message can stand alone

While social media writing presents difficult challenges, remember that you've learned rules of disciplined writing that can help. Understanding your audience, including how they use a medium and the rewards they want from a message, is critical to crafting a successful persuasive appeal. This truth anchors uses and gratifications theory, which you'll recall from Chapter 1, as well as the audience analysis and planning principles you learned in Chapters 3 and 4. And the need to quickly grab the audience's attention? Just another application of the TIPCUP + CAN filter and audience-centered writing.

So be confident. You're well equipped. Still, to successfully craft SNS messages we will ask you to remember old principles, introduce new ones and demand you unlearn other prose habits. We'll start with the CDC's excellent guidelines for their social media writers, which we adapted for Memory Memo 14.3.

## Using Plain Language

First thing to unlearn: the last end-of-semester paper you wrote. Maybe it was 10, or even 20 pages long. But honestly, did your 10-page paper include more than six or seven pages of actual information? To hit an arbitrary page-length requirement, you probably overexplained points, opted for unnecessarily complex argument structures, and used convoluted verb constructions.

Strategic communication isn't about flaunting your education, touting your organization's importance or fortifying your boss's ego. It's about communicating an idea so your audience can understand it and act accordingly. Your language should be plain, but that doesn't mean it should be dull or simplistic. That's what makes strategic writing—particularly for SNSs—difficult but also rewarding.

Let's look at some hypothetical scenarios. Suppose you work for a U.S. organization that favors legalizing medicinal marijuana. You might share polling data suggesting most doctors support this policy.[12] But doctors aren't exactly known for their communication skills (ever try to read their handwriting?), so we envision a top physician in this organization would write a post like this:

Among physicians, 76% support cannabis for pharmacological benefits.

How would you evaluate this message? Well, the doctor nailed brevity; the post is only eight words and 68 characters long. She also managed to squeeze in an active verb (*support*), as well as some statistical evidence backing the claim. And the words she chose have singular meanings: *physicians*, *76%*, *cannabis*, and *pharmacological* are exactly as in the dictionary.

The problem? Most of the audience would need a dictionary to even understand this post. Run these eight words through the Gunning-Fog readability index, and you get a score of 23.2. That means it reads at a 23rd grade level, so only audiences who've traded their youth for a doctorate will fully comprehend this message. Can you define *cannabis* or *pharmacological* without looking them up? Perhaps you know cannabis is the botanical name for marijuana, but *pharmacological* is a bit more difficult. You may have guessed it relates to drugs based on the *pharma-* root (e.g., pharmacy), but your posts should never require audiences to test their Latin (Scribo ergo sum?).

And what about *physicians*? You almost certainly know that one, but why not just use *doctors*? Most audiences are more familiar and comfortable with that term. And then there's the *76%*. Statistics can be great, and numbers can support your argument, but they're often abstract and difficult for people to comprehend. It's smart to make such numbers concrete and thus more relatable. So what if we, as professional communicators, were to rewrite this post?

> 3 out of 4 doctors want marijuana made a legal prescription drug.

We're at 12 words and 66 characters now, so the length is roughly the same. More importantly, these 12 words are easier for audiences to comprehend: the Fog Index dropped to 11.47. We replaced *physician* and *cannabis* with the more familiar *doctor* and *marijuana*, and the cryptic *pharmacological* with its layman cousin, *prescription drug*. Word choice remains solid. Each word is clear and simply defined. The verbs are arguably stronger and more action-oriented (*want* and *made* instead of just *support*). And though it may seem like a subtle change, shifting from *76%* to *3 out of 4* makes a huge difference. Picture 76% of doctors. Can you? We can't. But we can picture four of them, standing in white lab coats with stethoscope-laden necks. Now we can picture three out of four of them, easily comprehending a clear majority.

### Including Newsworthy Angles

This discussion helps you nail some of the linguistic basics. However, our message is still far from persuasive. Including links will carry most of the heavy lifting in retaining attention and persuading our audience. In fact, experts believe most SNS content you post shouldn't be original, but rather shared information relevant to stakeholders. So sharing a link to an article, photo, video or a snippet detailing one interesting factoid may prompt quick reactions from viewers, encourage higher comment rates and prompt shares.[13]

However, when supporting your message using only content you've produced, you don't have that advantage. To gain that social traction, you need to first consider why a given piece of information might be relevant to your audience (TIPCUP + CAN), then play up those angles, directing your audience's more active members to take a specific action. Revisiting the medical marijuana example, let's say we're trying to convince followers to pressure legislators on legalization. We'll need more than just a quick fact. Therefore, we might create this Facebook post:

> 3 out of 4 doctors want marijuana made a legal prescription drug. Medical marijuana helps those suffering from many diseases, from diabetes to PTSD. It also eases chronic pain, and because it's less addictive than alternative painkillers, legalizing prescribed marijuana could help our fight against the opioid epidemic. So what's the holdup? Contact your representatives today!

Most noticeably, this post extends our first version to 56 words and 379 characters. Considering we chose Facebook as our medium, the character count is appropriate. Facebook truncates posts, so everything after about 400 characters can only be seen by clicking "read more," which most people don't do.[14]

The readability has gotten a bit worse (13.77), but that's because the Fog Index scores multisyllabic words as adding complexity even if they're commonly understood. Our audience will probably know words like *addictive, alternative, painkillers* and *representatives,* so we're making defensible choices here.

It's worth noting we've also added an acronym, *PTSD,* which is shorthand for *post-traumatic stress disorder.* Be careful when using acronyms in social media posts. Acronyms slash the number of characters, but you shouldn't use them unless your audience knows their meanings. But knowing an acronym's meaning doesn't always guarantee the reader knows what the individual letters stand for.

However, your audience has been introduced to many such issues through their media use. Thus, your readers likely know *PTSD* refers to a mental health condition whose onset occurs after immensely stressful, harrowing or life-threatening experiences. Balance succinctness and understanding, then judge.

Looking beyond word choice, notice this new message employs several TIPCUP + CAN elements. *Impact* is clearly established, as is *timeliness.* When we wrote this chapter, the opioid epidemic was a major concern, and several states had recently held referenda to loosen marijuana laws. There's also a subtle element of *conflict*: Some people want to legalize medical marijuana, others don't. We've introduced conflict to the post merely by adding, "So what's the holdup?"

Evaluating the CAN filters, the post establishes *conversation* by using first- and second-person pronouns like *our* and *your* to bring the reader into the struggle. That's just like the emotional appeals that anchor focus features and some controlled media pieces. Lastly, you can see us *nurturing* relationships with conversational elements. By placing readers amid this struggle, we're hoping to convert them to the cause. For those already on board, this post signals our continued commitment to a cause they are passionate about.

### Adding the "Social" to Social Media

But we could stimulate more views without drastically changing the content. A quick look at trending topics on Facebook, Twitter and other social media identifies relevant *hashtags*

(#) we could include to ensure we're participating in the wider conversation about the issue. Look at these small changes we could make to the medical marijuana post:

> 3 out of 4 doctors want marijuana made a legal prescription drug. #MedicalMarijuana helps those suffering from many diseases, from diabetes to PTSD. It also eases chronic pain, and because it's less addictive than alternative painkillers, legalizing prescribed marijuana could help our fight against the #OpioidEpidemic. So what's the holdup? Contact your representatives today!

By mashing a few words together to create hashtags, social media searches will more likely include our content, so individuals interested in these issues become more likely to find it. Again, a small, mechanical change boosts our reach.

Beyond hashtags, *mentions* (using the @ symbol) are another productive tool you should employ. As you'll recall from Chapter 9, mentioning @partners, @experts or @Relevant-Organizations in your post means not only will your followers see your content, but so too will followers of these other groups. Your audience reach instantly expands with these simple additions.

Let's consider a different example. Say we're working for a nonprofit organization wishing to raise awareness about cancer risks and fund treatment research. Social media audience analysis, which we'll discuss in Chapter 15, shows Twitter is a great way to reach our defined audience: educated, relatively affluent men in their 30s, who at the moment feel impervious to the disease. Sure, they're healthy now, but persistent bad habits and the ravages of age will catch up to them (trust us). They'll help themselves by forming healthy habits now and investing in medical research so treatments improve as they age. At the very least, such a campaign could generate awareness now. We could later convert such awareness to action as our audience ages, perhaps feels more involved in the issue and perceives fewer constraints on their behavior.

Given our target audience, we might craft a Twitter post like this:

> Hey fellas, would you bet your life on a coin flip? According to the @AmericanCancer Society, you might be already. One in two American men contract cancer, and half of those who do, die. Don't leave your life to chance. Help us #beatcancer. Donate today. https://www.cancer.org/cancer/cancer-basics/lifetime-probability-of-developing-or-dying-from-cancer.html

This seems simple enough, but there's a lot going on here. Let's first focus on how we used mentions and hashtags to widen our reach. Our post includes a link from the American Cancer Society. Since we're citing data, it's good practice to attribute it, especially when it comes from such a prominent and respected source. But rather than simply citing the name in the tweet, we were smart. We included the American Cancer Society's Twitter handle, expanding our potential audience. We also researched popular hashtags related to cancer, specifically the fight against it. Including #beatcancer should boost views.

There's something else worth noting about these mentions and hashtags: they have an organic feel. You've probably seen social media posts in which users just cram a list of #EverythingUnderTheSun hashtags and @AnyoneWhoMightMaybeCare mentions at the end. That's arguably a viable strategy in some cases, but consider the drawbacks. First, in many ways, this is just a digital version of the shotgun approach to media relations we criticized in Chapter 11. Including more hashtags and mentions may draw a larger audience, but not necessarily the right audience. Duping people into viewing content irrelevant to them erodes what might otherwise be a useful relationship either now or in the future. Second, when audiences don't feel hashtags and mentions are integral to the message, they may interpret them as insincere attempts to latch onto some popular topic or opinion leader, instead of a genuine attempt to foster conversation.

Finally, there are spatial issues. Every SNS limits the length of posts, and for practical reasons, it's best to be brief. Chucking a barrage of hashtags at the end of a post consumes word count that could be devoted to more meaningful content. As of 2020, Twitter allows 280 characters per tweet; the post above has 278. The content accounts for 255 characters and the link 23 (Twitter treats all links as 23 characters, regardless of length). If you were to jam mentions and hashtags at the end, you'd have to make significant cuts elsewhere, which would likely remove some of the valuable persuasive prose elements the tweet includes.

> **MEMORY MEMO 14.4  J-School SNS Tips**[15]
>
> - Never forget your audience
> - Apply principles of lede writing
> - Make every word count
> - Use simple language
> - Link to your sources
> - Include graphics for complex information
> - Increase audience reach with @ and #

## Crafting Persuasive Prose for Social Media

Throughout this book, we've stressed that every prose element you include—indeed, every word—must enhance your message's persuasive appeal. The same truth governs social media messaging. Given its brevity, our cancer post lets us peer into the strategic thinking justifying each word choice we made. Let's look at our tweet sentence by sentence to judge each prose element. From the beginning:

Hey fellas, would you bet your life on a coin flip?

Think back to Chapters 10 and evaluate this as a lede sentence for a feature story, or even as the headline of a static ad we discussed in Chapter 12. The same principles explain what's happening in this truncated SNS message and why it works. Take the phrase "Hey fellas." Using *hey* is deliberate. We could have chosen *hello* or even *hi*, but *hey* conveys the more informal, conversational tone we're going for. The same could be said for using *fellas* instead of the Victorian English *fellows*.

Employing *fellas* also immediately screams, "Males! We're talking to you!" Sure, we could have used *men*, but again, that's too formal. And while *guys* sets an appropriate tone, it's often used colloquially to refer to groups of people that include women. Since we're targeting men, *fellas* is the best choice.

*[Handwritten margin note, left of upper text:]* Don't overload w/ hashtags, w/ it, like shotgun bksts, also, may

*[Handwritten margin note, left of lower text:]* undercut your ethos, your credibility, that you're reaching people on a wild goose chase

OK, so we just spent two paragraphs discussing two words, but that's how important these seemingly minor decisions are. Imagine how very different this post would be if it started out with *Hello men* as opposed to *Hey fellas*. Drastically. With just two words, we've signaled commonality with our target audience.

Now consider the rest of the lede: *would you bet your life on a coin flip?* Again, we communicated a lot in this phrase. First, *bet* is a strong action verb; not *make a bet* or *place a bet*, just *bet*. We could have gone with *wager*, another strong verb, but *bet your life* is a more common construction than *wager your life*, so we chose the former.

Our words are also concrete and relatable. Our audience members get it; they likely have made at least a few friendly wagers. Then there's our decision to use *coin flip*. Again, it's something concrete and relatable. While substituting *coin flip* with *50/50 odds* would preserve the meaning, we would lose the sensory experience. You can easily envision a *coin flip*. Imagine placing the coin on your thumb, flipping it, hearing the distinctive ting as it launches, and then feeling it smack back into your palm. You don't have that concrete, sensory experience with *50/50 odds*, a less powerful construction.

You may recall our earlier discussion of features in which we discouraged you from using question ledes. That's solid practice for features. However, when provocative, online question ledes can immediately generate interest with few words. In this case, what man knowingly takes a 50/50 chance with his life? The question's aggressive nature prompts audiences to keep reading. It makes the most of those first two seconds of attention, which we now try to retain through the next passage:

> According to the @AmericanCancer Society, you might be already. One in two American men contract cancer, and half of those who do, die.

What?! That's shocking! The tweet's lede poses a stimulating question, and the next sentence confronts the reader with an even more inflammatory answer. An estimated 42% of American men will develop some type of invasive cancer during their lives (fairly close to half), and about 23% will die from the disease (again, close to half the group who contract cancer).

Again, let's look at sentence construction. We've expanded the tweet's reach by seamlessly integrating @AmericanCancer Society into the text. Moreover, because "cancer" is in the organizational name, we've tightly targeted our audience and our topic. Again, we chose concrete terms like *one in two*, and *half*. These communicate our main idea more definitively than the precise though less comprehensible *42%* and *23%*.

More importantly, these concrete ratios explicitly remind readers of the lede's *coin flip* metaphor. It provokes a stark visual: heads, you develop cancer … tails, you don't. And if you unfortunately develop cancer? Heads, you live … tails, you die. Notice too we chose *die*. It's clear, direct and confrontational. Sure, we could have said *pass away*, but it doesn't deliver the same emotional weight.

Now that we've grabbed our audience's attention and held it long enough to evoke an emotional response, we close by channeling that emotion into reasoned action:

Don't leave your life to chance. Help us #beatcancer. Donate today. https://www.
cancer.org/cancer/cancer-basics/lifetime-probability-of-developing-or-dying-from-
cancer.html

Notice how this final portion is structured like the wrap and baseline of static advertising copy. It begins with a transitional sentence: *Don't leave your life to chance.* Just as you would structure the static ad's wrap, our word choice consciously reintroduces the opening hypothetical bet to our audience.

Now to the next sentence: *Help us #beatcancer.* We again see familiar strategic writing elements. We introduce the TIPCUP element of *conflict* by reframing the discussion of cancer. Our audience doesn't have to relegate themselves to chance—embodied by *don't leave*—but can take action, fight back, and *#beatcancer.* How? Simple: *Donate today* toward cancer research and treatment. The link here actually serves as a baseline and a call to action. It directs readers to the American Cancer Society for more information on the statistics we employed. Additionally, it offers readers an immediate mechanism by which they can convert their emotional engagement into action via the site's large "Donate" icon.

Finally, if you look at this tweet holistically, you'll notice yet more familiar writing elements. First, there's a clear, overarching rhythm. The sentences become gradually shorter, rhythmically pushing the reader toward donating. We accentuate that rhythm by using alliteration (*leave your life; do, die*) and near-rhymes (*don't* and *donate*).

The character count limitations imposed by many online platforms and social networks make prose choices even more critical. A feature story can run 5,000 words or more. Even a 60-second radio ad offers about 125. But the tweet in our example contains only 45 words—and it was a long tweet!

Notice though, not one choice was accidental. We spent pages anchoring the specific, strategic purpose of the tweet's 45 words within the journalism maxims influencing our media relations approaches.

Let's return to the contention with which we introduced this chapter. Yes, as children of the information age you've been breastfed on social media. But contrary to what you may think, the short-form writing distinguishing most online content is arguably more difficult to produce than you encounter in any traditional media.

In the next chapter we contend with the other side of social media writing: interaction. Social media is designed to spark a back and forth, but we too often have to deliver those responses without the careful parsing of language we devoted to the original post. Shortly, you'll learn about making split-second decisions on what to say, when to say it, where to say it, and how to say it. At times, you'll even have to decide whether you should say anything at all.

**SUMMARY**

- Online content is effective not simply because it exists but only when your audience can easily discover it and deem it useful.

- You can often repurpose content you develop for traditional media outlets to quickly create effective online content.

- Practicing brand journalism and reconceptualizing the organization as a publishing house helps build relationships with stakeholders that go deeper and last longer than simple business transactions.

- Creating thematic and tonal consistency across various elements of your online content (i.e., text, images, video, audio) helps drive its underlying message.

- Blogs are useful tools for establishing your organization as a thought leader within its industry and a valuable information source among its publics.

- Journalistic and traditional media writing conventions still matter, and they'll help you develop heuristic ways of creating engaging social media content.

### Scenario Prompts: Crafting Semicontrolled Messages

You'll find Scenario Prompts on pp. 367–386 of this textbook. While they vary in subject and difficulty, they help you hone your critical thinking and strategic writing skills. The following are best suited to this chapter's topics.

Management: **1.3** / Writing: 1.8, 2.6, 2.7, 2.9, 6.7, 9.5, 10.8

### *Figure Credits*

Fig. 14.2: kyforky.com. Copyright © by Kentucky for Kentucky.

Fig. 14.3: Copyright © 2013 Depositphotos/spotmatikphoto.

# Say Something, Then Be Ready for Anything

Delivering Semicontrolled Messages

OK, I don't hate the media. But statistically speaking, it would be a safe bet if you thought I did. In 2020, Gallup found just 40% of Americans claimed to have "a great deal" or "a fair amount" of trust in the media.[1]

Though I generally trust Gallup polling, I think this data is misleading. Closely examining the survey questions reveal a great deal about the data collected. Let's consider the media trust question respondents were asked:

> In general, how much trust and confidence do you have in the mass media—such as newspapers, TV and radio—when it comes to reporting the news fully, accurately and fairly—a great deal, a fair amount, not very much, or none at all?

So what's wrong with this question? It sounds reasonable, and you might expect people to view the media negatively. I'm sure at some point you've heard various people complain that the news media is terrible, the media is biased, the media is untrustworthy, or—Wait! There! Did you catch that?

Look again, and you'll see how poor grammar betrays us: Each *is* in that sentence above should be replaced with an *are*. Gallup joins too many of us in forgetting *media* is a plural word.

Most of us likely don't distrust the media wholly. We just distrust certain outlets. You may not believe *The New York Times* is fair but have complete confidence in *The Wall Street Journal's* reporting. You may loathe Fox News but treat every MSNBC utterance as gospel truth. Remember our Chapter 1 lesson on cognitive dissonance? Each of us is prone to tuning out sources challenging our worldviews and favoring those that align.

Theories of opinion leadership and uses and gratifications suggest each of us, depending on the topic, seeks out and trusts different sources. You may rely more on a local community blogger than a national newspaper concerning your city's affairs while reversing media preferences when exploring the latest congressional legislation.

And just to pile on, consider that individuals may use the same medium for different reasons and in different ways. For example, I use Facebook primarily to opine about current news and organize social outings. My mother shares family photos and recommends products to her friends. My retired father exchanges funny memes and taunts his friends and relatives.

We also use different platforms to accomplish the same thing. My father rarely uses Facebook to schedule events because it's easier to catch up with his hometown friends at church or sporting events. While my mother solicits and shares product reviews on Facebook, I trust Yelp or Wirecutter. It's just a matter of preference and convenience.

You must remember these considerations when you're delivering messages online, especially through social networking sites. Not only must you know which media your audience likely uses but how they use it and what they use it for ... hold on ... which media your audiences *are* most likely to use, how they use *them* and what they use *them* for. Damn, that's an easy mistake to make.

—*NB*

---

**What You Know**

- Audience research helps effectively target your messaging.

- Print, audio and visual platforms display strengths and weaknesses for which you must compensate.

- Persuasion occurs only if a message elicits a desired behavior.

- Accounting for gatekeepers' schedules and interests improves media relations success.

- Organizational ethics can be defined in the context of virtues.

**What You'll Learn**

- How to apply secondary audience profile data to conduct primary research, develop buyer personas and communicate through social media platforms your audiences actually use

- How to overcome the inherent message constraints when writing for specific social media platforms

- How likes, shares and comments predict pro-organizational behaviors

- How to communicate with journalists through social media channels

- How to apply virtues in online organization communication and action

## The Internets, With an 'S'

So you understand our frustration that the general public, as well as many practitioners, treat the media as a monolithic entity. Put simply, this is senseless. In past chapters, you've learned to target the right medium to the right audience and craft a message accentuating that medium's strengths.

But what if we took this fragmentation a step further. Here's a simple question: What is television?

The easy answer? Multichannel content transmitted to a television set. So when you're watching breaking news, a big game or a reality show on a flat-screen, that's television. But what if you streamed these exact same programs on your phone, tablet or computer? Is it still television?

Could we better define *television* by its content characteristics, maybe *multichannel content distributed through a device*? (However, that defines a streaming training bicycle, like a Peloton, as *television*. See our problem?)

Much like we stressed that *media* is a plural word, perhaps we might go even deeper to say that an individual medium might itself be just as fragmented. Perhaps referring to it as the medium of *televisions*—with an *s*—more honestly represents what we're dealing with.

As varied as television consumption patterns are, they don't compare with the internet—or should we say *internets*? As a professional communicator, you've got to answer a few, somewhat unique questions before you begin designing, developing or expanding an online communication plan.[2]

## What Devices Do They Use?

In June 2009, satirical news website The Onion posted a feature story regarding a fictitious university study, "Report: 90% of Waking Hours Spent Staring at Glowing Rectangles." Among the more tellingly predictive excerpts:

> Researchers were able to identify nearly 30 varieties of glowing rectangles that play some role throughout the course of each day. Among them: handheld rectangles, music-playing rectangles, mobile communication rectangles, personal work rectangles, and bright alarm cubes, which emit a high-pitched reminder that it's time to rise from one's bed and move toward the rectangles in one's kitchen.[3]

Good satire builds on truth. We do spend an inordinate amount of time staring at glowing rectangles, big and small. Increasingly, those devices are becoming internet enabled. In 2015, for the first time the majority of U.S. internet traffic came from mobile devices.[4]

While that may sound innocuous, it's momentous for the strategic communicator. Those rectangles are very different. Members of your audience will access your information on a 5-inch phone screen, a 60-inch flat-screen TV and everything in between. Devices run on numerous operating systems, and users gravitate toward different browsers and apps, with content displaying differently on each.

While you may be able to divert many of these design dilemmas to the IT department, you can make life easier on them and your end users. For example, smartphone screens are relatively small, so they can't display as much text as, say, a computer monitor. Keeping paragraphs short lets phone users view them in their entirety, improving the ease of reading. People also read less attentively on mobile devices, so you may choose to present shorter excerpts or simple images on mobile sites and apps while reserving long-form content for the full site.[5]

Similarly, many mobile devices rely on cellular data, which operates at lower download speeds than many Wi-Fi connections (particularly in rural areas). If your content is dominantly video, it may load slowly, meaning many users may abandon your message. You may need to alter your content, making mobile sites more "lightweight" to speed loading.

### Where and When Are They Online?

As of 2020, there were over 1.74 billion registered websites providing an array of choices for the world's 4.44 billion internet users.[6] But as you might expect, Google, YouTube and

Facebook are the dominant players, accounting for about 32% of global web traffic. The billions of other sites split the remaining two-thirds.[7]

The question for the strategic communicator: Where is your target audience most likely to spend its time? Equally important, *How* are they spending their time on that site?

Consider how your audience schedules its time on a given web source. While the internet offers 24/7 access, many individuals maintain a general routine, just as they would with traditional media. Back in the print-only days, people typically read the paper just before or after work. With digital, users can check newspaper sites or apps anytime, yet the average visitor to The New York Times website views the page twice a day, though sadly for only about four minutes total.[8]

Figure 15.1 shows how usage patterns for social media sites also vary. The Pew Research Center found Facebook users visit that site at least daily, while Twitter visits are less frequent. What does that mean for your messaging? Odds are, if you post a Facebook message today, your followers will see it today. However, your tweet could be buried in the week it takes a Twitter user to even check her feed. Therefore, to ensure users see your content, you may need to repeat Twitter content more frequently.

Among the users of each social media site, the % who use that site with the following frequencies

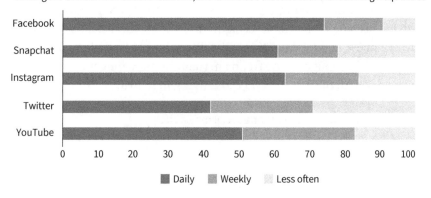

FIGURE 15.1  Social Media Use Frequency.

Note: Numbers may not add to 100 due to rounding.

**Social Media Fact Sheet**

https://www.pewresearch.org/internet/fact-sheet/social-media/

The social media stats from Pew we reference here just scratch the surface. Follow this QR code and poke around. There's a lot more to discover.

Thinking more broadly, it's likely your organization will distribute information through several online channels. These might include an official website, a blog, as well as a handful of SNSs. Each one requires its own publishing schedule driven by your audience's usage patterns and the nature of the content you're pushing. It's a challenge to manage multiple platforms, but software programs like Hootsuite help you schedule and monitor posts.

Generally, different content demands different scheduling. Organizing content along the 1-7-30-4-2-1 schedule outlined in Table 15.1 can help you effectively and efficiently disseminate information and respond to stakeholder feedback.[9]

**TABLE 15.1  The 1-7-30-4-2-1 Publishing Schedule**

| Timeframe | Commonly Distributed Content |
| --- | --- |
| 1—Daily | SNS posts |
| 7—Weekly | Blog posts |
| 30—Monthly | E-newsletters |
| 4—Quarterly | Employee webinar |
| 2—Biannually | Fundraising appeals |
| 1—Annually | Social responsibility reports |

## Parsing Social Media Audiences

### Battling Misperceptions

In the last 50 years, nothing has impacted strategic communicators more than the emergence of the internet. The World Wide Web became publicly available in 1991, and within 25 years, 287 million Americans were online, representing 88.5% of the total U.S. population.[10] Yet social media's growth has been more meteoric. As Figure 15.2 shows, social media use among U.S. adults ballooned from 5% in 2005 to 72% in 2019. According to Pew, all demographic groups reflected that growth, though usage trends higher among younger adults (18–29 years old), the college-educated, the affluent and those living in nonrural areas.[11]

**FIGURE 15.2  Social Media Use Over Time.** *"Social Media Fact Sheet." Pew Research Center, Washington, D.C. (June 12, 2019) http://www.pewinternet.org/ fact-sheet/social-media/.*

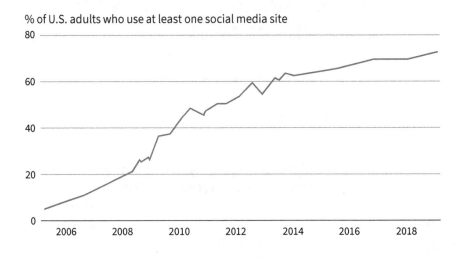

% of U.S. adults who use at least one social media site

That astonishing growth, however, has created misperceptions about social media among digital natives—like you, maybe. Our worldview is constrained by our own experiences. For example, what proportion of Americans 25 or older do you think have a college degree? Maybe you'd guess it's half or more.

Nope. In 2020, the U.S. Census Bureau reported just 36% of Americans age 25 or older held a four-year degree.[12] One way to explain your overshot: Who do you know who's gone to college? There's you. And because you're in college, so are most of your friends … and likely one or both of your parents … and your parents' friends … and your friends' parents.

You face a similar danger when implementing an organization's SNS strategy. Among ages 18–29, 90% are active on at least one social media platform. Yet older age groups sometimes have far lower usage rates (at this moment, particularly Instagram and Snapchat). Strategic communication challenges each practitioner to inhabit the world of people with whom, by definition, she cannot share a demographic. The media *you* use and the way *you* use them are irrelevant. This book's oft-repeated maxim is still true: The audience is all that matters.

## Targeting Social Media Messages

Believe it or not, this differentiated social media use pattern is actually good news. It means you don't have to be everywhere. Imagine if every adult used each of these platforms at an equally high rate. That would justify an organizational presence across the board, which would require you to produce and manage a staggering amount of content for an array of audiences across a multitude of outlets.

Fortunately, your organization doesn't need to be active on every social media outlet. In fact, it almost certainly shouldn't be. If your target audience doesn't patronize a particular platform, don't post content there. Content creation comes with opportunity costs, and maintaining a presence on one platform dilutes resources you could invest in another more promising venue—online or off.

Take Sweet'N Low for example. Sweet'N Low is an artificial sweetener brand introduced in 1957. The company has a fairly active web presence. The company website has a sleek look, is easy to navigate and features an impressive and easily searchable list of recipes for low-calorie foods. Additionally, Sweet'N Low has active Facebook, Instagram, Pinterest and Twitter accounts—but should it?

In Chapter 11, we discussed Simmons and other market research tools. Among the many products Simmons tracks is artificial sweetener usage. They do it by brand, so you can build a fairly reliable **buyer persona** from its data. For this social media test, we're comparing Sweet'N Low's basic demographics to Pew's social media data from Table 15.2.

**TABLE 15.2  Social Media Use by Platform**

% of U.S. adults who use each social media platform

|  | Facebook | Instagram | LinkedIn | Twitter | Pinterest | Snapchat | YouTube | WhatsApp | Reddit |
|---|---|---|---|---|---|---|---|---|---|
| **Total** | 69% | 37% | 27% | 22% | 28% | 24% | 73% | 20% | 11% |
| **Men** | 63% | 31% | 29% | 24% | 15% | 24% | 78% | 21% | 15% |
| **Women** | 75% | 43% | 24% | 21% | 42% | 24% | 68% | 19% | 8% |
| **Ages 18–29** | 79% | 67% | 28% | 38% | 34% | 62% | 91% | 23% | 22% |
| **30–49** | 79% | 47% | 37% | 26% | 35% | 25% | 87% | 31% | 14% |
| **50–64** | 68% | 23% | 24% | 17% | 27% | 9% | 70% | 16% | 6% |
| **65+** | 46% | 8% | 11% | 7% | 15% | 3% | 38% | 3% | 1% |
| **White** | 70% | 33% | 28% | 21% | 33% | 22% | 71% | 13% | 12% |
| **Black** | 70% | 40% | 24% | 24% | 27% | 28% | 77% | 24% | 4% |
| **Hispanic** | 69% | 51% | 16% | 25% | 22% | 29% | 78% | 42% | 14% |
| **High school or less** | 61% | 33% | 9% | 13% | 19% | 22% | 64% | 18% | 6% |
| **Some college** | 75% | 37% | 26% | 24% | 32% | 29% | 79% | 14% | 14% |
| **College graduate** | 74% | 43% | 51% | 32% | 38% | 20% | 80% | 28% | 15% |
| **Urban** | 73% | 46% | 33% | 26% | 30% | 29% | 77% | 24% | 11% |
| **Suburban** | 69% | 35% | 30% | 22% | 30% | 20% | 74% | 19% | 13% |
| **Rural** | 66% | 21% | 10% | 13% | 26% | 20% | 64% | 10% | 8% |

*Source: Survey conducted Jan. 8 to Feb. 7, 2019.*
*PEW RESEARCH CENTER*
*"Social Media Fact Sheet." Pew Research Center, Washington, D.C. (June 12, 2019) http://www.pewinternet.org/fact-sheet/social-media/.*

Recall that a Simmons index of 100 represents an average representation of a given category within the U.S. population. Therefore, when searching for higher-than-average users, large numbers (typically 120 or greater) designate demographic groups who buy Sweet'N Low at rates significantly higher than the average. Low numbers (typically less than 80) represent likely disinterested publics. Table 15.3 lists the index numbers for Sweet'N Low users based on commonly collected demographics.

**TABLE 15.3  Simmons Sweet'N Low Data**

| Demographics | Sweet'N Low Index |
|---|---|
| Male | 93 |
| Female | 107 |
| White | 101 |
| African American | 87 |
| Hispanic | 102 |
| Asian | 123 |
| Other | 94 |
| 18–24 | 107 |

| Demographics | Sweet'N Low Index |
|---|:---:|
| 25–34 | 78 |
| 35–44 | 59 |
| 45–54 | 109 |
| 55–64 | 110 |
| 65+ | 139 |
| Did Not Complete Grade School | 142 |
| No High School Diploma | 116 |
| High School Graduate | 111 |
| Some College | 83 |
| College Graduate | 94 |

*Source: MRI-Simmons.*

Sweet'N Low's target market data and social media platform user data lets us evaluate—at least to some degree—the company's social media strategy. While there are slight differences in gender and ethnic identification, age and education stand out. Sweet'N Low users tend to be middle-aged or older, with usage particularly high among those 65+. Also, as consumers attain higher levels of education, they become less likely to use Sweet'N Low.

This suggests you should communicate to the Sweet'N Low user through media attracting relatively older and less educated individuals. But in Table 15.2, you immediately see red flags. As income decreases and age increases, social media usage declines. These divergences make you question Sweet'N Low's social media choices.

The company's use of Instagram, Pinterest and Twitter seems especially suspect. Just 8% of the 65+ group, and 33% of those with a high school education or less, are active Instagram users. Similar patterns arise for Pinterest (15% and 19%, respectively) and Twitter (7% and 13%, respectively). Facebook, on the other hand, looks reasonable. It's the most popular social media platform among the 65+ demographic and the second-most popular among those holding no more than a high school diploma.

These data show us a potential oversight in Sweet'N Low's marketing strategy. The Pew data on YouTube users tell us that among Americans with a high school education or less, 64% are active on the platform, as are 38% of the 65+ demographic. That's a sizable chunk of the brand's target demographic. However, when we wrote this, Sweet'N Low lacked a dedicated YouTube channel.

This is troubling for at least two other reasons. First, Sweet'N Low maintains an excellent website featuring low-calorie recipes. The company frequently repurposes this content on its social media platforms. That's a sound strategy. But imagine how easy it would be to shoot a series of how-to videos that bring those same recipes to life. Because the core content already exists, adding a YouTube presence would be relatively easy.

What's worse, Sweet'N Low's competitor, Splenda, realized this. Splenda's dedicated YouTube channel features numerous recipes swapping sugar for artificial sweetener and maintains a video series called "Real Swaps, Real Stories." These short vignettes showcase individuals and businesses making the switch to Splenda, arguing you don't have to sacrifice flavor to cut calories.

Splenda has effectively undercut its competitor in this arena. Just as effective controlled and uncontrolled media relations strategies rely on solid research, so too does semicontrolled online communication.

## Delivering Social Media Messages
### The Confines of the Channel

When we first introduced the audience-centered model in Chapter 2, we described a three-step process: (1) identify a target audience, (2) develop a message addressing audience needs and (3) deliver that message through audience-appropriate channels. You've learned to identify target audiences by relying on market research, and you just saw how we applied that research to identify viable SNSs based on audience usage. In Chapter 14, you learned to modify social media messages by using specialized language, mentions, hashtags and more to draw a target audience. Moreover, the capabilities of social media platforms often prompt practitioners to modify their message strategies.

You've already been making such calculated decisions, though probably without recognizing it. In Chapters 8 and 9, we discussed the relative strengths and weaknesses of print vs. multichannel vs. interactive media. Once upon a time, just knowing each channel's characteristics was enough. In fact, until the early 2000s, strategic communicators typically specialized in a single media form. That doesn't cut it anymore.

Consider our analysis of Sweet'N Low's social media presence. We didn't advocate the brand create a dedicated YouTube channel just because market research identified prospective consumers active on this outlet. Instead, Sweet'N Low's branded content lent itself to multichannel communication. It's easy to picture a lower-calorie cupcake baking tutorial: a personable pastry chef walking novices through mixing milk, margarine, eggs, flour and Sweet'N Low, then pouring the batter into the pan. That's far more engaging than reading a recipe alongside still images of cupcakes.

But what if the messaging demands don't match the platform's format? Maybe you're working for a nonprofit offering shelter and assistance to domestic violence victims. Typically, women and their children suffer this abuse, so media used heavily by women of childbearing age seem like logical choices. Reviewing the Pew data in Table 15.2, we see that women 18–49 years old frequent Pinterest and Instagram. However, these could constitute disastrous media choices.

Both outlets are visual in nature. Your nonprofit could certainly capture compelling images of volunteers and social workers helping domestic violence victims. But do you really want to plaster those photos all over the internet, where these women's violent partners might see them? Your nonprofit has a moral (and likely legal) obligation to protect them, which supersedes every other organizational function. Without access to quality visuals, you can't produce successful Pinterest and Instagram pages, even if your target audience is active on these platforms.

## Liking

Once you've isolated a social media space where your target audience is active and your messaging fits, you must then consider how you're going to engage your audience and what you ultimately want them to do. Very often, practitioners wish to increase likes, favorites, etc. for particular posts or pages. OK. Fair enough. But here's a simple question: What is a like worth?

Both students and professionals seem to defer to this metric because it's easily measurable. PR practitioners once tracked press clippings to gauge media relations successes for the same reason, but both approaches simply measure potential exposure, not audience action.

Likes have some value. They let you pair some measure of message attention to an individual. However, most organizational goals depend on stakeholders taking more substantial actions than simply liking a post. You need to translate a like into something greater.

Some argue that likes signal support … and support may translate to behavior. Or maybe a like prompts others to act. But Harvard School of Business researchers reject this conclusion: "The mere act of endorsing a brand does not affect a customer's behavior or lead to increased purchasing, nor does it spur purchasing by friends."[13] A thumbs-up online carries less weight than an in-person recommendation. That makes sense given that liking a post or a brand requires minimal effort, and users often "like" organizations they're at best lukewarm about.

## Sharing

Rather than focusing on likes, many organizations instead strive to generate shares. When you share branded content, it pushes information to additional stakeholders whom an organization might not have otherwise reached. Sharing also creates a stronger sense of endorsement than a mere like, and when multiple people within your network share the same content, it creates a **social proof**.[14]

Social proof encourages us to trust the most shared and accessed information. Purchasing products through Amazon provides a ready example. Marketers have found new products struggle to gain traction because they have few or no reviews.[15] Reviewed products become more trusted, as does more frequently shared content.

Problematically, social media users are relatively passive when responding to most content. On average, just one of every 318 tweets is retweeted, and about one of every 200 Facebook posts is shared.[16] However, some posts are more likely to generate shares than others, based either on the content itself or the psychological rewards we gain from sharing. Memory Memo 15.1 summarizes some common reasons why we share.

> **MEMORY MEMO 15.1** Why We Share[17]
>
> - The information impacted us emotionally
> - The information was practical
> - The information was timely or novel
> - Sharing the information made us look good
> - Sharing the information made us feel useful
> - Sharing the information enhanced our relationships with others

Whether online or off, humans follow the tenets of interpersonal communication. We react to information that *impacts us emotionally*. When we delight in watching cute cats play in boxes or mourn a polar bear starving as its natural habitat melts away, we're drawn in.[18] Instinctually wanting to share that emotion, we share the content.

Of course, emotion is only half the human experience. We're creatures of logic as well. Therefore, when we encounter helpful information we tend to pass along that information, explaining why so many how-to and "life hack" videos make the rounds.

As we learned in Chapter 6, *timely* and *unusual* information engages human interest. Breaking news constitutes perhaps the best example but also helps explain why false information—or "fake news"—spreads faster than the truth: falsehoods are inherently more novel, so novel in fact that they never happened![19]

---

### PRINCIPLES IN PRACTICE 15.1   WTF, Wendy's!

By the end of 2020, @Wendys had amassed about 3.7 million Twitter followers, in large part because of the company's unusual approach. Brands are often tepid on social media because they fear alienating audiences, so they sometimes are perceived as impersonal, distant or even inauthentic. Wendy's is anything but.

Brands distinguish themselves by offering something unique or immediately identifiable. Wendy's branding has been its burgers' shape: square rather than round. That fact hasn't escaped some Twitter users:

Image 15.1

Wendy's Tweets: Copyright © Quality Is Our Recipe, LLC

Wendy's offers a response as unique as its square patty. Immediately you can see how such aggression might create negative backlash or be perceived as petty. Wendy's would disagree:

Wendy's has largely avoided upsetting its followers because it's generally agreed these little back and forths are all in good fun. In fact, many of the company's followers happily offer themselves up for ridicule, like these two guys on #NationalRoastDay:

Still, Wendy's fans aren't its only Twitter targets. The company regularly pokes fun of its rival, McDonald's:

Damn, that's cold! But as Wendy's might say, not as cold as their competitor's burgers:

WTF is Wendy's doing?! Hard work based on a well-considered marketing and social media strategy, that's what.

You'll notice the astounding number of retweets, comments and likes. Indeed, you can calculate an **engagement rate** for social media posts. Add all the engagement behaviors (in this case, retweets, likes and comments) and divide by the number of followers. Generally, engagement rates greater than 0.1% are considered high.[20] These five Wendy's tweets averaged nearly 2%.

While that rate is formidable, recall this measure includes likes, which have question-able value. For us, the truly impressive stat is how Wendy's gets so many retweets. If you consider why people share content, it's not all surprising. Its posts possess immediate emotional impact through their biting humor, and the novelty of a fast-food company bra-zenly roasting its competitors—and even its own customers—certainly helps.

In cultivating a unique organizational voice, Wendy's prompts its fans to share their con-nection with others both online and offline. In the end, this naturally leads to more sales of those "artificially" shaped burgers.

Beyond its raw information or usefulness, there are social and psycho-logical benefits to sharing. Sharing information helps us showcase our worth to those in our networks. Recall the major tenant of social exchange theory: relationships are stable when the people in them feel they continue to receive reciprocal rewards from their relationship partners. Through the information we share, we demonstrate our value. We *enhance our relationships* with those around us, constituting perhaps the greatest reward for inherently social beings.

> **Strategic Thought**
>
> What was the last thing you shared online? What prompted you to share that content? Why might others do the same?

### Engaging

This relational give and take lies at the heart of engagement. Unfortunately, engagement is a loosely defined term in social media contexts. For our pur-poses, **engagement** represents some level of involvement with or commitment to a product, brand, organization or issue. It's often measured by a level of interactivity or willingness to take actions that advance key goals.

For example, Wendy's high Twitter engagement rates in Principles in Prac-tice 15.1 comprise different levels of engagement. Many consider social media likes as a form of engagement. Perhaps, but at best it's low-level engagement because the minimal interactivity doesn't necessarily translate to action.

Shares, on the other hand, require the user to publicly endorse a message, validating its content to her wider social network and signaling greater com-mitment. This is considerably more likely to drive stakeholders to act.

Yet, stakeholders publicly conversing with an organization through a com-ment feature constitutes even higher interactivity. It provides the organization an opportunity to build a substantive relationship with a key stakeholder. Managing interactions with stakeholders through online comment sections and discussion boards is an incredibly difficult and delicate process, so much so that we'll devote an entire section to the practice at the conclusion of this chapter.

For now, we want you to consider ways you might foster engagement between your organization and its stakeholders or among stakeholders themselves. It may help to first reflect upon advice from David Meerman Scott, who believes stakeholders approach organizations online with these questions in mind: "Does this organization care about me? Does it focus on the problems I face? Does it share my perspective or push its own on me?"[21]

### Analytic Problem-Solving

Those three questions can be condensed to one: Are you meeting people where they are in relation to what they need or want from your organization? That's similar to what we've considered vital with other media, but social media introduces the added challenge of generating meaningful exchanges.

For some organizations, this ask is pretty easy. Recall Chapter 9's discussion of Home Depot. Consumers and DIY enthusiasts likely want information on home renovation products. That's fairly simple to provide. Consider Dollar Shave Club, discussed in Chapter 14. Obviously, its members want affordable razors, but what might they want in the way of content? Tips on grooming, fitness and other men's issues perhaps. Again, not difficult to supply but tougher for a strategic communicator to recognize.

But what if you make toilet paper?

Tough ask, but not impossible if you break it down. Let's say you're focusing on the U.S. market, and selling a product almost everybody uses, like toilet paper. While you've got a massive potential customer base, it's divided among dozens of name brands and countless generics. Then, of course, toilet paper isn't exactly a product we're excited to buy. It's a necessity we rarely think about until we assume the throne. And what's there to say? Every claim—the softest, thickest, gentlest, longest-lasting, eco-friendliest—has been made a thousand times before.

But if you recall our Chapter 12 discussion on controlled media, developing a novel claim represents most advertisers' biggest challenge: How do you make a familiar claim in a new and interesting way? Similarly, when managing social media communication for a toilet paper manufacturer, you have to consider how you can make something mundane seem marvelous, or at least mildly interesting.

### Getting Creative

That's what Charmin has managed to do, relying largely on the humor of shared experience. Perhaps the biggest thing Charmin has going for it is that we all have to … well … go. That arms the organization with an ability to reflect on common bathroom experiences across a variety of settings, which lies at the foundation of the #CharminAsks Twitter campaign.

---

**Strategic Thought**

So far we've discussed some fairly obscure or difficult products with which to prompt engagement, such as artificial sweeteners and toilet paper. Can you think of a similarly odd product or issue to discuss via social media? What are some creative ways to generate involvement or interactivity?

Image 15.6

Maybe we're oversharing here, but we're betting most of you have engaged in that awkward, one-foot flush balancing act to avoid touching the biohazard most concert venues call a toilet. If so, you join the 62% of Charmin's informal poll respondents who flush with their feet. Astonishingly, 14% of respondents possess both the snootiness and bladder control to exclusively use auto-flush toilets.

Image 15.7

Charmin Tweets: Copyright © 2016 by Procter & Gamble. Reprinted with permission.

Also, in this modern age, what public restroom is complete without someone both on the seat and on the phone? Well, #CharminAsks whether such behavior is taboo. Either way, we'd hate to be on the other end of that conversation.

**Charmin** ✔
@Charmin

Follow   ⌄

#CharminAsks: Share your bathroom? Which do you think most often?

**70%**  Why is the roll empty?!?

**30%**  Really? New roll on top?

104 votes · Final results

11:32 AM - 7 Oct 2016

**6** Retweets  **5** Likes

💬    ⟲ 6    ♡ 5    ✉

Tweet your reply

**Charmin** ✔
@Charmin

Follow   ⌄

#CharminAsks: The person who rolls under, is..

**20%**  100% right.

**80%**  all kinds of wrong.

175 votes · Final results

9:54 AM - 30 Sep 2016

**2** Retweets  **10** Likes

💬 6    ⟲ 2    ♡ 10    ✉

Image 15.8

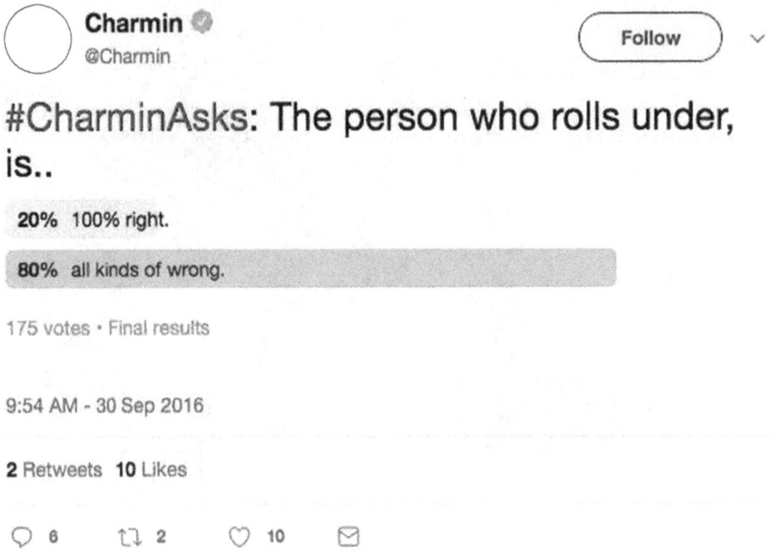

Image 15.9

And we haven't even touched on home bathroom etiquette. While we use them in private, bathrooms are shared spaces, which introduces disputes over barren rolls. Should you check first, or is it the moral duty of the person who used the last sheet to replace it? Then there's the granddaddy of all TP tussles: Why is the roll upside down? Whether you roll over or under, you've got a preference. Don't lie!

Before we launched into the toilet tissue tirade, we asked you to *think*. Now we're asking you to *feel*. Be honest: those images spurred emotions. Maybe you laughed, recalling a friend asking if you could spare a square because the neighboring stall had run out. Or you might have been enraged at your roommate, whose reptilian upbringing convinced her rolling the toilet paper under was acceptable in human society.

That's Charmin meeting you where you are in relation to them. The company can't engage you in these social media spaces by focusing on product attributes or "12 tips to get the most from your TP." But it can rely on humor and shared experiences to evoke emotion by connecting you to its product. Moreover, the playful nature of these tweets establishes an identity for the brand, attempting to sway you into viewing Charmin as something more than simply a toilet paper manufacturer—to see them as more human.

## Media Relations in the Internet Age
### Extra! Extra! Tweet All About It!

Beyond creating more personal relationships with consumers, there are other key publics active on social media. For many journalists and other influential media personalities, their job now requires an active presence on SNSs. Bylines often include social media handles along with the reporter's name.

That SNS presence doesn't exist just for media consumers to engage with journalists but also for those seeking to influence the media agenda to do the same. It's common practice not only for journalists to hunt for engaging information online, but also for strategic communicators to connect with reporters directly through SNSs, particularly Twitter.[22]

Twitter is a viable platform to pitch stories to journalists. It's usually done through direct messaging but sometimes through mentions or replies. It's basically a query letter in shorthand. Just as you should follow coverage from reporters who work beats related to your industry, you should also connect with them on SNSs. Target your Twitter pitch just like your letter: to a reporter whose audience might actually find your story interesting.

This message-crafting process should be familiar to you. The last chapter showed how easy it was to convert a media release to a blog. A social media pitch is a similarly downsized query letter. Shrinking **Click-Through 10.6**'s query letter might create this Twitter pitch:

> St. V's will employ a super-computer to assist doctors in diagnosing and treating diseases. We're one of the only rural hospitals with this technology to drastically improve patient outcomes. Thought this would interest your readers. Can connect you to doctors for interviews. DM for more information.

In 301 characters, we've captured the story's timeliness, impact and unusualness. If the reporter shows interest, we can provide greater detail via the reporter's preference, either Twitter, email or phone.

## Audience-Centered Pressrooms

Another common yet more passive way to interact with journalists is through online pressrooms, sometimes called digital newsrooms. An **online pressroom** is a publicly accessible storehouse for an organization's media relations materials—including press releases, media kits and contact information. It both archives an organization's communication efforts and offers access to current information.

The quality and content of online pressrooms vary widely across organizations. As you might now expect, we advocate an audience-centered approach to creating and displaying content in your organization's online pressroom. Start by understanding your audience. Easy. Journalists, right?

Well, yes and no. While reporters represent one target audience, there are numerous others: consumers eager to learn about new product releases, activists investigating your company's fair-hiring practices or potential investors curious about an upcoming merger.

And we say *attract* for a reason. An online pressroom stores lots of information. The problem is that many people don't know it's there. How to make that information easily accessible, discoverable and useful? Fortunately, avid reader of this book, you're well equipped to create this ideal online pressroom.

In Chapters 6 and 7, you learned how to exploit the inverted pyramid so arguments and information are clearly presented, with the most persuasive and newsworthy TIPCUP elements at the forefront. This style is not only familiar to journalists but also to the organization's other stakeholders. Moreover, the format lets visitors easily isolate a piece's main focus and quickly evaluate its relevance to them, making the search for information more efficient and less frustrating.

Still, there are several additional ways to improve that search. The first employs the SEO elements you learned in Chapter 9. You can push your online pressroom toward the top of Google searches—especially long-tail searches—by using keywords frequently and including several relevant incoming and outgoing links. It also helps to tag PDF pages of releases. This practice makes it more likely that those genuinely interested in your content will find it.

Remember too that once people land in your online pressroom, it needs to be easily navigable. Chapter 14's blog design principles are useful here. Be sure to tag and categorize news releases and other media relations content by topic and/or date so users can easily find what they're looking for, whether they're searching within or browsing through your online pressroom.

And by no means should you limit your online pressroom to a simple list of your outgoing press releases. Consider what your audiences might want beyond what a release provides. Recall from Chapter 8 that some messages lend themselves to multichannel media. Consumers might be more engaged by a video demonstrating a product than by a printed list of its specs; investors may prefer to listen to a CEO's keynote address rather than read a transcript; photos of employees volunteering to read to children at the local library speak louder than a more passive, written description.

Moreover, just as multichannel messages may generate more stakeholder engagement, they can also serve as needed tools for reporters. Because bloggers and independent journalists may lack the resources to produce their own photos, videos and infographics, they will welcome an opportunity to use organization-supplied media to supplement their coverage.[23]

Here's another tip focused on journalists' needs: Recall that inverted pyramid format calls for background or historical information as well. You can easily catalog information contained in various fact sheets and backgrounders to make it easily accessible in your online pressroom. This helps researching reporters add depth to their stories.

Finally, it's critical to make yourself accessible to these now-vested audiences. Basic contact information for members of your organization's PR team is the most obvious need. But you should also include links to your organization's various SNSs and blogs, as well as ensure your online pressroom has RSS capabilities. This will enable these highly valued information seekers to stay connected with your organization long after leaving the site.

### Breaking Your Own News
#### *Expanding Your Reach*

Cultivating relationships with journalists is an important part of a PR practitioner's job. The online strategy for media relations doesn't fundamentally differ from many offline approaches, but the web opens new opportunities to break your organization's news directly to key stakeholders without gatekeepers mediating your message.

This process often resembles the more controlled communication efforts of marketing and advertising discussed in Chapters 12 and 13. Product releases offer a nice example. In the days before the internet, strategic communicators might organize relatively small events at which the new product was announced, inviting reporters covering specialized beats or working for niche magazines to attend. Often these reporters even received the product early for trial and testing to inform their reviews.

In the internet age, many of these practices remain common, but there's an added dollop of fanfare targeting consumers more directly. Consider Apple's annual Worldwide Developers Conference. Apple assembles developers, journalists and other Apple enthusiasts to announce new products and updates to its popular lines, complete with a keynote address from its CEO. But there's

**Target's Online Pressroom**

https://corporate.target.com/press

Target hits the bull's-eye with its online pressroom, which features releases, fact sheets, corporate statements, FAQs, media contacts and a whole lot more.

**MEMORY MEMO 15.2** The Audience-Centered Pressroom[24]

- Cater information to the needs of target audiences
- Ensure easy navigation through both browsing and searching
- Provide background information for the organization
- Include multimedia content
- Link to your SNSs
- Enable RSS capabilities

no need to fret if you're not among the roughly 5,000 attendees who paid $1,600 a ticket for admission; Apple streams much of the event to its many eager stakeholders.[25]

This strategic approach allows Apple to dominate multiple tech news cycles. Articles anticipate the event, followed by long-form reports and reviews, many in widely circulated and respected media outlets. Additionally, the conference livestream allows Apple to control the initial messaging to its most ardent fans, with whom it communicates directly. And it's no coincidence the company website updates almost immediately with the new product's information, allowing consumers not only to take a deeper dive into its specs, but to place orders as well.

As you learned in Chapter 9, this approach is distinct from traditional advertising. Rather than a paid interruption, it's the persuasive message itself that attracts interest. Moreover, it enables Apple to reach consumers at a point in which they are most interested in the product, at a time when they're considering a purchase, and then immediately offer them a purchase mechanism. That's slick.

### Timing Your Shot

But breaking online news isn't limited to consumer audiences or major releases, and as more news breaks online, strategic communicators are increasingly calibrating information releases to maximally benefit their clients.

Much of that calculation concerns timeliness. Strategic communicators who manage blogs, update online pressrooms or pitch reporters online often time their content to align with some existing event or holiday to improve its news value (see Chapter 11). Such strategic choices increase your chances of gaining coverage.

However, there are other aspects of timing that enhance your content's relevance to reporters and other stakeholders. Assessing current events and anticipating what concerns they may provoke often lets you get ahead of your media relations competitors.

For example, the Tax Cuts and Jobs Act of 2017 marked the most sweeping change in the U.S. tax code in over three decades. Even before the bill's approval, organizations preemptively produced content framing the legislation within their own stakeholders' concerns. How would the new law affect taxes on various income brackets? Small business operations? Charitable giving? Employee contributions to retirement and health care plans? Housing affordability? Inheritances?

Strategic communicators use the same timing approach to proactively plan for those actionable moments when a social media effort has the best chance to be noticed and acted upon. Major media outlets prepare obituaries of prominent individuals so they can immediately respond to an unexpected death. We've done the same, prewriting news materials for an event we know will happen, just not exactly when. For instance, Professor Thompson waited until the season's biggest snowfall to drop an already-prepared release about a composer's newly released recording, which just happened to contain several songs about snowfall. Such strategies, which offer an expert immediately when the media needs one, can be invaluable to establishing your clients as authorities within their industry.

*Measuring Your Impact*

There's another advantage to social media relations approaches: Social media relations efforts foster precise valuation measures. Among the many benefits of placing stories in respected media outlets is expanding the reach of your message. Just as these outlets vary in the types and number of people they reach, so too do social media influencers—both institutions and individuals. In Chapter 2, we stressed how these opinion leaders can amplify your message. They not only spread it to larger audiences but enhance its credibility. As Figure 15.3 illustrates, you can employ **social network analysis** to determine the ways in which individuals online connect to and share messages with one another. Such analysis not only helps you to evaluate the reach of your message but also understand how information spreads on social media. That can help you target the proper influencers.[26]

Additionally, using social media metrics such as Google Analytics, Cision or Muck Rack lets you analyze messages more deeply. For instance, you can determine whether reaction to your messaging was largely positive or negative. You can also determine an audience member's action path: By analyzing the links through which donors accessed your nonprofit's website, you can track exactly what content prompted the donor's site visit. In turn, you can evaluate the relative strength of your persuasive messaging on Facebook compared to Twitter, Instagram, your organizational blog, a news article, etc. You could even employ the split-run tests commonly used in advertising, as discussed in Chapter 13—except in the social media world, you'd test different content on the same platform (say one long- and one short-form YouTube video) to determine which generates not only the most click-throughs but also the most eventual actions.

> **Strategic Thought**
>
> Think of the last organization for which you worked or interned. Referring to Figure 15.3, which conversation network(s) do you think most accurately represented the organization's interactions with its target audience(s). Why?

## Reactive Communication

Of course, you're not the internet's only breaker of news concerning your organization. Indeed, much online information is generated outside your control. Crisis communication responses best illustrate this truth. Think of the eyewitness videos users post to their various SNSs showcasing governments, corporations and even nonprofits abusing their stakeholders to varying degrees.

Those clips illustrate a broader reality—and challenge—in the everyday practice of strategic communication: Despite your best efforts and careful planning, unforeseen events occur, forcing you to shift from a proactive to a reactive stance. Rather than lamenting what you can't control, focus instead on what you can, and when an issue is resolved (one way or another), consider how you could prevent similar missteps in the future.

## The Six Structures of Twitter Conversation Networks

| Network Type | | | Groups | Examples |
|---|---|---|---|---|
| **Divided** **1** | | **Polarized Crowds** This type illustrates different groups of Twitter users who discuss polarizing topics. They often rely on different sources of information and commonly do not interact with groups that disagree with them. | **2 large** | Politics or divisive topics that display separate "echo chamber" structures |
| **Unified** **2** | | **Tight Crowds** This type captures close communities, such as conferences, professional topics and hobby groups, where participants strongly connect to one another for information, ideas and opinions. | **2–6 medium** | Hobbies, professional topics, conferences. No outsiders, all participants are members |
| **Fragmented** **3** | | **Brand Clusters** This type is formed around products and celebrities. These popular topics attract large fragmented Twitter populations, generating mass interest, but little connectivity. | **Many small** | Brands, public events, popular subjects |
| **Clustered** **4** | | **Community Clusters** These groups are created around global news events and popular topics. Communities form around multiple news sources. These community clusters are mostly disconnected from one another. | **Many small and medium** | Global news events |
| **In-Hub & Spoke** **5** | | **Broadcast Network** This type is often triggered by news media outlets and pundits who have loyal followers who retweet them. These communities are often star-shaped, as little interaction exists among members of the audience. | **1 large, some secondary** | News pundits and media outlets, famous individuals |
| **Out-Hub & Spoke** **6** | | **Support Network** This type is created when companies, government agencies or organizations respond to complaints and customer requests. The company, or hub, account replies to many disconnected users, creating outward spokes. | **1 large, some secondary** | Companies and services with customer support |

**PEW Research Center in association with Social Media Research Foundation**

**FIGURE 15.3  The Six Structures of Twitter Conversation Networks.** Some organizations command a degree of brand loyalty such that *brand clusters* form around them. Other organizations may position their products or services as part of broader lifestyles (e.g., athletic shoes in relation to marathon running) to manage relationships within *tight crowds* with niche interests. In the case of breaking news, you may find your organization amid a *broadcast network*. That's when relatively disconnected individuals share your messaging. Depending on the scenario, certain network structures are more likely.

## Managing Feedback

Throughout this text, we've defined online communication as semicontrolled. In the case of social media, you directly control what your organization says. However, you have no such power over what others say about you, spontaneously or in response to your organizational messaging.

Often, we think of this feedback in the simplest terms: an organization communicates a message or takes and action; an individual stakeholder responds. From there, the organization engages this stakeholder with a response, which may resolve the issue or continue the feedback loop through several exchanges (see Figure 15.4a). Consumer complaints or customer service concerns often follow this feedback pattern.

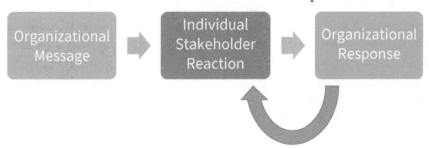

**FIGURE 15.4A  Simple Feedback.** When you think of feedback, you probably think of something relatively simple, in which an organization issues a message, a stakeholder reacts and the organization responds.

But there are numerous other ways in which stakeholders interact with your organization and one another. Let's illustrate these. Say your state's higher education administrators have steadily increased tuition and fees at public universities.[27] We also assume your state legislature maintains an active, online community forum on which these tuition hikes were announced.

It's likely university students will object to higher costs through a firestorm of reasoned complaints and downright fury posted on their legislators' social media page. The legislature's webmasters would likely engage not with the students individually but as a consensus stakeholder group (see Figure 15.4b).

**FIGURE 15.4B  Consensus Feedback.** Stakeholders can also interact with one another in response to an organizational action. In many instances, their individual reactions coalesce into some general consensus, which an organization must then address holistically.

Parents of younger children might also join this discussion, not simply to complain about the cost of college tuition but to address more wide-ranging concerns about elementary and high school education funding. Now the legislature must respond to multiple stakeholder groups with disparate concerns (see Figure 15.4c).

**FIGURE 15.4C Disparate Feedback.** On other occasions, stakeholders may draw multiple conclusions from an organization's actions requiring disparate concerns to be addressed separately.

Then of course there's the fact that virtually everything involving how tax dollars are spent sparks conflict. While some students and parents may want to see tuition lowered, there are most certainly sizable constituencies unwilling to pay the increased taxes necessary to implement such a policy. In this situation, the legislature's constituents may fight among themselves online. Now legislators face the difficult decision of not simply how to respond to such a heated issue but whether they want to attempt conflict resolution at all because (a) they may not view it as their place to intervene or (b) they're concerned about alienating a large swath of voters (see Figure 15.4d).

**FIGURE 15.4D Stakeholder Clash.** Sometimes stakeholders will respond to organizational actions not simply in disparate but also conflicting ways. In these instances, stakeholders clash with one another, and organizations face tough decisions about whether and how to intervene.

While each exchange involves unique strategic considerations, there are some general rules of thumb for responding to online, stakeholder feedback, particularly in the case of SNSs and blog comments.

### Read

The interactive nature of most online communication benefits your organization. Because your publics are telling you how they view the situation, they are in effect helping you craft your message and nurture important relationships. For much of your audience, simply validating the importance of their outlook can go a long way. So, your first step should be listening. Read the comments. Attempt to understand their concerns, needs or wants.

It sounds simple, but organizations surprisingly miss this mark quite often. Recall Professor Thompson's experience with Gibson Guitars related in Chapter 9's opening vignette. Rather than acknowledging his informed opinion, the company chose to actively silence him. Not only does this cavalier approach tarnish a possible relationship, but it also forfeits an opportunity to learn from and adapt to stakeholder feedback, which is a critical and easily accessible research tool.

### Respond

Still, listening is not enough. It takes two to tango, tweet and tumbl. Interaction requires two-way communication, which means managing social media requires not simply recording feedback but responding to it. It's true that in many cases responding to every stakeholder comment is impossible, but you can and should respond to some.

Typically you segment feedback based on valence (positive or negative) as well as topic. So, while you might conceivably be faced with hundreds or even thousands of public comments, that multitude likely voices similar concerns. You could therefore craft blanket responses to address the issue, or respond directly to the most influential stakeholders—i.e., those who first broached the subject or have the largest following. By communicating the organization's view to these online opinion leaders, you could improve your relationships with them, as well as boost your reputation for engagement among their followers.

### Resolve

Though they're more difficult to contend with, you should take particular care to respond to negative comments. Let's say a group of employees begins a thread on your organization's intranet forum discussing how management has discriminated against them. You should respond with a link to your organization's diversity and inclusion policies, reiterate your commitment to tolerance and describe the new management training program you will implement to resolve their issue. And always be sure to follow up with these individuals, asking whether these practices resolved their particular issues.

While this approach may not win over the firmest detractors, it at least demonstrates your organizational commitment. Going beyond response and toward resolution shows you're more than just talk. It signals sincerity and credibility. Ignoring negative feedback makes it seem like you're not listening or you don't care, damaging your organization's relationships with these particular individuals and signaling to others that you undervalue them as well.

### Remit

Still, there are a few instances in which abandoning the interaction or refusing to engage represents the best course of action.[28] Addressing such extreme detractors is a multistep process, which we've summarized in Memory Memo 15.3.

While you should absolutely do your best to resolve complaints and concerns, sometimes there's little you can do. Sometimes, stakeholders ask for more than you can give. In these situations, when a solution can't be reached, you have to recognize the cost of engaging is no longer worthwhile. Clearly explaining your efforts and reasoning for all to see and politely parting ways is a viable course of action. More reasonable stakeholders will at the very least see and respect your commitment and effort. In some cases, they may actually side with you in the conflict.

> **MEMORY MEMO 15.3** The Six A's of Handling Hecklers[29]
>
> 1. Acknowledge their right to complain
> 2. Apologize if you should
> 3. Assert your reasoning
> 4. Ask what they want
> 5. Accommodate them if possible
> 6. Abdicate if necessary

However, you sometimes may wish to ignore certain comments so as not to provide legitimacy to the commentators or stoke the flames of unrest. More often than not, this is the best approach to combat **trolling**. Understand that the internet troll behaves in fundamentally antisocial ways that are often easy to spot but hard to describe, so we'll lean on cinema to help us out. In the 2008 Batman film, "The Dark Knight," the villainous Joker's psychopathy is described thusly: "Some men aren't looking for anything logical … They can't be bought, bullied, reasoned or negotiated with. Some men just want to watch the world burn."

Though most internet trolls aren't interesting in destroying cities the size of Gotham, the principle is the same. These people have no interest in meaningful interaction; they only seek to sow discord and chaos. When facing trolls, you should catalog their activities and specify any organizational or platform policy violations they commit. If you have the capability, you can delete their comments. *This represents perhaps the only time such an action is justifiable.* If their behaviors do not violate set standards, simply ignore them. Nothing can be gained from an interaction initiated in bad faith with no real resolution in mind.

## Ethical, Effective and Efficient Communication Policies

When we start talking about deleting comments, we inevitably find ourselves debating the ethicality of such activities. After all, silencing stakeholders potentially violates several moral principles and virtues we discussed in Chapter 5, such as truthfulness, transparency and trust. In the case of trolling, however, to allow such behavior to continue unabated may itself violate other virtues, such as civility, decency and understanding.

Here again we remind you that your experience and behaviors as an individual social media user can't be explicitly transferred to your career. As an individual, you can block other users, dismiss members of out-groups or deride someone who does not agree with your views. When you make the transition to becoming a professional communicator, you must similarly professionalize your orientation toward social media.

Because ethics prescribe ideal practices governing our interactions with others, the interactive space of semicontrolled, online communication is an excellent forum for discussing how best to put organizational ethics into action. Indeed, by developing policies for managing an organization's online interactions with stakeholders, you glean insights into building ethical offline communication policies as well.

### Who Are You as an Organization?

The first step should be a step back, toward a moment of reflection. Consider who you are as an organization and what you strive to become. What do you do? What do you value? Who are your key stakeholders? What do they value? These are introspective questions you must answer if you want to behave sincerely and authentically—let alone morally. A close examination of the principles your organization hopes to embody serves as a good launch point.

## Which Organizational Values Should Manifest in Your Communications?

This subhead is a bit of a trick question. The answer is all of them. No matter the nature of your organization, its values form its conscience. That conscience can't exist in a vacuum. Over the years, many ethicists have harshly criticized organizational mission statements, and for good reason. Alone, they're completely meaningless. Any corporate toady can write a mission statement describing the organization's commitment to improving its stakeholders' lives. But if that organization proceeds to manufacture shoddy products, underpay its employees, poison the environment, or contribute nothing to the growth and well-being of the communities in which it operates, then that mission statement doesn't justify the time it took to write it.

Sincerity, authenticity and clarity of purpose mark the differences between a lived mission statement and a collection of empty words. And just as your organization's actions must embody that ethic, so too must its communication efforts to and with its stakeholders.

Let's examine issues through the virtues we established in Chapter 5. Would a *truthful* and *decent* organization steal others' content for its blog and claim it as its own? No. It would gain the proper permissions to reproduce the work and credit the creators.

Would a *courageous, just, transparent* and *prudent* organization delete negative comments from its Facebook account simply because they made the organization look bad? No. It would permit an open airing of grievances, consider those concerns and work diligently to correct its flaws and do right by its stakeholders.

Would a *wise* organization tune out stakeholders' online conversations about its actions? Would a *charitable* organization fail to engage with stakeholders in those conversations? Would a *trusting* organization bar its employees from communicating about its policies to others?

## How Do You Codify That Behavior?

In examining what your organization is and wants to be, you gain perspective on the values your organization must live to achieve that identity. From there, you can codify an ethical communication policy leading to that end. Not to oversell ethics, but such a policy would arguably be effective and efficient as well.

Just as we've conducted this discussion—and most topics within this text— we advocate beginning with a more general approach. While it's true that effective strategic communicators must anticipate eventualities and plan for them, it's impossible to account for all the dynamic variables semicontrolled channels present. Contingency planning for each specific and detailed communication act presents at least two problems.

**Strategic Thought**

Think of an organization you admire and one you loathe. Write a short list of reasons why you feel that way about both. Now visit their websites and read their respective mission statements. How, if at all, have your feelings changed or intensified? Why?

First, you're incapable of envisioning every contingency, especially considering the constant, rapid changes in the media landscape. Second, and perhaps more importantly, you won't see the forest by focusing on the trees. In Chapter 3 we asserted that a tactics-first approach to planning often fails. Why? Because it focuses on the minutia of day-to-day activities rather than the strategies, objectives and goals those tactics should advance. Similarly, if you submerge yourself in the nuances of different response strategies for the spectrum of publics across platforms, you can easily lose sight of the ethical and practical values such a policy was meant to promote in the first place.

Falls and Decker isolated excellent guidelines for establishing a more generalist social media communication policy that reflects the organization's larger values. We list the highlights in Memory Memo 15.4, which we'll build upon next.[31]

> **MEMORY MEMO 15.4**  A Guideline Policy for Social Media Communication[30]
>
> • Be prescriptive rather than restrictive
> • Focus on values
> • Obey the law
> • Encourage authenticity
> • Know your role
> • Determine who has final say
> • Spell out consequences

### Prescribe, Don't Restrict

Remember the first question we asked at the outset of this ethics discussion: *Who are you as an organization?* We didn't ask who you *weren't*. This proscriptive strategy isn't exactly new for us. Chapter 14's Ten Commandments of blogging tips focused exclusively on what you should do, not what you shouldn't. You don't become ethical only by avoiding wrong action. You must also seek to do right. Your guidelines for social media practice should predominately stress your values and the behaviors communicators should take to embody those values.

### Obey the Law

Still, from a more pragmatic standpoint, you'd do well to note some basic rules for both your social media management team and the stakeholders active on your various platforms. First and foremost, obey the law. Strategic communicators most often get themselves and their organizations in hot water by failing to adhere to libel, copyright and trademark laws. So make sure employees receive training in those areas. You should also establish basic restrictions promoting civility and respect, such as prohibiting content that is racist, sexist or homophobic on your organization's social media platforms.

### Encourage Authenticity

Some organizations also discourage anonymous posting. Requiring individuals to at least disclose a username can limit more insidious postings. Such transparency promotes civility, decency, understanding, truthfulness and trust. Whenever possible, you should similarly acknowledge the true author of organizational content. While SNS accounts will exclusively bear the organization's name, there's no reason blog posts, videos, podcasts and other website content should. Include the author's name and make her responsible for interacting with audiences.

First of all, she'll know the content better than anyone. More importantly, such practices foster authentic human connections. It's a real person, with a real life, with real thoughts, engaging in a real conversation. We've emphasized interpersonal communication because that's what a relationship is founded on, and that's what your organization is trying to build.

### Establish Roles and Empower Leaders

Nevertheless, overwhelming workloads compel most organizations to assign teams to effectively manage their social media communications. Prudent managers trust their team members to fulfill their roles and delegate responsibility accordingly. However, there will inevitably be moments of disagreement or even conflict. Therefore, it's critical someone has the final say. Input from team members should be respected and their expertise considered, but leaders must clearly establish themselves as the final arbiters regarding communication strategies and tactics.

### Spell Out Consequences

Lastly, you should clearly define the consequences of violating these policies for both internal and external publics. When a stakeholder behaves inappropriately and must therefore be reprimanded—which could range from a deleted comment to an employee dismissal—her peers must clearly perceive your organization behaved justly and in accordance with its guidelines.

## Lessons From Life: OK, So Now What?

So that's the book. And we could leave it there. The end. Thanks for playing the home version. See you for the Netflix reboot.

But that feels unsatisfactory to us, because now that you've read the text and hopefully absorbed its lessons, you may still be left with some burning questions: OK, so now what? What am I supposed to do with this knowledge? How can I apply this to improve my writing in other areas? Or to advance my career? To these questions, we offer one last lesson from life, a bonus round if you will.

Professor Browning's 15-page, single-spaced PR writing syllabus is proof that he's a bit of a stickler. He devotes nearly 1,000 words to outlining a three-step policy for emailing him questions: (1) Read the syllabus, (2) search online and (3) send an email demonstrating what you do know, not just what you don't. It's worth focusing on about a hundred of those words here:

> Once you graduate, you'll no longer have professors to lean on, and your bosses will not be pleased if you're constantly asking questions you should be able to answer for yourselves. Bosses delegate tasks to you and expect to see them accomplished. When you hit a snag and ask a barrage of easily answered questions, not only have you failed to solve the problem, you've become one. However, if you demonstrate initiative, it will be rewarded. Critical thinking and the ability to become your own teacher are the two most universally applicable skills you can learn while in college.

We know you have questions.

We're aware we've been stunningly general at times: Universal writing principles of audience and motive will be adaptable to whatever communication platforms you write for—even those that don't exist yet.

And we know we've been startlingly specific at other points in the text: Here's why your word choice should be *x* instead of *y*.

We know we haven't covered every detail of PR writing—let alone strategic communication practice—in this textbook. To our knowledge, no one has yet pulled off that miracle, nor will they. The field is too vast and changes too quickly.

Our goal—our *hope*—was to provide you with a foundation upon which you can build. You're going to face challenges in your career. You're going to encounter problems you've never faced before. But odds are they're not altogether different from something you've seen in the past.

Ideally, this book has armed you with some fundamental tools to help you leap over many such hurdles by answering basic reflective questions: What is my organization's goal? Which stakeholders must I engage to reach that goal? Why would they take a behavior that helps me reach that goal? Are any TIPCUP elements particularly powerful persuaders for this audience? Through which media can I reach them? How can I best structure my argument? We, decades into our careers, often return to such fundamental questions when we confront our own challenges.

We've repeatedly asked and answered questions like these in various settings so you can observe not only the nuts and bolts of how to *write* persuasively but also see the gears turning as we, as experienced practitioners, *think* strategically.

So, in regard to your question, "What now?" we have a simple answer: Figure it out. You're well equipped to do so.

## SUMMARY

- Data regarding the demographics and usage patterns of social media audiences is readily available to help you effectively target audiences.

- When you choose an online outlet, not only must it reach your target audience, but you must craft your message to take advantage of a given medium's strengths while minimizing its weaknesses.

- While generating likes and favorites isn't bad, to be considered successful, persuasive communication must ultimately lead to more concrete action.

- Journalists constitute an important online audience, and effectively managing an online pressroom, as well as connecting directly with reporters through social media, can build needed relationships.

- For an organization to be truly ethical, it must establish a standard for morality and adhere to it in both its communication with and actions toward its stakeholders.

**Scenario Prompts: Delivering Semicontrolled Messages**

You'll find Scenario Prompts on pp. 367–386 of this textbook. While they vary in subject and difficulty, they help you hone your critical thinking and strategic writing skills. The following are best suited to this chapter's topics.

**Management: 5.1, 10.2 /** Writing: 9.6, 10.11

### *Figure Credits*

Fig. 15.1: Source: http://www.pewinternet.org/fact-sheet/social-media/.

Fig. 15.2: Source: http://www.pewinternet.org/fact-sheet/social-media/.

Fig. 15.3: Copyright © 2014 by Pew Research Center.

# Scenario Prompts for Management Problems and Writing Assignments

The following case studies are designed to test many aspects of your strategic communication and writing ability. The information from which you'll be required to compose a coherent and well-structured document is often disorganized and haphazardly worded. That's similar to situations you'd encounter in professional life. They will contain information that would be boring or unnecessary to communicate to certain audiences.

Occasionally, the case studies will contain organizational information that, while vital for internal planning, might be better left unsaid to external audiences. The scenarios will sometimes require you to make judgments about objectionable language, idiomatic quotations, improper usage, and other problems inherent in a process that requires the practitioner to gather information from a variety of sources.

## Scenario Prompt 1: Announcing a Concert

You work as a public relations assistant for your local Fine Arts Council. The council is sponsoring a concert by Felipe Jones, a classical guitarist. He'll be playing "Fandanguilla," by Joaquin Turina; "Prelude No.2," by George Gershwin; and "Pleasant Despair," by Erik Satie. Jones, who is 87 years old, has performed in New York's Carnegie Hall, in the Kennedy Center in Washington, and, according to his press booklet, has just returned from a triumphant tour of seventeen European cities. The concert will be a month from Friday at 8:00 PM in the Midtown Community Auditorium. The site of the auditorium is 1756 Nall Avenue in your town. It's been 65 years since Jones first made his professional playing debut. Tickets to the show are $12. They are available at the door the evening of the show. Jones is a 1954 graduate of Central High School, the biggest high school in your town, and grew up on the west side of your community. Jones has been certified as the oldest active professional performer in the United States by the American Federation of Musicians. "I ain't seen anyone older than me playing for the last 20 years," Jones is quoted as saying in his publicity materials. Jones has only returned to your town to play one other time. That was in 1982. This concert is to raise funds for the arts council's annual Easter party so that the group can entertain your city council members two weeks before the vote on allocations to the city's arts budget.

### Management Problems

1. What are the possible audiences toward which you could direct your organization's marketing efforts?

2. How would the emphasis of your marketing communication change as you tried to reach each audience?

3. What are the implications of choosing to undertake a communication campaign that is limited to only social media channels?

4. How could information about the concert's proceeds be harmful to your organization's purpose? What would be your advice to the organization about this issue?

5. What combination of demographic factors might you choose to compile a targeted mailing list to attract concertgoers for this event?

### Writing Assignments

6. Write a news release announcing the concert to older adults in your community.

7. Modify the previous release to target classical music fans in your area.

8. Create a 280-character tweet to draw people to the concert.

9. Compose a print or radio ad for the concert.

10. Write a personal letter from the arts council director, Monica Torrence, to area art supporters to raise money to fund the Jones concert.

11. Prepare an outline of visuals and sound effects for a video news release that might help you tell the story and draw concertgoers for the event.

## Scenario Prompt 2: A Homebuying School

You work for a strategic communication firm employed by Paul Cremona, the owner of the Paul Creason Realty Company You work the Creason account. Cremona has noticed many first- time homebuyers are not very knowing about real estate. That causes two problems for him.

Often they waste his agents' time because they can't figure out if they can afford a home or not until they find that the down payment they can put on a house is way too inadequate. If this happens, by the time they abandon the search an agent has spent hours showing them houses. In addition, he finds the first-time buyer often is working with 3, 4 or even 5 agents, and Cremona often loses the sale to another agency, again after investing a lot of his agents' time in the quest. You suggest a home buying school, where people in a group could systematically learn about buying a house instead of having it given to them one-on-one by a real estate agent. You also suggest a gift or something like that would be nice to get people to join the program and would be especially appropriate if the students bought a home from Cremona's agency. Cremona is enthusiastic about your plan. The Creason Homeownership School, he calls it, and offers four weeks of night classes. He said the program will give help in explaining the disadvantages and advantages of fixed rate and adjustable mortgages, the No. 1 complaint Cremona says he hears homebuyers complaining about. The classes are every Monday night next month from

7-9 p.m. There won't be any cost for the class, and people can enroll by contacting the agency at (555) 875-3432. By the time the pupils get through they should know how to deal with home improvement contractors after they move into their home and movers and bankers before they move in. Among other things, the program, to be held at Creason's main office at 1763 Taylorsville Rd., will among many, many other things that will be of interest to people who have the potential to be homeowners, cover aspects of the homebuyer's relationship with real estate agents and what elements of a home's infrastructure should be examined in order to avoid later costly and complex jobs, such as replacing plumbing and other water outlets, electrical power wiring, roofing or even structural supports. In addition, the program, for which only first-time home-buyers are eligible, will tell persons how to manage a budget and save on taxes through the use of home equity loans in the years after you buy a home and have built some equity in the house. Participants will also learn how to read sales contracts. Cremona said he will teach the class himself. He has 23 years experience in the business and has been a speaker at many national real estate conventions. He said the program will even tell people how to figure closing costs when completing the purchase of a house. In addition, he agrees to rebate each graduating student the amount of $2,000 apiece off the cost of their home if they buy it from the Creason agency. The course is also intended, with luck, to help a person adjust their spending patterns so that they can keep up with their house payments and save enough for a down payment.

## Management Problems

1. How do the communication goals of the school help solve some of Cremona's organizational problems? How much should the release discuss the underlying organizational problems the school is supposed to solve?

2. How does the free gift help in the persuasive sequence?

3. What problems might a practitioner encounter in getting an editor to run an announcement of the school in his or her publication? How would this change if Cremona decided to charge for the school?

## Writing Assignments

4. Compose a news release to be sent to your local newspaper that announces the home buyers school. Be sure to target an audience and emphasize a benefit for that audience in the release's No. 1 position.

5. Compose a short oral presentation for Cremona to give to his sales agents that will help convince them of the program's value.

6. Write a 140-word tweet soliciting participation in the program from potential home buyers.

7. Compose a 20-second script for a social media video. Include instructions for visuals and sound effects.

8. Write a radio ad script for Cremona's program. Include sound effects and name an appropriate radio station for placement.

9. Write a 400-word post for Cremona's podcast program, which reaches past Creason clients.

## Scenario Prompt 3: Fashion House Introduces Hollywood Line

You work for April Apparel, a New York-based clothing company owned by April Ormand, a former cabaret dancer whose father was involved in the Algerian resistance against French rule in the 1960s. Ormand has been in this country since 1991. The company has developed a new clothing line that will be modeled after clothing worn by characters from major movies released by Calbaer Pictures. The clothing will be sold by better department stores. Calbaer Pictures has exclusive, multifilm contracts with some of Hollywood's major stars, including eight of last year's top-25 highest paid actors (by order of their earnings): Emma Stone; Ryan Gosling; Robert Downey, Junior; Samuel L. Jackson; Jennifer Aniston; Adam Sandler and Vin Diesel. The adult- audience pictures represent a further expansion of the apparel lines April Apparel already has established with the Cobalt Warriors and Deep Forest Baby Bunnies. Both lines, inspired by children's film franchises of the same names, were outrageously popular. As the exclusive licensed apparel manufacturer, April sold more than 300,000 apparel items linked with each of the two set of characters. Calbaer, with which April has entered into the agreement with, is run by Andy Borowitz and Susan Borowitz, a successful husband and wife team who created the popular 1990s TV show, "The Fresh Prince of Bel Air." April has already had a successful design history of converting movie looks into popular fashions. Her company developed a line of nylon jackets and pants in neon colors inspired by the film "Three Days of Thunder," released in 2012. Among the apparel April designers are creating as part of the Calbaer agreement are tight-fitting, naturally aged leather leggings inspired by the costumes Jennifer Aniston will wear in next summer's Calbaer release, "Foxtail," a comedy set in the old West. Another clothing line will be based on "sexy cowgirl" looks that figure prominently in scenes from the Margot Robbie movie "Rebel Ecstasy," a Civil War epic to be released at Christmastime next year. Other anticipated looks, according to Ormand, will be appropriate for office and formal wear.

Before beginning her own company, Ormand had been a designer for Clien Fashions, Gallante and Korbal, U.S.A. The first designs will be unveiled next spring.

Addendum: A letter you receive from the fashion firm's attorney indicated it has only obtained permission to mention the following Calabaer actors in April's publicity materials: Aniston, Diesel; Downey, Gosling, Hanks, Jackson and Robbie.

## Management Problems

1. To which print editors would you communicate in order to directly support the company's sales effort?

2. What general publication editors might be useful in helping to get your message to consumers interested in movies?

3. What are some specialized and more personal media that could let you communicate to a highly targeted audience of individuals interested in each of the contracted film stars?

4. What would be the learn-feel-do for the owners of the major retail store that is buying 15,000 of this company's items?

5. What are the implications of Calbaer's past successes adapting films into fashion? Explain how different age groups are likely to draw different conclusions?

## Writing Assignments

6. Ormand wants you to write a print news release that will help support the company's marketing effort.

7. Write a pitch letter to a television producer for a syndicated Hollywood entertainment news show.

8. Script a video social media post to support the company's sales effort.

9. Compose a print ad for the company's products.

10. Write a 15-second television commercial about the products.

# Scenario Prompt 4: Streamlining an Industrial Permit Process

In researching possible sources of information on the industrial recruitment process for your job at the Cornwell Chamber of Commerce, you find two cities that have apparently been very successful in recruiting new businesses: Norfolk, Virginia and Monmouth, New Jersey. The two cities are about the same size as Cornwell and have problems similar to those of Cornwell, their inner-city neighborhoods decaying after major heavy industries closed up. In an article in Manufacturing Quarterly, the development directors of both the two cities were interviewed. Each said they felt they had lost a couple of potential industries because of a long and lengthy permit process. Executives who had located in the cities complained that they had to go through between 14 and 20 different city and county agencies to connect utilities, get construction, zoning and sign permits, and other things like that. Both cities set up a business expansion clearinghouse, making it possible for executives to stop in one office and collect all the forms they needed for permits and licenses. The clearinghouse provided a central location where all the experts from each permit office were available so that people weren't bumped from office to office in search of answers for his questions. Obviously, shortening the review and application process enabled businesses to make money sooner and thus as it were, pay taxes sooner.

The new procedures gave the two cities a competitive advantage over other cities that they could push in their meetings with executives and in promotional materials. The two cities were also able to reduce their permit staffs by 85 people (38 in Monmouth and 47 in Norfolk), which meant quite a bit of savings on salaries. If Cornwell wanted to do this, you would immediately have to find and rent office space to house all the permit offices. In addition, all office personnel would have to meet to coordinate their application forms so that business people would not have to fill in the same information on application after application. At the very least, this policy might show a change in the city's attitude toward business and communicate that the city can provide a good environment for business.

There's also the possibility that businesses now in the city center would stay rather than move to adjacent rural counties where they think the bureaucracy will be lessened than from what it is here. That would mean more tax dollars would stay in the city. One problem is going to be that there are entrenched bureaucracies within all the permit offices that won't be glad to give up their accumulated powers. In addition, the mayor campaigned on this issue, that of reducing the bureaucracy. If the city payroll is reduced through the bureaucratic consolidation, the mayor stands to lose votes and support from the city bureaucracy but should gain support from non-city employees. Hopefully, these procedures will help reverse the decline of the city. The city, just last year, was in the running for three major industrial plants, but lost all three to other cities. Unemployment is now at 8.3 percent, up from 5.9 percent two years ago. In 2000, Cornwell was one of the nation's fifteen largest industrial centers, with auto, steel and other manufacturing plants located here in Cornwell. For the past 15 years, businesses located in the central city have increasingly been moving way out in the country in the areas surrounding Cornwell rather than expand in the city that gave them birth. Chamber of Commerce President Merle Bryant thinks the plan would be very popular with what he describes as "tough-minded, no-nonsense executives who want everything they do to run as efficiently as their businesses."

## Management Problems

1. What internal public may need prior notice before this policy change takes place?

2. What medium might be most effective in convincing this public of the need for the new policy? Describe the relative strengths and weakness of presenting the policy in a print format and a multichannel format.

3. What interaction might there be between external opinion about the changes and the internal public's acceptance of the policy?

4. Omitting the budget section, write a persuasion platform for the business owners the city hopes to attract to relocate to Cornwell.

5. Write a news release announcing the proposed changes in city procedures.

6. Write a pitch letter from the chamber's Bryant to bloggers who might influence businesses to move to Cornwell.

7. Write a short presentation for Bryant to deliver to a convention of business relocation experts. Specify the placement of illustrations to accompany the talk.

## Scenario Prompt 5: A Magazine's Recycling Effort

You're working as a public relations practitioner for Ballou, a big-circulation women's fashion magazine. In response to some environmental activists who happen to be Ballou employees, the company reluctantly put together a committee to examine ways the magazine could be involved in recycling and other environmental and social issues. The company's task force is comprised of administrative assistant Carol Underwood, production supervisor Jackson Norman and assistant vice president Linda Goodwin.

Among the programs they established is one that collects soft drink cans from offices and sells them to aluminum recovery firms. The company uses the proceeds, which were $950 during the first month, to help the homeless. The task force also recommended, among its many suggestions, that all internal communication, whether internal memorandums, story manuscripts, policy reports, announcements or letters, be placed on the company's electronic mail system that's been a part of its computer network for the past 17 years. In the past three months, the volume of messages transmitted on the email system has increased 32%. It's estimated that this one policy saves about one-half ton of paper each month. Among the e-mail messages is a 1-minute course, which employees can call up on their computer screens, explaining what materials can be recycled and procedures for recycling them. The magazine has also replaced its regular desk wastebaskets with green and gold wastebaskets that have three tiers. The tiers allow employees to separate trash into categories that aid recycling. Trash is still picked up every night but it's stored in three holding areas for later sale to recycling concerns.

Magazines, of course, use tremendous volumes of paper. Thus, there are many opportunities, many, many opportunities to save big amounts of paper. Through exact computer calibration of the magazine's photographs and layout boards, the production department has been able to reduce the number of spoiled and unusable magazines by 87 percent. That represents savings in the amount of one ton of paper each month. The designers have made the three outside margins of each page three-sixteenths of an inch smaller. By the time 400 million copies of the company's magazines are produced, printed and distributed every year, that tiny area will amount to nearly 90 tons of paper that the company will have saved. Following the lead of many other magazines, your company's publications will, starting this summer, be printed on lighter-weight paper. That's another 13 tons of paper saved over the next year. Following research, the magazine has discovered that not nearly as many subscriber-reply cards as estimated before are needed. Previously, the magazine has included four subscriber reply cards in each copy. Research found that although significant numbers of new subscriptions come from the cards bound into magazines sold at newsstands, only 1 percent of all new subscriptions come as a result of subscriber cards in home-delivered magazines. Knowing that, the magazine will no longer include subscriber reply cards in home-delivered magazines and will place only one reply card in newsstand copies. That action alone will save 95 tons of paper per year. The magazine's task force has also been instrumental in conceiving and implementing an industrywide effort to encourage paper manufacturers to produce even lighter-weight paper for color magazines. Among the magazines in this effort are Time, The New Republic, The National Review, Essence and The Atlantic. By starting an industrywide effort, the hope is that manufacturers will realize there is a market demand for new, environmentally sound products. The total savings in paper represent a sizable business advantage for the magazine. With the total paper savings, the company will save over $110,000 in paper costs this year. All told the recycling efforts cost the company about $8,000 for initial start-up costs and can be maintained for less than $3,000 each year. On an individual level, there have been some dramatic changes. Domika Lewis, who is a senior fashion writer for the magazine, is one of those people who has had to change her attitudes since the recycling effort started. During the orientation period two months ago, task force member Underwood passed through the editorial department at the magazine. Lewis, who has been with the magazine for 17 years, commented: "I'd been working at my desk all day transcribing interviews, so the floor around my wastebasket looked like there had been some sort of volcanic eruption in my trash can. Carol, who I didn't know at that time, came up to my desk trailing this line of blue-suited executives. So this woman I've never seen in my life is digging through my trash. At first I figured it was some rather indiscreet fashion house spy looking for the new spring designer lines. When Carol announced she was going to demonstrate how wasteful the company had been by using my trash, I was kind of offended. I figured she was going to give me some sort of holier-than-thou environmental sermon before pulling out a couple of pieces of paper that could be recycled. But Carol floored me when she separated all my trash into three recycling piles. There was cardboard in one, aluminum and plastic in another, and stationery paper in a third stack. By the time she got through, there were only two items left that couldn't be recycled. I was convinced. In those three minutes, she had reduced my part of the trash problem by over 90 percent. With these three-tier wastebaskets it's really easy to be involved in the program. After all, it's what the world is coming to. I don't like to sound like a sap, but each of us has got to develop a commitment to keeping the world in some kind of shape for our kids. It's got to be a part of how we live our lives forever."

## Management Problems

1. What additional media can we use to remind people at the point of action about the company's recycling program?

2. What's a possible danger of using traditional media targeted to employees to reinforce the company's recycling messages?

## Writing Assignments

3. Produce an advertisement to be placed in Ballou magazine that extols the company's commitment to environmental issues.

4. Compose a short feature story for the company's internal newsletter.

5. Write a release discussing the company's recycling effort that will be directed toward environmental group websites and bloggers.

6. Write an audio news release to be distributed to major-market news stations.

7. Write a multichannel spot directed toward Ballou subscribers that will be posted on the publication's website.

8. Write a lede sentence for a news release directed toward environmental magazines and another lede sentence for a release directed toward Ballou stockholders.

9. Design and write a advertisement that will be wrapped around employee recycling receptacles, urging employees to follow the company's policies when disposing of trash. Your design should include placement details to affix the wrap to the receptacles.

# Scenario Prompt 6: High-Temperature Engine Plastics

You work for an advanced technology plastics firm called Britlim Ltd. It's located in Indianapolis, Indiana, and its best-known work was fabricating specialty parts for Indianapolis 500 race cars. Britlim just successfully tested new plastic engine components and sold them to India's largest automobile manufacturer, Tata. Your scientists have been working on this concept for the last twelve years. The first parts of this series will be placed on Tata's cars during the next model year from now. The parts aren't the plastic parts that many manufacturers put in dashboards or bumpers and exterior things many auto manufacturers use plastic for.

Instead, the first batch of these new plastic parts is for plastic intake manifolds for Tata's gasoline-powered engines. These parts act as chambers in which the air needed to burn fuel is drawn into an engine. The problem with using plastics in cars before has been that they melt in the high temperatures that are within engines, which sometimes reach 250 degrees Fahrenheit in engine compartments.

That's why most engine parts were made of iron or steel. Plastics still aren't strong enough for moving parts within engines like camshafts and crankshafts. Recently, to save weight and thus save gas, manufacturers have been making more parts out of aluminum. Plastics are lighter than aluminum, however, and thus can save more gas. Britlim has already proved plastics will work. It has already produced plastic valve covers (a cover on the top of the engine that covers the valves, dummy) that have been installed in Tata-subsidiary Jaguar cars and its legendary Land Rover utility vehicles Just with the plastic valve covers, gas mileage is 1 percent or 2 percent better than with the aluminum covers. There are other advantages. It is much cheaper to make plastic parts than metal parts because plastic is smooth coming out of a mold, whereas metal parts are rough and often have to be machined to smooth out edges. That roughness hurts engine performance and gas mileage, too. It causes turbulence as air flows through the manifold. That causes friction and bad engine performance. That rough interior is caused by a difference in the way plastic and aluminum parts are cast. Aluminum parts are made out of melted aluminum that is poured into casts that have sand cores. After the aluminum hardens, the sand is flushed out. The sand leaves a rough surface inside the intake manifold. Because the sand casts are unstable, large metal parts normally have to be cast separately as two or more pieces and then joined together. That adds to the manufacturing costs. Plastic parts are different. They use metal cores that melt at between 150 degrees and 450 degrees Fahrenheit. The plastic resin is then injected into the mold, where it hardens. The metal core leaves much smoother edges than does the sand. The metal core is then melted out by submerging the entire mold in hot oil. The metal melts, leaving behind a one-piece plastic shape with very precise dimensions. That procedure demands plastics that can withstand very high temperatures. Such plastics are achieved by using a type of plastic resin called phenolic plastic, which actually undergoes a molecular change in the molding process. When the plastic is melted for the mold, the molecules link up differently. In fact, they bind together irreversibly so that once the plastic sets, it cannot melt again and can resist temperatures even higher than aluminum. The plastic parts weigh about 25 percent less than the metal ones they replace. The plastic parts put Britlim in a very lucrative position looking forward to the next few years. The company has already received contracts totaling $50 million from Tata, and if the other automakers also latch onto the parts, those figures could soar even higher. Company accountants estimate, for example, that if China's No. 2 car builder, SAIC Motor, converted exclusively to the plastic valve covers and intake manifolds, the total contract would be in excess of $950 million.

Britlim Ltd. President Benton Harlert is enthusiastic about the coming business: "We could bury everyone else in the business if we could get the SAIC contract. It's the wave of the future. While in the United States, electric cars are a cutting-edge force, in many parts of the world there's simply no infrastructure to recharge electrics. In Africa and a significant portion of Asia, gasoline engines are going to be dominant product. However, the car companies serving these areas have to drastically improve the mileage of their gasoline-powered autos. They've sliced the weight off the body and the interior. The only heavy thing left on a car is the engine, and Britlim has the solution to that problem." Britlim researcher Kyle

MacGlothlin developed the plastic-forming process and was present when Tata tested the product. "It's funny," MacGlothlin said. "Tata had all these tests lined up - there were steam rollers to try to crush it, explosives to try to tear it apart - all sorts of things. We were out on this airport runway, but it looked like a medieval dungeon with all its instruments of torture. They had a very negative attitude coming into the test, and they were really surprised when they couldn't destroy it. It validated all the work, all the years of backbreaking work we've put into this product. In fact, now that we've solved this initial problem of heat resistance, there's absolutely nothing that will prevent us from converting maybe 50 percent of every engine into plastic components. We could be a major force in meeting the developing world's contribution to global warming goals almost singlehanded. It's only in extremely high-temperature components, like pistons and piston wells where temperatures reach 260 degrees Celsius that we can't conceivably manufacture a replacement."

## Management Problems

1. What are some of the important messages about this new product to communicate to Britlim employees and stockholders?

2. How important will reliability be in helping establish consumer acceptance of these parts? What special events might you coordinate and publicize to communicate this property?

3. How would you recommend the company split its marketing resources between auto manufacturers and auto drivers?

## Writing Assignments

4. Compose a fact sheet pitch trying to interest an automotive editor in doing a feature story.

5. Write a news release to science editors about the new technology and the energy savings it represents.

6. Write a feature story for the company newsletter highlighting the research initiative and competitive advantages the company has gained with the new development.

7. Write a script for a 60-second video feature that will be distributed to cable television auto racing shows and posted on the company's website.

8. Write the lede sentence for a news release directed to a magazine read by automotive engineers and another lede for a release directed toward a newsletter that alerts investors to good stock buys.

9. Compose a list of five interactive features your company could install on its website to increase the time-on-task for visitors searching for information on the new engine parts.

## Scenario Prompt 7: A New Sick Leave Policy

Catharine Rios is a council member in your town who is approaching the end of her second 4-year term in office, already faces opposition from an anti-tax, anti-government spending group that has consistently labeled Rios as "free spending." After months of study she and her staff finished writing a 12-page report today. The report discusses sick leave and its use by city employees. The report notes that it cost city taxpayers $24,007,232 last year for the sick leave taken by employees of your municipality. In a city policy adopted in 2012, city employees accumulate sick leave at the rate of 2 hours for each week they work, or a total of 13 days of sick leave a year. The average city employee, according to the results of Rios' study, uses 10 of those sick days each year. Rios adds that that number is about twice the national average for all adult workers employed full time in the entire nation. In the report, Rios writes: "It must be suspected that much of the sick leave time claimed and used by city employees is used not to recuperate from illness, but to extend weekends or just to take time off. The problem is particularly acute on the days just before or after a holiday. It's also a serious problem on Mondays and Fridays, as many employees seem to take those days off in order to extend their weekends to a total of 3 or 4 days." Rios added that she is working on a possible solution to the problem and will present her corrective solution to the city council for its approval sometime during the next week. The solution she will propose is to pay retiring employees in cash (minus the employees' federally mandated social security contributions) for 1/2 of their unused accumulated sick leave so that they would have an incentive not to use sick leave but to save it. They might receive an extra payment totaling thousands of dollars upon their retirement. She noted that currently when city employees retire, they are not paid for their accumulated unused sick leave. "They lose it all," Rios claimed, "so there is an attitude among city employees that as long as it is given to them they should take as much of it as they can."

Rios explained that it would be cheaper to pay the employees a portion of their unused sick leave than to have to hire substitutes at full salary when someone is sick or to hire additional full-time city employees in order to have enough employees on hand at all times, as a number of city employees are likely to be out sick on any given workday during the year. Rios estimates that the plan could save the city ¼ of the costs it is currently spending on overtime.

### Management Problems

1. Why will the taxpayers group's preconception with Rios make your communication task more difficult? What aspects of social media will present concerns in Rios' use of Facebook posts in building support for her plan?

2. Will it be more effective to try to communicate this information to the taxpayer group's media channels before announcing it to the general public? Why or why not?

3. What are some of the other audiences with whom you will need to communicate about Rios' proposal?

4. Will you need to frame different arguments to convince city employees to support Rios' plan? What would those arguments emphasize?

5. Name at least three ways you could quantitatively measure success in this campaign.

## Writing Assignments

6. Write a media release for Rios' office to send to the 600 newsletter readers of the Better Government Association, the anti-tax group that has often criticized Rios.

7. Compose a personal letter from Rios to key individuals in the anti-tax group.

8. Create a 15-second video advertisement on this issue to support Rios' reelection campaign this November.

9. Write a 300-word article about Rios' position that will be posted on her official website.

10. Assemble a fact sheet concerning Rios' proposal that will be distributed to local editors and reporters.

## Scenario Prompt 8: Cooperating With a Strategic Partner

You work for BioloGene, a small, 4-and-one-half-year-old privately-held company that is working on gene-splicing technology. Started by three former researchers at Eastern Ontario University in Canada, Gopala Kanad, Solamane Adinkra and Portia von Neumann, your small biotechnology company has one very commercially viable idea, but ordinary product development procedures may mean another four to six years before the product can go on the market and start returning the company's investment. The company's idea, which the three women started on as high school students in your state or province's Governor's School of Science and Technology, is something called homologous recombination, which allows doctors and scientists to replace certain genes within cells. It also allows them to activate or deactivate specific genes within cells. All these actions permit the cells to react more favorably to drugs or allow the cells to accomplish some purpose themselves that will eliminate or fight a disease.

Unfortunately, company cash reserves are down to $2,826,500, which is much too little to finance the company during the developmental process. That process will consume about $3.345 million, and establishing a viable marketing effort will take even more money, maybe as much as $12.598 million, before the product is fully established.

Because of the company's high level of debt and uncertain short-term cash flow, taking out a bank loan is not likely to be a wise decision. Because of this need for financing, BioloGene is contemplating taking in a strategic partner, a larger, better-funded firm with which to share some of the product development costs and risks. Kanad, the firm's acting president, indicated those funds could come from either foreign or U.S. sources. The firm would like to hire a business broker by January 1 to help it discover five to eight possible partnerships. Obviously, by sharing those risks, BioloGene is losing equity, surely guaranteeing the three founders will lose a portion of the huge financial windfall that may come from selling the product. It's also true that the addition of a strategic partner is going to rob BioloGene's three founding partners of some of their autonomy and independence in making business decisions, because the strategic partner will want some significant control over company decisions in exchange for its capital contributions. The rather congenial environment the three partners (who are also friends) have enjoyed may be somewhat strained by the increased formality demanded by the strategic partner's bureaucracy. The alternative to all this are that BioloGene wouldn't have enough money to take the product to market, so that the company would probably go bankrupt before the product reached the market or would have to sell the homologous recombination idea to another firm. That would mean BioloGene would lose control of the technology and the potentially huge profits that could be made from it. There are other advantages to the strategic partner idea. A larger pharmaceutical firm as a partner could bring legal expertise and political contacts that might hasten the Food and Drug Administration approval process. That sort of firm could also bring marketing expertise and a distribution network to BioloGene's product. That's a definite weakness in BioloGene's business plan. The arrival of some marketing and business minds might also let BioloGene's three partners concentrate more on basic research, which seems to be their strength.

## Management Problems

1. What types of persuasion tasks will have to occur within the company's management hierarchy before this position is transformed into policy?

2. What are some of the possible consequences of not gaining full support of the present partners before undertaking a strategic partnership?

3. What further writing tasks are going to be necessary before BioloGene's offer is presented to potential partners?

4. What continuing communication is needed to smooth the business relationship if the strategic partnership is formalized?

## Writing Assignments

5. Draft a one- or two-page letter that could be used by the president of a potential strategic partner to inform and persuade key stockholders that the strategic partnership with BioloGene would be advantageous. Assume the letter is coming from Robert McKillip, president of McKillip Genetics, Inc.

6. Compose an outline for the middle section of an internal communication justifying this course of action to BioloGene employees. Compose another outline of a fact

sheet directed to stock market analysts. Does the order in which major persuaders are presented change between the two versions?

7. Prepare a one-minute A/V script for the company's website that explains how the process is expected to work in medical therapies.

8. Convert all the articles numbers into how they would appear in a print news story, and then into how they would appear in a broadcast script.

## Scenario Prompt 9: Announcing an Art Exhibit

You are the strategic communicator for your city's art museum. In "an artistic coup of tremendous proportions," as your museum's director terms it, your museum has snared an exhibit of paintings by the famous Russian painter of the early 20th century who was Jewish and eventually had to emigrate from Russia after the Communists took power in 1917, Marc Chagall. Your museum director got the chance to examine the paintings originally because he was a former student of an important Russian art curator, Benrikh Kalisniykov. Chagall was an enormously important figure in 20th century art as one of the pioneers of 20th-century fantastic art. His paintings, like "Self-Portrait with Seven Fingers" from 1912, melded brilliant colors and the delightful imagery of Russian-Jewish folk tradition with the fragmented forms of Cubism and led the way for artists like Salvador Dali, who would later found Surrealism. The exhibit will be shared with seven other museums in the United States (including the Metropolitan Museum of Art in New York City and the National Gallery in Washington, D.C.), Mexico, Belgium and the Louvre in France before going back to Russia. For your exhibit, tickets will be $60 each, and people wanting to see the exhibit must call for reservations by calling 555-889-1343. During the exhibit, the museum will not be open for general viewing, and only people who make reservations will be admitted to the museum's galleries. Tickets will probably be as rare for this exhibit as for the exhibit of Grecian gold that dated to Alexander the Great's time. That exhibit was mounted at the museum in 2008. There were 150,000 visitors to the museum during that 40-day exhibit, including a record of 11,000 visitors in a single day. Chagall was born in 1889, the same year as Adolf Hitler. Chagall, however, was born in Russia. He moved to Paris in 1910, but returned to Russia in the excitement over the Russian Revolution in 1917. He became disenchanted and returned to Paris in 1922. In fact, it is the nature of that disenchantment that led to the paintings that are going to be in the exhibit coming to your museum. The paintings were done as murals for the Moscow Jewish Art Theater. Chagall created the seven large panels in 1920 and 1921. The panels, Chagall said in a 1953 interview, "were a summation of the Jewish life of his youth in the White Russian town of Vitebsk." The paintings (each of which is 6 feet tall and 8 feet wide) portray a wedding scene, a Torah scribe, musicians, dancers and acrobats, in his usual pattern of bright colors and distorted perspective. They are meant, Chagall said, "as a metaphor for the travail of art in the Soviet Union, as well as the fate of that country's Jews." The paintings' history came to demonstrate that, according to your museum's director, Christian Kroner. Kroner said the paintings were taken from the theater's lobby in 1929 on Stalin's order. Stalin made the order because he viewed them as examples of decadent, non-Socialist art. They were moved to the theater's rehearsal hall. When the Germans attacked Moscow in 1941, the theater's actors carried the murals to safety in Siberia until the war ended. The scene was described in a book by one of the company child actors, Vladimir Kosrekov:

> It was a cold December night. The temperature was about minus twentyfive degrees Celsius. The German artillery flashed on the horizon like popping light bulbs at the edge of a stage. The three buildings on one side of our theater and the two buildings on the other side had already been destroyed. There were three hulking holes in our theater's backstage area already, and you could see these lacy, delicate sets done in pastels that we had made up for Cinderella through the blackened holes in the bricks. As an actor, it was hard for me to tell which was the reality and which was the fantasy, because the scenery was so much closer to what we had known as reality until just a few months before. But that was over now. We knew the paintings, these wonderful, priceless works of art that were the symbol of our theater and of our faith, would be immediately destroyed if the Germans reached the city. They knew it was of the Jews. We knew they might be destroyed by the artillery even if the Nazis never reached the city. We knew just as well that if we tried to get them from the theater we put our lives in danger too. But we were young and death meant nothing to us. Fifteen of us, four males and eleven women, waited until after midnight and then moved them from the theater. Our way was lit by the fires burning in the buildings. That night over 600 buildings in the city were on fire. We moved the paintings, two to each painting, the three blocks to the station. There, one of the actress's brothers, who was in the army and being sent to the Manchurian front, hid the paintings in camouflage screens for our own artillery pieces. After an eleven-day ride, he hid them in caves behind the battle lines and did not tell anyone where they were until after the war.

In 1947 the paintings were brought back to Moscow and placed back into the theater. But after the war, Stalin pushed his anti-Semitic campaign, and one night in 1952 the paintings were removed from the theater's rehearsal hall and taken to the cellars of the Tretyakov Gallery in Moscow. Although Stalin died in 1953, the paintings were never seen again until two years ago, when Kroner, after much pleading, was given access to the paintings. The exhibit at your gallery, from June 8 through July 21 of next year, results from that first viewing. Kroner said the paintings looked awful. "Paint was flaking from the paintings and you could see only the ghosts of these wonderful images that I had fallen in love with in art school. I was simply furious." Kroner spent that fury on Benrikh Kalisniykov, who is the chief of all fine arts in the Russian Republic. Kroner offered to have Western museums restore the paintings if the institutions could exhibit the murals. Kalisniykov initially refused, saying that it would be unfair to the Russian people to have them exhibited first in the West, because their people hadn't had a chance to see them since Stalin pulled them from the theater lobby in the 1920s. "I quickly put him straight about that," Kroner said. "I told him that it is the fault of the Soviet leaders that the Russian people haven't seen these paintings. Then I told him he had the choice of letting us restore them to again be a glory of the Russian people or watch them rot away in his cellars. The responsibility for destroying a glorious work of art would be his, and his alone." Kroner went on: "Kalisniykov eventually relented and the paintings were brought to New York where expert art restorers spent eight months getting them into shape for our show. We had the honor of exhibiting them first because I was the one, among all the other museum directors of the world, who had enough clout and moxie to get them out of Russia." You find that Vladimir Kosrekov is still alive and you call him. You discover he will be flown into your city by the museum to participate in the opening. He's now 96 years old.

You call him at his home in St. Petersburg and get this quote:

> I will be there for the opening day. It is my first trip into a western country and I will be seeing my sister-in-law in Boston on my way to your city. It will be nice to know that I'm still alive to see my paintings again. Stalin is dead. Hitler is dead. All those who tried to destroy them are dead. But the paintings and the hopes of little people like me still are alive. Is life all bad when this happens?

The exhibition is already drawing widespread attention from sources across the country. The New York Times art critic, who is named Mordikye Anton, wrote, "You've seen these pictures in art history books your entire life. They're considered treasures of the world.

And the surprising thing is that no one has seen them for seventy years. It will be an exciting time when they hit our shores."

## Management Problems

1. In addition to selling tickets to the Chagall exhibit, how could the museum take advantage of this show to build its institutional strength?

2. In addition to art lovers, what audiences are potential marketing targets for your communication campaign?

## Writing Assignments

3. Write a fundraising letter from Kroner to the museum's members and local corporate supporters to bring in money to stage equally impressive shows.

4. Compose a news release announcing the show to local and regional newspapers and television stations.

5. Script a multichannel overview of the paintings' creation and history to be posted on the museum's website.

6. Create a schedule of social media posts, specifying the subject of each post, that will promote the exhibit from the time of the announcement through its run.

7. Write a short introduction of the paintings' history that will be delivered orally by the museum's tour guides.

8. Script a television public service announcement for the exhibit.

9. Write a persuasion platform that will guide your efforts to draw members of your city's Russian Orthodox churches, which include a large number of recent Russian immigrants. Omit the budget section.

10. Which argumentation structure will you most likely use to present the paintings' history? Which one will be most appropriate for listing the other museums in which the paintings will be exhibited? What argumentation structure should you use to present the Russian museum director's rationale for sharing the paintings with western museums?

11. Write two lede sentences-one for a release directed to art historians and another directed toward local art museum members. Compare the vocabulary of the two sentences.

12. Prepare an outline of sound effects that might draw your receivers' attention to the lede of a radio story about the art exhibit as well as other sound effects that might help you tell the story.

## Scenario Prompt 10: An Industry Tries to Improve Its Image

As a freelance public relations specialist, you've been hired to coordinate a new program that is being started by a group of companies that make liquor, beer and wine. You have this conversation with John Clark, a one-time Hollywood actor whose most notable role was in the movie, "Psycho Clowns." He was president of the Screen Actors Guild, the same office held by Ronald Reagan before he became president of the United States. Clark later became ambassador to Uruguay and is now the chairman for this group of alcohol producers. Clark said:

> The company leaders recognize that they have been getting destroyed in the media and in public opinion during the past 10 years. Every drunk driving death spurs a whole new round of negative press attention to the problem.
>
> Fraternities, sororities and college students in general, and the sobbing stories about 'another young life cut short' and the grieving mother breaking down in tears at the funeral; that stuff has been a catastrophe for us. We wish we could just get those kids sunk into the ground before anyone knows about it, but we can't so we've faced increased taxes on alcoholic beverages and warning labels on packaging. This is cutting into our business, so we decided we need to become more proactive. We've also had this increased attention to alcohol's role in domestic violence. For God's sake, there are now anti-drinking programs in kindergartens. The manufacturers felt they had to do something to reinforce the idea that some drinking of alcoholic beverages isn't a bad thing and the liquor, beer and wine industry isn't against

arresting drunk drivers or sponsoring alcohol awareness programs. In fact, they hope that by becoming actively involved in sponsoring and funding alcohol awareness program that they can head off some of the most radical measures that some of the anti-alcohol lobbying groups are lobbying for, and point their efforts in more reasonable directions that accept that some drinking is OK but that alcohol abuse is not; that social drinking is fine but that getting drunk and hitting schoolchildren is not what alcohol makers are in favor of. We want responsible use of our products and we're tired of looking like the bad guys in this whole debate. We've got a big job ahead of us, because we know we've got to stimulate some fairly substantial changes in the way our society views drinking and driving. But I've got the commitment from the presidents of the largest liquor, beer and wine companies. We're dedicated to this task. We want to stop being against efforts to control alcohol and start being for responsible individual and social actions to encourage responsible drinking."

The coalition's goals are very ambitious, you find out, for they involve cutting drunken driving arrests in half within the next 10 years. That's a big job, because alcohol-related traffic deaths have gone down from 57.3 percent of all fatal accidents seven years ago to 49.2 percent today, which is about a 1 percent drop each year. But obviously, nine more years will only take the accident rate down to 40 percent, which is a heck of a long way from the 25 percent rate the council claims it wants to achieve. The coalition plans to run an extensive alcohol awareness advertising campaign. The first step in that campaign is a set of commercials due to run before Labor Day in September. The radio ads will be run in 77 cities. The time was chosen because over 400 Americans die in alcohol-related car wrecks each Labor Day. The council members have also agreed to not target advertising to anyone under the legal drinking age. That prohibits them from using characters, celebrities or active sports figures to promote alcohol or from sponsoring events on college campuses.

The council members have also agreed to work to enact into legislative law those state proposals that would immediately strip the licenses from drivers who are caught behind the wheel drunk and would urge states to issue driver's licenses and identification cards that are harder to forge to help stop the black market in illicit ID cards that underage minors use to get liquor. Gavin is going to be responsible for $80 million in expenditures for the coalition of makers of beer, liquor and wine, which is known as the Decade Coalition. The coalition's plans came from studying the successes that have already reduced deaths attributed to alcohol. Most experts attribute those successes to various lobbying citizen groups that have undertaken massive efforts to beef up drunken driving laws and enforcement and to heighten public awareness of alcohol abuse. The groups have worked hard to tighten enforcement of present laws forbidding alcohol sales to people under 21 years of age. The coalition plans to copy and reinforce these plans. In addition to the other measures outlined, the coalition also has agreed to fund community alcohol awareness and enforcement programs that work and then work to duplicate those programs in other places.

## Management Problems

1. What are some of the difficulties the Decade Coalition has to overcome to coordinate efforts with anti-alcohol lobbying groups? What might be the positive effect of that collaborative effort?

2. What are the industry group's complications in extending its communication efforts to younger people, many of whom who are affected by alcohol problems before they even enter high school?

3. How may the participation of this industry group change the way elected officials view groups trying to pass laws regulating alcohol use?

4. What are some of the consequences in the choice of this particular spokesperson for the industry group?

5. If the campaign were directed toward combating teenage drinking, would a different campaign kickoff date be more effective?

## Writing Assignments

6. Write a news release for metropolitan newspapers announcing the new program.

7. Write a news feature for an industry newsletter that discusses the philosophy for the new program.

8. Author a series of tweets for a popular music artist of your choice that incorporates the industry group's messages and reflects the prose style the artist uses in her own account.

9. Compose a print advocacy advertisement that would be placed in a political magazine read by state legislators. Your ad should highlight the alcohol manufacturers' efforts to regulate themselves and the use of their products.

10. Write a sample of a short speech that could be used to guide individual speakers at high school presentations.

11. Compose a minute-long, multichannel message urging appropriate alcohol use to be employed in a sponsored internet ad directed toward an under-21 audience.

12. Write an audio public service announcement to be placed at the end of recordings released by leading country music stars.

# Glossary

**5W1H System.** Traditional journalistic writing formula for a lede sentence. It recommends the lede include answers to all six questions of *Who?, What?, When?, Where?, Why?* and *How?* When converted to prose, it often buries information of immediate interest to the reader.

**Actuality.** A visual clip, sound effect and/or quote from prerecorded sources incorporated into a multichannel story.

**Adoption Process Model.** A five-step hierarchical persuasion model. First, people develop an awareness of an idea or product and then an interest in it. After evaluation and trial, they assert a preference and then a resolution of intention. Finally, they adopt the idea as their own.

**Advertising.** The use of paid media to communicate with target audiences, most often customers/consumers, to persuade those audiences to purchase a product or service, adopt an attitude, express an opinion or take some behavior benefiting the organization.

**Agenda-Setting Theory.** A theory asserting that issues and topics discussed in mass media channels gain importance in the minds of media consumers.

**Amoral.** A term used to describe decisions and issues that lack any deep ethical component related to moral rights and wrongs.

**Attribution Theory.** A theory asserting that interpersonal interactions and relationships may be judged not only by one party's behavior, but also by how that behavior is interpreted. For PR and strategic communication practitioners, this theory helps explain how miscommunication in organizational-public relationships occurs through misinterpretations of the actions of one or both parties.

**Audience-Centered Communication Process.** A general approach to persuasive communication that asserts a message's audience controls whether a communication act is completed. It considers the audience's capacities, needs and habits, then develops a strategy for engaging key publics by a conscious matching of audience to information.

**B-Roll.** Video footage acquired from any source other than principal photography.

**Back-End Performance.** An assessment of communication effectiveness that focuses not on responses to a message but whether individual stakeholders continue to support the company over time.

**Back-Through Run.** A tactic used to expand a list of prospects by assembling current stakeholder demographic and psychographic qualities. It then processes the typical adopter file "back through" a database to produce a list of prospects with characteristics like current stakeholders.

**Benchmarking.** An analysis tool that measures an organization's performance against the best-in-class, searching for methods the lower-performing organization could integrate into its own management procedures to strengthen its performance.

**Blog.** A website that houses original content in which posts are thematically connected. They comprise primarily short commentary, and while often hosted on independent sites, are sometimes embedded into larger organizational websites.

**Brand Journalism.** The practice of promoting some aspect of an organization, its brand or its products/services by applying journalistic writing principles to developing stories interesting to key publics.

**Break Points.** Places where readers, listeners or viewers decide whether to abandon the message or keep attending to it. By concentrating information at the beginning of sentences and paragraphs (typical break points), readers are encouraged to keep reading.

**Bridge.** An advertisement's equivalent of the media release's second paragraph. It explains the headline and directly states the main selling idea in terms the audience can understand.

**Browsing.** The act of looking for content or information online in a general, somewhat aimless sense.

**Bullshitting.** Communicating without knowledge of what is true or false to advance one's own ends. Bullshitting is distinct from lying insofar that to lie requires that the communicator actually know the truth in order to deny it.

**Buyer Persona.** A representation of either an average or ideal customer based on market research and/or organizational data about existing consumers.

**Cartograms.** A map scaled not on the physical dimensions of the geographic subdivisions it portrays but upon the intensity of another statistical unit.

**Category.** A section of a blog that delineates posts by topic, much like a table of contents. It's often used as a means of click-through navigation.

**Character.** The culmination of moral qualities possessed by an individual that drive her to habitual ethical action across varying situations.

**Clickbait.** The gratuitous use of compelling information to grab attention. Clickbait often features information that is misleading or off-topic.

**Cognitive Dissonance.** An uncomfortable mental state that results from holding two contradictory beliefs at the same time or from acting in a way that runs counter to a deeply held, preexisting belief.

**Complex of Personal Values.** An individual's layers of personal experiences influencing her interpretation of a communication act's meaning.

**Conceit.** In advertising, a creative method of presenting a persuasive claim to attract audience attention and introduce the benefits to be gained by buying a product, using a service or adopting an idea.

**Conscience.** Our cultivated, inner sense of morality that guides our judgment of behaviors or states as being wrong or right.

**Controlled Communication.** Messages, such as advertising, speeches or institutional webpages that don't have to pass through a media gatekeeper before reaching an audience.

**Convergence.** The merger of previously distinct media technologies and platforms as a result of digitization and computer networking.

**Corporate Social Responsibility (CSR).** An institutional approach to good corporate citizenship to ensure the company's attention to legal and ethical standards. CSR constitutes an organization's voluntary actions addressing stakeholder needs and wants. Its primary goal is managing reputations to help organizations achieve goals of self-preservation and long-term profitability.

**Cost-Effectiveness.** A measure of success calculated by determining a ratio of costs expended to a valuation of benefits received.

**Crisis Communication.** The efforts undertaken before a negative occurrence, such as a product recall, scandal or natural disaster, or invoked when an event occurs that could negatively impact the institution's standing among its customers, workers or other stakeholders.

**Cross-Tabulation.** A data report that shows information for an entire group and researcher-designated subgroups. It is often used to discover subgroup variations that may be hidden when examining data for the whole group.

**Cultivation Theory.** A theory asserting heavy media users—particularly of television—view the real world through that medium's lens, distorting their capacity to accurately observe the real world.

**CUS Information Model.** A strategic communication model that conceptualizes media content as either controlled, uncontrolled or semicontrolled by the sender.

**Customer Twins.** Individuals who display approximately the same spectrum of demographic or psychographic descriptors as those who have taken a desired action toward a message, product or service.

**Data-Driven Marketing.** Communication tactics and strategies predicated on tracking consumer behavior information and employing it to enhance desired behaviors of current customers or to solicit new customers.

**Data Visualization.** A visual representation of information through a chart, diagram or picture, which is intended to enhance audience comprehension and to discover additional research insights.

**Database Overlay.** A database research tactic that searches for duplicate information within entries from multiple databases in order to refine the characteristics in a final data collection.

**Demographics.** Nonattitudinal, difficult-to-change audience characteristics that include age, income, profession, geographic locality, gender and race. They generally define a public's capacity to act upon a message.

**Deontology.** An ethical theory that devises universal rules for right action based on moral obligations, asserting that the intentions of the agent—specifically whether she followed moral maxims and acted from a sense of duty—are of greater concern than the outcome of an action in determining its ethicality.

**Dialogue.** An open exchange of ideas between two parties (often an organization and a stakeholder) in which both possess the ability to influence the other's beliefs or actions.

**Earned Media.** Information transmitted via mediated channels through the initiation of media relations or publicity efforts.

**Elaboration Likelihood Model (ELM).** A theory asserting that people elaborate on messages in one of two different ways. Central route processing occurs when individuals are motivated and able to process messages; these messages are most persuasive when supported by strong rational and/or emotional arguments. Peripheral route processing occurs when individuals are less interested in the message content but might still be persuaded by heuristic cues, such as the speaker's credibility or charisma.

**Electronic Word-of-Mouth (eWOM).** Information spread or shared electronically from one person to another person or persons, often through email or social networking sites.

**Email Pitch.** See *query letter*.

**Engagement.** In social media contexts, involvement with or commitment to a product, brand, organization or issue typified by interactivity or the willingness to take some pro-organizational action.

**Engagement Rate.** A measure of audience engagement calculated by adding all audience engagement behaviors (likes, shares, comments, etc.) for a given post, and dividing by the number of followers.

**Ethics.** A process for making decisions and taking actions based on considerations of moral rights and wrongs.

**Evergreen.** Slang for content that is relevant or newsworthy for reasons other than timeliness.

**External Communication.** Communication conducted with a target public that is not part of the organization.

**Feature.** Nonfiction writing that showcases deeper research and more creative expression than spot news coverage.

**Focus Feature Lede.** A feature story introduction that concentrates on an individual's involvement in a critical incident exemplifying a larger issue.

**Gaslighting.** The cumulative process in which speakers create doubt and confusion among audiences to the point at which audiences no longer trust their own assessments about reality.

**Gatekeeper.** Any individual (e.g., editors, producers and reporters) who controls access to a media channel or can modify a speaker's message before it reaches its ultimate audience.

**Golden Mean.** The concept that virtues represent a balance between two opposing vices, and that such balance can only be reached through the exercise of practical wisdom. For example, courage is a virtue that balances cowardice (a deficiency of courage) and foolhardiness (an excess of courage).

**Heat Map.** An image that can visually display thousands of data points to indicate the intensity of a characteristic.

**Heuristic.** An approach to problem-solving that relies on research, experience, inductive reasoning and rules of thumb to efficiently address a given issue.

**Hierarchy Models.** Persuasion models asserting that when people decide upon adopting a new idea, their decision process moves through a non-varying sequence of steps.

**Infographic.** A display of information that helps communicate complex information through visuals that speed audience comprehension.

**Inoculation Theory.** A theory of persuasive communication based on the principle of immunization. It advocates exposing audiences not only to the position you want them to adopt, but to opposing viewpoints as well. By learning to defend a position early on, audiences are more likely to retain that position over time.

**Internal Communication.** Institutional messages directed toward stakeholders via forms of controlled communication working within the organization.

**Intranet.** A private, inward-facing website only accessible to an organization's employees.

**Inverted Pyramid.** A traditional journalism writing structure that recognizes audiences will remain in a communication event only as long as it satisfies their needs. It places information in descending order of importance to communicate the most important information to the reader first.

**Learn-Feel-Do Model.** A persuasion approach positing that people choose decision-making strategies depending upon the significance of consequences they attach to their decision and whether the decision satisfies an emotional or rational need.

**Lede.** The first sentence of a document, which establishes the basic structural outline that will be used to build the rest of the document. The first 10 words of a good lede define an audience, then provide a benefit that will be important for that audience.

**Lifetime Value.** A measurement of how much a given stakeholder will contribute to an organization's bottom line over the course of her relationship with an organization, not just within a single transaction.

**Limited Effects Model.** The conception that media messages affect our attitudes, opinions and behaviors, but they do so within the context of other influencing factors, such as individual personality, social relationships, cultural values and the nature of the messages themselves.

**Long-Tail SEO.** A method of optimizing multiple, specific keywords and phrases to improve search engine rankings for more engaged audiences.

**Marketing.** The use of controlled and semicontrolled media to communicate with customers/consumers to influence their opinions of organizational products and/or services and in turn persuade them to purchase those products or services.

**Maslow's Hierarchy of Needs.** A persuasion hierarchy model asserting people meet their needs in a definite sequence, beginning with basic needs—like food, water and shelter—and progressing toward more complex needs—like love, esteem and self-actualization.

**Media Relations.** The process of establishing respectful, mutually beneficial relationships between the media gatekeepers and an organization to help the organization communicate more effectively with key publics.

**Moral Exemplar.** An individual we regard as embodying virtuous character and thus turn to for guidance concerning moral matters.

**Multilogue.** An open exchange among three or more parties (often among stakeholders themselves) in which each party has the ability to influence the beliefs and actions of the others.

**Multichannel Advertising.** Advertising in which the message is supplemented with sound, visuals and/or motion.

**Multichannel Media.** Media that incorporates sensory channels beyond print, such as visuals, motions, sounds, voices and/or music. Examples include radio, television, film and when motion and sound are included in media distributed through the internet.

**Multichannel Writing.** Writing for electronic transmission channels that incorporates sensory channels beyond just print, such as radio, television, film, documentaries, audio, video news releases and blogs.

**Multimedia.** Media that engage multiple sensory channels (e.g., visual, auditory, olfactory and tactile senses).

**Multiple Insertion Points.** A strategic approach to campaign planning unrestricted to a sequenced brainstorming stage, instead being open to a single factor around which to organize the communication task and your persuasive message.

**Multivariate Descriptors.** Extensive information on individual consumers that includes demographic, psychographic, lifestyle and purchasing behaviors.

**New Media.** Any media message distributed through computer networks like the internet.

**News Hole.** A media outlet's available capacity for coverage, after deducting advertising and repetitive editorial components.

**News Release.** Also known as a *media release* or *press release*, a media relations tool directed to editors and producers that is structured to announce news, events, awards and other institutional information.

**Nut Paragraph.** The paragraph in a focus feature story that transitions from the opening scenario to define the story's main topic.

**Objective.** Part of the communication planning process that, if met, would contribute directly to solving an institutional problem. Objectives should be stated so practitioners and managers can agree on the precise conditions when they have been successfully met. Well-crafted objectives meet the SMARTO acronym qualifications: they are specific, measurable, actionable, relevant, timebound and outcome oriented.

**Online Pressroom.** A repository of an organization's media relations materials—including press releases, other print content, photos, videos, contact information—which serves as both an archive of the organization's actions and a source for current information.

**Opinion Leaders.** Trusted others to whom less attentive audiences turn for their insight and expertise on a given subject matter.

**Outcomes.** Audience actions prompted by communication efforts that help fulfill a company objective.

**Outlier.** Those data points appearing on a data set's extreme ends, which often contain valuable information about the process under investigation and more completely explain measures of central tendency.

**Outputs.** Communicator activities intended to prompt audience action.

**Owned Media.** Content distributed through channels the organization operates. These range from low-tech options, such as bulletin boards, fliers and direct mail; to online channels, such as organizational websites or blogs.

**Paid Media.** Coverage in outlets garnered for a fee. Traditional advertising is a prime example but sponsored social media content and marketing efforts such as point-of-purchase displays or product placements also fall into this category.

**Parallel Structure.** A prose organization tactic in which the argument is presented in the body copy in the same order as introduced in the lede sentence.

**Parasocial Relationship.** The perception that people know and have a relationship with a multi-channel presenter.

**Pareto Chart.** A data visualization process that progressively tracks increasingly narrow subsets of information concerning an issue.

**Persuasion.** The art and science of using communication to encourage a target audience to adopt a desired attitude, express a desired opinion or act in a desired manner.

**Persuasion Platform.** A nine-step planning system that enables users to identify and creatively confront organizational issues while providing a tactical framework guiding a later writing process.

**PESO Media Model.** A strategic communication model that categorizes media as belonging to one of four types: paid, earned, shared or owned.

**Photo Op Teaser.** A publicity tactic alerting media members to opportunities for photographic or multichannel coverage relevant to their audiences.

**Planning.** A communication effort that improves the probability of a communication campaign's success by guiding a practitioner to consider all elements of the communication process.

**Position-Evidence Relationship.** A prose organization tactic that suggests specific argument patterns for specific types of evidence. Order of importance is a good way to present lists. If a writer is offering a recommendation, problem-solution is recommended. A chronology is best in communicating sequences or histories.

**Post-Truth.** Generally, a description applied to communication acts that impair one's ability to determine with any accuracy what's happening in the world around us. Tactics like lying, bullshitting, hyperbole, distraction, evasion and silence are often deployed in its services.

**Powerful Effects Model.** A communication theory suggesting media have direct and immediate effects on audiences, who are in turn virtually unable to resist media's influence (aka, *hypodermic needle theory* or *magic bullet theory*).

**Practical Wisdom.** Knowledge of the virtues gained through experience and observation of moral exemplars that allow us, given the natures of the scenarios we face, to exercise virtues not only in concert but also appropriately.

**Press Agentry Model.** An approach to practice in which an organization communicates for its own ends, valuing dissemination of the organization's message more highly than the message's truthfulness.

**Primary Research.** An information-discovery process employing formally constructed experiments and surveys to test propositions and discover information not contained in previous research. Compare to secondary research.

**Pseudo-Event.** An event or activity created to foster publicity and conducted to satisfy the needs of the media.

**Psychographics.** Attitudinal traits that describe an audience by isolating probable emotional, self-image and lifestyle factors, such as hobbies, interests and opinions.

**Public.** A group of people or institutions that share common interests or concerns.

**Public Information Model.** An approach to practice in which the organization initiates and controls communication with a public, but in which the organization commits to be truthful when it does communicate.

**Public Relations.** An exercise of communication management in which practitioners employ persuasive messages in an attempt to influence public opinion and behavior to benefit the organizations for which they work and, ideally, its key stakeholders as well. Public relations often filters uncontrolled informational messages through news media, though messages are also communicated directly to and with stakeholders using controlled and semicontrolled platforms.

**Public Service Announcement (PSA).** A message urging changes concerning a social issue that is developed by nonprofit and governmental organizations with the intent of being disseminated without charge.

**Pun.** Wordplay that exploits multiple meanings of a term, or of similar-sounding words, for an intended effect.

**Query Letter.** Also known as a *pitch letter*, this media relations tool summarizes a projected story in a direct communication that demonstrates the story's value to a gatekeeper and her audience.

**Question Lede.** A story opening that immediately introduces a provocative inquiry pertaining to the story's theme.

**Relationship Management.** A process of understanding what each party expects from the other and then delivering on those expectations in a way that establishes trust through fostering continued commitment to the relationship. Organizations show that commitment by involving themselves in shared interests with key stakeholders, often investing time, money and other resources to add value to those stakeholders' lives.

**Relationship Marketing.** A valuation assessment approach that emphasizes the paybacks from a continuing relationship with an individual over an extended, defined time period.

**Resolution Focus.** The ending of a focus feature that returns the reader's attention to an individual affected by the issues discussed in the story.

**Resource Dependency Theory.** The theory that organizations depend upon external stakeholders to the degree that those stakeholders control resources necessary for organizational operations and survival. Organizations with the greatest access to needed resources and the ability to use them strategically are typically the most successful.

**Reversal.** Word play that contrasts an initial example in a headline with a second example, often in an oxymoronic way.

**RSS Feed.** Known as *rich site summary* or *really simple syndication*, an RSS format allows users to track and update online content through an aggregated feed, which pushes newly available content to users.

**Search Engine Optimization (SEO).** The process of producing, altering or overhauling content so search algorithms rank the site housing that content higher in search results.

**Searching.** The act of looking for content or information online in a specific, systematic way.

**Secondary Research.** An information-discovery process relying on previously collected data; it is the initial step of any research process, which helps guide the research design of any subsequent primary research. Compare to primary research.

**Selective Exposure.** A defense mechanism against cognitive dissonance in which people take preventative steps to avoid challenges to their beliefs or seek out information that confirms their existing viewpoints.

**Shared Media.** Interactive engagement in which the audience can initiate communication or contribute reactive content to an organizational message. This occurs frequently through word-of-mouth information spread via off-line (e.g., public forums) and online (e.g., social media) channels.

**Shotgun Approach.** A media relations approach characterized by an unfocused and overbroad delivery of information to media outlets regardless of each editor's interest in the issue.

**Signaling Theory.** A communication theory asserting that everything an organization says or does communicates perceived negative or positive value to stakeholders, be it the value of products or services, the value of the organization more broadly or what the organization itself values as important.

**Situational Theory of Publics.** A model stating that publics can be identified and classified based on their awareness of a problem, their involvement with that problem and their capacity to act. A cost-effective communication plan can be created by identifying people likely to communicate about and act on an issue, and those who likely won't.

**Social Exchange Theory.** The theory that social relationships and systems can be categorized by processes of resource exchange, and that relationship quality is governed by rules of perceived reciprocity, fairness and stability.

**Social Media.** A category that encompasses any website whose predominant function lets individuals share their viewpoints. Broadly speaking, social media include sites such as blogs, social networking sites, wikis, forums and message boards.

**Social Network Analysis.** The process of investigating the social structures through which individuals and institutions are linked, and messages and information are distributed among them.

**Social Networking Site (SNS).** A site on which individuals or groups create personal profiles and connect to and share information with other individuals or groups, typically those who share their interests, values or opinions.

**Social Proof.** A psychological phenomenon in which people, when faced with issues of uncertainty, take cues from those around them to guide their behavior. In social media contexts, the idea that multiple endorsements of content tend to lend credibility.

**Speaker-Centered Communication Process.** A general approach to persuasive communication that asserts communication happens when the sender transmits a message, irrespective of the audience's response. By focusing on the communication interests of a speaker rather than the needs of the audience, the audience assumes a passive role.

**Split-Run Test.** A communication evaluation strategy that tracks responses to different messages by statistically comparable groups to determine which option stimulates more responses.

**Spot News Story.** A media item that usually answers little more than the who, what, when, where, why and how of an event or issue.

**Stakeholder.** Any individual or group that affects or is affected by an organization's actions. Common examples include consumers, employees, investors and community groups.

**Static Advertising.** Advertising in which the message is presented in a still, fixed form. Examples include billboard, newspaper, magazine and web banner ads.

**Story Splitting.** A media relations tactic that helps practitioners obtain the broadest possible coverage. It crafts a separate release focused on each persuader comprising a story and matches each with gatekeepers most interested in that story element.

**Strategic Communication.** Communication based on research, planning and critical thinking that makes use of advertising, marketing and/or public relations strategies and tactics to persuade target audiences and help an organization achieve a stated goal or objective.

**Summary Lede.** A feature lede that closely resembles a TIPCUP-generated lede, which immediately identifies the story topic and involves the reader's interests or self-interests.

**Supertitle.** A print message integrated into and reinforcing a video image.

**Tag.** A keyword or key phrase attached to a blog post to index it for searches within the blog or through general search engines.

**Theory.** In the social sciences, a theory is a testable, organizing principle that, when applied in real-world settings, can explain and predict patterns of human behavior.

**TIPCUP Filter.** Acronym for *time, impact, proximity, conflict, unusualness* and *prominence,* which directs a writer to evaluate what information will or will not interest her target audience. It focuses on reader motivation rather than comprehensiveness of information to dictate lede sentence elements.

**Transitions.** Bridges between the sections of the story that show readers the relationship between what they just read and what they are about to read.

**Trend Analysis.** In this type of analysis, multiple data points representing related observations are plotted on a graph. If measurements from an extensive time period are available, practitioners can use the overall direction or slope of the trend line to predict changes.

**Trigger Word.** A specialized lede used in multichannel writing to overcome audience inattention. The trigger word(s) alerts the target audience that the story is intended for them by quickly suggesting the story's significance.

**Trolling.** Making deliberately offensive, upsetting or provocative statements through online platforms to elicit anger, resentment or self-defeating responses.

**Two-Step Flow.** A process through which attentive audiences internalize media messages and then pass along those messages—as well as their personal interpretations of them—to less-informed others. These attentive audiences are known as *opinion leaders.*

**Two-Way Asymmetric Communication.** An approach to practice in which the organization undertakes significant study of its publics and their needs in order to construct the messages it shares with those publics, but in which the publics are not anticipated to communicate meaningfully with the organization.

**Two-Way Symmetric Communication.** An approach to practice in which the organization undertakes significant study of its publics and their needs in order to construct the messages it shares with those publics. It incorporates methods by which those publics can easily communicate with the organization and thus directly shape organizational policy and action.

**Uses and Gratifications.** An approach to media effects arguing that audiences actively choose which media messages to attend to based on individual and social needs.

**Utilitarianism.** A consequentialist moral philosophy that evaluates the ethicality of an action based on its likely outcome, in which actions are deemed good if they generate greater happiness or well-being for greater numbers.

**Venn Diagram.** A data visualization tool that displays logical relations between a defined collection of different characteristics by detailing the degree to which characteristics are shared among audiences.

**Virtue.** A deeply ingrained trait that predisposes us to think, feel and act in characteristically ethical ways.

**Virtue Ethics.** An agent-based moral philosophy purporting that individuals must focus on *being* good if they wish to *act* well. Adherents assert that through a process of moral education, we internalize a virtuous character, and through exercising practical wisdom, learn to habitually act rightly for the benefit of ourselves and others.

**Word Cloud.** A data visualization method that visually summarizes a subject by illustrating the relative frequency of words appearing in a defined set of prose.

**Working Document.** Documents that contain information and are structured so as to become important references for stakeholders.

**Wrap.** Final section of body copy in an ad. It restates the main selling idea and offers a way of gaining all the benefits the advertisement promises.

# Endnotes

## Chapter 1

1. Walter Lippmann, *Public Opinion* (New York: Harcour, Brace and Company, 1922).

2. William F. Arens, *Contemporary Advertising*, 9th ed. (Boston: McGraw-Hill, 2001); Media Dynamics Inc., "Adults Spend Almost 10 Hours Per Day with the Media, but Note Only 150 Ads," news release, September 21, 2014, http://www.mediadynamicsinc.com/uploads/files/PR092214-Note-only-150-Ads-2mk.pdf; Louise Story, "Anywhere the Eye Can See, It's Likely to See an Ad," *New York Times*, January 15, 2007.

3. Elihu Katz and Paul F. Lazarsfeld, *Personal Influence: The Part Played by People in the Flow of Mass Communications* (New York: Free Press, 1955); Stephen W. Littlejohn and Karen A. Foss, eds., *Encyclopedia of Communication Theory* (Thousand Oaks, CA: SAGE Publications, 2009); Denis McQuail, ed. *McQuail's Reader in Mass Communication Theory* (London: SAGE Publications, 2002).

4. Elihu Katz, "Mass Communications Research and the Study of Popular Culture: An Editorial Note on a Possible Future for This Journal," *Studies in Public Communication* 2 (1959), 1–6; Harold Lasswell, "The Structure and Function of Communication in Society," in *The Communication of Ideas: A Series of Addresses*, ed. Lyman Bryson (New York: Harper, 1948), 32–51.

5. Katz, "Mass Communications Research," 2.

6. Lawrence Grossberg et al., *Media Making: Mass Media in a Popular Culture*, 2nd ed. (Thousand Oaks, CA: SAGE Publications, 2006); Katz, "Mass Communications Research"; Lasswell, "The Structure and Function"; Littlejohn and Foss, *Encyclopedia of Communication*; Denis McQuail, *Mass Communication Theory*, 6th ed. (Thousand Oaks, CA: SAGE Publications, 2010).

7. Nicholas Browning and Kaye D. Sweetser, "The Let Down Effect: Satisfaction, Motivation, and Credibility Assessments of Political Infotainment," *American Behavioral Scientist* 58, no. 6 (2014), 810–826.

8. Maxwell McCombs and Donald Shaw, "A Progress Report on Agenda-Setting Research," *AEJMC* (San Diego, CA, August 18–24, 1974).

9. Bernard C. Cohen, *The Press and Foreign Policy* (Princeton, NJ: Princeton University Press, 1963), 13.

10. Grossberg et al., *Media Making*; Littlejohn and Foss, *Encyclopedia of Communication Theory*; McQuail, *Mass Communication*.

11. Hannah Fingerhut, "Millennials' Views of News Media, Religious Organizations Grow More Negative." Pew Research Center, January 4, 2016.

12. Amy Mitchell, "Which News Organization Is the Most Trusted? The Answer Is Complicated." Pew Research Center, October 30, 2014.

13. Littlejohn and Foss, *Encyclopedia of Communication*; McQuail, *Mass Communication*; Richard E. Petty and John T. Cacioppo, "The Elaboration Likelihood Model of Persuasion," in *Advances in Experimental Social Psychology*, ed. Leonard Berkowitz (New York: Academic Press, 1986), 124–206.

14. Robert B. Cialdini, *Influence: Science and Practice*, 4th ed. (Needham Heights, MA: Allyn and Bacon, 2001).

15. Demetrios Papageorgis and William McGuire, "The Generality of Immunity to Persuasion Produced by Pre-Exposure to Weakened Counterarguments," *Journal of Abnormal and Social Psychology* 62, no. 3 (1961), 475–481.

16. Littlejohn and Foss, *Encyclopedia of Communication*; Arthur A. Lumsdaine and Irving L. Janis, "Resistance to 'Counterpropaganda' Produced by One-Sided and Two-Sided "Propaganda" Presentations," *Public Opinion Quarterly* 17, no. 3 (1953), 311–318.

17. Joel Cooper, *Cognitive Dissonance: 50 Years of a Classic Theory* (Thousand Oaks, CA: SAGE Publications, 2007); Leon Festinger, *A Theory of Cognitive Dissonance* (Stanford, CA: Stanford University Press, 1957); Littlejohn and Foss, *Encyclopedia of Communication*.

18. Festinger, *A Theory of Cognitive Dissonance*; Claude M. Steele, Steven J. Spencer, and Michael Lynch, "Self-Image Resilience and Dissonance: The Role of Affirmational Resources," *Journal of Personality and Social Psychology* 64, no. 5 (1993), 885–896.

19. Eliza Collins, "Poll: Clinton, Trump Most Unfavorable Candidates Ever," *USA Today*, August 31, 2016, http://www.usatoday.com/story/news/politics/onpolitics/2016/08/31/poll-clinton-trump-most-unfavorable-candidates-ever/89644296/; Harry Enten, "Americans' Distaste for Both Trump and Clinton Is Record-Breaking," *FiveThirtyEight*, May 5, 2016, http://fivethirtyeight.com/features/

americans-distaste-for-both-trump-and-clinton-is-record-breaking/.

20. Gregory J. Martin and Ali Yurukoglu, "Bias in Cable News: Persuasion and Polarization." *Stanford University*, May 27, 2016. http://web.stanford.edu/~ayurukog/cable_news.pdf.

21. Amy Mitchell, Jeffrey Gottfried, and Katerina Eva Matsa, "Facebook Top Source for Political News among Millennials," *Pew Research Center*, June 1, 2015. http://www.journalism.org/2015/06/01/facebook-top-source-for-political-news-among-millennials/.

22. Mostafa El-Bermawy, "Your Filter Bubble Is Destroying Democracy," *Wired*, November 18, 2016. https://www.wired.com/2016/11/filter-bubble-destroying-democracy/.

23. Jon Keegan, "Blue Feed, Red Feed: See Liberal Facebook and Conservative Facebook, Side by Side," *Wall Street Journal*, May 18, 2016, http://graphics.wsj.com/blue-feed-red-feed/#methodology.

24. Julia Carrie Wong, Sam Levin, and Olivia Solon, "Bursting the Facebook Bubble: We Asked Voters on the Left and Right to Swap Feeds," *The Guardian*, November 16, 2016, https://www.theguardian.com/us-news/2016/nov/16/facebook-bias-bubble-us-election-conservative-liberal-news-feed.

25. Festinger, *A Theory of Cognitive Dissonance.*

26. Em Griffin, *A First Look at Communication Theory*, 8th ed. (New York: McGraw-Hill, 2012).

27. R. Edward Freeman, *Strategic Management: A Stakeholder Approach* (Cambridge, England: Cambridge University Press, 2010), 46.

28. Brian L. Connelly, David J. Ketchen Jr., and Stanley F. Slater, "Toward a 'Theoretical Toolbox' for Sustainability Research in Marketing," *Journal of the Academy of Marketing Science* 39, no. 1 (2011), 86–100; Jeffrey Pfeffer and Gerald R. Salancik, *The External Control of Organizations: A Resource Dependence Perspective* (New York: Harper and Row, 1978).

29. Littlejohn and Foss, *Encyclopedia of Communication*, 895.

30. Littlejohn and Foss, *Encyclopedia of Communication*, 895; John W. Thibaut and Harold H. Kelley, *The Social Psychology of Groups* (New Brunswick, NJ: Transaction Publishers, 1959).

31. Connelly, Ketchen Jr., and Slater, "Toward a 'Theoretical Toolbox'"; Gregory E. Goering, "Corporate Social Responsibility, Durable-Goods and Firm Profitability," *Managerial and Decision Economics* 31, no. 7 (2010), 489–496.

32. Connelly, Ketchen Jr., and Slater, "Toward a 'Theoretical Toolbox'"; Littlejohn and Foss, *Encyclopedia of Communication*.

33. Littlejohn and Foss, *Encyclopedia of Communication Theory*, 61.

34. Littlejohn and Foss, *Encyclopedia of Communication Theory*, 61.

35. Gini Dietrich, "PR Pros Must Embrace the PESO Model," *Spin Sucks: Professional Development for PR and Marketing Pros*, March 23, 2015, http://spinsucks.com/communication/pr-pros-must-embrace-the-peso-model/; Gini Dietrich, *Spin Sucks: Communication and Reputation Management in the Digital Age* (Indianapolis, IN: Que, 2014); Alexandra Ritter, "PESO: The New-Age PR Model," *Pyxl (blog)*, January 26, 2015, http://thinkpyxl.com/blog/peso-model-pr; Mark Thabit, "How PESO Makes Sense in Influencer Marketing," *PR Week*, June 8, 2015, http://www.prweek.com/article/1350303/peso-makes-sense-influencer-marketing.

36. American Marketing Association, "Definition of Marketing," 2017, https://www.ama.org/AboutAMA/Pages/Definition-of-Marketing.aspx; Public Relations Society of America, "About Public Relations," 2021, https://www.prsa.org/aboutprsa/publicrelationsdefined/#.WD8TahIrLmE; Jef I. Richards and Catharine M. Curran, "Oracles on "Advertising": Searching for a Definition," *Journal of Advertising* 31, no. 2 (2002), 63–77; Dennis L. Wilcox, Glen T. Cameron, and Bryan H. Reber, *Public Relations: Strategies and Tactics*, 11th ed. (Boston: Pearson, 2015), 19–21.

37. PRSA Public Relations Society of America, "About Public Relations."

38. Robyn Blakeman, *Integrated Marketing Communication: Creative Strategy from Idea to Implementation*, 2nd ed. (Lanham, MD: Rowman & Littlefield, 2015); Don E. Schultz, Charles H. Patti, and Philip J. Kitchen, eds., *The Evolution of Integrated Marketing Communications: The Customer-Driven Marketplace* (New York: Routledge, 2011); Don E. Schultz, Stanley I. Tannebaum, and Robert F. Lauterborn, *Integrated Marketing Communications: Putting It Together & Making It Work* (Chicago: NTC Business Books, 1993).

**Chapter 2**

1. Michael D. Miller and Timothy R. Levine, "Persuasion." In *An Integrated Approach to Communication Theory and Research*, eds. Michael B. Salwen and Don W. Stacks (Mahwah, NJ: Erlbaum, 1996), 261.

2. Harold Lasswell, *The Structure and Function of Communication in Society: The Communication of Ideas* (New York: Institute for Religious and Social Studies, 1948).

3. Denis McQuail and Sven Windahl, *Communication Models for the Study of Mass Communications.* (New York: Longman, 1993).

4. Abraham H. Maslow, "A Theory of Human Motivation," *Psychological Review (1943)*: 370–96.

5. Everett M. Rogers, *Diffusion of Innovations* (Glencoe NY: Free Press, 1962).

6. William Thompson. *Targeting the Message: A Receiver-Centered Process for Public Relations Writing* (White Plains, NY: Longman, 1996), 10–12.

7. William J. McGuire, "Persuasion, Resistence and Attitude Change." In *Handbook of Communication*, eds. Ithiel de Sola Pool, Frederick W. Frey, Wilbur Schramm, and Edwin B. Parker (Chicago: Rand-McNally, 1973), 216–252.

8. Thom File, "Voting in America: A Look at the 2016 Presidential Election," *U.S. Census Bureau*, May 10, 2017, https://www.census.gov/newsroom/blogs/random-samplings/2017/05/voting_in_america.html.

9. Jacqueline Prescott, "Benetton Ads: Clashing Color," *Washington Post*, August 10, 1991.

10. Jame E. Grunig and Todd Hunt, *Managing Public Relations* (New York: Holt, Rinehart and Winston, 1984); Jame E. Grunig and Linda Hon, *Reconstruction of a Situational Theory of Communication: Internal and External Concepts as Identifiers of Publics for AIDS* (Portland, OR, s.n., 1988); James E. Grunig, "A Situational Theory of Publics: Conceptual History, Recent Challenges and New Research." In *Public Relations Research: An International Perspective, eds.* Danny Moss, Toby MacManus and Dejan Verčič (London: International Thomson Business Press, 1997), 3–48.

11. David M. Dozier and William P. Ehling, (1992). "Evaluation of Public Relations Programs: What the Literature Tells Us about Their Effects." In Excellence in Public Relations and Communication Management, ed. James E. Grunig (Hillsdale, NJ: Lawrence Erlbaum, 1992), 159–84.

12. Richard Vaughn, "How Advertising Works: A Planning Model," *Journal of Advertising Research* September/October (1980), 27–30.

13. Richard Vaughn, "The Common Mind: How to Tailor Ad Strategies," *Advertising Age*, 51 (1980), 45–46.

14. John W. Thibaut and Harold H. Kelley, *The Social Psychology of Groups.* (New Brunswick, NJ: Transaction Publishers, 1959).

15. Michael E. Roloff, *Interpersonal Communication: The Social Exchange Approach* (Beverly Hills, CA: SAGE Publications, 1981).

16. National Domestic Violence Hotline, "Get the Facts & Figures," 2020, https://www.thehotline.org/resources/statistics/.

17. "Why Don't They Just Leave?," 2020, https://www.thehotline.org/is-this-abuse/why-do-people-stay-in-abusive-relationships/.

## Chapter 3

1. Peter F. Drucker, *The Practice of Management* (New York: Harper, 1954); Norman R. Nager and Allen T. Harrell, *Public Relations Management by Objectives* (Lanham, MD: University Press of America, 1984).

2. Drucker, *The Practice of Management*; Bonnie L. Drewiniany and A. Jerome Jewler, *Creative Strategy in Advertising*, 11th ed. (Boston: Cengage, 2014); A. Jerome Jewler, *Creative Strategy in Advertising*, 5th ed. (Belmont, CA: Wadsworth, 1995); Nager and Harrell; William Thompson, *Targeting the Message: A Receiver-Centered Process for Public Relations Writing* (White Plains, NY: Longman, 1996).

3. Joe Garecht, "Making the Most of Year End Fundraising Appeals," *The Fundraising Authority*, 2011, http://www.thefundraisingauthority.com/strategy-and-planning/year-end-fundraising-appeals/.

4. James E. Grunig and Todd Hunt, *Managing Public Relations* (New York: CBS College Publishing, 1984); James E. Grunig, *Excellence in Public Relations and Communication Management* (Mahwah, NJ: Lawrence Erlbaum, 1992).

5. Ken Tracy, "Happy Meal Ads Target Kids," CBS News, November 8, 2010.

6. Karlene Lukovitz, "Mcdonald's Digital Promos Geotarget College Kids," *Marketing Daily*, December 15, 2011, http://www.mediapost.com/publications/article/164279/mcdonalds-digital-promos-geotarget-college-kids.html.

7. Mee Smit, "Cutest Mcdonald's Commercial," McDonald's, January 26, 2012.

8. Lisa Fall and William Thompson, "Psychographics." In *The Encyclopedia of Public Relations*, ed. Robert L. Heath (Thousand Oaks, CA: SAGE Publications, 2005), 656–660.

### Chapter 4

1.  John Keane, "Post-Truth Politics and Why the Antidote Isn't Simply 'Fact-Checking' and Truth," *The Conversation*, March 22, 2018; Harry G. Frankfurt, *On Bullshit* (Princeton, NJ: Princeton University Press, 2005).

2.  Keane, "Post-Truth Politics."

3.  Internal Revenue Service, "Form 990: Return of Organization Exempt from Income Tax: Wounded Warrior Project Inc.," 2011, https://www.woundedwarriorproject.org/media/1065/form-990-2009-2010.pdf; Internal Revenue Service, "Form 990: Return of Organization Exempt from Income Tax: Wounded Warrior Project Inc.," 2012, https://www.woundedwarriorproject.org/media/1065/form-990-2010-2011.pdf; Internal Revenue Service, "Form 990: Return of Organization Exempt from Income Tax: Wounded Warrior Project Inc.," 2013, https://www.woundedwarriorproject.org/media/1065/form-990-2011-2012.pdf; Internal Revenue Service, "Form 990: Return of Organization Exempt from Income Tax: Wounded Warrior Project Inc.," 2014, https://www.woundedwarriorproject.org/media/1067/form-990-2012-2013.pdf; Internal Revenue Service, "Form 990: Return of Organization Exempt from Income Tax: Wounded Warrior Project Inc.," 2015, https://www.woundedwarriorproject.org/media/1068/form-990-2013-2014.pdf.

4.  Jessica Semega, Melissa Kollar, Emily A. Shrider, and John F. Creamer, "Income and Poverty in the United States: 2019," U.S. Department of Commerce (Washington, DC: U.S. Census Bureau, 2020).

5.  DQYJ, "Average, Median, Top 1%, and All United States Individual Income Percentiles in 2020," 2020, https://dqydj.com/average-median-top-individual-income-percentiles/.

6.  Semega et al., "Income and Poverty."

7.  DQYDJ, "Average, Median."

8.  U.S. Department of Health and Human Services, "Poverty Guidelines," Office of the Assistant Secretary for Planning and Evaluation, 2020, https://aspe.hhs.gov/poverty-guidelines.

9.  DQYDJ, "Average, Median."

10. Office of the Assistant Secretary for Planning and Evaluation, "Poverty Guidelines," 2020, https://aspe.hhs.gov/poverty-guidelines.

11. Howard R. Gold, "Never Mind the 1 Percent: Let's Talk About the 0.01 Percent," *Chicago Booth Review* (2020), https://review.chicagobooth.edu/economics/2017/article/never-mind-1-percent-lets-talk-about-001-percent.

12. DQYDJ, "Average, Median."

13. Gold, "Never Mind."

14. U.S. Bureau of Labor Statistics, "CPI Inflation Calculator," 2020, https://www.bls.gov/data/inflation_calculator.htm.

15. Semega et al., "Income and Poverty."

16. U.S. Census Bureau, "Households by Total Money Income, Race," 2020, https://www.census.gov/data/tables/time-series/demo/income-poverty/historical-income-households.html.

17. U.S. Census Bureau, "Hispanic Origin of Householder: 1967 to 2019," 2020, https://www.census.gov/data/tables/time-series/demo/income-poverty/historical-income-households.html.

18. Federal Reserve Economic Data, "Gross Domestic Product," Economic Research: Federal Reserve Bank of St. Louis, 2020, https://fred.stlouisfed.org/series/GDP.

19. U.S. Bureau of Labor Statistics, "CPI Inflation Calculator," 2020, https://www.bls.gov/data/inflation_calculator.htm.

20. U.S. Bureau of Labor Statistics, "CPI Inflation Calculator."

21. Semega et al., "Income and Poverty."

22. U.S. Census Bureau, "Households by Total Money."

23. U.S. Census Bureau, "Hispanic Origin."

24. U.S. Census Bureau 2020, "Historical Household Table," 2020, https://www.census.gov/data/tables/time-series/demo/families/households.html.

25. Semega et al., "Income and Poverty."

26. U.S. Census Bureau, "Households by Total Money."

27. U.S. Census Bureau, "Hispanic Origin."

28. U.S. Census Bureau, "Quickfacts," 2020, https://www.census.gov/quickfacts/fact/table/US/RHI725219.

29. Semega et al., "Income and Poverty."

30. World Population Review, "Median Income by Country 2020," 2020, https://worldpopulationreview.com/country-rankings/median-income-by-country.

31. C. L. Illsley, "What Are the Biggest Industries in Norway?," *World Atlas*, 2019, https://www.worldatlas.com/articles/which-are-the-biggest-industries-in-norway.html.

32. The World Bank, "Gini Index," 2018, https://data.worldbank.org/indicator/SI.POV.GINI?end=2018&most_recent_value_desc=true&start=1967&view=map&year=2018.

33. Organisation for Economic Co-operation and Development, "Public Social Spending Is High in Many Oecd Countries," *OECD*, 2019, https://www.oecd.org/social/soc/OECD2019-Social-Expenditure-Update.pdf.

34. Kyle Pomerleau, "How Scandinavian Countries Pay for Their Government Spending," Tax Foundation, 2015, https://taxfoundation.org/how-scandinavian-countries-pay-their-government-spending/#:~:text=Norway's%20top%20marginal%20tax%20rate%20of%2039%20percent%20applies%20to,U.S.%20income%20(around%20%2424400%2C000).

35. Rocky Mengle, "What Are the Income Tax Brackets for 2020?," *Kiplinger*, 2020, https://www.kiplinger.com/article/taxes/t056-c000-s001-what-are-the-income-tax-brackets-for-2020-vs-2019.html.

36. Gold, "Never Mind."

37. Mengle "Income Tax Brackets."

38. Tax Foundation, "Taxes in Norway," 2020, https://taxfoundation.org/country/norway/.

39. Organisation for Economic Co-operation and Development. "Public Social Spending Is High in Many OECD Countries," *OECD*, 2019, https://www.oecd.org/social/soc/OECD2019-Social-Expenditure-Update.pdf.

40. Internal Revenue Service, "Form 990," 2011; Internal Revenue Service, "Form 990," 2012; Internal Revenue Service, "Form 990," 2013; Internal Revenue Service, "Form 990," 2014; and Internal Revenue Service, "Form 990," 2015.

41. Abridged from William Thompson and Pamela G. Bourland-Davis, "Wounded Warrior Project." In *Cases in Public Relations: Translating Ethics into Action*, ed. Brigitta Brunner and Corey Hickerson (Oxford, England: Oxford University Press, 2018), 292–302.

42. Organisation for Economic Co-operation and Development, "Health Spending," 2019, https://data.oecd.org/healthres/health-spending.htm.

43. Robert Reich, "Where Your Tax Dollars Really Go," *The American Prospect*, 2019, https://prospect.org/economy/tax-dollars-really-go/.

44. Michael E. O'Hanlon, "Is US Defense Spending Too High, Too Low, or Just Right?," Brookings Institute, 2019, https://www.brookings.edu/policy2020/votervital/is-us-defense-spending-too-high-too-low-or-just-right/#:~:text=The%20Trump%20administration's%20projected%20defense,during%20the%20Cold%20War%20decades.

45. Nan Tian, Alexandra Kuimova, Diego Lopes da Silva, Pieter D. Wezeman, and Siemon T. Wezeman, "Trends in World Military Expenditure, 2019," *SIPRI*, 2020, https://www.sipri.org/sites/default/files/2020-04/fs_2020_04_milex_0_0.pdf.

46. Todd Harrison and Seamus P. Daniels. "Analysis of the FY 2021 Defense Budget," *CSIS*, 2020, http://defense360.csis.org/wp-content/uploads/2020/08/Analysis-of-the-FY-2021-Defense-Budget.pdf.

47. Bonnie S. Glaser, Matthew P. Funaiole, and Brian Hart. "Breaking Down China's 2020 Defense Budget," CSIS, 2020, https://www.csis.org/analysis/breaking-down-chinas-2020-defense-budget.

48. Tian et al., "Trends in World Military."

49. Adapted from "An American Budget: Budget of the U.S. Government, Fiscal Year 2019," Office of Management and Budget, 2018, https://www.govinfo.gov/content/pkg/BUDGET-2019-BUD/pdf/BUDGET-2019-BUD.pdf; Bonnie S. Glaser, Matthew P. Funaiole, and Brian Hart, "Breaking Down China's 2020 Defense Budget," Center for Strategic and International Studies, https://www.csis.org/analysis/breaking-down-chinas-2020-defense-budget, May 22, 2020; International Institute for Strategic Studies, "Comparative Defense Statistics," https://www.iiss.org/publications/the-military-balance/military-balance-2020-book/comparative-defence-statistics; Siemon T. Wezeman, "Russia's Military Spending: Frequently Asked Questions," Stockholm International Peace Research Institute, April 27, 2020, https://www.sipri.org/commentary/topical-backgrounder/2020/russias-military-spending-frequently-asked-questions; The World Bank, "GDP Current US$," 2019, https://data.worldbank.org/indicator/NY.GDP.MKTP.CD; Global Fire Power, "Active Military Manpower," 2020, https://www.globalfirepower.com/active-military-manpower.asp; Global Fire Power, "Reserve Military Manpower," 2020, https://www.globalfirepower.com/active-reserve-military-manpower.asp; United Nations, United Nations Department of Economic and Social Affairs, "World Population Prospects 2019," August 19, 2020, https://population.un.org/wpp/Download/Standard/Population/; Tian et al., "Trends in World Military"; Armed Forces, "Compare Armed Forces," Armedforces.eu, April 20, 2019, https://armedforces.eu/compare/country_China_vs_USA.

50. Armed Forces, "Military Power of China & USA."

51. Paul D. Miller, "Why We Need to Move Beyond the 'Two War' Doctrine," Foreign Policy, 2012, https://foreignpolicy.com/2012/01/06/why-we-need-to-move-beyond-the-two-war-doctrine/.

52. Tian et al., "Trends in World Military."

**Chapter 5**

1. There are, admittedly, several options for people on these government plans as well, though their choices are fewer, and coverage tends to be more comprehensive than private plans.

2. U.S. Centers for Medicare & Medicaid Services, "Glossary," HealthCare.gov, 2017, https://www.healthcare.gov/glossary/.

3. George Cheney, "The Corporate (Re)Presents Itself." In *Rhetorical and Critical Approaches to Public Relations*, ed. Elizabeth L. Toth and Robert L. Heath (Hillsdale, NJ: Lawrence Erlbaum, 1992), 179.

4. U.S. Department of Labor, "Wages and the Fair Labor Standards Act Topical Fact Sheet Index," n.d., https://www.dol.gov/agencies/whd/fact-sheets.

5. Dartunorro Clark, "House Passes $15 Minimum Wage Bill," *NBC*, July 18, 2019.

6. Shannon A. Bowen, "A State of Neglect: Public Relations as 'Corporate Conscience' or Ethics Counsel," *Journal of Public Relations Research* 20, no. 3 (2008), 271–296.

7. PR practitioners and journalists scored roughly the same on the defining issues test (DIT), which measures moral reasoning capabilities. While these strategic communicators performed poorly in comparison to philosophers, as one might expect, they outperformed average adults and business professionals, which points to the ethical value that strategic communication practitioners bring to organizations. See Renita Coleman and Lee Wilkins, "The Moral Development of Public Relations Practitioners: A Comparison with Other Professions and Influences on Higher Quality Ethical Reasoning," 23 (2009), 318–340; Bowen, "A State of Neglect."

8. Adapted from N. Browning, "The Ethics of Two-Way Symmetry and the Dilemmas of Dialogic Kantianism," *Journal of Media Ethics 30*, no. 3 (2015): 1–18. https://doi.org/10.1080/08900523.2014.985295; Rosalind Hursthouse, *On Virtue Ethics* (Oxford University Press, 1999); Louis P. Pojman, *The Moral Life: An Introductory Reader in Ethics and Literature* (Oxford University Press, 2004).

9. Jeremy Bentham, *An Introduction to the Principles of Morals and Legislation* (Oxford, England: Clarendon Press, 1789/1907); John Stuart Mill, *Utilitarianism*, 2nd ed. (Indianapolis, IN: Hackett, 1861/2001); Henry Sidgwick, *The Methods of Ethics*, 7th ed. (London: Macmillan, 1907); Peter Singer, *Writings on an Ethical Life* (New York: HarperCollins, 2000).

10. Brooke Wolford, "CDC Says to Wear Face Coverings in Public. WHO Says Don't Bother. What's Going On?," *Miami Herald*, April 7, 2020.

11. Mayo Clinic Staff, "How Well Do Face Masks Protect Against the Coronavirus?," February 13, 2021, https://www.mayoclinic.org/diseases-conditions/coronavirus/in-depth/coronavirus-mask/art-20485449.

12. Thomas H. Bivins, *Mixed Media: Moral Distinctions in Advertising, Public Relations, and Journalism*, 2nd ed. (New York: Routledge, 2009); Larissa A. Grunig and Elizabeth L. Toth, "The Ethics of Communicating with and About Difference in a Changing Society." In *Ethics in Public Relations: Responsible Advocacy*, ed. Kathy Fitzpatrick and Carolyn Bronstein (Thousand Oaks, CA: SAGE Publications, 2006), 39–52.

13. Nicholas Browning, "The Ethics of Two-Way Symmetry and the Dilemmas of Dialogic Kantianism," *Journal of Mass Media Ethics* 30, no. 3 (2015), 1–18.

14. Walter Sinnott-Armstrong, "Consequentialism," *Stanford Encyclopedia of Philosophy*, 2015, https://plato.stanford.edu/entries/consequentialism/#Bib.https://plato.stanford.edu/entries/consequentialism/#Bib.

15. Immanuel Kant, *Ethical Philosophy* (Indianapolis, IN: Hackett, 1785/1994).

16. Nicholas Browning, "Ethics and the Profession: The Crystallizing of PR Practice from Association to Accreditation, 1936–1964," *American Journalism* 35, no. 2 (2018), 140–170; Public Relations Society of America, "Public Relations Society of America (PRSA) Member Code of Ethics," *PRSA*, 2000, https://www.prsa.org/wp-content/uploads/2018/04/PRSACodeofEthics.pdf.

17. Browning, "Ethics and the Profession."; Michael Parkinson, "The PRSA Code of Professional Standards and Member Code of Ethics: Why They Are Neither Professional nor Ethical," *Public Relations Quarterly* 46, no. 3 (2001), 27–31; Donald K. Wright, "Enforcement Dilemma: Voluntary Nature of Public Relations Codes," *Public Relations Review* 11, no. 1 (1993), 51–60.

18. Wright, "Enforcement Dilemma."

19. CNN Wire Staff, "Retracted Autism Study an 'Elaborate Fraud,' British Journal Finds," *CNN*, January 5, 2011, http://www.cnn.com/2011/HEALTH/01/05/autism.vaccines/.

20. Centers for Disease Control and Prevention, "Vaccines Do Not Cause Autism," August 25, 2020, https://www.cdc.gov/vaccinesafety/concerns/autism.html.

21. Autism Speaks, "No MMR-Autism Link in Large Study of Vaccinated Vs. Unvaccinated Kids," *Autism Speaks*, April 20, 2015, https://www.autismspeaks.org/science/science-news/no-mmr-autism-link-large-study-vaccinated-vs-unvaccinated-kids.

22. John W. Hill, founder of the PR agency Hill & Knowlton, was a strong advocate of this approach. See Karen Miller Russell, "Character and the Practic of Public Relations: Arthur W. Page and John W. Hill." In *Rhetorical and Critical Approaches to Public Relations*, eds. Robert L. Heath, Elizabeth L. Toth, and Damion Waymer (New York: Routledge, 2009), 315–327.

23. Oxford English Dictionary, "Murder," 2016.

24. Browning, "The Ethics of Two-Way"; Larry Alexander and Michael Moore, "Deontological Ethics," *Stanford Encyclopedia of Philosophy*, 2016, https://plato.stanford.edu/entries/ethics-deontological/.

25. Alasdair MacIntyre, *After Virtue*, 3rd ed. (Notre Dame, IN: Notre Dame University Press, 2007), 155.

26. Nicholas Browning, "Amoral Public Relations: A New Standard of Ethical Practice" (paper presented at the annual conference of the Association for Journalism and Mass Communication Ethics, Montreal, Canada, 2014).

27. Steve Mackey, "Virtue Ethics, CSR and "Corporate Citizenship," *Journal of Communication Management* 18, no. 2 (2014), 131–145; Aaron Quinn, "Moral Virtues for Journalists," *Journal of Mass Media Ethics* 22, no. 2&3 (2007), 168–186.

28. Rosalind Hursthouse and Glen Pettigrove, "Virtue Ethics," *Stanford Encyclopedia of Philosophy*, 2016, https://plato.stanford.edu/entries/ethics-virtue/.

29. Aristotle, *Nicomachean Ethics*, trans. Terence Irwin (Indianapolis, IN: Hackett, 340 BCE/1999).

30. Hursthouse and Pettigrove, "Virtue Ethics"; Kevin Timpe and Craig Boyd, eds., *Virtues and Their Vices* (New York: Oxford University Press, 2014).

31. Aristotle, *Nicomachean Ethics*; Hursthouse and Pettigrove, "Virtue Ethics"; Timpe and Boyd, *Virtues and Their Vices*.

32. Philippa Foot, *Natural Goodness* (Oxford, England: Oxford University Press, 2001); Hursthouse, *On Virtue Ethics*; Hursthouse and Pettigrove, "Virtue Ethics"; MacIntyre, *After Virtue*.

33. Stanley B. Cunningham, "Getting It Right: Aristotle's 'Golden Mean' as Theory Deterioration," *Journal of Mass Media Ethics* 14, no. 1 (1999), 5–15; David L. Martinson, "Ethical Decision Making in Public Relations: What Would Aristotle Say?," *Public Relations Quarterly* 45, no. 3 (2000), 18–21.

34. Philippa Foot, *Virtues and Vices* (Oxford, England: Oxford University Press, 2002); Hursthouse, *On Virtue Ethics*; Hursthouse and Pettigrove, "Virtue Ethics."

35. Wendy N. Wyatt, "Being Aristotelian: Using Virtue Ethics in an Applied Media Ethics Course," *Journal of Mass Media Ethics* 23, no. 4 (2008): 303.

36. Thomas Lickona, "What Does Moral Psychology Have to Say to the Teacher of Ethics?," in *Ethics Teaching in Higher Education*, ed. Daniel Callahan and Sissela Bok (New York: Plenum Press, 1980), 103–132; Martinson, "Ethical Decision Making?"

37. Wyatt, "Being Aristotelian."

38. Martinson, "Ethical Decision Making," 19.

39. Quaker Oats Company, "Aunt Jemima Brand to Remove Image from Packaging and Change Brand Name," news release, June 17, 2020, https://www.prnewswire.com/news-releases/aunt-jemima-brand-to-remove-image-from-packaging-and-change-brand-name-301078593.html.

40. "Aunt Jemima: Our History," 2020, https://www.auntjemima.com/our-history.

41. PepsiCo, "Aunt Jemima Rebrands As Pearl Milling Company," news release, February 9, 2021, https://www.pepsico.com/news/press-release/aunt-jemima-rebrands-as-pearl-milling-company02092021.

42. PepsiCo, "Pepsico's Journey to Racial Equality," 2020, https://www.pepsico.com/healthcheck/racial-equality-journey.&quot; https://www.pepsico.com/healthcheck/racial-equality-journey.

43. Browning, "Ethics and the Profession."; Browning, "The Ethics of Two-Way."

44. Richard S. Tedlow, *Keeping the Corporate Image: Public Relations and Business, 1900–1950* (Greenwich, CT: Jai Press Inc., 1979), 136.

45. Judy Foster Davis, "'Aunt Jemima Is Alive and Cookin'?" an Advertiser's Dilemma of Competing Collective Memories," *Journal of Macromarketing* 27, no. 1 (2007): 27.

46. Davis, "'Aunt Jemima," 28.

47. PRSA, "Public Relations Society of America (PRSA) Member Code of Ethics," 2000, https://apps.prsa.org/AboutPRSA/Ethics/CodeEnglish/#.WMK80hIrLmE.

48. Allstate Insurance Co., "Allstate College Football Sponsorships," 2020, https://www.allstate.com/national-sponsorships/college-football.aspx.

**Chapter 6**

1.  Silvan Tompkins, "Script Theory," in *The Emergence of Personality*, ed. Joel Arnoff and Albert I. Rabin (New York: Springer, 1987).

2.  Mikal E. Belicove, "A New Study Reveals the Power of First Impressions Online," *Entrepreneur*, March 14, 2012, https://www.entrepreneur.com/article/223150.

3.  William Thompson, "Motive-Based Publics: A New Approach to Public Relations Planning and Execution" (paper presented at the Annual Conference of the Religious Communicators Conference, Louisville, KY, 2007).

4.  Belicove, "A New Study Reveals."

5.  William Thompson, *Targeting the Message: A Receiver-Centered Process for Public Relations Writing* (White Plains, NY: Longman, 1996).

6.  Jesse L. Williams, *The Stolen Story and Other Newspaper Stories* (New York: Charles Scribner's Sons, 1899), 223.

7.  Joe Taksel, "Remembering the Pets Which Died on 9/11," *Opposing Views*, September 11, 2011, http://www.opposingviews.com/i/society/animal-rights/remembering-pets-which-died-911.

8.  Brian Scott, "Readability Formulas," n.d., http://www.readabilityformulas.com/search/pages/Readability_Formulas.

**Chapter 7**

1.  Elihu Katz and Paul F. Lazarsfeld, *Personal Influence: The Part Played by People in the Flow of Mass Communications* (New York: Free Press, 1955); Stephen W. Littlejohn and Karen A. Foss, eds., *Encyclopedia of Communication Theory* (Thousand Oaks, CA: SAGE Publications, 2009); Harold Lasswell, "The Structure and Function of Communication in Society," in *The Communication of Ideas: A Series of Addresses*, ed. Lyman Bryson (New York: Harper, 1948); Lawrence Grossberg, Ellen Wartella, D. Charles Whitney, and J. Macgregor Wise, *Media Making: Mass Media in a Popular Culture*, 2nd ed. (Thousand Oaks, CA: SAGE Publications, 2006); Denis McQuail, *Mass Communication Theory*, 6th ed. (Thousand Oaks, CA: SAGE Publications, 2010); Nicholas Browning and Kaye D. Sweetser, "The Let Down Effect: Satisfaction, Motivation, and Credibility Assessments of Political Infotainment," *American Behavioral Scientist* 58, no. 6 (2014), 810–826.

2.  Robert B. Cialdini, *Influence: Science and Practice*, 4th ed. (Needham Heights, MA: Allyn and Bacon, 2001); Richard E. Petty and John T. Cacioppo, "The Elaboration Likelihood Model of Persuasion," in *Advances in Experimental Social Psychology*, ed. Leonard Berkowitz (New York: Academic Press, 1986), 124–206.

3.  Christopher Scanlan, *Reporting and Writing: Basics for the 21st Century* (Oxford, England: Oxford University Press, 2000).

4.  James E. Grunig and Todd Hunt, *Managing Public Relations* (New York: CBS College Publishing, 1984); James E. Grunig, *Excellence in Public Relations and Communication Management* (Mahwah, NJ: Lawrence Erlbaum, 1992).

5.  Richard Vaughn, "The Consumer Mind: How to Tailor Ad Strategies," *Advertising Age*, 51, (1980), 45–46; Jay D. Lindquist and M. Joseph Sirgy, *Shopper, Buyer, and Consumer Behavior: Theory, Marketing Applications and Public Policy Implications*, 4th ed. (Cincinnati, OH: Cengage Learning, 2009).

6.  William Thompson, *Targeting the Message: A Receiver-Centered Process for Public Relations Writing* (White Plains, NY: Longman, 1996).

7.  William Strunk Jr. and E. B. White, *The Elements of Style*, 4th ed. (London: Pearson, 1999).

8.  Ryan Weber and Karl Strolley, "Writing Transitions," *The OWL at Purdue*, 2017, https://owl.english.purdue.edu/owl/owlprint/574/.

9.  Thompson, *Targeting the Message.*

**Chapter 8**

1.  William Thompson, *Targeting the Message: A Receiver-Centered Process for Public Relations Writing* (New York: Longman, 1996), 174.

2.  Em Griffin, *A First Look at Communication Theory*, 8th ed. (New York: McGraw-Hill, 2012).

3.  John C. Abell, "Aug. 31, 1920: News Radio Makes News," *Wired*, 2010, https://www.wired.com/2010/08/0831first-radio-news-broadcast/.

4.  Franklin D. Roosevelt, *The Fireside Chats of Franklin Delano Roosevelt: Radio Addresses to the American People Broadcast between 1933 and 1944* (Rockville, MD: Arc Manor, 2009).

5.  Mark Memmott, "75 Years Ago, 'War of the Worlds' Started a Panic. Or Did It?," *NPR*, 2013, http://www.npr.org/sections/thetwo-way/2013/10/30/241797346/75-years-ago-war-of-the-worlds-started-a-panic-or-did-it.

6.  New York Times, "Lowell Thomas, a World Traveler and Broadcaster for 45 Years, Dead," *New York Times*, August 30, 1981; Lowell Thomas, *So Long*

*until Tomorrow: From Quaker Hill to Kathmandu* (New York: William Morrow, 1977).

7. Jennifer Alejandro, *Journalism in the Age of Social Media* (Oxford, England: Reuters Institute for the Study of Journalism, 2010).

8. Terry Flew, "Media Convergence," in *Encyclopedia Britannica* (Chicago, IL: Encyclopedia Britanica, Inc., 2016).

## Chapter 9

1. Craig Havighurst, "Why Gibson Guitar Was Raided by the Justice Department," *NPR*, August 31, 2011.

2. Matthew M. Langer, "The Gibson Raid: When You Lie Down with Dogs, You Get up with Fleas," *Breitbart*, September 2, 2011.

3. 100.3 Jack FM, "The Craziest Things Ted Nugent Said at His Billy Bob's Show," *100.3 Jack FM Radio*, August 29, 2012.

4. James E. Grunig and Todd Hunt, *Managing Public Relations* (New York: CBS College Publishing, 1984).

5. James E. Grunig, Larissa A. Grunig, and David M. Dozier, "The Excellence Theory," in *Public Relations Theory II*, ed. Carl H. Botan and Vincent Hazleton (Mahwah, NJ: Lawrence Erlbaum, 2006), 46–7.

6. Marshall McLuhan, *Understanding Media: The Extensions of Man* (Berkeley, CA: Gingko Press, 2013/1964).

7. Kate Keib, Camila Espina, Yen-I Lee, Bartosz W. Wojdynski, Dongwon Choi, and Hyejin Bang, "Picture This: The Influence of Emotionally Valenced Images, on Attention, Selection, and Sharing of Social Media News," *Media Psychology* 21, no. 2 (2018), 202–221; Yagodina Kartunova, "Facebook Engagement and Its Relation to Visuals, with a Focus on Brand Culture," *Language & Semiotic Studies* 3, no. 3 (2017), 77–102.

8. Brett Nelson, "Do You Read Fast Enough to Be Successful?," *Forbes*, June 4, 2012.

9. David Meerman Scott, *The New Rules of Marketing & PR: How to Use Social Media, Online Video, Mobile Applications, Blogs, News Releases & Viral Marketing to Reach Buyers Directly*, 6th ed. (Hoboken, NJ: Wiley, 2017).

10. Mark W. Schaefer, *The Content Code: Six Essential Strategies for Igniting Your Content, Your Marketing, and Your Business* (Louisville, TN: Schaefer Marketing Solutions, 2015), 206–07.

11. Scott, *The New Rules of Marketing*.

12. Schaefer, *The Content Code*; Scott, *The New Rules of Marketing*.

13. Amy Gallo, "The Value of Keeping the Right Customers," *Harvard Business Review*, October 29, 2014.

14. John A. Ledingham, "Explicating Relationship Management as a General Theory of Public Relations," *Journal of Public Relations Research* 15, no. 2 (2003), 181–198.

15. Jason Falls and Erik Deckers, *No Bullshit Social Media: The All-Business, No-Hype Guide to Social Media Marketing* (Indianapolis, IN: Que, 2012), 48.

16. Ann Handley and C. C. Chapman, *Content Rules: How to Create Killer Blogs, Podcasts, Videos, Ebooks, Webinars (and More) That Engage Customers and Ignite Your Business* (Hoboken, NJ: Wiley, 2011), 70.

17. Mor Naaman, Jeffrey Boase, and Chih-Hui Lai, "Is It Really About Me? Message Content in Social Awareness Streams" (Association for Computing Machinery Conference, Savannah, GA, 2010).

18. Rebecca Ford, "How 'Straight Outta Compton' Viral Marketing Became a Sensation," *The Hollywood Reporter*, August 14, 2015.

19. Stacey Ritzen, "A Twitter Rally to Thank Donald Trump Predictably Goes Horribly Wrong," *Uproxx*, January 25, 2017.

20. Scott, *The New Rules of Marketing*, 258.

21. Neil Irwin and Quealy, "The Places in America Where College Football Means the Most," *New York Times*, November 8, 2014.

22. Scott, *The New Rules of Marketing*.

23. New York Times, "The Psychology of Sharing: Why Do People Share Online?," 2011.

24. Schaefer, *The Content Code*.

25. Kelly Yamanouchi, "Delta to Shut Down @Deltaassist Twitter Account, Assist Customers Via @Delta," *Atlanta Journal-Constitution*, April 4, 2016.

## Chapter 10

1. Tom Kelleher, *Public Relations* (New York: Oxford University Press, 2018); David W. Guth and James G. March, *Public Relations: A Values-Driven Approach*, 6th ed. (New York: Pearson, 2017).

2. Guth and Marsh *Public Relations: A Values-Driven Approach*, 149.

3. American Film Institute, "AFI's 100 Greatest American Films," 2007, https://www.filmsite.org/afi100films_2007.html.

4. Matt Rocheleau, "Oscar Nominations Often Lead to Boost in Movie Revenues," *Boston Globe*, January 14, 2016.

5. ChildFund International, "Be the Solution: Change the World, One Child at a Time," n.d., https://www.childfund.org.

## Chapter 11

1. Günter Bentele, "Parasitism or Symbiosis? The Intereffication Model under Discussion" (paper presented at the Spanning the Boundaries of Communication, Jyväskylä, Finland, 2002); Günter Bentele and Howard Nothhaft, "The Intereffication Model: Theoretical Discussions and Empirical Research," in *Public Relations Research: European and International Perspectives and Innovations*, ed. Ansgar Zerfass, Betteke van Ruler, and Krishnamurthy Sriramesh (Wiesbaden, Germany: VS Verlag für Sozialwissenschaften, 2008), 34–47.

2. Julia Hobsbawn, "Why Journalism Needs PR," *The Guardian*, November 16, 2003.

3. Robert Wynne, "What Journalists Really Think of Your Press Release," *Forbes*, February 24, 2014.

4. U.S. Census Bureau, "Quickfacts: Lincoln County, Georgia; Seattle City, Washington," 2020, https://www.census.gov/quickfacts/fact/table/lincolncountygeorgia,seattlecitywashington/PST045219.

5. Tumblr, "Tumblr Is Where Your Interests Connect You with Your People," n.d., https://www.tumblr.com/about.

6. Philip A. Napoli, *Audience Economics: Media Institutions and the Audience Marketplace* (New York: Columbia University Press, 2003); *Audience Evolution: New Technologies and the Transformation of Media Audiences* (New York: Columbia University Press, 2011).

7. Beki Winchel, "Report: Journalists Are Ditching the Press Release," *PR Daily*, December 28, 2018.

8. John Rampton, "Are Press Releases Dead?," *Forbes*, July 14, 2016.

9. Winchel, "Report: Journalists."

10. Robleh Jama, "The Press Release Is Dead. Hear Are Its Replacements," *Medium*, December 2, 2015.

11. Bureau of Labor Statistics, "Occupational Outlook Handbook: Reporters, Correspondents, and Broadcast Analysts" (Washington, DC, 2018); Career Trends, "Reporters, Correspondents, and Broadcast News Analysts," n.d., https://careertrend.com/reporters-correspondents-and-broadcast-news-analysts.html.

12. Christopher Ali and Damian Radcliffe, "Life at Small-Market Newspapers: A Survey of over 400 Journalists" (New York: Tow Center for Digital Journalism, 2017). https://www.cjr.org/tow_center_reports/local-journalism-survey.php.

13. Steve Dubb, "Where Local Media Falter, Nonprofit Models Step In," *Nonprofit Quarterly*, January 12, 2018.

14. Bureau of Labor Statistics, "Occupational Outlook Handbook: Public Relations Specialists," (Washington, DC, 2018). https://www.bls.gov/ooh/media-and-communication/public-relations-specialists.htm.

15. Jon Allsop, "Trump's Pointless Friday-Night News Dumps," *Columbia Journalism Review*, July 13, 2020.

## Chapter 12

1. Kate Taylor, "Bud Light Is Bringing Back a Controversial Mascot Who Once Helped Sales Soar 20%," *Business Insider*, February 7, 2017.

2. Sheree Johnson, "New Research Sheds Light on Daily Ad exposures," *SJ Insights*, September 29, 2014, https://sjinsights.net/2014/09/29/new-research-sheds-light-on-daily-ad-exposures/.

3. Al Ries and Laura Ries, *The Fall of Advertising & the Rise of PR* (New York: Harper Business, 2002).

4. Kim Bhasin, "Time Warner Cable Changes Its Name, and Suddenly People Love It," Bloomberg, June 13, 2017.

5. Betty Crocker, "Ultimate Chocolate Chip Cookies," January 13, 2021, https://www.bettycrocker.com/recipes/ultimate-chocolate-chip-cookies/77c14e03-d8b0-4844-846d-f19304f61c57.

6. Adapted by William Thompson and Nicolas Browning, from Richard Vaughn, "The Common Mind: How to Tailor Ad Strategies," *Advertising Age*, 51, (1980), 45–46; and Richard Vaughn, "How Advertising Works: A Planning Model," *Journal of Advertising Research* (1980), 27–30.

7. Bob Garfield, "If Only Inifiniti's Commercials Were as Appealing as Its Cars," *Ad Age*, June 18, 2007, http://adage.com/article/ad-review/infiniti-s-commercials-appealing-cars/117367/.

8. Hongmei Shen, "Organization-Employee Relationship Maintenance Strategies: A New Measuring Instrument," *Journalism and Mass Communication Quarterly* 88, no. 2 (2011), 398–415.

9. Jim Macnamara, *Organizational Listening: The Missing Essential in Public Communication Reprint Edition* (New York: Peter Lang, 2016).

10. Minjeong Kang and Minjung Sung, "To Leave or Not to Leave: The Effects of Perceptions of Organizational Justice on Employee Turnover Intention Via Employee-Organization Relationship and Employee Job Engagement," *Journal of Public Relations Research* 31, no. 5–6 (2019), 152–175.

11. Chuck Carney, "Indiana University Trustees Approve Operating Budget for 2020–21," *News at IU*, 2020, https://news.iu.edu/stories/2020/08/iu/inside/14-trustees-approve-operating-budget.html#:~:text=The%20Indiana%20University%20Board%20of,for%20the%20new%20fiscal%20year.&text=The%20fiscal%20year%202020%2D21,from%20the%20last%20operating%20budget.

12. Indiana University, "IU and Its Impact, by the Numbers," 2020, https://www.iu.edu/about/facts.html.

13. U.S. Census Bureau, "County Population Totals: 2010–2019," U.S. Department of Commerce, 2020, https://www.census.gov/data/tables/time-series/demo/popest/2010s-counties-total.html.

14. Indiana University, "The IU Master Brand Architecture," n.d., https://brand.iu.edu/messaging-strategy/brand-architecture/index.html.

15. "Color and the IU Brand," n.d., https://brand.iu.edu/design/colors.html.

16. "Indiana University Retirement Plans Transition Guide," Indiana University, 2019, https://hr.iu.edu/benefits/pubs/misc/IU_TransitionGuide_IU_FINAL.pdf.

17. "Indian University Retirement."

18. IU Bloomington Professional Council, "COVID-19 Survey Results II," 2020, https://iubpc.indiana.edu/resources/COVID-19-Results-2.html.

## Chapter 13

1. Aarian Marshall, "So Digital Billboard Ads Change Wit the Speed of Traffic Now," *Wired*, July 29, 2016.

2. GPS World, "GPS-Powered Advertising Geo-Targets Moving Vehicles," November 4, 2015, https://www.gpsworld.com/gps-powered-advertising-geo-targets-moving-vehicles/.

3. Tim Johnson, "Smart Billboards Are Checking You Out – and Making Judgments," *McClatchy*, September 20, 2017.

4. Gavin Weightman, "The History of the Bar Code," *Smithsonian Magazine*, 2015, https://www.smithsonianmag.com/innovation/history-bar-code-180956704/.

5. Ashley Rodriguez, "Best Practices: How to Create a Rewards Program That Really Works," *Ad Age*, June 17, 2015.

6. Equifax Inc., "Product Overview: Speed Decisions with Superior Data," n.d., https://www.equifax.com/business/consumer-reports.

7. Emre Soyer and Robin M. Hogarth, "The Illusion of Predictability: How Regression Statistics Mislead Experts," *International Journal of Forecasting* 28, no. 3 (2012), 695–711.

8. U.S. Census Bureau, "County Population Totals: 2010–2019," *U.S. Department of Commerce*, 2020, https://www.census.gov/data/tables/time-series/demo/popest/2010s-counties-total.html.

9. Politico, "Donald Trump Won in Texas," January 21, 2021, https://www.politico.com/2020-election/results/texas/.

10. U.S. Census Bureau, "National Population Totals and Components of Change: 2010–2019," U.S. Department of Commerce, 2020, https://www.census.gov/data/tables/time-series/demo/popest/2010s-national-total.html.

11. "2019 National and State Population Estimates," December 30, 2019, https://www.census.gov/newsroom/press-kits/2019/national-state-estimates.html.

12. Bureau of Labor Statistics, "Fatal Occupational Injuries for Selected Events or Exposures, 2011–16," December 16, 2020, https://www.bls.gov/news.release/cfoi.t02.htm.

## Chapter 14

1. Jason Falls and Erik Deckers, *No Bullshit Social Media: The All-Business, No-Hype Guide to Social Media Marketing* (Indianapolis, IN: Que, 2012), 34.

2. Adapted from Mark W. Schaefer, *The Content Code: Six Essential Strategies for Igniting Your Content, Your Marketing, and Your Business* (Louisville, TN: Schaefer Marketing Solutions, 2015), 10–11.

3. David Meerman Scott, *The New Rules of Marketing & PR: How to Use Social Media, Online Video, Mobile Applications, Blogs, News Releases & Viral Marketing to Reach Buyers Directly*, 6th ed. (Hoboken, NJ: Wiley, 2017), 258.

4. Ramona Sukhraj, "How Dollar Shave Club Grew from Viral Video to $1 Billion Acquisition," *Impact*, July 21, 2016.

5. Dollar Shave Club. (2012, March 6). *Our blades are f\*\*\*Ing great* [Video]. YouTube. https://www.youtube.com/watch?v=ZUG9qYTJMsI.

6. Gladstone Murray, "Canada a Century Hence: The High Destiny of Canada," *Vital Speeches of the Day* 13, no. 7 (1947), 213–216; Roland Marchand, *Creating the Corporate Soul: The Rise of Public Relations and Corporate Imagery in American Big Business* (Berkeley, CA: University of California Press, 1998).

7. Scott, *The New Rules of Marketing*, 87–97.

8. Thomas J. Johnson and Barbara K. Kaye, "Wag the Blog: How Reliance on Traditional Media and the Internet Influence Credibility Perceptions of Weblogs among Blog Users," *Journalism and Mass Communication Quarterly* 81, no. 3 (2004), 622–642; "Using Is Believing: The Influence of Reliance on the Credibility of Online Political Information among Politically Interested Internet Users," *Journalism and Mass Communication Quarterly* 77, no. 4 (2000), 865–879; "In Blog We Trust? Deciphering Credibility of Components of the Internet among Politically Interested Internet Users," *Computers in Human Behavior* 25, no. 1 (2009), 175–182; Scott, *The New Rules of Marketing*.

9. It's important to familiarize yourselves with some basics of web design, XHTML and cascading style sheets (CSSs). We highly recommend Elisabeth Robson and Eric Freeman's *Head First HTML and CSS* as a user-friendly guide for beginners, Elisabeth Robson and Eric Freeman, *Head First Html and CSS*, 2nd ed. (Sebastopol, CA: O'Reilly Media, Inc., 2012).

10. Lindsay Kolowich, "The Character Count Guide for Blog Posts, Videos, Twets & More," HubSpot, April 25, 2017, https://blog.hubspot.com/marketing/character-count-guide.

11. Centers for Disease Control and Prevention, "CDC's Guide to Writing for Social Media," 2012, https://www.cdc.gov/socialmedia/tools/guidelines/pdf/GuidetoWritingforSocialMedia.pdf.

12. Michelle Castillo, "Survey: 76 Percent of Doctors Approve of Medical Marijuana Use," CBS News, May 31, 2013.

13. Kolowich, "The Character Count Guide."

14. Liam Corcoran, "What's the Perfect Length of a Facebook Post?," *NewsWhip*, July 28, 2016, http://www.newswhip.com/2016/07/perfect-length-of-a-facebook-post/.

15. Adapted from Ann Handley and C. C. Chapman, *Content Rules: How to Create Killer Blogs, Podcasts, Videos, Ebooks, Webinars (and More) That Engage Customers and Ignite Your Business* (Hoboken, NJ: Wiley, 2011), 108–13.

**Chapter 15**

1. Megan Brenan, "Americans Remain Distrustful of Mass Media," Gallup, 2020, https://news.gallup.com/poll/321116/americans-remain-distrustful-mass-media.aspx.

2. Ann Handley and C. C. Chapman, *Content Rules: How to Create Killer Blogs, Podcasts, Videos, Ebooks, Webinars (and More) That Engage Customers and Ignite Your Business* (Hoboken, NJ: Wiley, 2011).

3. The Onion, "Report: 90% of Waking Hours Spent Staring at Glowing Rectangles," June 15, 2009, https://www.theonion.com/report-90-of-waking-hours-spent-staring-at-glowing-re-1819570829.

4. Greg Sterling, "Mobile Devices Now Driving 56 Percent of Traffic to Top Sites—Report," *Marketing Land*, February 23, 2016.

5. Michael S. Rosenwald, "Serious Reading Takes a Hit from Online Scanning and Skimming, Researchers Say," *Washington Post*, April 6, 2014; Naomi Baron, "Why Digital Reading Is No Substitute for Print," *The New Republic*, July 20, 2016.

6. Matt Ahlgren, "100+ Internet Statistics" Website Hosting Rating, 2020, https://www.websitehostingrating.com/internet-statistics-facts/#:~:text=How%20many%20websites%20are%20there,published%20on%20August%206%2C%201991.

7. SimilarWeb, "Industry Leaders," 2020, https://pro.similarweb.com/#/industry/topsites/All/999/1m?webSource=Total.

8. Alexa, "Top Sites in United States," 2020, https://www.alexa.com/topsites/countries/US.

9. Handley and Chapman, *Content Rules*.

10. Internet Live Stats, "United States Internet Users," 2016, http://www.internetlivestats.com/internet-users/us/.

11. Pew Research Center, "Social Media Fact Sheet," June 12, 2019.

12. U.S. Census Bureau, "U.S. Census Bureau Releases New Educational Attainment Data," news release, March 30, 2020, https://www.census.gov/newsroom/press-releases/2020/educational-attainment.html.

13. Leslie K. John, Daniel Mochon, Oliver Emrich, and Janet Schwartz, "What's the Value of a Like?," *Harvard Business Review* 95, no. 2 (2017): 110.

14. Mark W. Schaefer, *The Content Code: Six Essential Strategies for Igniting Your Content, Your*

*Marketing, and Your Business* (Louisville, TN: Schaefer Marketing Solutions, 2015).

15. Jason Cipriani, "Why You Shouldn't Trust All Amazon Reviews," *Fortune*, March 14, 2016.

16. Schaefer, *The Content Code*.

17. Adapted from Schaefer, *The Content Code*; The New York Times, "The Psychology of Sharing: Why Do People Share Online?" (2011).

18. Sarah Gibbens, "Heart-Wrenching Video Shows Starving Polar Bear on Iceless Land," *National Geographic*, December 7, 2017; Jessica Gall Myrick, "Emotion Regulation, Procrastination, and Watching Cat Videos Online: Who Watches Internet Cats, Why, and to What Effect?," *Computers in Human Behavior* 52 (2015), 168–176.

19. Soroush Vosoughi, Deb Roy, and Sinan Aral, "The Spread of True and False News Online," *Science* 359, no. 6380 (2018), 1146–1151.

20. Georgia Mee, "What is a Good Engagement Rate on Twitter?," *Scrunch*, November 19, 2020, https://scrunch.com/blog/what-is-a-good-engagement-rate-on-twitter.

21. David Meerman Scott, *The New Rules of Marketing & PR: How to Use Social Media, Online Video, Mobile Applications, Blogs, News Releases & Viral Marketing to Reach Buyers Directly*, 6th ed. (Hoboken, NJ: Wiley, 2017), 194.

22. Scott, *The New Rules of Marketing; Jason Falls and Erik Deckers, No Bullshit Social Media: The All-Business, No-Hype Guide to Social Media Marketing* (Indianapolis, IN: Que, 2012).

23. Scott, *The New Rules of Marketing*.

24. Adapted from Scott, *The New Rules of Marketing*, 331–37.

25. Katie Clark Alsadder and Stephanie Saffer, "Apple's Worldwide Developers Conference Kicks Off June 4 in San Jose," news release, March 13, 2018, https://www.apple.com/newsroom/2018/03/apples-worldwide-developers-conference-kicks-off-june-4-in-san-jose/; Jonny Evans, "Wwdc 2018: What to Expect at Apple's Developers Conference," *Computerworld*, March 14 2018.

26. Falls and Deckers, *No Bullshit Social Media*; Marc A. Smith, Lee Rainie, Itai Himelboim, and Ben Shneiderman, "Mapping Twitter Topic Networks: From Polarized Crowds to Community Clusters," Pew Research Center, 2014.

27. College Board, "2017–18 Tuition and Fees at Public Four-Year Institutions by State and Five-Year Percentage Change in in-State Tuition and Fees," 2020, https://trends.collegeboard.org/college-pricing/figures-tables/2017-18-state-tuition-and-fees-public-four-year-institutions-state-and-five-year-percentage.

28. Adapted from Falls and Deckers, *No Bullshit Social Media*, 100–01.

29. Adapted from Falls and Deckers, *No Bullshit Social Media*, 100–101.

30. Adapted from Falls and Deckers, *No Bullshit Social Media*, 202–04.

31. Adapted from Falls and Deckers, *No Bullshit Social Media*, 202–204.

# Index

CPSIA information can be obtained
at www.ICGtesting.com
Printed in the USA
LVHW062049090622
720912LV00001B/3